ARISTOTLE

D1027932

**Property of
UAB
University of Alabama at Birmingham
Department of Philosophy
Birmingham, AL
(205) 934-4805**

ARISTOTLE

*Fundamentals of the
History of His Development*

BY
WERNER JAEGER

TRANSLATED
WITH THE AUTHOR'S CORRECTIONS AND ADDITIONS
BY
RICHARD ROBINSON

η γαρ νογ ενεργεια ζωη

SECOND EDITION

OXFORD UNIVERSITY PRESS

Oxford University Press, Amen House, London E.C.4

GLASGOW NEW YORK TORONTO MELBOURNE WELLINGTON
BOMBAY CALCUTTA MADRAS KARACHI LAHORE DACCA
CAPE TOWN SALISBURY NAIROBI IBADAN ACCRA
KUALA LUMPUR HONG KONG

FIRST PUBLISHED 1934
SECOND EDITION 1948
REPRINTED LITHOGRAPHICALLY IN GREAT BRITAIN
AT THE UNIVERSITY PRESS, OXFORD
1950, 1955, 1960
FIRST ISSUED IN OXFORD PAPERBACKS 1962

PREFACE TO PAPERBACK EDITION

THIS book first appeared in Berlin in 1923; since then it has been reprinted many times and translated into many languages. A survey of the books and articles which its new approach to the study of Aristotle has provoked since its first publication would reflect the course that Aristotelian studies have taken during the period and the way in which they have been affected by the method of the book.

It goes without saying that at the end of my life I cannot contemplate entering a discussion of this whole literature nor could I, or anyone else, offer definite answers to all the problems raised in or prompted by my study. I gladly confess that I have learnt much, both from the discussions of others, and from my own efforts such as those contained in my book *Diokles von Karystos* (Berlin 1938) and the contributions now collected in my *Scripta Minora* (Rome 1960). This study is presented here once more in its original form, though between paper covers, in the hope that it may be the more easily accessible to every earnest reader of Aristotle who wants to keep alive the problems that formed the point of departure for our present-day discussions.

WERNER JAEGER

Harvard University,
Cambridge, Mass. 1961

THE TRANSLATOR'S PREFACE
TO THE SECOND EDITION

IN this edition I have made about a score of alterations, most of them suggested by two reviewers of the first edition, Professor Benedict Einarson in *Classical Philology*, 1935, and Professor Harold Cherniss in *The American Journal of Philology*, 1935. Of the two new appendixes, the first comes from *The Philosophical Review*, 1940, and was written in English by Professor Jaeger. The second comes from *Sitzungsberichte der preussischen Akademie der Wissenschaften*, Philosophisch-historische Klasse, 1928, and is translated by myself.

The edition has a new and more complete index, the work of Mr. James E. Walsh of Harvard University, to whom the author has asked me to make this acknowledgement.

R. R.

THE TRANSLATOR'S PREFACE

THIS is a translation of *Aristoteles, Grundlegung einer Geschichte seiner Entwicklung*, which was published at Berlin in 1923 by the Weidmannsche Buchhandlung. I have consulted the author on the meaning of numerous sentences, and he has made several alterations and additions to the German text as it appeared in 1923. The accuracy of the rendering has been criticized in part by Dr. Fritz C. A. Kölln. The propriety of the English has been criticized almost throughout by Dr. James Hutton. I am very grateful to these gentlemen.

This translation is intelligible to persons who know no Greek. All Greek is rendered into English, and the books of ancient writings are referred to not by Greek letters but by Roman numerals. The only exception to this rule is Aristotle's *Metaphysics*, where a peculiar situation makes any use of numerals confusing.

For ease of recognition I have adopted standard translations of Greek authors as far as possible. I thank the Trustees of the Jowett Copyright Fund and the Delegates of the Oxford University Press for permission to use their translation of the works of Aristotle, and Messrs. Heinemann, the publishers of the Loeb Classical Library, for permission to reproduce R. D. Hicks's translation of Aristotle's will. I have ventured to quote an occasional sentence from other translators without asking permission. Differences of interpretation between Professor Jaeger and the Oxford translators have sometimes obliged me to depart from their rendering. The quotations from Iamblichus are translated by myself.

R. R.

THE AUTHOR'S PREFACE TO THE
GERMAN EDITION

THIS book, being at once treatise and monograph, demands a brief word of explanation.

It does not seek to give a systematic account, but to analyse Aristotle's writings so as to discover in them the half obliterated traces of his mental progress. Its biographical framework is intended merely to make more palpable the fact that his previously undifferentiated mass of compositions falls into three distinct periods of evolution. Owing to the meagreness of the material the picture that we thus obtain is of course fragmentary; yet its outlines constitute a distinctly clearer view of Aristotle's intellectual nature and of the forces that inspired his thinking. Primarily, this is a gain to the history of philosophical problems and origins. The author's intention is, however, not to make a contribution to systematic philosophy, but to throw light on the portion of the history of the Greek mind that is designated by the name of Aristotle.

Since 1916 I have repeatedly given the results of these researches as lectures at the universities of Kiel and Berlin; even the literary form, with the exception of the conclusion, was established in essentials at that time. The literature that has since appeared is not very important for Aristotle himself anyhow, and I have noticed it only so far as I have learnt something from it or am obliged to contradict it. The reader will look in vain for the results even of earlier researches so far as they concern merely unimportant changes of opinion or of form; such matters have nothing to do with development. Still less has my purpose been to analyse all Aristotle's writings for their own sake and to complete a microscopic examination of all their stages. The aim was solely to elucidate in its concrete significance, by means of evident examples, the phenomenon of his intellectual development as such.

In conclusion I offer my profoundest thanks to the publisher, who, in spite of the unfavourableness of the times, boldly undertook the whole risk of publishing this book.

W. J.

BERLIN, *Easter, 1923*

CONTENTS

ARISTOTLE

THE PROBLEM

ARISTOTLE was the first thinker to set up along with his philosophy a conception of his own position in history; he thereby created a new kind of philosophical consciousness, more responsible and inwardly complex. He was the inventor of the notion of intellectual development in time, and regards even his own achievement as the result of an evolution dependent solely on its own law. Everywhere in his exposition he makes his own ideas appear as the direct consequences of his criticism of his predecessors, especially Plato and his school. It was, therefore, both philosophical and Aristotelian when men followed him in this, and sought to understand him by means of the presuppositions out of which he had constructed his own theories.

Such attempts, however, have not given us a vivid insight into the individual nature of his philosophy; and this cannot surprise the philologist, who is not accustomed to use a writer's own estimate of himself as an objective document, or to take his standards from it. It was especially unprofitable to judge Aristotle, as was actually done, by his understanding of his predecessors, as if any philosopher could ever understand his predecessors in this sense. Surely there can be only one positive standard for Aristotle's personal achievement, and that is not how he criticizes Plato but how he himself Platonizes (since that is what philosophizing means to him). Why he gave this particular direction to knowledge cannot be explained merely from previous history, but only from his own philosophical development; just as he himself does not simply derive Plato's position in the history of Greek thought from his predecessors, but explains it as the result of the meeting of those historical influences and Plato's own creative originality. In the treatment of intellectual progress, if we are to give full weight to the creative and underived element in great individuals, we must supplement the general tendency of the times with the organic development of the personality concerned. Aristotle himself shows the close relation between development and form; the fundamental conception of his philosophy is 'embodied form that lives and develops' (Goethe). The aim is, he holds, to know the form and the entelechy by means of the stages of its growth. This is the only way in which the element of law in an intellectual 'structure' can be directly intuited. As he says at the beginning of his lecture on the preliminary stages of political life, 'here and elsewhere we shall not obtain the best insight into things until we actually see them growing from the beginning'.

It is one of those almost incomprehensible paradoxes in which the history of human knowledge abounds, that the principle of organic development has never yet been applied to its originator, if we exclude a few efforts which, though praiseworthy, have been quite partial and therefore without influence. It is no exaggeration to say that, at a time when a whole literature has been assembled about the development of Plato, scarcely any one speaks of that of Aristotle and almost nobody knows anything about it. In fact, our failure to apply the evolutionary point of view to him has finally come to be taken for an indication of his objective difference from Plato! While the history of the latter's development threatens gradually to blind us to the constructive impulse that forms one of the fundamental elements of his thought, we have become accustomed to regard it as almost a sign of philosophical stupidity to inquire into the chronology and development of Aristotle's doctrine and its sources. For, we think, the monad, carrying timelessly within itself the germ of all particulars, *is* precisely the system.

The main reason why no attempt has yet been made to describe Aristotle's development is, briefly, the scholastic notion of his philosophy as a static system of conceptions. His interpreters were past masters of his dialectical apparatus, but they had no personal experience of the forces that prompted his method of inquiry, or of his characteristic interplay of keen and abstract apodictic with a vivid and organic sense of form. Aristotle's spiritualism is saturated with an intuitive vision of reality. The strict rigour of his demonstrations is only the salutary chain with which the fourth century restrained its overflowing energies. The failure to realize this goes back to the separation of the more specifically philosophical parts of his doctrine, the logic and the metaphysics, from the studies of empirical reality, a separation which was accomplished by the time of the third generation in the Peripatos. The service done later by the line of commentators beginning with Andronicus (first century B.C.), to whom we owe the preservation of the treatises, was very great. By clinging to the letter of the tradition they far surpassed the pitiable successors of Theophrastus and Strato in exactness of philosophical comprehension. But even they could not restore the original spirit. There was no steady advance of natural and mental science to serve as breeding-ground, and therefore none of that fruitful interaction between experience and conception from which Aristotle's speculative notions had drawn their flexibility and their adaptive power. Since then there has been no break in the continuity of our idea of Aristotle. Without a gap the Oriental tradition follows that of the commentators, and Occidental Aristotelianism follows the Oriental Each of them had an educational effect on its age that cannot be overestimated, but their peculiar characteristic is just that purely conceptual scholasticism which had already barred the ancient world from a living understanding of Aristotle. Men were unable to apprehend his philosophy as the product of his special genius working on the problems set him by his age, and so they confined their attention to the form in which it was expressed, without having any notion how it had grown to be what it was. In the meantime one of the main sources for his development, the dialogues and letters, had been lost, and the traditional attitude alone was to blame. This prevented all access to his personality. So it came about that the new love which the humanists aroused for antiquity did not make any difference to Aristotle, especially as he was accounted the prince of medieval scholasticism, which was thoroughly despised by Luther and the humanists alike. Aristotle is the only great figure of ancient philosophy and literature who has never had a Renascence. Everybody knew, indeed, that he was a power to be reckoned with, and one of the foundations of the modern world, but he remained a tradition, for the reason, if for no other, that even after the days of humanism and the reformation men still had far too much need of his *content*. Melanchthon and the Jesuits both built their theology on his *Metaphysics*. Machiavelli got his rules from the *Politics*, the French critics and poets theirs from the *Poetics*. Moralists and jurists have drawn on the *Ethics*, and all philosophers down to Kant and far beyond on the logic.

As to the philologists, what has prevented them from penetrating to the inner form of Aristotle's thoughts is not so much an excessively strong interest in the content as the narrow and superficial conception of ancient literary prose reintroduced by the humanists. They have made acute studies of the writings that remain, and attempted to determine the text. But with the new feeling for style the unfinished state in which these works have come down to us was aesthetically displeasing. They were judged by the standard of literary writing, which they constantly flouted and which is wholly alien to their nature. Men naïvely compared the 'style' of the treatises with Plato's dialogues, and then lost themselves in enthusiasm for the marvellous art of the latter. By all kinds of rationalizing interference, by declaring disturbing passages spurious and transposing sentences or whole books, they tried to force the Aristotelian writings into the shape of readable handbooks. The reason for this sort of criticism was the failure to understand that provisional form which, being thoroughly characteristic of Aristotle's philosophy, constitutes the inevitable starting-point for every historical understanding of it. Even in the case of Plato, the importance of the form for the understanding of his peculiar thought has often been overlooked for long periods ; departmental philosophers and students of literature, in particular, are always prone to consider it as something literary, which had no material significance for Plato, in spite of the fact that it is unique in the history of philosophy. By now, however, most persons know that the study of the development of the form of his writings is one of the main keys to a philosophical understanding of him. With Aristotle, on the other hand, they still devote themselves exclusively to the content, all the more so because they suppose that he 'has no form whatever'. The Hellenistic rhetoricians' narrow notion of what constitutes literary form almost lost us his treatises, and is actually responsible for the disappearance of the Stoic and Epicurean writings. As soon as we abandon it the question of historical development naturally arises, for it is absolutely impossible to explain the peculiar state of the extant writings without the supposition that they contain the traces of different stages in his evolution. Analysis of the treatises would lead us of itself to this conclusion, and the fragments of his lost literary works confirm it. The main purpose of this book must be, therefore, to show for the first time, by means of the fragments of the lost works and through the analysis of the more important treatises, that at the root of them there is a process of development. It is in fact out of the interpretation of these documents, for an edition of the *Metaphysics*, that the present work arose. Philological criticism, however, is here directly subservient to philosophical inquiry, since we are concerned not merely with the outward condition of the writings as such, but also with the revelation which this condition gives us of the driving energy of Aristotle's thought.

PART ONE
THE ACADEMY

CHAPTER I

THE ACADEMY AT THE TIME OF ARISTOTLE'S ENTRANCE

ACCORDING to the evidence of his biographer, which is reliable, Aristotle wrote to King Philip of Macedon that he had spent twenty years with Plato. Since he was a member of the Academy down to the time of the latter's death (348/7), he must have entered it during 368/7. At that time he was a youth of about 17 years.[1] When he left he was approaching his forties.

These acknowledged facts have aroused far too little remark. That a man of such profoundly original talent should have remained for so long a period under the influence of an outstanding genius of a totally different complexion, and should have grown up wholly in his shadow, is a fact without parallel in the history of great thinkers, and perhaps of all independent and creative natures whatever. There is no safer index to a disciple's powers of assimilation, and at the same time to the strength and sureness of his creative instinct, than his relation to a great master to whom he dedicates his youthful affections. The impersonal spiritual force that works through such a master frees the pupil's powers by constraining them, and ripens him until he is ready to stand alone. Such was Aristotle's intellectual development. It was his experience of Plato's world that enabled him to break through into his own. It was the two together that gave his intellect the marvellous tautness, speed, and elasticity, by means of which he reached a higher level than Plato had, in spite of the definite difference between Plato's unlimited and his own limited genius. Thereafter, to retreat from that level would have been to turn the wheel of fate backwards.

Right down to the present day, Aristotle's philosophical relation to Plato has frequently been supposed to be like that of a modern academic philosopher to Kant. That is to say, in a

---

[1] The letter is mentioned in the Vita Marciana (Rose, *Aristotelis Fragmenta*, p. 427, l. 18 ; see also Ps. Ammon, ibid., p. 438, l. 13, and the Latin trans., p. 443, l. 12). The figure 17 does not appear in this passage, but had been linked up with it at least as early as the Alexandrian biographer, cf. Dionys. Hal. *ad Amm.* 5 (R 728).

mechanical way, he accepted certain bits of his master's doctrine and rejected others. Plato's uniqueness, and his pictorial way of philosophizing, naturally gave rise to the suspicion that Aristotle failed to understand his archetype. It was supposed that he missed the mythical, the plastic, and the intuitive in Plato; and, because they omitted these fundamental aspects, his criticisms seemed almost entirely beside the point. Being thoroughly abstract, they really involved a transition to another genus (μετάβασις εἰς ἄλλο γένος).

What a shortsighted and pettifogging charge! It is clear from several passages that Aristotle was well aware of this feature in Plato's thought before he ever began to criticize him. How could the founder of psychology, and of its application to intellectual and aesthetic processes, possibly have been ignorant of it? It was precisely Aristotle who first described, in short and telling words, the poetic and prophetic elements which the moderns suppose they were the first to discover in Plato; and his definition of the aesthetic nature of the dialogues is better than most of theirs. He never for a moment imagined that in describing the logical and ontological difficulties of Plato's theory he had disposed either of its historical significance or of the absolute value of its contents. This assertion does not need to be supported by quotation. It is self-evident to any one who knows that Aristotle did not approach Plato's views in a cold and critical spirit, but was at first spellbound for many years by the overwhelming personal impression that they made on him as a whole.

It is, however, one thing to understand, and quite another to want to imitate and perpetuate in its entirety, such a complicated world as Plato's, so manifold in its intellectual tendencies and so individual in its presentation. Here is where profitable and unprofitable Platonism part company. It is unprofitable to cultivate an 'aesthetic' and insincere aping of the Platonic spirit, making great play with its favourite images and expressions. It is profitable to work at its problems; and this, which Plato himself recognizes as the most important thing, necessarily leads beyond him. It is also profitable to realize the onesidedness of our modern thought, inevitable though this onesidedness is, by surveying with Aristotle the contrast between our sciences and Plato's irrecoverable spiritual unity. Aristotle's attitude to this problem was different at different times. Beginning by naïvely trying to imitate and continue the Platonic manner, he came to distinguish between the abiding essence and the outward formulation, the latter of which is either determined by the accidents of the age or unique and so inimitable. He then sought to remove the form while retaining the essence. From being a perfected form the Platonic philosophy became to him the matter or ὕλη for something new and higher. He had accepted Plato's doctrines with his whole soul, and the effort to discover his own relation to them occupied all his life, and is the clue to his development. It is possible to discern a gradual progress, in the various stages of which we can clearly recognize the unfolding of his own essential nature. Even his latest productions retain some trace of the Platonic spirit, but it is weaker than in the earlier ones. His own notion of development can be applied to himself: however strong the individuality of the 'matter', the new form finally overcomes its resistance. It grows until it has shaped the matter from within in accordance with its own law, and imposed its own shape upon it. Just as tragedy attains its own special nature (ἔσχε τὴν ἑαυτῆς φύσιν) 'out of the dithyramb' by leading the latter through various forms, so Aristotle made himself out of the Platonic philosophy. The history of his development—and the order of the documents for this can be determined with certainty—represents a definite scale of graduated progress in this direction, although he never got beyond compromises in some matters. In these matters his pupils very often understood him better than he did himself; that is to say, they excised the Platonic element in him and tried to retain only what was pure Aristotle. The specific Aristotle is, however, only half the real Aristotle. This his disciples failed to grasp, but he himself was always conscious of it.

The Academy that Aristotle entered in 367 was no longer that of the time of the *Symposium*, around whose table Plato in the full tide of his enthusiasm had imagined the leaders of art and science and the representatives of Hellenic youth gathered to hear from the lips of the prophetess the great mystery of the birth of the intellect out of Eros. The essence of Plato's philosophy had long ceased to lie in the figure that he had created in his early works, the central figure of the philosopher Socrates. In content and method it was now far beyond the Socratic field of problems. It was only by reading, and not through any living presence of the Socratic spirit in the Academy of the sixties, that Aristotle learnt what Socrates had meant to Plato and his early disciples. The *Phaedo* and the *Gorgias*, the *Republic* and the *Symposium*, were now the evidences, already classical, of a closed chapter in the master's life; and they towered above the busy realities of the school like motionless Gods. Any one whom these dialogues had drawn from distant places to enjoy Plato's actual presence must surely have been surprised to find no mysteries celebrated among the philosophers. They certainly radiated a revolutionizing force and a new seriousness, and these Aristotle found in the Academy also; but their classic doctrines about the Ideas, about unity and multiplicity, about pleasure and pain, about the state, about the soul and virtue, were by no means inviolable sanctuaries in the discussions of the students. They were constantly being tested, defended, and altered, in the light of acute distinctions and laborious examinations of their logical validity. The distinctive feature was that the learners themselves took part in this common effort. The images and myths of the dialogues remained Plato's most characteristic and irrecapturable work; but, on the other hand, the discussion of conceptions became along with the Academy's religious tendency the essential principle of the school. These were the only two elements in Plato's thought that were transferable, and the more students he attracted the more they preponderated over the artistic side of his nature. Where the opposing forces of poetry and dialectic are mixed in a single mind it is natural for the former to be progressively stifled by the latter, but in Plato's case the school carried him irresistibly in this direction.

The set of Aristotle's mind was decided by the fact that he entered the Academy just as this momentous alteration, the development of Plato's later dialectic, was beginning to make headway. Thanks to the recent advances of research we can follow this process with chronological exactitude in the great methodological dialogues that Plato wrote during these years, *Theaetetus, Sophist, Statesman, Parmenides,* and *Philebus.* The first dialogue of the group, the *Theaetetus,* was written soon after the death in 369 of the famous mathematician whose memory it honours.[1] It is the more characteristic of the Academy at the time of Aristotle's entrance because in this and the following dialogues (*Sophist* and *Statesman*) the work of the school, which had been almost entirely concealed in the writings of the classical period, begins to press Plato's whole literary activity into its service, and has thus left a picture of itself that lacks no essential feature.[2] In order to understand Aristotle and his relation to Plato it is important not to set out from the vague notion of 'Plato' as a whole, but to substitute the precise conception of his last period, the abstract and methodological period that began about 369. This gave Aristotle a definite direction, and opened up a field of work suitable to his particular disposition.

Socratic thought always kept close to real life, and the early Plato was a reformer and an artist. In contrast to this, Aristotle's thought was abstract, and his attitude was that of the pure scientist. But these traits were not his private property; they were common to the whole Academy during the time when he belonged to it. In the *Theaetetus* we have the apotheosis of the un-Socratic philosopher of Plato's later days. The machinery of the dialogue gives the delineation of the type to Socrates, but the picture he draws has no resemblance to himself, according to his own faithful characterization of himself in the *Apology*, but to the mathematical recluse; and it is obvious that the new con-

---

[1] For the external reasons for this date see the conclusive arguments of Eva Sachs, *De Theaeteto Atheniensi Mathematico*, Berlin, 1914, pp. 18 ff. The main evidence, of course, comes from the stylistic and philosophical analyses of the dialogue, both of which confirm the external arguments for lateness. The *Sophist*, which is the positive development of the problem of the *Theaetetus*, retains its setting, as does the *Statesman*; but no one nowadays considers the *Sophist* an 'elementary' dialogue coming at the beginning of Plato's development, as did Zeller and those who preceded him. Campbell's fundamental researches took some time to make their way into Germany, but have since been confirmed on all sides by later investigations. The final touch has been given by the history of the development of Plato's dialectic, which is a later addition; see especially J. Stenzel's *Studien zur Entwicklung der platonischen Dialektik* (Breslau, 1917), to which I am much indebted.

[2] Since the appearance of the German edition of this book Friedrich Solmsen has tried to determine more exactly how far the picture presented by the dialectical dialogues agrees with the actual philosophical activities of the Academy, and how far it falls short of it. See his 'Die Entwicklung der aristotelischen Logik und Rhetorik' (*Neue Philologische Untersuchungen*, ed. by Werner Jaeger, vol. iv, Berlin, 1929), p. 240. His observations form a valuable addition to what is said above.

ception of the 'theoretical' life has helped to determine its features. Socrates had concerned himself solely with man, and not with that which is above the heaven or under the earth. The *Theaetetus*, on the other hand, speaks of the philosophical soul as 'geometrizing' and 'astronomizing'.[1] She is indifferent to what is near at hand; she despises precisely those practical activities that occupied the lives of Socrates' favourite hearers; and she roams in lofty distances, as is solemnly quoted from Pindar.

The *Theaetetus* unmistakably refers to the forthcoming appearance of the *Parmenides*. The latter was pretty certainly written before the former's sequels, the *Sophist* and the *Statesman*; hence it was probably finished when Aristotle entered the school, and cannot in any case be much later. Those who suggest that Aristotle was the author of the objections which this dialogue raises to the theory of Ideas, are making the unlikely supposition that he took the initiative in a revolutionary manner while he was still extremely young and had only just entered the society. The dialogue shows that before Aristotle the Academy had already gone far in criticizing the hybrid character of the Ideas, half substances and half abstractions. It could not be long before the two were separated. Plato himself, indeed, thought that he could overcome the difficulties; nevertheless he prepared the way for what happened when he recognized it as in principle correct to make laborious logical and ontological examinations of the Ideas, as is done in this dialogue and in later ones. Aristotle's speculations cannot be linked up with the *Phaedo* or the *Republic* and the Idea-theory as it appears in them.

In the *Theaetetus* Theaetetus and Theodorus are opposite types. One represents the young generation of mathematicians, who are interested in philosophy; the other the old, who will not hear of it, though they are experts in their own subject. It was not an accident that Plato's relations to famous mathematicians found expression in a dialogue precisely at this time. For about the year 367 Eudoxus of Cyzicus brought his school to Athens, in order to discuss with Plato and his followers the problems that interested both parties.[2]

---

[1] *Theaet.* 173 E–174 A.
[2] Tannery's conjecture (*Histoire de l'astronomie*, p. 296, n. 4) is confirmed by

This event attracted a good deal of attention, and from that time on we constantly find members of this school of mathematicians and astronomers in communication with the Academy. Helicon and Athenaeus are examples. As early as the *Republic* we can observe the effects of Theaetetus' discovery of solid geometry. After their intercourse with Eudoxus, Plato and his followers took a very great interest in the attempts of the Cyzicenian school to explain the irregular movements of the planets by simple mathematical suppositions. This was not the only way in which Eudoxus stimulated them. He tremendously enlarged their notions of geography and human culture by bringing exact reports of Asia and Egypt, and by describing from extended personal experience the status of astronomy in those parts. His contribution to ethical questions was also important. The problem of the nature and meaning of pleasure and pain, which was to be so central in Aristotle's ethics, led to one more great debate within the Academy in Plato's later years. Xenocrates, Speusippus, and Aristotle contributed works *On Pleasure* to it; Plato contributed the *Philebus*. Many years afterwards Aristotle, who met Eudoxus right at the beginning of his stay in the Academy, could still speak of his personal impression with real warmth, when he was recalling the stimulus that Eudoxus gave. Eudoxus also raised difficulties about the Ideas and suggested an alteration of the theory.[1] In every field Plato's school began to attract more and more strangers, some of them of the most diverse types. His travels had brought him into close connexion with the Pythagoreans gathered round Archytas at Tarentum. Their influence reached as far as Sicily, and in Sicily at this time there flourished the medical school of Philistion, whose importance was so great that we must reckon

the *Life* (Rose, p. 429, l. 1) according to which Aristotle entered the Academy under Eudoxus. Some excerptor must have misunderstood the statement and taken Eudoxus for an archon. What his authority told him was simply that Aristotle's entry coincided with Eudoxus' presence. Cf. Eva Sachs (who follows F. Jacoby), op. cit., p. 17, n. 2.

[1] For Aristotle on Eudoxus' character and theory of pleasure see *Eth. Nic.* X. 2. For the latter's proposed reformulation of the Idea-theory see *Metaph.* A 9, 991ᵃ 17; and at greater length in the second book *On Ideas* (Rose, frg. 189), which has been preserved by Alexander in his commentary on the passage. Eudoxus proposes to regard participation as the immanence of the Ideas in the things, and to this Aristotle strongly objects. That participation was the most debated problem of the time is clear from Plato's later dialogues.

among its spiritual members such an author and physician as Diocles of Carystus in Euboea. Plato must have had relations with Philistion. The author of the spurious second letter appears to know that Plato visited Philistion, and even seemingly that the latter was invited to Athens. If not Philistion himself, at any rate some real member of his school is concealed behind the unnamed 'Sicilian doctor' whose impatience at the logical hairsplittings of the Academy is described by a contemporary comic poet.[1] Incidentally this story shows that, although Plato was accustomed to converse with specialists in all fields, the result was often merely to reveal the unbridgeable gulf between Ionic or Sicilian science and what Plato understood by that word. The fact that he makes copious use of the latest researches in medicine, mathematics, and astronomy, in order to construct his story of creation in the *Timaeus*, must not blind us to the independent manner in which he handles this material.

The Academy of Plato's later days did indeed get through a great mass of material, and this environment no doubt made it possible for an Aristotle to learn by his own efforts the significance of empirical facts, which later became so integral to his researches; but the present universal custom of speaking of an 'organization of the sciences' in the Academy is wrong.[2] Modern academies and universities cannot claim Plato as their model. The notion of a systematic unity of all sciences was totally foreign to him, and still more so was its realization in an encyclopaedic organization of all subjects for purposes of teaching and research. Medicine, mathematics, astronomy, geography, and anthropology, the whole system of historical sciences, and that of the rhetorical and dialectical arts, to mention only the main channels of Greek thought, arose each by itself, though several were sometimes combined in one person, and went each on its own way undisturbed. To a Theodorus or a Theaetetus it would have seemed a very peculiar notion to combine into one universal system of sciences their mathematics and the researches that some sophists were making into Greek

---

[1] Epicrates frg. 287 (Kock). See also M. Wellmann's *Fragmente der sikelischen Ärzte* (Berlin, 1907), p. 68, and my article 'Das Pneuma im Lykeion' (*Hermes*, vol. 48), p. 51, n. 3.

[2] It has been universal since H. Usener's now famous article in vol. 53 (1884) of the *Preussische Jahrbücher*, reprinted in *Vorträge und Aufsätze*, p. 69.

culture or archaeology. The physicians also stood quite alone. Democritus, and after him Eudoxus, who to some extent anticipates the type that Aristotle represented, are abnormal phenomena. Eudoxus was marvellously manysided. To mathematics and astronomy he joined geography, anthropology, medicine, and philosophy; and was himself productive in the first four fields.

Plato was concerned exclusively with 'Being'. If we are to give him his place in the tradition of Greek thought, he is one of the representatives of the speculation about substance (οὐσία). With his theory of Ideas he gave it a new turn; in fact, he really restored it to life. Starting from the Ideas, and being concerned solely with unity and the supersensible, he does not at first touch the manifold and empirical world at any point. The direction of his inquiries is away from phenomena towards something 'higher'. The sheer necessities of his speculation about concepts did indeed lead him to develop the method of division, which later became enormously important for Aristotle's attempt to get an empirical grasp of plants and animals, as well as of the mental world. But Plato himself was not concerned to reduce individuals to a system. They lay below the realm of Ideas; and, being completely infinite (ἄπειρον), were unknowable. His notion of the individual (ἄτομον) was that of the lowest Form, which is not further divisible and lies on the border between phenomena and Platonic science and reality. The many classifications of plants, &c., that Epicrates speaks of, which were generally felt to be the most characteristic and peculiar occupation followed in the Academy (even Speusippus' great *Resemblances* was apparently concerned solely therewith), were pursued not from interest in the objects themselves, but in order to learn the logical relations of conceptions; this is illustrated by the quantity of books put forward in the school at this time with the title of *Classifications*. In classifying plants the members no more aimed at producing a real botanical system than Plato in the *Sophist* aims at a historical study of the real sophists.[1]

[1] In the fragment previously referred to Epicrates does not imply that the Platonists pursued botanical inquiries in a positive spirit. What he is laughing at is the enthusiasm for classification that led them to hold relations between conceptions more important than the things themselves. 'They were *defining* the world of nature and *dividing* the life (βίον) of animals and the nature of trees

It is no great distance from such classifications of the real to the notion of a single science embracing as many departmental sciences as there are departments of reality (ὄν). And although the articulation of the positive sciences was not effected until Aristotle's notion of reality had replaced Plato's transcendental being,[1] it remains a remarkable fact that the idea of a systematization of the departmental sciences, each of which had arisen independently, was an afterthought due to the Attic philosophy of conceptions and its enthusiasm for classification. It is almost too late now to estimate the advantages and disadvantages of carrying this systematization through in detail. Presumably both have been pretty large. At no period when research was truly flourishing has the general spirit of a particular philosophy ever thoroughly permeated all the sciences; and this is natural since each science has its own spirit and its own principle. Only through dual natures, or where the lead in philosophy has been taken by famous scientists who imbued it with the spirit of particular branches of research, has a partial permeation occurred. Aristotle, Leibniz, and Hegel, very different types, are the most important examples of this.

Plato himself had some specialized understanding of mathematical questions, which enabled him to follow the important contemporary developments of the science. He was also interested in astronomy so far as it could then be treated mathematically. In later life he devoted himself seriously to the physics of the elements, hoping to be able to give a mathematical derivation of the qualitative differences between the so-called

---

and the *species* of vegetables; and among these latter they were examining what is the species of the pumpkin.'

> Περὶ γὰρ φύσεως ἀφοριζόμενοι
> Διεχώριζον ζῴων τε βίον
> Δένδρων τε φύσιν λαχάνων τε γένη,
> κᾆτ' ἐν τούτοις τὴν κολοκύντην
> ἐξήταζον τίνος ἐστὶ γένους.

Here βίος does not mean the habits of animals, which would be δίαιτα. It is the same as 'nature' and 'genus', and these are actual terms from Plato's dialectic, as are 'definition', 'division', and 'examination', of conceptions. The fragments of Speusippus' Ὅμοια have been collected by P. Lang, *De Speusippi Academici scriptis* (Bonn, 1911, Diss.). The title itself shows what the aim of the book was.

[1] 'There are as many parts of philosophy as there are kinds of substances', Arist. *Metaph.* Γ 2, 1004ᵃ 2.

elements of Empedocles, which he regarded as mere phases. His only other interests in phenomena lay in the sphere of medicine and in that of ethics and politics. In the latter he collected, especially for the *Laws*, extensive material on criminal law and the history of civilization. It was thus during the period when Aristotle was a member of the school that he turned his attention to particulars. And the stimulus that his collection of new historical and political matter gave to Aristotle is clear from the numerous coincidences between the *Laws* and the *Politics*. On the other hand, Aristotle lacked the temperament and the ability for anything more than an elementary acquaintance with the Academy's chief preoccupation, mathematics; while the Academy, contrariwise, could not stimulate him in the field of biological science in which his own true genius lay.

Fruitful and congenial as was the youthful Aristotle's experience of the strict and methodical procedure of the various sciences, the impression made upon him by Plato's personality was the strongest of all. Plato surveyed all those fertile plains from the high vantage-point of his own creative spirit and inward vision, and Aristotle was wholly preoccupied with him.

It is not our purpose here to discuss the influence of Plato's personality on his contemporaries, or to reduce his position in the history of knowledge to a formula, although to a man like Aristotle this latter question was naturally the kernel of his whole attitude to Plato. The elements out of which his work arose did not include either Ionic ἱστορία (inquiry) or the rationalizing Enlightenment of the sophists, although these two, in spite of their disparity, together constituted the forms of knowledge *par excellence* at the time. The first of these elements was (1) the *phronesis* or wisdom of Socrates. This bore only a superficial resemblance to the rationalism of the sophists. Essentially it was rooted in the realm, hitherto undiscovered by Greek science and philosophy, of an ethical consciousness of absolute standards. It demanded a new and superempirical conception of intellectual intuition. The second and third elements, which were also foreign to contemporary thought, were two new additions to the Socratic philosophy, produced by giving *phronesis* a supersensible object and making this a 'form'. These were (2) the Idea, which was the result of a long process

of visual and aesthetic development in the Greek mind, and
(3) the long-neglected study of οὐσία or substance, to which Plato
gave new material by the problem of the one and the many, and
living and tangible content by the invention of the Ideas. The
last element was (4) the dualism of the Orphic myth of the soul,
to which his whole constitution inclined him, and which, watered
by his fertile imagination, took firm root in the new conception
of being.

When we consider these four elements it is not difficult to
suppose that he affected the ordinary educated person as a
mixture of poet, reformer, critic, and prophet. (The strictness
with which he imposed his new method on himself would not at
first make any difference to this impression.) Hence it is not
surprising that, in view of the gulf between him and all other
science, both ancient and modern, he has been called a mystic
and expelled from the history of thought. If this simple solution
were right, however, it would be very hard to understand why
he has had such a great influence on the destinies of human
knowledge; and the fact that he was the sun around which
revolved persons like Theaetetus, Eudoxus, and Aristotle, that
is to say, the most talented pioneers of scientific research that
the fourth century produced, is sufficient to condemn the cheap
wisdom whose notion of the complexity of intellectual currents
is so inadequate that it would strike the most revolutionary of
all philosophers out of the history of knowledge, because he
discovered not merely new facts but also new dimensions.

Aristotle saw as clearly as Eudoxus that Plato, in his philosophical work, had welded together scientific discoveries,
elements of myth, and mysterious spiritual realms to which the
eye of knowledge had never penetrated. This weld was by no
means the mere result of the creator's subjective inclination; it
was necessarily determined by the historical situation, the
elements in which were later analysed by Aristotle with a
profound understanding alike of the creation and of its creator.
At first, however, he abandoned himself without reserve to
this incomparable and indivisible world, as is shown by the
fragments of his early writings, and it was precisely the
non-scientific elements in Plato's philosophy, that is, the metaphysical and religious parts of it, that left the most lasting

imprint on his mind. He must have been unusually receptive for such impressions. It was their conflict with his own scientific and methodical tendencies that later gave rise to most of his problems; and their strength is beautifully shown by the fact that he never sacrificed them, although in scientific matters he went beyond Plato at every point. In Plato he sought and found a man to lead him in a new life, just as in his dialogue *Nerinthus* he makes the simple Corinthian countryman, enthralled by the *Gorgias*, abandon his plough to seek and follow the master.

Plato explains the connexion between knowing the good and following it in his seventh letter. The knowledge which according to Socrates makes men good, and that which is commonly called scientific knowledge, are distinct. The former is creative, and can only be attained by souls that have a fundamental affinity to the object to be known, namely, the good, the just, and the beautiful. There is nothing to which Plato right down to the end of his life was more passionately opposed than the statement that the soul can know what is just without *being* just.[1] This, and not the systematization of knowledge, was his aim in founding the Academy. It remained his aim to the end, as is shown by this letter that he wrote in his old age. Let there be a communion (συӡῆν) of the elect, of those who, once their souls have grown up in the atmosphere of good, are able by virtue of their superior equipment to share at last in the knowledge that is 'like a light kindled by leaping fire'. It seems to him, Plato says, that the search after this knowledge is a thing not for the mass of mankind, but only for the few who with a slight hint can find it for themselves.[2]

[1] *Ep.* VII. 344 A. [2] Ibid. 341 C–E.

CHAPTER II
EARLY WORKS

ARISTOTLE wrote a series of works in dialogue form. The fragments that remain of them are not studied as much as they should be, partly because it is pleasanter to leave such troublesome work to philologists, but also because of the conviction, which has always obtained in the Peripatetic school, that the true Aristotle is to be found in the treatises. Even if we only wish to understand the treatises, however, the fragments of the lost dialogues can teach us a great deal. If we knew nothing else about the relation between the two kinds of writing, it would be highly significant to be able to determine that the dialogues, modelled on those of Plato, belong almost entirely to Aristotle's early years, and that in his later period he practically abandoned literary activity (since the treatises are merely the written basis of his very extensive activities as teacher and lecturer). There are indeed exceptions to this statement. *Alexander or Colonization* must, to judge from its title, have been a dialogue belonging to the time when Alexander's racial policy in Asia obliged Aristotle to make public announcement of his disapproval to the Greek-reading world. This straggler therefore had a special reason in Aristotle's political position. *Mutatis mutandis*, the same is true of the collection of 158 Constitutions, which was intended for publication and was written in a clear and lively style, as we can tell from that of the Constitution of Athens. In spite of these exceptions, however, it remains true to say that in the course of his development Aristotle radically altered his views about the necessity of presenting science in literary form, and about the relation between literary and truly productive work.

With Plato the primary impulse was originally the formative one. He did not write in order to set out the contents of his doctrine. His desire was to show the philosopher in the dramatic instant of seeking and finding, and to make the doubt and conflict visible; and that not in a mere intellectual operation, but in the fight against pseudo-science, political power, society, and his own heart; for the spirit of Plato's philosophy necessarily collided with all these forces. According to his original view of it, philosophy is not a sphere of theoretical discoveries but a reorganization of all the fundamental elements of life. Consider, for example, the paradoxical picture of the philosopher in the *Theaetetus*, or the duel between the Socrates of the *Gorgias* and Callicles, who represents the egoistical, might-is-right view of state and society. These dialogues have nothing but the name in common with the didactic conversations of Giordano Bruno, Hume, or Schopenhauer. Plato was writing the philosopher's tragedy. Unlike his imitators he never gave mere theoretical differences of opinion under a stylistic veneer.

The *Theaetetus*, which is contemporary with Aristotle's entrance into the Academy, is the first of a group of dialogues that are radically different from the earlier ones both in form and in content; and it ushers in the transference of Plato's main philosophical interests to methodological, analytical, and abstract studies.[1] In this group the equilibrium between the aesthetic and the philosophical elements in Plato's mind is destroyed for the sake of the latter. The discords, clearly perceptible to delicate ears, begin to appear in the *Theaetetus*. They are due not so much to the lack of outward polish in the form as to the conquest of Plato's dramatic impulse by his abstract interest in method, to the consistent pursuit of a single question along a single level track. A man can indeed find Plato the dramatist even here, so long as he is able to detect reversal of fortunes (περιπέτεια) and complication (πλοκή) even in the development of methodological and abstract ideas. But in spite of the artistic elaborateness of its construction it remains significant that this very dialogue seems to most modern philosophers Plato's 'greatest philosophical achievement'. It is in fact almost a treatise, positive though critical; and it is not an accident that in the introduction Plato refers to his previous

---

[1] J. Stenzel was the first to give any thorough account of the connexion between Plato's philosophical development and his form. See his address 'Literarische Form und philosophischer Gehalt des platonischen Dialogs', *Jahresbericht d. Schlesischen Gesellschaft für vaterl. Kultur*, 1916; reprinted in *Studien zur Entwicklungsgeschichte der platonischen Dialektik*, &c., Breslau, 1917, pp. 123 ff. For the late dialogues see the chapter on 'Die neue Methode', pp. 45 ff.

method of writing dialogues, and announces simplifications the aim of which is to give greater scientific lucidity and directness to the exposition.[1]

The *Sophist* and the *Statesman* show more clearly the difficulty that Plato now has with the dialogue form. The application of the method of division to a particular conception, descending step by step from the universal to the particular, is such an undramatic and monotonous procedure that at the beginning of the *Sophist* the leader of the discussion is obliged to tell his interlocutors not to interrupt him too often, or preferably to listen to a continuous speech.[2] This amounts to openly abandoning Socrates' 'obstetric' method of discussion, and announcing that from now on the dialogue form is nothing but an unessential stylistic ornament. The *Timaeus* and the *Philebus* are not exceptions; what they offer to the reader as dialogue is merely a transparent veil of style thrown over a purely doctrinal content. It is not any vivacity in the conversation that gives the *Timaeus* its tremendous effectiveness. The *Philebus* could be transformed without difficulty into a methodical and unified treatise much like Aristotle's *Ethics*. In the *Laws* the last trace of scenic illusion is gone. The delineation of character (ἠθοποιία) is consciously renounced; and the whole is a solemn address or proclamation, not by Socrates but by Plato himself, the stranger from Athens.[3]

As was logical, the figure of Socrates, after having been rele-

[1] *Theaet.* 143 B. The *Theaetetus* retains the outward form of a Socratic dialogue, and frequently makes express reference to Socrates' midwifery. But this very selfconscious reflection on the nature and limits of the Socratic method, which is strongly emphasized, shows that Plato is now purposely using the old form of cross-examination (ἔλεγχος) merely to clear the ground for his question about the definition of knowledge. Stenzel rightly points out the close connexion between the *Theaetetus* and the *Sophist*; the latter solves the problems raised by the former, and it does not use 'midwifery'. Cf. Socrates' final words at *Theaet.* 210 C: 'These are the limits of my art; I can no farther go.'

[2] *Soph.* 217 D. It is true that they are still going to give remark for remark (ἔπος πρὸς ἔπος), it being assumed that the answerer will always say yes; but that is something quite different from the old 'obstetric' conversation 'by question and answer', where the questioner puts forward no views but only gets the answerer to do so.

[3] The author of the *Epinomis* judges the real state of affairs correctly in 980 D. He makes the Athenian remind the two others of a famous passage of the *Laws* in words that absolutely abandon all dramatic reality: 'if you remember; for, to be sure, you made notes (ὑπομνήματα) at the time'. Here we are suddenly in the middle of a lecture.

gated to minor roles from the *Sophist* onwards, is finally dropped
in the *Laws*. In the *Philebus* he appears once more, for the last
time, because this dialogue discusses questions that had been
raised by the real Socrates. (The answers are obtained, however,
by means of methods that would never have occurred to him.)
In this last period the separation between the historical Socrates
and Plato's own philosophizing is complete. And that is another
sign that his general tendency towards science, logic, and dogma
is seeking self-expression. The last fruit of the theory of Forms
was the methods of classification and abstraction, which are
what Plato means by dialectic in the narrow sense of his later
works. These methods had revolutionized the form of the
controversial dialogue that arose out of the Socratic cross-
examination. They had made it psychologically meaningless and
almost turned it into a treatise. No further progress was possible
in this direction. It was only a question of time before the great
art of the classical Platonic dramas died out, for its root was
dead. This was the moment at which the young Aristotle began
to take a hand.[1]

All members of the Academy wrote dialogues, though none
wrote more and weightier ones than Aristotle. This fact is
significant for the relation of the new generation to Plato. They
all used the dialogue as a ready-made form, without asking
themselves how far such an imitation was possible. The Greeks
naturally tended to imitate everything once it was 'discovered';
and they had not yet realized that Plato's dialogue in its
classical perfection was something absolutely inimitable, the
flower of a unique combination of historical necessity, individual
creative power, and particular experience. His pupils regarded
the dialogue as the established vehicle for giving living form to
esoteric philosophy, and hence every one desired to see the
master's effect on himself reproduced in such a medium. But
the more they realized that, because of the intimate unity
of his personality, life, and works, Plato was an indivisible

[1] No one has yet tried to connect Aristotle's dialogue with the development
of Plato's form. R. Hirzel (*Der Dialog*, p. 275) does not even put the question.
Using a merely general impression of Plato's dialogues, he can only see the
Aristotelian type as opposed to it. He regards the two kinds as due simply to
the difference in the characters of the two authors, and does not do justice to
the factors inherent in the situation.

magnitude that could not be taken over as a whole without producing either a dead scholasticism or a literary dilettantism, the more they consciously set themselves to find fundamentally new forms for that which was scientific and objective in him and so could be detached. These attempts properly took their departure not from the dialogues but from Plato's oral teaching. It is significant both of the youthful Aristotle's natural affinity to Plato and of his inability to view him objectively that he did not at once take this way, but began by continuing the dialogue. Clearly he found the essential Plato more alive, more powerful, and more objective, in the dialogue than in any other form.

The remaining fragments of his dialogues, together with the reports of antiquity and the imitations of later writers (he had an especially powerful influence on Cicero), enable us to infer that Aristotle invented a new kind of literary dialogue, namely the dialogue of scientific discussion. He rightly saw that the shadow-existence of the 'obstetric' question and answer must be done away, since it had lost its real function by becoming a mere cloak for 'long speeches'; but, while Plato in his later days was tending to replace dialogue by dogmatic lecture, Aristotle set speech against speech, thus reproducing the actual life of research in the later Academy. One of the speakers took the lead, gave the subject, and summed up the results at the end. This naturally put narrow limits to the delineation of personality. The art of writing the speeches was taken over from rhetoric and developed in accordance with the precepts of Plato's *Phaedrus*. The dialogue now depended for its effect more on its character (ἦθος) as a whole than on the *ethopoeia* of particular persons; and, while it lost in aesthetic objectivity, it presumably gained in unity of mood and tendency. It was, therefore, only logical for Aristotle finally to make himself the leader in his own dialogues.

This alteration, while it did not restore the original Socratic purpose of the dialogue (that was irretrievably lost), gave it once more a real content, one that corresponded to the new form of the conversations in which it had always had its root. Instead of the arena of arguments, with the dramatic thrust and counter-thrust of eristical duels, there were long theoretical examinations and demonstrations, conducted according to strict method. The change may be deplored; but it was inevitable, as Plato had recognized when he abandoned 'obstetric' conversation and the delineation of character. The historians of literature, who do not see what inner forces were at work, suppose themselves to have established that Aristotle brought about the decline of the dialogue. On the contrary, he merely performed the inevitable transition to another stage. The dialogue of discussion is simply an expression of the fact that the scientific element in Plato finally burst its form and remoulded it to suit itself. It was not a mere matter of aesthetics; it was a development of the philosophic mind, which necessarily produced its own new form.

It is customary to apply the casual remarks of later writers about the characteristics of Aristotle's dialogue to *all* of them, but the mere titles show that that is impossible. *Eudemus or On the Soul* and *Gryllus or On Rhetoric* cannot have been very different from the earlier Platonic type of which the *Phaedo* and the *Gorgias* are examples. One of the fragments of the *Eudemus* still retains the Socratic technique of question and answer.[1] Whether Aristotle appeared as leader of the discussion in dialogues of this type is to be doubted. Those in which we are told that he was the leader, the *Statesman* in two books and the *Philosophy* in three, were obviously almost didactic works, and thus entirely different.[2] Plato's example ought to be enough to

---

[1] Frg. 44. (I give the numbers of the fragments according to the Teubner edition of Rose's *Aristotelis Fragmenta*, 1886. They are different from those in the earlier Academy edition.) There is, however, no midwifery about this question and answer. It is the learner who asks questions, while the other gives him systematic information. The conversation is reported by a third person, as in the earlier Plato. Aristotle thus does not use the principle laid down at the beginning of the *Theaetetus*.

[2] Frgs. 8, 9, and 78. The last passage (Cic. *Ep. ad Quintum fr.* III. 5, 1) seems to refer not merely to the *Statesman* ('de praestante viro') but also to the books *On Justice* ('de republica', cf. next note), which Cicero must have known. As soon as we look at the passages concerned without presuppositions, it becomes obvious that there is no point in the attempts to explain the 'contradiction' in Cicero's statements about the *mos Aristotelius*. In *Ad Att.* XIII. 19, 4, he says it is Aristotelian for the author himself to lead the discussion. In *Ad fam.* I. 9, 23, he calls the style of his books *De Oratore* Aristotelian, although he is not himself the leader in them. In each place he is right. Aristotle did not take the lead in all his dialogues; in the *Gryllus* and the *Eudemus* he certainly did not appear at all. It is Aristotelian to have a series of long speeches; it is Aristotelian to have a special introduction to each book of a dialogue; it is Aristotelian to put oneself into the dialogue. But there is no passage which says that a dialogue is not Aristotelian unless it exhibits all three of these peculiarities at once. We must not try to squeeze a single and constant type of

prevent us from supposing that Aristotle had a fixed form which he never changed. As a matter of fact, his development as a writer of dialogue includes all stages from 'obstetric' conversation to the pure treatise. It runs parallel to his development as a philosopher, or rather is its organic expression.

It is often possible to show that particular Aristotelian dialogues are modelled on particular Platonic ones, especially in their contents. The *Eudemus* is related in this way to the *Phaedo*, the *Gryllus* to the *Gorgias*, and the books *On Justice* to the *Republic*.[1] The *Sophist* and the *Statesman*, like the *Symposium* and the *Menexenus*, were naturally suggested by Plato's dialogues of the same name. The *Protrepticus*, which was not a dialogue, reveals the influence of the protreptic passages in Plato's *Euthydemus*, even to verbal echoes. Plato may have appeared as a speaker in the dialogues.

The style also shows very close dependence. It seems indeed that Aristotle soon attained his own manner, a style whose only aim was to be pure and clear, such as naturally belongs to the pure scientist ;[2] but the *Eudemus*, for example, contained myths ; and it had other lively graces, such as frequent similes, partly based on well-known Platonic models, which were famous in later antiquity. In the simile of the subterranean men coming up into the light and seeing the heaven, the power of the language carries one away. The myth of Midas echoes the apocalyptic style of the Fates in the last book of the *Republic*. Cicero praises the golden stream of the prose in Aristotle's

---

Aristotelian dialogue out of our authorities. The same is true of the statement that Aristotle attacked the theory of Forms 'in the dialogues'.

[1] That the books *On Justice* are modelled on the *Republic* can be inferred with certainty from (1) the existence of so many corresponding dialogues and (2) the fact that Cicero in his *De Republica* makes use of both works. In Plato's *Republic* the political philosophy develops out of the problem of justice, just as it must have done in the books *On Justice*. The *Republic* must have already obtained the subtitle *On Justice* by the time of Aristotle, a fact important for the history of the origin of the subtitles of the Platonic dialogues.

[2] The only mark of good style laid down by previous rhetoricians that Aristotle recognizes is lucidity (*Rhet.* III, 1404[b] 1, 1414[a] 19; *Poet.* 1458[a] 18. Cf. J. Stroux, *De Theophrasti virtutibus dicendi*, Leipzig, 1912, p. 30). Lucidity is said to include everything. This ideal is intended not so much for practical oratory as for the creation of a pure and scientifically accurate style. It was dropped again by Theophrastus and all later students of rhetoric. They bowed to the taste of the times, but Aristotle thinks of knowledge as a force that must alter everything, language included.

dialogues. Rhetorical affectations are entirely absent; clear and exact in thought, fine and moving in character, these writings appealed to the best men of later antiquity. It is evidence of their intellectual breadth that Crates the Cynic and Philiscus the cobbler read the *Protrepticus* together in the shop, that Zeno and Chrysippus, Cleanthes, Posidonius, Cicero, and Philo, were strongly influenced in religious considerations by these works of Aristotle's youth, and that Augustine, who came to know the *Protrepticus* through Cicero's *Hortensius*, was led by it to religion and Christianity.[1] The Neo-Platonists lived by Aristotle's dialogues as much as by Plato's; and the *Consolatio* of Boethius sounds the last medieval echo of the religious element in them. As works of art antiquity did not mention them in the same breath with Plato's, though it valued them greatly; but their religious influence on the Hellenistic age was almost more important than Plato's thoroughly distant, objective, and non-inspirational art.

But what was Aristotle's *philosophical* relation to Plato in those works? It would be strange if the influence of his model had been confined to the choice of subject-matter, and to details of style and content, while the general attitude to Plato was one of rejection, as it later became. *Symposium, Menexenus, Sophist, Statesman*—were they really written to outdo Plato's dialogues of the same names, and to show how the questions discussed in them ought to have been handled? Did the disciple obstinately and pedantically dog the master's footsteps in order to reduce each one of his works to shreds in turn? Before ascribing to him such a malady of taste and tact men should have given more serious attention to the other possibility that the purpose of these dialogues was simply and solely to follow Plato, in philosophy as well as in all other respects.

The understanding of the dialogues has had a curiously unfortunate destiny ever since the recovery of the treatises through Andronicus in the time of Sulla. At that time they

---

[1] For the *Protrepticus* in the cobbler's shop see frg. 50. For Augustine's conversion by the *Hortensius* see *Confess.* III. 4, 7: 'Ille vero liber mutavit affectum meum et ad te ipsum, domine, mutavit preces meas et vota ac desideria mea fecit alia. Viluit mihi repente omnis vana spes et immortalitatem sapientiae concupiscebam aestu cordis incredibili et surgere coeperam, ut ad te redirem' (cf. also VIII, 7, 17).

were still much read and highly thought of; but they soon began to lose ground, when the learned Peripatetics undertook the exact interpretation of the long-neglected treatises and wrote commentary after commentary upon them. The Neo-Platonists made some use of them, in contrast to the treatises, as sources of uncontaminated Platonism; but a strictly Peripatetic interpreter like the acute Alexander of Aphrodisias does not know what to make of them, though he must have read most of them. More naïve in philological matters than was necessary at that time, he explained the relation between them and the treatises by saying that the latter contained Aristotle's true views, and the former the false opinions of other persons![1] It was therefore recognized at that time that there were contradictions between the two kinds. The unsuccessful efforts of the later Peripatetics to explain this puzzling state of affairs can be detected in the notorious tradition about the difference between the exoteric and the esoteric writings. Students naturally looked for an explanation of the dialogues in the treatises. They found it in the phrase 'exoteric discourses', which occurs several times and in some instances can easily be referred to the published dialogues. In opposition to these exoteric discourses, which were intended for the outside world, they then set up the treatises as a body of secret esoteric doctrine, although there is no hint of any such notion or expression in Aristotle. Thus the relation between the contents of the dialogues and those of the treatises appeared to be like that of opinion to truth. In some passages, indeed, Aristotle must have been purposely deserting the truth, because he thought that the masses were incapable of grasping it. Even the difficulty of the technical terms in the treatises, which gave later scholars many headaches, was pressed into the service of this mystical interpretation, and a letter was forged in which Aristotle wrote to Alexander that the terms were purposely made obscure in order to mislead the uninitiated.

[1] Elias in Arist. *Categ.* 24[b] 33: 'Alexander explains the difference between the lecture-notes and the dialogues differently, namely that in the lecture-notes he gives his own opinions and the truth, while in the dialogues he gives the opinions of others, which are false.' In spite of the *naïveté* of the expression the commentator surely represents the essence of Alexander's view correctly. Contradictions between the two kinds of writing were noted as early as Cicero (*De Fin.* V. 5, 12). In those days they were ascribed to the literary form of popular writing.

Modern criticism has been sceptical about this mystification, which is obviously a late invention originating in the spirit of Neo-Pythagoreanism.[1] Nevertheless it has not got rid of the prejudice against the dialogues.[2] This is, of course, more difficult for the moderns than it was for the ancients, because we now have only fragments to work with. Rather, therefore, than believe these few but precious remnants, scholars have relied on 'the authorities', and especially on two statements, one in Plutarch and one in Proclus, both coming from the same source, which speak of the criticisms of the Idea-theory that Aristotle made in his *Ethics*, *Physics*, and *Metaphysics*, 'and in his exoteric dialogues'.[3] These passages seemed to provide unshakable proof that in the dialogues Aristotle had already adopted the position in which he stands in the critical works. It was therefore necessary either to put his 'defection' from Plato early during his stay in the Academy or to put the dialogues later. It was not difficult to find another 'authority' for the first supposition. Diogenes Laertius says that Aristotle fell away while Plato was still alive, whereat Plato remarked, 'Aristotle has kicked me, as foals do their mothers when they are born.'[4] Under the influence of these passages Bernays, in his colourful book on Aristotle's dialogues, made a determined attempt to explain away every

[1] It was Andronicus' revival of the study of the treatises that first raised the problem of the relation between these sources of 'pure' Aristotelian doctrine and the exoteric writings, which up to that time had been almost the only Aristotle read. This revival occurred during the full tide of Neo-Pythagoreanism, which in accordance with its nature always looked for a special secret doctrine in all previous thinkers. This notion was then applied to Aristotle's writings.

[2] Just recently two works have appeared in which for the first time it is recognized that the contents of the dialogues are Platonic. In 'Über Aristoteles' Entwicklung' (*Festgabe für Georg von Hertling*, Freiburg, 1913), Dyroff has collected in a brief form numerous echoes of Plato in the dialogues. His point of view is mostly systematic. He does not go closely into the particular works, as indeed was impossible in his limits. His paper did not come into my hands until these studies had been written down. It confirms me in my view; yet we now need exact interpretation, as is shown by Dyroff's view of the dialogue *On Philosophy*. A. Kail's dissertation for the doctorate at Vienna (*Diss. Phil. Vindob.* XI. 67) also reached me subsequent to my own investigations. He discusses the *Eudemus* and the dialogue *On Philosophy* only. His general standpoints, which are von Arnim's, are right, and he gets good results in detail, but philosophically he is not profound. Neither of these works has any notion of linking up the problem of the dialogues with that of the growth of the treatises.

[3] Frg. 8.   [4] Diog. L. V. 2.

Platonic turn in the fragments as an outburst of lyrical feeling. Contrariwise, Valentin Rose fastened upon them eagerly as proofs of his fantastical view that all the lost dialogues were spurious.[1] What both scholars had in common was simply the irrational conviction that a man of such strict and systematic mind as Aristotle would never abandon opinions once formed. They supposed that from the very beginning his own writings were sharply critical of Plato, and the idea that he went through a Platonic phase seemed to them an intolerable contradiction of the sober, cool, and critical nature of his own understanding.

The conclusion is obvious. If this inwardly consistent view is untenable as a whole, if Aristotle began by going through a Platonic period that lasted a score of years, if he wrote works in Plato's spirit and supported his view of the universe, then our whole previous notion of the man's nature is destroyed, and we must hammer out a new conception both of his personality and its history and of the forces that moulded his philosophy. In fact, this myth of a cool, static, unchanging, and purely critical Aristotle, without illusions, experiences, or history, breaks to pieces under the weight of the facts which up to now have been artificially suppressed for its sake. It is not really surprising that the ancient Aristotelians did not know what to make of the dialogues, especially as it was to their interest to draw a clear distinction between Plato and Aristotle and make the latter's doctrine as much of a unity as possible. To them the collection of treatises was a single systematic unity without chronological distinctions. They had not yet learnt to apply the notion of development, which Aristotle himself could have given them, to the history of a philosophy or an individual. So there was nothing for it but to dismiss the dialogues as giving un-Aristotelian views, and to explain them as a piece of popular literary hackwork. In any case, even before we begin to interpret them, it is certain that the dialogues contradict the treatises. Where their affinities lie is shown by the fact that the Neo-Platonists and other admirers of Plato's religion and philosophy valued them and ranked them equal to Plato's own writings.

---

[1] J. Bernays, *Die Dialoge des Aristoteles in ihrem Verhältnis zu seinen übrigen Werken*, Berlin, 1863; Valentin Rose, *Aristoteles Pseudepigraphus*, Leipzig, 1863.

Examples of this will be given later. It only remains to consider the evidence of Plutarch and Proclus, which made Bernays feel obliged to deny *a priori* all traces of Platonism in the dialogues.

This argument also gives way as soon as we examine it closely. In the first place, it is not two different pieces of evidence; the correspondence in the expression makes it certain that both authors were following the same authority, since Proclus does not seem to have followed Plutarch. What the passage says is that Aristotle opposed Plato's theory of Forms not merely in his *Ethics*, *Physics*, and *Metaphysics*, but also in the exoteric dialogues. As evidence for this Plutarch and Proclus quote, both from the same source, a passage from one of the dialogues where Aristotle represents himself as saying that he cannot sympathize with the dogma of Forms, even if he should be suspected of disagreeing out of contentiousness.[1] This shows that both accounts are founded on a concrete historical situation in a particular dialogue (most probably that *On Philosophy*, in which we know that Aristotle attacked other parts of Plato's

[1] Frg. 8. Proclus (in his work *Examination of Aristotle's Objections to Plato's Timaeus* in Joannes Philoponus *De Mundi Aetern.* II. 2, p. 31, 17 Rabe): 'There is none of Plato's doctrines that that man [i.e. Aristotle] rejected more decidedly than the theory of Ideas. Not merely does he call the Forms sounds in the logical works, but in the *Ethics* he attacks the good-in-itself and in the physical works he denies that coming-to-be can be explained by the Ideas. This he says in the work *On Coming-to-be and Passing-away*; and much more so in the *Metaphysics*, for there he is concerned with first principles, and he makes long objections to the Ideas both in the beginning and in the middle and in the end of that work. *In the dialogues* also he exclaims unmistakably that he cannot sympathize with this dogma, even if he *should be suspected of disagreeing out of contentiousness* (κἄν τις αὐτὸν οἴηται διὰ φιλονεικίαν ἀντιλέγειν).'

Plutarch *adv. Colot.* 14 (1115 B): 'Aristotle is always harping on the Ideas, with regard to which he objects to Plato; and he raises all sorts of difficulty about them in his ethical, ⟨in his metaphysical,⟩ and in his physical notes, and also *by means of his exoteric dialogues*, ʃo that *some thought him contentious* rather than philosophical . . . these dogmas, as if he were proposing to undermine Plato's philosophy' (φιλονεικότερον ἐνίοις ἔδοξεν). The original source, which both follow, and which the later author, Proclus, reproduces more accurately, listed separately *all* the places in Aristotle's works that attack the theory of Forms. Thus three passages are mentioned from the *Metaphysics*, Books A, Z, and MN. The mention of *Post. Anal.* I. 22, 83ᵃ 33, like that of *Nic. Eth.* I. 4, recalls the actual words of the original. It is the same with the passage that I have printed in italics (which comes from the dialogue *On Philosophy*). This was the only passage that the author could discover in the dialogues, although his list is obviously very careful and complete. This catalogue is thus direct proof that this polemic was unique in the dialogues.

metaphysics). To universalize this and apply it to all the dialogues
is illegitimate. All it proves is, what we already knew, that there
were one or two dialogues in which Aristotle opposed Plato.
This gives us no justification whatever for explaining away the
Platonic views that we find in other dialogues. Rather we must
recognize that these works evince a development in philosophical
matters, precisely as we demonstrated that they do in form.

As a matter of fact, Plutarch himself, although he has hitherto
been supposed to show that Aristotle was completely opposed to
Plato even in his dialogues, gives us explicit and unmistakable
proof of the fact of Aristotle's philosophical development. In a
passage that has been entirely neglected[1] he actually mentions
Aristotle as the outstanding example of the fact that the true
philosopher will alter his views without regret, and indeed with
joy, as soon as he perceives his error. Aristotle, Democritus, and
Chrysippus all changed their earlier philosophical opinions in this
way; and the word that Plutarch uses for the change (μετατίθεσθαι)
proves that he cannot be referring to questions of minor importance, since it was a technical term in Hellenistic philosophy for
the passage from one school to another. Moreover he must have
known that the 'earlier views' in question (τὰ πρόσθεν αὐτῷ
ἀρέσκοντα) were expressed in Aristotle's dialogues. This becomes
clear if we look back once more at the other passage and examine
it carefully. 'Aristotle attacked Plato not merely in the treatises,
but also in the dialogues, as appears from this and that passage.'
The contrast obviously involves the tacit assumption that we
have here something remarkable and contrary to the ordinary
rule. As a general thing Plutarch must have considered
Aristotle's dialogues evidence of a Platonic point of view; this
is suggested also by the fact that he occasionally speaks of them
as 'Aristotle's Platonic works'.[2]

---

[1] Plut. *de virt. mor.* c. 7, pp. 447 ff.: 'In philosophical speculations why is it
not painful to have one's opinions altered by others and *to change one's mind*
(μετατίθεσθαι) frequently? *Aristotle* himself and Democritus and Chrysippus
gave up some of the opinions that formerly satisfied them without fuss or chagrin
and even with pleasure. . . . Therefore when the true appears reason gladly
inclines to it and abandons the false.' I have drawn attention to the passage
for the first time in *Hermes*, LXIV (1929), p. 22.

[2] Plut. *adv. Colot.* 20: 'as Aristotle said in his Platonic works (ἐν τοῖς Πλατωνικοῖς). This is usually referred to the dialogue *On Philosophy*. It is true that
an unimpeachable tradition informs us that this dialogue contained an attack

As we saw above, these facts were not so clear to everybody in later antiquity as they were to Plutarch. This is shown by an important statement of Eusebius' about the great polemical work written against Aristotle by Isocrates' pupil Cephisodorus.[1] This work must have been a product of the competition between the Academy and the school of Isocrates, belonging to the time when Aristotle, then a youthful member of Plato's school, was introducing the study of rhetoric there and thus causing the latent rivalry of the two institutions to break out into the open. Eusebius tells us that Cephisodorus took up arms against Plato's theory of Ideas and all his other doctrines in turn, and he expresses surprise that Cephisodorus should have saddled Aristotle with these opinions. In accordance with the prevailing notion Eusebius thought of Aristotle as the natural antipode of Plato. He (or his authority Numenius) did not know, and hardly could have known at that late date, that the Aristotle whom Cephisodorus had in mind was entirely different from the one that the treatises, not published until centuries later, made familiar to readers of imperial times. Cephisodorus knew Aristotle only through his literary publications, that is to say, through the dialogues that he wrote while still a member of the Academy; and since when he writes a book against Aristotle he attacks the theory of Ideas, we have simply got to learn that up to that time

on Plato; but if, as is likely, the phrase 'the Platonic works' had become an established name for the whole group of dialogues, there was nothing to prevent that *On Philosophy* from being also described in this way. The majority of these writings were really Platonic not merely in form but also in doctrine.

[1] Euseb. *Praep. Evang.* XIV. 6 (he tells us that he is here following Numenius): 'Now this Cephisodorus, when he saw his teacher Isocrates being criticized by Aristotle, *was ignorant of and unfamiliar with Aristotle himself*; but since he saw that Plato's views were celebrated, *and since he thought that Aristotle philosophized after the manner of Plato, he attacked Aristotle with criticisms that applied to Plato, and argued against him beginning with the Forms and ending with the rest*; about which he himself knew nothing, but merely guessed at the common opinion about them.' At the end of this section there is another passage to the same effect: 'This Cephisodorus argued not against the person he was attacking [i.e. Aristotle], but against some one he did not wish to attack' [i.e. Plato]. As to the explanation here given of why Cephisodorus in his polemic against Aristotle attacked the doctrine not of Aristotle but of Plato, it is a threadbare invention *ad hoc*, and cannot be taken seriously for an instant. To say that he was not acquainted with Aristotle's own philosophy, and attacked Plato's instead because it was more famous, is a solution that could occur only to some one who had not the faintest notion of the real situation during Aristotle's stay in the Academy.

all of Aristotle's writings had been based entirely on the philosophy of Plato.

Our interpretation of the surviving fragments of the dialogues must defend this view in detail; and the questions that we raise must concern the fragments that actually remain, and not be merely general. As starting-point we must take whatever chronological and philosophical matters can be definitely fixed by means of the fragments. Even the earliness of the dialogues can be adequately proved only by the interpretation of each one separately.

CHAPTER III

THE *EUDEMUS*

THE date of the Dialogue *Eudemus*, which is named after Aristotle's Cyprian friend, is given by the motive for its composition, which can easily be reconstructed from Cicero's account of the dream of Eudemus.[1]

This pupil of Plato's, banished from his country, became gravely ill during a journey through Thessaly. The physicians of Pherae, where he lay, had despaired of his life, when there appeared to him in a dream a beautiful young man who promised him that he would shortly get well, that soon afterwards the tyrant Alexander of Pherae would meet his death, and that when five years had elapsed Eudemus would return to his country. Aristotle related, obviously in his introduction, how the first and second promises quickly came true; Eudemus recovered, and soon afterwards the tyrant was assassinated by his wife's brothers (359). All the more fervent was the exile's hope that five years would see the third promise fulfilled and himself back in Cyprus. During the interval Dion, who had been banished from Syracuse, was at Athens. With the support of the Academy he assembled a company of resolute volunteers, prepared to risk their lives for the liberation of his city. Out of enthusiasm for Plato's political ideals, which Dion was supposed to be going to realize, some of the young philosophers joined the expedition. Among them was Eudemus; but he was killed in one of the engagements outside Syracuse, precisely five years after the dream (354). This unexpected fulfilment of the vision was interpreted in the Academy to mean that what the God had foretold was the return of the soul not to its earthly but to its eternal home.

In this dialogue Aristotle immortalized the memory of his beloved friend and sought comfort for his sorrow. He began by relating the story of the dream of Eudemus, in order to show

[1] Arist. frg. 37 (Cic. *De Div.* I. 25, 53). The *Eudemus* is mentioned as a desideratum in a catalogue of the third century A.D. (papyrus), edited by Medea Norsa in *Ägyptus*, vol. ii (1921), p. 16. Undoubtedly, therefore, it was still read at that date.

that by its fulfilment the deity itself confirmed the truth of Plato's doctrine of the heavenly origin of the soul and its future return thither. This provided the starting-point for a meta-physical conversation 'on the soul', the central portion of which was the question of immortality. The conceptions of the *Phaedo*, asceticism and the practice of death, live again in this early work of Aristotle's. The earthly life of the soul in the chains of corporeality, which the *Phaedo* likens to a prison, becomes for him a period of exile from an eternal home. In the picture of the fugitive in a foreign country, gazing towards the home from which he has been driven, there lies a fervour of longing for the peace and security of the heavenly plains. The *Eudemus* was a book of consolation. Not a word need be wasted on the singular insensibility that cannot see in it anything but a frigid stylistic exercise in the manner of the *Phaedo*. The only thing that could give genuine comfort was a living faith in that reversal of the values of life and death which Plato had accomplished in the *Phaedo*. The author of the *Eudemus* had surrendered himself absolutely to this belief in another life, and to the corresponding views of the world and the soul. Hence the Neo-Platonists use the *Eudemus* and the *Phaedo* as equally valuable sources for Plato's doctrine of immortality. We shall examine the frag-ments of Aristotle's work in the light of that doctrine.

Like Plato in the *Phaedo*, Aristotle in the *Eudemus* attacked the materialistic view that is opposed to the doctrine of im-mortality. And he attacked it in the same form as it has in the *Phaedo*, namely that the soul is nothing but the harmony of the body; that is to say, while different from the sum of the body's elements, it is the product of the right arrangement of them—this is also the modern materialist's account of the soul. Out of the criticism of this view in the *Eudemus* two counter-arguments remain. The first runs thus. 'Harmony has a contrary, namely disharmony. But the soul has no contrary. Therefore the soul is not a harmony.'[1]

Here we have the non-identity of two conceptions proved from the non-identity of their marks. Hence Aristotle is pre-supposing knowledge of the important fact that the identity of objects depends on the identity of their attributes. The

[1] Arist. frg. 45.

attribute that he here takes as a means of comparison is one belonging to formal logic—the possibility of producing a contrary opposite to the conceptions that are to be examined, namely soul and harmony. This is found to be possible with harmony, but the soul has no such opposite. Aristotle formulates his syllogism tersely and trenchantly, and is obviously pleased at its laconic cogency. It is not immediately obvious what led him to choose precisely this line of argument in order to demonstrate the non-identity of the two conceptions and their contents; but this becomes clear as soon as we consider the following proposition from his doctrine of the categories: 'substance (οὐσία) admits no contrary', that is, it is not possible to conceive of any contrary opposition to it.[1] In reality, therefore, this syllogism does not merely contain the proof that the soul is not a harmony; it also implicitly presupposes—and this is very important for the philosophical standpoint of the dialogue—that the soul is a substance. It is easy to see how a thinker for whom this was established doctrine might be led to use the above principle of formal logic in attacking the materialist view, and this principle undoubtedly takes the opponent on his weakest side.

It is interesting to observe the relation between the Aristotelian argument and that of Plato in the *Phaedo* (93 c ff.). The latter is more complicated. According to Plato the soul is either moral, rational, and good, or immoral, irrational, and bad. He shows that these opposed states or constitutions are a sort of order and harmony, or disorder and disharmony, in the soul. There can be various degrees of these attributes in the soul. Therefore harmony itself, or its opposite, can be harmonious in greater or less degree. If the opponent's proposition were true, and the soul were nothing but a harmony of certain states, it would be possible simply to replace the conception of harmony with that of the soul, which would give the absurdity that the soul could be more or less soul.[2] Hence harmony can be only an attribute of the soul, and not the soul itself. Aristotle's alteration of the proof—for his argument is nothing but a reformulation of Plato's—shows clearly what he as a logician took exception to in his original. The demonstration in the *Phaedo* has its own logical principle as basis, and this is formulated in the

---

[1] [Arist.] *Categ.* 3ᵇ 24 ff.　　　　　[2] Plato, *Phaedo* 93 B–D.

Aristotelian doctrine of the categories thus: 'substance (οὐσία) does not appear to admit of variation of degree (τὸ μᾶλλον καὶ τὸ ἧττον). I do not mean by this that one substance cannot be more or less truly substance than another, but that no substance can be more or less that which it is. For example, a man cannot now be man in a higher degree than he was, but he can well be paler than he was. The category of quality by its nature admits a more or less, but that of substance does not.'[1] It follows from this law, if one believes with Plato that the soul is a substance, that there cannot be variations of degree in the soul, while there can be in harmony and in disharmony, as in all relatives that have contraries, for example virtue and vice or knowledge and ignorance.[2] Thus Plato also infers the non-identity of soul and harmony from the impossibility of applying one and the same logical principle to both conceptions; or, in Aristotelian terms, from their belonging to different categories.

We can now see clearly why Aristotle altered the argument of the *Phaedo* as he did. On Plato's view a 'more or less', a variation of degree, can occur only in the indeterminate (ἄπειρον), never in anything absolutely determined (πέρας). Now we have a 'more or less', a variable scale of degrees, an intermediate between two extremes, wherever we have contrary opposites. Thus the proposition that the *Phaedo* employs, namely that substance admits no more or less, is referred by the *Eudemus* to the prior proposition on which it depends, namely that substance admits no contrary opposite. Hence the reduction of the proof to a single, simple syllogism, with which Aristotle achieves the same result.

At the same time he gets a second counter-argument out of what is left of Plato's proof after the extraction of its kernel. He sets this out in the following way. 'Opposed to the harmony of the body is the disharmony of the body, but the disharmony of the living body is disease and weakness and ugliness. Of these

[1] [Arist.] *Categ.* 3^b 33–4^a 9.
[2] [Arist.] *Categ.* 6^b 15: 'It is possible for relatives to have contraries. Thus virtue has a contrary, vice, these both being relatives; knowledge, too, has a contrary, ignorance.' From this it follows in 6^b 20 that 'it also appears that relatives can admit of variation of degree', just as the incompatibility of substance with the 'more and less' follows from its incompatibility with contrary opposition (ἐναντιότης).

disease is a lack of symmetry in the elements, weakness a lack of symmetry in the homogeneous parts (ὁμοιομερῆ), and ugliness a lack of symmetry in the members. If, therefore, disharmony is disease and weakness and ugliness, harmony is health and strength and beauty. But I say that the soul is none of these, neither health nor strength nor beauty. For even Thersites had a soul in spite of all his ugliness. Therefore the soul is not a harmony.'[1]

This argument follows directly from Plato's anthropology. Plato distinguishes virtues of the soul and of the body. Those of the soul are wisdom, courage, justice, and temperance, those of the body health, strength, and beauty. Parallel to these is the series of opposite qualities, the vices of body and soul. The virtues depend on the harmony (symmetry), the vices on the disharmony (lack of symmetry), of the soul or body as the case may be. This explanation of disease, weakness, and ugliness, as lack of symmetry in the body and its parts or their relations, was taken over by Plato from contemporary medicine, on which he based his whole science of ethics or therapy of the soul, and in which he saw the pattern of true science and strict method. His doctrine of virtue is a doctrine of the illness and health of the soul, modelled on medicine and having for principle the conception of measure (μέτρον) and of symmetry or harmony. But if it is established that harmony is the principle of the bodily virtues, health, strength, and beauty, it is not possible at the same time to explain the soul as a harmony of the body. This argument has the advantage of attacking the materialist opponent on his own ground. The explanation of health as the symmetry of the body, and of disease as the lack of it, might be expected to meet with approval from the representatives of natural science; not so the explanation of virtue as the symmetry of the soul, which was the starting-point of the *Phaedo*. This Platonic doctrine of the virtues of soul and body, which Aristotle here follows and develops in detail, is wholly foreign to the treatises. It is in the spirit of Pythagorean mathematics. According to Plato the correct ethical state of the soul, just like the normal and natural state of the body, is only a special case of the universal cosmic law of symmetry, as that is developed

[1] Arist. frg. 45 (Rose, p. 50, l. 13).

in the *Philebus* as a part of Plato's later view of the nature of things.[1]

The analysis of these two arguments has yielded a double result. In the first place, it has shown us that in the *Eudemus* Aristotle is still completely dependent on Plato in metaphysics, not only in the rejection of materialism, but also in positive matters. It has not indeed been previously recognized that his proofs rest on the same basis as Plato's metaphysics and doctrine of immortality, namely Plato's conception of substance and the soul; but this is to be ascribed merely to the lack of thorough interpretation. That Aristotle here still regards the soul as an absolute substance is clear from his later imitators. For example, Olympiodorus gives the first inference in this form: 'harmony has an opposite; but the soul has not, for it is a substance' (Arist. frg. 45). The assertion that there is a *petitio principii* in this formulation is true; but it is equally true of the original form, where the *petitio* is quietly presupposed.[2] It goes back to Plato himself, as we have shown, for the same presupposition is made in the *Phaedo*. The dogmatic character of the proof is brought out still more clearly by Plotinus, when he says simply: 'the soul is a substance but harmony is not'.[3]

[1] For the doctrine of the three virtues of the body see Plato, *Rep.* IX. 591 B; *Laws*, I. 631 C; and *Phil.* 25 D ff (especially 26 B), *et passim*. He is fond of drawing the parallel between them and the virtues of the soul. In *Phil.* 26 B they are reduced to a numerically determined relation between certain opposites; the origin of this theory is clearly revealed by the *Eudemus*. This dialogue also shows that the ethics of measure or μέτρον rest on a transference into the mental sphere of contemporary mathematical views in medicine. The Aristotelian mean (μεσότης) is a conscious return to this point of departure, and carries the analogy through still more strictly. The physicians' measure or μέτρον was itself a correct mean that had to be determined *subjectively*, and to be 'aimed at' (στοχάζεσθαι); this was medical doctrine as early as the Hippocratic school. The only other places in which the bodily virtues appear are the early *Topics* (116ᵇ 17, 139ᵇ 21, 145ᵇ 8) and the 7th book of the *Physics* (246ᵇ 4), which is known to have taken shape during or soon after Aristotle's time at the Academy (cf. E. Hoffmann, *De Aristotelis Physicorum L. VII*, Diss., Berlin, 1905). The picture is completed by the doctrine of the four virtues of the soul in the *Protrepticus*, which is also entirely Platonic. Incidentally, there is no difference between the definition of health as the symmetry of the elements in the *Eudemus*, and as the symmetry of the cold and the warm in the *Topics*; for the elements arose out of the warm, the cold, the wet, and the dry, considered as the fundamental opposites, and Aristotle often calls these qualities elements even in his treatises.

[2] Bernays, op. cit., p. 145, n. 15.

[3] Plotinus, *Enn.* IV, 7, 8 (p. 133, l. 19—p. 134, l. 18, in the Teubner text

Aristotle's later doctrine lies midway between the materialistic view that the soul is the harmony of the body, and the Platonic view of the *Eudemus* that it is a substance of its own. The soul is substance only as being 'the entelechy of a natural body potentially possessing life'.[1] It is not separable from the body, and therefore not immortal; but in connexion with the body it is the formulative principle of the organism. To the soul in the *Eudemus*, on the contrary, can be applied the remarks that Plotinus makes in his rejection of Aristotle's entelechy-soul from the Platonic point of view. 'The soul does not possess being because it is the form *of something*; on the contrary, it is absolute reality (οὐσία). It does not take its existence from the fact that it is in a body; it exists before ever it belongs to a body.'[2] Now, since we find the doctrine of pre-existence in the *Eudemus*, this alone is enough to show that the soul is there a substance (οὐσία); and hence it is not surprising that Plotinus, who combats the Aristotelian conception of the soul, can nevertheless make the argument in the *Eudemus* completely his own; while contrariwise this syllogism is attacked by the supporters of the 'genuine' Aristotle, such as Alexander and following him Philoponus. According to these latter the soul has an opposite, namely privation, and so the argument falls to the ground. This view presupposes the conception of entelechy, and is a correct deduction therefrom. In rejecting the inference Alexander connects it with the argument in the *Phaedo*, out of which it is developed.[3] What distinguishes Aristotle's early view of the soul is in fact that the soul is not yet the form *of something*, but a form in itself (not yet εἶδος τινός but εἶδός τι), an Idea, or

of 1884, edited by Volkmann). It is clear that Plotinus is using the *Eudemus* and not the *Phaedo*, because he breaks up the one proof of the *Phaedo* (93 B ff.) into the two arguments that Aristotle gets out of it. He silently substitutes them for Plato's proof, while he reproduces †he first two arguments of the *Phaedo* (92 A–C and 93 A) without change.

[1] 'Εντελέχεια σώματος φυσικοῦ δυνάμει ζωὴν ἔχοντος, *De An.* II. 1. 412ᵃ 19 ff. In the whole chapter Aristotle examines his earlier view of the soul as a substance, and qualifies it with the doctrine that the soul is not separable from the body, but is simply 'substance as notion or form' (ἡ οὐσία ἡ κατὰ τὸν λόγον, 412ᵇ 10).

[2] Plotinus, *Enn.* IV. 7, 8. (Volkmann, p. 134, l. 19; and esp., p. 135, l. 31 ff.).

[3] Alex. in Arist. *De An.* apud Philop. comm. in Arist. *De An.*, p. 144, ll. 25 ff. (Hayduck). Form and privation are the opposition whose substratum is matter (cf. *Metaph.* Λ 2, 1069ᵇ 3 ff., esp. ᵇ32–34 and 1070ᵇ 18; *et passim*). Thus the soul as an Aristotelian form has an opposite just as much as harmony.

something of the nature of an Idea. We are expressly told this, and it is now for the first time possible really to understand it.[1] Aristotle himself has left us an important piece of evidence that throws light on the facts of his development. When attacking the theory of harmony in his work on the soul he quotes his earlier writing. He takes from the *Eudemus* the second and scientific argument, which he develops somewhat, but he silently abandons the argument from the substantiality of the soul.[2]

The second fact that we discover by our analysis is that the young Aristotle was completely independent of Plato in the sphere of logic and methodology. Though dependent on him for his view of the world, he is here quite free, and perhaps even has a slight feeling of superiority. His reduction of Plato's proof to its elements, and the technical excellence of the two proofs that he constructs out of them, reveal long experience in these things; and the knowledge embodied in the doctrine of the categories forms the presupposition of his corrections. It is nothing against this that the work which we have on the categories cannot have been written before the days of the Lyceum, and is not by Aristotle himself at all. (It is characteristic of the period of naturalism and empiricism, which arose in his school after his death.) The fundamental attitude embodied in the doctrine of the categories, and the main portions of the doctrine itself, had been developed before Aristotle dared to shake the metaphysical foundations of Plato's philosophy.[3]

[1] Arist. frg. 46 (Rose, p. 52, l. 19): 'And in the Eudemus he shows that the soul is a Form' (εἶδός τι). The important point is the absence of any genitive such as 'of a body' or 'of something'; and we must not follow Bernays (op. cit., p. 25) in supplying one and then explaining that the expression was purposely made ambiguous in order to conceal a secret opposition to Plato. Simplicius thought it contrary to Aristotle's usual view.

[2] Arist. *De An.* I. 4, 408ª 1 ff.

[3] The *Categories* cannot be an early work because the Lyceum is given as an example of the category of place; and this undoubtedly refers to the school, which also provided several other examples of logical conceptions. One need only think of Coriscus; the point of the frequent use of his name as an example becomes clear when one imagines the lectures in Assos, at which he was present. In the *Categories* Aristotle's doctrine of first and second substance is made nominalistic; this cannot be removed or explained away; and the very form is un-Aristotelian. The importance of these slight and unintentional verbal indications must not be underestimated. Moreover, the author assumes that the doctrine of the categories is already known; he takes up only a few questions. All this, however, does not prevent us from seeing that most of the details are Aristotelian in content; the *Eudemus* shows how early in his develop-

This shows how weak was the original connexion between logic and metaphysics in Aristotle's mind, as opposed to Plato's. He is the real father of logic and devoted an immense amount of acute thinking to it. But he never recognized it as a part of philosophy and as having its own proper object; he always treated it merely as an art or faculty (Δύναμις) with special formal rules, more or less like rhetoric. He had already become the first specialist in logic before he deduced from his new doctrine of abstraction consequences that ran counter to the theory of Ideas.

The influence of his studies in logic can also be seen in some of the other fragments of the argument for immortality in the *Eudemus*, and especially in his fondness for what he called dialectic. By this word Aristotle means, in contrast to Plato, all those arguments that rest on merely probable premisses and have only subjective cogency. Plato himself makes extensive use of them in his dialogues. Alongside the strictly apodictic arguments they serve to support the proof as peltasts serve alongside hoplites. (The eristic side of Plato's and Aristotle's logic must always be kept in mind.) They do not possess complete scientific exactitude (ἀκρίβεια). Nevertheless, who could despise the weight of the arguments for an after-life that Aristotle makes out of the religious beliefs of nations, the customs of ritual, and the most ancient myths?[1] Even in his treatises he usually starts from the general view or from the opinions of great men. He tries to combine rational and purely philosophical knowledge with the kernel of truth that lies hidden in those sources. Because of this he has been accused of a tendency towards 'common sense' by those who love the radical and the extreme (and since the Romantic revolution we have generally reckoned such persons as the most profound thinkers, at any rate in the intellectual sphere). As a matter of fact this dialectic conceals a peculiar theory of experience, in the historical and concrete sense of the word. In giving a hearing not merely to his own

---

ment they must be placed. Ernst Hambruch shows in his 'Logische Regeln der plat. Schule in der arist. Topik' that a large number of important items of logical knowledge contained in the *Topics* were discovered during Aristotle's time in the Academy (*Wissenschaftliche Beilage zum Jahresbericht des Askanischen Gymnasiums*, Berlin, 1904).

[1] Arist. frg. 44 (Rose, p. 48, ll. 11–22).

reason, but also to what has historically been believed, to the
collective experience of men or to the ideas of famous persons,
Aristotle is not so much lazily relying upon the general opinion
as displaying insight into the limitations of every merely
intellectual argument about such matters.

To sound the metaphysical depths of the *Eudemus* we must go
to the myth of Midas and Silenus. When the king asks him what
is the highest good (τὸ πάντων αἱρετώτατον), Silenus unwillingly
reveals the misery and wretchedness of man's estate. The style
shows the influence of the speech of maid Lachesis, daughter of
Ananke, in the tenth book of the *Republic* (617 D ff.). In word
and shape Silenus breathes the melancholy humour of nature's
earthbound stupor. A cleverly disguised Platonic terminology
conveys the principles of the dualist philosophy. 'It is altogether
impossible that men should attain to the highest good; they
cannot share in the nature of the highest (μετασχεῖν τῆς τοῦ
βελτίστου φύσεως). For the highest good for all men and women
is not to be born (τὸ μὴ γενέσθαι). But, if they are born, the best
—and *this* men can attain—is to die as quickly as possible.'[1]

The special attraction, the real oracle, of these elevated words
lies in their intentional ambiguity. Popular wisdom recommended torpid resignation; the best thing is to die. In this
naïve pessimism there is no hope whatever of another and a
perfect world, or of a higher existence beyond the grave.
Aristotle, on the contrary, introduces into Silenus' words the
fundamental conception of Plato's metaphysics. Τὸ μὴ γενέσθαι
is not merely 'not to be born'; it also means 'not to enter into
Becoming'. To Becoming the *Philebus* (53 C ff.) opposes the
pure Being of the world of Ideas as at once its complete opposite
and its highest aim. All that is valuable, all that is perfect, all
that is absolute, belongs to Being; all that is bad, imperfect, and
relative, belongs to Becoming. Whereas Aristotle in his later
ethics differs from Plato in that he seeks not for an absolute
good but for the best for man (ἀνθρώπινον ἀγαθόν), in this dialogue
he is completely on Platonic ground. It is still self-evident to
him that when we discuss the highest value we must think of the
transcendental Being or the absolute Good, and not of what the
Greeks called happiness (εὐδαιμονία). In the absolute Good no

[1] Arist. frg. 44 (Rose, p. 48, l. 23—p. 49, l. 11).

earthly activity can share. We must get back as quickly as possible out of the realm of Becoming and Imperfection into the unseen world of Being.

Aristotle's Platonism comes out most clearly in the main subject of the dialogue, the doctrine of immortality. Later on he held that the essential problem of psychology was the connexion between the soul and the bodily organism, and he claims to have been the first to recognize the psycho-physical nature of mental phenomena. The first result of the discovery of these psycho-physical relations was inevitably to undermine the Platonic belief in the permanence of the individual soul, and the only part of his original conviction that Aristotle could retain was the belief that pure *Nus* is independent of the body. All the other functions of the soul, such as reflection, love and hate, fear, anger, and memory, involve the psycho-physical unity as their substratum and disappear together with it.[1] This disbelief in the immortality of 'the whole soul' (this is the only historically accurate way of describing what moderns often anachronistically call individual immortality) appears quite early in Aristotle. Among the treatises Book Λ of the *Metaphysics* tends to limit survival to *Nus*, and this was written soon after Plato's death.[2] And even in an excerpt made by Iamblichus out of Aristotle's *Protrepticus* we read: 'Man has nothing divine or blessed except the one thing worthy of trouble, whatever there is in us of *Nus* and reason. This alone of what we have seems immortal and divine.'[3] This limitation causes him to value *Nus* all the higher; it is actually God in us—which recalls the doctrine of '*Nus* entering from outside'. His ethical doctrine of happiness and his theological doctrine of the thought of thought depend on this view. It is therefore comprehensible that as early as the Neo-Platonists men began to try to refer the arguments of the *Eudemus* to *Nus* alone. Themistius connects up this difficult question with the problem of how to understand the conception of the soul in the *Phaedo*, which likewise contains certain ambiguities.

---

[1] For the inseparability of the mental functions from the body see *De An.* I. 1, 403ª 16, *et passim*. For the difference between the separate *Nus'* and the psycho-physical functions see I. 4, 408 ᵇ 18–30.

[2] Arist. *Metaph.* Λ 3, 1070ª 24.

[3] Arist. frg. 61.

Themistius indeed, or his source, ascribed to the *Phaedo* the secret intention of making only *Nus* eternal, but here he is confusing the intention of Plato's arguments with their consequences.[1] The myths of the punishment of sins and of the rewarding of souls in the after-life inevitably involve the survival of 'the whole soul', and lose all sense if applied to Aristotle's *Nus*. Nevertheless, it cannot be denied that the more 'earnest' of the proofs in the *Phaedo* (to use Themistius' expression) prove the eternity of reason only, for instance that from recollection and that from the soul's kinship with God. The fact is that Plato did not clearly distinguish the two problems in his dialogues; they were first mastered in the discussions in the Academy, which gave rise to Aristotle's cautious later formula. In the *Phaedo* we can still clearly discern the original currents of thought that were united in Plato's religion of immortality. The one comes from the Anaxagorean speculations about pure *Nus*; this rested on an apotheosis of scientific reason, and constituted the philosophical high-water mark of fifth-century rationalism. The other current is of opposite origin. It arises out of the Orphic belief in another life, out of the cathartic religion that preaches repentance and purification in order that the soul (ψυχή) may not suffer the most frightful penalties on the other side. In this there is no speculation; it is the ethical and religious feeling of the independence and indestructibility of the soul's essence. In Plato these two currents coalesced into a seeming unity. This unity was based, however, not on a real kinship in its elements, but on the marvellous combination of rational clarity and fervent religious longing in Plato's own soul. Beneath the probe of the analytical intellect the creation breaks up again into its original parts.

After all this it cannot surprise us that in the *Eudemus* Aristotle follows the view of the *Phaedo* even in holding that 'the whole soul' is immortal.[2] This realistic view is the only one that can give religious comfort to the heart of man, which cares nothing for the eternity of the impersonal reason, without love

---

[1] Arist. frg. 38.

[2] This is perfectly clear from Themistius' words, which imply that it would need 'interpretation' to apply the *Eudemus*' proofs of the survival of the soul to *Nus* alone.

and without memory of this life. But Aristotle has wrestled with doubts, and they have left traces in his notion of Platonic recollection. We know that in his psychology he rejects recollection along with the Idea-theory and the survival of 'the whole soul'.[1] The *Eudemus*, on the other hand, is still based on this theory. But at the time of writing it Aristotle had already put to himself, and attempted to answer by Plato's methods, the psychological question whether consciousness is continuous in the life after death. This is the question on which immortality in the sense meant in the *Phaedo* later seemed to him to founder. The continuity of consciousness depends on memory. Whereas he later denies that *Nus* possesses this, in the *Eudemus* he tries to save it for the soul that has returned to the other world. He does this by enlarging Plato's recollection into a doctrine of the continuity of consciousness in all three phases of the soul's existence—its former existence, its life on this earth, and its life after death. Alongside the Platonic view that the soul remembers the other world he sets his thesis that it remembers this one. He supports this by an analogy. When men fall ill they sometimes lose their memories, even to the extent of forgetting how to read and write; while on the other hand those who have been restored from illness to health do not forget what they suffered while they were ill. In the same way the soul that has descended into a body forgets the impressions received during its former existence, while the soul which death has restored to its home in the other world remembers its experiences and sufferings (παθήματα) here.[2] Life without a body is the soul's normal state (κατὰ φύσιν); its sojourn in the body is a severe illness. Our Lethe of what we beheld in our previous lives is only a temporary interruption and obscuration of our memories and of the continuity of our consciousness. Since nothing of this kind is to be feared when we grow well again, i.e. when our souls are freed from their bodies, this view appears to guarantee the immortality of 'the whole soul'. The validity of the proof depends on the correctness of its presupposition, that man's knowledge is a recollection of 'the visions there' (τὰ ἐκεῖ θεάματα). The personal immortality that the *Eudemus* teaches necessarily stands or falls along with this Platonic dogma. Plato

---

[1] *De An*. III. 5, 430ᵃ 23; Metaph. A 9, 993ᵃ 1.   [2] Arist. frg. 41.

had supported his great logical discovery, the *a priori*, with the myth of recollection. At first the young Aristotle followed along the lines of this myth, and we should not be justified in regarding this way of thinking, which is a fundamental dogma in the *Meno* and the *Phaedo*, as a mere metaphor in the pupil. But the moment that he had clearly grasped the specifically logical nature of pure thought, and realized that memory is a psycho-physical phenomenon, he denied that *Nus* was capable of recollection and dropped pre-existence and immortality. In the *Eudemus*, however, he has not yet reached the instant at which Plato's realistic myth was to fall apart into its two elements, poetry and conception.

The circle of Platonic views that surrounds the fortunes of the soul in the *Eudemus* is now closed but for the last link, namely the Forms. A sober and unprejudiced critic will certainly feel that it would be unreasonable to strike out of Proclus' account, which he describes as authentic Aristotelian doctrine, just that link in the chain of conceptions which alone gives meaning and logical connexion to the whole exposition, or to declare it an addition of his own. This is the theory of Forms. It is precisely the Forms of the *Phaedo* that are hidden behind 'the visions there'. Quite apart from the language, which is pure Plato, Aristotle could never have spoken in this way on the basis of his later psychology and epistemology. And even if Proclus' quotation did not explicitly guarantee the occurrence of the Forms in the *Eudemus*, the adoption of the doctrines of pre-existence and recollection would be enough by itself to make them necessary. As Plato says in the *Phaedo*, you can admit or deny the Forms, but you cannot separate them from recollection and pre-existence. These doctrines stand or fall together, and the necessity for both of them is one and the same.[1] Later on, when Aristotle abandoned the theory of Forms, he inevitably dropped recollection along with it.

This then is the relation in which Aristotle stood to Plato at about the year 354/3, after at least thirteen years of study

[1] Plato, *Phaedo* 76 D. Bernays's main argument to prove that the outlook of the *Eudemus* cannot be based on the doctrine of Forms is once again the testimony of Proclus and Plutarch, that Aristotle attacked the Forms even in the dialogues (op. cit., p. 25). Against this see p. 35 above.

under him. His Platonic period extends nearly down to the death of his teacher. In so far as early works give us any information about the nature of a writer, it is quite possible to infer some of Aristotle's typical characteristics from the *Eudemus*. The peculiar thing is that he was already a master in the realm of method and logical technique at a time when he was still completely dependent on Plato in metaphysics. This dependence was obviously rooted in the depths of his unreasoned religious and personal feelings. The corrections that he undertakes to introduce into his Platonic archetype are cautious and conservative. He even attempts to follow along Plato's own most individual path, into the realm of the myth of the soul's progress. This is the home of one of Plato's greatest philosophical powers, the power of shaping a *Weltanschauung*. In the *Eudemus* it is already clear that Aristotle's capacity in this matter is less, in spite of the intensity of his inner need for it, than his genius in science in the narrower sense.

CHAPTER IV

THE *PROTREPTICUS*

1. FORM AND PURPOSE

NEXT to the *Eudemus* the *Protrepticus* is for us the most important work of all those written before Plato's death, both because of the extent to which it is preserved and because of its actual significance. First, however, we require a proof that it *was* written before Plato's death, for as yet scarcely the shadow of one has been offered. Even the problem of its literary form, though much discussed until recently, has not been completely explained. Still less has any attempt been made to determine its philosophical contents.

The *Protrepticus* holds an exceptional position among Aristotle's early writings. It is addressed to Themison, a prince of Cyprus. Although we know nothing further of this man and his circumstances, it is easy to imagine what sort of person a small enlightened despot would be at the beginning of the Hellenistic age. We know two other Cyprian princes from Isocrates' encomium to Evagoras and his open letter to Evagoras' son Nicocles. The address to Nicocles is a protreptic; it prescribes to the young ruler the best principles of just and intelligent government. In the fourth century the schools competed in this way for the attention of the temporal powers, in order to obtain influence in politics. We do not know whether it was through his Cyprian friend Eudemus that Aristotle came to know Themison. We must certainly suppose that the purpose which his letter served formed part of the far-reaching political activities of the Academy at that time.

Aristotle addressed Themison in the introduction. He there said that Themison's wealth and position made him peculiarly suitable for philosophy.[1] This is not a piece of flattery, as it seems at first sight. We must remember that on Plato's view the only persons who can hope to realize the greatest good in the state, and to give help to suffering humanity, are philosophers who obtain political power, or kings who devote themselves

[1] Arist. frg. 50.

seriously to philosophy. Thus Plato too holds that riches and power are indispensable instruments of the Idea.[1] Themison is to help to realize the political philosophy of the Academy.

The form of the work is closely connected with this purpose, and this is one of the matters in which we suffer from having usually treated the two questions separately. The protreptic form took its origin in the new educational method of the sophists. It is not a development of the Socratic method. It by no means necessarily demands the dialogue dress, although that has often been regarded as the natural thing for Aristotle's exoteric writings.[2] When Cicero in his *Hortensius* put the ideas of Aristotle's *Protrepticus* into dialogue form, he thought it necessary to announce the alteration even in the title. And the form of the protreptics that are preserved, although they belong to the time of the emperors, allows us to infer that a protreptic was an exhortation, something like the Hellenistic proselytizing sermon, which is connected with it in form and spirit, and which has been taken over by the Christian church. Probably protreptic ideas were often converted into dialogues, as has happened in the *Tablet* of the so-called Cebes. Whether this was so with Antisthenes' *Protrepticus* is not certain, but everybody knows that Plato did it with Socratic arguments in the *Euthydemus*. In that dialogue Socrates gives to the sophists who are taking part in the conversation examples of a protreptic discussion with a pupil, in his own peculiar form of question and answer, just as he often makes fanciful play with the sophistic forms of expression. Aristotle expressly follows this classical example of Platonic protreptic—but only in content. In form he here for once takes the path not of Plato but of Isocrates.

The form of a personal letter is not the only thing that Aristotle borrowed from this source; for exhortation (παραίνεσις)

---

[1] The author of the second Platonic letter is expressing a thoroughly Platonic notion when he says (310 E): 'It is a natural law that wisdom and great power attract each other. They are always pursuing and seeking after each other and coming together.'

[2] In our catalogues of Aristotle's works, both in Diogenes and in Hesychius and Ptolemy, the *Protrepticus* is listed among the exoteric writings, which are given first. But this implies nothing about its form, since it is possible that other writings besides the dialogues were exoteric. The *Protrepticus* would be reckoned exoteric just as much if it were in the form of a speech or an open letter.

was a standing part of the Isocratean method of education. To address oneself to a particular person is a very ancient point of style in every kind of moral maxim and didactic speech. In the period during which the accepted means of exerting a spiritual influence on mankind was poetry, we can follow the address to an individual from Hesiod's exhortations to Perses down to the didactic poem of Empedocles and the maxims that Theognis addressed to Cyrnus; the schools were still using the latter for the moral education of boys at the time of Socrates and the sophists. The sophists replaced this old-fashioned maxim-poetry with a new prose form, which began to compete successfully with the traditional method.[1] The pattern of a prince that Isocrates gives us in his *Ad Nicoclem* is the sophistic counterpart of the pattern of chivalry in Theognis. Both belong to the same genus. Aristotle's *Protrepticus* is, however, more than a philosophical pattern for princes. It proclaims the new ideal of the purely philosophic life, which Plato demanded from the man of action as much as from any one (for to exhort a practising politician to cultivate the 'theoretic life' is a Platonic trait, foreign to the later Aristotle). Incidentally this work is not, as is generally said, 'dedicated' to Aristotle's princely friend. The dedication of dialogues and treatises belongs to the literary customs of Hellenistic courtesy; no such artificial usage was known to the better period. With Aristotle the address to a particular person is still the living expression of the mood of earnest ethical exhortation. It is organic to the protreptic style as such.

There are other traces of the imitation of the Isocratean exhortation or παραίνεσις. It is true that even here we find the peculiar form that stamps everything coming from Aristotle, the predominance of the arrangement of chains of thought in apodictic syllogisms. It is true that precisely here this form could win easy and ingenious victories. ('Ought we to philosophize?' was the question that preoccupied every exhortation to the study of philosophy. Aristotle's answer came pat. Either we ought to philosophize or we ought not. If we ought, then we

---

[1] P. Wendland gives the true account of the development of the prose protreptic out of the maxim-poetry of the Ὑποθῆκαι in his *Anaximenes von Lampsakos* (Berlin, 1905), pp. 81 ff. Cf. Isocr. *Ad Nicocl.* 3.

ought. If we ought not, then also we ought (in order to justify this view). Hence in any case we ought to philosophize.[1] Most of the remaining fragments have a similar syllogistic form.) Nevertheless, the ideas of the older exhortations often shine through this veil of dialectic. The interplay between the old store of ideas and the new and striking way of supporting them comes out particularly clearly in one of the longer fragments. This passage survived long enough to get into the Byzantine anthologies; its original, unabridged form has lately been discovered in a papyrus from Oxyrhynchus.[2]

'Believe that man's happiness lies not in the magnitude of his possessions but in the proper condition of his soul. Even the body is not called blessed because it is magnificently clothed, but because it is healthy and in good condition, even if it lacks this decoration. In the same way only the cultivated soul is to be called happy; and only the man who is such, not the man who is magnificently decorated with external goods, but is himself of no value. We do not call a bad horse valuable because it has a golden bit and costly harness; we reserve our praise for the horse that is in perfect condition.'

Or again:

' Just as a man would be a ridiculous figure if he were intellectually and morally inferior to his slaves, in the same way we must believe a man miserable if his possessions are more valuable than himself. . . . Satiety begets wantonness, says the proverb. Vulgarity linked with power and possessions brings forth folly.'

These ideas are not peculiar to Platonic wisdom, but the apodictic form of exposition is new. The frequent 'we must believe' is itself one of the technical devices of sophistic exhortation. Isocrates in his address to Nicocles, and the author of the protreptic *To Demonicus*, begin their maxims in this way no less than fifteen times. Our philosophical analysis will show that Aristotle effectively transformed not merely the inexhaustible storehouse of ancient Greek proverbial wisdom, but also Plato's ethics and metaphysics. He makes the hortatory content of the *Gorgias* and the *Phaedo* coalesce with the uniform prose of the Isocratean protreptic. This synthesis is the fruit of the young Platonist's efforts to make technical rhetoric at home in the Academy, and to turn it into a scientific discipline.

In this way the *Protrepticus* comes to be a manifesto on behalf of Plato's school and its notion of the aim of life and culture.

[1] Frg. 51.   [2] Frg. 57. Cf. *Pap. Oxyrh.*, vol. iv, pp. 83 ff.

C

Isocrates had been combining mind-training, by means of formal exercises in writing and speaking, with instruction in the principles of ethics and of practical statesmanship. His circle now found itself publicly opposed by a new competitor. The *Protrepticus* showed that the Academy could hold its own in the sphere of rhetoric. Besides this, its contents must have seemed to the followers of Isocrates an open attack on their ideal of culture. Isocrates' polemical remarks on the Platonic ideal of educating the young by means of pure philosophy, and his recommendation of the banal viewpoint of utility in education, designed to suit the psychology of the average Philistine—these things had long called for an answer from the Academy. In the *Protrepticus* Aristotle refuted the trivial proposition that the value of knowledge is to be measured according to its utility in practical life. But what refuted banausic persons even more convincingly than the acuteness of his syllogisms was the demonstration, renewed in every line, of his own intellectual superiority. He showed that neither a good style of writing, nor a sensible disposition of one's life, nor a productive statesmanship—the aims towards which Isocrates professed to lead—is possible without solidity in the ultimate principles of human conviction.

It appears that the school of Isocrates did not fail to produce a rejoinder, and that an accident has preserved it for us among the speeches of Isocrates. It is the anonymous exhortation *To Demonicus*, a wretched piece of work by an inferior mind, betraying the spirit of sheer envy and competitiveness. The author can be recognized as a pupil of Isocrates by the arsenal from which he draws his intellectual weapons—the arrangement and the commonplaces of the speech show that it cannot have been written appreciably later. Presumably it is preserved simply because it was commissioned by the school. In the introduction the author explains his intentions in the following manner.[1]

'Those who compose protreptic discourses addressed to their own friends are, no doubt, engaged in a laudable employment; yet they do not occupy themselves with the most vital part of philosophy. Those, on the contrary, who point out to the young, not by what means they may cultivate skill in mere dialectic (Δι' ὧν τὴν Δεινότητα τὴν ἐν τοῖς

[1] [Isocr.] *Ad Demon.* 3.

λόγοις ἀσκήσουσιν),[1] but how they may win repute as men of sound character, are rendering a greater service to their hearers, in that, while the former exhort them to proficiency in argument, the latter improve their moral conduct.'

This appears to be directed against a protreptic addressed to a friend from a philosophical point of view, consciously theoretical, and calling for the study of dialectic. Surely no such work can have become sufficiently famous to seem dangerous to the Isocratean circle, except the *Protrepticus* of Aristotle. This fits in specially well with what the follower of Isocrates says about his opponent's hostile attitude towards life and the world, as displayed in his view of the aim of education. It was the first philosophical protreptic, and so far as we know the only one, definitely to put the controversial question whether we really ought to educate merely for 'life'. Against the bourgeois world of Isocrates it set up its bold demand for 'the theoretic life'. We need not, however, content ourselves with general considerations; it is possible to give more tangible proof of its influence on the *Ad Demonicum*.[2]

Ad Demon. 19: 'Do not hesitate to travel a long road to those who profess to offer some useful instruction; for it were a shame, when merchants cross vast seas in order to increase their store of wealth,	Arist. frg. 52 (Rose, p. 62, l. 7). 'We ought not to shun philosophy, if philosophy is as we think the possession and use of wisdom, and wisdom is one of the greatest goods. We ought not to sail to the pillars

---

[1] The author's notion of philosophy is that of Isocrates, which resembles our notion of general culture. The 'skill in argument' that he condemns, and the 'cultivation' of this, is, as Wendland saw, not the cleverness of the rhetorician. He is not opposing protreptics on behalf of rhetoric, but logical or dialectical philosophy; cf. Isocr. *Hel.* 2, where the same things are again described as 'excessive interest in arguments' (περιεργία ἐν τοῖς λόγοις). In the *Antidosis* (258 ff.) dialectic, geometry, and astronomy are associated as forming the opponent's characteristic educational programme. As in the speech *To Demonicus*, they are said to be useful indeed as intellectual disciplines (265), but not helpful for great actions and ideals.

[2] In his excellent discussion of the *Ad Demonicum* P. Wendland (op. cit., pp. 92 ff.) calls attention to its relations to Aristotle's *Protrepticus*, and points out the parallel given in the text. Although he does not draw it, it seems to me the inevitable consequence of these observations that the *Ad Demonicum* is mainly aimed at the *Protrepticus*, and was actually written with the intention of setting up another goal against the ideal of that work. It is not of course necessary that the echo followed immediately on the appearance of Aristotle's work, but it was certainly written while he was still alive. During the next hundred years the influence of the *Protrepticus* was constantly increasing (cf. Arist. frg. 50), which makes such a criticism of it perfectly comprehensible.

that the young should not endure even journeys by land to improve their understanding.'

Cf. the beginning of this section: 'Believe that many precepts are better than much wealth; for wealth quickly fails us, but precepts abide through all time; for wisdom alone of all possessions is imperishable.'

of Hercules and run many dangers for the sake of wealth, while we spend neither labour nor money for wisdom. Verily it is slavish to long for life instead of for the good life, and to follow the opinions of the many instead of demanding that the many follow our own, and to seek for money but pay no attention whatever to the noble.'

The correspondence between the two passages cannot be accidental, for the following reason. In Aristotle the picture of the sailors risking all dangers in their hunger for wealth provides a very good contrast to the men who must make sacrifices in order to cultivate the highest goods. The pupil of Isocrates, on the other hand, brings it in loosely, just as a rhetorician would collect tricks of style in his reading and afterwards make use of them. He is unable to get the proper effect with it. His antithesis seems strained and frigid. To the borrowed image of the seafaring merchants he opposes the safe travel of the student overland, going to Athens to attend the university. His surprising admonition that 'many lectures' are worth more than 'much wealth' is for once not altogether lacking in originality, for in the school of Isocrates instruction was expensive.

2. PRESERVATION AND RECONSTRUCTION

In his penetrating book on Aristotle's dialogues Bernays directed the attention of philologists to the works of the Neo-Platonists, by giving some examples of their predilection for these dialogues.

This brought forth excellent fruit in 1869, when Ingram Bywater showed that there are large portions of Aristotle's *Protrepticus* in Iamblichus' work of the same name, where they lie buried under numerous excerpts from Plato's dialogues.[1] As luck would have it, Bernays had by that time completed his researches; and his conclusion, that Aristotle never had a Platonic period, barred him from understanding the new discovery. Even Bywater himself remained entirely convinced by Bernays's argument. His delight at his find led him to hasty

[1] *The Journal of Philology*, vol. ii, pp. 55 ff.

publication, without any careful attempt to make sure of what he had got, or to establish the limits of the new fragments.

The *Protrepticus* of Iamblichus is a reader for beginners in philosophy. It is put together out of such works as taught a genuinely Pythagorean doctrine according to the Neo-Platonists subsequent to Porphyry. These were (1) their own, (2) the writings, mostly spurious, of the older Pythagoreans whom they quote, and above all (3) those of Plato and the early Aristotle, who were regarded as genuine esoterics. The sacredness of these writings is an example of the tremendous power then exercised by tradition as embodied in books; we see it also in contemporary Christianity and Judaism, and later in Islam. Out of loosely connected passages from Plato's dialogues, mostly well-known ones, Iamblichus weaves a variegated carpet. The transitions are inadequate and stereotyped, so that the seams are everywhere visible at first sight. The conversational parts are transformed into continuous prose, not without serious inaccuracies. Although it is not explicitly said that Plato and Aristotle are being quoted, there is no question of an attempt to deceive, for every scholar was familiar with the passages. Even so, it is a sorry piece of work, and gives evidence of the fact that literary culture and scientific independence were steadily declining at the time. Iamblichus took account of Aristotle's *Protrepticus* because it was the archetype of this form of writing, if for no other reason; and he got his excerpts from his own reading of it. The Neo-Platonists were attracted by the ascetic and religious character of the book. They considered it evidence of Aristotle's supposed Platonism, or at any rate a means of reconciling the contradictions between Plato and the Peripatetic doctrine. One may go so far as to say that the Neo-Platonists caused a revival of the book, for almost every one of them reveals traces of it.

We now come to the determination of the extent of the excerpts in Iamblichus, a task already attempted by Bywater, Hirzel, and Hartlich.[1] The main portion of his book, chapters 5–19, is made up of quotations from Plato's dialogues. In chapters 6–12 this series is interrupted by passages from Aristotle.

[1] Hirzel, *Hermes*, vol. x, pp. 83 ff. Paul Hartlich, 'De exhortationum a Graecis Romanisque scriptarum historia et indole' (*Leipz. Studien*, vol. xi, Part 2, Leipzig, 1889).

They all come from a lost work, and that this is the *Protrepticus* was first recognized by Bywater himself. Identification was not difficult, because portions of these chapters are to be found in Cicero, Augustine, Proclus, and Boethius, either verbally the same or nearly so, and either ascribed to Aristotle or in obviously protreptic passages and in writings that can be proved to be dependent on his *Protrepticus*. Impressed by the lack of order in the excerpts, Hirzel and Hartlich asserted that Iamblichus must have used other writings of Aristotle's as well; but this has not been proved. In addition to Plato and Aristotle another writer is used in chapter 5, and to him are ascribed the parts of that chapter that cannot be referred to Plato. The end of it is generally reckoned along with the demonstrably Aristotelian excerpts beginning in chapter 6 (as in the latest edition, that of Pistelli), but I hope to show in another place that it comes from Porphyry. This would make it probable that Porphyry is also the author of the three other unidentified sections of chapter 5, since they are clearly Neo-Platonic in origin.

The excerpts from Aristotle begin with some loosely connected arguments on behalf of the value of philosophy. They are based on Plato's *Euthydemus*, being taken over more or less verbally from Socrates' protreptic conversation (278 E ff.), a fact that has escaped notice. What is more important is that this is the very part of the *Euthydemus* that Iamblichus also uses as the beginning of his quotations from Plato (p. 24, ll. 22 ff.). Since it is improbable that the repetition of it here is an oversight, and since the words are not a plain citation from the *Euthydemus*, but a compression of Plato's exposition into several fairly long syllogisms, in which there are some Aristotelian terms, it is obvious that Iamblichus is here using not Plato directly, but an intermediate source. That source is Aristotle's *Protrepticus*. Just as in the *Eudemus* Aristotle took the *Phaedo* for model, so in the *Protrepticus* he frequently followed the work that contained Plato's criticism of the sophists' protreptics, namely the *Euthydemus*.

This brings us another step forward. Bywater compared the following passages together:

Cic. *Hortensius* (ed. Baiter) frg. 26; (ed. Mueller, frg. 36):	Iambl. *Protr.* (ed. Pistelli) p. 24, l. 22:
Beati certe omnes esse volumus.	All we men wish to fare well.

That Cicero made use of Aristotle's *Protrepticus* in his protreptic dialogue is so indubitably certain on other grounds that it scarcely needed the support of this verbal agreement. Bywater supposed that here again Aristotle was the common source. The passage in Iamblichus, however, along with its whole context (p. 24, l. 22,—p. 27, l. 10), belongs to a direct quotation from the *Euthydemus*; and this makes Bywater's inference invalid for Iamblichus. On the other hand, the view that Cicero also made direct use of the *Euthydemus* imputes to him a more piecemeal method of working than he had. This sentence, which formed the beginning of a syllogism, was doubtless really taken from Aristotle's *Protrepticus*, and it was Aristotle and not Cicero who got it out of the *Euthydemus*, along with all the passages that we have recovered above. He was unwilling, it seems, to leave out the famous opening sentence of the protreptic conversation in the *Euthydemus*. Iamblichus, on the other hand, omits it when quoting Aristotle, because a few pages earlier he has copied it directly out of Plato. It is this method of making excerpts that is responsible for the complete lack of connexion in the first series of arguments (p. 37, ll. 3–22) that he takes over from the *Protrepticus*.

The next passage reveals Iamblichus' method still more decisively (Arist. frg. 52).

It consists of a single complete argumentation, extending over several pages (p. 37, l. 22—p. 41, l. 5). At first sight it seems to be all of a piece. Since ll. 15–24 of p. 40 are also quoted by Proclus, and by him expressly ascribed to Aristotle, it has been inferred that not merely this passage but the whole proof is borrowed from the *Protrepticus*. That work must certainly have discussed the possibility of philosophy as a department of human knowledge, its importance for life, and the rate of its advance. Besides this, the whole proof reappears in another book of Iamblichus', where it is incongruously used as a defence of mathematics. There it is preceded by a criticism of philosophy from the side of its enemies, those who are opposed to all mere theory on principle; and this passage also bears all the marks of Aristotelian origin. Rose therefore connects the two versions (frg. 52).

Inner evidence shows that there can be no doubt of the

rightness of this ascription. The only question is whether Iamblichus took over the proof as a whole, or put it together for himself out of Aristotelian material. In the first place, while the excerpts from Plato are throughout laid side by side without any connexion, we notice that those from Aristotle evince an inner relation. In his Aristotelian source Iamblichus found a complete train of protreptic thought, which he naturally desired to imitate. But the hope that he has preserved to us undamaged whole trains of argument from Aristotle's *Protrepticus* unfortunately turns out to be illusory. His model has indeed instigated him to attempt a connected proof of the independent value of philosophy. But the chapters in which he has articulated this train of thought, though outwardly polished, are a pretty crude and violent combination of Aristotelian materials. Their outward conjunction does not allow us to infer that they are undamaged, or that they really belong together.

Fragment 52 will serve as an example of the point. The whole is a tripartite defence of philosophy. The opening and closing words, and those in the middle, by means of which the three parts are held together, are reminiscent of Aristotle's manner in his treatises. But if we compare the other version of this excerpt in Book III, we find that Iamblichus there omits the introduction altogether and gives the conclusion in another form. It follows that it is he who is responsible for the structure of the proof and for the words that indicate it. He has used Aristotle's ideas as building stones, and crudely forced them into his own miserable framework. No trace of the original architecture remains. The same conclusion follows from the words that both Iamblichus and Proclus have preserved at the end of the fragment. It is clear from their close and detailed correspondence that they are throughout the original words of Aristotle. The only difference lies in the point of view from which the quotation is introduced in each case. Proclus uses it to prove that philosophy is an end in itself (δι' αὐτὸ αἱρετόν), a thesis that received exhaustive treatment in the *Protrepticus*. Iamblichus wishes to demonstrate by its means that philosophy cannot be a very difficult study, which was certainly not Aristotle's intention. This arouses the suspicion that the rest of the construction of the proof is equally un-Aristotelian. Iamblichus' arrangement of his material is superficial, and we should be equally superficial in our analysis of it if we divided it by chapters, and still more so if we assigned them to different writings of Aristotle's. There is no ground for the supposition that he used more than one work. It has been urged that such and such a chapter cannot be from the *Protrepticus* because it mentions things that have already been partly discussed in another chapter. Such arguments are not cogent. The 'chapters' are phantom buildings. They crumble as soon as one taps the brittle mortar that holds their members in place. Only the members themselves, falling out of their settings, will stand investigation without pulverizing. Their substance is bound together by the stony logic of Aristotle's syllogisms.

Through parallels in Cicero or Augustine and Boethius[1] the following passages are also proved to be excerpts from the *Protrepticus*: chap. 8, p. 47, l. 5—p. 48, l. 21 (frgs. 59, 60, and 61); and chap. 9, p. 52, l. 16—p. 54, l. 5 (frg. 58). To these must be added the beginning of chap. 8, p. 45, l. 6—p. 47, l. 4 (frg. 55). This whole portion is derived from a single source. It is characterized by dialectical inferences ('from the things that seem clear to all'), which Aristotle is especially fond of using in his literary works, and by a peculiar use of the conception of wisdom (φρόνησις), of which we shall speak hereafter. But there are still further excerpts. I begin with chapter 7, which is especially important and has up to now been held not to come from Aristotle's *Protrepticus*.

The opening words are Iamblichus' own (p. 41, ll. 6–15). He proposes to show (1) that thinking (τὸ φρονεῖν, which is here a genuinely Platonic term meaning the whole of pure philosophy) is valuable for men in itself; (2) that it is useful in life, because without thought and inference man cannot attain to anything profitable; and (3) that philosophy is essential to the attainment of happiness, whatever outlook on life you may have, and whether you understand by happiness a maximum of pleasant sensations (ἡδονή), or a life completely imbued with ethical

---

[1] Usener's expectation (*Rhein. Mus.*, vol. 28, p. 400) of finding substantial portions of the *Hortensius* in Boethius has not been fulfilled. In fact, Boethius cannot have used the *Hortensius* at all, as Usener himself was later obliged to admit (*Anecd. Holderi*, p. 52). Augustine, on the other hand, was an assiduous reader of the dialogue.

principles and occupied in their realization (ἀρετή), or the life of the pure intellect (φρόνησις). These three points correspond exactly to the sequence of the chapters: (1) chaps. 7–9, (2) chap. 10, and (3) chaps. 11–12. Now it is possible to doubt how far these chapters are copied from an Aristotelian source (it is shown below that as a matter of fact they are all excerpts from the *Protrepticus*); but no one is going to believe that in the order given to them in Iamblichus they constitute a single continuous fragment of Aristotle. Therefore Iamblichus himself must be responsible for the introductory words in which the scheme of the six following chapters is announced. What he does is to take this outline and fill it out with selected passages from his source (although no doubt the three divisions of the outline are themselves copied from the same source). This is clear at the start; after announcing his plan he makes no attempt to smooth over the transition to verbal quotation, but begins with Aristotle's schematic phrase ἔτι τοίνυν (p. 41, l. 15). The proof thus inaugurated extends down to p. 43, l. 25, and forms on the whole a single train of thought, though p. 42, l. 5, is undoubtedly abbreviated. At l. 25 of p. 43 some more excisions begin, but the conclusion of the preceding part (p. 43, ll. 22–5) shows how close was its original connexion with the argument that follows (p. 43, l. 27, to the end of chapter 7). It is obvious that all this consists of disconnected quotations from an earlier author, and the style and the ideas reveal at every turn that that author is Aristotle. It was a very unmethodical proceeding to exclude these pages merely because there seemed to be no external evidence for them, when they are surrounded on all sides by demonstrably Aristotelian passages.

The main thought of the first section (p. 41, l. 15—p. 43, l. 25) is specifically Aristotelian, and so is the way in which it is developed. In order to determine what is favourable and advantageous for each nature, the author makes use of the notion of τέλος. The 'aim' of every nature must be sought in some significant activity, some living effectiveness that it has. In the mass of its effects or functions (ἔργον) one will stand out as its peculiar strength (οἰκεία ἀρετή) over against all other individuals or species; this is the work that is essential to it and constitutes its τέλος. The task of every nature is determined by its inborn capacity. The scale of functions according to their value is given by nature, for the instrumental ones are always biologically the lower, and the governing ones the higher. Such is the relation, for example, of the bodily to the mental functions. In this sense the ἔργον of the mental capacities has greater value than that of the bodily. The highest of all is that capacity of the soul whose value does not lie in effecting a mere result (ἔργον) distinct from its own activity (ἐνέργεια). This capacity does not aim at the production of any external object, and in it activity and product are one. Its name is *phronesis*, which is perhaps to be rendered as 'pure reason'. *Phronesis* has only itself for object and aim, and produces nothing but itself. It is pure intuition (θεωρία). In the conception of intuition being, action, and production, are resolved into a unity. The highest form of life is neither ordinary production nor ordinary action, but the contemplative vision of the intellect, which is active and productive in a higher sense. The following elements in this can be seen at a glance to be Aristotelian in content: the comparison of the pleasures of contemplation with those of the disinterested use of the eyes; the importance of the notion of function and work (ἐνέργεια, ἔργον); the distinction between functions performed *in* activities and those that are merely performed *through* them; the distinction between the productive, the practical, and the theoretical activities; and the identity of subject and object in the active intellect.[1] In the doctrine of levels, which is presupposed here and receives express mention somewhat further on, we have the fundamental principle of Aristotle's teleology, namely that in every sphere of reality the higher levels include the lower. Lastly, Aristotle was familiar with the doctrine of the three lives and three points of view, the hedonistic-sensual, the ethical, and the intellectual.

Besides this internal evidence we have a convincing external proof. In the chapter on the original form of the *Ethics* it will be shown that large and connected portions of the *Eudemian Ethics* correspond exactly in content and language to the excerpts that Iamblichus has preserved. Some of them are

---

[1] The conception of ἔργον, which is one of the most important elements in Aristotle's theory of value, is present throughout the passage. It appears in the following places: p. 42, ll. 5, 15, 19, 20, 22; p. 43, ll. 6, 9, 18, 21.

passages of which the author of the *Eudemian Ethics* expressly says that he is taking them from 'the exoteric works'. Now if we compare these passages with the excerpts in Iamblichus we find that the latter are the archetypes. It follows that the work from which Iamblichus took these quotations was one of those lost works of Aristotle the application to which of the word 'exoteric' was so long in dispute, but is now beyond doubt. Now Iamblichus' seventh chapter is one of these excerpts. Therefore it must be Aristotelian. It is equally certain that it must be from the *Protrepticus*, since this is true of the other passages in the *Eudemian Ethics* that are known to be borrowed, and since the whole train of thought is protreptic in tone.

In his later lectures Aristotle frequently touched on the question of the value of the different kinds of life, and put the choice before his hearers. In such places he invariably distinguished the life of pleasure and gain, the life of action, and that of the student and philosopher. The *Protrepticus* is the origin both of the question and of the answer, which is that the life of pure knowledge is preferable to all other modes of human existence, even from the ethical point of view.

But the significance of the quotation in Iamblichus' seventh chapter is still not exhausted.

Every reader of the *Metaphysics* has been carried away again and again by the force of its opening pages. Aristotle there develops with irresistible power the view that, far from its being contrary to man's nature to occupy himself with theoretical studies, the pleasure of seeing, of understanding, and of knowing, is rooted deep within him, and merely expresses itself differently at the different levels of his consciousness and culture. It is really the fulfilment of man's higher nature; it is not a mere means to the satisfaction of the rising standards of civilized life, but the highest absolute value and the summit of culture; and of all studies the highest and most desirable is the one that produces the most exact science, and realizes in its perfect form the disinterested vision of pure knowledge. The protreptic power of these ideas will be felt by all who have learnt through experience the supreme value of this activity when pursued for its own sake. Knowledge has never been understood and recommended more purely, more earnestly, or more sublimely;

and it is still a dead letter to-day for those who cannot pursue it in this spirit. Now to teach us to understand it in this profound sense was what Aristotle aimed at in the *Protrepticus*, and the famous introduction to the *Metaphysics* is in essence nothing but an abbreviated version of his classical exposition of the matter there. This is shown by a comparison of Iamblichus' seventh chapter (p. 43, l. 20), which develops the same idea at greater length, and carries the argument into more detail. We find that the introductory chapter of the *Metaphysics* is simply a collection of material extracted from this source for the purpose of a lecture, and that it is not even quite firmly cemented into place.

Protr., p. 43, l. 20	*Metaph.* A 1, 980ᵃ 21

Protr., p. 43, l. 20

Thought and contemplation . . . is *the most desirable of all things for men*, as is (I think) the sense of sight, which a man would choose to possess *even if nothing were going to come of it except the sight itself*.

Again, if we *love* sight *for itself*, this is sufficient proof that all men *love* thought and knowledge exceedingly. . . . But what distinguishes life from non-life is perception, and life is determined by the presence of this capacity. . . . *The power of sight differs* from the other senses *by being the clearest, and this is the reason why we prefer it*

Metaph. A 1, 980ᵃ 21

All men by nature *desire* to know. An indication of this is the *delight* we take in our senses; for even apart from their usefulness *they are loved* for themselves; and above all others the sense of sight. For not only with a view to action, but *even when we are not going to do anything, we prefer seeing* (one might say) *to everything else*. The reason is that this, *most of all the senses, makes us know and brings to light many differences between things*. By nature animals are born with the faculty of sensation. . . .

to all. If then life is to be chosen because of *perception*, and if *perception is a kind of knowledge* which we choose because it enables the soul *to know*, and if *as we have said above the preferable one of two things is that which has more of the same thing*,[1] it necessarily follows that sight is the most desirable and honourable of the senses, but that wisdom is more desirable than this and all the other senses, and even than life itself, since it has *a better grasp of truth*.[2] Therefore all men seek wisdom above all things; for they *love* wisdom and *knowledge because they love life*.

The meaning of the concise word ἀγάπησις in the second sentence of the *Metaphysics*, namely the love of an activity for its own sake, receives much clearer expression in the

---

[1] Reading ὅτι instead of ὅτιπερ. [2] Reading κυριωτέρα οὖσα.

corresponding passage of the excerpt from the *Protrepticus*, as was necessary in an exoteric exposition. Every word is obviously Aristotelian; but the excerptor has put together several distinct passages from the *Protrepticus* because of the similarity of their contents, and as the weld is pretty roughly made the whole gives a tautologous effect. It is, however, quite impossible to suppose that we have here a mere paraphrase of the passage in the *Metaphysics*. These excerpts definitely go beyond what is said in that work. This is especially clear in the emphasis put on correct logical reasoning, which corresponds to the picture of Aristotle's early manner that we have received from the *Eudemus*. Examples are the use as a premiss of the topical principle that of two objects that which possesses a valuable quality in a higher degree is itself valuable in a higher degree;[1] and the use of definitions in order to prove that wisdom is good by means of the conception of life. Both in the *Metaphysics* and in the *Protrepticus* the method of proof is dialectical, and this also agrees with what we observed in the *Eudemus*.

The first two chapters are of this nature throughout, and since they teach the same fundamental principle as the *Protrepticus*, namely the self-sufficiency of pure theoretical knowledge, it is natural to suppose that they are substantially or wholly borrowed therefrom. This can easily be demonstrated in detail. In both writings the conception of pure knowledge is developed by contrasting it with the activity of the practical man, which rests on mere experience or routine. It is not the empirical and practical man who stands higher, but the theoretical and contemplative one; for empiricism never attains that insight into the causes and reasons for phenomena which the theoretical man possesses owing to his mastery of the universal. The more empirical you are, and the more you rely on perception (πρόσ-θεσις), the less exact your knowledge. The only truly exact knowledge is that of what is most knowable, namely those most general principles (τὰ πρῶτα) which form the subject-matter of the highest theoretical studies. It may well be that in practice

---

[1] In the *Eudemus* the logical proposition that the identity of the object depends on the identity of the attributes was employed to refute the doctrine that the soul is a harmony of the body. In referring the greater value of the object to the presence (ὑπάρχειν) of more valuable attributes Aristotle is here proceeding in a similar manner.

the mere empiric will have more success than a theorist who has had no actual experience, but the former never attains to action that really depends on secure principles and on insight into the necessities of the case; he remains 'banausic'. The concealed polemic against banausic persons and their contempt for theory, which is continuous throughout the first chapters of the *Metaphysics*, was modelled on the *Protrepticus*, in which Aristotle had refuted the attacks of the empiricists in detail. Fortunately we still possess a fragment that goes deeply into the arguments of the opposite side (frg. 52; Rose, p. 59, ll. 17 ff.).

'That philosophy is useless in practical life may be seen in the following manner. The best example that we have is the relation between the theoretical or pure studies (ἐπιστῆμαι) and the applied disciplines that are subordinate to them (ὑποκείμεναι δόξαι). For we notice that the geometricians are quite unable to apply their scientific proofs in practice. When it comes to dividing a piece of land, or to any other operation on magnitudes and spaces, the surveyors can do it because of their experience, but those who are concerned with mathematics and with the reasons for these things, while they may know how it *ought* to be done, cannot do it.'

The demand for exactitude (ἀκρίβεια) in scientific knowledge is another thing that is strongly emphasized in the *Protrepticus*. It is there brought into connexion with the doctrine that science is knowledge of reasons and first principles, for only the universal and the principles can be known with exactitude. In some passages there is even a verbal correspondence. The parallel between the two writings is equally complete in the derivation of the higher and the highest levels of knowledge from the lower and naïve ones. But naturally we must not expect Aristotle to repeat himself mechanically page after page; verbal echoes remain the exception. The most decisive consideration is that these ideas were originally intended for the *Protrepticus*. They belong there by their essential nature, whereas in the lectures on metaphysics they are an external addition, arbitrarily tailored to suit the requirements of an introduction.

Immediately after the long passages of Iamblichus' third book referred by Rose to the *Protrepticus* there follows a description, also from the *Protrepticus*, of the gradual development of philosophy out of the other 'arts' (frg. 53). Presupposing Plato's theory of catastrophes, this work taught that after the

devastations of the great flood men were at first obliged to
devote themselves to the discovery of the mere necessities of food
and life (τὰ περὶ τὴν τροφὴν καὶ τὸ ʒῆν πρῶτον ἠναγκάʒοντο
φιλοσοφεῖν). When things were going better they invented the
arts that serve for recreation, such as music and the like. It was
later still, when their need of necessaries was fully supplied, that
they turned their attention to liberal studies and pure philosophy. Aristotle no doubt has the mathematical disciplines
especially in mind when he speaks of the enormous advances
made by the pure sciences in recent times (i.e. during Plato's
generation). The same observation reappears in the *Metaphysics*
(A 1, 981^b 13–982^a 2). There it is strangely out of relation to
its context, whereas in the *Protrepticus* it served to show that,
once the stimulus to philosophical studies has been given, they
exercise an irresistible attraction over men's minds. The original
reference to mathematics still obtains in the *Metaphysics*, where
the mathematical inquiries of the Egyptian priests are cited as
the beginning of the third era. The distinction between necessary and liberal arts also comes from the *Protrepticus*. In fact,
everything in the first two chapters of the *Metaphysics* is taken
therefrom. We must assume that this is true also of the out-
standingly Platonic theological section 982^b 28–983^a 11, although
our material fails us here.[1]

With regard to Iamblichus' ninth chapter, the end of it (p. 52,
l. 16—p. 54, l. 5, frg. 58) is recognized as certainly belonging to

---

[1] In two famous places where he is praising the divine blessedness of pure
philosophical contemplation (*Metaph.* A 2, 982^b 28, and *Eth. Nic.* X. 7, 1177^b 31)
Aristotle exhorts men not to be afraid of setting their thoughts on divine and
immortal things, thus contradicting the ancient Greek precept. It is notorious
that in both these passages he borrows a number of ideas and descriptive
formulae from the *Protrepticus*; and his reversal of the ancient exhortation
is protreptic in the highest degree. Now the author of the protreptic *Ad
Demonicum*, who (as was shown above) made polemical use of Aristotle's
work in several places,.writes in § 32 as follows: 'Think immortal things by
being lofty of soul, and mortal things by enjoying in due measure the goods
that you possess.' Although he here understands 'thinking immortal things'
in a purely moralistic and non-speculative sense, he does at any rate allow
it a certain value; and this shows that he has been induced by Aristotle to
correct the traditional exhortation, which would hear nothing of such high
thinking. Hence it is as good as certain that the famous call 'to make ourselves
immortal as far as we can' (*Eth. Nic.* 1177^b 33) originally appeared in the
Protrepticus, and was borrowed thence for the *Ethics* and the introduction to
the *Metaphysics*.

the *Protrepticus*. In content it forms part of Aristotle's reply to the objection that philosophy is useless for life. We know from Cicero that he actually used the division of goods into necessary and valuable in themselves (ἀναγκαῖα and δι' αὐτὰ ἀγαπώμενα or ἐλεύθερα), and also the beautiful description of the isles of the blest, whose inhabitants, having no earthly needs, are wholly devoted to pure contemplation.[1] Nevertheless, Iamblichus has largely obliterated the force of the passage. Aristotle was not merely painting a pleasant picture. He also intended to show mankind isolated, as it were, from the needs (χρεία) of life. In using an image for such a purpose he was following Plato in the *Republic*, where the story of Gyges is employed in order to observe the behaviour of a man who can do whatever he likes, without having to take any account of other men and their judgements. It is commonly held that Iamblichus gives the original more truly than Cicero. This is wrong. Cicero says: supposing we were on the islands of the blessed, what need should we have of oratory, since there are no judicial proceedings there? What need should we have of the virtues of justice, courage, temperance, and even ethical prudence? Only knowledge and pure contemplation would still be desirable. It follows that we love knowledge for its own sake, and not because of its usefulness or of any need of ours. Iamblichus omits all this, and thereby obscures the point of the picture. Cicero has preserved the tenor of the original on the whole pretty accurately. His only alteration is the addition of eloquence to the four cardinal virtues adduced in the *Protrepticus*. This was obviously done because of Hortensius, who reckoned not philosophy but eloquence the highest good.

The proof of Cicero's superior accuracy is to be found in the tenth book of the *Nicomachean Ethics*. Here again a reminiscence of his early work has influenced Aristotle's pen.[2] The subject is the same as that of the *Protrepticus*, namely pure contemplation. He contrasts it with the life of action. The latter requires many external aids for the realization of the ethical disposition (ἡ ἐκτὸς χορηγία ἡ ἠθική). Generosity requires money. So does justice, if you wish to return equals for equals. Courage requires strength. Temperance can be tested only by the

---

[1] Frg. 58.   [2] *Eth. Nic.* X. 8, 1178ᵃ 24–ᵇ 5.

opportunity to abandon one's self-control. How else can a good disposition be exercised? And without exercise it never reaches fulfilment. The knower, on the other hand, needs no external aid in order to exercise his virtue; on the contrary, such aids could only be a hindrance to him. There, moreover, Aristotle represents contemplation (θεωρία) as isolated and independent of the necessities of life. The idea is somewhat differently turned; Plato's doctrine of the four virtues is consciously rejected; through the inclusion of generosity the whole regains in effectiveness what it loses in enthusiasm through the suppression of the isles of the blest. In spite of retouching, however, the original picture is still recognizable, because the old method of presenting the thought is retained. The essential point, both here and in Cicero, is the disappearance of the 'ethical virtues' in the state of pure bliss that belongs to intellectual vision. This proves that Cicero's version is the more complete.

The first part of the ninth chapter also comes from the *Protrepticus*. This is as certain from the contents as it is from the style. Aristotle starts by dividing the causes of becoming into nature, art, and chance, a distinction that he makes in other places as well, though nowhere so pregnantly as here.[1] It is a characteristically Aristotelian view that nature is purposive in a higher degree even than art, and that the purposiveness that rules in handiwork, whether art or craft, is nothing but an imitation of the purposiveness of nature. The same view of the relation between these two things is often briefly expressed in the second book of the *Physics*, which is one of Aristotle's earliest writings. It is occasionally alluded to in other places also, but never so well developed and articulated as here. An expression like the following is strikingly original: 'Nature does not imitate art,[2] but art nature; and art exists to help and to make up what nature leaves undone' (p. 49, l. 28). The means

[1] We shall meet this tripartite division of the causes of becoming again in the dialogue *On Philosophy*. There its authenticity has been doubted, but in reality it is a part of the mechanistic physics that obtained before Plato. In *Laws* X. 888 E, Plato had already used it precisely as Aristotle does in the *Protrepticus*, to show that nature (φύσις) is not behind art (τέχνη) in intellect and resourcefulness, and to develop his new conception of φύσις by this means. The realistic manner in which the idea is worked out in the *Protrepticus* shows how closely Aristotle followed the later Plato even in his philosophy of nature.

[2] That it did was the view of the Presocratic sophists, who were thoroughly

taken to recommend this view are again indubitably Aristotelian. He offers examples from agriculture and from the care that the higher organisms require before and after birth. He establishes the proposition that there is a universal purposiveness in organic nature by examples from the mechanics of the human body and its self-protecting devices.[1] Everything comes into being for the sake of an end. An end is that which always appears as the final result of a development, in accordance with natural law and by a continuous process, and in which the process attains its completion. Thus in the process of becoming the mental is later than the physical, and in the mental realm the intellectual element in its pure form is again the later. Therefore Pythagoras was right in calling pure contemplation the end of man, i.e. the completion of human nature. To the question what we are born for he replied, 'to gaze upon the heavens'. Anaxagoras also expressed himself to the same effect.

Anaxagoras' apophthegm reappears in the *Eudemian Ethics*,

---

imbued with the rationalist spirit, and taught the existence of a mechanical adaptation of means to end in nature, and especially in the human organism. Traces of such a system are preserved in Xen. *Mem.* I. 4, 6 ff., and Arist. *Part. Animal.* II. 15. Aristotle's philosophy of nature depends on an entirely different attitude, as he himself says here. It is *teleological*. Far from nature's exhibiting 'incipient' tendencies to rival the art of our machines, all arts are merely man's attempt to compete with organic and creative nature; and this competition necessarily takes place in another medium (that of artificial construction), in which it is never possible to speak of an end (τέλος) in the highest or organic sense.

[1] Bernays (*Gesammelte Abhandlungen*, vol. i, p. 23) believed Heraclitus to be the originator of the proposition that art is an imitation of nature, because the author of the *De Mundo* (5, 396^b 7 ff.) explains the process of natural becoming as being a harmonious amalgamation of opposites, and proves this from the example of the arts, which he declares to be nothing but imitations of nature; but what the *De Mundo* quotes from Heraclitus in this connexion ('that which agrees and that which differs, that which produces harmony and that which produces discord') shows no trace of such a view. So far as concerns the inference from art to nature, and the conclusion that the latter is the archetype, this view is Peripatetic and has nothing to do with the sage of Ephesus. Democritus has a similar but distinct doctrine when he calls men the pupils of the animals, of the spider in weaving and mending, of the swallow in building, and of the songbirds in song (frg. 154). (With the last cf. Lucretius V. 1379. Lucretius also derives cookery (l. 1102) and sowing and grafting (l. 1361) from the imitation of nature, which he certainly got from Democritus by way of Epicurus). But Aristotle is concerned with something entirely new. He refers the proposition that art is an imitation of nature to the teleological character of all human construction, and grounds it in the teleological view of nature.

and the verbal correspondence is such that either Iamblichus must have got it thence or he must have preserved for us the source from which it came to the *Eudemian Ethics*. Later on, when we analyse the whole train of thought of the *Ethics*, it will appear that the latter is the fact. Here again, therefore, the *Eudemian Ethics* reproduces the *Protrepticus*, and this proves that the latter is the source from which Iamblichus took not merely the apophthegm of Anaxagoras but the whole argument of which that is a part.

This can be substantiated indirectly. The doctrine that art imitates nature is further developed in Posidonius' theory of the origin of civilization. What this was we know in outline from Seneca's ninetieth letter; Posidonius held that the advances of civilization are philosophical discoveries. He did a great deal to spread in later antiquity the Aristotelian doctrine that the arts arose in stages, first those necessary to life, then those of pleasure, and lastly pure contemplation. It has been plausibly suggested that he expressed this view in his *Protrepticus*.[1] If this hypothesis is correct, we have here another of the many points in which he attached himself to the doctrine of Aristotle's work of the same name. With the particular nuance that he gives it we are not concerned; the important thing is that the Aristotelian archetype lends substantial support to the view that Posidonius' expression of it was to be found in his *Protrepticus*.

The demonstration that the rest of Iamblichus' excerpts from Aristotle (chaps. 10–12) are also from the *Protrepticus* need not take so long. Chapter 10 begins with the proposition that art is an imitation of nature, which has already been shown to come from the *Protrepticus*. From this it is deduced that even the science of politics needs a philosophical foundation, since it requires, still more than medicine and the like, to take its start from nature in the proper sense of the word, that is, from true being. Nothing but the knowledge of this can give the statesman insight into the ultimate norms (ὅροι) in accordance with which he must direct his activity. Politics can become an exact art only when it becomes through and through philosophy. As was remarked above (p. 71), this passage on the ideal of exacti-

[1] See Gerhäusser, *Der Protreptikos des Poseidonios* (a Heidelberg thesis), Munich, 1912, pp. 18 ff.

tude in pure science is one of the parts of the *Protrepticus* that
are reproduced in the first book of the *Metaphysics*. Its Platonic
colouring in Iamblichus, which is intentionally removed in the
Metaphysics, fits the *Protrepticus* very well, as the philosophical
interpretation of the fragments (pp. 90–91) will show in detail;
Hirzel and Diels recognized that this colouring constitutes no
reason for assigning the passage to the Neo-Platonic excerptor;
the thoughts are too original for that. Aristotle points out that
only when politics is studied on scientific principles and regarded
as a normative discipline will it be freed from its present un-
fruitfulness and instability (a remark especially suitable in a work
addressed to a practical statesman). This train of thought culminates in the proof that in the long run politics is theoretical in
character. The only foundation for creative statesmanship is,
not the mere analogies of experience, but theoretical knowledge
of the ultimate standards. Here again Aristotle's main purpose is to refute the mere empirics, who know of nothing better
than the so-called model constitutions (εὐνομίαι) of Sparta and
Crete. (He seems to mean Isocrates and the sophistic theory of
the state.) From this we learn that the critical discussion of
the three ideal states (Sparta, Crete, Carthage), which now constitutes the second book of the *Politics*, goes back in content to
Aristotle's Academic period. We thereby obtain a very interesting fragment of his early views on politics. For all its Platonic
presuppositions no other Platonist could have written it, because
of its predominantly methodological interests. It shows that
the *Protrepticus* took direct account of the Academy's political
aims. The fact that chapter 10 is 'political' in content has been
supposed to prove that it must come from some purely political
work of Aristotle's; but this is superficial. The decisive thing is
not the content but the point of view from which it is presented;
and the point of view of this fragment—the emphasis on the
theoretical character of normative politics—shows that it belongs to the praise of pure 'theory' in the *Protrepticus*.

The eleventh chapter is concerned with the relation between
wisdom (φρόνησις) and pleasure. This topic has been held in-
appropriate for a protreptic, on the ground that it does not
appear in the later ones. But such a method of argument is
fundamentally unsound. What was fitting in a protreptic

emanating from Plato's school cannot be mechanically deduced from the commonplaces of the later protreptics of imperial times. The method has been used only too enthusiastically in literary research; but it can never be successful when we have to deal with writers like Plato or Aristotle, whose form is the individual and organic result of the necessities of their matter. It is really self-evident that the relation between wisdom (φρόνησις) and pleasure, a traditional subject of discussion in the Academy, would be in place in a protreptic which attempted to show that true happiness is Platonic knowledge (φρόνησις). The thesis positively could not be proved in any other way. Aristotle was unable to conceive of happiness without pleasure; it was therefore necessary to inquire what kind of pleasure wisdom can give. If the ideal of pure contemplation was to be established, this problem had to be faced. It is discussed as early as the *Republic*,[1] and then more thoroughly in the *Philebus*. The *Nicomachean Ethics* again, in the tenth book of which the 'theoretic life' is shown to be true happiness, examines both the relation of pleasure to perfect activity and, more especially, the sensation of pure pleasure accompanying knowledge. We have already shown that this portion of the tenth book is partly dependent for its content on the *Protrepticus*, and has the same theme. Hence the pleasure of contemplation was a necessary part of the subject-matter of the *Protrepticus*, as will be proved once more when we show that the *Eudemian Ethics* makes use of the *Protrepticus*. Both in the *Protrepticus* and in the *Ethics* wisdom, pleasure, and virtue are listed as the three possible kinds of happiness. In the *Protrepticus* the demonstration culminates in the proof that the life of pure contemplation affords the most complete satisfaction of the demands of all three of these ideals. Contemplation is there found to be not merely the climax of philosophical knowledge, but also the completion of man's ethical development and the pure happiness of uninterrupted intellectual joy. No element in this construction can be removed without destroying the whole. This proves that the first part of the twelfth chapter is also an extract from Aristotle's work.

It is certainly not too bold to imagine that the *Protrepticus*, like the later examples of this kind of literature, culminated in a

[1] Plato, *Rep*. VI. 506 B.

description of the *vita beata*. Both its matter and its form demand such an arrangement, so that the inference from the later
and derivative to the earlier and original is here free from danger.
What would we not give to possess that epilogue in which
Aristotle rose to the heights of his ultimate convictions! But to
suggest that he is the author of the conclusion actually found in
Iamblichus (p. 60, l. 7—p. 61, l. 4) is to let desire stifle critical
reflection.[1] Enthusiastic the sentences may be, and even inspired; but it is not the controlled enthusiasm of Aristotle, who
never forgoes the strict rhythm of his apodictic advance, and
values form higher than the highest inspiration, often as his
arguments perceptibly overflow with the latter. Most of the
details of Iamblichus' passage could indeed well have been taken
from the *Protrepticus*, and they may be so. Such are the unnaturalness of our earthly and corporeal existence, the nig-
gardliness of all our knowledge and apprehension, the contrast
between our present unstable abodes and that place from which
we come and towards which we strive, and the disproportion
between the labour required to obtain the mere necessities of
life and the time that we are able to devote to the only valuable,
the eternal things. But the loose and merely associative conjunction of these notions into an edifying summons to the other
world, the confusion of ideas that can be detected in them, the
sacerdotal unction with which the writer introduces some of
Plato's ceremonial words, the presence of certain distinctly Neo-
Platonic phrases like 'the heavenly path' and 'the realm of the
gods', and lastly the excessive loquacity of the conclusion, with
its inability to come to an end—all these things betray retouching by Iamblichus. Then follow excerpts from Plato.

3. THE PHILOSOPHY OF THE *PROTREPTICUS*

The *Protrepticus* has no single problem. Its importance
reaches beyond the limits of departmental philosophy, and lies
in the universality of the question that it raises about the conduct of life—the question of the meaning and justification of
philosophy and of its place in man's life as a whole.[2] Not that it

[1] Hartlich, op. cit., pp. 254 ff.
[2] With regard to the philosophy of the *Protrepticus* I find myself in opposition not merely to Bernays's attempt at harmonization, but also to the view

was Plato's philosophy which first confronted men with this question; it persistently recurs in the legends about Thales, Anaxagoras, Pythagoras, and Democritus. But every new generation of genuine students revives it and argues passionately about it against the mass of mankind; for in its most thorough-going form 'the theoretic life' remains a postulate of the born student, which, though its rightness is always being re-experienced, can presumably never be made to seem justifiable to the common sense of the generality. It demands a strong and abounding faith in the power of knowledge to lift its finder higher than men are otherwise privileged to attain. Out of this faith, which is utterly different from the intellectual pride of the pedant, Aristotle's *Protrepticus* is written. The experience of which it gives evidence is no commonplace idyll of scholarship, but the beatitude of the man who has learnt to see the world through the eyes of Plato. Thus it becomes a manifesto for the Platonic life, and for Platonic philosophy as the means thereto. For us it has the advantage of being the confession that we are looking for out of Aristotle's own mouth.

It was not an accident that one of the younger generation of Academicians undertook to justify the ideal of the scholarly life to the outer world. This generation suffered the old conflict between theory and practice with renewed violence. Plato himself never denied, even in his most theoretical periods, that he had been to school under Socrates, who put his painful questions to his fellow-men at the bidding of conscience and of the needs of life. Plato's own philosophy was equally rooted in the needs of the time and of practical life; only its culmination, the apprehension of the Forms, reaches up into the region of pure theoretical knowledge. In his hands the Socratic demand that we shall

expressed in the *Archiv für Geschichte der Philosophie* (vol. i, p. 493) by Diels, who at that time wished to explain away the obvious traces of Platonism in the fragments as mere stylistic ornaments. The real state of affairs had been suggested by Hirzel (*Hermes*, vol. x, p. 98). He was too timid, however, to oppose the reigning prejudice, as would have been logical; and Diels put him to silence. Since then Diels has changed his view about the development of Aristotle, as is clear from the *Zeitschrift für vergleichende Sprachforschung*, vol. xlvii, p. 201, n. 4. He there recognizes that my *Entstehungsgeschichte der Metaphysik* has demonstrated that Aristotle had a Platonic period. But the exoteric writings are in part still earlier than the oldest passages in the treatises, and in contents they constitute the stage prior to the critically revised Platonism of those works.

know the nature of virtue becomes a doctrine of the primacy of the creative intellect, which contemplates pure being and reorganizes life accordingly. He disputes the right of every other kind of life to this position. This is not an attempt to prove to the incorrigibly practical that a 'gift' for theory has a certain justification for existing along with other activities, because it does no one any harm; it is the bold belief that nothing but the knowledge of the highest truth can form the foundation of a life that is worthy of its name. Plato never relaxed this claim, even when he had given up trying to reform reality and was devoting himself exclusively to research; but the younger generation was obliged to ask itself the question afresh, just because it had never experienced anything but the theoretical life; and it had to find the value of this life in the inner man, in the pure bliss of contemplation, and in the union of the intellect with the eternal. Thus the Platonic ideal, originally so full of reforming zeal, took a contemplative and religious turn.

This exuberant ideal of contemplation can be justified only by means of some conception that implies the identity of theoretical knowledge and practical conduct. Such a conception is that of *phronesis*.[1] *Phronesis* is central to the *Protrepticus*, which is concerned with the possibility, subject-matter, use, growth, and happiness, of theoretical knowledge. It may be interpreted as the creative apprehension of pure goodness through the inner intuition of the soul and at the same time as an apprehension of pure being, and also as the derivation of valuable activity and true knowledge from one and the same fundamental power of the mind. It is one of the 'innate ideas' of the Greek spirit. It went through a long development, but no period brought it nearer to its fulfilment than that from Socrates to Aristotle. In the *Protrepticus* its meaning is purely Platonic. For a long time it had been split into two systems, one predominantly practical and economic, the other moral and religious. This very split made it suitable to be the crystallizing point of the thought of Socrates. It was then taken over by

[1] [Translator's note. The word φρόνησις is usually translated by 'wisdom' in Plato. In Aristotle's *Nicomachean Ethics* W. D. Ross renders it by 'practical wisdom'. Sometimes the best translation is 'prudence'. The corresponding verb means 'to take thought'.]

Plato, who strongly emphasized the element of intellectual knowledge in it, and examined the special nature of this 'knowledge'.
It now took to itself the Form or standard as its object, and thus
became the intellectual intuition of the good and the beautiful
in themselves. The Form had first occurred to Plato in connexion
with Socrates' problems, that is to say, in the ethical sphere; but
as it widened its sway until it finally became the general principle
of all being, *phronesis* received more and more content. It became
the Eleatic science of being. It became the Anaxagorean *Nus*.
In a word, it became pure theoretical reason, the opposite of what
it had been in Socrates' practical sphere. At this point Plato
divided his system into dialectic, ethics, and physics. From then
on there were several *phroneseis*. Frequently the word meant no
more than 'special science'; gymnastics and medicine, and all
disciplines whatsoever, were *phroneseis*. This development can be
understood only by means of the development of Plato's philosophy as a whole, and its final division into three philosophies.
At the same time a development took place in the theory of the
first principles, in the course of which the Form became mathematical, and ended in a theology and a monadology. In the
Protrepticus phronesis has this meaning almost exclusively. It is
Nus, metaphysical speculation, that which is really divine in us,
a power wholly distinct from the other faculties of the soul; as it
is in the *Timaeus* and the *Philebus*, in the *Laws* or the *Epinomis*.

Whereas the *Protrepticus* understands *phronesis* in the full
Platonic sense, as equivalent to philosophical knowledge as
such, when we come to the *Metaphysics* the conception has disappeared. The *Nicomachean Ethics* also presents a wholly
different picture. In this work the *phronesis* of the *Protrepticus*
is definitely rejected. In the sixth book considerable space is
devoted to the question of the position of *phronesis* among the
intellectual faculties. Everywhere a polemical intention appears
between the lines. Aristotle reduces the word to its meaning
in ordinary usage, i.e. to the sense that it had before Plato.
He deprives it of all theoretical significance, and sharply distinguishes its sphere from that of *sophia* and *Nus*.[1] In common

---

[1] *Eth. Nic.* VI. 5 ff. Ordinary usage is emphasized in 1140^a 25 and 29; ^{b} 8, 10,
and 11; and 1141^a 25, 27, and ^{b} 5. [Tr.—Σοφία is practically identical with
'wisdom'.]

usage it is a practical faculty, concerned both with the choice of the ethically desirable and with the prudent perception of one's own advantage. Such is Aristotle's later terminology. He is at the farthest remove from the standpoint of his early period when he concedes *phronesis* to animals.[1] In connexion with ethics it now means an habitual disposition of the mind to deliberate practically about everything concerning human weal and woe[2] (ἕξις πρακτική). He insists that it is not speculation but deliberation, that it is concerned not with the universal but with the fleeting details of life, and that it therefore does not have the highest and most valuable things in the universe for object, and in fact is not a science at all.[3] What all this amounts to is the public recantation of the Platonic views in the *Protrepticus*. Whereas he there described metaphysics as 'the *phronesis* of the kind of truth that was introduced by Anaxagoras and Parmenides and their followers', he here expressly lays it down that such persons as Anaxagoras and Parmenides are not called *phronimoi* but *sophoi*, precisely because while they inquired into the eternal laws of the universe they did not understand their own advantage.[4]

Beneath this change in terminology lies a change in the fundamental principles of Aristotle's metaphysics and ethics. To Socrates *phronesis* had meant the ethical power of reason, a sense modelled on the common usage that Aristotle restores to its rights in the *Nicomachean Ethics*. Plato analysed the nature of this ethical insight more exactly, and derived it from the contemplation of eternal Norms, and in the last resort from the Good. This changed it into the scientific apprehension of independent objects; but Plato was justified in retaining the name *phronesis*, in as much as the knowledge of true being was in fact a knowledge of the pure Norms by reference to which man should order his life. In the contemplation of the Forms being and value, knowledge and action, coalesce. When the theory of Forms was abandoned being and value fell apart, and dialectic thereby lost its direct significance for human life, which to Plato was an essential feature of it. The distinction between

---

[1] *Eth. Nic.* VI. 7, 1141ᵃ 27.   [2] *Eth. Nic.* VI. 5, 1140ᵇ 4 and 20.
[3] *Eth. Nic.* VI. 8, 1141ᵇ 9 and 14; 1141ᵃ 21 and 33 ff.; 1142ᵃ 24.
[4] Frg. 52 (p. 59, l. 3, in Rose). *Eth. Nic.* VI. 7, 1141ᵇ 3–5.

metaphysics and ethics became much sharper than before.[1] To one looking backwards from this point of view Plato appears 'intellectualist', because he based ethical action entirely on the knowledge of being. Aristotle drew a line between the two. He discovered the psychological roots of moral action and evaluation in character (ἦθος), and from then on the examination of ἦθος took the foremost place in what came to be called *ethical* thought, and suppressed transcendental *phronesis*. The result was the fruitful distinction between theoretical and practical reason, which had lain together as yet unseparated in *phronesis*.

From this sketch of the historical development it follows necessarily that in the *Protrepticus* Aristotle based himself on a different metaphysics. It was the abandonment of the Idea-theory that led to the break with Plato's doctrine of the primacy of *phronesis*, and with his onesidedly theoretical derivation of the ethical life. Therefore the *Protrepticus*, which is still completely dominated by the conception of *phronesis* in the old sense, must have been based on Plato's ethical metaphysics, that is, on the unity of being and value. All the essential parts of it are in fact Platonic, not merely in language but also in content. Nowhere else does Aristotle sanction the Academic division of philosophy into dialectic, physics, and ethics (except in the *Topics*, but there it is merely mentioned in passing, and the *Topics* is presumably one of his earliest efforts).[2] Moreover,

---

[1] This is true of all specifically human values, but not of absolute value or good. Aristotle believed as much as Plato that being and value in the absolute sense coincide in the conception of God. In that respect he remained a Platonist to the day of his death. The highest being is also the highest good. At the point that is farthest removed from human affairs metaphysics penetrates into ethics and ethics into metaphysics. The perspective, however, has shifted completely. It is only in the far distance that the motionless pole appears, an ultimate sign-post, on the horizon of existence. The connexion of this metaphysics with particular actions is too loose to justify its being called *phronesis*.

[2] In frg. 52 (p. 60, l. 17, in Rose), in the course of a proof that we can attain to real knowledge, Aristotle clearly distinguishes knowledge (1) 'of the just and the beneficial', (2) of 'nature', and (3) 'of the rest of truth'. He does not yet possess an expression for 'first philosophy' (cf. p. 59, ll. 1-4, in Rose, where the conception of it is again linked with the knowledge of the just and unjust and the knowledge of nature, and again expressed by a periphrasis). At any rate, Plato's word 'dialectic' seems to him not to be characteristic enough; it fails to distinguish ontology from ethics and politics, and it does not contain any reference to an object. For the latter reason Aristotle limits it to formal logic, which has no object. In harmony with the tripartite division of philosophy is the proof (1) about substance (p. 60, l. 21—p. 61, l. 1, in Rose),

there is as yet no trace of what we find in the *Ethics*, the supplementation of the doctrine of virtue by psychological analysis; instead of that we have Plato's architectonic doctrine of the four virtues.[1] The decisive thing, however, is what the *Protrepticus* says about the method of ethics and politics.

The opponents of philosophy are there made to describe ethics in accordance with Plato's notion of it, as if the correctness of that notion were self-evident. It is a science of the just and unjust, of the good and bad, like geometry and its related sciences.[2] Aristotle is here calling attention to a point that had obviously aroused severe criticism, the view that ethics is an exact science. In another place he describes politics (which he considers inseparable from ethics) as a science that seeks for absolute norms (ὅροι). To philosophical politics he opposes the 'arts', which use merely second-hand knowledge. He reckons ordinary empirical politics as one of them, because its decisions are based only on the analogies of experience and it is therefore incapable of ever giving rise to creative action. Philosophical politics has 'the exact in itself' for object. It is a purely theoretical science.[3]

This ideal of mathematical exactness is contrary to everything that Aristotle teaches in his *Ethics* and *Politics* about the method of those studies. In the *Nicomachean Ethics* he explicitly opposes the demand for an exact method, as being incompatible with the nature of the material. In this respect he equates ethics and politics with rhetoric rather than with mathematics.[4] Their propositions are merely typical, never universal; their inferences are valid at best as a general rule, and not without exception. To the ideal of method that he stood for in the *Protrepticus* Aristotle here replies that the more general ethical propositions are the more empty and ineffective they are.[5] Virtually every

---

(2) about the virtues of the soul (p. 61, ll. 2–8, in Rose), and (3) about nature (p. 61, ll. 8–17, in Rose). In *Top.* I. 14, 105^b 20 ff., Aristotle distinguishes between ethical, physical, and logical premisses; here again 'dialectical' is avoided, cf. Xenocrates frg. 1 (Heinze).

[1] For the four Platonic virtues see frg. 52 (p. 62, l. 1, in Rose) and frg. 58 (p. 68, ll. 6–9).

[2] Frg. 52 (p. 58, l. 23, in Rose).

[3] Iambl. *Protr.*, p. 55, ll. 1 and 6 ff., in Pistelli.

[4] *Eth. Nic.* I. 1, 1094^b 11–27; I. 13, 1102^a 23.

[5] *Eth. Nic.* II. 7, 1107^a 29.

word that the *Nicomachean Ethics* contains about this matter is written with a polemical implication, and we must learn to read it with this in mind. In the *Protrepticus* it was said that the philosophical statesman is distinguished from the common run of politicians by the exactness of his knowledge of the norms; he beholds things in themselves, and does not rest content with their variegated reproductions in empirical reality. There is an intentional reminiscence of this passage, almost to the very same words, in the *Nicomachean Ethics*; but there the view is converted into its exact opposite. We read that one must distinguish between the way in which a geometer and the way in which a carpenter (i.e. an empiric) measures a right angle. The former beholds truth itself; the latter inquires into the nature of rectangularity only so far as it is necessary for his practical purposes. And it is with the latter, not with the geometer, that Aristotle compares the science of ethics or politics! Plato's ideal of an ethics proceeding *more geometrico* is here emphatically rejected, whereas in the *Protrepticus* it still holds undisputed sway;[1] and when Aristotle here insists that for the statesman, and even for the student listening to lectures on ethics, practical experience is far more important than theoretical equipment, that also is polemic against his own earlier Platonic view.[2] Of late origin again is the declaration that philosophy is not necessary for a king, but rather a hindrance; he should, however, give ear to truly philosophical councillors. This appears to come from a work addressed to Alexander, and to refer to a particular situation, which may be dated during the Asiatic expedition.[3] Between the time of the letter to Themison, which invited him to theoretical statesmanship based on the Forms, and the time when Aristotle wrote this piece of advice, a change had occurred in the fundamentals of his thought.

[1] *Eth. Nic.* I. 7, 1098ª 26: 'And we must also remember what has been said before, and not look for precision in all things alike, but in each class of things such precision as accords with the subject-matter, and so much as is appropriate to the inquiry. For a carpenter and a geometer investigate the right angle in different ways; the former does so in so far as the right angle is useful for his work, while the latter inquires what it is or what sort of thing it is; for he is a spectator of the truth. We must act in the same way, then, in all other matters as well, that our main task may not be subordinated to minor questions.' Cf. Iambl. *Protr.*, p. 55, ll. 1–14, in Pistelli.

[2] *Eth. Nic.* X. 10, 1181ª 1 and 10; I. 13, 1102ª 19 ff.   [3] Frg. 647.

The ideal of geometrical ethics could have been conceived only on the basis of the later theory of Ideas. To Plato knowledge was measurement. By an exact science he understood one that measures things in accordance with an absolute and completely determinate measure. Hence the indeterminate (ἄπειρον), the manifold of the sensible world, is never an object of pure science. The *Philebus* shows how in his old age he tried to make ethics an exact science on the mathematical pattern by means of the principles of limit (πέρας) and measure (μέτρον). In that dialogue the notion of measurement is constantly recurring; it is the sign of the mathematical stage of the Idea-theory. Since all that is good is measurable and determinate, while all that is evil is immeasurable and indeterminate, both in the cosmos and in the soul, Plato's later politics and ethics are really nothing but a theoretical science of measure and the norm. In the second book of his lost *Statesman* Aristotle wrote: 'the good is the most exact measure'.[1] The Platonist Syrianus quotes these words against their author, and argues from them that Aristotle understood Plato's doctrine better at other times. Aristotle meant precisely the same thing in the *Protrepticus* when he demanded exactness and described politics as a science of pure norms. This is the philosophy of the *Philebus*, which gives the first place in the table of goods to measure (μέτρον), the second to the measurable (σύμμετρον), and the third to the reason that apprehends measure (*phronesis*).[2] In the *Republic* the Form of the Good had been the ground of the being and knowability of the whole real world. According to the *Philebus* and to Aristotle's *Statesman* the reason why it is so is that it is the highest and universal measure, the absolute unity that makes the world of Forms determinate, 'symmetrical', and thereby real, good, and knowable. All that is indeterminate is excluded from it. We need not here inquire what part Plato's later view that the Forms are numbers has to play in this doctrine   Aristotle mentions it frequently in the *Protrepticus*. His later ethics is an intentional contradiction of the view represented there and in the *Statesman*; according to it there are no universal norms, there is

---

[1] Frg. 79. Syrian's remarks on this statement, which Rose does not reproduce, are important because they show that he was fully conscious of the contradiction between it and Aristotle's later view.   [2] *Phil.* 66 A.

no measure except the individual living measure of the autonomous ethical person, and *phronesis* is concerned not with the
universal but with the particular.[1]

'The good is the most exact measure' means precisely the
same as Plato's dictum in the *Laws*, 'God is the measure of all
things'. This pointed attack on Protagoras' statement that man
is the measure of all things was intended to set the absolute
norm on the throne of the universe;[2] God is the good in itself,
the pure monad, the measure of measures. Thus politics and
ethics become theology and take their stand at the head of
theoretical philosophy; what is and what ought to be are
identical in the absolute sense; and human action is done with
immediate reference to the highest value and meaning in the
world. In accordance with its principles the *Nicomachean Ethics*
denies that politics has this leading position; politics can no
more be the highest wisdom than the aims of human life can
aspire to the highest good, which is glimpsed only by the wise
man in his intuition of the divinity.[3]

The view of the *Philebus*, that philosophy ought to be made
an exact and mathematical science,[4] did not influence the *Pro-*

[1] 'The good man judges each class of things rightly, and in each the truth
appears to him. . . . And perhaps *the good man* differs from others most by
seeing the truth in each class of things, *being as it were a norm and measure of
them*', *Eth. Nic.* III. 6, 1113ª 29 ff. 'The refined and well-bred man, therefore,
being as it were a law to himself', IV. 14, 1128ª 31. 'If virtue and the good man
as such are the measure of each thing, those also will be pleasures which appear so to him, and those things pleasant which he enjoys', X. 5, 1176ª 18.
Incidentally, these remarkable sentences prove once more, if only we look at
them in the light of the *Protrepticus*, that Aristotle's ethical inquiries were
originally entirely dominated by Plato's problem of the measurability and
measure of moral phenomena; his change consisted simply in rejecting the
universal norms, and recognizing no measure but the autonomous conscience of
the ethically educated person ('the good man'), a measure which can claim no
'exactness' in the epistemological sense. Thus he refers every man to himself,
and recognizes the inexhaustible variety of the conditions of individual moral
action without undermining the inviolability of the inner norm. The famous
notion of virtue as a mean between excess and defect is also treated as a problem
in the measurement of continuous quantities (II. 5, 1106ª 26); and it is this
treatment that gives sense to the method employed, a fact which is usually
completely misunderstood, because everybody ignores the actual historical
connexions out of which Aristotle's problem arose.
[2] Plato, *Laws* IV. 716 c: 'God ought to be to us the measure of all things,
and not man as men commonly say.'
[3] *Eth. Nic.* VI. 7, 1141ª 20 ff.
[4] For exactness (ἀκρίβεια) as the sign of a discipline's being scientific in
character see *Phil.* 56 B-C, 57 C-E, 58 C, 59 A, 59 D, and so on.

trepticus merely with regard to the nature of ethics and politics. It is also the underlying reason for the account there given of the relation between empirical and pure science. Plato's later doctrine took from mathematics not merely the conception of measure and the ideal of exactness, but also the problem of drawing the line between pure and applied science. In the *Protrepticus* the opponents of pure philosophy and science are represented as coupling geometry and surveying, the theory of harmony and music, astronomy and the sailor's knowledge of sky and weather, in order to prove that theory is actually a handicap in any department of practical activity, because it prevents the student from getting practice and often even impairs the certainty of his natural instinct.[1] We should like to know how Aristotle replied to this criticism, but unfortunately his answer is lost. The idea of coupling together pairs of pure and empirical sciences was naturally not invented by his opponents; it was first used by Plato. The *Philebus* distinguishes an arithmetic of the philosophers from the arithmetic of the many;[2] it is science in a greater or less degree according as the units with which it operates are like or unlike. Similarly there are two 'arts' of computation and two of mensuration; in fact, there are many 'arts' where such a twin brotherhood exists, without their being distinguished by name.[3] Those with which the true philosophers are occupied are incomparably superior to the others because of their exactness and truth in matters of measure and number. Presumably Aristotle's answer to the empiricists was similar to Plato's in the *Philebus*: it does not matter which 'art' is most serviceable and which is of the greatest use, but which aims at the greatest accuracy, clarity, and truth. 'A little pure white is whiter and fairer and truer than a great deal that is mixed', and the lover of pure colours will therefore prefer it unconditionally.[4] This view, that knowledge ought to be made exact even if it thereby becomes useless, is also the conviction of the *Protrepticus*. It arises out of the artistic attitude to mathematics that is characteristic of Plato's

---

[1] Frg. 52 (p. 59, ll. 18 ff., in Rose).   [2] *Phil.* 56 D.
[3] *Phil.* 57 D. Cf. *Epin.* 990 A, where the mathematical astronomer is contrasted with the empiric and the man who is weatherwise.
[4] *Phil.* 53 A.

later theory of Ideas; and without this artistic feeling for method Aristotle is inconceivable.

The *Protrepticus* gives clear expression not merely to the consequences of the theory of Forms but also to its actual contents.[1] Just as in the arts and crafts man's best tools, by which he measures and tests the straightness or smoothness of perceptible things, are copied from nature, so too the statesman according to Aristotle has definite norms (ὅροι), which he receives 'from nature *itself* and from the truth', and by reference to which he judges what is just, noble, good, and advantageous. Just as the tools that are taken from nature are superior to all others, so the best law is that which most accords with nature. It is, however, impossible to produce this law without first having learnt to know being and truth by means of philosophy. Neither the tools of the other arts nor their most accurate calculations are directly derived from the highest principles (οὐκ ἀπ' αὐτῶν τῶν πρώτων); they come from sources once, twice, or many times removed, and their rules are obtained by mere experience. Only the imitation (μίμησις) of the philosopher is exercised directly upon the exact *in itself* (ἀπ' αὐτῶν τῶν ἀκριβῶν); for he is a contemplator of things in themselves, and not of imitations (αὐτῶν γάρ ἐστι θεατής, ἀλλ' οὐ μιμημάτων).

Both the language and the philosophical content of this passage are pure Plato, a fact which had already been noticed in the days when the idea that Aristotle had a Platonic period was inconceivable.[2] So long as it was considered in isolation it may have seemed a sufficient explanation to say that it was an imitation of Plato's style, and that the pupil's own opinion lay hidden discreetly and cautiously beneath; but the meaning of these words can be really understood only by reference to their organic connexion with the philosophy of the *Protrepticus*, and the latter necessitates the dualist metaphysics of the Forms as

---

[1] Iambl. *Protr.*, p. 54, l. 22–p. 55, l. 14 (not in Rose).

[2] In *Hermes*, X. 99, Hirzel rightly compared this fragment, where the ruler and statesman is called upon to study philosophy, with Plato's demand that kings philosophize or only philosophers be kings. Hirzel also says that Iamblichus' tenth chapter belongs not to the *Protrepticus* but to some purely political writing of Aristotle's early period; but we have already shown that this is an error.

the theoretical basis of the above-described doctrines of values. The 'first things' that are here spoken of are not the same as those in Aristotle's *Metaphysics* and *Analytics*. It is true that in the *Metaphysics* as well as here we read that the philosopher apprehends the highest principles, the things that are most universal (πρῶτα);[1] and we have shown that its first two chapters are closely dependent on the *Protrepticus* throughout; but this only makes it the more significant that Aristotle there purposely avoids the Platonic expression 'the first things in themselves' (αὐτὰ τὰ πρῶτα) by excising the 'in themselves' (αὐτά)—that is to say, by excising the very word that makes the expression 'first things' in the *Protrepticus* a piece of specifically Platonic terminology. Even apart from that the expression 'first things' cannot here refer to the abstract universal in Aristotle's later sense, because the abstract universal is not contrasted with any 'imitations' (μιμήματα). 'Imitations' is again a specifically Platonic term, and cannot be significantly used apart from the doctrine that the Forms are archetypes (παρα-δείγματα) in which the things of sense participate. To suppose that such an acute logician and stylist as Aristotle could use 'imitation' merely in the etiolated sense of 'perceptible things' is simply impossible.[2]

---

[1] *Metaph.* A 2, 982ª 25.

[2] The expression 'imitation' is meant to emphasize the greater reality of the archetype. Hence it can no longer be used as soon as the Forms have ceased to be substances and become merely the highest universals. Still less would it be possible to say that on Aristotle's view the particular things of visible nature, which are made up of matter and form, are 'imitations' of the entelechies or forms that are active in them. 'Imitations' presuppose Platonic transcendence, the 'separateness' of archetype and copy. The question is decided by the fact that Aristotle also uses Plato's technical term when criticizing the Forms in later works; he often calls them simply 'themselves' (αὐτά) without any accompanying words, just as he does here when he says 'for he is a contemplator of *themselves*, and not of *imitations*' (αὐτῶν γάρ ἐστι θεατής, ἀλλ᾽ οὐ μιμημάτων, Iambl. p. 55, l. 13). Here the pronoun does not refer to anything that has gone before; it is used absolutely. This way of writing is not lucid unless the Forms are being contrasted with the corresponding sensible phenomena or copies, and hence we find it only when this is so. Cf. *Metaph.* 991ª 5, 'in itself and in the particular' (ἐπί τ᾽ αὐτῆς καὶ τῆς τινός); ª 30, 'not only of sensible things, but of themselves also' (οὐ μόνον τῶν αἰσθητῶν . . . ἀλλὰ καὶ αὐτῶν); ᵇ 30, 'between the things here and themselves' (μεταξὺ τῶν Δεῦρό τ᾽ ἔσται καὶ αὐτῶν); 997ᵇ 14, 'besides themselves and the sensible ones' (παρ᾽ αὐτάς καὶ τὰς αἰσθητάς); ᵇ 24, 'between themselves and the perishable ones' (μεταξὺ αὐτῶν τε καὶ τῶν φθαρτῶν). This peculiar usage of Plato's has obviously escaped the notice of scholars.

Such a way out of the difficulties that entangle every Aristotelian interpretation of the passage would be desperate, and there is still another fact that precludes it. These Platonic expressions are equated with the phrase 'nature itself and the truth'. Now this cannot be the Aristotelian conception of nature. In the first place, the addition of 'itself' would not be justifiable. Secondly, this nature is the source of absolute and exact standards for politics and ethics, which Aristotle's is not.[1] Lastly, Aristotle could not say that the philosopher who investigates nature is investigating 'the first things themselves', while the other arts, whose instruments and rules are equally obtained from visible nature, are concerned only with copies two, three, or many degrees removed; for if both have nature in the same sense as the subject-matter of their imitation, what distinguishes philosophy from the other arts in this respect?

This comparison between philosophy, which contemplates things in themselves, and the arts, which merely imitate copies of copies, brings us a little farther. It comes from the account of the theory of Forms in the tenth book of the *Republic*.[2] The *tertium comparationis* is the fact that both of them have their archetype in something objective and external to themselves, from which they as it were read off the law of their subject-matter. For the arts and crafts the archetype is the nature that is perceptible. For philosophers it is 'nature itself', which can be grasped only by pure thought. It is real being, and it can also be described as 'the first things themselves' (αὐτὰ τὰ πρῶτα)[3]. It follows that these 'first things' cannot possibly be the highest universals, because, whereas their equation with 'nature itself' gives them objective reality, Aristotle in his maturity denied that universals possess this. The only possible inference from these facts is that in this passage the highest universals and the

[1] Plato's *Statesman*, 297 C and 300 C ff., is the origin of the application of the terms 'imitation' and 'copies of the truth' to a politics that proceeds by earthly models and in accordance with written laws and constitutions, and is not creative because not based on the eternal norm. In that dialogue it occurs frequently, as does the comparison of the true statesman with a helmsman (cf. 297 E). The problem itself also comes from the same place. In 308 C Plato's ideal politics is called 'the true and natural art of statesmanship'.

[2] Plato, *Rep.* X. 599 A, 600 E, 602 C, 603 A, 605 B.

[3] Plato, *Parm.* 132 D: 'the Ideas are, as it were, patterns fixed in nature.' The equation of nature, being, and truth, is Platonic.

most 'exact' things are still considered identical with the essentially real—and that is true only of the Platonic Idea. Only of the Idea could one say that it is nature itself, the divine, the steadfast, the abiding, and the eternal, by the sight of which the philosophical statesman lives, and to which like a good helmsman he moors his ship.[1]

The main function of the Forms in the *Protrepticus* is to support its theory of knowledge by providing an exact object for pure knowledge, and secondarily to provide ethical norms. This is the direction in which Plato's development finally took him, and Aristotle follows. It leads to greater emphasis on method, and to the suppression if not to the denial of the existential character of the Forms. The very proof that they do possess real existence is now made to rest mainly on the requirements and presuppositions of conceptual knowledge. If the only real objects were sensible phenomena, conceptual thinking, which alone is exact, would have no real object; and in that case it would not be knowledge at all, according to the outlook of the time. The view that pure knowledge is exact thus becomes really the cardinal point in Plato's later thought. The Form is the pure object revealed by exact thinking. This was one of the Academy's main arguments. Aristotle reproduced it in his lost work *On Ideas*, and Alexander of Aphrodisias has preserved it therefrom.[2] It explains why the *Protrepticus* calls the Forms 'the exact in itself'. Even the technical term that was used in the Academic proof reappears here, namely 'the absolutely determinate' (τὰ ὡρισμένα).[3] In later days it was one of Aristotle's hardest problems to decide whether we can have any scientific knowledge of the supersensible; if Plato's Forms do not exist, it is not clear how the essences of things can be grasped by general conceptions. The *Protrepticus*, on the other hand, argues with remarkable determination, and obviously from quite different presuppositions, that it is possible to have a science of the just and the good, of nature, and of 'the rest of truth' (i.e. the 'really real', ὄντως ὄν). For its author that which is first in order of being coincides with that which is most knowable; and the latter, which is also called the determinate

[1] Iambl. *Protr.*, p. 55, ll. 21 ff. [2] Frg. 187.
[3] Frg. 52 (p. 60, l. 21, in Rose). Cf. *On Forms*, frg. 187 (p. 149, l. 22, in Rose).

and the orderly, coincides with the good and the cause.[1] It is
true that expressions like 'prior by nature', and 'prior with
reference to us', and 'first things' in the sense of 'ultimate
grounds', occur elsewhere also in Aristotle's philosophy. But
there is no doubt that they arose originally out of Plato's arguments for the Forms. They fit them best, and must have been
invented primarily for them. Their meaning is clear only so
long as they are applied to a transcendental reality such as Plato
believed in; they become ambiguous if referred to immanent
essence. Hence Aristotle is obliged to differentiate their meaning
and to add qualifications (such as 'by nature' and 'with reference to us'). They cannot be used absolutely, as they are in the
Protrepticus, unless truth and being and value coincide in the
most perfect object of knowledge (as they do on the theory of
Forms). The amalgamation of ethics and ontology, which also
occurs in this argument, is explicable only on the supposition
that the words 'prior' and 'good' refer to the Forms.

The final proof is given by the view taken in the *Protrepticus*
of the elements (στοιχεῖα) of reality, a view which the *Metaphysics* combats in detail.[2] In the earlier work Aristotle writes as
follows: 'the prior is cause in a greater degree than the posterior;
for when it is destroyed the things that receive their substance
(τὴν οὐσίαν) from it are destroyed along with it, lines along
with numbers, planes along with lines, and solids along with
planes'. The *Metaphysics* on the other hand denies all substantiality to the objects of mathematics, numbers, points, lines,
planes, and solids; while it mentions that the Platonists held
this view. We read there: 'We call that substance (οὐσία) . . .
also by whose destruction the whole is destroyed, as the body is
by the destruction of the plane, as some say, and the plane by the
destruction of the line; and in general number is thought by
some to be of this nature'. In the oldest portions of the *Metaphysics* the criticism of Platonism is mainly directed against
this, the final form of the theory of Ideas, according to which the
Ideas either have mathematical objects existing as substances
alongside of them, or actually are numbers themselves. Aristotle there calls this 'a remarkably weak argument'. This only

[1] Frg. 52 (p. 60, ll. 17 ff., in Rose).
[2] Frg. 52 (p. 60, l. 26, in Rose), cf. *Metaph*. Δ 8, 1017^b 18; N 3, 1090^b 5.

makes it the more significant that he himself had formerly maintained the doctrine he here attacks. It stands or falls together with the Platonic view of substance, and with the doctrine that the Ideas and the objects of mathematics possess transcendental actuality.

Aristotle allows it to be seen that there was controversy in the Academy about the elements of reality. 'It is impossible to know anything else until we know the causes and principles of things, whether they are fire or air [i.e. the elements of the physicists] or number or some other natures [φύσεις, i.e. the Ideas].'[1] Plato himself gives similar hints in his later dialogues, without actually lifting the veil. In the *Philebus* he speaks openly of the 'strong feeling' (πολλὴ σπουδή) about the theory of Forms, and the 'controversy about division' (μετὰ Διαιρέσεως ἀμφισβήτησις) in connexion with them.[2] Aristotle took a lively share in these discussions, which only makes it more remarkable that in the *Protrepticus* he subordinates his private opinion to the prevailing Academic doctrine. Two conclusions may be drawn with certainty. First, even in those early days he did not maintain the theory of Forms as a static dogma; he was an adherent of it, but he spoke of it with full consciousness of its difficulties. These difficulties, however—and this is the second conclusion—did not yet seem to him sufficiently fundamental to enable him definitely to refute Plato's doctrine, as he did in his work *On Philosophy* and in the *Metaphysics* soon after 348. And so perhaps we may say that neither in the *Protrepticus* nor in Plato's later dialogues does the Academy's literary portrait of itself quite reveal the true state of its esoteric discussions. It is significant that the most interesting thing in Aristotle's early works and in the later dialogues of his master is often precisely that which they do not say.

This gives the more value to this confession of the representative of the young generation, as an addition to Plato's own embodiment of the spirit of the Academy in his writings. We learn from it what seemed to him essential in the work of the Academy.

When he mentions with enthusiasm the recent rapid advance (ἐπίδοσις) of philosophy along the road of exact science, we

---

[1] Frg. 52 (p. 61, l. 13, in Rose). [2] *Phil.* 15 A. Cf. *Parm.* 130 B ff.

feel ourselves directly transported into the midst of Plato's community of students. In the Academy men felt that they were swimming in the main current of progress, in comparison with which the other 'arts' were stagnant water. Aristotle speaks of the pace of the movement, and he believes that the completion of knowledge is at hand. He shares in the confidence which his generation derived from the conviction that it possessed creative power and had made unexampled progress. Men believed that genuine inquiry can make men happy, and this belief arose not from any artificial arguments but from actual good fortune and intensified experience; if it ever has been true it was true then. The outsider may think it thankless work, exclaims Aristotle, but he who has once tasted of it can never be satiated.[1] It is the only form of human activity that is not restricted to any time or place or instrument. It does not require any encouragement from external gain. He who lays hold of it is laid hold of by it; thenceforward he knows of nothing pleasanter than 'sitting down to it' (προσεΔρεία). It was this circle of students that gave birth to Aristotle's ideal of 'the theoretic life'—not, that is to say, the animated gymnasium of the *Lysis* or the *Charmides*, but the cabin (καλύβη) in the secluded garden of the Academy. Its quietude is the real original of the isles of the blest in the *Protrepticus*, that dreamland of philosophical otherworldliness.[2] The new type of philosopher models himself not on Socrates but on Pythagoras or Anaxagoras or Parmenides. The *Protrepticus* names these three as founders.

This change is important enough to require our attention a little longer.

This seems to have been the moment at which the Academy first raised the problem of the historical and the Platonic Socrates, because the members were becoming more and more conscious of their distance from the Socratic type. In their earliest attempts to distinguish his share from Plato's they naturally denied to the historical Socrates almost every piece of philosophical knowledge that is ascribed to him in Plato's

---

[1] Frg. 52 (p. 62, l. 20, in Rose).

[2] Frg. 58 (p. 68, l. 3, and p. 69, l. 1, in Rose). The literary model for this was Plato, *Gorg.* 526 C, and *Rep.* VII. 540 B. The Platonists referred these two passages to life in the Academy. The *Epinomis* (992 B) takes over the same idea.

dialogues. Later on this radicalism was followed by a reaction, so that Aristotle obtained the following result: 'Two things must in fairness be ascribed to Socrates, inductive arguments and universal definition.'[1] In any case there is no connexion between Socrates and the theoretical philosophy of the *Protrepticus*. In that work metaphysics, which has not yet received the name 'first philosophy', is described as 'speculation of the type introduced by Anaxagoras and Parmenides', and the ancestor of Plato's philosophy is considered to be Pythagoras.[2] Even in the first book of the *Metaphysics* Aristotle still holds that Plato's doctrine was essentially Pythagorean in origin, though it added 'some peculiarities of its own'.[3] This view, which must often have astonished the reader, is not intended to belittle Plato. It was the official view of the Academy; and Aristotle still held it when he wrote these words about 348/7. The Platonic Socrates had been the result of the artist's desire to mould and create; the Academy's cult of Pythagoras, one of the most remarkable examples of religious auto-suggestion there have ever been, was a projection of the Academy itself and its number-metaphysics into the half-mythical personality of Pythagoras, whom the Platonists venerated as the founder of 'the theoretic life', and whom they soon freely credited with the views of their own time and school.

The tale about Pythagoras in the *Protrepticus*, unimportant as it is, enables us to see with our own eyes how story-telling developed and came to have its fateful influence on the history of Greek philosophy. Pythagoras is asked what is the purpose of human life. He replies, 'to contemplate the heavens'.[4] In

---

[1] *Metaph.* M 4, 1078^b 27. This cautious formula seems to me to be still the fairest account of the historical facts. Maier (*Sokrates*, Tübingen, 1913, pp. 77 ff.) was no doubt right in denying that Socrates had any logical *theory* of the universal and induction; it is high time that we ceased calling Socrates the first logician on the strength of Aristotle's statement. But his actual words give no sanction whatever to such a view; he merely describes the logical operations that Socrates *practised*. He considers Socrates, however, from his own *point of view*. His aim is not in the least to give 'a picture of the man', but to discover in him, as in Democritus and the Pythagoreans, the primitive origins of logical method (cf. 1078^b 20).

[2] Iambl. *Protr.*, p. 51, ll. 8 and 11; frg. 52 (p. 59, l. 4, in Rose).

[3] *Metaph.* A 6, 987^a 30.

[4] Iambl. *Protr.*, p. 51, l. 8. The dictum of Anaxagoras at l. 13 is a variant of this.

answer to a second question he describes himself as such a contemplator (θεωρός). With this story let us compare the classical account of the origin of the word 'philosopher' in Cicero's *Tusculan Disputations*, which comes from Heraclides of Pontus, a fellow-student of Aristotle's.[1] Here again Pythagoras is being questioned. He calls himself a philosopher, and to explain this new name he tells the following story. He compares human life with the great festival at Olympia, where all the world comes together in a motley throng. Some are there to do business at the fair and to enjoy themselves; others wish to win the wreath in the contest; others are merely spectators. The last are the philosophers, of whom there are but few. After reading the *Protrepticus* one recognizes in the first two groups the representatives of pleasure and virtue, that is of the 'apolaustic' and the 'practical' lives. The philosopher lives entirely for 'theory', for pure *phronesis*. Attractive as this story sounds it is neither a unity nor original. Heraclides, the most assiduously Pythagorean of all the Platonists, has obviously been stimulated by the *Protrepticus*. He projects the distinction of the three lives into the dim past. The kernel of the tale lies in the word 'theory', which inevitably suggests a double meaning. The *Protrepticus* had already drawn the parallel between the philosopher's contemplation of reality and the sacred spectacle of Olympia, and had done so in a passage close to that describing the answers of Pythagoras.[2] Heraclides simply combined these two elements into a short story and gave it a little embellishment. What to Aristotle was merely a stylistic device now becomes a simile of the three lives (since not every one who goes to Olympia is a spectator), and is ascribed to Pythagoras himself (αὐτὸς ἔφα). In reality the tale presupposes the fundamental notions of Plato's later ethics and metaphysics.

Lastly, we must consider what the *Protrepticus* can tell us about Aristotle's early attitude towards life and relgion. In this respect it is supplementary to the *Eudemus*; it shows that the view that he had there established about the other world made a radical difference to his opinion of this one. In both works he is thoroughly pessimistic about earthly life and temporal goods and interests. He exhorts us to throw away life of our own

[1] Cic. *Tusc.* V. 3, 8.　　　　　　[2] Iambl. *Protr.*, p. 53, l. 19.

accord, in order to obtain a higher and purer good in exchange. But whereas the *Eudemus*, with its doctrine of the soul and immortality, is predominantly speculative, the *Protrepticus* introduces us to a more personal atmosphere.

Following Plato's example and doctrine, Aristotle is convinced that there are higher, imperishable values; and that there is a truer world, towards which genuine knowledge leads. For the sake of that good he abandons all the seeming goods of power, possessions, and beauty.[1] The worthlessness of all earthly things has never been more contemptuously denounced. As to the dream of the aesthetic eighteenth century—harmony, cloudless serenity, and the enjoyment of beauty—the *Protrepticus* feels nothing but the profoundest disgust for it. Probably it never really appealed to the Greek spirit. There were moments, as in the fourth century, when the aesthetic attitude seemed to be triumphant in life and in art; but they were soon overtaken by the reflection that 'strength, beauty and stature are but a laughing stock, and utterly valueless'. When these words were written the beauty of the body in its sublime austerity had long ceased to seem divine; and the art that should have interpreted it was living on a mere semblance, the empty cult of form. In the *Protrepticus* Aristotle lays hands on the beautiful Alcibiades, who was the idol of that age, and in whom it delighted to find its own image. He puts his finger on the weakness of the time when he says that if a man could see into the inside of that much-admired body 'with the eyes of Lynceus', he would find a picture of ugliness and nausea.[2] He himself is using the Lynceus-vision of another attitude towards life when he penetrates this visible material partition that surrounds us and discovers behind the scenes of appearance a new and hitherto invisible world, the world of Plato.

On this view the perfection of all the imperfections of human life must lie in the transcendental world. Thus life becomes the death of the soul, and death the escape into a higher life. Aristotle borrows the language of the *Phaedo* and declares that the life of the true philosopher must be a continual practice of death.[3] He will find nothing harsh in that, for to him the

---

[1] Iambl. *Protr.*, p. 53, l. 19.   [2] Frg. 59 (p. 70, l. 11, in Rose; cf. ll. 7 ff.).
[3] See Diels, *Archiv für Geschichte der Philosophie*, vol. i, p. 479.

imprisonment of the soul in the body is an unnatural state full
of inexpressible suffering.[1] This is pictured in horrible colours
in the simile of the Etruscan pirates. In order to torture their
prisoners, these pirates bound their living bodies face to face
with corpses and left them to perish slowly, thus constraining
life and putrefaction into an unnatural union. In spite of the
self-tormenting crassness of this simile, it bears the marks of
genuine personal experience and sensitive emotion. The young
Aristotle had really felt the pains of man's dualistic existence,
as Plato and the Orphics had felt them before him. It is an
absolutely intolerable and blasphemous notion that this Platonic
imagery is nothing but a conventional mask, concealing a spirit
in reality playful and easy-going. We must simply relearn our
history. The fact is that there was a time when these ideas
seemed to Aristotle an inseparable part of his own ego. He uses
every kind of phrase and metaphor to inculcate them. He is fond
of taking words from the vocabulary of the mysteries, because
only by means of religion can he understand and overcome the
constraint of man's dualistic existence. As the ancient mystic
doctrines whisper, the whole of human life is a penance for some
heavy guilt that the soul has incurred in an earlier existence.

The supersensible process of the soul's home-coming is made
to include man's moral obligations as well. Ethics is thus deprived of its absolute validity and independent worth. Far
removed though Aristotle is from reducing the various aspects of
actual moral life to the single gaze of the mystical vision, or from
having recourse to ecstasy, he nevertheless does unconditionally
subordinate the realm of will and action to the contemplation of
the eternal good.

---

[1] The final section of the excerpts from the *Protrepticus*, which was worked
over by Iamblichus (see page 79 above), is contaminated with Neo-Platonism;
but the following passage seems to me unmistakably genuine. 'Here, however,
because it is perhaps unnatural to our race to be here, it is hard to learn and to
examine anything, and only with difficulty would a man perceive anything,
because of the awkwardness and unnaturalness of our life; but if ever we can
get safely back whence we came [the *Eudemus* again!], it is obvious that we
shall all do it more pleasantly and easily' (Iambl. *Protr.*, p. 60, ll. 10–15).
Ἀλλ' ἐνταῦθα μὲν διὰ τὸ παρὰ φύσιν ἴσως εἶναι ⟨?⟩ τὸ γένος ἡμῶν χαλεπὸν τὸ μανθάνειν τι
καὶ σκοπεῖν ἐστι καὶ μόλις ⟨ἄν⟩ αἰσθάνοιτο ⟨?⟩ διὰ τὴν ἀφυΐαν καὶ τὴν παρὰ φύσιν ζωήν, ἄν
δέ ποτε δυνηθῶμεν σωθῆναι πάλιν ὅθεν ἐληλύθαμεν, δῆλον ὡς ἥδιον καὶ ῥᾷον αὐτὸ ποιήσομεν
πάντες. The repetition of παρὰ φύσιν shows that here, too, the original has been
clumsily abbreviated.

The philosopher must keep himself as free as possible from the distractions of practical life. The *Protrepticus* warns us not to become too deeply involved in mortal affairs, and not to lose ourselves on the false trails that humanity follows. All such things only hinder our return to God. Our sole aspiration should be that we may one day die in peace, and so return from this close imprisonment to our home. We ought either to seek truth and devote ourselves to it, or to have done with life altogether; for all else is but folly and idle talk.[1]

[1] Frg. 61 (p. 72, l. 20, in Rose). Cicero put this passage at the end of his *Hortensius*, along with similar thoughts also borrowed from the *Protrepticus*. Presumably they came at the end in the original too.

PART TWO
TRAVELS

CHAPTER V

ARISTOTLE IN ASSOS AND MACEDONIA

IN 348/7 Plato died, and at almost the same instant Stagira was destroyed by the ravaging and burning troops of Philip of Macedon, who was attacking the commercial cities of the Chalcidic peninsula. Thus at one stroke Aristotle was deprived both of his ancestral and of his spiritual home (for such had Plato's presence made Athens to him). In spite of his increasing independence in intellectual matters he had refused to leave Plato, so long as the latter lived; but, the master's eyes once closed for ever, the tie that bound him to his fellow-students was soon broken. In the very same year he departed for Asia Minor, leaving his circle of friends and the scene of twenty years of en-nobling experience and devoted common work.[1] In the absence of any information about the true reason for this momentous step, which was perhaps decided even before Plato's death, wild suggestions have been put forward. In his writings Aristotle frequently applies sharp criticism to Plato's doctrines; hence it was not difficult to find supporters for the conjecture that he had broken away from his teacher, and that his departure from Athens was the expression of the break. His character was scrutinized in the hope of discovering personal reasons. His mocking way affected delicate nerves unpleasantly (although it always gives place to the greatest respect when he speaks of Plato), and he was particularly obnoxious to those who took his all-commanding intellect and his insistence on logical purity for the signs of a destructive spirit. He himself protests against the insinuation that a criticism must always have personal motives, even if it happens to be true. In late antiquity gossip openly charged him with malice and ingratitude, and the motives of his departure were shrouded in a thick fog of suspicion, the express dispersion of which, although we have become more sceptical about conventional moral judgements, is not yet superfluous, especially as the real reasons for the step are still unexplained.[2]

---

[1] Apollodorus in Diog. L. V. 9 (cf. V. 3, where the chronology is hopelessly confused); Dionys. Hal. *ep. ad Amm.* 5.

[2] Aristotle protests against charges initiated by Plato's followers in *Eth. Nic.*

A clever and cultivated scholar of imperial times, Aristocles of Messana, had the moral force to tear down this veil of legend. He put an end to the persistent tradition of the compilers by going back to the primary sources and demonstrating the miserable insufficiency of the grounds on which the gossip rested. Chance has kindly preserved to us the part of his critical inquiry where, after triumphantly destroying the threadbare tissue of lies, he shows that the rumours of a break between Plato and Aristotle rest on a crying misinterpretation of a passage in the latter's pupil Aristoxenus of Tarentum.[1] In all probability it was Aristocles who, after demolishing these apocryphal tales, restored to light that precious personal document which gives us Aristotle's real attitude to his master better than all the hypotheses of alien malice, namely the altar-elegy dedicated to Eudemus.[2] The assertion, that the man to whom Aristotle is enthusiastically testifying in this fragment is not Plato but Socrates (whom Aristotle had never seen in his life), is self-contradictory and psychologically improbable.[3] It would never have been put forward if scholars had kept steadily in mind the fact that this rare jewel owes its rediscovery solely to a critical biographer's search for first-hand information, and therefore must have contained Aristotle's own explicit account of his relation to Plato and his reply to the malicious critics of that relation. The later Neo-Platonists took the poem from a learned work on this subject, where it was quoted only so far as it threw a direct light thereon. It is therefore clear that by the man 'whom bad men have not even the right to praise' is meant in this elegy none other than Plato; and that the 'bad men' whose praise Aristotle thinks

I. 6, 1096[a] 11–16, and frg. 8. Our information about the gossip in the schools has been critically examined by Stahr (*Aristotelia*, Halle, 1830, vol. i, pp. 46 ff.). He takes his material from Franciscus Patritius (*Discussiones peripateticae*, Basle, 1581). The latter, a Platonist of the Renascence, was quite blinded by his hate of Aristotle; he put implicit faith in any accusation however absurd.

[1] Aristocles in Euseb. *praep. ev.* XV. 2, 3.

[2] This is the view of Immisch (*Philologus*, vol. lxv, p. 11). It is rendered probable by the fact that, as Stahr has shown (ibid. vol. i, p. 61), what the Ammonius-life of Aristotle tells us about his relation to Plato must be referred, on account of its verbal echoes, to the fragment of Aristocles preserved in Eusebius.

[3] Bernays, *Gesammelte Abhandlungen*, vol. i, pp. 143 ff. Rightly rejected by Wilamowitz (*Aristoteles und Athen*, vol. ii, p. 413), and more recently by Immisch (loc. cit.).

damaging to the master are not just any *misera plebs*, but those
mistaken admirers who thought it their duty to defend Plato
against Aristotle's criticism of his doctrine.[1] A literal translation
may be added here:

> Coming to the famous plain of Cecropia
> He piously set up an altar of holy Friendship
> For the man whom it is not lawful for bad men even to praise,
> Who alone or first of mortals clearly revealed,
> By his own life and by the methods of his words,
> That a man becomes good and happy at the same time.
> Now no one can ever attain to these things again.

The dedicator of the altar, here spoken of in the third person,
is unknown to us. The statement that the poem was addressed
to Eudemus is no help, because we cannot determine whether the
Cyprian or the Rhodian is meant. The latest Neo-Platonists, in
their confused version of the life of Aristotle, professed to be
able to describe the inscription on the altar; and according to
them the dedicator was Aristotle. It is quite unsafe to make this
the basis of an interpretation. Fortunately, the various remaining versions of the biographical tradition enable us to follow the
growth of the legends so clearly that we can detect the stages in
the gradual development of this supposed inscription.[2]

Though there is some obscurity in the outward situation as
depicted by Aristotle, there is none whatever in the inner, and

---

[1] Only so can we give concrete meaning to this passionate repudiation of the
profane. In Aristotle's style an empty rhetorical hyperbole is unthinkable; and
to refer it to Diogenes the Cynic (as is done by Gomperz, *Griechische Denker*,
vol. ii, p. 539; and by Immisch, loc. cit., p. 21), because he also taught the self-
sufficiency of virtue, seems altogether too strained. Diogenes could perhaps
have appealed to Socrates in support of his own doctrines, but never to a
thinker so theoretical and so far removed from himself as Plato.

[2] Immisch considers the inscription genuine (loc. cit., p. 12); but in the *Vita
Marciana* the spurious hexameter, 'Aristotle set up this altar for Plato', is
quoted by itself, as is right (p. 432 in Rose); and then we read, 'and *in another
place he says* of him, "a man whom it is not lawful for bad men even to praise"'.
This second line is a pentameter, and what happened is that the careless compiler
of the so-called *Life According to Ammonius* put the pentameter and the hexameter together (p. 439 in Rose), supposing that 'man' was in apposition to
'Plato', and that the two lines formed a single distich, although they were given
separately in his source. It is inconceivable that things can have gone the other
way, namely that the author of the *Vita Marciana* can have had the distich
before him as a whole, and then broken it up and said that the pentameter came
from another poem. Originally the quotation probably included the whole of
the fragment of the elegy, for it is obvious that it was obtained from Aristocles
(see above, p. 106, n. 2).

that is what we are concerned with. The first line tells of a man, presumably a pupil of Plato's, who came to Athens and set up an altar there. That this was an altar to Plato, i.e. that the latter was accorded divine honours, I cannot admit. At first sight we may be confused by the fact that 'altar' governs two genitives, 'Friendship' and 'man'; but a Greek would surely have assumed without question that what was meant was that he set up an altar to most honourable Philia, in honour of the friendship of the man whom bad men may not even praise.[1] The adjective 'holy' puts it beyond all doubt that the divinity in whose name the altar was set up was Philia. On the other hand, the second genitive makes it equally certain that this altar of friendship was to be sacred not to any rationalistic allegory, not to any bloodless and lifeless abstraction, but to the man in whose person and actions the goddess had revealed herself to his disciples as a very present help.[2] The apotheosis of the human person is impossible in Plato's concept of religion, and the examples of Alexander, Lysander, and Epicurus, are inapplicable here. Only that which is of the nature of a Form can be fully divine.[3] For an example of this specifically Platonic religious feeling we may take Aristotle's hymn to Hermias (below, p. 118). Here too we find that neither is the poem addressed to the dead human being nor is the abstract notion of virtue

---

[1] Wilamowitz (loc. cit., pp. 413 ff.) takes ἱδρύσατο βωμὸν ἀνδρός together ('set up an altar to a man', i.e. to Plato), and regards 'of holy Friendship' as a genitive of cause, or as an Ionicism, though he thinks this less good; but either would be somewhat far-fetched for the simple and prosaic speech that had been the rule in elegiac poetry since the days of Evenus and Critias. Immisch, feeling this, but wanting to preserve the altar dedicated to Plato, emended the text to εὐσεβέων σεμνὴν φιλίαν ('in worship of holy Friendship he set up an altar to the man whom', &c.), which is simply impossible. (In his commentary on Hesiod's *Works and Days* Wilamowitz has since called Ζηνὸς φύλακες ἀνθρώπων (v. 253) 'a *locus classicus* for one noun governing two genitives'.)

[2] Aristotle, Xenocrates, Speusippus, and Philip of Opus, all wrote works *On Friendship* in the Academy. A whole literature of the subject arose round Plato in his old age. It is true that 'erotic theses' were still discussed in the traditional fashion, but Eros was no longer the unifying symbol of the group. Aristotle projected him into metaphysics, where he lived on as the *amor Dei* that moves the world. 'It moves the world by being loved.' The neuter is significant of the change.

[3] Wilamowitz's conception of Plato the God, to whom he supposes the altar to be dedicated (loc. cit., vol. ii, pp. 413 ff.), is certainly fine, but it scarcely fits the temper of the stern and pious men of Plato's circle. To Aristotle Plato does indeed hold an exceptional place among 'mortals' (l. 4), but he always remains the mortal who leads towards the divine goal.

personified. Virtue here means the divine Form of human virtue (he twice uses the word μορφή) striving for the greatest prize of existence, such as Aristotle and his friends experienced it in the life and death of Hermias; and therefore it is 'the virtue of Hermias'. The hymn sings the praises of an invisible goddess, never to be seen by man, but it sings them in honour of her latest visible embodiment on earth. In fine, the altar carried only one word, 'To Friendship'; but Aristotle, who is here interpreting the inscription in the manner of a pious exegete before a sacred object, rightly refers it to 'The Friendship of Plato'. We do not miss the second name, although friendship involves two persons, for in the band of 'friends' (φίλοι, as the members of the Academy called themselves) which one of them could lay exclusive claim to this position? Plato's friendship was holy to them all, because it was the innermost bond of their community.

There is a close connexion between the dedication and the attributes which the last lines ascribe to Plato in the manner of a hymn. The fundamental principle, both of Plato's theory of friendship and of the actual life of the Academy, was that the true friend is simply the perfectly good man. Hence the last lines praise Plato as the mortal through whom this transcendental Form has been realized.[1] He alone has shown us, or he first at any rate, that man is the free master of his own life and fate if he is good; and he did not merely teach it in theory, but was a living example of it to his friends. No one will ever be able to do so again—so says Aristotle, if we are to conclude from the uncompromising 'he alone of all mortals'; but who can tell the future, or say what is possible to man? So Aristotle modifies 'alone' with 'or first'; and in the last line he modifies 'ever again' with 'now'—at any rate it is impossible for the *present* generation ever to equal him.[2] In this contrast between the

---

[1] Since this book was written I have again discussed the poem in detail in the *Classical Quarterly* (vol. xxi, 1927, pp. 13 ff.), and shown that κατέδειξεν ('revealed') is commonly used of founders of religions and such persons. This makes it quite unmistakable what position Aristotle assigns to Plato in the elegy.

[2] On the understanding of the final line depends the understanding of the whole poem. In content it is unexceptionable. Its interpreters have failed to notice that οὐκ ἔστι λαβεῖν ('it is impossible to attain') is a standing expression in Aristotle's treatises for the unattainability of the ideal. In *Pol.* VIII. 1332ᵇ 23 he says of a political ideal, 'since this is not easy to attain' (οὐ ῥᾴδιον

present generation and the superhuman leader there is a tragic resignation, in virtue of which this memorial poem is not a mere piece of exalted praise but a human and moving confession. The fact is that Aristotle in his *Ethics* denies Plato's doctrine that man's happiness depends only on the moral power of his soul.[1] He would prevent the chatterers from copying this sublime dictum. But to Plato, its originator, it was absolute truth. Where is the man that can follow up his steep path?

> Earth's insufficiency
> Here grows to Event;
> The Indescribable,
> Here it is done.

Nevertheless, Aristotle's departure from Athens was the expression of a crisis in his inner life. The fact remains that he never came back to the school in which he had been educated. This was presumably connected with the question of Plato's successor, which would inevitably determine the spirit of the Academy for a long time to come, and the decision of which could not meet with Aristotle's approval in any event. The choice, whether Plato's own or that of the members, fell on Plato's nephew Speusippus. His age made it impossible to pass him over, however obvious Aristotle's superiority might be for all who had eyes to see. The decisive consideration was perhaps certain external circumstances, such as the difficulty of convey-

λαβεῖν). III. 1286ᵇ 7, 'aristocracy would be more desirable than monarchy, . . . if it were possible to obtain many men of the same kind' (ἂν ᾖ λαβεῖν, i.e. to discover in reality, or to make real). Objection has been taken to the juxtaposition of 'ever again' and 'now'. This manner of speech is due to the compactness that compresses two possible expressions into one, namely 'never or at least not now' and 'none of those now living' (οὐδενὶ τῶν γε νῦν). Aristotle writes his own language, and it cannot be reduced to a set of rules. He is interested solely in the accuracy of the intellectual nuance that he wishes to convey, and not in the smoothness of the diction; e.g. the precise distinction of 'or first' in the fourth line is more suitable to a lecture than to an elegy. The master has shown us the goal—such is the meaning of the conclusion—but we men of the present cannot fly so high. It follows that the poem was written after Plato's death, and is addressed to Eudemus of Rhodes. The feeling is too direct, however, for it to have been written during Aristotle's latest period. It seems to be the offspring of strong emotion and inner conflict. If, as I believe, it was at Assos that both Theophrastus and Eudemus became students of Aristotle's, the elegy may have been written shortly after Plato's death. At the moment when Aristotle was abandoning the master in matters of doctrine, the impulse of his heart drove him to declare his inner relationship to him in the form of an intimate personal confession.

[1] Immisch rightly emphasizes this, loc. cit., p. 17.

ing the Academy to a metic, although this was afterwards overcome. The choice of Speusippus continued Plato's family in the possession of the property. Whether, in addition to such reasons of external expediency, personal antipathies also played a part, it is no longer possible to say; but on general grounds it is practically self-evident that they must have done so. One thing, however, is certain; it was not Aristotle's criticism of Plato's fundamental doctrines that prevented him from succeeding to the headship of Plato's Academy. Speusippus himself had declared the theory of Ideas untenable during Plato's own lifetime, and had also abandoned the Ideal numbers suggested by Plato in his last period; he differed from him in other fundamental particulars as well. And that Aristotle was not meanly but highly thought of in the school when he left Athens is proved by the person who accompanied him, namely Xenocrates, the most conservative of all Plato's students with regard to alterations of the doctrine, but at the same time a thoroughly upright man. The departure of Aristotle and Xenocrates was a secession.[1] They went to Asia Minor in the conviction that Speusippus had inherited merely the office and not the spirit. The spirit had become homeless, and they were setting out to build it a new place. For the next few years the scene of their activity was Assos on the coast of the Troad, where they worked in common with two other Platonists, Erastus and Coriscus from Scepsis on Ida.

The importance of this period has not been recognized. Plato's sixth letter, the genuineness of which has been convincingly demonstrated by Brinckmann,[2] is addressed to Erastus and Coriscus, two former students now in Asia Minor, and to their friend Hermias, lord of Atarneus. The two philosophers are to put themselves under the protection of Hermias, since, while persons of excellent character, they are devoid of worldly

---

[1] Strabo XIII. 57, p. 610.

[2] *Rheinisches Museum*, N.F., vol. lxvi, 1911, pp. 226 ff. In our views of the external events connected with Hermias we agree almost entirely (see my *Entstehungsgeschichte der Metaphysik des Aristoteles*, 1912, pp. 34 ff.); and this is all the stronger evidence because Brinckmann started from a quite different point, and we reached the same conclusion independently of each other. Although my book was not published until 1912, it had already been submitted as a thesis to the philosophical faculty at Berlin when Brinckmann's miscellany appeared.

experience; Hermias on his part is to learn to appreciate their steadfast and trustworthy friendship. This remarkable relation between the two companions of Plato and the prince of Atarneus has been illuminated by an inscription first published by Boeckh,[1] in which 'Hermias and the companions' (the formal phrase Ἑρμίας καὶ οἱ ἑταῖροι occurs five times in the original) make an alliance with the people of the city of Erythrae. The newly discovered commentary of Didymus on Demosthenes' *Philippics* leaves no doubt that the companions who here appear along with Hermias as legal parties to the contract are none other than the two philosophers from the neighbouring town of Scepsis, as was already probable from Plato's letter.

Hermias was a man of lowly origin. That he was a eunuch is not to be denied. Even the story that in earlier years a bank had employed him as money-changer at the counter presumably rests on fact, although it is related by Theopompus, who describes him as unpleasantly as possible.[2] He began by getting possession of some mountain villages in the neighbourhood of Ida.[3] Later he obtained public recognition from the Persian administration, and was allowed to adopt the title of prince, presumably after the payment of an adequate sum. His residence was at Atarneus. His steadily growing political influence extended the area under his control to an astonishing size. In the end he must have maintained a substantial contingent of mercenaries, for he reduced rebellious places to obedience by military raids, and he afterwards withstood a siege by the Persian satrap.

Erastus and Coriscus had lived for a long time in the Academy, and then returned to their native town of Scepsis. Hermias' original reason for entering into relations with them was certainly not theoretical enthusiasm for Plato's philosophy. They must

---

[1] Boeckh, 'Hermias von Atarneus' in *Abhandlungen der Berliner Akademie*, 1853, Historisch-philosophische Klasse, pp. 133 ff. (*Kleinere Schriften*, vol. v, p. 189). The inscription appears in Dittenberger's *Sylloge*, vol. i³, p. 307.

[2] He was certainly a Greek, or Aristotle in his hymn could never have represented him as the upholder of the true tradition of Hellenic virtue, in contrast to the barbarians who treacherously killed him (cf. the epigram, Rose, frg. 674). In the letter to Philip Theopompus says (Didymus *in Demosthenem*, col. 5, 24, Diels-Schubart, Berlin, 1904): 'Though a barbarian he philosophizes with Platonists, though he has been a slave he competes with costly chariots at the meetings.' Here the first statement at any rate is either a lie for the sake of rhetorical antithesis or merely a reference to his being a eunuch.

[3] Didymus *in Demosthenem*, col. 5, 27, Diels-Schubart.

have been persons of importance in that little city. The community was proud of its two learned sons. It was not uncommon for small Greek cities to call for laws from citizens who had become famous. The mathematician Eudoxus, who returned to Cnidus as a great scholar, was highly respected there; he was voted an honorary decree and entrusted with the task of writing new laws for the city.[1] Erastus and Coriscus no doubt tried to introduce in Scepsis various political reforms that had been suggested in the Academy, as other Platonists did in other places, some as dictators or the advisers of princes, others as communists and tyrannicides. Presumably Plato wished to institute a friendship between the two companions and their 'neighbour' Hermias, because, while he recognized their noble disposition, he was afraid they might be somewhat doctrinaire. The letter that we possess is the solemn record of this peculiar pact between *Realpolitik* and theoretical schemes of reform. The spirit of Plato hovers over the institution, and, although he is not acquainted with Hermias,[2] whom he supposes to be an unphilosophical and purely practical man, he exhorts the three parties to read the letter in common whenever they come together; and, if there should be any disagreement, to have recourse to the arbitration of the Academy at Athens. The movement towards reform thus appears as the result of a philosophic political system, which is to be realized throughout Greece wherever the opportunity occurs, and in which the Academy intends to retain the lead.

When this oligarchy of wise men was established the philosophers naturally demanded that Hermias study geometry and dialectic,[3] just as Plato had once demanded it of Dionysius, his pupil Euphraeus of Perdiccas king of Macedon, and Aristotle of Themison of Cyprus; and, like those other knowledge-hungry men of a busy and enlightened but inwardly vacillating century, Hermias applied himself to study with increasing zeal; and, what

---

[1] Diog. L. VIII. 88.

[2] See Plato, *Letter* VI, 322 E. Strabo, on the contrary (XIII. 57, p. 610), wrongly makes Hermias a philosopher and one-time student of Plato's, in order to explain his connexion with the Academy. For some inexplicable reason this contradiction was formerly supposed to prove the letter spurious, although Strabo's account contains many other inaccuracies (Brinckmann, loc. cit., p. 228).

[3] Plato, *Letter* VI. 322 D.

is more, directed his life on moral principles, which Theopompus, perhaps not without some justification, declares that he had not done during the first years of his rise. From the contradictory judgements of the Chian, who considered him absolutely unscrupulous, and of the Platonists, whose honest admiration for him is reflected by Aristotle and Callisthenes,[1] we may conclude that he was an unusual person, a mixture of natural intelligence, enterprising energy, and great will-power, but at the same time full of unresolved contradictions. At any rate the benefit that he received from the men of Scepsis was not merely in regard to the health of his soul; we now know from Didymus that they gave him correct political advice, for which he presented them with the town of Assos. On their recommendation he voluntarily changed his tyranny 'into a milder form of constitution'. This step conciliated the Aeolian peoples of the coast, and the consequence was that the territories from the Ida-range down to the coast of Assos came over to him of their own free will. In the milder form of constitution we may recognize the idea of Plato and Dion, who had intended to consolidate the Syracusan tyranny by the adoption of a constitutional form, and then to unite the city-states of Sicily, for purposes of foreign politics, under its strictly monarchical leadership. What could not be realized in Sicily became a political reality in miniature in Asia Minor.[2]

[1] See the juxtaposition of favourable and unfavourable judgements in Didymus, col. 4, 60 ff. He quotes in turn Book XLVI of Theopompus' *Philippic Histories*, his letter to Philip, Callisthenes' encomium on Hermias, Aristotle's poem to him, Hermippus' life of Aristotle, and Book VI of Anaximenes' *Philippic Histories*.

[2] Didymus, col. 5, 52, Diels-Schubart. I have added some tentative restorations at the beginning:

καὶ ε]ἰς [τὴν π]έριξ· ἐ-
στρατήγ[ησε, φίλους Δ' ἐποιήσατο Κορίσκον] καὶ Ἔ-
ραστον καὶ Ἀριστοτ[έλην καὶ Ξενοκράτην]· Διὸ καὶ
πάντ[ες οὗ]τοι παρὰ ['Ερμίᾳ Διῆγον. . . . .] ὕστε-
ρον . . [. . . .] ἥκο[υσεν αὐτῶν. . . . .]. Ἔδωκεν
αὐτ[οῖς Δ]ωρεὰ[ς.] . . [. . . . .] ἐπιτηδ]ὲς Δὲ τὴν
τυραν[νίδ]α μ[ετέ]στη[σεν εἰς πραιο]τέραν Δυ-
ναστείαν· Διὸ καὶ πάσ[ης τῆς σύν]ε[γγ.]υς ἐπῆρ-
ξεν ἕως Ἀσσοῦ, ὃτε [Δὴ καὶ ὑπερησ]θεὶς τοῖς εἰρημένοις φιλοσόφοις ἀ[πένειμεν] τὴν Ἀσσίων
πόλιν, μάλιστα Δ' αὐτ[ῶν ἀποδεξ]άμενος Ἀρι-
στοτέλην οἰκειότατα [Διέκειτο πρ]ὸς τοῦτον.

The text, together with the restorations, may be translated as follows: 'And into

The reforms of Erastus and Coriscus must have occurred before Plato's death, because, since in 347 Aristotle joined them not in Scepsis but in Assos, Hermias' gift must have been an accomplished fact at that time. Didymus expressly tells us, what we did not know before, that Hermias heard the philosophers and lived with them for a considerable period; and, in fact, Plato could not have referred in his sixth letter to such purely theoretical questions as the doctrine of Forms (322 D) unless he had known that each of the three recipients was interested therein. The language of Didymus compels us to imagine not merely casual philosophical discussions but actual lectures. In this group the lead naturally fell to Aristotle, and the fact that Hermias felt specially obliged to him seems to show that he took the outstanding part in the lectures. Nothing less than a colony of the Athenian Academy was taking shape in Assos at this time, and there was laid the foundation of the school of Aristotle.

It must have been here that Callisthenes enjoyed the instruction of his uncle, for he did not hear him in Athens; in any case we have to assume that he was personally acquainted with Hermias, because he wrote an encomium on him. In later days Neleus, the son of Coriscus, was one of the most active and important Aristotelians; and Theophrastus came from the neighbouring town of Eresus on Lesbos. When, at the end of three years, Aristotle left Assos and settled himself at Mytilene in Lesbos, it was probably the influence of Theophrastus that led to the decision.[1] He it was also, as is well known, who bequeathed

the surrounding country; he made expeditions, and he made friends of Coriscus and Erastus and Aristotle and Xenocrates; hence all these men lived with Hermias . . . afterwards . . . he listened to them . . . he gave them gifts . . . he actually changed the tyranny into a milder rule; therefore he also came to rule over all the neighbouring country as far as Assos, and then, being exceedingly pleased with the said philosophers, he allotted them the city of Assos. He accepted Aristotle most of all of them, and was very intimate with him.'

[1] That Theophrastus joined Aristotle at least as early as the Macedonian period is proved by his personal knowledge of Stagira and by the fact that he owned property there (Diog. L. V. 52; *Historia Plantarum*, III. 11. 1; IV. 16. 3). This can have been acquired only by means of a fairly long stay in that place, and such a stay can have occurred only during the period prior to the founding of the school at Athens (335), when Aristotle, together with the little group that had followed him to Macedon, was often away from the court for long intervals; and especially during the years immediately preceding Alexander's accession, when the latter was already taking part in affairs of state. If this is

Aristotle's papers and library to Neleus, who in turn left them to his relatives in Scepsis. The close connexion between Aristotle and the friends in Scepsis and Assos, for the sake of studying philosophy, finally removes all appearance of romance from the oft doubted story of the rediscovery of his papers at Scepsis in the cellar of Neleus' descendants;[1] and it is now clear that the frequent use of the name Coriscus as an example in Aristotle's lectures goes back to a time when its owner was actually sitting on the bench of the lecture-room in Assos. In this connexion it is important to observe a tradition found in the Jewish writer Josephus (c. Apionem 176), which has apparently never received any notice. He mentions a work of Clearchus, one of the better-known earlier Peripatetics, on sleep. Aristotle himself appeared as a figure in this dialogue, and told of a Greek-speaking Jew who came to him during his residence in Asia Minor in order to study philosophy 'with him and some other members of the school'. Whether this story was Clearchus' own invention or an actual piece of tradition which he used for his own purpose, in either case he must have been convinced that there had been a time when Aristotle was teaching in Asia Minor together with other Platonists, and that can only have been the time when he was teaching in Assos. In every respect the experiences of this stay in Asia Minor were decisive for Aristotle's later life. Hermias gave him Pythias, his niece and adopted daughter, to wife. We know nothing about this marriage except that of it was born a daughter who received the same name as her mother. In his will Aristotle directs that the bones of his wife, who had

so, it follows that Theophrastus' acquaintance with Aristotle dates from the master's stay in Asia Minor, and that Theophrastus followed him thence to Macedon. It is not indeed impossible that he had even heard Plato, gone through the same process of development as Aristotle (Diog. L. V. 36), and left Athens along with him; but it is very improbable. He died in the 123rd Olympiad. If he was twenty years old when he came to Aristotle at Assos in 348/7, he would be at least eighty when he died, even supposing that it was the first year of the Olympiad (288), and may have been anything up to eighty-four. Hence it is scarcely possible that he was Plato's pupil for long. It is much more natural to think that he was attracted from Lesbos to the neighbouring Assos by the teaching of Aristotle and the other Academicians there. His friendship with Callisthenes (to whom Theophrastus dedicated Callisthenes, or On Grief after his death, Diog. L. V. 44) must also belong to a time before the founding of the school at Athens, since this man followed Alexander to Asia in 334 and never returned.

[1] Strabo XIII. 54, p. 608.

died before him, shall be laid beside his own, as was her last wish. Strabo's account is as usual romantically exaggerated; he tells a sensational story of Aristotle's flight with the tyrant's daughter, which he supposes to have taken place after the capture of Hermias. Here as elsewhere the new Didymus discovery has corrected and enlarged our knowledge. After three years of activity at Assos Aristotle went to Mytilene in Lesbos, where he taught until 343/2. He then accepted King Philip's invitation to go to the court of Macedon as tutor of the prince.[1]

Soon after entering on this new work he received news of the terrible fate of Hermias. Mentor, the Persian general, after shutting him up in Atarneus and unsuccessfully beleaguering him there, treacherously enticed him into a parley and carried him off to Susa. There he was questioned under torture about his secret treaties with King Philip, and when he steadfastly preserved silence he was crucified. Under the torture the king caused him to be asked what last grace he requested. He answered: 'Tell my friends and companions (πρὸς τοὺς φίλους τε καὶ ἑταίρους) that I have done nothing weak or unworthy of philosophy.' Such was the farewell greeting delivered to Aristotle and to the philosophers at Assos.[2] Aristotle's attachment to his friend, and the deep emotion that he felt at his death, are still living to-day in the cenotaph at Delphi, for which he himself composed the dedicatory epigram, and in the beautiful hymn to Hermias. While the nationalist party at Athens, led by Demosthenes, was blackening the character of the deceased, while public opinion was dubious about him in Hellas and feeling ran very high throughout the land against Philip and his partisans, Aristotle sent out into the world this poem, in which he declared himself passionately on the side of the dead man.

---

[1] Cf. my *Ent. Met. Arist.*, p. 35. For an example of the wrong view see Gercke in *Realenzyklopädie der klassischen Altertumswissenschaft*, vol. ii, col. 1014. He regards the fall of Hermias as the reason for Aristotle's 'flight', and hence assigns it to the year 345, since it is established that Aristotle spent only three years in Assos (348–5); but Didymus has shown that he left Assos while Hermias was still alive, and that the latter did not fall until 341. Some (including Gercke, loc. cit.) have conjectured that Aristotle was in Athens for a short intervening period, during which he taught in the Lyceum; but this rests on a rash misinterpretation of Isocrates XII. 18.

[2] Didymus, col. 6. 15.

Virtue toilsome to mortal race,
Fairest prize in life,
Even to die for thy shape,
Maiden, is an envied fate in Hellas,
And to endure vehement unceasing labours.
Such fruit dost thou bestow on the mind,
Like to the immortals, and better than gold
And ancestors and languid-eyed sleep.
For thy sake Heracles the son of Zeus and Leda's youths
Endured much in their deeds
Seeking for thy potency.
Through longing for thee Achilles and Ajax came to the house of Hades.
For sake of thy dear shape the nursling of Atarneus also
Has left the sun's beams desolate.
Therefore his deeds shall be famous in song,
And he shall be declared immortal by the Muses,
Daughters of Memory,
As they magnify the guerdon of steadfast friendship and the worship of
   Zeus the hospitable.

The unique value of this poem for our knowledge of Aristotle's philosophical development has never been exploited. For the most part it has been regarded merely as a human document, but it shows that when Aristotle had completed his destructive criticism of Plato's Idea, exact thinking and religious feeling went separate paths in him. To the scientific part of himself there was no longer any such thing as an Idea when he wrote these lines, but in his heart it lived on as a religious symbol, as an ideal. He reads Plato's works as poetry. Just as in the *Metaphysics* he explains the Idea, and the participation of the sensible world in its being, as the free creation of the contemplative imagination, so here in his poem it appears to him again, transfigured into the shape of a virgin for whom in Hellas it is still exquisite to die. The words 'in Hellas' must not be overlooked. Callisthenes also, in the encomium which he wrote on him at this time, uses Hermias' brave death as a picture of Greek virtue (ἀρετή), in contrast with the character of the barbarians (ὁ τῶν βαρβάρων τρόπος);[1] and Aristotle's dedicatory epigram at Delphi reveals hate and contempt for the 'Medes', who did not overcome Hermias in open fight but craftily broke their word and cruelly murdered him. The juxtaposition of Hermias with Heracles and the Dioscuri, with Achilles and Ajax, is not a trick

---

[1] Didymus, col. 6. 10–13.

of the panegyric style; Aristotle does not intend to deck out his friend in the pathetic paraphernalia of Homer's heroes. On the contrary, all Hellenic heroism, from Homer's naïve kind down to the moral heroism of the philosopher, appeared to him as the expression of one single attitude towards life, an attitude which scales the heights of life only when it overcomes it. He found the soul of the Greeks' power in this Platonic virtue or heroism, be it military prowess or steadfast silence in pain; and this he instilled into Alexander, so that in the middle of a century of enlightenment that proud conqueror long fought and carried himself as if he were Achilles. On his sarcophagus the sculptor represented the deciding battle between Hellenes and Asiatics as an example of the same contrast—on the visage of the Orientals the marks of deep physical and spiritual suffering, in the forms of the Greeks the original, unbroken, mental and bodily might of heroes.

The unfriendly attitude of Aristotle and his companions towards Persia was at that time universal in the Macedonian court. Now that the testimony of Didymus has rehabilitated Demosthenes' fourth *Philippic*, we know for certain that as early as 342/1 Philip was already seriously thinking of a plan for a national war against the hereditary foe, a war such as the Pan-Hellenic propaganda of Isocrates and his circle had long been brewing. Only this could justify the brute force by which the king of Macedon was ruling over the free Greek cities. By means of his secret agents Demosthenes knew that Hermias had made agreements with Philip, and thereby put himself in a serious position as regards Persia. This military treaty opened the way for a Macedonian attack on Persia. Hermias, being a far-sighted politician, had been well aware that the time was ripe to invoke Philip's protection for his hard-won position in northwest Asia Minor. The clash between the Persian empire and the military power of Macedon seemed to him inevitable, and he hoped to preserve his independence by giving Philip the Asiatic bridgehead and assuring him of a strong base in Aeolia. We do not know who told the Persians of these plans. However that may be, when the Persian general had taken Hermias prisoner, Demosthenes rejoiced to think that the great king would soon extract from him, under torture, confessions such as to throw a glaring light on Philip's plot, and to make Persia ready for the alliance with Athens on behalf of which Demosthenes had long striven in vain.[1]

It is scarcely conceivable that Aristotle knew nothing of the high affairs of state which Philip, at whose court he was living, was arranging with his own friend and father-in-law. He removed to Pella in 342; Hermias fell in 341. We do not know whether the secret treaty was made during this year, or was already in being when Aristotle went to Macedon; but it is probable that it did not remain secret for long, and therefore was concluded not very long before the catastrophe. At all events Aristotle went to Pella with the approval of Hermias and not without some kind of political mission. The conventional tradition has it that King Philip was searching the world for a man to educate his important son, and therefore lit upon the greatest philosopher of the age; but at the time when Aristotle was lecturing in Assos and Mytilene he was not yet the intellectual leader of Greece, and Alexander was not yet an historic figure. Nor can the choice have been decided by the fact that Aristotle's father Nicomachus had been the personal physician of Amyntas at the court of Macedon, for since then four decades had passed. Everything indicates that it was the connexion between Hermias and Philip that really suggested this remarkable symbolization of world-wide historical events, the association of the thinker and the great king. Merely to play private tutor would not have suited Aristotle's virile character, and there was never much outlook in Macedon for a part such as Plato had taken at the court of Dionysius and Aristotle himself towards his princely friend in Atarneus. Hence it is important that when we analyse the *Politics* we observe a gradual transition from Plato's ethical radicalism, and from his speculation about the ideal state, towards *Realpolitik*; and that we are led to the conclusion that this change was accomplished mainly under the influence of the experienced statesman Hermias. Aristotle did not recommend to Alexander the Platonic ideal of the little city-state, such as it is preserved in the oldest portions of his *Politics*; although this

[1] Demosthenes, *Orations*, X. 31. Cf. the scholia ad loc. They refer the mysterious hints of the fourth *Philippic* to Hermias, and this has been confirmed by Didymus' commentary.

ideal still had its importance for the Greek cities, which had remained formally autonomous, and although he afterwards recognized it again when he lectured at Athens. He was well aware
—and that he undertook the work is more significant of his
character than all his political theories—that he was forming
the ideas of the heir of the leading state in Greece, the most
powerful European kingdom of the age, and that he was at the
same time a diplomatic link between Philip and Hermias. The
death of the latter gave an unexpected turn to everything, but
the anti-Persian sentiment of the coalition thus destroyed became a part of Aristotle's emotional life, and in that atmosphere
Alexander grew up.

It was a matter of faith with Aristotle that Greece could rule
the world if it were politically united. As a philosopher he recognized the cultural leadership of this people, which, wherever
it found itself, penetrated and dominated the surrounding
nations with astonishing power. No race could vie with the intellectual compactness of the urban Greek; both in war and in
commerce he conquered by his mere technical superiority and
personal self-reliance. On the other hand, the traditional narrow-
ness of political life in the autonomous city-state put in the
way of any organic union difficulties that Aristotle, born in Chal-
cidice, was unable to appreciate with the Attic democrat's long-
standing passion for freedom. Being the son of a family that had
lived at the Macedonian court, it was easy for him to accustom
himself to the thought of Greece united under Macedonian leadership. But in such an unstable form of state there would inevitably be an antinomy between the patriarchal or agricultural
kingship on the one hand, and the freedom of the city-demo-
cracies on the other. This would make for inner disunion and
could be overcome only by the outstanding personality of a real
king, in whom Greece could see its own embodiment. Aristotle
knew that such a man is a gift of the Gods. He was not a supporter of monarchy at all costs; Greek thought in fact never
possessed—or at least that of the fourth century did not—the
juristic insight necessary to appreciate the value of legitimacy and
a fixed succession. The less, however, that the Greeks regarded
a monarch as ruling by legal right in our sense, the more ready
they were, even in the century of the greatest enlightenment,

to bow before the natural inborn kingliness of a superior individual, if he appeared as a saviour in chaos, and imposed upon their world of outworn political forms the law of inexorable historical Ananke.

Aristotle hoped to find such a born king in Alexander, and it is due to him that the young monarch, although he always remained enough of a *Realpolitiker* to base himself on his solid household troops, his descent from Heracles, and his position as commander-in-chief, did sometimes honestly think of his historical mission as a Hellenic project. The tremendous difference between him and Philip comes out most clearly in their attitude towards the Greeks. Philip knew how to make an intelligent use of Greek civilization, as is shown by his invitation to Aristotle, for example; and he could not imagine a modern state without Greek technical skill and military science, or without Greek diplomacy and rhetoric. But inwardly he was just a cunning barbarian; and his genial power only made the fact more grossly obvious, more insulting. By nature Alexander was a true scion of this wild stock; and his Greek contemporaries, who were deceived by his excellent education into supposing that he might be measured by Greek standards, could never understand his combination of great qualities with demonic incalculability, mad desire for pleasure, and, in later days, increasing outbreaks of brutality and cruelty. Nevertheless, his remarkably high degree of personal and historical self-consciousness is a clear sign of the influence of Aristotle. His favourite plan, to set out for Asia like a second Achilles, is characteristic of the peculiar mixture in him, and of the clearness with which he himself apprehended it. He was Greek in his literary and moral schooling. He was Greek in striving for 'virtue', i.e. for a higher and more harmonious individuality. But his defiant imitation of Achilles expresses his romantic and passionate conviction that there was a contrast between himself and the excessively civilized culture and politics of the fourth century, and also perhaps expresses a certain feeling of half-barbarian knighthood that made it impossible for him to merge himself in Greek enlightenment. He marches to Asia surrounded by historians and scholars; in Ilium he seeks out the grave of Achilles and pronounces him fortunate because he found Homer to be the herald of his deeds. Of such a youth Aristotle might well expect that he would lead the Greeks to unity and establish their dominion in the east over the ruins of the Persian empire (the two things were inseparably connected in his mind). The community of ideas between the two men was obviously very close, not merely while Aristotle was living in Macedon, but down until long after the beginning of the Persian wars. Only when the expedition into Asia had immeasurably extended the horizon of the Iliadic landscape did Alexander begin to confound the bearing of Achilles with other and oriental roles. Then his Greek mission gave place to the new aim of reconciling peoples and equalizing races, and Aristotle opposed him strongly. This end of their intimate connexions, however, must not be allowed to cast any shadow over the time when Alexander, as heir to the throne of Macedon, laid the foundations of his political thought under the tutorship of Aristotle, and the latter made a close friendship with Antipater, which in some respects took the place of that with Hermias, and which lasted even after the death of the philosopher. When Philip died Alexander fulfilled his teacher's dearest wish by rebuilding his birthplace Stagira, which had been devastated by Philip's troops during the Chalcidic war. Theophrastus' mother-city, Eresus on Lesbos, was also spared when the Macedonians took the island. Callisthenes accompanied Alexander to Asia as historian.

CHAPTER VI

THE MANIFESTO *ON PHILOSOPHY*

THE history of the most productive epoch in Aristotle's life has previously been a blank sheet. Of the period from his thirty-seventh to his forty-ninth years, that is, from the time when he left the Academy to the time when he returned to Athens from Macedonia and founded the Peripatetic school (347–335), nothing has been known. No essential connexion could be traced between his 'travels' and the secluded life in the Academy that had preceded them. In any case they seemed to have no special importance for the understanding of Aristotle as a thinker. Since his writings could not be accurately dated there appeared to be a complete vacuum between his Academic and his Peripatetic periods, it being supposed that the treatises were all written during the latter. Since nothing precise was known about his teaching and writing previous to the foundation of his school, it is not surprising that scholars imagined his thought as having reached a final shape, and regarded the treatises as its systematic and definitive expression. Within this system the highest place appeared to belong to metaphysics, the study of pure being, an overarching dome beneath which all departmental sciences were included, presupposed, and thereby cancelled.

We now know from the newly discovered work of Didymus that Aristotle resumed his teaching immediately after 347, and that his first independent appearance occurred while he was still at Assos. What we hear of his activity during these years shows that it had come to be his desire to exert a widespread public influence. At the same time, everything points to the conclusion that his close affinity with Plato and Plato's preoccupations continued undisturbed. He went on living and teaching among Plato's pupils. As we have seen, his departure from the school at Athens was in no sense a break with the Academic community as such; and it would be an intolerable contradiction to suppose that, after having remained a true disciple throughout his master's life, he broke away from him the instant he was dead.

On the contrary, his development took on more and more of the public character that had always determined Plato's personality and influence. He founded schools and sowed the seeds of philosophy in various places. He took part in political affairs, as Plato had done, and came to have influence at the courts of the most powerful rulers of the age. For the first time he began to number important men among his pupils.

It is *a priori* probable that this was also the time of his first appearance before the general public as a critic of Plato, since he now had to explain the Platonic philosophy on his own responsibility and according to his own conception of its nature. Starting from this reflection, we must try to penetrate farther into the mysterious darkness of these decisive years, during which he reached the first comprehensive formulation of his own point of view. We discover that between the early, dogmatically Platonic, stage of his development, and the final form of his thought in its maturity, there was a period of transition whose nature can be definitely ascertained in many particulars; a period when he was criticizing, rearranging, and detaching himself; a period, previously wholly overlooked, which was clearly distinct from the final form of his philosophy, although it reveals the entelechy of the latter in all essential points. The advantage of examining this situation is not merely to obtain a picture of the gradual growth of his principles. Only when we know what he emphasizes as time goes on, what he suppresses, and what he introduces, can we form a clear conception of the determining forces that were working to bring about a new *Weltanschauung* in him.

At the head of this development I place the dialogue *On Philosophy*. It is generally reckoned along with the earlier writings,[1] but its doctrine is obviously a product of the transition. The numerous fragments remaining, some of them quite substantial, make the attempt at reconstruction more hopeful than it is with any of the other lost works. Here again we shall have to go into the minutiae of interpretation in order to extract

---

[1] Bernays and Heitz see no difference between this and the other exoteric writings, because they assume that Aristotle attacked Plato in all of them. Dyroff, on the other hand (op. cit., p. 82), universalizes his correct view that the contents of the dialogues and the *Protrepticus* were mostly Platonic, and assumes that the same was true of that *On Philosophy* also.

the essential from our material. Up to the present it has been very little understood. In style, in content, and in purpose, it holds a unique place in Aristotle's development.

On Philosophy is expressly mentioned as having attacked the doctrine of Ideal numbers; and it is in fact the sole literary work of which we definitely know that its contents were anti-Platonic. This criticism apparently formed part of a general refutation of the doctrine of Ideas, for it deals not with Speusippus' view that the mathematical numbers were independent substances, but with Plato's own later form of the doctrine, according to which the Ideas were numbers. 'If the Ideas were another kind of number, and not the mathematical, we should have no understanding of it. For who understands another kind of number, at any rate among the majority of us?'[1] Syrianus has preserved these words for us from the second book of the dialogue. The speaker is Aristotle himself, expressing his aporia about Plato's doctrine half in protest and half in mockery.

The same attitude seems to me to be expressed in another fragmentary criticism of the Idea-theory, the origin of which, though not definitely recorded, is more than probable. This is the passage taken by Proclus and Plutarch from a common source to prove that Aristotle attacked Plato in the dialogues as well as in the treatises.[2] Since the tradition does not inform us of a criticism of Plato in any dialogue except that *On Philosophy*, and since this unidentified criticism agrees surprisingly well with the attitude expressed in the fragment quoted by name from this dialogue, it would be unnatural not to assign both to the same work, especially as the mere title of this work, so unusually informative for a dialogue, suggests a thorough examination of the fundamental problems of philosophy. Here again Aristotle himself was the speaker. We do not know the exact words he used, but both accounts preserve the remarkable expression, 'he cannot sympathize with the theory of Ideas, even if he should be believed to be disagreeing out of mere contentiousness'. This protest illuminates even more clearly than the other fragment the fact that in his picture of the stubborn conflict of opinions Aristotle was representing the actual situation. Something had to give way. Finally he appeals to the respect that all inquirers

[1] Frg. 9.   [2] Frg. 8. See above, page 35.

owe to every honest and reasoned conviction. He emphatically repudiates the malicious suggestion, which of course had been made in the Academy, that his divergence of view was due to personal reasons. This imputation was obviously one of the main reasons why he published his criticism, which no doubt had already been a matter of discussion for some time within the Platonic circle. When at length he announced to the world, 'I cannot but maintain my objection', he had ceased to be greatly concerned about recovering the good will of those former friends from whom he now dissented. He was ready to submit his arguments to the verdict of the public.[1]

If we may judge from the title and the fragments, the dialogue was peculiar in form as well as in content. Cicero, when appealing to Aristotle to justify his own procedure, tells us that the latter appeared in his own dialogues and led the discussion. We have shown, however, that this probably occurred only in a few dialogues, in fact only in the *Statesman* and the *Philosophy*.[2] In the latter the prominence of Aristotle himself is surely connected with the nature of the work as a kind of personal manifesto. The title suggests a fairly systematic treatise, and this the fragments confirm. No doubt a supporter of the Platonic view made a long speech in opposition to Aristotle. Cicero tells us, moreover, that Aristotle wrote a separate introduction for each of the books when his dialogues had more than one; from this we may infer that each book was complete in itself, as in Cicero's dialogues.[3] Thus both formally and philosophically the work is midway between the early Platonic works and the treatises, and in spirit it approximates to the latter.

The date of composition is indicated by the relation between this criticism of the Idea-theory and that in the first book of the

---

[1] The passage owes its preservation to its peculiar importance for the development of Aristotle's critical attitude to Plato. It was unique. Hence to universalize such an individual and irretrievable situation, and apply it to all the dialogues, is a procedure that refutes itself.

[2] See above, p. 29.

[3] Cic. *Ep. ad Att*. IV. 16. 2; 'quoniam in singulis libris utor prooemiis, ut Aristoteles in eis quos ἐξωτερικούς vocat.' The introductions must therefore have been very loosely connected with what followed. According to Proclus (*in Parmen.* I. 659, Cousin) the same was true of the dialogues of Theophrastus and Heraclides Ponticus, which were modelled on those of Aristotle. In the *Eudemus*, on the contrary, the discussion arises naturally out of the introductory setting, as it does in Plato.

Metaphysics. One of the few points that can be firmly established about the chronology of the treatises is this: shortly after
Plato's death Aristotle produced a happy sketch of the main
results of the mass of discussion that had been going on about
the Forms within the Academy, in which he attempted to outline his new system of improved Platonism; the introduction to
this early sketch is contained in the first book of the *Metaphysics*.[1] Now it is inconceivable that the criticism in the
dialogue *On Philosophy*, which was addressed to the public and
cast in literary form, came before this esoteric discussion; that
criticism was not the first but the final step   For the sake of the
Academy Aristotle would avoid as long as possible a public
examination of the internal controversies of his school on logical
and metaphysical questions, which few persons were capable of
judging; and the remaining fragments prove that he did so only
when self-defence obliged him. It follows that the dialogue was
written at the same time as the criticism of the Forms in the
first book of the *Metaphysics*, or slightly later, and certainly
after Plato's death. Aristotle enters the lists armed not merely
with destructive criticisms but also with a view of his own.
Until Andronicus published the *Metaphysics* this dialogue remained the chief source of information about Aristotle's general
philosophical opinions in the ancient world, and from it the
Stoics and Epicureans took their knowledge of him. It was,
however, an undeveloped Aristotle with whom they had to
content themselves.

He began with the historical development of philosophy. He
did not confine himself to the Greek philosophers from Thales
onward, who display a real continuity, and who were pure
inquirers, proceeding without presuppositions along definite
lines. Contrary to his procedure in the *Metaphysics*, he went
back to the East, and mentioned its ancient and tremendous
creations with interest and respect. In the first book of the
Metaphysics he touches only on the Egyptian priests and their
services to mathematics, for the sake of the example of philosophic leisure and contemplation that they gave to the Greeks.
In his dialogue, however, he penetrated to the earliest times—if
we follow his own chronology—and spoke of the Magi and their

[1] See *Ent. Met. Arist.*, pp. 28 ff., esp. p. 33.

teaching.[1] Then came the venerable representatives of the oldest Hellenic wisdom, the theologians, as he calls them; then the doctrines of the Orphics, and no doubt Hesiod, though he does not appear in the fragments; and finally the proverbial wisdom traditionally ascribed to the Seven Wise Men, the preservation of which was specially cared for by the God of Delphi. This gave occasion to mention the old Apolline worship. It is worth noticing that Aristotle was the first successor of Plato to rid himself of Plato's contemptuous opinion of the Sophists. He restored the name to its rightful meaning as a title of honour; and he had the historical insight to put the Seven Wise Men at the head of this succession of commanding intellects, whose influence on the development of Greek thought seemed to him so important that he included it in the history of philosophical wisdom.[2]

This mass of facts was critically sifted and reduced to order. Aristotle raised the question of the genuineness of the remaining Orphic poems. He denied that Orpheus wrote verse; and he distinguished between the religious ideas and the form in which they were handed down, correctly assigning the latter to a fairly late period, about the end of the sixth century. This is the origin of the view, which still holds the field, that the mystification of the Orphic poem was invented by Onomacritus, theologian to the Pisistratids, who were interested in Orphic mysticism.[3] Aristotle also inquired into the antiquity of the proverb 'Know thyself', which was inscribed over the entrance to the temple at Delphi. He sought to determine its date by means of the history of the building.[4] Similarly, instead of naïvely admiring the hoar antiquity of Egyptian wisdom and of Iranian religion, he attempted to assign to them the most definite possible dates.[5]

This strict chronology is the result not of a mere antiquarian

---

[1] Frg. 6.

[2] The evidence for these details in the dialogue *On Philosophy* is as follows. Apart from the dating of the religion of the Magi, only the calculation about the antiquity of the Delphic proverb 'Know thyself', which led on to the question of the date of the Seven Wise Men, is definitely ascribed to this dialogue (frg. 3). Aristotle assigned the proverb to a time prior to Chilon. It follows that fragments 4 and 5 come from the same context. That the theologians must have been mentioned is obvious from the fact that in the *Metaphysics* too he makes philosophical reflection begin with them.

[3] Frg. 7. [4] Frg. 3. [5] Frg. 6.

interest but of a philosophical principle. His doctrine was that
the same truths reappear in human history, not merely once or
twice, but indefinitely often.[1] He therefore laid the foundation
of a collection of Greek proverbs, on the ground that these
laconic and striking empirical precepts are the survivals of a
pre-literary philosophy, and have preserved themselves by word
of mouth, through all the changes in the nation's spirit, in virtue
of their brevity and pregnancy. His keen eye perceived the
value of proverbs and proverbial poetry in the study of the origins
of ethical reflection. To the educated Greek the detailed labour
of making such a collection seemed banausic, and Aristotle's
attempt evoked open scorn from Isocratean circles.[2] In examining the antiquity of the Delphic maxim 'Know thyself' he tried
to determine the question from which of the Seven Wise Men it
came. By means of his deductions from the building he settled
this rather empty controversy with a judgement of Solomon;
since the maxim is older than Chilon it comes from none of the
Wise Men, but was revealed by the Pythia herself. The point
of the argument becomes clear when we consider Plutarch's
statement, according to which Aristotle 'in the Platonic works'
held that 'Know thyself' is the most divine of the precepts at
Delphi, and that it was this same precept that gave Socrates his
problem. The peculiar phrase 'in the Platonic works' (ἐν τοῖς
Πλατωνικοῖς) is parallel to 'in the Socratic works', which
means Plato's Socratic dialogues; it must refer to the form, not
the content, and it must mean Aristotle's Platonic dialogues.
The relation here established between the old Delphic maxim
and the new Socratic search for ethical knowledge fits better
into the dialogue *On Philosophy* than into any other. It is an
example of the doctrine that philosophical truths are redis-
covered throughout the course of history. Thus Socrates became
the restorer of the ethical principle of Apolline religion; in fact,
as Aristotle tried to show by the tale of the visit to Delphi, it
was from this ancient centre of revelation that he received the

---

[1] *De Caelo* I. 3, 270^b 19; *Meteor.* I. 3, 339^b 27; *Metaph.* Λ 8, 1074^b 10;
Pol. VII. 10, 1329^b 25.
[2] For Aristotle's interest in proverbs see παροιμία in Bonitz's *Index Aristote-
licus.* For the view that proverbs are 'remnants of ancient philosophy' see
frg. 13. For collections of the proverbs see Diog. L. V. 26 and Athenaeus
II. 60 D.

external impulse leading to those questions that agitated all the ethical problems of his age.[1]

The connexion thus discovered between religion and philosophy extends throughout the dialogue. Socrates' Apolline mission had already been touched on by Plato in the *Apology*; here the doctrine of cycles is used to broaden it into a renascence of Delphic wisdom. Apollinism and Socraticism are the two foci in the development of Greek ethics. The inquiry into the date of the origin of Orphism must have been part of the same idea. Aristotle never doubted the historicity of Orpheus; he emphasized the lateness of the literary formulation solely in order to replace the Pisistratid versifier and oracle-monger with a genuine prophet of Greek antiquity. He was certain that the Orphic poems were late; there was nothing, however, to prevent the religious teaching itself from being of great antiquity. What led him to inquire into the date of its origin was doubtless its recent return in a more spiritualized form in Plato's doctrine of the after-life and the soul's progress.

Another example of this method is to be found in the following fragment. In his *Natural History* Pliny says (30. 3): 'Eudoxus, who wished it to be thought that the most famous and most beneficial of the philosophical sects was that of the Magi, tells us that this Zoroaster lived 6,000 years before the death of Plato. Aristotle says the same.' We know that Eudoxus, the astronomer and friend of Plato, interested himself in Oriental and Egyptian learning during his stay in those parts. He brought with him to Greece the lore that he had gathered from the representatives of a world still more or less closed to the Hellenes.

At that time the Academy was the centre of a very strong interest in the Orient. As an omen of Alexander's expedition and the consequent *rapprochement* between Greek and Asiatic this interest is of great and by no means sufficiently recognized significance. The channels through which the Eastern influence

---

[1] That fragments 1 and 2 belong with 3 cannot be doubted, as soon as it is perceived that the key to the whole is the theory of the periodic return of all knowledge. We are not concerned here with the question whether the Delphic precepts really belong to the ethics of Apollo, or are pieces of foreign wisdom availing themselves of the god's protection. The parallel between Socrates and the Delphic maxim also appears in Ps.-Plato, *Alcib.* I. 124 b: 'taking the advice of myself and of the Delphic maxim "Know thyself".'

forced its way can be traced only to a small extent. From a fragment of the Academy's list of students, preserved on a papyrus from Herculaneum, we happen to know that a Chaldaean was a regular member of the school.[1] This appears to have been during Plato's last decade. Other signs of Oriental influence point to the same period. Such are the parallel in *Alcibiades* I between Plato's four virtues and the ethics of Zarathustra, and the astral theology put forward as the highest wisdom by Plato's pupil and secretary, Philip of Opus, in his postscript to the *Laws*. To recommend the new religious views which he is earnestly proclaiming 'to the Greeks' Philip openly appeals to Oriental sources.[2] These tendencies undoubtedly originated during the time when Eudoxus was present in the Academy, although our material unfortunately does not permit us to evaluate to its full extent the tremendous influence exercised upon the Platonists by this man. They are connected in part with the Academy's admiration for Chaldaean and 'Syrian' astronomy, from whose ancient empirical acquaintance with the heavens it had obtained its reckoning of the times of revolution and its knowledge of the seven planets, a knowledge that appears in Philip of Opus for the first time in Europe. In part, again, these tendencies are connected with the appeal of the religious dualism of the Parsees, which seemed to lend support to the dualistic metaphysics of Plato's old age. The bad world-soul that opposes the good one in the *Laws* is a tribute to Zarathustra, to whom Plato was attracted because of the mathematical phase that his Idea-theory finally assumed, and because of the intensified dualism involved therein.[3] From that time onwards the Academy was keenly interested in Zarathustra and the teaching of the Magi. Plato's pupil Hermodorus discussed astralism in his *Mathematics*; he derived the name Zarathustra from it, declaring that it means 'star-worshipper' (ἀστροθύτης).[4]

---

[1] *Index Acad. Herculan.* col. iii, p. 13 (Mekler).

[2] *Epin.* 986 E, 987 B, and 987 D–988 A. Ps.-Plato, *Alcib.* I. 121 E–122 A.

[3] *Laws* X. 896 E. '*Ath.* And as the soul orders and inhabits all things that move, however moving, must we not say that she orders also the heavens? *Cle.* Of course. *Ath.* One soul or more? More than one—I will answer for you; at any rate, we must not suppose that there are less than two—one the author of good, and the other of the opposite.'

[4] For Hermodorus *On Mathematics*, used by Sotion in the *Diadoche*, see Diog. L. I. 2 and 8; cf. Schol. on Ps.-Plato, *Alcib.* I. 122 A.

These influences gave rise to Aristotle's interest in the Magi in the dialogue *On Philosophy*. Even the attempt to determine Zarathustra's date had already been made by other Academics. Hermodorus, for instance, had put him 5,000 years before the fall of Troy. The researches of this Platonist were still the main authority on the matter when the learned Alexandrian Sotion wrote his history of the philosophical schools. Besides Hermodorus he mentioned the suggestion of Xanthus, according to which Zarathustra lived 6,000 years before the invasion of Xerxes.[1] The date given by Aristotle and Eudoxus, as reported by Pliny, differs from the other traditional dates in its peculiar point of reference. When we compare '6,000 years before Plato's death' with figures reckoned from the fall of Troy or from the expedition of Xerxes (which later gave way to that of Alexander), it becomes obvious that this manner of statement is due not to chronological convenience but to the desire to connect Zarathustra and Plato as two essentially similar historical phenomena. The point of the comparison, and of Aristotle's interest in the round thousands of the interval, is clearly the view put forward in *On Philosophy* that all human truths have their natural and necessary cycles. Now in a fragment that is known to belong to the first book of this dialogue Aristotle speaks of the teaching of the Magi, namely the Iranian dualism, according to which there are two principles, a good and a bad spirit, Ormuzd and Ahriman; and these he identifies with the Greek divinities Zeus and Hades, the god of heavenly light and the god of chthonic darkness. Plutarch, also, compares Plato's doctrine of the good and the bad world-souls with the dualism of the Chaldees and Magi. It is natural to suppose that the same consideration was actuating Aristotle in the fragment where he draws a parallel between Zarathustra and Plato.[2] This supposition is rendered certain by the only other passage where he mentions the Magi, namely one of the oldest parts of the *Metaphysics*, which must be assigned on other grounds to the time when *On Philosophy* was being written. Here again the subject is Platonic dualism. As the earliest forerunners of this view Aristotle mentions in Greece Pherecydes, in Asia the Magi.[3] The Academy's

---

[1] Diog. L. I. 2.   [2] Frg. 6. Plutarch, *Is. et Osir.* 370 E.
[3] *Metaph.* N 4, 1091[b] 8.

enthusiasm for Zarathustra amounted to intoxication, like the rediscovery of Indian philosophy through Schopenhauer. It heightened the historical self-consciousness of the school to think that Plato's doctrine of the Good as a divine and universal principle had been revealed to eastern humanity by an Oriental prophet thousands of years before.

This explanation is confirmed by the number 6,000. We know from Theopompus, who perhaps had it from Eudoxus himself, that the generation of Eudoxus and Aristotle was aware of the great cycle in Iranian religion, and of the world-wide drama of the struggle between Ormuzd and Ahriman.[1] Ormuzd and Ahriman rule in turn (ἀνὰ μέρος), each for 3,000 years. For another 3,000 years they fight, and each tries to injure the other and destroy what he has created. Finally the good spirit gains the day. The length of this eschatological drama is variously estimated in Iranian tradition, sometimes as 9,000 years (this is apparently the figure that Theopompus' source follows), and sometimes as 12,000. The significance of each three-thousand-year act in the world-cycle varies accordingly. For this reason the means at our disposal will perhaps not allow us to determine unambiguously the precise points at which Zarathustra and Plato are supposed to appear;[2] but it is certainly not an accident that the figure 6,000, which according to Aristotle and Eudoxus is the number of the years between the two, is divisible by 3,000. Zarathustra and Plato are obviously two important

---

[1] Theopompus, frg. 72 (Mueller). Cf. Jackson, 'The Date of Zoroaster', *Journal of the American Orient. Soc.*, vol. xvii (1896), p. 3; F. Cumont, *Textes et monum. de Mithra*, vol. i, p. 310, n. 6; and recently Gisinger, *Erdbeschreibung des Eudoxus* (Leipzig, 1907). Since the creation of the good God is completed in 6,000 years, the Christian fathers and philosophers of history identify this period with the six days of creation according to the Mosaic story.

[2] In the original German edition of this work I tried to fix more accurately the probable positions of Zarathustra and Plato in the world-drama of Iranian religion. Since then my assertion that the assignment of Zarathustra to a date 6,000 years before Plato implies some inner connexion between them, or rather between their principles, has been largely taken up by orientalists and is perhaps generally accepted. In view of recent Iranian researches, however, I now prefer not to attempt the harmonization of the Greek and Persian traditions, since for my purpose the only important thing is to establish *the fact that* shortly after his death, and even while he was still living, Plato was brought into connexion with Zarathustra and with Iranian teaching about the struggle between the good principle and the bad. On Plato as the founder of a religion, as Aristotle's altar-elegy regards him, see my article 'Aristotle's Verses in Praise of Plato', *The Classical Quarterly*, vol. xxi (1927), p. 13.

stages in the world's journey towards its goal, the triumph of the good.

The main reason for assigning Pliny's fragment to the first book of the dialogue *On Philosophy* is that only in this context can it be fully understood; but since Rose included it among the fragments of the spurious *Magicus*—for no discoverable reason —it may be well expressly to dissipate the shadow of suspicion that has thereby fallen upon it.[1] Pliny did not get his information from the *On the Magi* of Apion, as Rose unreasonably conjectures, but from the learned work of the same title by Hermippus, the follower of Callimachus. In the next line he unmistakably indicates Hermippus as his source, and expresses naïve wonder at his wide reading in the original texts, which is very proper in view of his own lack of it. It was not Pliny but Hermippus who consulted Eudoxus and Aristotle. We may confirm this by comparing the passage with fragment 6, a statement about the Magi which is definitely known to belong to the first book *On Philosophy*. This also comes from Hermippus, and here again he mentions Eudoxus and Aristotle as his sources. We give the two excerpts side by side.

Pliny, *Natural History*, 30. 3.

Without doubt it began with Zoroaster in Persia, as the authorities agree. It is not so clear whether there was only one man of this name, or another one later on. *Eudoxus*, who held it to be the most excellent and valuable of all philosophical sects, said that this Zoroaster lived six thousand years before the death of Plato. *Aristotle says the same. Hermippus*, who

Diogenes Laertius I, Prologue 8.

Aristotle in the first book of his dialogue On Philosophy declares that the Magi are more ancient than the Egyptians; and further, that they believe in two principles, the good spirit and the evil spirit, the one called Zeus or Ormuzd, the other Hades or Ahriman. This is confirmed by *Hermippus in his first book about the Magi, Eudoxus in his Voyage round the World*, and

[1] Arist. frg. 34. Cf. Rose, *Arist. Pseudepigraphus*, p. 50. The reason why Rose assigned the fragment to the *Magicus* is presumably that in Diogenes Laertius (I. 1 and I. 8) this work is mentioned as one of Aristotle's in the immediate context of the quotation from *On Philosophy* about the Magi. Precise examination shows, however, that Diogenes is not following the same source in quoting each of the two works as Aristotle's. The spurious *Magicus* was given as main source by Sotion and Hermodorus, for Diogenes mentions all three names both in I. 1–2 and in I. 7–8 (the excerpt extends down to 'and Hermodorus agrees with him in this'); whereas the information from Aristotle's *On Philosophy* and Eudoxus was obtained from Hermippus, as has been shown above.

wrote copiously about all that art, and commented on two million lines written by Zoroaster, affixing an index to every book, says . . . that his teacher was Agonaces, and that he himself lived five thousand years before the Trojan war.[1]

Theopompus in the eighth book of his *Philippica*.

It is evident that Hermippus used the same sources for both these accounts of the Magi, namely the dialogue *On Philosophy* and the *Voyage* of Eudoxus. He must have quoted them exactly each time. Diogenes preserves his quotation in full; but Pliny, as often, names only the authors without the books. Pliny's fragment fits excellently with the theory of cycles, and with the chronological discussions in the first book *On Philosophy*, which contained other statements about the Magi; in future, therefore, it is to be included among the fragments of this dialogue. The parallel position of Plato and Zarathustra in the cycle does not give the impression of having been invented during Plato's life. It was certainly not to be found in the *Voyage* of Eudoxus, who died long before him. The originality of Eudoxus lay solely in putting Zarathustra '6,000 years ago'. It was Aristotle who, led by his doctrine of the periodical return of all human knowledge, first specifically connected this figure with the return of dualism, and thereby put Plato in a setting that corresponded to his profound reverence for him. There can be no doubt that the dialogue in which he thus directed the light of the centuries upon his master was written after the latter's death.[2]

---

[1] On the correct form of the name 'Agonaces' see Fr. C. Andreas in Reitzenstein, 'Die Göttin Psyche', *Sitzungsberichte der Heidelberger Akademie der Wissenschaften*, Philosophisch-historische Klasse, vol. viii (1917), Abh. 10, p. 44. On the significance of the above discussion of Aristotle's statements about Zarathustra's teaching for the oriental tradition and its chronology see Reitzenstein-Schaeder, *Studien zum antiken Synkretismus aus Iran und Griechenland* (Leipzig, 1926), p. 3.

[2] If Pliny's words 'sex milibus annorum ante *Platonis mortem*' do not come from the intermediate source Hermippus—it is true, as Eduard Fraenkel has pointed out to me, that in technical chronology 'ante mortem . . .' sometimes means no more than 'ante aliquem'—but from Hermippus' authority, they can only be from Aristotle, since Eudoxus died before Plato. (It is impossible to follow Gisinger, op. cit. p. 5, n. 1, in supposing on the basis of the passage in Pliny that Eudoxus died later than Plato.) Merely on internal grounds, however, it seems to me certain that such a comparison could never have arisen

The doctrine that truth returns at certain intervals assumes that men are incapable of permanently retaining it once it has been discovered. It was not supposed, however, that humanity cannot maintain itself for long upon a high spiritual level, and for that reason continually loses again even truths that have been known for a long time. The theory was that the tradition, and in fact civilization as a whole, is periodically destroyed by violent convulsions of nature. In other words, Plato's doctrine of catastrophes was applied to the history of philosophy. Bywater has given convincing reasons for believing that this doctrine occurred in Aristotle's dialogues.[1] In the *Timaeus* it is suggested that all the more ancient traditions of the Greeks have been annihilated by overwhelming natural events. Such myths as those of Phaëthon and of the flood are there interpreted as traces of these events in human memory. The same method of interpretation is applied to the oldest records of culture in the *Laws*, just as Aristotle in the *Metaphysics* explains the stories of the Gods as remnants, distorted by tradition, of an early stage of his own theory of the movers of the spheres.[2] This rationalizing procedure certainly cannot have originated in Plato's imaginative brain. It bears the stamp of Ionian science, and presumably it comes from Eudoxus himself, together with the theory of catastrophes. Aristotle made free use of it. In the *Meteorologica*, for example, he argues from the mythical tradition to the prehistorical existence of the hypothesis of ether, which as a matter of fact was invented by himself.[3] On the other hand, Eudoxus is certainly not the author of the view that all intellectual things recur. This, however, only brings out more clearly

while Plato was still alive, and the same is true of the attitude of the dialogue as a whole to Plato and his philosophy.

[1] Bywater (*Journ. of Philology*, vol. vii, p. 65) assigns to the *On Philosophy* portions of Philoponus *In Nicom. arithm.* The theory of cataclysms is there connected with the growth of knowledge, and this is an idea that Aristotle took over from Plato and developed. The form of the theory that Bywater analyses is, however, Stoic, especially the notion of the development of the arts, and of the continual change that this causes in the meaning of 'wisdom'. See my *Nemesios von Emesa, Quellenforschungen zur Geschichte des älteren Neuplatonismus und zu Poseidonios* (Berlin, 1914), pp. 124 ff. See also Gerhäusser, *Der Protreptikos des Poseidonios* (Heidelberg thesis, 1912), pp. 16 ff.

[2] Plato, *Timaeus* 22 A–C, *Critias* 109 D ff., *Laws* III. 677 A; Arist. *Metaph.* Λ 8, 1074^b 1–13.

[3] *Meteor.* I. 3, 339^b 20 ff., *De Caelo* I. 3, 270^b 16 ff., *De Animal. Mot.* 3, 699^a 27, *Pol.* VII. 10, 1329^b 25.

the effect of contemporary natural science on men's thought about
the history of culture, on their use of the myths, and on their
conception of the human spirit, which, like nature with her forces,
is ever bringing forth anew that which lies hidden within itself.

By representing Plato in the first book as a man of the ages,
out of the reach of every petty contradiction, and as the culmination of all previous philosophy, Aristotle gave the proper
perspective to the criticism that followed. The second book was
a destructive criticism of the Ideas. The third gave his own view
of the world; it was a cosmology and a theology; like the second,
it took the form throughout of a criticism of Plato, for the simple
reason that it was dependent on him at every step. Its general
contents are described by the Epicurean in Cicero's *De Natura
Deorum*. In essentials Aristotle adopted the stellar theology of
Plato's later days. This, it seemed to him, must be the point of
departure for metaphysics now that the theory of Forms had
collapsed. Plato conceived that behind the sidereal story of his
later years there lay the supersensible world of Ideas, of which
the visible heavens were a copy. Aristotle, however, was concerned exclusively with the cosmological side of this dual world.
(So, though in a different manner, was that other pupil of Plato's,
Philip of Opus, in the *Epinomis*.) In this way he became the real
founder of the cosmic religion of the Hellenistic philosophers,
which, emancipated from popular beliefs, sought its objects of
worship solely in the heavenly bodies. The threads connecting on
the one hand Aristotle's stellar religion with the Academy, on
the other Stoic theology with Aristotle's early views, have not
yet been laid bare. In particular, the importance of Aristotle in
this connexion has not been clearly recognized, because scholars
have taken their start too exclusively from the treatises, which
were totally unknown to the Hellenistic age.

According to the unfavourable account in Cicero, which comes
from some Epicurean source also used by Philodemus, Aristotle
in his third book *On Philosophy* declared now that God was
mind, now that he was the world, now that he was the ether,
and now that he was some other being, to whom the world was
subordinated, and who guided its movement by a kind of backwards turning (*replicatione quadam*).[1] By applying the dogma of

[1] Frg. 26 (Cic. *De Natura Deorum* I. 13, 33).

the Epicurean school the critic discovers gross contradictions in these statements; but, however superficial his judgement of them may be, the correctness of the account as such cannot be doubted. The God to whom the world is subordinated is the transcendental unmoved mover, who guides the world as its final cause, by reason of the perfection of his pure thought. This is the original nucleus of Aristotelian metaphysics. Besides this, Aristotle described the ether as a divine body, or as a more divine body, as he does in the treatises; he certainly did not call it God.[1] The divinity of the ether does not seem to fit very well with a strict transcendental monotheism, but below the un- moved mover were the stargods, whose matter was ethereal. There is no real contradiction in the fact that Aristotle called now the world and now the ether God, i.e. first the whole and then the part. 'World' here does not mean what the Epicurean takes it to mean. It is not the Hellenistic conception of the cosmos filled with living creatures and containing all things, but the heavens, the mere periphery. This was the way in which the old Academy used the word, as the *Epinomis* also shows. In this work it is said to be indifferent whether we call the highest God, who is the heaven, Uranus or Olympus or Cosmos. In another passage we read that the truest description of him is Cosmos.[2]

The influence of the later Plato on the dialogue *On Philosophy* was not confined to terminology. In the main features of theo- logy, also, it corresponds almost perfectly with the *Epinomis*. It is noteworthy that the Epicurean, who is looking for points of attack, says nothing whatever about the fifty-five sphere- gods of the later metaphysics. In this dialogue Aristotle obviously had not yet adopted that view.

This is confirmed by a statement of Pseudo-Philo's in the work *On the Eternity of the World*. Aristotle is there said to have im- puted terrible atheism (Δεινὴν ἀθεότητα) to the philosophers who declared that the world had a beginning or an end, because

---

[1] Cicero translates 'ether' by *caeli ardor*. This is usual, and the description of it as divine is further evidence that what is meant is Aristotle's hypothesis of ether as the fifth element (cf. Cic. *De Natura Deorum* I. 14, 37; *ardorem, qui aether nominetur*, to which Plasberg refers in commenting on our passage). Aristotle must therefore have put forward the hypothesis while he was still in the Academy. It became fairly general there, though it suffered some excisions and modifications. Its first presentation to the public was no doubt that in the *On Philosophy*.   [2] *Epin.* 977 A, B and 987 B.

they thereby implied that this great and visible God (τοσοῦτον ὁρατὸν θεόν) was no better than a work made with hands. He called the cosmos a pantheon comprehending sun, moon, fixed stars, and planets. He derisively observed that, whereas formerly he had feared that his house might collapse only through tempest or old age or careless construction, there was now a far greater danger impending, if we believed the thinkers who destroyed the whole universe in their statements.[1]

We recognize the tone. Where Aristotle is attacking the physicists' view of the destruction of the world it is bitingly sharp. It is distinctly milder and more respectful when he is rejecting Plato's account of creation in the *Timaeus*—for that is what 'a work made with hands' refers to. Here we have the same personal air as we found in the criticism of the Forms in the second book. The third book too, as we learn from Cicero's account, was written with polemical reference to Plato throughout. This must apply mainly to the doctrine that the world is eternal, for that was Aristotle's greatest innovation ;[2] and since the passage does not come from any of the existing treatises, and is undoubtedly taken from a dialogue in view of its style, the only source that can possibly be suggested for it is the dialogue *On Philosophy*. It was this work, now lost but much read in antiquity, that contained the two philosophical views then considered most characteristic of Aristotle: the adoption of the ether as the element of the heavens, and the assertion that the cosmos is indestructible and uncreated. The doxographers commonly mention the two together as his distinctive additions to Plato's cosmology, and this is correct.

In spite of the divergence in details the doctrine of the dialogue is still completely Platonic in its positive views, and above all in the fusion of theology and astronomy. The *Laws* is the origin of the accusation of atheism against those whose astronomical views are unorthodox. In that work Plato converted this science, previously very atheistical, into the essence of

---

[1] Frg. 18. Ps.-Philo, *De Aet. Mundi* 3, 10 (p. 53 in Cohn-Reiter).

[2] Frg. 26 (Cic. *De Natura Deorum* I. 13, 33) 'Aristotelesque in tertio de philosophia libro multa turbat a magistro suo Platone dissentiens'. Manutius inserted a *non* before *dissentiens*, and Rose follows Lambinus in adopting it; but this gives an unacceptable meaning, and Vahlen has shown that it is also stylistically impossible (cf. Plasberg, large edition, p. 218).

theology.[1] It agrees with Cicero's account that the above-mentioned passage of Pseudo-Philo also uses the word 'cosmos' in the sense of heaven. For what is the doctrine of the cosmos 'comprehending within itself' sun, moon, and stars, but a reflection of the picture of the universe in the *Timaeus* (30 D)? 'The Deity, intending to make this world like the fairest and most perfect of intelligible beings, framed one visible animal *comprehending within itself* all other animals of a kindred nature.' It is true that for Aristotle the heavens are no longer the visible image of the highest Form, which contains within itself all other Forms and the whole intelligible cosmos. The world of Forms is gone, and with it the demiurge who made the visible world on the pattern thereof. But this only increases the religious and metaphysical dignity of the image, i.e. of the heavenly bodies and of the cosmos itself as the visible unity of the world, the sole empirical guarantees of Plato's demand that there should be something permanent and enduring in the flux of becoming. The expression 'visible God' is itself Platonic; and the comparison of the heavens with a pantheon including all the particular gods, though the words may belong not to Aristotle but to Philo, is Aristotelian in intention and reappears in the *Epinomis* when the sky is described as Olympus.[2] The old theory of Olympus gives place to the feeling that there is divinity in the cosmos, and the word thus symbolizes this decisive change in the history of Greek religion. The stars are living, rational beings, inhabiting the cosmos in divine beauty and unchangeableness. This is the theogony of Hellenistic and late antiquity, and Plato stands at its fountain-head.

In Aristotle's later metaphysics, as we know, the principle of the unmoved mover was no longer isolated; a special transcendental mover was assigned to each of the spheres that produce the apparent progressions, retrogradations, and stationary points, of the heavenly bodies. Of this view there is no trace in our dialogue. The unmoved mover hovers above all other gods, immaterial and separated from the world as pure Form. The

---

[1] *Laws* 821 D–822 C, 898 C, and 899 A. The pact between astronomy and atheism is dissolved in 967 A ff.

[2] For the sky as Olympus see *Epin.* 977 B; for the stars as images of the gods within it see *Epin.* 984 A.

unity of the world is anchored in that Form. The stars and the heavens, however, have souls within them and follow their own inner laws spontaneously and consciously. This theory of immanent star-souls excludes the other method of explanation. The causes of the heavenly motions had long been discussed in the Academy. In the *Laws* Plato mentions three hypotheses as reasonable, without definitely deciding in favour of any one. They are to be valid for all heavenly bodies without distinction. Either we must think of the stars as bodies with souls inside them (to Plato the soul is the principle of spontaneous movement), or the soul, not being inside the star, makes itself an external body of fire or air and therewith propels the star, or finally the soul has no body at all, but guides the motion of the star 'by some extraordinary and wonderful power'.[1] Plato's own theory is probably that of the immanent souls, for this fits best both with his view that the soul is the principle of all movement and with the plastic simplicity and vitalizing power of his thought. He describes the second as 'the view of certain persons' (λόγος τινῶν), presumably astronomers; one thinks of the spheres of Eudoxus, although he is almost certainly too early to have believed that the spheres had souls. The bodiless soul of the third hypothesis is obviously a transcendental Form, moving the star as final cause, as the beloved moves the lover. It is the principle of the unmoved mover. The wonderful power of which Plato speaks may be imagined as similar to the longing of sensible things for the Idea, or to Aristotle's *orexis*.

It will presumably always remain impossible for us to determine whether it was Aristotle himself or some other Academic who first conceived the theory of the unmoved mover and applied it to the problem of stellar motion. The communal nature of their studies prevents us from distinguishing the precise share of each person. The spirit of the idea is Platonic; that is to say, it is one that could not have arisen by itself, but only within the Platonic universe of thought, whoever its acute inventor may have been. Aristotle used it only for the highest principle, which is distinct from the world and has absolutely no motion; the stars and the heavens, on the other hand, were moved by immanent souls. We know this not merely from the

[1] *Laws* X. 898 E.

passage in Philo, but above all from the Aristotelian arguments preserved by Cicero, which must now be examined. According to Plato one of the three hypotheses had to be true of all heavenly motions without distinction. The fact that Aristotle combines the first and the third perhaps indicates that he was not the originator of either.

In the second book of his work on the Gods Cicero gives us proofs of their existence from Cleanthes, from Chrysippus, from Xenophon, and several from Aristotle, which he obviously obtained not from his own reading but from a ready-made collection.[1] Many of the arguments simply repeat what has already been said. Even the collection itself did not derive everything from the originals, any more than Sextus, who also made a collection of arguments for the existence of Gods, largely similar to this one in content.[2] Hence Cicero's account must be used critically. Nevertheless, it is authentic in essence. Both points can be demonstrated from the very first argument. All elements give rise to living things, earth to some, water to others, air to others. Hence it seems absurd to Aristotle to suppose that there are no living things in the element that by its purity and power of movement is most suited for their production, namely the ether. Now in the region of the ether we find the stars. Presumably, therefore, the stars are living beings of keen intelligence and extremely rapid motion.

This argument has been correctly assigned to the dialogue *On Philosophy*, but it cannot have appeared there in its present form. We have seen that in that work Aristotle was already maintaining the doctrine of ether as a fifth element. The argument preserved by Cicero presupposes only four. It cannot belong to a period prior to the introduction of the fifth, and therefore cannot be assigned to any earlier work of Aristotle's; it is an adaptation of his argument to the Stoic theory of the elements, the latter being a compromise between the traditional and the Aristotelian view, by which fire and ether were regarded as a single element. The only thing that Cicero's Stoic authority correctly reproduces is the formal analogical nature of the reasoning. Aristotle began with the universal validity of the

[1] Cic. *De Natura Deorum* II. 15, 42–44 (partly reproduced in Rose as frgs. 23 and 24).   [2] Sext. Emp. *Adv. Phys.* I. 49.

proposition that there are living things in every element of which
we can have experience. From this he inferred that there are
also living beings in the ether, although that element is not
directly open to scientific inquiry. The original sense of the
argument must therefore have been this: since it can be demonstrated that living things occur in all the elements, some in
earth, others in water, others in air, still others in fire, there must
certainly be some in the ether as well; now the stars are in the
ether; therefore they are living things. This was suggested by
the *Timaeus* (39 E), where the four elements are peopled with as
many kinds of divine being. The *Epinomis* takes account of
this theory of ether, which had appeared in the meantime, by
assuming five kinds of elemental God instead of the four of the
Timaeus; but the author shows, by the mere order in which he
puts the elements, that his intention is not to follow Aristotle
implicitly, but to make a conservative adaptation of his hypothesis to that of the *Timaeus*. According to Aristotle ether takes
the highest place in the world; then follow fire, air, water, earth.
Philip retains fire in the highest position; then follow ether and
air, then water and earth; thus the only change in Plato's
doctrine is that in the place of air, the highest and purest level of
which had already been called ether by Plato himself,[1] we have
two separate elements.[2] Thus the *Epinomis*, while outwardly
assimilating the theory of ether, intentionally evades the really
essential element in the idea. Aristotle's argument, unlike
Plato's, is not meant to demonstrate the existence of any mythic-
ally conceived gods or spirits. It is intended to be a strictly
empirical proof, and as such it presupposes that Aristotle thought
he could empirically demonstrate the existence of his fire-
animals. As late as the *Historia Animalium* he was still in-

[1] *Phaedo* 109 B; *Tim.* 58 D.

[2] The position of the five elements in the world is given in *Epin.* 984 D ff. In
981 C the ether is called the 'fifth body'. This is the Aristotelian expression,
but here it means merely the fifth and last body to be discovered, not that
which is farthest away from the earth. That the ether was called the 'fifth
body' or the 'fifth substance' in the *On Philosophy* follows from the fact that
the doxographers, whose source is always this dialogue, universally employ
this mode of referring to the specifically Aristotelian view. In the treatises it is
the 'first body'. The *Epinomis* is the earliest of the many works to which the
On Philosophy gave the expression 'fifth body'; there are also numerous other
respects in which it is dependent on it. Since Isocrates (V. 12) mentions the
Laws in the year 346, Aristotle's dialogue must have appeared in 348/7.

terested in insects that were supposed to fly through fire without being damaged, and speaks of observations made upon such creatures in Cyprus.[1] The most significant passage, however, is one in Apuleius, not included in the collection of fragments, where the doctrine of 'fireborn animals' is expressly attributed to Aristotle. It will be worth while to look closely at this passage, not for the sake of the miraculous fire-dwellers, but for the train of thought that they enable us to follow.

In his work on Socrates' divine sign Apuleius has an argument superficially similar to Aristotle's, but actually quite different both in purpose and in premises. Since there are living beings in the earth and the water; and since in fire (as Aristotle says) there are creatures that are born in this element and remain in it continually; and since lastly there are also living things in the ether, namely the stars—whose possession of souls had in the meanwhile become such an established dogma that it could be treated as a matter of experience—it follows that there are living things in the air, too, although they are invisible, namely the spirits of the air.[2] The only Aristotelian elements in this argument are those which Apuleius, following his source, directly attributes to Aristotle, that is to say, the fire-animals. That it was not Apuleius but his authority who remodelled the argument is shown by several passages in Philo, where the same inference occurs with the same emphasis on the proof of the existence of spirits in the air, i.e. angels. Philo remarks, also parenthetically, that these fire-animals are to be found in Macedonia; that is to say, he avoids letting his readers know of his heathen source, and names the country instead of the man.[3] This correspondence between two authors widely separated in time shows that some Stoic philosopher, living before the days of Christianity or of Philo, changed the real Aristotelian argument from a proof of the divinity of the cosmos into a proof of the existence of angels. The two forms are completely and hopelessly confused in the parallel passage of Sextus.[4]

---

[1] *Hist. An.* V. 19, 552b 10.

[2] Apul. *De Deo Socr.* VIII. 137, p. 15, l. 12, in Thomas.

[3] Philo, *De Gig.* 2. 7–8; *De Plantat.* 3. 12; *De Somn.* I. 22, 135. In the last passage he omits the fire-animals; in the altered form of the argument they were really only a nuisance.

[4] Sext. Emp. *Adv. Phys.* I. 86, p. 410, l. 26. It is there inferred both that

Without further inquiry concerning the author of this alteration, we may content ourselves with the conclusion which alone is important for the argument preserved by Cicero, namely that it originally included the fire-animals and the five elements, and that these were afterwards suppressed by Cicero's Stoic authority.[1]

In any case the fire-animals and the whole argument must come from a dialogue. It is impossible to refer the passage in Apuleius to the insects that are said to fly through fire in the *Historia Animalium*, although this is done by the commentators, because the essential point, which is required for the argument in *On Philosophy*, namely that the animals are born in fire and live their whole life in it, occurs only in Apuleius and Philo, and not in the *Historia Animalium*. The passage comes from the work that Hellenistic philosophers and doxographers used more than any other writing of Aristotle's.

there are spirits in the air and that the stars have souls. The Aristotelian and the angelological arguments have been confused.

[1] The source of the argument in Philo and Apuleius is obvious at first glance. In remodelling Aristotle's argument, in order to obtain a proof of the existence of spirits in the air, the author was following *Epinomis* 984 D ff., where the existence of star-souls is *assumed*, and that of aery beings is *demonstrated*. Aristotle, on the contrary, must have meant by the aery beings certain animals known to experience, since otherwise his analogy breaks down. Presumably he meant the birds. If so, it fits excellently that Apuleius' authority opposes this very supposition in detail. He rightly remarks that birds are 'terrestrial animals'. Moreover, they occupy only the lower region of the air. No bird can fly over Olympus (he gives mathematical measurements of its height, but the number of the stades has unfortunately disappeared from the manuscripts), whereas the atmosphere stretches far above it 'from the lowest turnings of the moon to the highest peak of Olympus'. This region cannot be wholly without inhabitants. Furthermore, the author, in order to obtain the four Stoic elements instead of Aristotle's five, regards the fire-animals and the stars as both fire-dwellers. His only concession to Aristotle is to separate the ether, not as a distinct element, but merely as the purest upper level of fire. This baroque mixture of angelology, empirical observation, and exact scientific thinking, corresponds to my idea of Posidonius, who has already been suggested as Apuleius' source by Rathke (*De Apulei quem scripsit de deo Socratis libello*, p. 32; thesis, Berlin, 1911). Rathke has failed to observe, however, that Posidonius makes use of the dialogue *On Philosophy* in his argument, and combines it with the *Epinomis*. Reinhardt's fine book on Posidonius (Munich, 1921) seems to me far too sceptical about the religious and mythical element in his thought; for instance, it wrongly denies that he believed in fire-animals. Nowadays we underestimate the influence of the old Academy and of the early Aristotle on Posidonius and the Stoics in general. The fact that in *Doxographi* 432. 4, only four kinds of living thing are ascribed both to Plato *and* to *Aristotle* is merely one of the many confusions of that textbook-wisdom (cf. Diels in the Proleg., p. 64).

It is also possible to show how the original form of the argument influenced the literature evoked by *On Philosophy* about the eternity of the world. We can follow step by step the process by which this literature obtained its weapons from the armoury of this dialogue. We have already mentioned in this connexion the work traditionally attributed to Philo on the eternity of the world, which uses not merely Aristotle but also other good Peripatetic authors like Theophrastus and Critolaus. Since the appearance of Aristotle's book the Stoics had come forward with their doctrine that the world is continually destroyed and regenerated, and the Peripatetic view required to be defended against the counter-arguments of the Porch. Because of this element in the author, who lived at about the beginning of the Christian era and shared the contemporary tendency to harmonize Plato and Aristotle, the form of the arguments, which he uses without mentioning their originator, has been greatly altered, and we are by no means justified in ascribing to Aristotle everything that is included among the fragments. On the other hand, just as Rose omits the fire-animals in Apuleius and Philo, so in the present work he omits an argument which, while not itself Aristotelian, is nevertheless formulated in words borrowed from Aristotle's 'zoogonic' argument—to use the expression in the *Epinomis*. Whereas, according to our hypothesis, Aristotle argued by analogy from the living creatures in the known elements to the existence of star-souls in the ether, Pseudo-Philo presupposes this and converts the argument into one against the transitoriness of the world. If all the living creatures that maintain themselves in the regions of the various elements are one day to disappear, both those on the earth and those in the water and those in the air and those in fire (πυρί-γονα), it follows by analogy (κατ' ἀναλογίαν) that the heavens also, the sun, the moon, and all the stars (i.e. the living things in the ether), are dedicated to destruction. This, however, conflicts with their divinity, with which their eternity stands or falls.[1] It is obvious that we have here a conflation of two classic arguments from Aristotle *On Philosophy*. His inference from the divinity of the heaven to its eternity is mechanically applied to all celestial bodies. (By a verbal imitation of the passage in

[1] Pseudo-Philo, *De Aet. Mundi* 14. 45, in Cohn-Reiter.

which he called the heaven 'this great visible God'[1] they are described as 'this great and blessed army of visible Gods acknowledged of old', ὁ τοσοῦτος αἰσθητῶν θεῶν εὐδαίμων τὸ πάλαι νομισθεὶς στρατός). With this the author conflates the zoogonic argument: if in the four known elements all living things pass away, they must do so in the ether also, by analogy. The logic, which is decidedly not his strong point, is not improved by the change. It is in fact an empty verbalism and a mere truism, incomprehensible until we see that he is attempting to carve something apparently new and original out of the famous arguments of his source. To us, however, he does the service of confirming the occurrence of the fire-animals, the five elements, and the inference from analogy, in the Aristotelian argument that we have recovered by examining Cicero. His testimony is all the weightier because in other parts of his work, where he is obviously using a Stoic source, he recognizes only four elements.[2]

In order to separate the original from the subsequent additions and alterations, it has been necessary to go into the historical effects of the dialogue. With regard to those arguments for the divinity of the stars which are next cited by Cicero, and which seem to be closely connected with the previous one, the problem of distinguishing the original from the accretions and distortions has recently been raised for the first time. It has been suggested that only the last argument (§ 44), which indeed is expressly described as such, is Aristotelian.[3] Strictly taken, its opening words ('Nec vero Aristoteles non laudandus est in eo, quod . . .') imply that the preceding ones also belong to him, but in case of necessity it is possible to understand them as referring back to the first, which was expressly ascribed to him. The intermediate matter would then belong to another author, and be inserted here merely because of its similarity to Aristotle's arguments. It is thought that Posidonius' theory of heat can be detected in it, and certainly, in view of what has been said in connexion with the first argument, the possibility of Stoic colouring cannot be excluded. The various arguments

---

[1] Frg. 18.
[2] Pseudo-Philo, *De Aet. Mundi* 11. 29.
[3] K. Reinhardt, *Poseidonios*, pp. 228 ff.

form such a connected and significant series, however, that we ought not to tear them apart unless we have to. The train of thought is as follows.

Since all the other elements contain life the ether must do so too. Hence the stars that we see there must be living things; and, in keeping with the fineness and mobility of the ether, they must be of the highest intelligence and velocity. To extend this relation between the elements and the character of the beings living in them, the relation between the intellectual quality of the stars and the vital powers of the ether is parallel to that between the intelligence and temperament of man and the food-supply and climatic conditions of his dwelling-place. Where the air is pure and thin the inhabitants are more intelligent and think more keenly and quickly than those who live in a thick and heavy atmosphere. The same applies even to the effects of light and heavy foods on the human mind. Since therefore they live in the region of the ether, which is the finest of all elements, and since they are nourished by the exhalations of earth and sea, which are reduced to extreme thinness as they traverse the great intervening space, the stars must possess intelligence of the highest sort. The correctness of this inference is confirmed by a fact of external experience—the inviolable order and regularity of their motions. This cannot be the product of Nature, since Nature does not behave like a conscious rational being; nor can it be explained by chance, for incalculability and merely average results exclude constancy and design. It must therefore be the result of a conscious intention and an inner purpose. With the final argument this train of thought culminates in the demonstration that, as their order and constancy imply reason and purpose, so the circularity of their motion implies effective free will, since the natural movement of bodies is always in a straight line upwards or downwards, and since no overruling external force is present here.

In the first argument Cicero expressly ascribes to Aristotle the statement that, since living things occur in all the other elements, it is absurd to suppose that they do not also occur in the ether, which is 'most suitable' of all 'to beget animate things'. According to Aristotle the pneuma of life is analogous to the element of the stars, which contains in its purest form the heat that is essential to life.¹ In this argument the vitalism of the (professedly Stoic) doctrine of heat is derived from Aristotle's doctrine of the pneuma, which was the historical germ of the Stoic view. The theory that the stars are moved by souls is carefully developed to its farthest consequences. The seriousness with which the argument takes Plato's semi-mythical view, and its conscientious application of the categories of psychology, zoology, and physics, show that its author is the early Aristotle. He is too respectful and dogmatic to doubt the correctness of the view; but the more seriously he takes it, and the more acutely he presses it, the quicker he will outgrow it. Plato, again, is responsible for the theory that climate and diet influence man's body and mind; and the expression of it here is verbally similar to a passage of the *Laws*. The *Epinomis*, also, detects a causal connexion between the material constitution of earthly creatures and the irrationality and disorderliness of their motions, and between the ethereal matter of the stars and their physical beauty and spiritual perfection. Either this reflects the general Academic view, or it is borrowed from Aristotle's work, which appeared just prior to the *Epinomis*.²

The dialogue *On Philosophy* carries out the analogy in more detail. The stars are surrounded by the purest atmosphere. Their food is the fine exhalations of earth and sea—Aristotle here uses this old physical doctrine to support his view of the heavenly beings and their physiological processes; later he abandoned it. From this dialogue Cleanthes took it over, together with all the rest of Aristotle's early theology, and made it at home in the Stoic school.³

---

¹ *De Gen. An.* II. 3, 736ᵇ 29 ff.   ² *Laws* V. 747 D; *Epin.* 981 E.

³ In *Meteor.* II. 2, 354ᵇ 33 ff., Aristotle opposes the physicists' theory that the sun feeds on the exhalations of the sea. The theory must have been quite old, since on the basis of it some physicists naïvely explained the solstice as a change of 'pasture'. Though Aristotle might smile at this anthropomorphic account, the general theory was quite consonant with his own view that the hot feeds on the wet (e.g. *Metaph.* A 3, 983ᵇ 23). When he objects that the supporters of the theory ought to have provided, not merely for the sun, but also for the stars (355ᵃ 19), that is simply the consequence that he himself had formerly developed in the dialogue *On Philosophy*. Cleanthes took it over from this work (Cic. *Nat. Deorum*, II. 15, 40. Arnim, frg. 504). He also appropriated the explanation of the solstice (*Nat. Deorum*, III. 14, 37. Arnim, frg. 501). In comparison with the level attained by Aristotle Stoic physics presents many examples of this sort of atavism, namely the conflation of Aristotle's early cosmological theology with Pre-Aristotelian theories.

The *Epinomis* also contains the argument for the existence of star-souls from the regularity of the heavenly motions, at somewhat greater length but with less dialectical power; and here as in Aristotle it is directly connected with the 'zoogonic' argument. This hitherto unnoticed correspondence obliges us to infer that Philip and Aristotle both give the ruling Academic doctrine.[1] Aristotle's formulation of it was directly suggested by Plato. In the *Laws*, at the beginning of the argument that the stars have souls, we read that some say 'that all things do become, have become, and will become, some by nature, some by art, and some by chance'. The elements and 'the bodies which come next in order—earth, and sun, and moon, and stars—' 'all exist by nature and chance, and none of them by art', for they are totally and absolutely without soul.[2] The physicists whom Plato is attacking meant by nature the same as Aristotle in these arguments (for he is here using their trichotomy and refuting them with their own weapons), namely an aggregation of matter without mind or soul. Plato, on the contrary, makes the soul the chief principle of becoming, and hence demands a new conception of nature.[3] There are, however, countless passages in Aristotle where this lower conception of nature, having once become familiar to him, is used without hesitation; in the very next argument, for example, the tendency of fire and air to go upwards, and of earth and water to go downwards, is said to be a natural movement. The division of all becoming into natural, fortuitous, and intentional, also occurs in his *Protrepticus*. The method of the argument, namely the establishment of one possibility by the elimination of all others, is connected with Plato's later dialectic of division, and is characteristic of Aristotle.

The same method is used in the last argument, a refinement of the previous one, which is expressly stated to come from Aristotle. All motion is produced either by nature or by force or by free will. So far as it is natural, the motion of bodies is always in a straight line upwards or downwards, and not circular like the motion of the heavenly bodies. Nor can this circular motion be explained by external force, for what force can be greater than that of those bodies themselves? The only

[1] *Epin.*, 982 ff. [2] *Laws* X. 888 E ff. [3] *Laws* X. 892 C, 891 C.

remaining possibility is motion by free will. For this inference too there is a parallel in the *Epinomis*, where mention is made of a most perfect deliberation (ἀρίστη βούλευσις) on the part of the star-souls.[1] This is the ground of the unalterable necessity that guides the revolutions of the stars. Their perfection consists in the fact that the circular path, which the star-soul at the same time contemplates and wills, is the ideal mathematical form. This act of will can never alter, because all true perfection excludes the tendency to deteriorate. Thus the law that the soul of the star imposes on its matter necessarily involves that the star has free will, since without this there could be no reflection with a view to action.[2] To this extent Aristotle's notion of free will is the exact complement of the notion of most perfect deliberation in the *Epinomis*; they are adjacent elements in a single thought-construction.[3] The doctrine that the stars move of their own free will, being an obvious contradiction of Aristotle's later views, has compelled those who deny his development to institute the most desperate *ad-hoc* conjectures. It is said that Cicero has simply grossly misunderstood his authority.[4] It is not worth while to refute these extravagances in detail; our analysis of the theory of star-souls seems to have made it clear that, even if this intermediate stage in Aristotle's development were not so unquestionably recorded, we should be practically obliged to reconstruct it *a priori* in all its parts.

The last argument also throws much light on the origin of

---

[1] *Epin.* 982 c.   [2] *Epin.* 982 B.

[3] The motion of the stars can be due to free will only if it rests on conscious purpose (προαίρεσις). The latter, however, is 'deliberative desire', and therefore presupposes deliberation (*Eth. Nic.* III. 5). In 1112ᵃ 21 Aristotle expressly denies that there can be deliberation about things eternal. Thus he rejects his earlier doctrine that the stars have wills. In his later period the only remnant of the old view is the use of the word 'action' (πράττειν) in connexion with the heavenly motions. This early doctrine that the stars have conscious wills must not be confused with the view that God, as the final cause, moves the world by means of the desire with which all things strive towards him (cf. Zeller, vol. ii. 2³, p. 375, n. 3). The latter involves neither that matter is an independent principle of action which strives towards Form, nor that all things including the inorganic world possess souls. According to Aristotle everything seeks to perform its function perfectly, and that is its good (καλόν). Because of this it is connected with everything else (cf. *Metaph.* Λ 10, 1075ᵃ 16, 'all things are ordered together somehow'). The connexion of all things with each other is the order (τάξις) of the world, whose 'end' is God, the most perfect being. Thus every thing seeks God in so far as it realizes its own 'end'.

[4] Bernays, *Die Dialoge des Aristoteles*, p. 104.

Aristotle's celestial physics, i.e. his doctrine of ether. Were it not that we have already proved it, it might be doubted whether in this dialogue the ether was assumed without demonstration, on the ground that he here reckons as 'natural' only the motions of heavy bodies downwards and of light ones upwards in a straight line, whereas he derives the circular motion of the stars not from their material constitution but from their free will. Contrariwise, he tells us in the *De Caelo* that there are five elements and a special kind of motion is natural to each of them, motion downwards to water and earth, upwards to fire and air, and in a circle to ether.[1] He expressly calls the latter the body that moves in a circle, thus making this an essential property of it. Here again those who deny his development are driven to the desperate expedient of reducing the account in the dialogue *On Philosophy* to mere poetry;[2] but the arguments are far too acute and serious for that, and apparently it has escaped notice that the two views are mutually exclusive. The derivation of circular motion from the material nature of the ether reveals the intention to explain all phenomena of movement whatever by the natural laws of matter; but this can be done only by means of a double physics, one terrestrial and the other cosmic, the latter being exempt from the former's law of gravitation. The double-entry book-keeping thus established was not abolished again until modern physics. At any rate it was a scientific improve-

---

[1] *De Caelo* I. 2–3.

[2] Bernays (op. cit., p. 104) was unable to conceive how Aristotle in this dialogue could have so utterly repudiated the fundamentals of his cosmology (presumably this means the derivation of all becoming from 'natural' causes), and could have so unhesitatingly accepted 'the vulgarly anthropomorphic deification of the heavenly bodies'. Such a misconception was possible only at a time when insufficient attention was paid to Plato's *Laws* and to the *Epinomis*, before the effect of Zeller's rejection of the former had altogether ceased. Plato's doctrine of star-souls has nothing to do with the naïve popular belief in Helios and Selene. To derive the circular motion of stars and sky from an immaterial cause was the most natural thing for a Platonist, since Plato thought of *Nus* as a circular movement, and since the new discovery of the regularity and simplicity of the heavenly motions favoured the suggestion that they were produced by a mathematical intelligence, cf. Plat. *Tim.* 34 A, 37 C, and often. According to the *Timaeus Nus* and Necessity divided the creation of the cosmos between them (47 E). In *De An.* I. 3, 406^b 26 ff., Aristotle attacks in detail the doctrine of the continuous circular motion of *Nus*. With his abandonment of this Platonic view, and with his change in the notion of the psychological functioning of *Nus*, there inevitably followed the fall of the theory of immanent star-souls.

ment on the procedure of the Academy and of Aristotle in his early years, which had given an anthropomorphic account of the relation between the mathematical law and the inert matter of the stars by introducing psychophysical analogies—the *Epinomis* even ascribed legislative functions to the will of the stars.[1] We now see that the original purpose of the ether must have been something other than to derive the celestial motions from the nature of the matter of the stars, since it was already in existence as a hypothesis before it was endowed with the attribute of circular motion. What first gave rise to it was obviously the new and precise calculations, undertaken by the school of Eudoxus and by Philip of Opus, about the size and distance of sun, moon, and the other heavenly bodies. These calculations rendered untenable the old physical doctrine that the upper heavens and the stars are composed wholly of fire; in view of the smallness of the earth and the infinite extent of the universe there was no longer any proportion between the quantity of fire and the other elements, and in fact it would have consumed them all. Thus the new discoveries upset the theory of the mutation of the elements and thereby removed one of the foundations of contemporary cosmology.[2] Later on Aristotle used his hypothesis to construct a cosmic physics without star-souls or mythical additions. We now have the later view fully developed in the first book of the *De Caelo*, which makes an impressive beginning with the new doctrine; it is not too rash, however, to assert that this lecture has undergone later alterations, and that in its original form it belongs to the period when the notion of ether was new. In favour of this it may be said that in content it is concerned almost entirely with Plato's later cosmology and criticizes that alone, that parts of it are still quite theological in colouring, and that large portions are taken over verbatim from the third book of the dialogue *On Philosophy*.

The doctrine of the star-gods and of the divinity of the cosmos (i.e. the sky), which received its first complete statement in this dialogue of Aristotle's, constitutes, together with Plato's cosmology as a whole, the permanent expression of the great intel-

[1] *Epin.* 982 B, 'the necessity which belongs to the soul which possesses intelligence . . . legislates as ruling and not as ruled'.

[2] Arist. *Meteor.* I. 3, 339^b 2 ff., esp. 340^a 1 ff.

lectual stimulus given to the philosophical world of the fourth century by the new astronomical discoveries. The hypothesis that the planetary motions are circular and perfectly orderly, and that the original configuration of the whole heavens periodically returns when the Great Year[1] is complete, threw the most astonishing light on Plato's fundamental principle that the material phenomena of the sensible world are controlled by mind and order, and opened up fruitful relations between philosophy and the study of facts. The first attempt to illustrate on a grand scale the 'rule of reason' over matter was the doctrine of star-souls. This went far beyond the needs of mere natural science, but its myth of the soul opened up unsuspected opportunities for the construction of a *Weltanschauung*. It is clear that to Plato the important part of the doctrine was its mythical and spiritualistic element. Its appeal to the early Aristotle, on the other hand, rested on the fact that speculation, whose insoluble problems the human mind cannot perpetually avoid, could here base itself on solid empirical facts, even if they were facts that admitted of more than one explanation. Thus, while the views of both coincide in content, Aristotle's close-knit argumentation breathes a new scientific spirit, according to which all myths, however overflowing with emotional values, are simply material for methodical inquiry. This spirit reveals itself most clearly in his positively insatiable desire for proof. If we compare the account in the *Epinomis*, where Plato's doctrine is swallowed dogmatically and full rein given to the taste for edification and religious mystery, we perceive still more clearly that, in dealing with the Platonic myth, the choice lay between scholasticism on the one hand and critical science on the other. Plato himself understood himself in this way, and gave his pupils the right to apply this realistic measure to himself, when he introduced his myth as one of several possible hypotheses.[2] But what great thinker ever understood himself correctly? The old controversy whether Aristotle understood Plato shows a

[1] The 'Great Year' is mentioned in Arist. frg. 25. Rose can scarcely be right, however, in including this among the fragments of *On Philosophy*, since Tacitus (*Dial.* 16, 10 ff.) tells us that it was referred to in Cicero's *Hortensius*. Cicero took it presumably from the main source, which was Aristotle's *Protrepticus*; but with this question we are not concerned.

[2] Plato, *Laws* X. 898 E.

complete lack of comprehension. He appears to stand upon the same ground and wrestle with Plato for better insight; but his victory consists not in refuting him but in impressing the stamp of his own nature on everything Platonic that he touches.

The same is true of the second main division of the dialogue, namely the philosophy of religion; for in this work Aristotle founded not merely Hellenistic theology,[1] but also that sympathetic but at the same time objective study of the inner religious life for which antiquity had no name and no independent discipline apart from metaphysics. It did not vindicate its independence until the modern age gave it the name of 'philosophy of religion'. This is another aspect of the early Aristotle which, in spite of its inestimable importance for the history of the human mind, has been overlooked or ignored down to the present day—perhaps because the conventional picture of him (as a purely intellectualist metaphysician) might have been disturbed if it had appeared that his dialectical operations were inspired from within by a living religion, with which all the members of the logical organism of his philosophy were penetrated and informed. The history of the philosophy of religion, in the modern sense of the phrase, begins with the sophists and their first great attempts to give a psychological explanation of its nature and origin. Rationalism, however, can never advance more than a little way along this road, because it lacks the organ

[1] What he worked out under this name as an independent discipline derives, indeed, in content from the later form of Plato's general view of the world; but his foundation of a separate discipline indicates an intense concentration of the spirit on the problem of God, which was something entirely new, and had an epoch-making significance for Hellenistic philosophy. The Stoic theology developed the Aristotelian. It is true that owing to its monistic tendency it abandoned Aristotle's transcendent God, but coincidence of content is not the decisive thing in the evaluation of his influence. What is decisive is the whole inner attitude of the new age towards the problem of theology, and the position assigned to it in the very centre of philosophy. In content Aristotle's theology, with its sharp distinction between the highest God and the star-gods, did not exert its full influence until the beginning of the Christian era. This age demanded a *deus exsuperantissimus*, who, unseen, guides the world from a sublimely distant throne, high above the courses of the stars. Aristotle then began to have a strong effect on contemporary Platonism; his view was combined sometimes with Oriental religious beliefs, and sometimes with the so-called negative theology, which was the climax of religious experience in the Hellenistic East, whether pagan or Christian.

by which the phenomena of the religious life are properly perceived; and hence the philosophy of religion did not enter on its classical period until the time of the early Aristotle and the Academy in the later days of Plato. Here were supplied the two conditions essential for a study at once psychologically penetrating and religiously productive—on the one hand increased theoretical insight into all the phenomena of the spirit, on the other hand a piety, arising out of Plato's power of constructing myths and symbols, which opened fresh sources of religious inspiration to a community imbued with a new feeling for the values of life. It is a fact, though the accepted history of philosophy may ignore it, that almost the entire stock of later and modern ideas about the philosophy of religion can be traced to this society.

The main question concerns the natural sources, and the theoretical justification, of our inner certainty about the objects of religion, that is to say, it concerns the reality of the numinous. To the naïve religious consciousness this is no problem at all. It becomes one only when popular faith has been destroyed, and the intellect has been specifically directed towards the sphere of religious ideas. Then comes the period of arguments for the existence of God. After the hasty triumph of criticism with its destructive rationalism, the religious instinct, homeless but ineradicable, seeks shelter with its conqueror. The Xenophontic arguments for God's existence arise from this need for the aid of rationalism. Now Plato in his early and middle periods had no objective and theoretical attitude towards the question, such as is implied in the existence of a philosophy of religion. He was engaged in creating new worlds, in which the only proper demeanour was that of pious contemplation. The Form of the Good was not merely an eternal ideal for the state, but also the symbol of a new consciousness of God. It was in fact religion itself, for with Plato's philosophy religion entered on the stage of speculation and science entered on that of the creation of religious ideas. Not until his later days do we find reflection on the roots of faith and on its compatibility with natural science. In the theology of his old age the ruling thought is that of the priority of soul to body, and of spirit and law to blind matter. The Ionian conception of nature as mechanical causation gives way to a view according to which everything is derived from spiritual forces and is once more 'full of Gods'.[1]

The real argument for God's existence first appears with the early Aristotle. He it was who, in the third book *On Philosophy*, demonstrated the reality of a highest being with strictly syllogistic arguments, and thus gave the problem the sharp, apodictic form which has continually goaded keen religious thinkers, in all later centuries, towards new attempts to make our experience of the ineffable visible even to the eye of the understanding. 'In general, wherever there is a better there is also a best. Now since among the things that are one is better than another, there is also a best thing, and this would be the divine.'[2] Here we stumble upon the root of the ontological argument, though bound up, as Aristotle's physics require, with the teleological one. Wherever there is a series of comparable things displaying gradual differences of value there is also a most perfect thing or maximum, even when we are concerned not with mere imaginary series, but with the actual series from less to more perfect in reality. In nature, which to Aristotle possesses a form and purpose that work and create from within, all is gradation; every lower thing is related to something higher and ruling. To him this teleological order is a law of nature and can be empirically demonstrated. It follows that in the realm of existing things (i.e. among the real Forms of nature) there is a most perfect thing, which, naturally, must also be a real Form, and which, as the highest final cause, is the principle of everything else. This is what is meant by the last sentence, that the most perfect being would be identical with the divine. Within the Aristotelian view of nature as a realm of strictly graded Forms this argument is valid; and it avoids the later mistake of supposing that the existence of the most perfect being is a predicate involved in the very idea of perfection, so that it could be obtained from this idea by mere analysis without the aid of experience. The Form of all real Forms must necessarily be itself real. When Aristotle equates this with the divine he does not, of course, thereby prove the truth of the popular notion of God.

[1] Plato, *Laws* X. 899 B; *Epin.* 991 D.
[2] Frg. 16. The argument reappears in the great schoolmen as the *argumentum ex gradibus*.

What he does is to give a new interpretation of this notion, which like all human things is subject to change, in the spirit of the teleological view of the world. No doubt the dialogue also contained the arguments with which we are familiar from the treatises, that from the eternity of motion, and that from the necessity of supposing a limit to the series of causes in order to avoid an infinite regress. It was the first great attempt to render the problem of God amenable to scientific treatment, by basing dialectically cogent inferences on a consistent interpretation of nature. Circumstances imposed the task on Aristotle, but only the greatest logical architect of all time would have dared to compress the whole result of his immense efforts into these few simple-sounding sentences. The one thing that we must not do is to separate them from his physics and examine them by themselves. They are the necessary conclusion of the detailed development of an eidological theory of nature; and they enable us to be sure that Aristotle's physics was already completed in principle at the time when he wrote the dialogue, from which it follows that it was conceived while he was still in the atmosphere of the Academy.

Aristotle also examined in this work the psychological sources of belief in God, not out of cold scientific curiosity, but in order that others might experience what he had experienced. He was thus well aware that even the most gifted logic can never attain to that irresistible force of inner conviction which arises out of the inspired presentiments of the soul.[1] Nobody in the ancient world ever spoke more beautifully or more profoundly about the personal and emotional side of all religious life than Aristotle during the years when religion was the central problem in his mind. In the dialogue *On Philosophy*, when he was preparing to discuss the divinity of the stars, he spoke of the feeling of awe in the presence of that which is higher than men. He recognized

[1] *De Caelo* II. 1, 284ᵇ 3, also speaks of the co-operation of scientific speculation and the inner sense of God (μαντεία περὶ τὸν θεόν) which rests on immediate feeling; thus it distinguishes clearly between the two. Presumably it was Plato who first took the notion of inner divination (μαντεύεσθαι), which the poets were already using in the sense of the presentiment of external events, and stamped it with the philosophical meaning of a divination not of the future but of deep and hidden affinities. Aristotle then applied it for the first time to the problem of faith and knowledge, and made knowledge and divination two commensurable and complementary forms of religious consciousness.

that inner composure is the essence of all religious devotion.[1] Just as we do not venture to enter a temple until our feelings are composed, so, he declares, whenever we inquire into the nature of the stars, we ought to enter the temple of the cosmos in a devotional manner. No doubt the words were intended to prepare for the accusation of godlessness which he then launched against those who denied that the heavens and the stars were divine and indestructible.[2] Towards the end of his work *On Prayer* he wrote, 'God is either *Nus* or something beyond *Nus*'. Why write a book on prayer, if not to show that we shall not think it unworthy of a philosopher to approach Godhead in prayer so long as we take it to heart that God is *Nus*, or higher than all reason, and that only through *Nus* can a mortal approach Him?[3] Neither Schleiermacher nor Kant distinguished more sharply between faith and knowledge, between feeling and understanding, than did the originator of speculative argument for God's existence in his classic pronouncement: 'Those who are being initiated are not required to grasp anything with the understanding (μαθεῖν), but to have a certain inner experience (παθεῖν), and so to be put into a particular frame of mind, presuming that they are capable of this frame of mind in the first place.'[4] It is not accidental that he formulates this epoch-making discovery in connexion with the mystery-religions. The cults of the old gods lacked the personal relationship between the righteous man and his God, whereas the mysteries gave it the foremost place by their mere exclusiveness, and encouraged it still further through the various grades of initiation, and through the differences in fervour with which the individual members of the faithful received them. It is this spiritual factor, and not the 'intellectual significance' of their content, which accounts for the keen interest accorded to these cults, from the end of the fifth century onwards, in all quarters where religion was

[1] Frg. 14. [2] Cf. pp. 139–140 above.
[3] Frg. 49. The purpose of emphasizing God's transcendence at the end of a work on prayer must logically have been to apply it to the question how we ought to pray. The demand that we should pray in *Nus* and in truth arose in the Platonic community, and through it the philosophical spirit of Attica restored religion to the men of the fourth century. The fact that the gospel according to St. John gave it a new content (iv. 24) by writing *Pneuma* (spirit) instead of *Nus* (certainly without knowledge of Aristotle's works) in no way diminishes the significance of this demand for the history of the mind. [4] Frg. 15.

alive. How often do Plato and the early Aristotle borrow their language and symbols to give colour and form to their own new religious feeling! The mysteries showed that to the philosopher religion is possible only as personal awe and devotion, as a special kind of experience enjoyed by natures that are suitable for it, as the soul's spiritual traffic with God; and this insight constitutes nothing less than a new era of the religious spirit. It is impossible to estimate the influence of these ideas on the Hellenistic world, and on the spiritual religion that was in process of formation.

Aristotle derives the subjective conviction of God's existence from two sources; from man's experience of the inspired might of the soul, which, in the instants when it rids itself of the body, in sleep or at the approach of death, takes on its own 'real nature' and pierces the future with prophetic eye; and from the sight of the starry heavens.[1] This derivation is not to be understood historically; it does not refer to the men of primitive times; it is a pregnant juxtaposition of the two great wonders that all the enlightenment of the enlightened cannot explain, the residue that the system of rationalistic physics cannot reduce. Prophecy and the irrational and obscurer elements of the soul's life had always aroused great interest in the Academy, and the emotional religious feeling for the cosmos had taken its origin there. What Aristotle here compresses into a formula is simply the religious attitude of Plato's circle towards the universe. Even the formula is borrowed from Plato; for in the *Laws* he derives the belief in God from the same two sources, the everflowing being (ἀέναος οὐσία) of the inner life of the soul, and the sight of the eternal order of the stars.[2] No other formula could express so fitly the timeless truth of the religious element in Platonism, free from all temporary dogmatic details. Again and again it reappears in history as the symbol of the ultimate unassailable postulate with which the spirit confronts the inexorable forces of matter and chance. We naturally think of Kant's words at the end of the *Critique of Practical Reason*. 'Two things fill the spirit with ever fresh and increasing wonder and awe, the more often and the more persistently they are reflected upon, the starry heavens above me and the moral law within me.' The transformation of the first source, the everflowing being of the

[1] Frg. 10.   [2] *Laws* XII. 966 D.

soul (as Plato calls it), into the moral law, is characteristic of the difference between the Platonic and the Kantian spirit, although it really goes back to the Stoics. Kant does not definitely say so, but it is clear from his words that this 'wonder and awe' are of a religious nature, and were originally introduced precisely as sources of the belief in the existence and government of God.

Aristotle preserves the original form of the second argument also. Instead of the marvel of the soul as such, he speaks of the prophetic powers that slumber within it, awakening only when it has rid itself of the body. This is the Platonic view. The recognition of occult phenomena, inaccessible to science, is also contrary to Aristotle's later doctrine; he refutes it in detail in his work on dreams.[1] Will any one offer to explain all this as a mere concession to the dialogue-style? It is the same attitude towards divination as that in the *Eudemus*. There is no clearer sign of the depth to which spiritualism had driven its roots in Aristotle than this fact, that, even after he had abandoned the theory of Ideas, he still retained for some time Plato's conception of the soul, and no doubt his doctrine of immortality also. Among those who have found this doctrine in our passage is Posidonius.[2]

---

[1] Arist. *De Divinatione per Somnum*, c. 1, 462ᵇ 20; there are no truth-telling dreams sent by God; cf. 462ᵇ 12. In *Timaeus* 71 A–E and *Epin*. 985 C, on the other hand, the position is the same as that of *On Philosophy*, frg. 10.

[2] Posidonius took over the passage on the prophetic power of the soul (frg. 10) in his book *On Divination*, and Cicero makes this book the basis of his account in *De Divinatione* I. 63, as he does frequently in this work.

Sextus Empiricus, *Adversus Physicos* I. 20–21 (p. 395, l. 6).

Cicero, *De Divinatione* I. 63.

Aristotle said that the notion of gods came from two beginnings . . . from the phenomena of spiritual life by reason of the ecstasies and prophecies which the soul experiences in sleep. (21) For, *he says*, when the soul is by itself in sleep, then it puts on its proper nature and foresees and foretells the future. The same thing occurs also in the separation from the body at death. At any rate he believes that the poet Homer had observed this when he made Patroclus, as he was being killed, foretell the killing of Hector, and Hector foretell the death of Achilles.

(63) When therefore sleep has removed the mind from the society and contact of the body, then it remembers the past, perceives the present, and foresees the future . . . and thus when death approaches it is much more divine. (64) That dying men have foreknowledge is also proved by the example which Posidonius adduces.... An instance of this . . . is Homer's Hector, who when dying declares the approaching death of Achilles.

Aristotle's expression 'foresees and foretells the future' was adopted by

The two sources of belief in God were also borrowed from this dialogue by the Stoics. Cleanthes, who puts them side by side with the hypotheses of Prodicus and Democritus about the origin of religion, thereby shows that he wrongly took them in the historical sense.[1]

The great influence of the work on the Hellenistic age appears again in a famous passage which recurs at second hand in all Stoic theologies. This passage has been preserved by Cicero, and certainly belongs to the proof of God's existence in the third book *On Philosophy*.[2] For the sake of the power with which it suggests the overwhelming experience of the divinity of the cosmos it may be translated here.

'If there were men who had always lived beneath the earth in good and shining habitations, adorned with statues and pictures and supplied with all the things possessed in abundance by those who are considered happy, and if, however, they had never gone out above the earth, but had heard by rumour and report that there is a certain divine presence and power, and then if at some time the gorges of the earth were opened and they were able to escape out of those hidden places and to come forth into these regions which we inhabit, then, when they suddenly saw the earth and the seas and the sky, when they had learnt the greatness of the clouds and the power of the winds, when they had gazed on the sun and recognized his greatness and beauty and the efficacy with which he causes day by spreading his light through the whole sky, when moreover, night having darkened the lands, they perceived the whole sky laid out and adorned with stars, and the variety of the lights of the moon, now waxing now waning, and the risings and settings of them all and their courses ratified and immutable to all eternity—when they saw this they would straightway think that there are gods and that these are the mighty works of gods.'

The first thing that we notice is his dependence on the cave in Plato's *Republic*. The latter is a magnificent representation of the fundamental experience of Plato's philosophy, namely the reduction of the visible world to a realm of mere shadows, and

Posidonius in his definition of divination as 'praesensio et praedictio futuri'. He also increased the number of examples out of his own unmistakable wealth of learning. The dream of Eudemus is included among them (53). As was to be expected, special attention is paid to Plato, the Pythagoreans, and Heraclides of Pontus (46 and 60–62). Here again Posidonius has been greatly influenced by the early Aristotle.

[1] In *De Natura Deorum* II. 5, 13 (frg. 528 in Arnim), Cicero reports that Cleanthes gave four reasons for the 'origin' of the belief in God. The first and fourth come from Aristotle *On Philosophy*, the two others from Democritus and Prodicus.   [2] Frg. 12.

the vision of true being by which the philosopher is separated
from his brothers and rendered lonely. Aristotle's simile also
breathes a new attitude towards the world. His men, however,
have not lived in caves. They are modern, cultivated, satiated,
miseducated persons, who bury themselves like moles in the
sunless and comfortless splendour in which they are seeking
their dubious happiness. He makes them ascend one day into
the light, there to perceive the drama that he himself sees, the
immeasurable marvel of reality, the divine structure and motion
of the cosmos. He teaches them to contemplate, not a super-
natural world, but that which is visible to all and yet seen of
none. He is conscious of being the first Greek to see the real
world with Plato's eyes, and his intentional alteration of Plato's
simile is a sign of this view of his historical mission. What he
gives us instead of the Ideas is the contemplation of the wonderful shapes and arrangements of the cosmos, a contemplation
which, intensified until it becomes religion, leads up to the intuition of the divine director of it all.

By means of the *Epinomis*, which is equally emphatic in
assigning to theology the central position in philosophy, we
know that these lofty speculations met with energetic opposition from the Greeks. According to the popular Greek view the
knowledge of the divine, the Gnosis of the Orientals, is a thing
that must be for ever unattainable to mortals; and unhappy is
the man who plagues his head with the search for the forbidden
fruit. Aristotle himself, at the beginning of the *Metaphysics*,
deprecates the deeply-rooted Hellenic dislike of extravagant
(περιεργία) and high-flown audacities of thinking. He often
opposes the ancient wisdom according to which a mortal should
think mortal things; and he earnestly invites us to live in
eternity.[1] Theology became possible to the Greeks only when
the discovery of laws in the heavenly motions had led to the
assumption of star-souls, and when assured knowledge of the

---

[1] *Epin.* 988 A: 'Let none of the Greeks fear that it is not right for mortal
men ever to busy themselves with matters divine; they must hold entirely the
opposite view'; 988 B, the divine power is free from jealousy. The same ideas
reappear with verbal echoes in Aristotle's *Metaph.* A 2, 982^b 28 ff. Cf. also
Eth. Nic. X. 7, 1177^b 31; 'we must not follow those [e.g. Epicharmus (frg. 20 in
Diels), and Euripides (*Bacchae* 395 and 427 ff.)] who advise us, being men, to
think of human things, but must, so far as we can, make ourselves immortal.'

'visible Gods' had brought within measurable distance the possibility of an exact and astronomical theology based on experience. To this we must add the influence of the East, as the *Epinomis* tells us and other evidence confirms. The Socratic 'know thyself', the quintessence of Apolline wisdom, was now converted into its opposite. In his *Life of Socrates* Aristoxenus the Peripatetic related that an Indian, meeting Socrates in Athens, asked him about his philosophy. When Socrates answered that he was attempting to understand human life, the Indian represented to him the hopelessness of such an undertaking, since man cannot know himself until he knows God.[1] This sounds apocryphal, but it is simply the legendary formulation of the view, universal in the later Academy and summed up in the *Epinomis* as a programme for religious reform, that in future Oriental astralism and theology would have to be combined with the Delphic religion of Hellas, if the Greeks were to make religious progress.[2] In the opinion of the author, who gives us the ruling tendency in the Academy (he could hardly represent merely personal preferences as the conclusion of Plato's *Laws*), the way to this combination is through mysticism. Aristotle shares with him, and with all Academics whatever, the view that *cognitio dei* is conceivable only if it is God Himself

[1] Aristoxenus, frg. 31 in Mueller. The visit of the Indian to Athens is also mentioned in the fragment of Aristotle (frg. 32) preserved in Diogenes Laertius II. 45. If this were genuine it would presumably have to be assigned to the first book of the dialogue *On Philosophy*; but Rose was probably right in including it under the remains of the spurious *Magicus*, since its contents do not accord with Aristotle. The nearest parallels to the theology of the supposed Indian (it is really that of the later Plato) are Aristotle's *Protrepticus* (whose demand that human action be based on the knowledge of God reappears in *Eth. Eud.* VIII. 3, 1249b 13–21) and the *Alcibiades Major*, which Friedländer has recently attempted to rehabilitate, and has assigned to Plato's early period (*Der grosse Alcibiades ein Weg zu Plato*, Bonn, 1921). This dialogue culminates in the thesis, elaborately and somewhat pedantically developed, that the Delphic maxim 'know thyself' can be realized only through the self-contemplation of *Nus* in the mirror of the knowledge of God (132 E–133 C). The attainment of this thereby becomes the real focus of all the ethical, political, and educational problems that Plato's school inherited from Socrates. The *Epinomis* also stands for this reduction of all ethical questions, both of happiness and of virtue, to the question of the knowledge of God. The *Alcibiades* is obviously an attempt, undertaken by some disciple at the same time as the above-mentioned works, to apply theology to the problems of Plato's early days, and to anchor them in a firm dogmatic principle, to wit, the mysticism of Plato's later doctrine of *Nus*.

[2] *Epin.* 987 D–988 A.

knowing Himself. He pictures this activity as something transcendental and beyond the merely human standard. The self is the *Nus*, which is said to 'come in from without' and to be 'the divine in us'; and it is through *Nus* that the knowledge of God enters into us. The author of the *Epinomis* goes so far as to speak of the participation of the one contemplator in the one *phronesis*, whereas Aristotle never emphasizes God's unity with human *Nus* more than His transcendence.[1] In any event it is impossible to understand Aristotle's influence on posterity unless we realize that he breathed this atmosphere for many years, and that his metaphysics is rooted in it, however far it may have developed beyond it on the logical side. The establishment of the worship of the stars, which are confined to no land or nation but shine on all the peoples of the earth,[2] and of the transcendental God who is enthroned above them, inaugurates the era of religious and philosophic universalism. On the crest of this last wave Attic culture streams out into the Hellenistic sea of peoples.

[1] In *Metaph.* A 2, 983^a 5–11, the knowledge of God is identified with God's knowledge. For the union of the human spirit with the divine see *Epin.* 986 D.
[2] *Epin.* 984 A.

CHAPTER VII

THE ORIGINAL *METAPHYSICS*

I. THE PROBLEM

THE importance of the dialogue *On Philosophy* is not exhausted by the light it throws on the period between the Academy and the Lyceum. It gives us for the first time a fixed point in the development of Aristotle's opinions, and a historically accurate starting-place from which to analyse his metaphysical treatise. The earlier works obviously rest on an entirely different basis; but what is the relation between the doctrines of this classical dialogue, in which he made it public that henceforth he dissented from Plato's views, and the traditional Aristotelian metaphysics? Naturally, we must not take what we have learnt from the fragments and read it into the text of the treatise—itself, indeed, fragmentary, but still incomparably fuller. Our recovered picture of the lost work would, however, become important, if analysis of the *Metaphysics* were of itself to lead us along the same lines.

The fundamental conceptions of the *Metaphysics* were undoubtedly already determined when Aristotle wrote the dialogue. Even if we knew nothing else but that it contained the doctrine of the unmoved mover, we should thereby be assured that he had already established the conceptions of matter and form, of potency and act, and his own conception of substance. Moreover, the three separate inquiries of which the dialogue was composed, the historical, the critical, and the theological, have their counterparts in the *Metaphysics*, the first in the first book, the second in the concluding books and throughout, the third in Book Λ. A more difficult question is how far the dialogue contained any parallel to the so-called central books of the *Metaphysics*, those which develop the theory of substance and of potency and act. We may say either that Aristotle considered these investigations too hard and too esoteric for publication, or that it is simply an accident that no fragment of this portion remains. In any event it cannot have occupied so large a space as in the *Metaphysics*, where it outweighs everything else, especially if we omit the introduction (A–E). Theology, on the contrary, was developed much more thoroughly than it is in Book Λ, for our accounts tell us much of which the *Metaphysics* by itself would have given no inkling. With the doctrine of star-souls we are transported into a distinctly earlier stage of Aristotle's development, and there is much to indicate that, if we had more of the dialogue, its divergence would probably appear still greater. That would seem to be a proof of the late origin of the *Metaphysics*, which would thus have to be assigned to Aristotle's last period; and this would agree thoroughly with the view that has obtained up to now, for ever since the Roman empire it has been a widespread opinion that the *Metaphysics* was written late and left unfinished.

This picture alters entirely, however, as soon as we analyse the *Metaphysics*. The origin of the *book* bearing this name now becomes important for the origin of Aristotle's metaphysical *speculation* itself.[1] It is totally inadmissible to treat the elements combined in the *corpus metaphysicum* as if they were a unity, and to set up, for purposes of comparison, the average result of these entirely heterogeneous materials. As I have shown in another place, internal analysis leads to the view that various periods are represented; and this is confirmed by the tradition that the collection known as the *Metaphysics* was not put together until after its author's death. Previous investigations, however, have concerned only the history of the text *subsequent* to Aristotle's death, i.e. the history of his literary remains. The clarification of these matters was undoubtedly the first step; but it was directly important only for the history of Aristotle's influence, and the labour expended was out of all proportion to the advance made in knowledge of his own thought and personality. Criticism did not regain its meaning and importance until it sought to understand the actual state of the text as the organic result of the inner form of its author's thought.[2] This at once led away from the question of the external literary unity of the surviving metaphysical papers to that of their inner philosophical unity, and thus to chronology and the analysis of development. I took the first steps along this road in my *Entste-*

[1] See my *Entstehungsgeschichte der Metaphysik des Aristoteles*, Berlin, 1912.
[2] Cf. *Ent. Met. Arist.*, pp. 150, 161.

hungsgeschichte der Metaphysik, but at that time I was too much under the influence of the old philological attitude (whose pro- blem is, 'In the *Metaphysics* as we have it, can we justify the division into books and the order of the parts?') to pursue my own findings to their logical conclusions. The question of chronology, on one point of which I had already reached an assured result at that time, must now be taken up again in the light of Aristotle's philosophical development. This will neces- sitate some repetitions in detail, which the course of the inquiry itself must justify.

Before beginning to discuss the chronology we may once more briefly remind ourselves what, in the present condition of the *Metaphysics,* is to be ascribed to the editors of Aristotle's literary remains. Here it will be best to omit all arguments and rely on the results of the previous investigation.

The aim of the modern philologist, to make the external order reflect the order of composition, even at the cost of the general impression, was quite foreign to ancient editors. Aristotle's literary executors were philosophers. They would have given much to be able to construct, out of the precious papers that they found, as true a picture as possible of the whole intellectual system of 'first philosophy' as Aristotle had intended it to be; but their desire was thwarted by the incomplete and disparate character of the material. For one thing is certain; the editors themselves did not believe that with the order which they established they were giving posterity the complete course of lectures on metaphysics. They realized that they were offering an unsatisfactory makeshift, which was all that the condition of their materials allowed. The postscript to the introductory book, the so-called little α, comes after big A simply because they did not know where else to put it. It is a remnant of notes taken at a lecture by Pasicles, a nephew of Aristotle's disciple Eudemus of Rhodes.[1] ABΓ belong together; Δ, on the other hand, was still known as an independent work in Alexandrian

[1] Asclepius, in his commentary on the *Metaphysics* (p. 4, l. 20, in Hayduck), refers this information, which reached him as a tradition handed down in the Peripatetic school, to A; but this is a confusion. His account must come from notes taken at a lecture by Ammonius, and obviously he misheard. The true account is given by the scholiast on little α in the codex Parisinus (cf. *Ent. Met. Arist.,* p. 114).

times, as a sound bibliographical tradition informs us. Ε is a short transitional passage leading to ΖΗΘ. These three form a whole, but their connexion with the previous books seems to be problematical. Ι, a discussion of being and unity, stands entirely alone; and from this point onwards all inward and outward connexion disappears. Κ simply contains another form of ΒΓΕ, to which are appended some excerpts from the *Physics*, in themselves just as Aristotelian as any other part of this collection of manuscripts, but out of all relation to their surroundings. Similarly, a passage from the *Physics* has been inserted into Δ. Λ is an isolated lecture, giving a general view of the whole metaphysical system, entirely complete in itself, and presenting no trace of connexion with the rest. The concluding books ΜΝ have no relation to the preceding; this was remarked even in antiquity, and has led to their insertion before ΚΛ in many manuscripts, which, however, does not produce a more plausible train of thought. Their closest relationship is to the first two books.

Nothing but exact inquiry can determine in detail at what time and in what connexion this material arose, and how it is to be used in reconstructing Aristotle's philosophy. On no account must we, by assuming that it is philosophically homogeneous, cover up the problems which its content as well as its form presents at every step. We must reject all attempts to make a literary whole out of the remaining materials by rearranging or removing some of the books, and we must condemn the assumption which overhastily postulates their philosophical unity at the expense of their individual peculiarities. Each of these papers is the result of decades of untiring reflection on the same questions; each is a fruitful instant, a stage in Aristotle's development, an approach to the solution, a step towards new formulation. It is true that all the details are supported by that potential unity of the whole system which is active in every particular utterance of the philosopher; but no one who is content with that has the right to call himself familiar with the Aristotelian temper in its actuality. Aristotle has a dour, austere form; no wide-ranging survey, no genial, comfortable intuition, can really understand him. Rarely does he offer us a whole on which the eye can rest with pleasure. Only in the concrete details, only by intensive concentration, can his essence be grasped. 'For the actuality of *Nus* is life.'

II. THE INTRODUCTION AND THE EARLIEST DRAFT OF THE CRITICISM OF IDEAS

The piety of the editors has preserved the famous criticism of Plato's doctrine of Ideas in two versions, one in the ninth chapter of Book A, and the other in chapters 4–5 of M. These two versions, which correspond almost letter for letter, cannot both have been intended for the same draft of the *Metaphysics*. If the version in M, which fits perfectly into the whole argument of that book, was meant to remain where it is, this can only have been because Aristotle intended either to write a new introduction, or at the least to omit the partly duplicated chapters at the end of the introduction as we have it (A 8–10). Now M frequently refers to the first two books[1] and this shows that somehow and somewhere it was meant to follow them. Hence Aristotle must have intended to delete the critical matter at the end of the first book. This proves that he used parts of Book A as raw material for a subsequent reconstruction.

This conclusion, that the two versions differ in date, is confirmed by the few respects in which their language disagrees. If we exclude a new argument which the later passage introduces against the Ideas,[2] their only difference lies in the systematic removal of the *first* person plural, which the earlier version consistently uses to represent the supporters of the theory of Ideas. This characteristic 'we' shows that the first book was written at a time when Aristotle could still call himself a Platonist and a recent supporter of the theory.[3] Hence the interval between the two books must have been considerable, for in M his separation from the Platonic community is an accomplished fact. More-

---

[1] M 2, 1077ª 1 (= B 2, 997ᵇ 12–34); M 9, 1086ª 34 (= B 6, 1003ª 6); M 9, 1086ᵇ 2 (= A 6, 987ᵇ 1); M 10, 1086ᵇ 15 (= B 4, 999ᵇ 24, and B 6, 1003ª 6).

[2] M 4, 1079ᵇ 3–11; cf. *Ent. Met. Arist.*, pp. 29–30.

[3] The result of our inquiry into the doctrines of the *Eudemus* and the *Protrepticus* is thus placed beyond all doubt; up to the moment when he first made such a criticism of the Ideas Aristotle himself supported the theory. The passages are collected in *Ent. Metaph. Arist.*, p. 33. 'We' also occurs in the first book outside the duplicated section, wherever the doctrine of Ideas is mentioned. Thus A 9, 992ª 11, 'we state', 25 'we have given this up' and 'we say', 27 'we assert', 28 'our account', 31 'we assert'.

over, in contrast to the considerate treatment of the first book, the tone of the later polemic is often sharp or positively contemptuous.

As the date of the earlier version only one single fleeting instant in Aristotle's life can be suggested. Plato himself was dead; this is the unmistakable meaning of the imperfect tense in which he is spoken of, and which appears several times.[1] In general, this criticism does not give the impression of having been Aristotle's first utterance on the subject in the Academy. The means by which Plato's arguments for the existence of 'separate' Ideas are here referred to—mostly abbreviated terminological descriptions—presuppose that the hearers were constantly occupied with them. Aristotle even assumes that they are acquainted with the objections to them. We should scarcely be able to understand his account, or to infer from his words exactly what argument he is criticizing, if the commentary of Alexander of Aphrodisias had not preserved their meaning for us from Aristotle's lost work *On Ideas*.[2] He is using mere formulae when he refers to 'the arguments from the sciences', 'the "one over many" argument', 'the third man' (a counter-argument that does not come from himself at all, but from Polyxenus the sophist,[3] and that Plato himself had already puzzled over in the *Parmenides*); also to 'the more accurate arguments', some of which assumed Ideas of relatives, and to 'the argument that there is an object for thought even when the thing has perished'.[4] Thus the original form of the criticism presupposes a group of *Platonic* philosophers, for whom Aristotle once more sums up, in a rapid survey, all those objections to the doctrine of the now dead master that had occupied the Academy in the course of the years, in order to infer the necessity for a complete reorganization of Platonism on the basis of these criticisms. The bereaved school is now standing at a decisive turning-point of its career. Outside of Athens, which he very soon left, Aristotle was surrounded by such a group of Platonists, after Plato's death, only in Assos, and then never again. In Athens he can

[1] A 9, 992ª 20 'he used to object', 21 'he used to call', 22 'he often posited'.
[2] Frgs. 187–189.
[3] According to Phanias 'in the speech in reply to Diodorus' (frg. 24 in Mueller), quoted by Alex. Aphr. *In Arist. Metaph.*, p. 84, l. 16, in Hayduck.
[4] A 9, 990ᵇ 12 ff.

scarcely have been sufficiently composed in mind to work out, before his departure, a new lecture embracing all the criticisms of Plato's doctrine and all his own reflections on the problems of metaphysics. In Assos, on the other hand, he had not merely the necessary leisure, but also an audience of sound philosophical judgement, including Plato's best-known disciples, men who were either objective enough to listen to an opponent's reasons, like Xenocrates, or themselves full of doubt about Plato's doctrine, as Erastus, Coriscus, and their convert Hermias, seem to have been. At any rate Plato himself, in his letter to them, had thought it necessary to explain that 'even in his old age' he could not give up the theory of Ideas. He assumes that the men of Assos also have their controversies about 'this noble lore'; perhaps they had consulted him on some point. He exhorts them to have recourse to the Academy in every difficulty; if dissensions threaten he will exorcize them.[1] After his death the men of Assos invited the two representatives of the conservative and the critical tendencies respectively to visit them, and this is the group to whom the earliest version of the *Metaphysics* was read. It was contemporary with the dialogue *On Philosophy*.

We can still detect that the first book is a boldly sketched improvization. The famous opening chapter is borrowed in all essentials from the *Protrepticus*, as our examination of the latter showed;[2] in other words, Aristotle's fundamental attitude to knowledge had not changed. The aetiology which follows it, the doctrine of the four causes, is taken, along with the other main conceptions—form, matter, potency, act—from the *Physics*; Aristotle expressly refers to that work as the foundation of what he says here. It is new, however, when he develops his doctrine of causes genetically out of the history of earlier philosophy, as the completion and fresh beginning of which he represents Plato. The criticism of the Ideas, itself also hastily thrown together,

---

[1] Plato, *Letter VI*, 322 D: 'In addition to the love of Ideas (a noble lore, as I maintain, even in my old age) Erastus and Coriscus have need also of the lore of self-defence against the base and wicked, and of a sort of faculty of self-preservation.' (The words τῇ καλῇ ταύτῃ φήμ' ἐγώ καίπερ γέρων ὤν go together. The usual view, that φημί goes with προσδεῖν, makes nonsense of the intervening concessive participle. Hence we must emend προσδεῖν to προσδεῖ.) Thus this statement, when we restore its original meaning, becomes highly significant for the controversies about the Ideas within the Academy during Plato's last years, and for his own point of view.   [2] Above, p. 69.

then paves the way for his own formulation of the problems in
the second book, which is equally conditioned by the situation
that we have described, and cannot be fully understood apart
from this historical background. This result completes the
picture of Aristotle's relation to Plato and his school that we
obtained from the dialogue *On Philosophy*. It confirms the view
that the publication of his criticism was the very last step in a
long process, the beginnings of which are lost in the darkness of
the esoteric communal studies of the Academy. It is no longer
possible to distinguish Aristotle's own special objections from
those of other critics, for what he gives us in the *Metaphysics* is
obviously a collection of *all* the essential arguments, irrespective
of origin. At the same time as he publicly attacked the official
Academic doctrine, he attempted, by means of an esoteric
lecture on metaphysics in Assos, to convert such of his fellow-
students as were more favourable to his critical attitude to a
certain conviction, namely that the essence of Plato's legacy
could be preserved only by the absolute abandonment of dualism
and of the 'separateness' of the Ideas. What he proposed
seemed to himself to be pure Platonism, and was meant to be
nothing else; it was to be the philosophical consummation of
what Plato had aimed at but failed to attain. The most remarkable thing about this estimate of his own position, which
enabled him to preserve his reverence in spite of violent alterations of Plato's doctrine, is his feeling that he is responsible for
the organic development of the doctrine, and his determination
to acquit himself well. His contemporaries, however, judged him
otherwise. Beneath the conservative covering they recognized
a new and revolutionary attitude towards the world, and hence
they no longer considered him a Platonist. He himself, however,
was not yet sufficiently detached from his own development to
perceive the truth of this opinion. Only in his latest period did
he become wholly free and independent. Whether his earlier or
his later estimate of himself seems truer to us, will depend on
whether we look more to the historical presuppositions of his
philosophy, or to his individual way of regarding reality and
reflecting upon it. We must call to mind how difficult Plato
found it to distinguish his own identity from that of Socrates,
if we are to understand, from the *irrationale* of his discipleship

with Plato, Aristotle's modest repudiation of all and every claim to originality.

The next question is how far this earliest version of the *Metaphysics* extends and what its members are. In the first place, it includes, besides the criticism of the Ideas (where the 'we' very clearly denotes the transitional period), the complete first book; for, since the unity of this book is above suspicion, the chronological inferences that can be made about a part of it must apply also to the whole. It appears that Aristotle's frequent reference to himself as a Platonist was already a stumbling-block in the days of antiquity. Alexander of Aphrodisias and Syrian tell us that some ancient scholars rejected the book. According to a remark of Albert the Great the Middle Ages sometimes ascribed it to Theophrastus, and apparently it was lacking in the Arabic translations.[1] Both facts are to be explained as the result of a tradition among learned persons in antiquity; obviously some late editor actually omitted the book because of the assertion that it was spurious. A comment of Alexander's on the second book shows that this assertion was suggested precisely by the objectionable 'we' of the first, which seemed to mark it off from all the others. Aristotle says (B 2, 997^b 3): 'It has been explained in the introduction that we hold (λέγομεν) the Ideas to be both causes and self-dependent substances; while the theory presents difficulties in many ways, the most paradoxical thing of all is our statement that there are certain things besides those in the material universe, and that these are the same as sensible things except that they are eternal while the latter are perishable.' From this passage Alexander infers that it is wrong to reject the first book, since it is here expressly referred to, and since its 'ethos' agrees precisely with that of this passage; in both places Aristotle treats the theory of Ideas as his own. This argument presupposes that it was that 'ethos' which had rendered the first book suspicious. At that time no one understood how Aristotle could call the Ideas his own doctrine, and even Alexander can only suppose that it is a device to give vividness.[2]

[1] Albertus Magn. I. 525^b: 'et hanc probationem ponit Theophrastus qui etiam primum librum qui incipit "omnes homines scire desiderant" metaphysicae Aristotelis traditur addidisse; et ideo in Arabicis translationibus primus liber non habetur.'

[2] Alex. Aphrod. *In Ar. Metaph.* B 2, 997^b 3 (p. 196, l. 19, in Hayduck):

The rejection must therefore be due to the orthodox Peripatetic scholars of the empire, who erased all signs of connexion between Aristotle and Plato because the theory of Ideas was a heresy in which the master could have had no part. To us this kind of criticism simply shows, once more, how little we can trust the Peripatetic tradition when it comes to the question of Aristotle's development. The fact is that this, our chief witness, is through and through a biassed source of information. We have already seen (p. 32 above) how the dialogues, which protest loudly against this distortion of the truth, were reduced to silence. As a matter of fact, the passage in the second book, which Alexander brings into play against the rejection of the first, shows how close is the genetic relation between the two. To this quotation from the beginning of the second book he might have added a similar one from the end, which also has not yet been used in the inquiry into chronology, incomprehensible as that may seem (B 6, 1002^b 12): 'In general one might raise the question why after all, besides perceptible things and the intermediates, one should have to look for another class of thing, i.e. the Forms which we posit.' These two passages allow us to assign the whole second book with certainty to the earlier version of the *Metaphysics*. It was written in the same breath as the first. Later on we shall find that its content also leads to this conclusion.

III. THE EARLIER AND THE LATER CRITICISM OF THE ACADEMIC THEORY OF NUMBERS

Books M and N are usually considered a unity, mainly because of the uniformity of their content, the criticism of the Academic theory of Ideas and numbers. In the opening chapter (M 1) Aristotle explains the purpose of the inquiry. He raises the question whether, besides the things of the phenomenal world, there is another kind of being, unmoved and eternal. He proposes to begin by examining the thinkers who have main-

---

' Being about to speak of [the Ideas] he begins by referring to what he said in the first book to remind us what the doctrine was. Hence it is plain for many reasons that this book is also Aristotelian and belongs to the same treatise. Moreover, the "ethos" with which he spoke of them there is the same as that with which he reminds us of them here. In both places he writes as if he himself held the theory of Ideas.' Cp. Syrianus, *Comm. in Metaph.* ad loc. (p. 23, l. 9, in Kroll); he, however, is probably merely following Alexander.

tained such a kind of being, namely Plato and his school. He lays down a fixed plan of procedure, the mere arrangement and method of which would invite the closest attention. First we are to consider the constructions of mathematics, simply as such, i.e. without reference to the metaphysical doctrines that have been attached to them, such as the view that they are Ideas, or that they are the principles and essence of all things. In the second place we must examine the Ideas; here again we must consider them not with reference to Plato's later interpretation of them as numbers, but in their original and genuine form. Thirdly there must be a critical study of the mathematical philosophy of Speusippus and Xenocrates.

In this scheme the first two parts, the discussion of the being (οὐσία) of mathematical objects and the criticism of the original theory of Ideas—with both of which we are familiar from Plato's dialogues—have really no independent significance. They are simply stages in Aristotle's methodical exposition of that which was their historical consequence, namely the doctrines of Speusippus and Xenocrates. The latter are the main objects of interest in the inquiry, as would be clear merely from the length of their treatment. They obviously constituted the actual problem at the time when M was in the writing, whereas the Platonic Ideas are mentioned only for the sake of completeness. Aristotle definitely tells us this in the passage where he is giving the Idea-theory its place in the book. Not because it still has supporters in the Academy is he going to include it in this discussion, but merely 'for form's sake as it were'.[1] Speusippus abandoned the Ideas entirely, replacing them with numbers as a higher kind of reality. Xenocrates, conservatively attempting to save Plato's later theory, identified the mathematical 'essences' with the Ideas which Plato had regarded as numbers; that is to say, he compromised between Plato and Speusippus. Aristotle calls this the 'third mode' of the theory, and naturally it must have been the last to appear.

This shows that M was written much later than the first books. It is true that Aristotle mentions speculation about

---

[1] Ὅσον νόμου χάριν, *Metaph.* M 1, 1076ᵃ 27. [W. D. Ross translates: 'only as far as the accepted mode of treatment demands.' Tr.] For the expression see Bernays, *Die Dialoge des Aristoteles*, p. 150.

numbers a great deal earlier—in the *Protrepticus*; but during the period immediately after Plato's death, in which the original *Metaphysics* took shape, his manner of criticizing the Idea-theory had been the very opposite. In the first two books this theory is still the acknowledged centre of philosophical interest; he there regards it as the starting-point for all metaphysical and logical speculation whatever. In M, on the other hand, we can already detect clear signs of the Academy's reaction to his criticisms. He is now able to treat the classical form of Plato's metaphysics as admittedly superseded. To refer to it he merely appeals to his own earlier, detailed criticism—not to the first book, but to his exoteric writings, which, as they are widely known, he need not here repeat.[1] In this reference we recognize the dialogue *On Philosophy*, which was not mentioned in the criticism in the first book, and presumably did not come into existence until shortly thereafter. Since then a long time had elapsed, thirteen years or more. In accordance with the new situation Aristotle no longer gives first place to the criticism of the Ideas, which, during the period immediately after Plato's death, had no doubt still found many supporters. The altered situation is the real reason why, in the new version, he entirely deletes the criticism of Plato in the first book, which had been the burning question of his earliest metaphysics. With the necessary alterations, which are again caused wholly by the new external and internal situation,[2] he incorporates it into his new work against the mathematical philosophy of Speusippus and Xenocrates; as the forerunners of this doctrine the Ideas still possessed some historical interest. His earlier companions are now sharply attacked; their theory of numbers is declared a hallucination.

Everything points to the time when the Peripatetic school was hostile to the Platonic. We may begin by running over the structure of the book.

A. INTRODUCTION, M 1, 1076ᵃ 8–32.

B. PART ONE. The objects of mathematics (purely as such), 1076ᵃ 32–1078ᵇ 9.

    1. *They cannot be in sensible things*, 1076ᵃ 33–ᵇ 11,

---

[1] 1076ᵃ 26–31. [W. D. Ross's translation is scarcely consistent with Professor Jaeger's interpretation. Tr.]   [2] See above, p. 171.

2. *nor separate from them*, 1076^b 12–1077^b 11.

3. *The manner of their existence is peculiar* (they are sensible things *qua* quantitative), 1077^b 12–1078^b 9.

C. PART TWO. *Ideas* (purely as such, without reference to numbers), 1078^b 9–1080^a 11.

   1. *Historical analysis of the origin of the theory*, 1078^b 12–32.

   2. *Dialectical refutation*, 1078^b 32–1079^b 11.

   3. *Refutation by means of physical considerations*, 1079^b 12–1080^a 11.

D. PART THREE. *Numbers as separable substances*, 1080^a 12–1085^b 34.

   1. *Derivation of all possible forms of the theory*, 1080^a 12–^{b} 36.

     (*a*) Three forms are conceivable, 1080^a 18–^{b} 5.

       (i) Numbers are inassociable.

       (ii) They are associable.

       (iii) Some are associable and others not.

     (*b*) Each form has found supporters (except i), 1080^b 6–36.

       (i) Ideal number and mathematical number—Plato.

       (ii) Mathematical number only—Speusippus.

       (iii) Ideal and mathematical number are the same—Xenocrates ('another thinker').

   2. *Refutation of these forms*, 1080^b 37–1085^b 34.

     (*a*) Refutation of Plato, 1080^b 37–1083^a 17,

       (i) if all units are associable, 1081^a 5–17.

       (ii) if they are all inassociable, 1081^a 17–^{b} 35.

       (iii) if those in different numbers are differentiated, but those in the same number undifferentiated, 1081^b 35–1082^b 1.

       (iv) There is no possibility whatever of differentiating units and hence none of making them Ideas, 1082^b 2–1083^a 17.

     (*b*) Refutation of the other number-metaphysicians, 1083^a 20–1085^b 34.

       (i) Distinction of three possible forms, 1083^a 27–^{b} 18.

         (α) Speusippus, 1083^a 27–^{b} 1.

         (β) Xenocrates ('the third version'), 1083^b 1–8.

         (γ) The Pythagoreans, 1083^b 8–18.

       (ii) Refutation of these doctrines, 1083^b 19–1085^b 34.

E. CONCLUSION, 1085^b 35–1086^a 20.

    1. *The disagreement between these thinkers makes their doctrines suspicious.*

    2. *The modern representatives of the doctrine have not improved on Plato.*

    3. *Their failure is due to the falsity of their first principles.*

This train of thought shows a strictness of construction that we do not often find in Aristotle. His lecture-notes are usually too liable to continual alteration for any polish of form to appear, but this book is arranged on one plan throughout, and has obviously been carefully elaborated. It is a whole with beginning, middle, and end. Its originality lies not so much in the details as in the totality. Aristotle wishes to unify into one last great critical survey all his reflections on Ideas and numbers, that is, on the problem of supersensible reality. He conceives the plan, typical of his logical genius, of systematically developing and refuting, not merely the doctrines actually reigning in the Academy, but all possible forms of the Academic 'fiction' whatever. Into this framework he fits those versions of the theory which had found historical representatives, reducing them to a few fundamental presuppositions which he shows to be false. The introduction, and more especially the conclusion, are carefully polished; towards the end the sober language takes on an almost oratorical tinge. The end, of course, is not the end of the book, but M 9, 1086^a 20. The succeeding words are the beginning of a new discussion; this had already been noticed in ancient times, and, following Schwegler, I have demonstrated it in detail.[1] It is especially clear from the sentences just preceding the break (M 9, 1086^a 15–20); they are wholly in the manner of an epilogue. Aristotle loves to conclude a lecture with a line of poetry; as in Λ, or in the lecture on *Friendship* which was later incorporated into the *Nicomachean Ethics* (Books VIII and IX), so here he finishes with a quotation from Epicharmus; and just as he takes leave of his audience at the end of the *Sophistical Refutations*, or completes a lecture on the ideal state by referring those listeners who are still unconvinced to another occasion,[2] so here he has a parting word for his hearers, who included apparently students of the opposite persuasion, not yet shaken

[1] *Ent. Metaph. Arist.*, pp. 41 ff.　　　　[2] *Pol.* VII. 1, 1323^b 36.

in their faith. 'He who is already convinced might be further convinced by a longer discussion. But one still not convinced'—the train of thought breaks off.

Original as this lecture is in its method, it is not so in the material that it uses. Aristotle appears to have worked into it every note that he had previously made about the problem. It is not probable that nothing but the criticism of the Ideas in chapters four and five was borrowed from the earlier version of the *Metaphysics*. The whole book is a rapid sketch; everywhere it bears the marks of different styles. It is significant that perfect smoothness appears only in the introduction, the conclusion, the detailed programme, and the transitions—in a word, in all the passages written specially for the present formulation and necessarily late in origin. The style of the criticism of the Ideas, which comes from the older sketch, is wholly distinct from that of the framework, and this alone would betray its disparate character.

It is also quite inconceivable that the long rows of counter-arguments, monotonously linked together with 'again' (D 2(*b*) (ii)), which I have not tried to systematize in the above analysis, were ever worked over for the purposes of the present composition. They seem to have been adopted without alteration from an earlier work.

Clear proof that such was the origin of the book is afforded by the passage attached to it at the end (M 9, 1086ᵃ 21, to the end of M 10). Some of the ancient commentators wanted to include this in the following book, thinking that it was a preface, as indeed it is.[1] Its connexion with Book N would have been very superficial, however; the editors responsible for our manuscript tradition displayed more insight. They recognized that there is no direct transition. They therefore followed the procedure which they have adopted in other similar circumstances, and inserted this preface, which had been handed down by itself, as a loosely connected addition to M. They thereby expressed their belief that it is closely related to the book to which they attached it. What the relation is becomes clear when we compare this preface with that at the beginning of M.

[1] Syrian *In Ar. Metaph.*, p. 160, l. 6, in Kroll.

Preface, M 1, 1076ᵃ 8.

We have stated what is the substance of sensible things, dealing in the treatise on physics with matter, and later with the substance which has actual existence. Now since our inquiry is *whether there is or is not besides the sensible substances any which is immovable and eternal,* and, if there is, what it is, we must first consider what is said by others . . .

Two opinions are held on this subject; it is said that the objects of mathematics—i.e. numbers and lines and the like—are substances, and again that the Ideas are substances. *And since* (1) *some recognize these as two different classes*— the Ideas and the mathematical numbers, and (2) some recognize both as having one nature, while (3) *others say that the mathematical substances are the only substances, we must consider first* the objects of mathematics, not qualifying them by any other characteristic—not asking, for instance, whether they are Ideas or not. . . . Then *after this we must separately consider the Ideas* themselves in a general way, and only as far as the accepted mode of treatment demands.

Preface, M 9, 1086ᵃ 21.

Regarding the first principles and the first causes and elements, *the views expressed by those who discuss only sensible substance have been partly stated in our works on physics,* and partly do not belong to the present inquiry. But the views of *those who assert that there are other substances besides the sensible must be considered* next after those we have been mentioning.

Since, then, some say that the Ideas and the numbers are such substances, and that the elements of these are elements and principles of real things, we must inquire regarding these what they say and in what particular form they say it.

Those who posit numbers only, and these mathematical, *must be considered later;* but as regards *those who believe in the Ideas* one might survey at the same time their mode of thinking and the difficulty into which they fall.

The subject-matter envisaged by the preface in M 9 is precisely what has already been discussed in the previous part of the book. The reference to numbers as 'principles' and 'elements' is a piece of Academic terminology that Aristotle can be shown to have used from the *Protrepticus* on. We are not to suppose that in M 1–9 he has treated numbers as independent substances, and is now going on to consider their character as principles and elements of all being.[1] The sequel shows clearly

---

[1] Ancient commentators explained the difference between the two discussions as being that in M 1–9, 1086ᵃ 20, Aristotle treats of the Platonic substances (οὐσίαι) as separate essences, while from M 9, 1086ᵃ 21, to the end of N, he treats of these same essences as principles and elements of reality; but the second treatment is in no way and at no point based on the first, and does not

that in M 9 he means, exactly as he did in M 1, the separate existence (χωρισμός) of the Ideas, of numbers, and of the other mathematical quantities such as points, lines, planes, and solids. With this in mind, let us read the following words (M 9, 1086ᵃ26):
'Since, then, some say that the Ideas and the numbers are such substances, and that the elements of these are elements and principles of real things, we must inquire regarding these persons, first, what they say and, secondly, in what particular form they say it.' That is exactly the content of Book M. Aristotle could not possibly have spoken so if M had preceded; he could not possibly have begun to discuss Ideas and numbers afresh, as if he had so far said nothing about them. Moreover, he speaks in M 9 of the 'mode' and of the 'difficulty' of Plato's doctrine, two things which he wishes us to keep separate. This distinction rests on the same method of critical inquiry into the views of other philosophers as that employed in M 1–9. First the doctrine itself is stated; then follows a criticism in which its difficulties are developed. The correspondence extends even to the verbal details. For example, each preface starts by appealing to the *Physics* for the theory of sensible substances. Each has the expression, we must begin by 'considering' the kinds of supersensible essence that are 'asserted' by 'other' thinkers. Thus both the content and the language clearly show that we have here two parallel versions of the preface to a critical discussion of Academic metaphysics.

Now what is the relation of these two versions to each other in time? At first we are tempted to suppose that M 9 is simply a verbal variant that Aristotle afterwards rejected.

The possibility of a merely stylistic difference is, however, excluded by the fact that, in spite of all their correspondences, the two prefaces diverge in one decisive respect, the arrangement which they propose to give to the subject-matter of the work. In M 9 we read: 'Those philosophers who hypostasize numbers, and these the mathematical numbers, must be con-

recognize its existence at all. It really handles *both* questions together, and criticizes Plato's supersensible essences both as separate substances and as 'elements and principles of real things'. As we shall see in the course of our inquiry, it agrees with the history of Aristotle's metaphysical views that the emphasis here lies more on the significance of these essences as elements of reality than on their substantiality.

sidered later. But as regards those who believe in the Ideas we can survey at the same time their mode of thinking and the difficulty into which they fall.'[1] The preface in M 1 is far more careful in the arrangement of the same matter. Aristotle there enumerates not merely Ideas and numbers, but also their sub-divisions, and before both of them he places mathematical magnitudes as such; thus the introduction displays the same gradual and cautious method as we have seen to permeate the book as a whole. In the preface in M 9, on the other hand, the inquiry is in a somewhat more inchoate stage, and what is lack-ing is precisely this distinctive detail in the differentiation of the problem.

We have here, therefore, not a merely verbal variant, but the introduction to an earlier criticism of Academic number-meta-physics, in which the subject was treated according to a distinctly less developed method.[2] As already suggested, there are pre-sumably other portions of this older writing also embedded as raw material in the new construction, the present Book M, but we are no longer able to separate them.

In order to determine the date of the earlier version we must make a detour, which will involve the interpretation of an obscure passage that has not yet been rightly understood. Here again the opportunity which the passage offers for exact dating has been overlooked as completely as in the decisive portions of Books A and B.

In M 10, 1086[b] 14, Aristotle begins his refutation of the Idea-theory with a difficulty which he had formulated in B 6, 1003[a] 6.

'Let us now mention a point which presents a certain difficulty both to those who believe in the Ideas and to those who do not, *and which was stated before, at the beginning, among the problems.* (1) If we do not suppose substances to be separate, and in the way in which particular things are said to be separate, we shall destroy substance, as may be admitted for the sake of argument; (2) but if we conceive substances to be separable, how are we to conceive their elements and their principles?

[1] M 9, 1086[a] 29.

[2] In my *Ent. Metaph. Arist.*, pp. 42 ff., I recognize that the passage from M 9, 1086[a] 21, to the end of the book is a subsequent addition, which the editors attached to the complete discussion M 1–9, 1086[a] 20. Strangely enough, how-ever, I failed to see that M 1 and M 9, 1086[a] 21 ff., undoubtedly form a doublet, the two parts of which must have arisen at widely separated times. This dis-covery alters my whole treatment of Books M and N, as the following pages will show.

'(A) If they are individual and not universal, real things will be just of the same number as the elements, and the elements will not be knowable.... (B) But if the principles are universal, [either the substances composed of them are also universal, or] non-substance will be prior to substance; for the universal is not a substance, but the element or principle is universal, and the element or principle is prior to the things of which it is the principle or element.'

Immediately before this passage Aristotle has explained the difficulties involved in the Idea-theory by means of its origin (1086ª 35–ᵇ 14). The main difficulty arises from the fact that the Ideas are regarded both as universal (καθόλου), and at the same time as existing independently and hence to a certain extent as a new kind of particular (τῶν καθ' ἕκαστον). The cause of this peculiar duality in their nature was the fact that Plato had asserted the unreality of phenomenal things, because he had been led by Heraclitus to the view that all perceptible things, all sensible particulars, are in continual flux and have no permanent existence. On the other hand, the ethical inquiries of Socrates had indirectly given rise to the new and important discovery that science is of the universal only, though he himself had not abstracted conceptions from real objects nor declared them separate. Plato then went further—according to Aristotle's retrospective account—and hypostasized universal conceptions as true being (οὐσία).

Then follows the important passage. Aristotle here develops the question whether the principles are universal or in some sense particular. This is difficult both for the supporters of the Ideas and for their opponents. He tries to show that either answer seems necessarily to lead to absurdities. If the principles are particular they are unknowable, since only the universal is knowable. If, on the other hand, they are universal, not-substance would be prior to substance, and we should have to derive substance, whose principles they are, from the universal; which is impossible, since the universal is never a substance. These are the logical consequences, Aristotle continues, of deriving the Ideas from elements, and of assuming alongside things of one kind a transcendental unity like the Ideas. This summary would by itself suffice to show that what he has in mind is really the theory of Ideas, and not specially its opponents, in spite of his introductory words; only, he needs them both in order to formulate his question as a dilemma. He regards the dilemma, whether the elements and principles are particular or universal, as a part of a more general one, namely the following. If we do not assume that substances (τὰς οὐσίας) exist separately as we say that particulars do, we destroy substance (τὴν οὐσίαν); if, on the other hand, we assume that they do exist separately and independently, we have the above-described difficulty whether their principles are particular or universal.

The first part of the more general dilemma seems to contain a tautology; but it only seems to. The plural 'substances' and the singular 'substance' evidently indicate some difference of meaning. The 'substances' to which Aristotle is here referring cannot be those 'recognized by every one', namely sensible things; for then it would have been meaningless to add 'and in the way in which particular things are said to be separate'. On the contrary, the particular mode of existence that sensible things exhibit serves here simply as an analogy to illuminate the manner of the independent existence of the 'substances'. Now this is precisely Aristotle's usual way of describing Plato's Ideas in their character as real essences; hence it cannot be doubted—this is also the view of Bonitz—that behind these 'substances' lie the Ideas, or some supersensible reality corresponding thereto. If we refuse to follow Plato and his school in assuming permanent realities, we destroy all 'substance' (Aristotle allows this for once); if, on the other hand, we assume any independent and separate being, we are faced with the above-mentioned difficult consequences about the derivation of its principles.

So far we have not considered the words 'as may be admitted for the sake of argument'. This is Bonitz' translation of ὡς βουλόμεθα λέγειν, and others have followed him, as they usually do in difficult circumstances.[1] He bases this rendering on the correct view that in the first alternative Aristotle is granting something that he does not really believe. Aristotle's dilemmas always take this form, and we need have no uneasiness about the thought. Nevertheless, his translation is impossible. The idea 'as we will admit for once' cannot be expressed in Greek by ὡς βουλόμεθα λέγειν. Pseudo-Alexander is another

---

[1] *Aristoteles' Metaphysik übersetzt von Hermann Bonitz* (edited from his remains by Eduard Wellmann, Berlin, 1890), p. 298.

person who obviously did not understand these three words. His foolish and hasty paraphrase ὅπερ οὐ βουλόμεθα ('which we do not admit') is simply a sign of complete helplessness. It gives almost the opposite of the real sense, and the suggestion that it is actually the better reading was properly rejected by Bonitz.

The commentators have failed to observe that ὡς βουλόμεθα is a frequent idiom. In A 9, 990ᵇ 17, we read: 'And in general the arguments for the Forms destroy the things whose existence we [Platonists] think more important (μᾶλλον βουλόμεθα) than that of the Ideas themselves', namely the principles of the Ideas. The manuscript Aᵇ reads βούλονται and inserts οἱ λέγοντες εἴδη ('those who believe in the Ideas think' instead of 'we think'), the latter being adopted by the Byzantine mixed version E. This change was suggested by the parallel passage in M 4, 1079ᵃ 14, where it is guaranteed by the train of thought. In our passage, however, the context supports precisely the first person plural. The main reason for Bonitz's misinterpretation of βούλεσθαι was the addition in this passage of the infinitive λέγειν, which seems to be otiose on this rendering. If it had been simply ὡς βουλόμεθα or ὡς λέγομεν he would scarcely have misunderstood. Yet this very combination, βούλεσθαι λέγειν, is not unusual as an expression for *that which a philosopher 'understands' by his conceptions*. Thus in Plato's *Laws*, x. 892 C, we have, 'by "nature" the physicists understand coming-to-be in reference to the elementary principles', where 'understand' is βούλονται λέγειν.

Strangely enough, this usage has been frequently mistaken in Aristotle. In *Metaph.* N 2, 1089ᵃ 19, he speaks of the meaning of non-being in Plato's *Sophist*: 'He means by (βούλεται λέγειν) the non-being . . . the false and the character of falsity.' Bonitz writes λέγει in accordance with Pseudo-Alexander's interpretation, and Christ follows him. Λέγειν should be restored, as being the only accredited reading; λέγει is a bad conjecture of Pseudo-Alexander's, who erroneously takes it with καὶ ταύτην τὴν φύσιν. Exactly the same interpretation applies to N 4, 1091ᵃ 30. 'A difficulty, and a reproach to any one who finds it *no* difficulty, are contained in the question how the elements and the principles are related to the good and the beautiful; the

difficulty is this, whether any of the elements is such a thing as
we mean by (βουλόμεθα λέγειν) the good itself and the best,
or this is not so, but these are later in origin than the elements.'
Here again Christ suspected λέγειν of being a spurious addition,
because he did not understand the idiom.

Let us now apply this knowledge to the passage with which
we started, 1086^b 18–19. The true translation must be: 'If we
do not suppose substances to be separate, and in the way in
which particular things are said to be separate [as Aristotle himself does], we shall destroy substance in the sense *in which we
Platonists understand it*.' Only when we see this are we in a
position fully to comprehend the singular 'substance' (τὴν
οὐσίαν), which is significant for Plato's terminology. In the
first horn of the dilemma Aristotle shows the difficulties into
which he, *as a Platonist*, falls owing to his rejection of the Ideas
and their 'separateness'; the second gives the difficulties involved in the theory of 'separateness'. So long as we do not
realize that in the first horn the opponents of 'separateness' are
judged according to Plato's notion of substance, we do not in
the least understand the point of the dilemma. It now becomes
clear that the opponents of the Ideas here are not the spokes-
men of materialism or of common sense—how could Aristotle
ever refute them with a conception of substance which they
must inevitably reject as begging the question from the start?
The dilemma is logically valid only for those who stand on
Platonic ground. The truth is that Aristotle here distinguishes
two sorts of Platonist, those who maintain the Ideas and those
who do not. Both are involved in contradictions, because both
presuppose Plato's conception of substance. The conclusion is
obvious: the contradictions can be resolved only by a new notion
of substance. Aristotle is thinking of the idea that the real is the
universal *in* the particular. He cannot, however, express it here
(the problematic form of the passage entirely forbids it); he can
only hint that merely to abandon the Ideas is not enough; this
inroad on Plato's first principles carries with it the obligation to
reconstruct completely the whole view of being on which the
doctrine of 'separateness' rests.

This answers the question of the date of the preface M 9–10.
Like the first two books, it is a part of the original *Metaphysics*,

and written at the same time, namely during the critical period in Assos, when Aristotle was attacking the theory of Ideas as a Platonist among Platonists. Hence it is not surprising that there are still closer relations between these two books and this newly-recovered fragment. The central books of the *Metaphysics*, ZHΘ, strangely enough, contain absolutely no quotations from the first two, not even from the problems in the second. Altogether different is this new portion of the matter that originally followed A and B. In spite of its shortness, M 9–10 contains more references to A and B than all of Z–Λ put together.[1] The next question is, do we possess only the preface of this part of the original *Metaphysics*, or are there some traces of the body of it? This leads us to the examination of Book N. May there not be a true idea at the bottom of the view of those ancient critics who separated M 9–10 from M 1–9, and regarded it as an introduction to the following book? We showed above that a perfectly smooth transition is not to be found; hence the question cannot be answered mechanically by means of the conventional device of redividing the books. Nevertheless, these dissenters from the traditional division may have based their experiment on a kernel of correct observation, even if their means of explaining it were violent and wrong. And this is actually so. Just as M 9–10 contains the old preface that was replaced by M 1, so in Book N a lucky chance has thrown into the hands of the editors of Aristotle's remains the very portion of the original *Metaphysics* which he meant to replace, in his last version, with the much improved and perfected discussion of M 1–9.

Here again we may take as an external criterion the signpost that has guided us correctly before. As in A and B, we find in N an allusion to the fact that Aristotle, when he was outlining these lectures, felt himself still a member of the Academy. The passage in question, which has not yet been noticed in this connexion, comes in the criticism of Speusippus (N 4, 1091ᵃ 30–33). 'A difficulty, and a reproach to any one who finds it *no* difficulty, are contained in the question how the elements and the principles are related to the good and the beautiful; the difficulty is

---

[1] 1086ᵃ 34 cites B 6, 1003ᵃ 6; 1086ᵇ 2 refers to A 6, 987ᵇ 1; 1086ᵇ 15 to B 4, 999ᵇ 24, and to B 6, 1003ᵃ 6.

this, whether any of the elements is *such a thing as we mean* by
the good itself and the best, or this is not so, but these are later in
origin than the elements.' The idiom has already been explained.
It only remains, therefore, to draw from this passage the same
conclusion about the date of Book N as we did about M 9 and 10.
Not only is the expression that of a Platonist, but the whole
attitude also corresponds exactly to the ticklish situation in
Assos. We Platonists, says Aristotle, put at the head of philosophy and at the beginning of the world the Good in itself (αὐτὸ
τὸ ἀγαθόν) or the Highest Good (τὸ ἄριστον). Speusippus, on
the other hand, supposes an evolution of the Good and Perfect,
which forces its way into reality only at the end of a gradual
process of becoming (ὑστερογενές).[1] In this fundamental
problem of *Weltanschauung* Aristotle feels himself the more
genuine Platonist, because he puts at the beginning, not indeed
Plato's Good in itself, but the *ens perfectissimum*, making it the
principle and starting-point of all movement. He thereby preserves the essential nerve of Plato's thought, whereas Speusippus
entirely reverses it.[2] Surely we detect a note of self-justification
in these words.

If this book was really written in Assos, like A, B, and M 9–10,
we should not expect it to attack Xenocrates, who had accompanied Aristotle thither, in the same unsparing manner as
happened later in M 1–9, after the final breach with the Academy.
It is true that there too Aristotle's main adversary is Speusippus,
but it is Xenocrates who receives the roughest treatment; with
the minimum of flattery, his hybrid compromise is said to be the
worst of the three versions. That was written in the Lyceum,
when Xenocrates had assumed the headship of the Academy, and
his opinions were beginning to exert a wider influence. On the other
hand, the earlier version of the preface mentions, besides the
theory of Ideas, *only* that of Speusippus; and, correspondingly,
the discussion in Book N refers to the view of Xenocrates only

[1] Speusippus, frgs. 34a ff. and 35e (Lang).

[2] The dialogue *On Philosophy* also represents the permanent essence of
Platonism as consisting in the view that the Good (ἀγαθόν, ἄριστον) is the
governing principle of the world (see above, p. 134). This central doctrine there
earns Plato a place besides Zarathustra. It formed the point of departure for
Aristotle's new 'theology', which attempted to preserve the Good as a substance by anchoring its transcendental reality in the teleological structure of
nature.

once, and then briefly and considerately.[1] This very natural deference to the view of his fellow-worker in Assos is a welcome confirmation of our dating.

Inspection shows that Book N as a whole really is the discussion announced in the earlier preface. In M 9, 1086ª 29, we read: 'Those who posit numbers only, and these mathematical [i.e. Speusippus], must be considered later'; first we shall examine the theory of Ideas. The latter is undertaken immediately, and is completed by the end of M 10. It must be what is referred to in the first words of the next book ('regarding this kind of substance, what we have said must be taken as sufficient'), which then goes on to speak only of the mathematical essences and their derivation. We have to admit, however, that the discussion of the Ideas in M 9–10 is somewhat brief, even considering that in the earliest version of the *Metaphysics* the real criticism of the theory had already been given in the first book. We seem also to need a connecting passage; the above-quoted opening words of the last book give the impression of being a merely external transition, inserted by an editor for want of anything better. Hence it is probable that in this oldest version of the criticism as well as in the later ones Aristotle took account not merely of the Ideas and of Speusippus' mathematical substances, but also of the intermediate stage, namely Plato's later doctrine of Ideal numbers. This might very well have stood in the gap; and would then, presumably, have been incorporated into Book M when the *Metaphysics* was reconstructed. However that may be, it is impossible to doubt that N belongs with the older preface, since it contains the detailed refutation of Speusippus which was there announced. As in the preface the emphasis lies on the significance of the Ideas and numbers *as elements and principles* (στοιχεῖα καὶ ἀρχαί) of reality, so the same point of view determines the exposition throughout Book N.[2]

[1] N 3, 1090ᵇ 28; whereas M 8, 1083ᵇ 2, reads 'it is evident from this that the third version [that of Xenocrates] is the worst'.

[2] See above, pp. 182–183. This book shows that by the elements and principles of reality Aristotle understood the doctrine of the Great and Small, or Indefinite Dyad, and the One, from which Plato derived the Ideas. This later form of Plato's speculation was upheld also by Speusippus and other Academics, in many versions, the niceties of which we need not here consider. It makes it certain that to Aristotle in his *early* days metaphysics was a science of the

This is connected historically with the importance which the question about the elements and principles of the Ideal numbers had for Plato's later thought. It also agrees with the nature of the two opening books, where first philosophy is always defined as the theory of the highest principles and causes of being. It may be stated here, although the inevitability of the assertion will not be clear until we have analysed the later passages, that the view of metaphysics as a study of first principles, an aetiology of the real—a view which is connected with Plato's latest phase —is a sign of the earliest version of the *Metaphysics*, whereas the later formulation always devotes more attention to the problem of substance as such. Even in the doctrine of supersensible reality (M 1-9) we can clearly detect the aspect of principles yielding place in the later version to that of substance itself.

It is obvious that in the original *Metaphysics* the attack was directed mainly against Speusippus. At that time he was the leader of the Athenian school, and Aristotle threw his whole weight against the false direction in which he was seeking salvation. Speusippus was fully convinced of the necessity of reconstructing Plato's philosophy, but he took his start, according to Aristotle, from the one point in which the Idea-theory was not capable of fruitful development. He abandoned the notion of form and the relation to the sensible world; he retained the untenable 'separation' of the universal, merely replacing Plato's Ideal numbers with the objects of mathematics themselves as the fundamental reality. Aristotle makes the same criticism of 'modern thinkers' (i.e. Speusippus) in the first book, when he says that they have substituted mathematics for philosophy;[1] and whereas in the later criticism of M the tone is cool and con-

elements and principles of reality. Since he later viewed it as anything but this, at least in so far as it is an account of substance, he can have retained the traditional definition of it only so long as it was for him exclusively theology. The latter study, though not indeed a doctrine of elements, is one of principles. In fact, the description 'about elements' fits nothing whatever but a mathematical metaphysics such as, according to Aristotle, Plato put forward in his final lecture on the Good (Aristoxenus, *El. Harm.* II init.). Thus, whereas Book N, in thoroughly Platonic fashion, examines both the reality of the supersensible *and also* its elements and principles, later on, in Book M, Aristotle confined himself to an inquiry into the *reality* of the supersensible substances maintained by Plato and his school.

[1] A 9, 992ᵃ 32.

descending, in the oldest version it is frequently emotional or, as in the dialogue *On Philosophy*, bitingly sharp; as when he exclaims about Plato's doctrine of the Great and Small 'the elements—the great and the small—seem to cry out against the violence that is done to them; for they cannot in any way generate numbers'.[1]

[1] N 3, 1091a 9.

CHAPTER VIII

THE GROWTH OF THE *METAPHYSICS*

THE prevailing view that the *Metaphysics* is a late work has been rendered untenable by our discovery that it contains large portions of an earlier version belonging to the first half of the forties. The doctrine that we must now hold—and it is really obvious in itself—is that even during the years immediately before and after Plato's death metaphysics was the true centre of Aristotle's critical activity. On the other hand—and this is a no less important result—he returned to the matter again during his last period and undertook a reorganization that introduced fresh ideas into the old material, excising parts of it and reshaping others to fit their new surroundings. The traces of this last alteration enable us to guess the direction in which he wished to develop his philosophy. The individual peculiarities of the earlier and later portions cannot be clearly grasped, naturally, except through the knowledge of their 'alternating harmony' within the final structure that includes them both.

Our analysis must start from that purified torso of the *Metaphysics* which we have obtained by examining the history of its origin, and the inner relationships of which, as Aristotle meant them to be, we have rendered more visible through removing the loose pages appended by the editors. This is the compact body of books down to I, excluding α and Δ; Bonitz himself disentangled it correctly in the main.[1] He also established the fact that the series is unfinished—in particular, the theology as we have it (Λ) is not the intended conclusion—and this statement needs to be emphatically asserted in view of recent attempts to throw doubt on the convincing arguments in its favour. Only in the account of the last two books does Bonitz require supplementing; he obviously took less interest in them, because his attention was directed mainly to the doctrine of substance. We have shown that Book M was meant to replace N in the later version; it therefore belongs to the torso established by Bonitz.

---

[1] See the introduction to his *Kommentar zur Metaphysik d. Ar.*, vol. ii. He, in turn, was following Brandis (cf. *Ent. Metaph. Arist.*, pp. 3 ff.).

The metaphysics that Aristotle here offers us in sweeping strokes is the famous doctrine of substance in general, the philosophy of substantial forms, which served so many later centuries as the framework of their views of nature and being. To discover how this incomplete but mighty structure grew up we must start from its centre, that is from the doctrine of substance.

In Book B, which develops the problems of 'the science that we are seeking', Aristotle is aware of the problem of substance only in the specialized form of the question whether the super-sensible world is real. After four introductory problems concerning the nature of the new science he places this question, like a 'far-beaming countenance', at the head of the eleven problems that carry us into the real arena of the discipline. Thus he emphasizes its fundamental importance by the position he assigns to it.[1] Ever since Plato created the Ideas it had been absolutely *the* problem of philosophy. In formulating the task of metaphysics as he does, therefore, Aristotle starts directly from Plato's fundamental question. He expresses it, in fact, precisely as a Platonist would: the transcendental realities that we believe to exist in separation from sensible phenomena, such as the Ideas and the objects of mathematics—do they truly exist? And if not, can we posit, over and above sensible things, any other kind of supersensible reality? About the sensible world (αἰσθητὴ οὐσία) he says nothing whatever. The very first sentence goes straight to the central question, that of transcendence; the succeeding problems rise out of this root like trunk, boughs, and branches. A mere glance will show that they too originated without exception on Platonic territory. What are the first principles? Are they the genera, as Plato maintains, or, as natural science teaches, the elements of visible things? If the former, are they the highest or the lowest genera? What is the relation between the universal, which Plato regards as sub-stance (οὐσία), and Being or Reality? Is the 'truly real' the most abstract of abstractions, or do we approach the real more nearly the more we descend from the heights of abstraction to

---

[1] The four introductory problems are treated in *Metaph*. B 2, 996ᵃ 18–997ᵃ 33. The problem of the supersensible follows in 997ᵃ 34. For the distinction between essential problems, and those which merely introduce and define the science of metaphysics, see *Ent. Metaph. Arist.*, p. 100.

concreteness, to particularity, to the individual? Is each of the first principles one in number, as an individual, or in kind, as a genus? Are the principles of perishable and of imperishable things the same? Can we make being and unity the principle and origin of all things, as Plato does, or are they mere abstractions void of all real content? Are Plato and his disciples right in making substances (οὐσίαι) out of numbers, lines, points, planes, and solids? Since the abstract is not real or essential, but only something common to many things, what has led men to assume the existence of Ideas? Are we to think of the first principles as mere matter and potency, after the fashion of natural science, or as something that from the very beginning works and is active? (This was the question in dispute between Plato and Speusippus, in which, as we have already mentioned, Aristotle sided with Plato.) In fine, what Book B develops is simply and solely the problems of the Platonic doctrine, and in the earliest period of his *Metaphysics* Aristotle appears as the improver of that doctrine. The questions here raised lie without exception in the sphere of the supersensible. In their totality they make up a type of philosophy that not merely *derives* wholly from Plato, but is Platonic in its very nature, in spite of the fact that it presupposes and is actuated by a sceptical attitude towards the Ideas. All the problems of 'the science that we are seeking' arise out of the crisis in Plato's doctrine, and consist in efforts to rehabilitate the assertion of supersensible reality.

We naturally look for discussion of these problems in the main body of the work, which is contained, according to the prevailing view, in Books ZHΘ. The four introductory problems, which determine the conception, subject-matter, and extent, of metaphysics, are dealt with in the books immediately succeeding the list (Γ and E). We should expect Aristotle to follow it further, which would bring him to the question of supersensible reality in Book Z. We should also expect to find, conformably to Γ and E, some explicit reference to the fact that we were now approaching the central problem of metaphysics. Instead, however, of the question about the existence of the supersensible, Book Z unexpectedly confronts us with the theory of substance in general. From this point onwards, throughout the next three books, the list no longer has any significance at all. Not only does it cease to dictate the order of the exposition, but there is not even a single mention of it. This simultaneous disappearance both of the references to it and of the actual discussion of it is clear proof that either Aristotle abandoned in mid composition the original plan as he had contemplated it in Book B—which, in a work that was one both in outline and in performance, would be strange to the point of inconceivability—or the books on substance (ZHΘ) are not the execution of the original plan at all, but something new and later which either replaced it or was inserted into it.

That Book B really does belong to a distinctly earlier version than the books on substance can very easily be shown. As we demonstrated above (p. 176), it was written at the same time as Book A, during the years immediately after Plato's death. Now the 'we', with which Aristotle here designates himself a Platonist, is no longer to be found when we come to his criticism of Plato's doctrine in Book Z.[1] On the other side, we recovered a large part of the oldest *Metaphysics* in M 9–10 and Book N, and the assertion, that originally Z did not belong to the *Metaphysics* as outlined in B, is convincingly demonstrated by the facts (1) that this part of the oldest version, which is also characterized by the use of 'we' in its polemic, concerns itself, as was to be expected, exclusively with the problems stated in B, that is, with the question about the reality of the supersensible; and (2) that as soon as we re-enter this field—the field

---

[1] Namely Book Z, chapters 13 ff. In this book Aristotle examines the question of the nature of substance on the broadest possible basis, starting from the distinction of four different meanings of the word, as matter, as Form, as universal, and as essence. His object is to show that in the true conception of substance the three last meanings are united. In connexion with the question how far matter contributes to the reality of the Form and the essence, he develops his double conception of substance. The same question leads on to the assertion of an immaterial and highest Form. The inquiry whether the universal also possesses reality leads to an examination of the theory of Ideas (Z 13 ff.), which reproduces the essential notions of the refutation in the first book, though in another dress and from another point of view. The two refutations can hardly have appeared in one and the same course of lectures. Their relation to each other becomes intelligible if we suppose that Book Z was not originally intended for insertion within the larger discussion in which we now find it, but was an isolated treatment of the question of substance. This whole work *On Substance* must be later than the oldest parts of the *Metaphysics*, since there is no 'we' in the criticism of the Ideas in Z 13 ff.

of metaphysics in the narrower sense—the references back to Book B begin again.[1]

This result, that the books on substance had no place in the original plan, seems to undermine the fundamental notion of Aristotelian metaphysics. I must, therefore, take account of the objection that it is the essence of this type of speculation not to grasp the supersensible directly but to reveal it indirectly—to make it not the starting-point but the conclusion. Must not the theory of the being of the highest principle, which cannot be grasped by any experience, base itself on a theory of substance built up step by step with the help of the realities that can be experienced, and rising steadily from the known to the unknown? And do not the inquiries about substance and actuality (ZHΘ) expressly lead us to the threshold of the doctrine of supersensible being? It is certainly true that this part of the *Metaphysics* is preparatory, and it is obvious that in his last version Aristotle intentionally gave it its present place. The theory of substance in general was now to form the doorway to that of the immaterial substance of the prime mover. We shall inquire later how the specific character of his metaphysics was insured prior to this definitive arrangement, but here it is essential to establish the fact that the present version was preceded by one in which this gradual development of the conception of being was not to be found. The sketch of the problems of metaphysics in B does not envisage the excursus into the general theory of substance and actuality in ZHΘ, and these books themselves reveal at every step that they cannot have been originally written for the systematic purpose to which they are devoted in the final scheme as we have it.

In view of the importance of this point I will here establish it in still greater detail. It is true that Book Z begins by emphasizing that the best method will be to start from the substances that are perceptible to sense. It is true that this is followed by a fine and justly famous digression on the nature of human apprehension, and on the advisability of starting always from what is known 'to us', namely that which is guaranteed by perception, in order to proceed to that which is knowable 'by nature', namely the object of pure thought as such. But now this ex-

[1] See above, p. 171, n. 1.

planation of the reasons leading Aristotle to prefix to his account of the supersensible an examination of substance in general occurs in all manuscripts in the wrong position. Bonitz was the first to discover the displacement (though he drew no conclusions), and ever since his day our editions have given us this wandering passage at the point where it belongs. The error cannot be due to a confusion in a late manuscript, for it occurs in both classes of the tradition, and therefore appeared in all ancient manuscripts. The only possible explanation is that it was an afterthought written on a loose sheet, and inserted into the wrong part of the text by the very first editor.[1] There is a second reference to the merely preparatory nature of the inquiry about sensible reality, and this also is so loosely connected with the adjacent words that it seems to have been added subsequently by Aristotle.[2]

One thing is certain. Books ZH do not discuss substance in the way in which one would expect from these passages. They

---

[1] *Metaph.* Z 3, 1029^b 3–12. These words have got into the beginning of the discussion of essence, where they are quite meaningless. They really continue the words 'Some of the sensible substances are generally admitted to be substances, so that we must look first among these' (1029^a 33), which also belong to the subsequent addition. Clearly the first words of the insertion were written between the lines of the old manuscript, and hence occur in their proper place in our copies. The rest, for which there was no room, was written on a separate sheet. Another example of an addition on a loose sheet is the passage 'Regarding . . . intelligible', Z 11, 1036^b 32–1037^a 5.

[2] *Metaph.* Z 11, 1037^a 10 ff., seems to me to be such an addition, intended to represent the work *On Substance* as a preliminary to the theory of supersensible substance, and to call attention to this function at an early stage of the discussion. If it had been included from the beginning, Aristotle would surely, when speaking of matter, have made some reference, however slight, to the matter which Plato postulated even in supersensible substance. Yet there is not a single syllable here about the Great-and-Small, although in the *Metaphysics* it would necessarily interest him much more than matter in the physicists' sense, of which Z says so much. We can understand how, when inserting ZHΘ, he would add these words at the end of the first part of the inquiry: 'Whether there is, apart from the matter of such substances, another kind of matter, and one should look for some substance other than these, e.g. numbers or something of the sort, must be considered later. For it is for the sake of this that we are trying to determine the nature of perceptible substances as well, since in a sense the inquiry about perceptible substances is the work of physics, i.e. of second philosophy.' That these words are a later addition of Aristotle's is also proved by the next sentence (1037^a 17–20), which is a reference, inseparably connected with this passage, to the addition about definition which composes H 6. This addition and the reference to it were, like other alterations of the same kind, introduced into the scheme of the later *Metaphysics* on the occasion of the insertion of Books ZHΘ.

do not keep steadily in view their supposed purpose of leading
up to the proof of the existence of supersensible reality. On the
contrary, they give the impression of being written simply in
order to refute Plato's conception of being, according to which
the highest being is the highest universal, and in order to con-
front this exaggerated immaterialism with a proof that matter
and substratum have a positive significance for our conception
of reality. We here find Aristotle's combination of logic and
concreteness giving rise to a new conception of substance as
form and entelechy, the question of the 'separableness' of which,
though decisive for the metaphysician, receives no particular
attention. In fact, Plato's constant effort always to abstract
from matter is here rejected as one-sided, and attention is called
to the importance of matter for our notion of essence.[1] In view
of all this it is not surprising that the means which Aristotle uses
to develop his notion of form actually consist in an analysis of
becoming, and that he brings out very clearly the fundamental
significance of his notion for the proper comprehension of this
physical conception.[2] The way in which Book Z discusses the
various meanings of 'substance' one after the other, and the
result of the inquiry, prompt the suggestion that we have here
an originally independent work on the problem of substance, the
fundamental importance of this subject having already been
shown by the criticism of the Ideas even in the earliest version of
the *Metaphysics* (above, p. 188). It cannot be denied, of course,
that even in the earliest period of Aristotle's physical speculation
his new conception of substance, or rather of being, must be presupposed as such; but this conception took its origin just as
much in physics and in logic[3] as in metaphysics; and it is per-

---

[1] *Metaph.* Z 11, 1036b 22, 'And so to reduce all things thus to Forms and to
eliminate the matter is useless labour; for some things surely are a particular
form in a particular matter'.   [2] *Metaph.* Z 8, 1033a 24 ff.

[3] Aristotle's interest in the problem of substance often comes out in the
book, and metaphysics and 'analytics' are also very intimately concerned
with it (for the latter see Z 12 and H 6). It belongs to physics because of its
connexion with the theory of becoming and of change; to metaphysics because
of the conception of immaterial Form and because of the problem of 'separateness'; and to 'analytics' because of 'essence' and its relations with the theories
of definition, of abstraction, and of the classification of conceptions as genera
and species. We need only realize this manysidedness in order to understand
why this work stood 'between' the above-mentioned disciplines until Aristotle
incorporated it into the *Metaphysics*.

fectly possible that his earliest metaphysics (which, as we learn from the dialogue *On Philosophy*, was still pure theology), while it made clever use of the conceptions of entelechy and actuality in attacking the problem of God, nevertheless did not include any general discussion of substance, much less make it the central consideration.

The conjecture that the discussion of substance did not originally stand in its present position can be further supported by a number of weighty external indications.[1] In the first place, there is no reference whatever to ZHΘ in the older books. On the other hand, I refers to ZH, and describes them as 'the discussions about substance'; this by itself indicates their relative independence. Aristotle mentions them in the same way in Θ 8, 1049^b 27 ('it was said in the discussions about substance'). It appears from this that the two Books Z and H, which form a single whole—H begins with a recapitulation of Z, and offers a series of appendices thereto—are regarded both in Θ and in I as independent. What is still more important is that the introduction of Z is often referred to as the beginning, as in Z 4, 1029^b 1 ('since at the start we distinguished the various marks by which we determine substance'). Usually the words 'at the start' mean the beginning of the whole course of lectures, namely Book A, as they do, for example in B and in M 9–10, passages which belong to the original *Metaphysics*. We have an example of 'at the start' used in a central book to refer to its own beginning in the discussion of friendship in the *Nicomachean Ethics* (VIII–IX), and there is no doubt that this was originally an independent work. Z was also at one time the beginning of an independent work; it was in fact the first of a whole series of lectures. This is shown by Θ 1, 1045^b 31, where again 'in the first part of our work' means the beginning not of A or of Θ, but of Z. It follows that this series began with Z; then came H;

---

[1] Since it is here important to assemble all the proofs, I may be allowed to recapitulate briefly the inferences that can be drawn from the reciprocal references in the books of the *Metaphysics*, although I have already emphasized them (*Ent. Metaph. Arist.*, pp. 90 ff. and 106). It is precisely with regard to the matter of chapter four of the first part of my earlier book, namely the connected and continuous portions of the *Metaphysics*, that I now believe it possible to push the analysis far enough to obtain a complete understanding of the author's intention, whereas I have nothing important to add to my previous remarks about the passages that are isolated and independent additions.

H was presumably followed by Θ, as now. Whether I also belonged to the original series, or was added later when Aristotle removed ZHΘ from their isolation and inserted them into the *Metaphysics*, is difficult to decide. On the whole, it seems to have been added later. I 2, 1053^b 16, refers to Z, 13–17, thus: 'if, then, no universal can be a substance, as has been said in our discussion of substance and being'. Here ZH are still thought of as independent, and it does not appear that they come at the beginning of a series to which I also belongs. On the contrary, another passage, in which I refers to B, makes against it: 'with regard to the substance and nature of the one we must ask in which of two ways it exists; this is the very question that we reviewed in our discussion of problems, viz. what the one is' (I 2, 1053^b 9). This indicates that the original independent work consisted only of ZHΘ, that I was added when Aristotle was working on the final version of the *Metaphysics*. That is why it regards B as the introduction.

If we now consider the relation of Book Z to what precedes it, we find that this once more confirms our view that it was introduced into its present place after having been originally intended as a complete work in itself. As we have seen, Books Γ and E contain the discussion of the first four problems, concerning the nature of 'the science that we are seeking'. This discussion ends with E 1. Then comes something new, viz. the theory of the various senses of 'being', and the theory of the most fundamental of these, namely essence (οὐσία). In other words, this is the beginning of the main part of the *Metaphysics*. Aristotle starts by enumerating all the relevant meanings of 'being' in the widest sense of the word. 'Since the unqualified term "being" has several meanings, of which one was seen to be the accidental, and another the true ("non-being" being the false), while besides these there are the figures of predication (e.g. the "what", quality, quantity, place, time, and any similar meanings which "being" may have), and again besides all these there is that which "is" potentially or actually—since "being" has many meanings, we must first say regarding the accidental, that there can be no scientific treatment of it.'[1] He then discusses the accidental, and thereafter being in the sense of the truth or

[1] *Metaph.* E 2, 1026^a 33.

falsity of judgements. This short passage extends to the end of E. Z begins the examination of being in the fundamental sense, that is, of the categories, and especially of substance (οὐσία), which is the main object of the science concerned.

Strangely enough, the new book opens with almost the identical words that have immediately preceded, and with the same enumeration of the senses of being. 'There are several senses in which a thing may be said to "be", as we pointed out previously [here we expect at the least a reference to the list that was given in E 2, but a surprise awaits us] in our book on the various senses of words; for in one sense the "being" meant is "what a thing is" or a "this", and in another sense it means a quality or quantity or one of the other things that are predicated as these are.'

Here it is perfectly clear that, if E 2 had preceded, either Aristotle would have referred his readers to the full and detailed account of the meanings of 'being' there given, or he would not have enumerated these meanings at all, because every one would have them in mind. If, on the other hand, Z was written independently of the other books of the *Metaphysics* as a discussion of substance we can at once understand why it would have to begin by briefly determining the relation of substance to the other possible meanings of 'being', using the table of categories as its starting-point. For this purpose he referred to the lecture *On the Various Senses of Words*, which no doubt he often gave. This did not form part of the lectures on *Metaphysics* at that time, but was an independent inquiry. It is our so-called Book Δ, which received its present unnatural position not from Aristotle but from his editors. When, during the later rewriting, the book on substance and the account of potentiality were introduced into the places that they now occupy, this brought about an alteration in the whole structure of the *Metaphysics*; to put it more correctly, Aristotle introduced them with the intention of changing the structure in a definite fashion. The pattern of the new plan was the method followed in the discussion of substance (ZH), where the various senses of 'substance' (matter, form, universal, essence) provided the guiding thread by means of which Aristotle's conception of it was gradually built up, through its various historical and logical levels, before the reader's eyes. In the second version of the *Metaphysics* he applied this method to the conception of 'being' in its widest sense; and 'substance' now became just one of a whole series of meanings of 'being' in this broad sense. To the theory of pure, immaterial form he prefixed that of form in general, as the true reality and substance; in front of this again he put the doctrine of the various senses of 'being', from which he selects 'substance' as the only one that affects metaphysics. The selection consists in starting with the senses that signify nothing existential or independent, but only the accidental modifications *of* being or the attitudes of consciousness *to* being. In view of its merely preparatory nature this part is given very summarily (E 2–4). In the present version of the *Metaphysics* it forms the connexion between the earlier introduction (A–E 1) and the new body (ZHΘIM). Leading up to the main discussion, and sketching the structure of what is to follow, it was naturally the last part to be inserted. Its introduction converted the list of the senses of 'being' into the outline of the whole composition. We must realize, however, that this composition is the final stage in a long process of development—incomplete and provisional, indeed, even in this last version, but nevertheless bearing all the marks of the determination to make a great synthesis. The additions, insertions, and excisions, which originated mostly in this final stage, evince a unitary aim that was perfectly foreign to the original version—the construction of a theory of the manifold senses of 'being', a sort of ontological phenomenology, within which the old Platonic doctrine of transcendent and immaterial Form still remains as conclusion, but no longer holds the centre of interest.

I may here introduce a paragraph on the last chapter of Book Θ, which I have discussed in detail in a previous work.[1] This passage deals with the two meanings of truth; first, truth and falsity in the ordinary sense, when we call a judgement true or false according as it joins the predicate to the right subject or not; and secondly the truth of metaphysical statements of being, which do not arise from discursive thinking and hence are never true or false as discursive judgements are. The truth of metaphysical statements expressing a being that is not an object of

---

[1] *Ent. Metaph. Arist.*, p. 49.

experience rests, according to Aristotle, on a special intuitive form of apprehension, which resembles sense-perception more than discursive thinking in that it is a sort of intellectual vision, a pure 'contact and assertion'. This is the only remnant of Plato's contemplation of the Ideas that has survived in Aristotle's metaphysics. Why he discusses it here is explained by himself in E 4, where he shows that being in the common sense of the truth or falsity of a proposition is not part of the metaphysician's problem about being. Into this passage he inserted a later reference, which can be very simply recognized as such by the disturbance of the sentence-construction to which it has given rise; there is also, he says, a second kind of truth, intuitive apprehension, on which all general views of the universe depend, and this he is going to discuss later. The discussion is the final chapter of Book Θ. I have shown in my earlier book, following Schwegler, that this chapter is a subsequent addition to Book Θ, and that the reference to it in E 4 must have been inserted at the time when the chapter itself was attached. Aristotle introduces his account of intellectual intuition, and of the metaphysical sort of truth, at a fitting place, namely between the end of the doctrine of potentiality and the beginning of that of the reality of the supersensible, which was intended to follow immediately. This insertion, which must also have been made on the occasion of the introduction of ZHΘ, shows once again the attempt to arrange a gradual ascent up the scale of being to immaterial essence, and to make the whole work single in its aim, though constructed of such disparate materials. That was the spirit of Aristotle's final recension.

By good fortune our discovery of two separate versions of the preface to the theory of the supersensible, the earlier in M 9, and the later in M 1, enables us to test our hypothesis that the *Metaphysics* originally did not contain the doctrine of material sensible form.[1] If this supposition be correct, the later version must presuppose the books on substance, with their detailed analysis of sensible being and of immanent form (ἔνυλον εἶδος); whereas the earlier must proceed directly to the problem of transcendental being, as we should expect according to the early plan in Book B, and regard the world of sense (αἰσθητὴ οὐσία) as in no respect an object of 'the science that we are seeking'. It is necessary to examine these parallel versions once more from this point of view, and I print them side by side again for this purpose.

Later Version (M 1)	*Original Version* (M 9, 1086ᵃ21)

Later Version (M 1)

We have stated what is the substance of sensible things, dealing in the treatise on physics with matter, *and later with the substance which has actual existence.* Now since our inquiry is whether there is or is not besides the sensible substances any which is immovable and eternal, and, if there is, what it is, we must first consider what is said by others.

Original Version (M 9, 1086ᵃ21)

Regarding the first principles and the first causes and elements, the views expressed by those who discuss only sensible substance have been partly stated in our works on nature, and partly do not belong to the present inquiry; but the views of those who assert that there are other substances besides the sensible must be considered next after those we have been mentioning.

The original version, starting from the definition of metaphysics as the theory of the first principles and causes (which is usual in the oldest parts of the work), begins the doctrine of substance with Plato's division into sensible and supersensible. As in A and B, so here the discussion starts with the views of other thinkers. The materialistic teaching of the Presocratic philosophy of nature ('the views expressed by those who discuss *only* sensible substance') is partly referred to the *Physics*, and partly declared not to belong to the present inquiry. Here it is important to notice that Aristotle is not speaking of sensible substance itself, as he does in the later version. The view that sensible substance as such has any concern with metaphysics is still utterly foreign to him. Sensible reality belongs to physics; 'the views expressed by those who discuss only sensible substance have been partly stated in our works on nature.' Furthermore, these *views* 'do not belong to the present inquiry'; that is to say, they have already been criticized in Book A. To suppose that Aristotle is referring here to Books ZH is impossible; those books contain nothing whatever about the thinkers who admit no reality but what is perceptible to sense; and besides, it is not to be supposed that Aristotle would have confined himself to such a negative mode of expression, if he had previously given a detailed account of this very sensible reality in ZHΘ. The underlying view of this version is rather the simple alternative: either there is only sensible reality, and then there is no metaphysics, and the first science is physics; or there is something supersensible, and then there is also a science of that, namely metaphysics. Hence Aristotle turns at once to the philosophers who maintained the reality of the supersensible; that is to say, the school of Plato.

Between this stage of his development, when the problem still appeared to him as a simple dualism, and that represented by the version in M 1, comes the insertion of ZHΘ, which in large part opened metaphysics to sensible substance, and the expansion of this discipline into a science of the manifold senses of being. It is true that Aristotle still tells us, obviously borrowing the language of the oldest version, that sensible substance has already been discussed in the *Physics*; but he makes a qualification: 'dealing in the treatise on physics *with matter, and later with the substance which has actual existence.*' Whereas in the earlier version physics includes all being that is perceptible by sense, it is here confined to the examination of matter. This means that form and actual existence (ἡ κατ' ἐνέργειαν οὐσία) are to be assigned mainly to the science under consideration, which is metaphysics. Aristotle therefore removes the words 'and partly do not belong to the present inquiry', and replaces them with a reference to the newly introduced discussions of ZHΘ, which concern precisely the 'actual existence' of things perceptible by sense. This backward reference corresponds to the forward one inserted in Z 11, 1037ᵃ 10 ff., which calls attention to the account of supersensible reality to be given in Book M (see above, p. 199). Both of them belong to the later version, and are meant to unite what was originally separate. This also shows, though it scarcely needed proof, that the later version of the discussion of the supersensible (M 1–9) was intended for the latest *Metaphysics*, as enlarged by the introduction of ZHΘ. This is also indicated by the fact that both these parts are connected with the insertion of Book I.

But were these new passages simply 'interpolated'? Could Aristotle simply juxtapose a theory of sensible substance and an introduction originally intended to lead to an account of the supersensible? Would not insoluble contradictions necessarily follow? And since the transition from the introduction BΓE to the 'interpolated' portion has seemed smooth to all readers down to the present day, what is the principle that enabled him to connect the metaphysic of the transcendental with the doctrine of immanent entelechies? There really is such a link between the two stages, viz. the conception of being as such (ὂν ᾗ ὂν), by means of which he defines the object of metaphysics in the introduction. We have been accustomed to think of this conception as the seed out of which the manifold senses of being developed in Aristotle's mind like a flower; for does it not embrace both the pure act of divine thought and those lower forms of changing nature that are subject to becoming and dissolution, and is not he who studies being *as such* exempt from the necessity of confining himself to absolute being, and able to include in his researches the being of every sort of thing, even of the abstractions of the understanding? This is what the final form of the *Metaphysics* actually does, and that has betrayed us into supposing that the conception *could not have been* realized in any other way. We now see, however, that this is a mistake, though a very natural one. We can, in fact, show from the *Metaphysics* itself that there was an earlier stage in his development when he had not yet drawn this conclusion from the conception of being as such, when he did not regard metaphysics as the dialectical development of the manifold senses of being, and when he thought of its subject-matter simply and exclusively as the imperishable and eternal. The proof of this is K 1–8, a passage often declared spurious, but vindicated once and for all by our results.

I have shown in my earlier discussion of this invaluable document that certain tiny words, the frequent use of which betrays a stranger's hand, although the style is otherwise thoroughly Aristotelian, are the unconscious additions of a disciple who was taking down the lectures of the master. But as a source for Aristotle's doctrine the book is crystal-pure. It reproduces the three introductory books, ΒΓΕ, point for point throughout, usually in the same words, though in a much shorter form. It cannot be explained either as a preliminary sketch of the fuller version, or as a mere excerpt from it; it is distinct and independent. It must be a note taken of this part of the lectures on metaphysics during an earlier stage of their development; for, in spite of large resemblances, it differs characteristically from the fuller version in some respects.

When we examine the connexion between this earlier introduction and the main body of the work, which is what interests us mostly here, it becomes clear that this version belongs to a time before the interpolation of the books on substance, ZHΘ, when the introduction was followed immediately by the theory of the supersensible. In the later form of the *Metaphysics* we find a transitional passage (E 2–4) between the end of the introduction (E 1) and the beginning of the main part (Z 1). The same is true of the earlier (K 8, 1064^b 15–1065^a 26), but the characteristic feature of the later transition is absent here, namely the enumeration of the senses of being, which provide the framework of Books ZHΘ. It is true that here also Aristotle discusses, as he does in E 2–4, the two senses of being that he sets aside before entering on the main problem of metaphysics, (1) accidental being and (2) the truth or falsity of judgements, the former because it is not being proper at all, the latter because it is only an act of consciousness. But the classification that he announces in E 2, and carries out in the later version of the *Metaphysics* as we have it, receives no mention whatever in the older introduction. We are tempted at first to explain this by the brevity of the excerpt; but now that we have discovered in M 9, 1086^a 21 ff., the oldest version of the preface to the central portion of the work, and seen that it presupposes a *Metaphysics* not containing Books ZHΘ, it is no longer possible to imagine that we have here a mere play of chance. Moreover, there is another unmistakable sign of later revision in E 2–4, which is also absent here, and that is the reference that we find in E 4, 1027^b 28, to the subsequent insertion of the inquiry into the conception of metaphysical truth (Θ 10); this naturally does not occur in the parallel passage in K 8, 1065^a 24, because there was no Book Θ in the original *Metaphysics*.

Natorp considered K 1–8 spurious, on the ground that the conception of metaphysics therein contained is not to be found in the main part of the traditional *Metaphysics*.[1] He goes so far as to speak of a Platonizing author, and of the un-Aristotelian tendency of this work to exclude matter and all that is connected

[1] *Archiv für Geschichte der Philosophie*, vol. i, p. 178. The standard that he uses is the customary one, i.e. the conception of metaphysics in the books added during the composition of the second version (ZHΘ).

with it from the investigation. To him, with the presuppositions of that time, this observation was a serious ground for suspicion. To us the very same fact becomes a convincing proof of genuineness.[1] Metaphysics is here viewed as a science of the immaterial, and we have shown from the remains of the earliest version that this was the original notion. Nothing could be a more reliable test of the correctness of our conclusion than this restoration of the oldest of the introductory books to its true rights. Even the most secret doors of the enchanted castle spring open of their own accord, after long and hopeless efforts to break into them by force, now that we have discovered that the principle of development is the real key.

If we compare K 1–8 step by step with the later version, we find that in all the changes which he introduced in BΓE, Aristotle was actuated by the single purpose of adapting the old introduction to the new structure of the *Metaphysics*, which included material being as well as the other sort. This concession to the material world appears in the formulation of the very first fundamental problem (fifth in the whole list of problems), concerning the reality of the supersensible. We previously remarked that the antiquated impression made by Book B is due to the Platonic manner in which the problems are expressed; but we now see that in this matter K is still more antiquated and strict.[2] While even B passes beyond the boundaries of the phenomenal world in the very first problem, by asking whether, *apart from* the sensible, there is also a supersensible substance such as the Ideas, the version in K is more exclusive still. Aristotle here asks whether 'the science that we are seeking' deals with perceptible substances '*or not with them, but* with certain

---

[1] In my *Ent. Metaph. Arist.*, pp. 63 ff., I defended the genuineness of K 1–8 in detail against Natorp's rejection, and reached the conclusion that its philosophical content is worthy of Aristotle in every particular. The frequent use of the particle γε μήν, which perhaps reveals a hand other than Aristotle's, is nothing against the genuineness of the *content*; it is no doubt due to the disciple who took notes on Aristotle's lecture and prepared the present version. Nevertheless, I must withdraw my criticism of Natorp in so far as its aim was to explain away the traces of Platonism that he discovered. From the point of view of Aristotle's historical development they are completely unobjectionable, and in fact precisely·what our previous analysis would lead us to demand.

[2] Cf. pp. 195–196 above. The antiquatedness of B is therefore a characteristic that has survived *in spite of* the revision.

others'.[1] This excludes all possibility whatever that sensible substance should belong to metaphysics. On the contrary, sensible and supersensible being here constitute, just as we found them to do in M 9–10, a simple dualistic either-or.[2] In the revision this either-or becomes a not-only-but-also, as the latest state of the *Metaphysics* presents it to us in the co-ordination and superordination of the immanent and the transcendent forms.

We find the same emphatic either-or in the part of K where Aristotle discusses the aim of his ontological inquiry. 'It is in general hard to say whether one must assume that there is a separable substance besides the sensible substances (i.e. the substances in this world), or that these are the real things and Wisdom is concerned with them. For we seem to seek *another kind of substance*, and this is our problem, i.e. to see if there is something that can exist apart by itself and belongs to no sensible thing.'[3] By the 'something that can exist apart by itself' (χωριστὸν καθ' ἑαυτό) Aristotle here does not mean the concrete, particular existence of the phenomenal world, although this too is often spoken of as 'existing apart'; he is using the expression in the sense in which Plato's Ideas 'exist apart', as is shown by the qualification 'and belongs to no sensible thing' (μηδενὶ τῶν αἰσθητῶν ὑπάρχον). By this addition he explicitly eliminates all thought of the immanent forms (ἔνυλον εἶδος); in the same connexion the latter are said to be, so far as concerns their existence, perishable (φθαρτόν). On the other hand, it is *a priori* certain to him as a Platonist that the object of metaphysics—if there is such a science—must be an eternal,

---

[1] *Metaph.* B 2, 997ᵃ 34 = K 1, 1059ᵃ 39. I previously supposed that this dilemma was meant to indicate that the truth lies in the middle—metaphysics is the study of the Form, which includes both the substance of the world of sensible things and also supersensible reality, existing in the second without matter. But the passages that we are about to discuss seem to render this interpretation impossible (see especially K 2, 1060ᵃ 7), and it must be acknowledged that the exclusive formulation, 'either the sensible world or the supersensible', is absolutely essential to the general view implied in K. If Natorp had pursued throughout the whole *Metaphysics* the divergences of doctrine that he observed in K, he would not have declared this book spurious, but would have discovered the chronological and the inner differences between the two distinct sets of material, differences that can be satisfactorily explained only through supposing that Aristotle gradually developed away from Plato.

[2] See pp. 206–207 above.   [3] K 2, 1060ᵃ 7–13.

transcendent essence, having its being in itself (ἀΐδιος οὐσία χωρι-
στὴ καὶ καθ᾽ αὑτήν). He tells us that we must think of it as
analogous to Plato's Ideas, not to the objects of sense. Unless
there really is something of this sort, all that the best minds have
thought out must be mere sound and smoke. How could there
be any order in the world without it? Order implies something
eternal, transcendent, and enduring.[1] The emphatic nature of
these expressions differentiates them sharply from the later
version. Aristotle is here still quite close to Plato, and they
breathe a passionate advocacy of Plato's demand for a supersensible world—all the more impressive because it arises directly
out of the conviction that the reigning theory of Ideas is impossible.[2]

The eternal, unalterable reality, and the eternal laws of the
cosmos depending thereon, form, according to K 1–8, the presupposition of the possibility not merely of 'the science that we
are seeking', but even of any consistent logical thinking and any
absolute and enduring truths, since the world of sense is in
perpetual flux, and affords no foothold.[3] Thus the law of contradiction is established in an essentially ontological manner,
whereas the later version seems to omit the ontological passages

---

[1] K 2, 1060a 21: 'It would seem rather that the form or shape is a more important principle than [the matter]; but the form is perishable, so that there is
no eternal substance at all which can exist apart and independent. But this is
paradoxical; for such a principle and substance seems to exist and is sought by
nearly all the most refined thinkers as something that exists; for how is there
to be order unless there is something eternal and independent and permanent?'
See also K 2, 1060b 1–3.

[2] See the immediately preceding rejection of Plato's version of the supersensible, K 2, 1060a 13–18. This passage perhaps preserves more directly than
any other the Platonic postulate that lies at the root of Aristotle's metaphysics,
the postulate of the reality of the transcendental. It also shows that his
starting-point for the rehabilitation of the doctrine was that order in nature
which seemed to him inexplicable without the assumption of a transcendent
'good' as the first principle.

[3] K 6, 1063a 11. In my *Ent. Metaph. Arist.*, p. 82, I pointed out that Natorp
went too far when he ascribed to the author of K the view that in the earthly
and perishable there is no truth whatever; but I went too far in the opposite
direction when I denied that there was any difference at all between this and
Aristotle's usual account of truth. It must be allowed that this passage
emphasizes the eternity of cosmic reality, and bases the possibility of enduring
truths chiefly on that; whereas in Γ 5, 1010a 1 ff., on the contrary, the main
emphasis is on the possibility of obtaining definite propositions even about the
world of sense, and the cosmos and 'the nature that is changeless' are mentioned
only in second place (1010a 25).

for the most part. It is true that the conclusion of Book Γ says something about the connexion between the possibility of knowing permanent truths and the eternity and immovability of being; but, since this passage was lacking in some of the ancient manuscripts, it is obvious that we have here a section deleted by Aristotle during his recension, but discovered among his papers by the editors and published along with the rest. In any event, this section itself shows that the original version of Γ laid more emphasis on the metaphysical bases of the law of contradiction.[1] Both the ontological proof of the law, and the inclusion of these fundamental logical problems in metaphysics, were pieces of Platonic tradition. So was the question where one should discuss the matter of the objects of mathematics, and whether it belongs to first philosophy.[2] Actually, the discussion of it occurs in Book N, the close relation of which to K 1–8 is another sign of the age of both.

We have already seen that in Book B the nature of the problems is determined by the problems and content of Plato's metaphysics. Aristotle was somewhat superficial in altering this part, and hence it has not lost its fundamentally Platonic character. Apart from the fact that in two places he actually left the old 'we' of his Platonic days,[3] of which no other trace remains in the new version, he obviously did not alter or modify any passages except those that explicitly contradicted his new view

---

[1] Γ 8, 1012ᵇ 22—end of the book, was lacking in some of the ancient manuscripts according to Alexander *In Arist. metaph.*, p. 341, l. 30 (Hayduck).

[2] K 1, 1059ᵇ 15–21. I have discussed the conception of 'the matter of the objects of mathematics' in *Ent. Metaph. Arist.*, p. 74, and shown, contrary to Natorp, that it belongs to Plato's later metaphysics. I did not, however, fully answer the question why this problem is stated only in K, and not also in B. This can be explained if we observe that, as I had already recognized at that time, the discussion of the problem comes in N 2, 1088ᵇ 14. Both N and K belong to the original *Metaphysics*, and the one is therefore the fulfilment of the promise given in the other. Now the later version of these matters (B and M 1–9) largely suppresses the question about the elements of supersensible substance, as has been shown above (p. 192). This question was bound up with Plato's late doctrine of the existence of numbers, &c., as separate substances. In his mature period Aristotle rid himself of this doctrine, and he then deleted the whole complex of which it was a part.

[3] See p. 175 above. The fact that Book B was revised in order to appear as part of the introduction to the later version of the *Metaphysics*, whereas the criticism of the Ideas in A 9 was meant to disappear entirely, constitutes a complete explanation why so few traces of this 'we' remain in B. Those that do are simply oversights.

of metaphysics. The number and nature of the problems remained in general untouched. There is just one place where he
inserted a new one, and this is characteristic, for it concerns the
content of the inserted books, ZHΘ. Just before the last problem (B 6, 1002^b 33) he raises the question of matter and of the
actuality and potentiality of the principles, and here he also
takes account of perceptible reality. Now since, as Natorp
observed, this question does not appear in K 1–8, we can only
conclude that Aristotle inserted the new problem when he was
altering the three introductory books to make them lead up to
the theory of immanent form and of potentiality and actuality.
Book K, on the contrary, is still strictly Platonic in so far as it
divorces the notion of pure being from all matter and equates it
with that which is selfexistent, unmoved, and transcendent.
Moreover, whereas in the last version the criticism of the Ideas
was removed from A 9 to the new Book M, the earlier form of
the introduction presupposes the original state of affairs, in
which the criticism was still in the first book, since it refers us
for the refutation of the Ideas to what has preceded![1] This
proves that the three introductory books, BΓE, also underwent
alteration and had a new notion of metaphysics introduced into
them. We have now recovered the earlier and the last version of
almost the whole *Metaphysics*.

It can be shown, however, that even the earlier version of the
introduction (K 1–8) is not the original form of the *Metaphysics*.
We have seen that in K 1–8 metaphysics is described as the
science of that which is unmoved and eternal and transcendent.
We also find there, however, the definition of it as the science of
being as such (ὂν ᾗ ὄν), though not developed, as it is in the later
version, into a science of the manifold meanings of being including the perceptible being of movable nature. This combination of the two definitions in K 1–8 is a serious difficulty, and
becomes only too painfully obvious in the later version of E,
which in its present revised form is meant to introduce the
science of the manifold meanings of being. Since the earlier and
the later versions do not differ in this respect, but only in the

[1] K 1, 1059^b 3, presupposes the refutation of the Ideas in A 9. B 2, 997^b 3,
on the other hand, the corresponding passage in the later version, presupposes
only the historical explanation of the Idea-theory in A 6, which remained in
place when the refutation was removed to M 4–5.

extension that they assign to the notion of being, we shall not fall into error if we use them both together in what follows.

In E 1 (= K 7) Aristotle explains what he understands by a science of being as such. All sciences inquire into certain causes and principles of things. As examples he mentions medicine and gymnastics, and—to take one with a more developed method—mathematics, i.e. the examples usual in Plato's theory of science and method. Each of these sciences marks off systematically a definite sphere of reality (ὄν τι) and a definite genus (γένος τι) and studies the resulting limited complex of facts. None of them discusses the being of its object; they all either presuppose it on the ground of experience, as do natural science and medicine; or, like mathematics with its axioms, they start from particular definitions. Their demonstrations, which differ from each other only in degree of accuracy, deal solely with the properties and functions following from these definitions or from facts evident to sense. The metaphysician, on the other hand, inquires about being precisely as being. He examines the presuppositions of these sciences, of which they themselves are neither willing nor able to give an account.

Aristotle supplements this explanation at the beginning of Book Γ (= K 3), where he brings out even more fully and clearly the distinction between first philosophy as universal science and the special sciences, between being as such and its particular realms. Here he treats being not as a sort of object separate and distinct from others, but as the common point of reference for all states, properties, and relations, that are connected with the problem of reality. As the mathematician, according to him, looks at all things solely from the point of view of quantity, so the philosopher studies everything that belongs to being as such, whereas the physicist, for example, considers it only as in motion. Many things 'are' only because they are the affection or the state or the motion or the relation of some one being— they derive from something that 'is' simply. In Plato's school the method of referring (ἀναγωγή) all the affections (πάθη) of being to something single and common (ἕν τι καὶ κοινόν) was division in the form of oppositions (ἐναντιώσεις), which were referred to certain most general or 'first' distinctions in being. Aristotle presupposes a knowledge of the special work of the school in this field, and of its literature. He means the opposition between the one and the many, the same and the other, the like and the unlike, in short the whole sphere of Platonic dialectic, as we find it in the inquiries about being and the one (ὄν καὶ ἕν) in Book I, or again an inquiry like that on the ultimate principles of thought, the laws of contradiction and of excluded middle, which he treats in Γ. It is true that the connexion of these questions with his own theory of substance is only mediate, but obviously he was trying to find a definition of metaphysics that would make room for the traditional dialectic. To Plato dialectic was as such ontology. To Aristotle it was rather a practical and historical question whether this whole logic of being was under all circumstances to be included in first philosophy. His original metaphysics was theology, the doctrine of the most perfect being; it was hard to combine abstract dialectic with this once the Ideas were gone. But he tried to link them up by means of their common relation to being as such (ὄν ᾗ ὄν).

Whereas in this connexion the highest form of philosophy appears as the universal science, it is immediately followed by a different picture in E 1 (= K 7), where Aristotle is trying to distinguish metaphysics, physics, and mathematics, by their objects. He here divides sciences into theoretical, practical, and productive. Physics is a theoretical science; it studies the being that is capable of motion, and therefore regards the conceptual essence and form only in so far as it is joined with matter. To abstract from the matter would always be a mistake in physics. Even psychology must be pursued in this manner, so far as we are concerned with the realm of the psychophysical. Mathematics is also a theoretical science. Aristotle raises the question, indeed, whether its objects really have an unmoved, separate, and independent reality, as the Academy maintained. (He here decides against this doctrine, while at the same time adopting the Academy's tripartite division of theoretical philosophy and its assignment of mathematics to a place between ontology and physics.) But, however that may be, mathematics at any rate *regards* its objects *as* unmoved and independent (ᾗ ἀκίνητα καὶ ᾗ χωριστὰ θεωρεῖ), which only makes it clearer that the study of real unmoved and transcendent being (if there is any such) will be the task of a theoretical science. But what is this science?

It cannot be physics, for the objects of that, although independent (χωριστά) are not unmoved; nor can it be mathematics,
for its object, while partly unmoved, is not independent and
separate. Only the highest form of philosophy studies a sort of
being that is both independent and unmoved.[1] This definition
by itself would suffice to conclude that Aristotle is thinking of
the unmoved mover, and he says himself in the next sentence
that the principles he means are the causes of the visible divine
things (αἴτια τοῖς φανεροῖς τῶν θείων), in virtue of which he
calls metaphysics theology (θεολογική).

But now this determination of the nature of metaphysics
purely by means of its subject-matter, namely unmoved and
transcendent being, makes it one special science among others.
Whereas elsewhere it is considered as the universal science of
being as such, and sharply contrasted with the sciences that
examine only a special kind of being (ὄν τι καὶ γένος τι),[2] here
it is itself merely the knowledge of the highest kind of being
(περὶ τὸ τιμιώτατον γένος). Its object is said to be being of
this kind (τοιαύτη φύσις), and it is to be looked for in a particular genus of reality, namely in the cosmic region of what is
visible but imperishable. The contradiction is undeniable, and
Aristotle himself observed it. In a note that obviously breaks
the train of thought, and must therefore be a later addition, he
makes the following remarks.

'One might raise the question whether first philosophy is universal, or

[1] *Metaph.* E 1, 1026ᵃ 13, as corrected by Schwegler: 'For physics deals with
things which exist separately [the MSS. have 'inseparably'] but are not immovable, and some parts of mathematics deal with things which are immovable
but presumably do not exist separately, but as embodied in matter; while the
first science deals with things which both exist separately and are immovable.'
The conjecture of some reader has found its way into the manuscripts—a reader
who took 'separately' as meaning 'transcendentally', and realized that this
would not be true of the forms 'embodied in matter' of which the visible world
consists. But 'separately' means here merely 'independently', and Aristotle
uses the word in this sense even of perceptible things. The object of metaphysics, however, since according to this definition it is both independent and
unmoved, must exist 'separately' in the sense of 'transcendentally', because
only the supersensible exhibits both characteristics at once.

[2] *Metaph.* E 1, 1025ᵇ 8: 'all these sciences mark off some particular being—
some genus, and inquire into this, but not into being simply nor as being.'
Contrast 1026ᵃ 19 on metaphysics as the science of divine things: 'it is obvious
that if the divine is present anywhere, it is present in *things of this sort*. And the
highest science must deal with the *highest genus*', i.e. the divine.

deals with one genus, i.e. some one kind of being (φύσιν τινὰ μίαν) ; for not even the mathematical sciences are all alike in this respect—geometry and astronomy deal with a certain particular kind of thing, while universal mathematics applies alike to all. We answer that if there is no substance other than those which are formed by nature, natural science will be the first science; but if there is an immovable substance, this is 'prior' to the world of sensible appearances, and metaphysics is the first science, and *universal* just because it is *first*. And it will belong to this to consider being *as being*—both what it is and the attributes which belong to it as being.'[1]

This gloss does not remove the contradiction. On the contrary, it only makes it more obvious. In attempting here to combine the two definitions he understands by a universal science a science of the 'first' object, which is a principle in a more comprehensive sense than are the other kinds of being; but in Γ 1 and the beginning of E universal meant that which does not refer to any particular part of being at all, and Aristotle could not and does not assert that the immaterial movers of the stars are not 'particular beings' nor 'one sort of being'. One might perhaps be inclined to suspect that neither the problem nor its solution, which looks so much like an observation made *en passant*, comes from Aristotle himself; but since it also appears in the other version in K 8, and since it expresses a contradiction that is really present, there is nothing for it but to admit that the philosopher did not find the solution of the problem, or at any rate that it did not occur to him until after the two versions were already fused together.

These two accounts of the nature of metaphysics certainly did not arise out of one and the same act of reflection. Two fundamentally different trains of thought are here interwoven. It is obvious at once that the theological and Platonic one is the older of the two, and this not merely on historical grounds but also because it is far more schematic and less developed. It is a product of the Platonic tendency to make a sharp division between the sensible and the supersensible spheres. When metaphysics is defined as the study of being as being, on the other hand, reality is regarded as one single, unified series of levels, and this therefore is the more Aristotelian account of the two, that is to say, the one

---

[1] E 1, 1026ᵃ 23–32. Bonitz points out the contradiction in his commentary. He finds no explanation.

that corresponds to the last and most characteristic stage of his thought. At first he proceeded strictly in the direction indicated by Plato, that is, he retained the supersensible world as the object of first philosophy, as we learn from the manifesto *On Philosophy*, and merely replaced the transcendental Ideas with the first mover, which, being unmoved, eternal, and transcendent, possessed the properties that being must have according to Plato. This, his earliest, metaphysics was exclusively a science of the being that is unmoved and transcendent, i.e. theology. It was not the science of being as such.

This result is further confirmed by the treatise commonly referred to simply as 'the theology', namely Book Λ of the *Metaphysics*. Bonitz saw that, whereas one would expect this book to give us the conclusion of A–Θ, it actually stands in no relation to the others. This is because it is really a small independent work. The style and the choice of ideas show that it is an isolated lecture, composed for a special occasion, giving us not merely the part of metaphysics that is called theology but something much more comprehensive—a complete system of metaphysics *in nuce*. Aristotle here offers us a compact sketch of his whole theoretical philosophy, beginning with the doctrine of substance and ending with that of God. It is obviously his intention, not to introduce his hearers to technical inquiries, but to lift them out of themselves with the selfcontained swing of his great picture of the whole. With confident blows of the hammer he chisels magnificent sentences, which even to-day we involuntarily read aloud, in spite of the abbreviated nature of notes made for oral delivery. 'The creative activity of thought is life.' 'All things are ordered towards an end.' 'On this principle hang the heavens and nature.' The conclusion, where he addresses the Platonic dualists in the words of Odysseus ('the rule of many is not good; one ruler let there be'), is positively stirring in effect. It is a document unique of its kind, for here, and here alone in his lectures, Aristotle boldly sketches his picture of the universe in its totality, disregarding all questions of detail. At the same time it is invaluable as a source for the history of his development, for in date it belongs to the theological period whose existence we have demonstrated. It enables us to see what relation the doctrine of immanent forms had to that of the transcendental mover before the first-named became a part of metaphysics itself.

The lecture is sharply divided into two unequal portions. The first of these (cc. 1–5) discusses the doctrine of sensible reality; its analysis results in the conceptions of matter, form, potency, and act. The second (cc. 6–10) begins straight away with the speculative idea of the unmoved mover and with the assertion of a supersensible reality. Unlike the second, the first part is not an end in itself; it is there simply for the sake of the second, to which it serves as foundation. From the world of moving things, which he describes as forms developing and realizing themselves in matter, Aristotle ascends to the unmoved source and end of their motion, the form of all forms, pure act, the form that is creative and free of all matter. With this subject he therefore spends almost twice as much time as with that of the first part. To a casual glance the construction seems to be the same as in the later presentation of metaphysics. In both the doctrine of substance and of actuality precedes theology, and the earlier part of Λ is in essentials parallel to the content of Books ΖΗΘ. But the decisive consideration is that in Λ the notion of metaphysics is confined to the later part; the earlier is not reckoned as belonging thereto. The conclusion of the first part runs 'We have stated, then, what are the principles of sensible things and how many they are'.[1] The second begins 'Since there were three kinds of substance, two of them physical and one unmovable, regarding the latter we must assert that it is necessary that there should be an eternal unmovable substance' (οὐσία). Whereas later Aristotle describes the two kinds of sensible reality as 'in a sense' the concern of physics,[2] he here calls them 'physical' without qualification. The unmoved and eternal, on the other hand, is the object of metaphysics without qualification, just as it is in the earlier version of the introduction and in Book Ν, which we have shown to be early.[3] In exactly the same

[1] *Metaph.* Λ 5, 1071ᵇ 1.

[2] *Metaph.* Ζ 11, 1037ᵃ 14: 'Since in a sense the inquiry about perceptible substances is the work of physics, i.e. of second philosophy.'

[3] The determination of 'the science that we are seeking' by means of the qualities of eternity, independence, and permanence, which must belong to its object in accordance with the example set by the theory of Ideas, appears, as we have seen, not merely in the older version of the introduction (K 2, 1060ᵃ 26),

way he here says simply that sensible reality is perishable, and infers that, if there exists nothing but the forms immanent in sensible things, everything in the universe is necessarily subject to the Heraclitean flux.[1] Books K and Λ also agree in recognizing as the object of 'the science that we are seeking' only the transcendental, that which is not immanent in any sensible thing.[2] The three original kinds of being are clearly apportioned between physics and metaphysics. The two kinds that belong to the sensible world, the imperishable substance of the heavenly bodies and the perishable substance of plants, animals, &c., are assigned to physics without any limitation, because they are bound up with matter and motion; unmoved substance is the object of 'another science', metaphysics.[3]

Joining all these observations together, we may say that Book Λ represents the stage that we have discovered to come before the traditional metaphysics, a stage that was still purely Platonic and did not recognize the doctrine of sensible substance as an integral part of first philosophy. In Aristotelian language, metaphysics as Λ understands it does not study the whole category of substance, but takes a particular part of it. Its object is confined to the part of the category of substance that is perfect and good, namely God or reason.[4] It seeks for a tran-

but also in the early A 2, 982ᵇ 28–ᵃ 11, where this science is from the first assumed to be theology, as it is in the dialogue *On Philosophy*. That Book N belongs to the oldest stratum of the *Metaphysics* was proved above, pp. 189 ff. Hence it is especially important that in its opening sentences (1087ᵃ 30) this book is just as definite as Book Λ in contrasting the conception of metaphysics as the science of the 'unchangeable substances' with physics as the theory of the world of motion. Aristotle is referring to the metaphysics of the Platonists, the doctrine of Ideal Numbers (hence the plural 'substances'); but the contrast between the two sciences, based on the absolute distinctness of their objects, is obviously entirely accepted by him.

[1] Sensible substances, with the exception of the heavenly bodies, are described simply as perishable in Λ 1, 1069ᵃ 31, and 6, 1071ᵇ 6; cp. K 2, 1060ᵃ22. The later account in Z 8, 1033ᵇ 5, and H 3, 1043ᵇ 15, is much more complex: 'must be destructible without being ever in course of being destroyed, and must have come to be without ever being in course of coming to be'. Here the world of appearances, which to Aristotle was originally just changeable, has been thoroughly penetrated with the idea that it too partakes of the unchangeable because of the forms that hold sway in it.

[2] *Metaph.* K 2, 1060ᵃ 12: 'existing apart by itself and belonging to no sensible thing.' Cf. Λ 6, 1071ᵇ 19, and 7, 1073ᵃ 4.

[3] Λ 1, 1069ᵃ 30 and 36.

[4] For the view that the good in the category of substance is God or reason see *Eth. Nic.* I. 4, 1096ᵃ 19 ff., esp. ᵃ 24, and cf. *Eth. Eud.* I. 8, 1217ᵇ 30, and

scendental entity such as Plato's Idea, combining absolute reality (οὐσία) with absolute value (ἀγαθόν). According to Λ values and realities are two separate ascending series, converging towards the top. They meet at the point where the highest value (ἄριστον) coincides with the purest reality (οὐσία). This is the Platonic notion of the most perfect being (*ens perfectissimum*), which we have already found set out in the proof of God's existence in the dialogue *On Philosophy*.

The second and still more important thing to notice is the position of the doctrine of immanent forms. In Book Λ we can at last see clearly how this vital part of Aristotle's philosophy was related to theology while it was still a part of physics. The gradual ascent from sensible to pure supersensible form, which later took place within metaphysics, is effected in Λ by the primitive device of letting metaphysics, as the science of the unmoved and transcendental, simply rest externally on physics, the science of the movable and immanent. By the logical manipulation of the objects of sensible experience physics obtains the conceptions of form and entelechy, which it distinguishes from matter and potency, and the relations of which to these other conceptions it determines. It then hands them over to metaphysics. Whereas physics, however, is never able to abstract from the moment of matter and motion, which in experience are always found along with the form, metaphysics, standing on its shoulders, reaches up to the conception of a highest and immaterial form, on which nature, as a totality, 'depends' and in which alone physics receives its completion. With reference to its function as the summit of the system of physical movements this form is called the first mover. Here we come upon the earliest form of Aristotle's theology—the doctrine that physics is to be completed by a transcendent 'end' (τέλος), towards which all the visible motion in the world is directed, and by which the phenomena of nature are 'saved'.

Although the real proof of the early date of Λ is its form, which exactly fits the results of our analysis of the other books,[1]

Metaph. Λ 7, 1072ᵃ 34. Thus the original metaphysics was the science of pure and perfect being and of the highest good, not, like the later, of all kinds and senses of being.

[1] Chapter 8, which was inserted later on, is treated below in a separate discussion.

confirmation is to be found in certain of its external relations to them. Whereas its relation to the final version of the *Metaphysics*, as we have it, is entirely negative, it evinces the closest connexion with the fragments of the original version, to which it stands near in time, and especially with Book N. Bonitz failed to notice this because he was looking only for connecting links between Λ and the unified series of books that precedes it. This series, however, and the plan of it, are later than Λ, whereas we have shown that N, although in position it comes afterwards, is part of the earliest state of the *Metaphysics*, and obviously precedes Λ in time. In any event it would be natural to conjecture that in a merely occasional discourse, intended to give only a short summary of his whole metaphysical view, Aristotle would make use of his lecture-notes. And in fact Λ is little more than an extract from his more detailed esoteric lecture, so far as the remains of the original *Metaphysics* enable us to judge. It is true that we do not possess the really positive part of the philosophy of the supersensible, i.e. the doctrine of God, either in the earlier or in the later version; but the preceding critical portion, which was directed against the metaphysics of the other Academicians, was used liberally as a source of this discourse, and presumably the positive part of Λ's theology had exactly the same relation to the lost theology of the original *Metaphysics*, that is, was simply an excerpt therefrom. We may make the relation between Λ and N clearer by setting side by side some of the passages that are dependent on each other.

N 4, 1092ᵃ 9

If, then, it is equally impossible *not to put the good among the first principles* and to put it among them in this way, evidently the principles are not being correctly described. . . . *Nor does any one conceive the matter correctly if he compares the principles of the universe to that of animals and plants,* on the ground that *the more complete* always comes from the indefinite and incomplete—which is what leads this thinker to say that this is also true of the first prin-

Λ 7, 1072ᵇ 30

Those who suppose, as the Pythagoreans and Speusippus do, *that supreme beauty and goodness are not present in the beginning, because the beginnings both of plants and of animals* are causes, but beauty and completeness are in the effects of these, *are wrong in their opinion.* For the seed comes from other individuals which are prior and complete, *and the first thing is not seed but the complete being; e.g. we must say that before the seed there is a man,* —not the man produced from the

ciples of reality, so that the One it-self is not even an existing thing. This is incorrect, for even in this world of animals and plants the principles from which these come are complete; *for it is a man that produces a man, and the seed is not first.*

seed, but another from whom the seed comes.

It is obvious at first glance that one of these passages must have been influenced by the other. Although Λ mentions Speusippus by name, while N attacks him anonymously, there can be no possible doubt that N is the original and more complete version. It is much more precise. It brings out more clearly the fact that the 'principles of animals and plants', of which both accounts speak, were held by Speusippus to provide an analogy to the 'principles of the universe', and that this is not a strict inference but a mere comparison (παρεικάζειν). The argument from the evolution of organisms to a corresponding evolution of the universe appears to Aristotle as a 'transition to another genus'. The account in Λ does not even mention the questionable logic of this argument; it only remarks in passing, 'because the beginnings both of plants and of animals', &c. But the evolutionist theory is not true even of organisms—this is the second part of the account—because the first thing is not the seed but the actual living man, he being prior to the seed. At the beginning, therefore, comes pure actuality, not potency or matter. The influence of N also appears at the end of the lecture.

N 3, 1090^b 13

Again, if we are not too easily satisfied, we may, regarding all number and the objects of mathematics, press this difficulty, *that they contribute nothing to one an-other, the prior to the posterior;* for if number did not exist, none the less spatial magnitudes would exist for those who maintain the exis-tence of the objects of mathe-matics only, and if spatial magni-tudes did not exist, soul and sen-sible bodies would exist. *But the ob-served facts show that nature is not a series of episodes, like a bad tragedy.*

Λ 10, 1075^b 37

And those who say mathe-matical number is first and go on to generate one kind of substance after another and give different principles for each, *make the sub-stance of the universe a mere series of episodes (for one substance has no influence on another* by its existence or non-existence), and they give us many governing principles; but the world refuses *to be governed badly.* 'The rule of many is not good; one ruler let there be.'

This makes it clear that the whole concluding portion of Book Λ was influenced by the polemic against Speusippus in N 3. While writing this part of his sketch Aristotle had his earlier technical work before him, or at any rate it was very present to his mind. Here too there can be no doubt that the original version was N and not the much briefer passage in Λ. In Book N 'the prior contribute nothing to the posterior' is more clearly put. Its vivid expressions for the various levels of being according to Speusippus degenerate in Λ into the obscure statement: 'for one substance has no influence on another by its existence or non-existence.' We know that Speusippus held that every kind of being has its own principles, one for numbers, another for magnitudes, another for the soul, and so on, and that between these principles there is no further connexion.[1] These fine distinctions are clearly reproduced in N: on Speusippus' view numbers might wholly disappear, although they are the highest principle, without affecting the existence of magnitudes, which come next, and similarly magnitudes could go without in any way changing the existence of consciousness or of the extended world. Aristotle aptly calls this a nature composed of disconnected scenes like a bad tragedy. In Λ the omission of the last phrase makes the picture of 'a nature without connexion between its scenes' obscure to the point of incomprehensibility. Instead of it he here switches over to the magnificent simile of the monarch and the many rulers, which makes an equally striking picture of the structureless anarchy of Speusippus' theory of the first principles. Why does he drop the simile with which he began? Precisely because he no longer feels it vividly enough to do it full justice. He simply produces it from his store as something ready-made and quite familiar.

Chapters one and two of Book N were also used in the composition of Λ. The keynote of N 1 is the same as that of the last chapter of Λ—polemic against Plato's dualism of first principles. The rest will be obvious if we juxtapose them.

N 1, 1087ᵃ 29	Λ 10, 1075ᵃ 25
All philosophers make the first principles contraries. . . . But since there cannot be anything prior to	We must not fail to observe how many impossible or paradoxical results confront those who hold

[1] *Metaph.* Z 2, 1028ᵇ 21.

the first principle of all things, the principle cannot be the principle and yet be an attribute of something else. To suggest this is like saying that the white is a first principle, not as anything else but as white, but yet that it is predicable of a subject, i.e. that its being white presupposes its being something else; this is absurd, for then that subject will be prior. *But all things which are generated from their contraries involve an underlying subject*; a subject, then, must be present in the case of contraries, if anywhere. All contraries, then, are always predicable of a subject, and none can exist apart. . . . *But these thinkers make one of the contraries matter, some making the unequal*—which they take to be the essence of plurality—*matter for the equal,*[1] *and others making plurality matter for the One.*

different views from our own, and what are the views of the subtler thinkers, and which views are attended by fewest difficulties. *All make all things out of contraries.* But neither 'all things' nor 'out of contraries' is right; nor do these thinkers tell us how all the things in which the contraries are present can be made out of the contraries; for contraries are not affected by one another. *Now for us this difficulty is solved naturally by the fact that there is a third element. These thinkers however make one of the two contraries matter; this is done for instance by those who make the unequal matter for the equal, or the many matter for the one.*

N 4, 1091^b 35

It follows, then, that *all things partake of the bad except one—the One itself* . . . (^{b}30) These absurdities follow, and it also follows that *the contrary element . . . is the bad—itself.*

Λ 10, 1075^a 34

Further, all things, except the one, will, on the view we are criticizing, partake of evil; for the bad itself is one of the two elements.

Book Λ concludes with an impressive account of the devious consequences of dualism as upheld by the Academy, which serves as a foil to the strict monarchy of Aristotle's doctrine of the thought that thinks itself. This part is nothing but a mosaic of isolated sentences and ideas from N 1. It is true that it slightly popularizes and simplifies the highly differentiated material of Book N, but the main argument of that book against the dualist theory of the principles remains visible everywhere: the contraries must inhere in a third thing as a substratum, in accordance with the Aristotelian doctrine of form and privation, which require matter in order to change into each other. Λ

[1] Omitting τῷ ἑνί.

simply asserts the *tertium dabitur*; N proves it. For us, Aristotle triumphantly exclaims, the problem is solved without difficulty, for there is a third thing: and that is not matter, the substratum of contrary states, but absolute thought, the form that is without matter and hence not liable to any change or to any contrary. The inevitable consequence of the rejection of dualism is not materialism but the absolute monarchy of mind.

CHAPTER IX

THE ORIGINAL *ETHICS*

THE key to the understanding of Aristotle's ethics lies in the problem of the relation between the *Nicomachean* and the *Eudemian* versions. The so-called *Magna Moralia* may be disregarded. It is simply a collection of excerpts from the two other works; its author was a Peripatetic who used the longer presentations in order to make a brief handbook for lectures. In practice the *Nicomachean Ethics* has always predominated over the other main treatise almost without interference. The *Eudemian* has remained entirely in the background; its only use has been to help occasionally in the interpretation of difficult passages. There is good reason for this procedure, for the *Nicomachean Ethics* is decidedly superior in completeness of construction, clarity of style, and maturity of thought. Even in antiquity men discussed the *Nicomachean* only, and neglected the *Eudemian*, and the latter is still almost virgin soil. Recent years have seen a commendable move towards better things, but, so far as can be observed, it has not yet had much effect.

In the last century an event occurred which reinforced the natural preference of scholars for the better work: Spengel, the celebrated Aristotelian and reviver of ancient rhetoric, declared the *Eudemian Ethics* to be spurious.[1] His famous article, which immediately obtained universal acceptance and still holds the field for the most part to-day, expressed the view that this work was not merely published by Aristotle's pupil Eudemus of Rhodes, but also written by him. While its frequent and remarkable correspondences with the *Nicomachean Ethics* could only be explained as due to a close following of Aristotle's doctrine and of its formulation in that work, he held that in its deviations, which are considerable, the *Eudemian Ethics* betrays the individuality of Eudemus. The *Nicomachean Ethics* was so much better in many respects, and so much richer and riper as a whole, that it was impossible to imagine what could have caused Aristotle to write such a much less happy replica. The

[1] *Abh. d. bayr. Akad. d. Wiss.*, vol. iii (1841), pp. 534 ff.

deterioration was therefore ascribed to the pupil. Above all, the theological derivation of morality in the *Eudemian Ethics* seemed incompatible with the prevailing idea of Aristotle.[1] Its differences from the other work in this respect certainly do require explanation. It was thought that they should be connected with the personal devoutness of Eudemus, about which, however, nothing was known except that he was presumed to be the author of a history of theology,[2] which is scarcely to be taken as an expression of living, personal religion, especially as he also wrote a history of mathematics and astronomy. Mainly because of the belief that he is the author, there has grown up a notion of 'the pious Eudemus' which agrees very badly with the positive spirit of the Peripatetic school after Aristotle.[3]

However that may be, the two German editions now available, that of Fritzsche in 1851 and that of Susemihl in 1884, both entitle this work *Eudemi Rhodii Ethica*; and the valuable English commentaries on the *Nicomachean Ethics* by Grant, Stewart, and Burnet, as well as the German text by Apelt, all regard the other *Ethics* as a work of Eudemus.

The tradition gives no support to this supposition. It is true that the problem of the three books common to both *Ethics* gave rise in antiquity to the theory that they belong to Eudemus and were transferred to the *Nicomachean Ethics* to fill a gap;[4] but the usual view was the opposite, since they do not appear in the manuscripts of the *Eudemian Ethics*. This must have been so as early as the Alexandrian period, for the list of Aristotelian works known (and presumably actually in the library) at Alexandria during the time of Callimachus' pupil Hermippus mentions only an *Ethics* in five books, which is obviously the *Eudemian* with-

---

[1] Zeller, *Aristotle and the Earlier Peripatetics*, vol. 2 (1897), pp. 422–7. Grant, *The Ethics of Aristotle*, vol. i, pp. 23 ff.

[2] Zeller, op. cit., p. 417, n. 3. If Eudemus discussed in this work the cosmogonies of Orpheus, Homer, Hesiod, Acusilaus, Pherecydes, and Epimenides, and of the Zoroastrian and other oriental theologies, he did so owing to the stimulus of Aristotle's remarks on the subject in his first book *On Philosophy*.

[3] For 'the pious Eudemus' see C. Piat, *Aristoteles*, authorized German edition by Emil Prinz zur Oettingen-Spielberg (Berlin, 1907), p. 394. Gercke finds him remarkably religious for a Peripatetic (*Einl. i. d. kl. Alt.*, vol. ii³, p. 407).

[4] Aspasius, *Comm. in Arist. eth. Nic.*, p. 151, l. 24, and p. 161, l. 9, in Heylbut.

out the three that were taken over later from the *Nicomachean*.[1]
Two of the traditional hypotheses to explain the two versions
and titles betray their lateness by their mere ignorance. Thus
Cicero suggested that the *Nicomachean* might well be by Nicomachus—a conclusion which indeed would be inevitable if the
Eudemian were by *Eudemus*.[2] This is a mere invention, as his
threadbare argument for it shows: why should not the son of a
famous father have been himself a capable man for once?
Equally late and amateurish is the interpretation of the two
titles as meaning the *Ethics to Nicomachus* and *to Eudemus*. In
Aristotle's day the dedication of treatises was unknown, as is
clear when we contrast his genuine works with the spurious
Rhetorica ad Alexandrum, to which some naïve and unhistorical
person, completely mistaking the literary custom of the fourth
century, has prefixed a foreword and dedication. Not to mention that the two *Ethics* have no dedications and are not published works at all, but lecture-notes

The general view of earlier antiquity seems to favour simply
the publication, by Nicomachus and Eudemus, of two sets of
Aristotle's lecture-notes. There is nothing against the supposition that Aristotle left behind him more than one version of his
lecture on ethics, as we have discovered that he did with metaphysics. Here as there it is *a priori* probable that the earlier of
the two versions is the one of which only fragments remain. The
decision of the question must come in the main from the discovery of the inner logic that controls the development of Aristotle's ethical problems. Kapp has made a beginning of this
kind of inquiry in a keen and careful piece of work that is far
the best thing written on the *Eudemian Ethics* and their philosophical position during recent years.[3] He compares the two

---

[1] In spite of recent doubts, this seems to me to be proved by the mention of
'five books of ethics' in Diogenes' list, which goes back to Hermippus. That
Hesychius' list mentions ten books is no contradiction, even if both lists derive
from Hermippus' catalogue. Hesychius is obviously referring to the *Nicomachean
Ethics*, and either Hermippus himself mentioned this as well as the *Eudemian*
or else the five was later altered to ten. The statement in Diogenes is confirmed
by the fact that the manuscripts of the *Eudemian Ethics* give only five books.

[2] See the references for this and the following theory in Susemihl's edition of
the *Eudemian Ethics*, pp. xviii ff., and in Von der Mühll's dissertation *De. Ar.
eth. Eudem. auctoritate* (Göttingen, 1909), pp. 25 ff.

[3] E. Kapp, *Das Verhältnis der eudemischen zur nikomachischen Ethik*,
Freiburg, 1912. Dissertation.

Ethics afresh, and comes to the conclusion that the *Eudemian* is to be restored to Aristotle and to be regarded as the earlier. Von der Mühll had reached the same result a few years previously, taking his start from the special relations of the *Eudemian Ethics* to the *Politics* and to some other works.[1]

My own results, which partly agree with and partly go beyond those of my two predecessors, were reached along another path and without knowledge of their observations. Since their view, that the *Eudemian Ethics* is early and genuine, does not seem to have gained general acceptance, and since I hope to be able to make the matter clear once and for all, I will set out my own method here. It was a disadvantage of their work that it was not related to Aristotle's development as a whole. In particular, by confining their comparisons to the two great *Ethics* they gave a handle for many objections, since they had no fixed point of temporal reference. Such an immovable criterion is to be found in Aristotle's earliest ethics, which has never yet been seriously considered. By means of the fragments of the *Protrepticus*, including the newly recovered matter, it is possible to make a picture of the development of his ethics in three clearly separated stages: the late Platonic period of the *Protrepticus*, the reformed Platonism of the *Eudemian*, and the late Aristotelianism of the *Nicomachean*. For us the most important form of the inquiry will be the question which of the two *Ethics* is to be regarded as the immediate product of the problems of the *Protrepticus*, and whether it is possible to demonstrate a continuous advance at all.

[1] Von der Mühll, op. cit. The special value of this erudite work is that it traces out very completely the relations that Bendixen (*Philologus*, vol. x (1856), pp. 575 ff.) had already shown to exist between the *Eudemian Ethics* and the *Politics*, and adds some further observations of the same kind. We shall return to this question in the chapter on the *Politics*, a subject for which it is important; but I would rather not make it the foundation of my inquiry into the *Eudemian Ethics*, because the correspondences do not perhaps constitute a complete proof by themselves alone, in spite of the fact that those who favour the authorship of Eudemus might find it hard to give a satisfactory explanation of the method of work which Von der Mühll proves the author to have used. Von der Mühll finds a number of philosophical inaccuracies in the treatise, and explains them by the assumption that it is a set of somewhat careless notes made by Eudemus from Aristotle's lectures; but Kapp's acute interpretation has cleared them up (op. cit., pp. 8 ff.), and therefore the question whether the work is Eudemus' notes or Aristotle's original still remains open.

1. THE PHILOSOPHICAL RELATION OF THE *EUDEMIAN*
ETHICS TO THE *PROTREPTICUS*

The *Nicomachean Ethics* begins its inquiry into the aim of human life with a bold sketch of the system of ends. Thus from the start the problem is put into relation with Aristotelian teleology as a whole, and the nature of what follows is indicated. The beginning of the first book of the *Eudemian Ethics* introduces the same inquiry in a much less systematic, but more vivid and personal, form. On the propylaeum of the temple of Leto on Delos, the lecturer begins, these lines appear:

> Most noble is that which is justest, and best is health;
> But pleasantest is it to win what we love.

To this apodictic expression of popular Greek sentiment he opposes, not without feeling, his own thesis. 'But for ourselves, let us not agree with this author; for happiness is the noblest and best and at the same time the pleasantest.' This places the question of happiness at the summit of ethics, and the whole of the first book is concerned with it. The connexion between ethics and happiness had been traditional since Socrates and Plato, and the *Nicomachean Ethics* also retains it as starting and closing point. But the latter work is much more modern in prefixing to the discussion of happiness a chapter which derives from the general system of ends the formal conception of a necessary supreme end of all human effort. Not until the beginning of the next chapter is this equated with happiness.

The second point that Aristotle deals with in the *Nicomachean Ethics* before entering on the discussion of happiness is the question of method. Our study of the *Protrepticus* has shown that in the *Nicomachean Ethics* he had arrived at a view about method diametrically opposite to that of his early days. As early as the proem he gives it clear formulation.[1] Here again the *Eudemian*

---

[1] For the contrast between the *Protrepticus* and the *Nicomachean Ethics* in point of method see above, pp. 85 ff. The application of the name 'proem' to the part which in the *Nicomachean Ethics* precedes the place where the *Eudemian* begins (i.e. *Eth. Nic.* I. 2) comes from Aristotle himself: 'These remarks about the student, the sort of treatment to be expected, and the purpose of the inquiry, may be taken as our proem.' He then returns to the idea of the supreme end, using almost the same words as in the first chapter, and declares it, as in the *Eudemian Ethics*, to be happiness. The emphasis on the contrast with Plato's and with his own earlier method, and its insertion

Ethics is less definite. It contains no reflections on the peculi-
arity of ethical method. Instead the author discusses the difference between the philosophical and the unphilosophical treatment of ethical and political questions, a point that had already
received detailed examination in the *Protrepticus*.[1] In that work
empiricism was sharply opposed to the rational knowledge of
the pure norms, and to dialectic as the only philosophical method.
The *Eudemian Ethics* does not, like the *Nicomachean*, meet this
view with an absolute repudiation of the demand for exact geometrical treatment; on the contrary, it smoothes over the contrast on which the *Nicomachean* version purposely throws a
bright light. 'One must try to obtain conviction from reasoning
(λόγοι), but to use the phenomena as evidence and as examples.'
Further, it is necessary to bring the philosophical norm into
harmony with the prevailing ethical views by revealing their
underlying kernel of truth through conceptual manipulation.
Thus the conceptual analysis of experience replaces the soul's
spontaneous knowledge of the Ideas as we find it in the *Protrepticus*, although emphasis is still laid on the fact that experience by itself is 'confused', that only the Logos can lead to a
clear insight into the causes of things. The contrast between the
philosophical and the unphilosophical treatment is no longer the
same as that between the normative or logical and the empirical.
It now corresponds to two species of concern with experience:
a lower one that merely ascertains facts, and a higher that seeks
for the reasons of the facts. The way in which the standpoint
of the *Eudemian Ethics* has been influenced by the *Protrepticus*
can also be seen in its attitude towards the assertion that the
politician needs theoretical knowledge of the ethical norm. It
sounds almost like the defence of a half-abandoned doctrine
when we hear that such a knowledge is 'not superfluous' even to
the politician, because he must understand the reasons of ethical
and political facts. On the other hand, however, the *Eudemian*

before the beginning of the inquiry proper, is therefore wholly intentional in
the *Nicomachean Ethics*.

[1] Von der Mühll (op. cit., p. 21) suggests that *Eth. Eud.* I. 6 is directed against
Plato and the Academy; Kapp doubts this. The truth is that Aristotle is here
referring to the remarks on method in his own *Protrepticus* (Iambl. *Protr.*, c. x),
which were Platonic in essence, and is partly emending and partly rejecting
them. Cf. above, pp. 85 ff.

Ethics deprecates the philosophers who burden this discipline
with wide-ranging abstract discussions (this means the theory
of Ideas and of Ideal numbers), and stigmatizes their thoroughness as due to misunderstanding or to pomposity (ἀλαζονεία).
Between the *Protrepticus* and the *Eudemian Ethics* Aristotle had
in fact abandoned the theory of Ideas and separated ethics from
metaphysics. The eighth chapter of the first book contains the
refutation of the Idea of the good, which also occurs in the first
book of the *Nicomachean Ethics*; but whereas the latter prefaces
its criticism with a sharply aggressive statement of the revolution that this step had produced in method, the *Eudemian
Ethics* tries rather to show that *in spite of* the criticism of the
Ideas and of the earlier method very substantial portions of the
Protrepticus retain their validity.

Closer inspection of the first book of the *Eudemian Ethics*
shows that its formulation of the problems is throughout determined to a striking extent by the *Protrepticus*, and indirectly by
Plato's way of thinking. One of the permanent parts of Plato's
theory of 'virtue', and especially of its introductory statement
of problems, was the question whether men are 'virtuous' by
nature or through habituation or knowledge or divine gift or
luck; and since it was usual to subordinate the question of the
nature and value of virtue to that of true happiness, the *Eudemian Ethics*, at the beginning of its inquiry into happiness, combines both questions in the form: Does happiness arise through
natural constitution or through insight or through habituation, &c.? We are already familiar with the answer from the
Protrepticus: whether it depends on one or more or all of these
causes, men are essentially agreed that happiness (which is here
suddenly equated with 'living well') is made up of three factors,
the relative importance of which however in securing the end is
variously estimated. These are *phronesis*, virtue, and pleasure.
Men place the happy and perfect life sometimes in one of them
and sometimes in the correct mixture of them. Thus Plato in
the *Philebus* puts it in the mixture of *phronesis* and pleasure,
while Aristotle's *Protrepticus* decides for the union of all three
faculties.[1] The end of life (σκοπὸς τοῦ καλῶς ζῆν), which ethics
has to establish, depends on the decision of this question. In

[1] Plato, *Phil.* 22 A; Iambl. *Protr.*, p. 41, l. 11, and p. 59, l. 26 (Pistelli).

every event the problem of happiness leads to that of the best life (περὶ βίου τοῦ κρατίστου καὶ ζωῆς τῆς ἀρίστης). To speak of 'living divinely' (μακαρίως) is perhaps less desirable than to speak of 'living well and nobly'; the first expression might raise objection. The correction shows once more that this part of the *Eudemian Ethics* is dependent throughout on the *Protrepticus*, for the latter spoke without misgiving of the divine (μακάριον) in man, and proclaimed that he should live for that alone.[1]

The fourth chapter, which contains the comparison of the three 'lives', is also based on the *Protrepticus*. As in that early work, three typical forms of life are here derived from the three fundamental forces that are the source of all human values, the knowing mind, the moral character, and the experience of desire. The life that is based on knowledge has its roots in *phronesis*, that of practical politics in virtue, that of enjoyment in pleasure.[2] The example of Anaxagoras, who, when asked who is the happiest man, answered 'None of those that you think so, but someone who would seem extraordinary to you', also appears to come from the *Protrepticus*; for the statement that Anaxagoras himself held that man's happiness lies not in wealth or beauty, but perhaps in a just, pure, and painless life enjoying divine contemplation (τινὸς θεωρίας κοινωνοῦντα θείας), corresponds exactly to two passages in the *Protrepticus*, where the same philosopher describes the contemplation of the heavens as man's true aim, and assigns a share of the divine to human life in virtue of Mind.[3] Thus we find in the derivation of the three lives, as we have already found in the accounts of the right method for ethics, that the *Eudemian Ethics* is nearer to the *Protrepticus* in thought than is the *Nicomachean*. The latter is indeed familiar with the three lives that vie for the prize of happiness, and mentions them in the same connexion;[4] but it mentions them in passing only, and as if they were an established

---

[1] The distinction between 'living' and 'living well (perfectly truly, nobly)' is developed at length in the *Protrepticus* (Iambl. *Protr.*, c. xi, cf. especially p. 46, l. 25; p. 58, l. 1; p. 60, l. 9). For the 'divine' (μακάριον) and 'living divinely' see *Eth. Eud.* I. 1, 1214ᵃ 30; 3, 1215ᵃ 10; and cp. Iambl., p. 48, l. 9.

[2] *Eth. Eud.* I. 4, 1215ᵃ 26–b 6.

[3] *Eth. Eud.* I. 4, 1215ᵇ 6–14. Iambl. *Protr.*, p. 51, ll. 11–15, and p. 48, ll. 13–18.

[4] *Eth. Nic.* I. 2, 1095ᵇ 17.

topic, whereas the other work lays great weight precisely on the systematic derivation of them from the three conceptions of *phronesis*, virtue, and pleasure. This derivation reveals the origin of the theory of the three lives; it arose out of Plato's later ethics. The *Philebus* begins by asking what is the highest good for man, and makes the two lives of *phronesis* and pleasure compete for the position.[1] The *Protrepticus* adds virtue, and declares the best life to consist in the correct admixture of the three. The *Eudemian Ethics* takes its start from this stage of the development.

The fundamental reason why the *Nicomachean Ethics*, while retaining the lives, abandons the derivation of them from the trichotomy *phronesis*-virtue-pleasure, lies in the change in Aristotle's attitude towards *phronesis* in this work.[2] We need mention this point only briefly, since we have already discussed the contrast between the notion of *phronesis* in the *Protrepticus* and in Plato, and that in the *Nicomachean Ethics*. The two formulations of this notion express the two answers that Plato and Aristotle gave to the question of the ultimate standard and sanction of morality. In the *Protrepticus*, *phronesis* retains the full Platonic sense of the *Nus* that in contemplating eternal being is at the same time contemplating the highest good. There only the philosopher lives the life of *phronesis*. The *Nicomachean Ethics*, on the other hand, does not make moral insight dependent on knowledge of the transcendental; it looks for a 'natural' foundation of it in practical human consciousness and in moral character. *Phronesis* and the whole trichotomy of the *Protrepticus* are accordingly deleted from the first book. The *Eudemian Ethics*, on the other hand, not only retains it in the

---

[1] Plato, *Phil.* 20 E.

[2] In *Eth. Nic.* I. 2, 1095b 14, the three lives are no longer derived from the three goods. On the contrary, we are supposed to learn from the lives what men think good. In the life of enjoyment this is pleasure; in that of politics it is honour (not virtue). When he comes to the contemplative life Aristotle is in a difficulty (1096a 4), since he cannot mention *phronesis*. He therefore refers to the account to be given later: 'Third comes the contemplative life, which we shall consider later.' To this he adds the life of money-making, the aim of which is wealth. He thereby purposely removes all trace of the old trichotomy. The new lives are simply the result of the psychological observation of life, whereas the old ones were ideal points of reference. We have already noticed this procedure of obliteration in the treatment of the four Platonic virtues of the *Protrepticus* in *Eth. Nic.* X. 4, 1178a 24 (above, pp. 73–74).

earlier sense, as we have shown, but develops the outline and plan of the whole ethical system from it.[1]

It announces the plan in the following way: 'Let us first consider virtue and *phronesis* [notice the order; it corresponds to the actual order of treatment in the *Ethics*], inquiring into the nature of each of them, and whether they are, either themselves or the actions that proceed from them, parts of the good life.' Pleasure is to be dealt with later.[2] Since the central books of the *Eudemian Ethics* are lost, we must use the *Nicomachean* to see whether this proposal is actually carried out. The later version has preserved the original construction, although the role played by *phronesis* in it is essentially different from that assigned to it in the former. The first part, 'on virtue', is contained in Books II—V. Book VI follows with the theory of reason and knowledge, which the *Eudemian Ethics* would describe as 'on *phronesis*'. The nomenclature used in the *Nicomachean* is 'moral' and 'intellectual virtue' (which also occurs in the earlier work), 'moral virtue' being equated with the part 'on virtue', and 'intellectual virtue' with that 'on *phronesis*'; but in spite of the change of name in the latter version *phronesis* still remains the chief subject of the part. Book VII discusses pleasure, which is also treated of in X. In the last part of X Aristotle performs the synthesis of the three lives. The intervening books on friendship (VIII and IX), though found in the *Eudemian Ethics* too, cannot have been originally intended for this place, since they go beyond the original conceptual structure of the *Ethics*.[3] Without the *Eudemian* version it would now be impossible to see that the system of Aristotle's *Ethics* is an organic development, in three

---

[1] In *Aristotle Nicomachean Ethics Book VI* (Cambridge, 1909) Greenwood points out that with regard to the meaning of *phronesis* there is the same contrast between the *Nicomachean* and the *Eudemian Ethics* as we have shown (pp. 81 ff. above) to exist between it and the *Protrepticus*. Kapp makes use of this observation (op. cit., p. 48).

[2] *Eth. Eud.* I. 5, 1216ᵃ 37.

[3] I have shown in my *Ent. Metaph. Arist.* (pp. 150 ff.) that Aristotle's treatises arose by the combination of isolated and self-contained monographs (λόγοι, μέθοδοι, &c.) This does not mean that there is never an idea uniting a large group of such monographs, or that their relationship is one of loose juxtaposition in thought as well as in expression. It is simply an aid to the understanding of the way in which Aristotle's 'works' were composed, and it enables us to explain their incoherences and apparent irrelevancies by recalling the philosopher's manner of working and teaching.

separate branches of inquiry, of the tripartite division in the *Protrepticus*. The goal towards which each leads is the theory of happiness in the final book, which is supported by all three together. The *Nicomachean Ethics* does not give this derivation in its introductory book, but leaves the origin of the actual structure obscure. This is another indication of the comparative earliness of the Eudemian version.

What light do these considerations throw on the question of authorship? It now appears inconceivable that after the master's death Eudemus should have deliberately gone back to a stage that the master had long passed, especially when we consider the close unity of the school. On the basis, therefore, of the insight that we have obtained into the gradual development of the ethical problem we must declare it an untenable assumption that Eudemus is the author of the *Ethics* named after him. In the study of the history of Greek philosophy it has often happened that men have tried to explain by means of biographical and personal considerations facts that were necessitated by a law inherent in the matter itself. The series *Philebus, Protrepticus, Eudemian Ethics, Nicomachean Ethics*, evinces an irrefutable historical logic. No member can be exchanged with any other. Previously it was possible to be in doubt about the position of the *Eudemian Ethics*, but now that we have fixed the two end-points of Aristotle's development, namely the *Protrepticus* and the *Nicomachean Ethics*, whose genuineness is undoubted, it is easy to see that the *Eudemian* version falls, not on a continuation of this line, but within it. It is 'the original *Ethics*', if one may use this phrase to mean the earliest form of independent Aristotelian ethics, dating from the period after the break with Plato's metaphysics.

The original *Ethics* holds the same place in the development of Aristotle's moral theory, morphologically speaking, as the original *Metaphysics* does in the development of his metaphysical thought. The two agree in their unmistakable determination to find a tenable substitute for Plato's main doctrine, now that it has been refuted—a substitute that should also satisfy religious needs, and generally take the place of the contemplation of the Ideas in every particular. Criticism of Plato had to be subordinated to the effort to create a new form of Platonism which, while conforming to the facts of experience, should remain as conservative as possible. In content the original *Ethics* is related to the original *Metaphysics* by the exclusively metaphysical basis that it assigns to morality. Just as Aristotle was still so to speak bodily attached to Plato's metaphysics through theology, so, during this period when his own philosophy was being born, was he attached to Plato's ethics through his theonomic morality, this being what the conception of *phronesis* meant to Plato.

By *phronesis* the *Eudemian Ethics* understands, like Plato and the *Protrepticus*, the philosophical faculty that beholds the highest real value, God, in transcendental contemplation, and makes this contemplation the standard of will and action; it is still both theoretical knowledge of supersensible being and practical moral insight.[1] Anaxagoras is still the pattern of this contemplation of truth, as he was in the *Protrepticus*. *Phronesis* is still the essence of the philosophic and contemplative life. Hence it is still regarded as ruling over all the sciences (κυρία πασῶν ἐπιστημῶν) and as the most valuable knowledge (τιμιωτάτη ἐπιστήμη).[2] All this is clearly opposed to the *Nicomachean Ethics*.

Phronesis is the transformer that converts the knowledge of the eternal Good into the ethical movement of the will, and applies it to the details of practice.[3] In the *Nicomachean Ethics* it is *the* 'state of capacity to act', and no man ever does anything without it. The philosophical knowledge of God is no longer its essential condition. That knowledge is a source of higher

[1] The difference between this contemplation (θεωρία) and discursive scientific thought is discussed by Aristotle in *Metaph.* Θ 10. It is an affair not of truth in the sense of empirical judgements, but of an immediate vision that actually touches (θιγγάνει) its object (which is a νοητόν); compare the *Protrepticus* (Iambl., p. 58, l. 14), where the man who possesses *phronesis* is defined as ' contemplating the most knowable parts of reality'. The difference also appears in the fact that according to *Eth. Eud.* VIII. 1, 1246ᵇ 35, *phronesis* is not a science (ἐπιστήμη) that can be turned either to good or to bad use, but a virtue of *Nus*, which changes one's whole character and consists in 'another sort of knowledge' (γένος ἄλλο γνώσεως). It is a virtue of *Nus* in the *Protrepticus* too (Iambl., p. 41, ll. 22 ff.). This is not contradicted by the fact that it is there (p. 43, ll. 5 ff.) called a science (ἐπιστήμη). This means here that 'other sort of knowledge'.

[2] For the 'contemplation of truth' see *Eth. Eud.* I. 4, 1215ᵇ 2, and Iambl. *Protr.*, p. 42, ll. 15–25. For 'ruling over all the sciences' see *Eth. Eud.* VIII. 1, 1246ᵇ 9, and Iambl., p. 43, ll. 2–7.

[3] *Eth. Eud.* VIII. 2, 1248ᵃ 29: 'virtue is the instrument of *Nus*'.

insight revealed to few mortals, but this does not mean that practical wisdom is confined to the narrow circle of philosophers. Thus Aristotle tries to understand the fact that unphilosophical morality exists by reference to the autonomous conscience and its inward standard. Only at the end does he add the contemplative life to this picture, and even then he does not make moral virtue completely dependent on it.[1] In the *Eudemian* version he is still far from any such concession to what Plato calls bourgeois morality (Δημοσία ἀρετή). There *phronesis* is still strictly confined to the contemplation of the divine principle, and without it ethical action is impossible; the only innovation is that the objects of contemplation are no longer Plato's Ideas but the transcendental God of the original *Metaphysics*, who is a metamorphosis of the Idea of the Good. In the *Eudemian Ethics* the central notion is still God, just as it is the unmoved mover in the *Metaphysics*; ethical action is striving towards God. The *Protrepticus* also recognizes only one aim of life—to escape from the sensible and earthly world to God. 'There is a principle beyond which there is no other', says the original *Ethics* with regard to the processes that go on within the soul. 'As in the universe God moves everything, so is it in the soul. In a certain sense it is the divine in us [namely *Nus*] that moves everything. For the principle of reason is not reason but something higher. And what could be higher than knowledge but God?'[2] This is the same thought as Aristotle had expressed at the end of his work *On Prayer* (see p. 160 above). His earnest interest in 'enthusiasm' in the *Eudemian Ethics*, the great value that he sets on prophecy, fortune, and the instinctive, so far as it comes not from nature but from divine inspiration, in brief his emphasis on the irrational, belongs to the same stage as the view in the dialogue *On Philosophy*, where the irrational clairvoyant powers of the soul are described as one of the two sources of belief in God. He here

---

1 In *Eth. Nic.* X. 7 the life of wisdom and reason is called divine and superhuman. In X. 8 'the life in accordance with the other kind of virtue' is set against this highest ideal as taking the second place, and as being the really human life. About this non-philosophical virtue we read as follows (1178a 16): 'Practical wisdom, too, is linked to virtue of character, and this to practical wisdom, since the principles of practical wisdom are in accordance with the moral virtues and rightness in morals is in accordance with practical wisdom.' Thus ethical virtue stands on its own base and has its happiness in itself. It also has its own reason.   2 *Eth. Eud.* VIII. 2, 1248a 23.

sets inspiration above reason and moral insight, not because it is irrational—on that ground Plato, in genuinely Socratic fashion, had put reason above 'enthusiasm'—but because it comes from God. Rational morality misses infallibility. It is the product of mere sober reflection. The sureness of inspiration, on the other hand, is like lightning; as a blind man, no longer seeing what lies before his eyes, has a far better memory and sees everything clear before him within, so the man whom God inspires, though blind, is surer than those that see. This description of the melancholic and inspired person, full of personal experience, is of inestimable value for the understanding of Aristotle in his middle years.[1]

In the *Eudemian Ethics* Aristotle is still expressing the direct relevance of knowledge of God to moral action, as he had done earlier, by means of the Platonic conception of the absolute norm.[2] In the later *Ethics* this recedes very much. into the background; for the instinctive rightness (εὐστοχία) of morally educated persons, which is a law to itself, is not an aim that can be focused clearly at a single point, unlike the highest Good by reference to which the *Eudemian Ethics* directs us to live. The description of the morally good life as the imitation of absolute norms is to be found in the *Protrepticus*. In the *Nicomachean Ethics*, on the other hand, we have the famous definition of moral behaviour as a mean determined by insight in the way in which the man who possesses *phronesis* would determine it. This has given rise to much controversy, since it is somewhat abstract, and since its purpose is not clear at first sight.[3] Now at the end of the

[1] For 'enthusiasm' see *Eth. Eud.* VIII. 2, 1248ᵃ 30 ff., for prophecy ᵃ 35 and 38. The whole of VIII. 2 is devoted to fortune. Aristotle distinguishes physical and metaphysical good fortune. Line 1248ᵃ 39 is connected with *On Philosophy*, frg. 10.

[2] The Platonic conception of the ὅρος, sometimes compared with or equated to κανών, is developed in the *Protrepticus* (Iambl., p. 54, l. 22—p. 56, l. 2). It is fundamental for the method and the metaphysics of Plato's later and Aristotle's earlier ethics. This notion of an absolute norm occurs also in *Eth. Eud.* II. 5, 1222ᵇ 7; VII. 9, 1241ᵇ 36 and 1243ᵇ 29; and VIII. 3, 1249ᵃ 21, ᵇ 1, 19, 22, and 24. After the disappearance of the Ideas, which had been the aim of all normative judgement and effort, the conception of God took over this role. Most of the above-mentioned passages refer to this. Throughout the *Nicomachean Ethics* the word ὅρος has a different meaning, and the conception of God is not brought into the problem of the norm.

[3] *Eth. Nic.* II. 4, 1107ᵃ 1: 'Virtue, then, is a state of character concerned with choice, lying in a mean, i.e. the mean relative to us, this being determined by a

Eudemian Ethics there is a long discussion of the norm by reference to which the good man recognizes and pursues the morally
good. This passage enables us to see how Aristotle originally
conceived the relation between theoretical and practical reason,
and what he understands by 'right reason'. The physician also
makes use of a norm, we read, in order to determine what is
healthy for the body and what is not. It is possible to say, therefore, that the healthy is that which medicine and the reason
employed in medicine prescribe; but this is as indefinite as it is
true. The conception of the reason employed in medicine must
take its content from the objective principle to which it is relative, namely health and its unalterable law. Thus medicine is
on the one hand the knowledge of health and on the other the
application of this knowledge to the particular case. In the
same way moral reason is partly the knowledge of an objective
value (θεωρητικόν), and partly the application of this knowledge
to human behaviour, the moral imperative (ἐπιτακτικόν). Now
the absolute value or highest good, which reason thus grasps, is
God.[1] God is to be thought of not as issuing laws and commands,
not as duty or will, but as the highest Being, sufficient to Himself. Will and command arise only when reason or *phronesis*
devotes itself to the contemplation of this Being. Hence our

rational principle, and by that principle by which the man of practical wisdom
would determine it.' Here, for once, the idea of the norm reappears. This is the
most pregnant expression that could possibly be found of the change in Aristotle's attitude towards this problem. The fact is that there is no universal norm
for him any more. 'State of character in accordance with right reason' was
included in the definition of virtue by all Platonists (see VI. 13, 1144[b] 21). In
VI. 1, 1138[b] 25, Aristotle declares that this, though true, is anything but clear; in
this book, therefore, he gives a more accurate account of the share that *phronesis*
has in choice. Its function is no longer to apprehend the universal norm, as
it was in the *Protrepticus*, but to discover the right means of attaining the end
(τέλος, σκοπός) determined by the moral will (VI. 13, 1144[a] 8 and 20, 1145[a] 5).

1 *Eth. Eud.* VIII. 3, 1249[a] 21 to the end. Here too he is objecting to the
obscurity of the Academic definition of the norm as 'determined by a rational
principle' (1249[b] 3), as in *Eth. Nic.* VI. 1, 1138[b] 25. The problem remained with
him throughout his life, but the solution here is different from that in the later
Ethics. The comparison between *phronesis* and medicine had been used in the
Academy. Aristotle modifies it in his earlier *Ethics* by distinguishing between
theoretical and practical medicine. *Phronesis* apprehends the norm (health or
God) and then applies it. In *Eth. Nic.* VI. 13, 1144[a] 4, he calls the first process
wisdom and only the second *phronesis*. As early as the *Protrepticus* we find:
'Moreover what canon of goods have we, or what more accurate norm, than
the man who has *phronesis*?' (frg. 52, p. 61, l. 25, in Rose). But here *phronesis*
is still a general kind of knowledge without any differentiation at all.

most pressing duty is to choose all the occupations and activities and goods that further the knowledge of God. Theoretical philosophy is the means to man's moral education. Everything, whether possession or action, is morally bad and reprehensible if it hinders a man from serving and knowing God (τὸν θεὸν θεραπεύειν καὶ θεωρεῖν).[1] We know that *deum colere et cognoscere* is still a common definition of religion. The conclusion of the *Eudemian Ethics* is the *locus classicus* for theonomic ethics as taught by Plato in his later days. God is the measure of all things. In preserving this much from the wreck of the Idea-theory Aristotle believes he is retaining the abiding essence of Platonic morality, the notion of the absolute norm and of the metaphysical transcendence of the Good, which had given to the Platonist a new experience of God. No wonder that Eudemus, the supposed author of this *Ethics*, has always been looked on as a pious man! All this was incompatible with men's idea of Aristotle. This first lecture on ethics exhales the religious fervour of his youthful Platonic faith. Against such an ethics of pure devotion to God the famous picture of the contemplative life in book ten of the *Nicomachean Ethics* fades, and becomes little more than an objective if idealized description of the life of the scholar devoted to research, rising at the end to the intuition of the ultimate force that guides the spheres. Some of the old notes sound again in this picture, but not quite with their old power. The strength of the later *Ethics* lies rather in its parts, with their analysis of concrete moral types, and in its rich and humane urbanity.

The contemplation of God was originally closely connected with the theory of friendship, which in the *Nicomachean Ethics* is expanded into a general sociology of the manifold forms of human relationship. In this complex phenomenology of society we should be hard put to it to detect the close connexion between Aristotle's philosophy of friendship and Plato's theory of Ideas, had we not the older *Ethics* to give us a clear picture of the method that Aristotle originally had in mind. He here replaces the transcendental and universal Idea of the Good with ideal types, as he does throughout his earlier ethics and politics. These ideal types are immanent in experience, and yet they are normative and not

[1] *Eth. Eud.* VIII. 3, 1249b 20.

mere descriptive averages simply read off from experience. The most important of them is 'first friendship' (πρώτη φιλία), from which in the *Eudemian Ethics* all forms of friendship are 'derived'. This arises directly out of the conception of the 'first principle of friendship' (πρῶτον φίλον) as developed in Plato's *Lysis*.[1] But whereas the latter was the highest metaphysical value (αὐτὸ τὸ ἀγαθόν), in contrast with which all that seems dear on earth is nothing but a shadow, in 'first friendship' Aristotle is constructing the picture of the ideal friendship. He retains the kernel of Plato's notion—the basing of friendship on the ethical principle of the Good—but he makes the Good a concrete moral value developing within the character of the man himself. The suprapersonal ground of the value of the human relationship no longer diverts attention from the personality of the friend; on the contrary, it is concentrated and incarnated therein. Aristotle's idea is therefore not just another way of referring all social values to the general problem of value; its aim is rather to establish the independent worth of the moral personality, and in the last resort of human morality in general, as opposed to the cosmic Good that is based on the idea of God.

The derivation of the various forms of friendship from 'first friendship' is accomplished in the earlier *Ethics* by means of purely Platonic conceptions. The distinction between will (βούλεσθαι) and desire (ἐπιθυμεῖν) corresponds to Plato's distinction between the absolute Good, which is the natural goal of the will, and the apparent good, which is the goal of the desires. Plato is also the origin of the separation of the good from the pleasant, and of the doctrine that the good without qualification is identical with the pleasant without qualification, so that the friendship of the really good man is at the same time pleasant. The main part of the discussion in the *Eudemian Ethics* is devoted to showing that 'first friendship' combines in itself all the marks that have ever been declared characteristic of the essence of friendship, even those that seem to be mutually exclusive—a classical example of early Aristotelian dialectic. The *Nicomachean Ethics*, on the other hand, writes 'perfect friendship' instead of 'first friendship', because the latter expres-

[1] Plato, *Lysis*, 219 c. For the development of the ideal of 'first friendship' see *Eth. Eud.* VII. 2, and for 'the first friend' VII. 2, 1236b 28.

sion clearly recalls the theory of Ideas, and leads one to expect a purely deductive method.[1] It retains, indeed, the Platonic doctrine that the other kinds of friendship are not co-ordinate and can be called 'friendship' only *per accidens*, and the derivation of them from the ideal conception of perfect friendship; but the important thing for Aristotle now is the psychological and sociological analysis, which far outweighs the other even in bulk. We shall see later that a similar development occurs in the *Politics* also. A mass of facts gathered from experience, governed essentially by their own laws, and becoming more and more an independent object of interest, has been introduced into the framework of what was previously an ideal Platonic construction.

If the basis of true friendship is personal goodness, the ethical relation of the ego to the non-ego must be determined by that of the ego to itself. By distinguishing the rational part of the soul from the inferior parts, which nevertheless can be moved by reason, Aristotle is able to represent the ethical relation of the ego to itself by means of the conception of self-love (φιλαυτία), by which he understands not selfishness, which popular morality rightly condemns, but the kindred affection of the lower part, which is spoken of as if it were actually a second ego, for man's higher self (αὐτό).[2] By the self the *Protrepticus* meant *Nus*, the 'divine in us', in accordance with Plato's later doctrine; and Plato's view of the right relation of the soul that is ruled by *Nus* towards itself can be learnt from the *Timaeus* (34 B), where the highest visible God is said to be 'able to converse with itself, and needing no other friendship or acquaintance'. Thus the selfishness of the natural man is cancelled and made to serve his will to be his true self. The psychological problems connected with this view are not formulated sharply enough for our requirements, but this objection applies to the whole of Aristotle's theory of *Nus*, which is in fact a legacy from Plato's later speculations. In the religious atmosphere of the *Eudemian Ethics* the mysticism of the doctrine of self-love, from which

---

[1] *Eth. Nic.* VIII. 4.

[2] *Eth. Eud.* VII. 6, and *Eth. Nic.* IX. 4 and 8. We here have speculation developing a piece of popular Greek wisdom that often found expression, as in Soph. *O.C.* 309, 'What good man is not friendly to himself?', Eur. *Med.* 86, frg. 460, and Men. monost. 407. For *Nus* as man's self see Iambl. *Protr.*, p. 42, ll. 3 and 14, and *Eth. Nic.* IX. 8, 1168b 35, and X. 7, 1178a 2.

Aristotle derives the characteristics of true friendship,[1] is directly
intelligible. Its commandment, 'to serve and contemplate God',
also rests on Plato's theory of *Nus*.

Our result requires, naturally, to be supported in detail by a
comparative interpretation of the two *Ethics*. This, however,
cannot be undertaken here. Philology must first make good its
negligence with regard to the *Eudemian Ethics* and give us a
serviceable commentary, and above all a real text, which as yet
is completely lacking. For our purposes it must suffice if we
have succeeded in showing that we can clearly detect in the
development of Aristotle's ethical thought the same stage as is
characterized by theology in his metaphysics, and that the
original *Ethics* is closely connected with the original *Metaphysics*.[2]

2. THE *EUDEMIAN ETHICS* AND THE PROBLEM OF
THE EXOTERIC DISCUSSIONS

The above conclusions about the development of Aristotle's
ideas are confirmed and augmented when we discover that the
Eudemian Ethics displays a close verbal dependence on his early
works. Most important of all are its relations to the *Protrepticus*, which here too casts a wholly new light upon our problems.
The fact is that between the *Eudemian Ethics* and the parts of
the *Protrepticus* that we have recovered from Iamblichus there
are remarkable correspondences extending over long passages.
Apparently they have never before been noticed, and yet they
suffice, even apart from the question of the place of the *Eudemian
Ethics* in the history of ideas, to refute the prevailing view that it
was written by Eudemus and is a late work. Their importance
as evidence of the way in which Aristotle worked, and of the
relation between his teaching and his literary production, is so
great that we must here discuss them in detail. A welcome by-
product of our inquiry will be the decisive solution of a problem
that apparently has been despaired of, and that yet is constantly

---

[1] *Eth. Eud.* VII. 6, 1240ª 23.

[2] Bernays' statement, that Aristotle's theology permeates his philosophy as
little as his God permeates the world (*Dialoge des Aristoteles*, p. 82), must now
be abandoned as regards the early and middle periods. It remains a noteworthy fact, however, that the writings of his latest period could suggest such
a view.

being reopened because it is fundamental to the understanding of Aristotle—the problem of the so-called exoteric discussions.

We may start from the beginning of the second book of the *Eudemian Ethics*, where the author lays the foundation of his theory of virtue and gives a derivation of the conception of it. We do not need to examine in detail the content of this passage, which is the core of the work; a short survey of the train of thought will suffice. Having completed the introduction, which is contained in the first book, the author tells us that we are now to make a fresh start in our inquiry. This consists in dividing all goods into several classes. For the division he expressly appeals to the 'exoteric discussions', in order to avoid establishing it in detail here. The kinds of value enumerated in the first book (*phronesis*, virtue, and pleasure) are all 'in the soul', whether they are permanent states of character (ἕξεις) or faculties (ᾶυνάμεις) or activities (ἐνέργειαι) and movements (κινήσεις). Now the same assumption, he continues,—namely that we have to deal with either a state or a condition or a faculty in the soul—also applies to virtue, and must therefore form the basis of the following development of the conception.

The text has come down to us in poor condition, for the manuscripts have a lacuna in the division of goods: πάντα ᾶὴ τὰ ἀγαθὰ ἢ ἐκτὸς ἢ † ψυχῇ. The corresponding passage of the *Nicomachean Ethics* gives a *threefold* division of goods: 'Goods have been divided into three classes, and some are described as external, others as relating to soul or to body; we call those that relate to soul most properly and truly goods, and psychical actions and activities we class as relating to soul.'[1] This is immediately preceded by the statement that we must get clear about the nature of happiness not merely by means of general principles but also by using 'what is commonly said about it'. Finally, the same division reappears in the *Politics*: 'Assuming that enough has been already said in the exoteric discussions concerning the best life, we will now only repeat what is contained in them. Certainly no one will dispute the propriety of that partition of goods which separates them into three classes, viz. external goods, goods of the body, and goods of the soul, or deny', &c.[2] Here again we have the same division borrowed

---

[1] *Eth. Nic.* I. 8, 1098b 12.   [2] *Pol.* VII. 1, 1323a 21.

from the exoteric discussions—and not merely the division as such, but also its application to the inquiry concerning the best life, for the passage expressly refers to 'exoteric discussions concerning the best life', the fundamental notions of which are to be adopted in the present discussion.[1]

Zeller, who supposed Eudemus to be the author of the *Eudemian Ethics*, tried to explain this reference to the exoteric discussions by saying that Eudemus is really only reproducing the passage of the *Nicomachean Ethics* in which it is said that we must consider happiness in the light of 'what is commonly said about it', and that in changing this vague phrase to 'this distinction we make even in our esoteric discussions' he was copying the passage in the *Politics*.[2] This interpretation leaves it obscure how Eudemus could come to speak of one of Aristotle's writings in the first person ('we make').

We can now see, as earlier scholars could not, that so long as they assumed Eudemus to have been the author of the *Eudemian Ethics* it was simply impossible to solve the problem of the exoteric discussions. For either they followed a sound philological instinct for style and understood by these discussions actual works of Aristotle, as did Bernays (and then they came into irreconcilable conflict with the reference to exoteric discussions in the *Eudemian Ethics*[3]); or else they started from this passage and constructed with reckless logic as empty a sense as possible for 'exoteric', which was not so much an explanation as a way of escaping the dilemma, and which violated all the laws of philological interpretation.[4] Now that we have restored the

[1] The Oxford translators sometimes render ἐξωτερικοὶ λόγοι by such phrases as 'discussions outside our school', thus implying a view different from that maintained in this book. While preserving their versions as much as possible, for the sake of easy reference, I have been obliged to bring them into line with the theory of this chapter. Tr.

[2] *Hermes*, vol. xv, p. 554.

[3] Oddly enough Bernays took no notice of this passage (*Eth. Eud.* II. 1), so far as I can see, although he systematically examined all the places where Aristotle mentions exoteric discussions. On the presuppositions of those days it would have toppled his whole edifice.

[4] H. Diels, 'Über die exoterischen Reden des Aristoteles', *Ber. Berl. Akad.*, 1883, pp. 477 ff. (the passage in the *Eudemian Ethics* is discussed on p. 481). His arguments appear to have found general approval, which is comprehensible in view of the situation. To-day there is nothing for it but to admit that his trail was the wrong one. The sincerity of his work, however, has prevented it from being useless.

Eudemian Ethics to Aristotle there is no longer anything against Bernays' conjecture that the exoteric discussions were definite writings, and in fact the literary works of Aristotle. It is confirmed by the new material, without which it would have remained a mere hypothesis. The only alteration required is that in the present case we are concerned not with a dialogue, as Bernays supposed, but with the *Protrepticus*.

Protr., p. 52, l. 12.	*Eth. Eud.* II. 1, 1218^b 32.
So other things [that is, external things] should be done for the sake of the goods that have their seat in the man himself; and of the latter those that are in the body should be done for the sake of those that are in the soul, and virtue for the sake of *phronesis*. *Phronesis* is the supreme good. [Then comes a definition of goods.]	All goods are either outside or ⟨in the body or⟩ in the soul, and of these those in the soul are more desirable; *this distinction we make even in our popular discussions.*

Protr., p. 59, l. 26.	
We assume that happiness is either *phronesis* and some kind of wisdom, or virtue, or the greatest possible amount of pleasure, or all three. [Then follows a more detailed account.]	For *phronesis*, virtue and pleasure are in the soul, and some or all of these seem to all to be the end.

Protr., p. 41, l. 20.	*Eth. Eud.* 1219^b 28.
One part of the soul is reason. This is the natural ruler and judge of things concerning us. The nature of the other part is to follow it and submit to its rule.	Let it be assumed that the parts of the soul partaking of reason are two, but that they partake not in the same way, but the one by its natural tendency to command, the other by its natural tendency to obey and listen.

Elements that have been taken over ready-made into the *Eudemian Ethics*, and somewhat hastily put together, are to be found in the *Protrepticus* not merely in a form that for the most part verbally echoes them, but also, which is more important, in the context to which they were originally organic.

Protr., p. 41, l. 22.	*Eth. Eud.* II. 1, 1218^b 37.
The good state of everything is that which is in accordance with its proper *virtue*. To attain to one's	Let this then be assumed, and also that *virtue is the best state* or condition or faculty of all things

proper virtue is good. A thing is in a good state when its most essential, commanding, and valuable parts have their virtue. From this it follows that the natural virtue of a thing *is better when the thing itself is better* by nature. The better by nature is that which has more of the commanding and leading element in itself, as man has compared with the other animals. *Now the soul* is better than the body (because it is more commanding), and within the soul itself the rational and intellectual part is better than the rest. . . . *It necessarily follows, therefore, that the virtue of this part, whatever it is, is the most desirable of all things*, not merely for us but also absolutely or for everyone; and everyone would hold, I presume, that we are constituted, either wholly or chiefly, by this part. Furthermore, when a thing accomplishes *its work* as well as possible, then, provided that it is its work essentially and not just accidentally, *we must declare that such a state of affairs is also good, and that this accomplishment is the most perfect virtue, in accordance with which it is the nature of each thing to perform its work.*

A complex and divisible thing has several *different activities*; but if a thing is naturally *simple*, and is not relative in essence, it must have only one true and proper virtue. If therefore *man* is a simple animal, *and if the essence of his substance is reason and intellect, his work can be nothing whatever* but perfect truth —the discovery of the truth about things; but if his nature is compounded of several faculties, it is clear that when a thing naturally fulfils more than one function its

that have a use and work.‖ This is clear by induction; for in all cases we lay this down: e.g. a garment has an excellence, for it has a work and use, and the best state of the garment is its excellence. Similarly a vessel, house, or anything else has an excellence.‖ *Therefore so also has the soul, for it has a work. And let us assume that the better state has the better work*; and as the states are to one another, so let us assume the corresponding works to be to one another. And the work of anything is its end; it is clear, therefore, from this that the *work* is better than the state; for the end is best, as being end; for we assume *the best, the final stage, to be the end for the sake of which all else exists.* That the work, then, is better than the state or condition is plain.

Eth. Eud. II. 1, 1219ᵇ 32.

It makes no difference whether the soul is *divisible or indivisible*, so long as it has *different faculties*, namely those mentioned above, just as in the curve we have unseparated the concave and the convex, or, again, the straight and the white, yet the straight is not white except incidentally and is not the essence of the white.[1] We also neglect any other part of the soul that there may be, e.g. the vegetative, *for the above-mentioned parts* [*i.e. the rational ones*] *are peculiar*

[1] Omitting τοῦ.

work is always the best of these functions; for example, health is the work of the doctor and safety that of the navigator. *Now it is impossible to mention any better work of the intellect, or of the think-* ing part of our soul, *than truth.* Truth is therefore the essential work of this part of the soul.

to the human soul; therefore the virtues of the nutritive part, that concerned with growth, are not those of man. For, if we speak of him *qua* man, he must have *reason and moral action* as governing prin- ciples. . . . And just as general good condition of the body is com- pounded of the partial excellences, so also the excellence of the soul, *qua* end. But of virtue or excel- lence there are two species, *the moral and the intellectual.*

The *Ethics* considerably alters the order of the ideas. The logical structure is more luminous and more systematic in the *Protrepticus.* For good measure the *Ethics* adds examples explaining 'by induction' the connexion between virtue and work. The application of all this to the soul is performed in the *Protrepticus* with exemplary lucidity, beginning with the words 'now the soul'; but the *Ethics* merely indicates it with 'therefore so also has the soul', and leaves all details for oral elaboration. Possibly, indeed, Iamblichus found the examples in his source but left them out; yet since they are extremely trite and peda- gogical it is more probable that Aristotle did not cite them at all in his literary work, but introduced them only when he came to write his lecture. We must say the same of the examples of convex and concave by which the inseparability of the parts of the soul is explained in the second paragraph. There, incidentally, the difference in man's aim as envisaged by the two works comes out clearly. In the *Protrepticus* the sole aim of human life was the theoretical knowledge of reason (*phronesis*). The theoretic life hung high above all other aims and was sharply sundered from them. The soul, which was described as man's essence, was there conceived as the indivisible unity of the pure rational soul (after the manner of Plato's later theory of *Nus*), which has rid itself of animal and vegetable existence as well as of will and desire. In the lectures, on the other hand, we read that it makes no difference whether the soul is a unity or has parts, and prac- tice (πρᾶξις) now takes its place beside thought (λογισμός) as equally worthy. Aristotle now holds that happiness depends upon the interaction and equilibrium of the rational and irrational powers in the soul. In saying this he is not merely paying attention to the claims of ordinary life; he is establishing a new ideal, and seeking to overcome the harshness of his previous purely intellectual attitude (see especially 1219^b 39–1220^a 5). He was therefore obliged to suppress the passage in which the *Protrepticus* had represented pure contemplation as the only valuable and essential occupation of the human soul (p. 42, l. 22— p. 43, l. 25). All the alterations that he introduces in the *Ethics* are logical consequences of this fundamental change in his ideas.

The *Protrepticus* is also the root of what we read in the first book of the *Eudemian Ethics*. We have already shown this of the first four chapters by analysing the train of thought in them. The sixth discusses the new method in ethics, and we have seen that it is throughout directed against the *Protrepticus* (above, p. 233). That the greater part of the fifth also comes directly from this work is clear from the following juxtaposition. Aristotle is here giving the proof that life by itself is not the greatest good, but receives its value from *phronesis*.

Protr., p. 45, l. 6.

It is obvious to everybody that *no one would choose to live*, even if he had the greatest wealth and power that man has ever had, *if he were deprived of his reason and mad*, not even if he were going to be constantly enjoying the most vehement pleasures, as *some insane persons do*. It seems therefore that everyone shuns folly as much as possible. Now the opposite of folly is *phronesis*, and of opposites one is to be shunned and the other to be desired. As disease is to be shunned health is to be desired. According to this argument too, therefore, it appears that *phronesis* is *the most desirable of all things....* For if a man had everything, but the thinking part of him was *corrupted and diseased*, life would not be desirable for him. The other goods would be no benefit to him. This is why all men belittle all

Eth. Eud. I. 5, 1215^b 15.

About many other things it is difficult to judge well, but most difficult about that on which judgement seems to all easiest and the knowledge of it in the power of any man—viz. *what of all that is found in living is desirable. . . . For there are many consequences of life that make men fling away life, as disease*, excessive pain, storms, so that it is clear that, if one were given the power of choice, not to be born at all would, as far at least as these reasons go, have been desirable. Further, *the life we lead as children is not desirable, for no one in his senses would consent to return again to this*. Further, many incidents involving neither pleasure nor pain or involving *pleasure but not a noble kind* are such that, as far as they are concerned, non-existence is preferable to life. And generally, if one were to bring together all

other goods so far as they know what reason is and are capable of tasting it. This is also why *none of us could endure to be drunk or to be a child throughout life*. This again is why *sleep, though extremely pleasant*, is not desirable, even if we suppose that the sleeper experiences all the pleasures.

Cp. *Protr.* p. 40, l. 6: 'It is thoroughly slavish to long for mere life instead of for the good life', a favourite position of Aristotle's.

that all men do and experience but not willingly because not for its own sake, and were to add to this an existence of infinite duration, *one would none the more on account of these experiences choose existence rather than non-existence*. But further, neither for the pleasure of eating alone or that of sex, if all the other pleasures were removed that knowing or seeing or any other sense provides men with, *would a single man value existence, unless he were utterly servile*, for it is clear that to the man making this choice there would be no difference between being born a brute and a man. . . . We may say the same of *the pleasure of sleeping*. For what is the difference between sleeping an unbroken sleep from one's first day to one's last, say for a thousand or any number of years, and living the life of a plant ?

It is not chance that these parallel trains of thought are so like each other. It is inconceivable that Aristotle unconsciously formulated a view that was familiar to him in the same way in two different places. All doubts are removed by the quotation from the *Protrepticus* that follows a few lines lower.

Protr., p. 51, l. 11.

They say that when Anaxagoras was asked why one should choose to be born and live he answered the question thus, 'for the sake of viewing the heavens and the things in it, stars and moon and sun', implying that everything else is worthless.

Eth. Eud. I. 5, 1216ᵃ 11.

And so they tell us that Anaxagoras answered a man who was raising problems of this sort and asking why one should choose rather to be born than not—'for the sake of viewing the heavens and the whole order of the universe'.

Since the *Eudemian Ethics* connects this representative of the theoretic life very closely with those of the two others, and since this passage is dependent on the *Protrepticus* almost to the very words, we are justified in also ascribing what follows to the same source, down to 1216ᵃ 27. We here find Sardanapallus set against Anaxagoras as the representative of the life of pleasure, along with

Smindyrides the Sybarite 'and others who live the voluptuary's life'. All these persons believe that happiness and the pleasures of the senses are one and the same. Even if we had no evidence, it would be probable that the *Protrepticus* named these representatives of the voluptuous life, who are merely touched on in the *Eudemian Ethics*, and also those of the life of politics, of which the *Ethics* mentions no examples. The plastic force of the idea fits the style of a literary work better than a lecture, and in the *Ethics* Aristotle gives it merely as a bald narrative, without the full vividness and effectiveness of which it is capable. As a matter of fact, however, Cicero twice quotes a passage from Aristotle which proves conclusively that this passage too comes from the *Protrepticus*.[1] In rejecting Sardanapallus' view of life Cicero quotes his epitaph, translating it into Latin hexameters.

> Haec habeo quae edi quaeque exsaturata libido
> hausit, at illa iacent multa et praeclara relicta.

He expressly says that he gets from Aristotle both the epitaph and the witty method by which he punctures its frivolous view of life. The resemblance of these passages to that in the *Eudemian Ethics* must not mislead us into supposing that Cicero or his source made use of this work. The two main characteristics of these passages do not appear in it or in any of Aristotle's treatises; and since during those times only his literary works were read, there can be no doubt that Cicero is quoting from one of them. His agreement with the *Eudemian Ethics* is simply due to the fact that both used the *Protrepticus*.

This becomes still clearer when we examine more closely the remaining words that Cicero quotes from Aristotle. 'Quid aliud, inquit Aristoteles, in bovis, non in regis sepulcro inscriberes?' It is no longer possible to determine whether Aristotle really said that Sardanapallus' epitaph might just as well have been written on the tomb of a bull. To me the sentence seems unmistakably to reveal his lightly mocking air, but to have been

---

[1] Cic. *Tusc. Disp.* V. 35, 101; *De Fin.* II. 32, 106. Rose prints both as coming presumably from the dialogue *On Justice* (frg. 90). Bernays also supposed that they were fragments of an Aristotelian dialogue, and suggested the *Nerinthus*, of which we know nothing (op. cit., p. 84). He did not compare them with *Eth. Eud.* I. 5, 1216ᵃ 16, but with the passage derived from this one in *Eth. Nic.* I. 3, 1095ᵇ 19. The latter is only a faint echo of the *Protrepticus*, like most of the traces of that early work remaining in this late one.

somewhat vulgarized. In the immediately preceding passage of the *Eudemian Ethics* (1215^b 35), on the life of the pure pleasures of sense, we read: 'No one would value existence for the pleasure of eating alone or that of sex, if all the other pleasures were removed that knowing or seeing or any other sense provides men with, unless he were utterly servile; for it is clear that to the man making this choice there would be no difference between being born a brute and a man; at any rate the ox in Egypt, which they reverence as Apis, in most of such matters has more power than many monarchs.' Since the preceding and the following sentences (1215^{b}15–34, 1216^{a}2–10 and 1216^{a}11–16) are taken more or less verbally from the *Protrepticus* it is probable that this one is too. The comparison between the Apis-animal and the monarchs seems somewhat strange here in the *Ethics*, and is difficult to understand, since previously Aristotle had merely said that only a slave would choose such a life; but Cicero shows that in the original a comparison was drawn between the divine bull of the Egyptians and the royal voluptuary Sardanapallus, and this explains the point of saying that in sensual enjoyment Apis has more freedom than all the monarchs in the world (1216^{a}2). Aristotle has selected his quotations from the *Protrepticus* rather disjointedly. We have now traced the larger part of the fifth chapter to the *Protrepticus* (down to 1216^{a}27, and as far as the thought goes down to ^{a}36).

Thus the *Eudemian Ethics* contains many more extracts from and elaborations of the *Protrepticus* than are indicated by explicit references to exoteric works. And there are yet more passages in which it has undoubtedly been used, especially in the so-called Book VIII, whose gospel of the 'contemplation and service of God' is borrowed from the deep religious feeling of that early work. VIII. 3, 1248^b 27–34, also reminds one of the *Protrepticus* (cp. frg. 57 in Rose). Finally, there remain to be explained certain remarkable passages that have never yet received sufficient attention. Two of them are in the eighth chapter of the first book. Aristotle there shows that the Idea of the Good cannot be the highest good for which we are seeking; in other words, he draws the ethical consequences of the refutation of the theory of Ideas. For the refutation itself he refers to a published work. 'This has been considered in many ways both in our exoteric and in our philosophic discussions.'[1] By the many 'ways' he means the refutation of the theory from the logical, from the ontological, and from the physical, points of view, which are clearly distinguished in the *Metaphysics*. By the 'exoteric' refutation of the Ideas he does not mean something 'popular' as opposed to philosophical, as has been supposed;[2] on the contrary, the *Metaphysics*, which also assumes this refutation, expressly describes it as the most detailed and complete discussion of the question available. He is referring to the second book of the dialogue *On Philosophy*, which had just been published at the time when he was lecturing on ethics in Assos.[3] By the 'philosophic discussions' he means his formal lectures, especially those on metaphysics, which were also composed at that time. The second reference in this chapter is to the same dialogue. 'Further, there is the argument written in the discourse (λόγος)—that the Idea itself of Good is useful to no art or to all arts in the same way. Further, it is not practicable', &c.[4] The following arguments against the Idea of the Good, which are only mentioned and not

---

[1] *Eth. Eud.* I. 8, 1217ᵇ 22.

[2] And as the Oxford translation reads. Tr.

[3] We must assign the *Eudemian Ethics* to this period for the following reasons: (1) Its very close relations to the above-mentioned early works. Later on, in the *Nicomachean Ethics*, these relations were obliterated as far as possible. (2) Its parallelism with the earlier and theological phase of the *Metaphysics* in ideas and problems. (3) The loose way in which the parts criticizing Plato are worked in in I. 6–8. The passages that agree with the *Protrepticus* are apparently remnants of a lecture written while Aristotle was still in the Academy. (4) The dialogue *On Philosophy*, mentioned in I. 8, is the *terminus post quem*. It appeared in 348/7. (5) Coriscus of Assos, who is purposely omitted or erased from the *Nicomachean Ethics*, appears as a conventional example in II. 1, 1220ᵃ 19, and VII. 6, 1240ᵇ 25, in each place obviously with a humorous purpose. There is nothing in the train of thought that obliges Aristotle to call him 'the darkest man in the market-place'. It can be explained only by the situation in which he uttered these words.

[4] *Eth. Eud.* I. 8, 1218ᵃ 36. This reference, together with that in Book VII, which is discussed in the next paragraph, was declared spurious by Wilson and thereafter by Susemihl. The manner seemed unusual. But in view of the number of references to exoteric works in this early period, and of the systematic reciprocal influence of writing and teaching that they display, there is really nothing surprising in it. Aristotle also refers to oral discussions in the Academy, as in *Eth. Eud.* VII. 6, 1240ᵃ 22 ('By a man's attitude to himself the other modes of friendship, under which we are accustomed to consider friendship, are determined'); and to an inquiry, obviously dialectical in character, conducted by means of the accepted definitions: 'the various definitions of friendship that we give in our discourse' (VII. 11, 1244ᵃ 20).

developed, are also part of the extract from this dialogue. That which is 'written' is available to all, and may be found in 'the discourse'. Aristotle must therefore be referring to a work that had received literary publication, and that was too well known in the circle to which he was lecturing for him to mention its name. This confirms the conclusion that we should draw from his copious use of the *Protrepticus*: when he first began to lecture he constantly referred to his dialogues and to the *Protrepticus*, and presupposed that his hearers were familiar with them.

There is a similar reference in Book VII: 'as it is written in the discourse' (1244[b] 30). And a few lines lower we read ([b] 34): 'We must put together two statements made in the discourse, first that life is desirable, and secondly that the good is so . . .' (Δεῖ γὰρ ἅμα συνθεῖναι Δύο ἐν τῷ λόγῳ, ὅτι τε τὸ 3ῆν αἱρετόν, καὶ ὅτι τὸ ἀγαθόν . . .). The words that follow are corrupt. Now these two statements were actually made in the *Protrepticus*. It was said there that the affirmation of the will to live is at the same time the affirmation of the desire for knowledge, since the life of men, in contrast to that of animals and plants, is consciousness and knowledge (αἰσθάνεσθαι, γνωρίζειν).[1] But this is exactly what we find a few lines higher up in the *Eudemian Ethics* ([b] 23). It is followed immediately by the sentence containing the phrase 'as it is written in the discourse'. Here too the text is corrupt, a word having fallen out, but the sense is clear: if one could make the experiment of cutting consciousness and knowledge out of a man, and if this man nevertheless retained the power of observing his state of mind, or what was left of it, he would find himself observing a totally different being, as if somebody else were living in his stead. The corresponding passage of the *Protrepticus* is not preserved, but it certainly must have existed, for this very method of excision, abstraction, and isolation, for which Aristotle appeals to 'the discourse', is constantly used in that work,[2] and the view that knowledge and intellect are man's true self is used there to establish the injunction that we should live only for this higher part. We see then that during the time when the earliest lectures

[1] Iambl. *Protr.*, p. 56, l. 22, and p. 44, l. 11.
[2] Ibid., p. 44, l. 11; p. 45, ll. 8, 18, and 25; p. 53, l. 3. Cp. *Eth. Eud.* I. 5, 1215[b] 32; VII. 12, 1245[a] 14; and VII. 14, 1248[a] 39, 40, and [b] 2.

on ethics were being written philosophical discussion in the school at Assos turned mainly on these writings.

The ancient problem of the exoteric discourses is now settled once and for all. We have not merely demonstrated the fact that Aristotle used his literary works in his lectures—this would hardly have needed proving, since he himself frequently speaks of so doing in an unmistakable manner (χρῆσθαι)—but also revealed, by means of our new material, exactly what writings it was that he used, and what is the philosophical explanation of this remarkable fact. It is bound up with his development. In the earliest period after his break with Plato's theory, when it became necessary completely to rewrite all the main branches of philosophy, he took from his early compositions whatever he could still use, and constructed the new with the help of the old. At the end of the first book of the earlier *Ethics*, for example, the criticism of the Ideas, borrowed from the dialogue *On Philosophy*, stands somewhat isolated between older passages taken from the *Protrepticus*; the *Nicomachean Ethics*, on the other hand, provides a whole new scheme, which naturally presupposes his new point of view from the outset. The part played by the *Protrepticus* in the earliest *Metaphysics* has already been discussed. In Assos Aristotle could still think that his distance from Plato was not so great but that he might everywhere connect with his Academic period. Later on he discovered more serious consequences in his new ideas. They led him farther and farther away from the old. His early Platonic writings then dropped entirely out of sight; and it seems that he even abandoned the beginnings of his emancipation from Plato, his own first attempts at a critical philosophy, as being still too penetrated with the presuppositions of his dogmatic period. This appears to be the explanation of the fragmentary condition of the earliest *Ethics* and *Metaphysics*.[1]

[1] I cannot leave this subject without mentioning the three books that are common to the two versions of the *Ethics*. *Eth. Nic.* VI cannot belong to the *Eudemian Ethics* because of its view of *phronesis*, which is essentially later than that in *Eth. Eud.* I and VII, and argues against it. We must suppose that these three books entered the *Eudemian* version together and at a later time, and therefore that they come from the *Nicomachean* edition; but this does not prove that the latter is all of a piece. The absence of connexion between the two accounts of pleasure, in Books VII and X, remains a problem. That in Book VII is presumably somewhat earlier than that in Book X. It presupposes a different conclusion.

CHAPTER X

THE ORIGINAL *POLITICS*

IF we possessed the writings that the ancients knew of we should have a picture of Aristotle's political development reaching from his Academic beginnings down to his old age. The series starts with the two books on the *Statesman*, suggested by Plato's work of the same name, and the four 'bulky' books *On Justice*.[1] While these writings would have given us exacter knowledge of the connexion between Aristotle's politics and Plato's, *Alexander or On Colonization*, a memoir in the form of a dialogue, also lost, would have introduced us to the late period when the royal pupil was breaking and making empires in Asia, while the ageing philosopher followed the dizzy flight of his fortunes from afar with anxious eyes. The loss of this work has hidden from us what we should most of all have liked to know—what effect this world-wide change in the historical scene had on Aristotle's political thought.[2] The work *On Monarchy*, whose genuineness we have neither the material nor (in view of the testimony of the Alexandrian catalogue of Aristotle's works) the right to doubt, must belong to the time when he was preparing Philip's son for his high office, or, rather, must be the sign of the close of that period. We shall not doubt for an instant that in this book the philosopher, who wrestles with the problem of monarchy so seriously in his *Politics*, tried to give new ethical and spiritual content to the traditional idea of a king.[3]

[1] Cic. *De Rep*. III. 8, 12.

[2] A sidelight is thrown on his views of the problem of the relation between Greeks and Asiatics, which was necessarily decisive as regards methods of colonization, by the fragment of a letter to Alexander in which he advises him to behave towards the Greeks as a leader and towards the barbarians as an absolute and unlimited monarch, to which they were accustomed; to treat the former as friends and equals, and the latter as 'animals or plants' (frg. 658). The dissent of Eratosthenes and Plutarch shows how emphatically the humane Hellenistic cosmopolitans rejected this view. Although it is typically Greek, in Aristotle's case it was certainly the result of sober reflection on the facts. The attempt to assign this fragment to the work *On Monarchy* (Heitz, *Die verlorenen Schriften des Aristoteles*, p. 206) does not seem to me successful.

[3] It must have been a communication sent to Alexander on his ascending the throne, somewhat like the *Protrepticus* and Isocrates' *Nicocles*; that is to say, of a more general and ethical nature. To a king standing at the summit of

All these are serious losses as regards the history of the time and the personality of the thinker; but the disappearance of that monument of Peripatetic scholarship, the collection of 158 constitutions, has dealt our knowledge of Greek history and culture an incurable wound. The fortunate recovery of the first book of the collection, the *Constitution of Athens*, written by Aristotle himself as a sort of canon for the whole, has at any rate made it certain that the undertaking was not organized until those last decades in which he reached his maturity. Nothing is more significant of the form his development took than the fact that he did not pile up this gigantic mass of material until the systematic foundations of his political thought had long been laid, whereas theoretically it ought to have preceded them. The two points furthest removed from each other in time, the books *On Justice* and on the nature of the *Statesman* at the beginning, and the collection and classification of constitutions at the end, make the general direction of his development certain.

Our prime object of interest is the beginning, the breaking away from Plato. Our main source of knowledge must always be the analysis of the extant eight books of the *Politics*; but this analysis can hope for results only if, here as with the *Ethics* and the *Metaphysics*, we take what remains of the early writings as a criterion by which to estimate the extent of Aristotle's continually increasing distance from his starting-point. Here again the newly recovered fragments of the *Protrepticus* give us some valuable material, and make good to some extent the irreparable loss of the main political works of his early days.

Plato's aim was to make politics a science by uniting it inseparably with the theory of individual virtue and basing it on knowledge of the Idea of the Good. The *Republic* is built upon the inquiry into justice. This was the model for Aristotle's

power and success one does not send philosophical advice as to the way in which he should regard his office. This agrees with what Cicero says (*Ad Att.* XII. 40, 2 and XIII. 28, 2) of a 'hortatory' letter of Aristotle's written at Alexander's request and dealing among other matters with the question of true fame. The communication *On Monarchy* informed the Greeks of the ethical and political principles in accordance with which Alexander had been taught, and by asking his tutor to set them down and publish them in a 'hortatory' letter the young prince clearly indicated his intention of ruling in the spirit of them.

books *On Justice*, which Cicero in turn names as his models in his *Republic*. In Aristotle's first independent *Ethics* the Good was no longer the real object of all ethical and political science; but in his earliest period it was the kernel of politics, just as it is the central theme in Plato's *Republic*. We know this from the important fragment of the second book of the *Statesman* in which the Good is described as the most exact of all standards. This presupposes Plato's later theory of Ideas, which, as we have already seen, was chiefly concerned, as regards ethics and politics, with the problems of exactitude and of the norm, and emphasized the notions of measure and measuring.[1] The point is confirmed by the *Protrepticus*, which brings out in a noteworthy manner the exactitude of political science and contrasts it, as a new form of theoretical knowledge, with the politics of practical statesmen. Its purpose, we there learn, is not to treat a particular state by all the methods that experience suggests; such a procedure—the sole one that the Aristotle of the fourth and fifth books of the *Politics* admits at all for general practice[2]— is expressly condemned. 'Just as no man is a good builder if he uses no line or other such tool, but imitates other buildings, so perhaps if a man who is making laws for a city or practising politics looks to and imitates other human actions or constitutions, whether Spartan or Cretan or other such, he is not a good and perfect lawgiver. For the copy of a thing that is not ideal (καλόν) cannot be ideal, and the copy of a thing that is not divine and permanent cannot be divine and permanent.'[3] Only the pure philosopher, who rids himself absolutely of empiricism

[1] See above, p. 87.

[2] In *Pol.* IV. 1, 1288b 21–1289a 7, the conventional theory of the ideal state is criticized for concerning itself only with the construction of a state in accordance with ideal standards, and not with the question, usually more urgent in actual politics, how to better a given state that does not conform to the ideal standard, but is perhaps thoroughly inferior and rotten. This cannot be done, indeed, without the erection of a standard, but still less can it be done without copious experience and the knowledge of analogous cases in reality, as is shown by Books IV–VI of the *Politics*.

[3] Iambl'. *Protr.*, p. 55, ll. 7–23. It is interesting to note that the sophistical theory of the state, which held that the perfect constitution was realized at Sparta or in Crete, is rejected in the *Protrepticus* because it is too close to empirical reality or takes its standards therefrom; whereas in *Pol.* IV. 1, 1288b 41, it is rejected for the opposite reason that it proceeds too schematically and refers everything to a norm, instead of adapting itself completely to the actual given case.

and looks to the law of nature and of being as the highest archetype, who, like a good helmsman, casts anchor only on an eternal
and permanent bottom—only he can give enduring laws, and
only his practice is right and normative.[1] The notion of nature
here, occurring several times, is unambiguously distinguished
from Aristotle's later conception of φύσις by the synonyms used
for it. It means that which at once *is* and *ought to be*, in accordance
with Plato's metaphysics. Its peculiar colouring is obtained by
the emphasis of its archetypal character. The banausic arts construct their canon—this example must be taken symbolically—
in accordance with nature. In the same way the most exact of
all arts, philosophical politics, takes its canon from nature itself
(φύσις αὐτή), which is the being of the Ideas. It is in fact a
canonic of values, concerned exclusively with absolute standards
(ὅροι). The relation between this theoretical politics and the
practical kind is described by means of the clever simile of the
eye, which does nothing and produces nothing, except to distinguish visible things and make them clear, and without which
nevertheless we should be practically helpless and unable to
move.[2] This is politics as developed in Plato's *Statesman*. The
sluggish mechanism of a system of abstract law is there contrasted with the royal artist in statecraft, whose living knowledge of the Ideas gives him an adaptability in face of difficult
cases of practical politics such as can never be obtained by mere
chapter-and-verse booklearning, but is to be compared rather
to the art of the physician, because it arises from living and
productive knowledge.[3]

[1] Iambl. *Protr.*, p. 55, l. 24.

[2] Iambl. *Protr.*, p. 56, l. 4. 'For just as sight makes and constructs nothing
(for its only function is to distinguish and reveal each visible thing), and yet it
enables us to act and helps us very greatly in our actions (for we should be
almost completely unable to move if we were deprived of it), so it is plain that,
though this knowledge is theoretical, we nevertheless do thousands of things
in accordance with it, and choose some things and shun others, and in general
get all good things by reason of it.' This passage of the *Protrepticus* has influenced *Eth. Nic.* VI. 13, 1144^b 11, where Aristotle elucidates the function of
phronesis with the example of 'a strong body that moves without sight' and
hence 'stumbles badly'.

[3] The Greeks called the sciences 'arts' because they never for an instant lost
sight of the cultural products of theoretical activity. Art or τέχνη really includes
both the whole content of the theoretical knowledge (and in this sense Plato
and Aristotle contrast it with experience, because by knowledge they mean
something conceptual) and the power that makes this knowledge fruitful in life.

Thus the sole form of political thought originally recognized by Aristotle was that handed down by Plato, the Utopia. He sought for the absolute standard, which is not to be found in experience.

With this insight let us approach the extant eight books of the *Politics*. The characteristic feature of their construction is that the whole culminates in an account of the ideal state (ἀρίστη πολιτεία) in the last two books (VII and VIII).[1] This high point rests, however, on the broad empirical basis of a theory of the manifold forms of actual political life, with their varieties and their transformations into one another, to which is added a casuistry of the diseases of the state and the methods of treating them (IV–VI). The preceding book (III) determines the elementary presuppositions of politics by developing the conceptions of city and citizen, and by deriving the various forms of constitution from the various modes of allotting political rights in the particular states. We are here giving only a rough outline of the content, in order to make the main features of the construction appear as clearly as possible. In Book II Aristotle prefixes to this theory of the elements a critical survey of the systems of previous political theorists. To this again the first book provides a still more elementary introduction, discussing the fundamental kinds of government (ἀρχή) more from the sociological or economic point of view, and thus taking its start genetically from the simplest components of political life.

There is a thoroughgoing inner logic in the combination of these books into a whole. Everything appears to lead up, in methodical progress, to the crowning aim, the ideal standard of a state fulfilling all wishes. But for centuries, ever since the *Politics* has been systematically studied, close critical examination has revealed difficulties that make it improbable, and in fact impossible, that the treatise as we have it was ever planned as a whole or sprung from a single creative act of the mind. Up to the present scholars have spoken mainly of the difficulties in the literary composition; but we must not apply literary

---

[1] I follow the traditional numbering of the books, as found in the manuscripts, and not the alteration preferred by most editors. I do not mean to deny that there is a kernel of correct observations at the basis of their procedure, but the difficulties cannot be wholly removed by changing the order of the books.

standards here, and the fact is that the problems of composition have a deeper root; the philological *aporia* arises out of a difficulty in the philosophical method and structure. For the present, therefore, we will not enter into detailed analysis, or follow Aristotle book by book, only to lose ourselves, as has so often happened, in purely external questions about the correct position of passages and books. We must begin by observing the peculiar Janus-face that the *Politics* presents as a whole, gazing on the idealists as if it were a Platonic Utopia and on the realists as if a sober and empirical science, and yet obviously being really both at once.

In boldness of creative fancy and in legislative magnificence Aristotle's ideal state is not to be compared with Plato's *Republic* or even with his *Laws*. It has been truly said that in the *Laws* Plato moderates his state in order to bring it closer to reality, and that Aristotle relaxes it still further. In doing this he is following the path taken by Plato in his old age, but much more is he following his own inward tendency, which seeks to reconcile the Idea and the reality at all costs. He tells us himself that for an imaginary ideal state we may assume conditions as favourable as we please, but not impossible.[1] The Utopian part of his *Politics*, however, is not its real strength, although the ideal state gives the mark by reference to which the external organization of the whole structure is determined. The really original and characteristic feature of the work is the way in which it takes over Plato's notion of an ideal state and supports it with a broad empirical foundation amounting to a descriptive science of constitutions, the method of which it develops with profound insight. The important thing for Aristotle is the welding together of the two forms of politics, the combination of Books VII and VIII, containing the ideal state, with IV–VI, which develop the theory of actual historical states, or rather of the manifold varieties, diseases, and treatments, of actual states. The principle of this arrangement is clearly expressed by himself at the end of the *Nicomachean Ethics*, where he joins politics to ethics in order to unite the two into a single comprehensive science of man, including both the individual and the

---

[1] *Pol*. II. 6, 1265ᵃ 17 (in the course of the criticism of Plato's Utopias), and VII. 4, 1325ᵇ 38.

social aspects (ἡ περὶ τὰ ἀνθρώπινα φιλοσοφία). 'First, if any-thing has been said well in detail by earlier thinkers, let us try to review it; then in the light of the constitutions we have collected (ἐκ τῶν συνηγμένων πολιτειῶν) let us study what sorts of influence preserve and destroy states, and what sorts preserve or destroy the particular kinds of constitution, and to what cause it is due that some are well and others ill administered. When these have been studied we shall perhaps be more likely to see with a comprehensive view which constitution is best, and how each must be ordered, and what laws and customs it must use, if it is to be at its best.'[1]

This programme obviously implies a turning-point in the development of Aristotle's *Politics*. In unambiguous language he here abandons the purely constructive method that Plato and he himself had previously followed, and takes his stand on sober empirical study. What he says is in fact—and nothing but his extreme explicitness has prevented his being under-stood—: 'Up to now I have been using another method. I have made my ideal state by logical construction, without being sufficiently acquainted with the facts of experience. But now I have at my disposal the copious material of the 158 constitu-tions, and I am going to use it in order to give to the ideal state a positive foundation.'[2] This was written at the end of the latest

[1] *Eth. Nic.* X. 10, 1181ᵇ 13 to the end.

[2] We must always remember that the statements of Aristotle's point of view, as we have them in the treatises or rather in the surviving versions of the treatises, can be understood only as stages in the living whole of his unresting intellectual development. Hence there is often something relative about them, which is not fully comprehensible to those who do not bear the other moments of the process in mind. Many passages in the *Ethics* and the *Metaphysics* must be taken as self-polemic, in which the philosopher transcends his earlier views. Among such is the conclusion of the *Ethics*, 'when these have been studied we shall perhaps be more likely to see with a comprehensive view which constitution is best', which refers to an earlier stage when the idea of such a painstaking and wearisome detour through the empirical facts had never entered his head. That the expression ἐκ τῶν συνηγμένων πολιτειῶν refers to the collection of 158 constitutions—συναγωγή in this sense is common in Aristotle, compare συναγωγή τεχνῶν—has been conjectured from time to time, and much useless ingenuity has been expended on denying it, most recently by Heitz (*Die verlorenen Schriften des Aristoteles*, pp. 231 ff.). It was, of course, impossible to draw conclusions from these words about Aristotle's development when the *Constitution of Athens*, which belongs to his latest period, had not been re-covered, and the *Nicomachean* had not yet been recognized as the latest edition of his *Ethics*.

version of the *Ethics*, that is to say, in his last decade. The collection of constitutions came into being at the same time. It was the period during which he gave to his early theological metaphysics the broad foundation of a theory of being in general, while in ethics the psychological and descriptive element began to oust the speculative mode of treatment. Some may find it surprising that this development took place so late. We have imagined Aristotle as being on that road from the beginning. The fact that his progress was gradual, however, is completely proved by the contrast between the last paragraph of the *Nicomachean Ethics* and the method of the *Protrepticus* and the *Statesman*, while the temporal indications are unambiguous. The remark about the introduction of a new and empirical part to precede the theory of the best constitution refers to Books IV–VI, whose content he there clearly describes; and it has long been inferred that these books are composed of the material contained in the collection of constitutions, because, quite apart from this passage, their attitude towards the subject is different and they display an inexhaustible wealth of historical examples.[1] They are the only books of the *Politics* that mention recent historical events. The allusion to the murder of King Philip (336) proves that they were written during Aristotle's second stay in Athens.[2] That he took this opportunity to rewrite the whole *Politics* is not said and is in itself unlikely. We must therefore inquire how far it is still possible to distinguish earlier and later levels. In doing this we may start from the results obtained by those who have investigated the proper order of the books.[3]

[1] W. L. Newman, *The Politics of Aristotle*, vol. i (Oxford, 1887), p. 491. Wilamowitz, *Aristoteles und Athen*, vol. i, p. 359.

[2] *Pol*. V. 10, 1311ᵇ 2. The murder is not mentioned as a recent affair, nor for its own sake at all, but as one of a series of similar assassinations quoted as examples of the murder of princes for revenge (τιμωρίας χάριν). Hence the passage may have been written much later. Zeller, *Aristotle and the Earlier Peripatetics*, vol. i, p. 154, n. 4, infers from it that the whole *Politics* was written late, but the question is precisely how far its chronological implication can be extended. Only Books IV–VI, which Aristotle describes at the end of the *Ethics* as based on the collection of constitutions, and which have this origin unequivocally stamped on their faces, can be assigned with certainty to the last period in Athens. They are contemporary with the production of the *Nicomachean Ethics*. That the rest is earlier will be demonstrated below. The first book, however, is an exception.

[3] Wilamowitz was the first person to put forward the conjecture that in the *Politics* later layers are superimposed on earlier (*Aristoteles und Athen*,

Ever since the Italian humanists of the Renascence interested themselves in the *Politics* critics have attacked the traditional order and tried to restore the 'genuine' by means of more or less violent alterations. In the nineteenth century these theories forced their way into the editions. The two concluding books, VII and VIII, were placed after the third, and IV–VI were made the end. Within this latter group, again, the fifth and sixth books were sometimes made to change places. In recent years Wilamowitz has protested energetically against this rage for alteration, and certainly such a mechanical operation is unlikely to reduce the tradition to 'order'. Our first task must be to obtain an understanding of the historical necessity of the actual state of affairs. In this, however, we can get substantial help from the facts that the critics have brought to light. Books II and III are not an introduction to a general theory of the state. It is clear from their method, from their problems, and from some explicit utterances, that they are meant to introduce an ideal state in the manner of Plato.[1] Those who wished to make the last two books, containing the ideal state, follow immediately on this introduction, were able to appeal to the fact that II and III are closely connected to VII and VIII by mutual references, whereas they do not mention the intervening Books IV–VI. Their connexion with the latter is quite loose.[2] Observant readers

---

vol. i, pp. 356 ff.), and it was his keen historical sense that first gave Aristotle his just place in the development of the fourth century as a man and as a student of politics.

[1] It is clear at the first sight that Book II is a historical and critical introduction to a theory of the ideal state, and not to a theory of the state without qualification. Book III, on the other hand, appears to introduce more general questions, the conception of the city and the citizen as such, and the classification of all possible forms of constitution, the bad as well as the good. The normative character of this classification shows, however, that Aristotle is working up to the best state. The latter is really in his mind throughout, see III. 3, 1276a 30 ff. (and cp. VII. 4, 1325b 39); III. 4 (where he asks whether the virtue of a man and of a citizen are the same or not, for ex. 1276b 37 and 1277a 2 and 5); III. 5, 1278a 8 and 17 (the inquiry into the political rights of artisans); III. 9, 1280b 5, 31, 39, and 1281a 2 (the determination of the correct view of the state as an organization for public education, and the rejection of the 'Manchester state'); III. 13, 1284a 1 and b 25; III. 14, 1284b 38; III. 15, 1286a 8 and 15; and III. 18, 1288a 33 to the end.

[2] For references to VII and VIII in III see the previous note. Contrariwise, VII. 4, 1325b 34, refers back to III. 6–8; and VII. 14, 1333a 3, refers to III. 6, esp. 1278b 32 ff., with the words 'as I observed in the first part of this treatise'. VII. 16, 1335b 4, refers forward to VIII. This makes it the more remarkable that

could not fail to notice that these intervening books positively interrupt and disturb the construction of the best state. For, although the end of the *Nicomachean Ethics* says that they are to form the foundation of it, this arrangement never got beyond the mere intention, and in point of fact they do not in any way prepare for and establish the ideal state, or at least not directly. The final consideration was that in the manuscripts the first sentence of VII also appears, with slight verbal alterations, at the end of III. At the beginning of VII it is given the style appropriate to the opening of an independent monograph, while at the end of III its form is such as to connect directly with the concluding reflections of that book. Aristotle's writings contain several examples of such technical indications of the order of the rolls. The fact that Book VII once followed III was thus no longer an hypothesis but an express tradition.

If we supposed that the closing words of the *Nicomachean Ethics*, which give the outline of the *Politics*, were not written by Aristotle himself—as has actually been suggested—but by his editor, whether Nicomachus or Theophrastus, then it would be the latter who interrupted the genuine Aristotelian order by inserting Books IV–VI. If, however, this outline comes from Aristotle, which seems to me the only trustworthy interpretation, he himself inserted them, and the words at the end of Book III are a rudiment of the original state of affairs. In either case it is proved that VII and VIII originally followed on II and III, but if Aristotle himself made the insertion we have no right to undo his step. What we have to distinguish, therefore, is not a true and a false, but an earlier and a later, order of the books. The difficulty has arisen out of Aristotle's development, and, instead of making order by force, we ought to be thankful that the tradition still allows us a glimpse of the growth of his ideas, a glimpse possible, however, only because the final enlargement does not arise organically out of the earlier *Politics*, and because the parts are merely tacked, not sewn, together.

Reviewing our results so far, we have first the original *Politics*

III, VII, and VIII take no account of IV—VI, especially as IV—VI, on the other hand, do not lack references to III and VII. These latter, however, are not such as to demand the insertion of IV—VI between III and VII—VIII. In fact, such an insertion appeared to be excluded by the connexion between III and VII—VIII and their references to each other. (See below, pp. 273–274.)

of the ideal state, directly connected with Plato in virtue of its aim. It begins in Book II with a historical survey of the earlier theorists about the ideal state, including Plato, and with a criticism of their Utopias. Apparently this book was originally the beginning, just as the historical part is the beginning of the *Metaphysics*, of the dialogue *On Philosophy*, and of the books *On the Soul*. It was useless, however, as an introduction to anything but a discussion of the ideal state, and hence a more general introduction had to be prefixed to it when the discussion developed into a general theory of the state.[1] In Book III we have the transition to the fundamental conceptions involved in the state. Its main content is the derivation of the six archetypal constitutions from the amount of the share in the government enjoyed by their citizens. Here again we have the characteristic search for absolute norms and standards, especially in the distinction between the true and the degenerate forms. The attitude is just as theoretic and conceptual as that of the actual description of the best state in Books VII and VIII, to which it often refers. We shall return to the latter.

Over against this speculative picture stands the empirical part in Books IV–VI. It shows no trace of the old Platonic spirit of constructions and ideal outlines. Aristotle does, however, expressly define his attitude towards the older part when, at the beginning of IV, he explains that in addition to the construction of the ideal it is a no less important task of the political theorist to examine what is good or bad for a particular state in given conditions. The constitution of an absolute ideal, and the determination of the best politics possible under given conditions, are parts of one and the same science. His remarks on this point show that he felt a certain difficulty in combining Plato's Utopian speculations with this purely empirical treatment, although he believed himself able to overcome it. He tried to escape by pointing to the analogy of a double form of medicine and gymnastics, the one concerning itself with the pure standard and the other applying the knowledge thus gained to the given case. Throughout the introduction to the empirical part one can scarcely help feeling that there is an undertone of polemic against the mere construction of ideals, and that Aristotle was

[1] For the vindication of the view that Book I is late see below, p. 272.

very proud of his innovation. The uncompromising assertion of
the unattainable ideal could not help the rent and riven actuali-
ties of Greek politics.

The main point, however, is that in the empirical inquiries of
the inserted books the ideal state is no longer the norm that
determines what is attainable and desirable in given circumstances. The standard there is immanent and biological. It is
obtained by immersing oneself sympathetically in the manifold
possible forms of the state, and not by looking to a single, fixed,
ideal goal. Hence Aristotle is never weary of insisting that there
are not one kind of democracy, one kind of oligarchy, and so on,
but very divergent varieties, and whereas in Book III democracy
and oligarchy are regarded as merely degenerate and contrary
to the norm, in IV they are the two types to which almost all
actual constitutions are in practice to be referred, although
Aristotle still retains his old systematic division into two categories of value, good constitutions and perversions. The essential thing for the understanding of Books IV–VI is not what he
preserves of the old, but his new method, which could never
have been derived from speculation about the ideal state. In
that speculation the rule was logical division, but here it is the
feeling for biological form. This comes out clearly in the detailed
methodical comparison between the theory of the forms of
state and that of the morphology of animals, which Aristotle
places at the beginning of his new inquiry.[1] This is tangible and

---

[1] *Pol.* IV. 4, 1290^b 25: 'If we were going to speak of the different species of
animal, we should first of all determine the organs that are indispensable to
every animal, as, for example, some organs of sense and the instruments of
receiving and digesting food, such as the mouth and the stomach, besides
organs of locomotion. Assuming now that there are only so many kinds of
organ, but that there may be differences in them—I mean different kinds of
mouth, and stomach, and perceptive and locomotive organ—the possible combinations of these differences will necessarily furnish many varieties of animal.
(For animals cannot be the same which have different kinds of mouth or ear.)
And when all the combinations are exhausted there will be as many sorts of
animal as there are combinations of the necessary organs. The same, then, is
true of the forms of government that have been described.' Then follows the
parallel between the particular parts of the social organism and those of the
living thing. By the way in which he works it out Aristotle shows that he
regards this not as an ingenious analogy but as a revolution in method; and the
result, which he emphasizes again and again in what follows, is important
enough: the few forms of constitution distinguished in Book III do not exhaust
the list, for each of them is divisible again according to the way in which the
parts are combined, and this can vary very widely.

unmistakable evidence of the influence exerted on the constructive way of thinking that he inherited from Plato by the descriptive sciences of nature, especially biology and morphology, which underwent development on all sides during his later period. It is not a question merely of the control of conceptual construction by experience. That had always been his tendency; even in the old account of the ideal state he had had recourse to experience to confirm or overthrow Plato's speculations. But in these late books the unbiased observation of empirical reality has led him to a wholly different mode of treatment, which starts from the particular phenomena and seeks to discover their inner law, like a scientist observing the characteristic motions and emotions of a living thing. The theory of the diseases of states and of the method of curing them is modelled on the physician's pathology and therapy. It is scarcely possible to imagine a greater contrast to the doctrine of an ideal norm, which constituted Plato's political theory and that of Aristotle in his early days, than this view, according to which no state is so hopelessly disorganized that one cannot at least risk the attempt at a cure. Radical methods would certainly destroy it in short order; the measure of the powers of recovery that it can exert must be determined solely by examining itself and its condition.

We must here content ourselves with this general characterization, and not enter further into the detailed analysis of these three books. It is necessary, however, to say one more word about the first. As already remarked, it was added when the existing structure was enlarged into a general theory of politics by the insertion of the purely empirical part. It sets out the plan of the whole as Aristotle conceived it while working on the later version. He intended to develop in the introduction the fundamental natural conditions of all political existence, in order to construct the state from nature, out of its simplest presuppositions. These presuppositions are the three fundamental elements of all social life, master and slave, man and wife, parent and child.[1] The way in which he carries out, or rather fails to carry out, the resulting threefold division of his material shows that there were certain difficulties in his path.

[1] *Pol.* I. 3, 1253^b 4–8.

The first book discusses only the first of these three fundamental relations, the question of slaves and its connexion with the economy of social life. As to the two other subjects proposed, marriage and children, Aristotle consoles his readers by remarking at the end that these had better be discussed in connexion with the problem of the family, 'when we speak of the different forms of government' (ἐν τοῖς περὶ τὰς πολιτείας). At first sight this looks like an incomprehensible failure in consistency and lucidity, and it makes the close of this book very unsatisfactory. The explanation is that he was in an awkward position, and only violent means could help him out of it. Marriage and the family had already been liberally discussed in the earlier version of the *Politics*, on the occasion of the criticism of Plato's demand that wives and children should be common. He was therefore obliged either to delete this earlier treatment, thereby destroying the main attraction of his criticism of Plato's *Republic*, or to abandon the account of it in Book I and content himself with a reference to that in II.[1] He chose the latter. The muti-

---

[1] *Pol.* I. 13, 1260b 8–13. It is not permissible to omit the article before πολιτείας or to change it from τὰς to τῆς. This would make the passage refer to the part of the *Politics* that contains the ideal state, which, however, does not mention the problem of the family; and it would be poor consolation to suppose that the missing discussion appeared in the final part of the last book, which is lost. It is surely a dubious proceeding to alter the tradition on the ground of a passage that may never have existed. The expression 'when we speak of the different forms of government' (ἐν τοῖς περὶ τὰς πολιτείας) is ambiguous. In IV 2, 1289a 26, 'our original discussion about governments' means the classification of constitutions into six kinds in the third book. In II. 1, 1260b 29, Aristotle understands by the 'other constitutions', in contrast to his own ideal state, the Utopias proposed by other theorists, which he criticizes in that book; at the end of the same book he again sums up this inquiry under the name of 'our inquiry into the various constitutions' (1274b 26). Now the problem of the family is fully discussed in the criticism of the community of wives and children in Plato's *Republic* (II. 3–4); and, although Aristotle there develops his own view somewhat indirectly, by contrast with what seems to him a mistake, this very indirectness is mentioned in the preliminary announcement in I. 13, 1260b 10: 'The relations of husband and wife, parent and child, their several virtues, *what in their intercourse with one another is good and what is evil*, and how we may pursue the good *and escape the evil*, will have to be discussed when we speak of the different forms of government.' He here indicates a treatment of the question in the form of a criticism of the wrong view. If he had meant to discuss it in the same way as he does the problem of slavery, it would be impossible to conceive any reason why he should not have done so immediately after the former; but Book I was written to precede a pre-existing treatise in which the question had already been discussed, as is proved by the brusque transition to Book II, where we are told

lated structure of the first book is thus the consequence of its adaptation to the older version. The concluding passage, which is intended to make the transition to the older part with its problem of the ideal state, also betrays the difficulty of doing so by its remarkable tortuousness—this has even been made a reason for denying that it is genuine; and yet it does not succeed in disguising the abrupt change of thought which strikes the reader of the opening sentence of Book II.

These results may be confirmed by examining the system of references. There are in fact two distinct sets, imposed one on the other, and partly contradicting each other. At first, naturally, the scholar treats them as all on a level and tries to harmonize them. Then he sets them against each other and declares one half to be interpolations. But the only way to untie the knot is to bear the facts of Aristotle's development in mind, and so to distinguish the references that must have occurred in the old sketch of the ideal state (because they presuppose that alone) from the later ones, which presuppose the whole *Politics* as it now stands. The only directly demonstrative references, naturally, are those that conflict with the present state of the *Politics*. Those presupposing it may belong to the latest version, and hence prove nothing. If we make a division into two groups on this principle, we find that what is presupposed by the group conflicting with the present state of the treatise is that the books containing the ideal state (II, III, VII, VIII) were originally united and independent. Book III was once the real beginning of the treatise, since the contents of II are merely negative. Hence it is often referred to with the phrase 'at the commencement of our inquiry' (ἐν τοῖς πρώτοις λόγοις). Even Book IV refers to III in this way, although it belongs to the later version; and this shows that IV–VI were inserted before the first book was prefixed to the whole.[1] Before the first book was written

without warning that the aim of politics is to set up an ideal state, although until that moment the discussion had been concerned solely with the state in general.

[1] For Book III or the beginning of it referred to as 'at the commencement of our inquiry' see III. 18, 1288ᵃ 37 (= III. 4); VII. 14, 1333ᵃ 3 (= III. 6); IV. 2, 1289ᵃ 26 (= III. 6); IV. 7, 1293ᵇ 2 (= III. 4–5); and IV. 10, 1295ᵃ 4 (= III. 14–17). If Susemihl is right, it also conflicts with the present state of the *Politics* when IV. 3, 1290ᵃ 1, refers to VII. 8–9, with the words 'which were mentioned by us when treating of aristocracy'; but we cannot absolutely

Aristotle used to refer to his exoteric dialogues for the matters now treated there, namely slavery and the doctrine of the three forms of rule obtaining within the household (master, husband, and father). They were fully treated in those works, and so we read in III. 6, 1278^b 30: 'There is no difficulty in distinguishing the various kinds of authority; they have often been defined already in the exoteric works.'[1] He then gives the classification exactly as we find it in the first book: the kinds of authority are master and slave, husband and wife, father and child. That he nevertheless refers to a dialogue for this classification can fail to be surprising only if Book III belongs to a version in which I did not occur. In the final version he conceived the plan of filling up this gap by giving a full discussion of the matter in an introductory book. It then became necessary to insert in the passage quoted a reference to the fact that the subject had already been treated in the first book. But the older reference to the dialogues was not removed, and the juxtaposition of the two is a strange contradiction.[2] Aristotle introduced another reference to I at a passage in VII where he touches on the subject of master and slave;[3] and the remarkable relation obtaining between the references in II, III, VII, and VIII, and those in IV–VI, already discussed, can also be satisfactorily explained if we bear the development of the work in mind.[4] The reason why II, III, VII, and VIII, the books con-

exclude the possibility that the reference here is to III. 4. Newman (*The Politics of Aristotle*, vol. iv, p. 155) suggests III. 12, 1283ᵃ 14 ff. See the next note but one.

[1] The Oxford translation, 'in discussions outside the school', presupposes another view of the meaning of 'exoteric', but see p. 249 above. Tr.

[2] *Pol.* III. 6, 1278^b 17. If this reference to Book I had been present from the beginning, and I itself therefore were as old as III, it would be impossible to see why Aristotle here finds it necessary to repeat all over again what he had already said there about the forms of authority, and to appeal to the exoteric works for support. It is clear from the other references to exoteric works that we have here an extract from a dialogue, and that Aristotle introduces it *for the want of anything better*; but this presupposes that at the time of writing III was not preceded by I.

[3] *Pol.* VII. 3, 1325ᵃ 30: 'about which I have said enough at the commencement of this treatise.' Here, as in III. 6, 1278^b 18, 'the commencement of this treatise' does not mean Book III, which is its usual sense in the *Politics*, but Book I. That is to say, it presupposes the latest revision. Both references were introduced on that occasion. That the *Politics* contains any references not inserted by Aristotle himself I cannot admit.

[4] See p. 267 above.

taining the account of the ideal state, are tied together with a network of mutual references, while they do not mention the intervening Books IV–VI, is that they were written as one and at an earlier time. The same fact also explains why the latest and empirical part, and especially IV, frequently takes account of the old.

Let us now attempt to determine more exactly the date of the sketch of the ideal state, as against that of the later books and of the collection of constitutions. As with the *Ethics* and the *Metaphysics*, we must start from its connexions with Aristotle's early writings—and it is significant that only the older part of the *Politics* shows any such connexions; the later books, IV–VI, evince not the slightest trace of a relation to the dialogues. Unfortunately the material at our disposal for comparison is extremely poor. The *Protrepticus*, the only work that we can use, helps us solely in matters where the *Politics* is directly based on the *Ethics*. The surviving remains contain little that is wholly political. This misfortune is to some degree counterbalanced, of course, by the fact that the connexion between the *Politics* and the *Ethics* was much closer in the early period than afterwards. Later on, while Aristotle still formally preserved the unity of the two disciplines, and even systematized them externally into one great whole, the ethics of the individual had nevertheless been practically completely separated, beneath the surface, from its traditional Platonic yokefellow, and a way was already open to the independence that it obtained in Hellenistic times.

We start with the beginning of Book VII, which lays the foundation of the ideal state. It is thoroughly Platonic in identifying the end of the state with the ethical end of the individual; for this is the meaning of the proposition from which the inquiry proceeds, that the best state is that which assures its citizens of the best life (αἱρετώτατος, ἄριστος βίος). In saying this Aristotle is by no means subordinating the state to the welfare of the individual, as a liberal would do, but is deriving, as Plato does, the categories for judging the value of the state from the ethical standards that apply to the soul of the individual. To say that the 'best life' of the state and of the individual are one and the same does not mean for him that things are well with the state if everybody has good food and feels comfortable, but that the spiritual and moral value of the state is based on that of its citizens. Its ultimate source is the evaluating soul of the individual. On the other hand, the highest ethical conception to which that soul attains is the state, towards which man is by nature predisposed.

Plato performs the derivation of the best state from ethical standards within a single science. With Aristotle, however, the differentiation of ethics and politics has advanced so far that at this point he is obliged to remind his readers of the fundamental importance of the ethical doctrine of the 'best life'. Now the form that the ethical question here takes ('What is the best life?') is by itself a sign of the date of this picture of the ideal state; for, although its influence can still be detected even in the later *Ethics*, it there constitutes merely the traditional framework within which Aristotle develops his realistic and psychological doctrine of character, whereas in the *Philebus* and the *Protrepticus*, and even in the original *Ethics*, it is still the centre of the whole problem of value. When, therefore, we find that Aristotle, when he has to determine the question of the best life in order to establish his ideal state, appeals to his exoteric works, we shall not be surprised, but shall give the matter our serious attention, and shall not merely consider the literary form, as had been done up to now, but also examine the content. His language unmistakably implies that he is basing himself on a particular work on the 'best life', and this must be the *Protrepticus*.[1] Bernays, who was the first to recognize this passage as a self-quotation, conjectured the reference to be to the totally unknown dialogue *Nerinthus*,[2] which is an incomprehensible view; but he did lasting service in drawing our attention to the change of style that takes place in the following chapter.[3] From the unusualness of such elevated writing in the treatises, and from its coincidence with the reference to the exoteric works, he concluded that we have here an extensive reproduction of one of Aristotle's dialogues, down even to the details. Diels afterwards put the problem of style into a more general setting, and explained the striking rise in tone, which

---

[1] *Pol.* VII. 1, 1323ᵃ 21. Here again the Oxford translation implies a different view. Tr.

[2] Bernays, *Die Dialoge des Aristoteles*, p. 89.   [3] Bernays, op. cit., p. 77.

occurs in several passages of the treatises, as a sort of διατριβή intended to produce an ethical effect by working on the hearer's subjective feelings. He did not believe that any of these passages were borrowed from the dialogues.[1] After what has been said, however, the fact that the treatises frequently make use of the exoteric works requires no further confirmation, and the introduction to Book VII of the *Politics* is a case in point. Nevertheless, the elevated style is certainly not to be explained by saying that Aristotle has failed to remove all traces of the original tone, for it is thoroughly suitable to an introduction to the ideal state, and recurs in similar places where borrowing from the dialogues is not to be assumed.[2] The fact is that this passage happens to combine both elevation of style and borrowing from an early work. Aristotle takes from his exoteric source not merely the ideas, but also the attempt to make them protreptically effective by means of a particular style.

The first thing that he takes over from the *Protrepticus*, as in the beginning of the second book of the *Eudemian Ethics*, is the division of all goods into external, bodily, and spiritual. Happiness depends on the possession of all three kinds, although it is naturally not so much the philosopher's business to demonstrate the necessity of the external or of the bodily goods as of those of the moral and spiritual personality. 'No one would maintain that he is happy who has not in him a particle of courage or temperance or justice or *phronesis*, who is afraid of every insect that flutters past him, and will commit any crime, however great, in order to gratify his lust of meat or drink, who will

[1] Diels, review of Georg Kaibel's 'Stil und Text der 'Αθηναίων Πολιτεία des Aristoteles' in *Gött. gel. Anz.*, 1894; and 'Zu Aristoteles' Protreptikos und Ciceros Hortensius' in *Arch. f. Gesch. d. Philos.*, vol. i, p. 478. In my *Ent. Metaph. Arist.* I followed Diels (p. 137); and I still hold it impossible to impute to Aristotle such a manner of using his dialogues as to fall into involuntary reminiscences of their style like a late compiler. If the style changes it is always because he intends to produce a particular effect. But whereas formerly I believed with Diels that this was a reason for dispensing entirely with the supposition that Aristotle borrowed from his exoteric works, this inference must now of course be abandoned. Vahlen's discussion of the opening of the sixth book of the *Politics* (*Ber. Wiener Akad. d. Wiss*, vol. lxxii, pp. 5 ff.), though admirable for its fine linguistic observations, does not help to solve Bernays' problem of the origin of the ideas in this chapter.

[2] As, for example, in the first book *On the Parts of Animals*, which is the introduction to a long series of lectures on animals, and is very general in character.

sacrifice his dearest friend for the sake of half-a-farthing, and is as feeble and false in mind as a child or a madman.' The age of this passage is clear from its mention of the four Platonic virtues, including *phronesis*, which is substituted for *sophia* in accordance with Plato's late view. We have seen the same four-fold scheme in the *Protrepticus*.[1] The importance assigned to it is shown by the four examples. That given for the value of *phronesis* can still be found in our fragments of the *Protrepticus*. 'No one would choose to live, even if he had the greatest wealth and power that man has ever had, if he were deprived of his reason and mad, not even if he were going to be constantly enjoying the most vehement pleasures.' And later on we read: 'If a man had everything, but the thinking part of him was corrupted and diseased, life would not be desirable for him. The other goods would be no benefit to him. This is why all men belittle all other goods so far as they know what reason is and are capable of tasting it. This also is why none of us could endure to be drunk or to be a child throughout life.'[2]

This, however, is universally acknowledged, the *Politics* continues. Men differ only about the degree, that is, about the question which sort of good we need most of. 'Some think that a very moderate amount of virtue is enough, but set no limit to their desires of wealth, property, power, reputation, and the like.' Yet 'happiness, whether consisting in pleasure or virtue or both [this was the problem of the *Philebus* and the *Protrepticus*],[3] is more often found with those who are most highly cultivated in their mind and in their character, and have only a moderate share of external goods, than among those who possess external goods to a useless extent but are deficient in higher qualities.' These words reproduce ideas and phrases characteristic of the *Protrepticus*. The man 'most highly cultivated in mind' is the counterpart of the man in the *Protrepticus* who is 'decked in shining raiment' but whose soul is 'in evil state'.[4]

---

[1] Frg. 52 (p. 62, ll. 2–4 in Rose) and frg. 58 (p. 68, ll. 6–9 in Rose). Compare *Pol.* VII. 1, 1323^b 33–6, and 15, 1334^a 22.

[2] Frg. 55 (p. 65, ll. 4–7 and 15–21 in Rose).

[3] Iambl. *Protr.*, p. 41, l. 12, and p. 59, l. 27, in Pistelli.

[4] *Pol.* VII. 1, 1323^a 36 ff.; cp. frg. 57. The method of determining the parts played in happiness by external possessions and by the state of the soul is the same in both passages.

Aristotle mentions this inner 'state' a few lines lower down in the *Politics*. 'The best state of one thing in relation to another corresponds in degree of excellence to the interval between the natures of which we say that these very states are states.'[1] The *Protrepticus* expresses the same thing more simply. 'If the state of a man's soul is bad neither wealth nor strength nor beauty is a good for him. On the contrary, the more the excess in which these states are present the more and the greater the harm they do to the man who possesses them without *phronesis*' (frg. 57 end).

External goods must have a limit (πέρας); for they are means, and every means is useful for something. Treated as an end in itself, a means becomes harmful to the man who makes himself its slave, or at the least it becomes useless. The more we increase inner goods, however, the more useful they are, if the epithet 'useful' as well as 'noble' is appropriate to such subjects.[2] Here again the *Protrepticus* is the source. In that work we read: 'To look for some result from every piece of knowledge, and to demand that it be useful, is to be absolutely ignorant of the fundamental difference between goods and necessities, and this difference is very great. Such things as we desire for the sake of something else, and without which we could not live, should be called necessary conditions (ἀναγκαῖα καὶ συναίτια); while what we desire for its own sake, even if nothing else comes from it, is good in the strict sense. For it is not the truth that one thing is desirable for the sake of another, and that for the sake of another again, and so on to infinity; there is a stop somewhere' (cp. *Pol.* 1323ᵇ 7, 'external goods have a limit'). In general one must not be always asking 'What use is it?' or 'How does that help us?'; there is an ideal ('the noble and good') that stands above base usefulness.[3] 'Each one has just so much of happiness as he has of virtue and *phronesis*'—the formula of the *Eudemian Ethics*. 'God is a witness to us of this truth, for he is happy and blessed, not by reason of any external good, but in

---

[1] For Aristotle's tendency in the *Protrepticus* to express conclusions in the manner of formal logic see Iambl. *Protr.*, p. 43, l. 28, and p. 44, l. 21. Both of these examples also refer to the eligible and the more eligible.

[2] *Pol.* VII. 1, 1323ᵇ 7–12.

[3] Frg. 58 (p. 68, l. 19, in Rose). At l. 1 of p. 69 in Rose three lines have fallen out after λέγομεν through a printer's error, cp. Iambl. *Protr.* p. 52, ll. 28 ff.

himself and by reason of his own nature.'[1] (This sort of argumentation belongs to the period shortly after Aristotle's emancipation from Plato, when the theological element still had the
upper hand and still penetrated ethics and politics. Later on
he avoided introducing such metaphysical matters.) That this
too is copied from the *Protrepticus* is shown by the fragment that
Cicero has preserved about the *beata vita* on the islands of the
blest. 'Una igitur essemus beati [scil. si nobis in beatorum
insulis immortale aevum degere liceret] cognitione naturae et
scientia, qua sola etiam deorum est vita laudanda.'[2] Here too
the true nature of human happiness is inferred from the reason
of God's happiness. This inference, together with the distinction between happiness and good fortune, which is developed
in the next line of the *Politics*, is found both in the early works
and in the oldest form of the *Ethics* and in the *Nicomachean
Ethics*; but the whole manner in which it is here treated is that
of the earlier period.[3] The first chapter of Book VII ends with
these words: 'Thus much may suffice by way of preface; for I
could not avoid touching upon these questions, neither could
I go through all the arguments affecting them; these are the
business of another lecture' (ἑτέρας σχολῆς). The hearer who is
not satisfied is thus expressly promised another discussion of the
question. In the Platonic circle in which these lectures were
written Aristotle expected opposition to his identification of the
happiness of the state with that of the individual. It would not
be difficult for a philosopher to merge himself in Plato's city
of philosophers and serve its ends, but Aristotle's new ideal state
is not to be ruled by Platonic kings. When, in the first chapter,
he speaks of the identity of the best life for the state and for the
individual citizens, it is significant that he recognizes as possible
kinds of life only two: a maximum of pleasure or a life of ethical
and practical goodness. He does not mention the life of pure
reason (*phronesis*).[4] To this a Platonist would have to reply,
'Then there is nothing for the philosopher but to withdraw
entirely from political life'; and this would be the necessary
consequence of Aristotle's own view in the *Protrepticus*, where
philosophy alone could determine the highest political norm,

[1] *Pol.* VII. 1, 1323b 21–26.   [2] Frg. 58 (p. 68, l. 10, in Rose).
[3] Cp. *Eth. Eud.* VIII. 2.   [4] *Pol.* VII. 1, 1323b 1.

and was the lawgiver in the state. Now, however, that the ideal state had been approximated to reality what room was there for the contemplative life of the philosophical individual? Here for the first time the antinomy between state and individual becomes a scientific problem, though as yet only in a very restricted sense, since it is only the philosophical ego, the ego of *phronesis*, that may have interests higher than the state's to represent. For the ordinary citizen who is simply the product of the reigning political principles there is no such problem in the ancient world. His membership in the state exhausts his nature.

But Aristotle demands that in the ideal state the community and the individual shall never have irreconcilably divergent aims; and so in the next two chapters of the *Politics* we have the spectacle, the interest of which is more than historical and bio-graphical, of the author of the *Protrepticus*, who has now aban-doned Plato's city of philosophers, working out the resulting inevitable conflict between his philosophical and his sociological conscience. Like the antinomy between faith and knowledge in metaphysics, and that between character and the speculative mind in ethics, this between the state and the individual (the latter being equivalent to cultural values) is not theoretically possible until we come to Aristotle's mutilated version of Plato. The original undivided unity of the active forces in Plato's romantic myth of the state could no longer restrain the tendency of these factors more and more to separate and diverge. Aris-totle tries to reconcile them once again into a higher unity. The thoroughgoing upholders of the contemplative life had long seen that the ultimate conclusion of Plato's ideal was to shun all actual states and live as a metic (ξενικὸς βίος), for where was the philosophically adjusted state in which their ideal could find a place? All actual constitutions, it seemed to them, were just might, nothing but might, tyranny, and slavery. The solu-tion was not to act, not to rule, not to incur the reproach of taking part in the despotic horror of political activity, with its selfishness and its hunger for power. With such thinkers Aris-totle contrasts those who hold that to act forcibly and to rule is the only thing worthy of a man. There are states whose whole constitutions and laws are aimed solely at breeding a proud, masterful, and warlike spirit in their citizens. And so far as

K

constitutions are not lifeless products of chance, which most of them are, they are without exception of this character according to him.[1] Now his new ideal is constructed as a mean between these two radical extremes. The boundless individualism of the thoroughgoing Platonist, who prefers absolute freedom to taking part in a despotic state, and wishes neither to rule nor to be ruled, is indeed ethically better than the modern state's ideal of power, he says, but rule is not necessarily despotism, and a large number of men are simply born to be dependent. It is also unjustifiable to condemn action and praise inactivity. He is incomparably Greek when he declares that there must be truth in the view that 'he who does nothing cannot do well'. To the Hellenic mind this was a certainty that required no discussion. Clearly Aristotle can combine the philosopher's ideal life with this view of the purpose of state and society only by representing philosophic contemplation as itself a sort of creative 'action'. Here again he is opening up new roads, and making a new tie to replace Plato's shattered mythical synthesis of knowledge and life. The activity of the creative mind is—building. Aristotle has abandoned the lonely heights of the *Protrepticus*. He now places himself in the midst of active life, and comes forward as an architect of thoughts (ὁ ταῖς Ζιανοίαις ἀρχιτέκτων), to build a state in which this intellectual form of action may obtain recognition and become effective as the crown of all the human activities that further the common good.[2] Thus he wrestles with the reality, whose nature he now sees more clearly, and preserves his youthful ideal. His criticism of the fundamental ethical and political principles of the *Protrepticus*, and of its theory of the best life, is as much to the fore in his early account of the ideal state as we have found it to be at every step in the original *Ethics*; and this fact not only proves the early date of that account, but also allows us, for the first time, to give it its right place in the history of his development. The original *Politics* comes, in fact, at the same stage as the original *Ethics* and the original *Metaphysics*.[3]

---

[1] The two types are described in *Pol.* VII. 2, 1324ᵃ 35 ff.

[2] *Pol.* VII. 3, esp. 1325ᵇ 15 ff.

[3] The dependence of Book VII on the *Protrepticus* is by no means confined to the first three chapters, which are analysed above. For example, it can be clearly detected in chapter 15 also. The mention of the four Platonic virtues

This gives a fresh meaning to the numerous passages where the old sketch of the ideal state refers to the *Ethics*. They have usually been supposed to apply to the *Nicomachean* version, even when the *Eudemian* was perfectly possible. There remained, indeed, the peculiar fact that some of the chief ones would fit the *Eudemian* only, which was supposed to be by Eudemus;[1] but since in these passages the *Ethics* is not expressly quoted but tacitly made use of (which is the ordinary thing), it was possible to maintain that it was Eudemus who had the *Politics* before him while writing, and not the other way about. Now that we have disproved his authorship and determined the age of the *Ethics* called after him, the real relation becomes clear. If the sketch of the ideal state must, in view of its close relation to the *Protrepticus*, have been written during the forties of the fourth century, it is self-evident that it cannot have used any *Ethics* but the original one. In VII. 13, for example, it quotes a long account of the right relation between means and end.[2] The source of this admittedly cannot be the *Nicomachean Ethics*. Nor is it possible to suppose that these ethical reflections first appeared in the *Politics*, where they are only mentioned in passing, whereas the *Eudemian Ethics* gives them in their original

there (1334ᵃ 22 ff.) is sufficient to show that this whole sketch of the state belongs to a very early date, and the topic on the necessity of philosophy and of the moral virtues upon the islands of the blest is directly borrowed from the *Protrepticus* (frg. 58). Thence comes also the invective against persons who are unable to use the goods of life (frg. 55), which follows this topic. So do the statements at the end of the chapter about the relation between body and soul, and about the parts of the soul (Iambl. *Protr.* p. 51, l. 18—p. 52, l. 2). 'The deficiencies of nature are what art and education seek to fill up' (VII. 17, 1337ᵃ 2) is verbally copied from Iambl. *Protr.*, p. 50, ll. 1–2. 'Nature has given older men wisdom' (VII. 9, 1329ᵃ 15) comes from p. 51, ll. 24 ff.

[1] Bendixen was the first to point out (*Philologus*, vol. xi (1856), pp. 575 ff.), against Spengel's view that the *Eudemian Ethics* was written by Eudemus, that there are several passages where the *Politics* shows a remarkable connexion with the *Eudemian Ethics*. He did not, however, venture to infer definitely that Spengel's declaration of spuriousness was untenable. In the Göttingen dissertation (1909) that I have already mentioned Von der Mühll reopened the discussion of Bendixen's observations (p. 19), but did not examine them in detail. Now, however, that we have adequately established the Aristotelian origin of the *Eudemian Ethics* by another path, and determined that it was written while he was moving away from Plato, it is necessary to take a new view of Bendixen's material.

[2] *Pol.* VII. 13, 1331ᵇ 26. Cp. *Eth. Eud.* II. 11, 1227ᵇ 19. That the passage is borrowed from the *Ethics* is rendered certain by the fact that this chapter expressly refers to 'the *Ethics*' in two other places (1332ᵃ 8 and 21).

context. It is equally impossible that, either by chance or by an accident of memory, Aristotle formulated the same ideas in the same language in two independent passages. Such an explanation is excluded by the existence of numerous other similar correspondences with the *Eudemian Ethics*, some of which have very characteristic details. They all go to show the same fact, namely that when he wrote the oldest parts of the *Politics* Aristotle had the *Eudemian Ethics* before him and frequently quoted it; and the correctness of this view is decisively proved by the fact that these remarkable borrowings all occur in the oldest books of the *Politics*, those concerning the ideal state.[1] Like the *Nicomachean Ethics* and the later version of the *Politics*, the original *Politics* and the original *Ethics* arose in close connexion with each other.

This same thirteenth chapter makes use of the original *Ethics* in several other passages. That at $1332^a 8$ is too general to permit definite inferences,[2] but ^{a} 21 ff. can refer only to the original and not to the *Nicomachean* version, because the manner in which it is expressed exactly reproduces the relevant passage in the former, while there is nothing corresponding to it in the later. (The passage that the editors refer to in the *Nicomachean* version does not fit.[3]) That the *Eudemian* is meant is also shown

[1] Taken in connexion with our whole inquiry this point is final. It has never previously been remarked. Up to the present the connexions between the *Politics* and the *Eudemian Ethics* have been examined only in order to determine whether the latter is genuine, and this they must be allowed to be incapable of doing. Besides the striking borrowings from the *Eudemian Ethics* in Books II and VII of the *Politics*, and also in III, the distinction between two meanings of 'use', as we find it in *Eth. Eud.* III. 3, 1231^b 38, also occurs in *Pol.* I. 9, 1257^a 5, that is to say, in one of the later parts; and similarly two passages of the late Book V contain proverbial maxims that also appear in the original *Ethics* (Bendixen, op. cit., p. 580). These faint echoes are not real proofs, however, and cannot be put on the same level as the borrowings in II, III, and VII. Some of them are reminiscences, and some, like the two senses of 'use', are things that would necessarily be repeated.

[2] The passage concerns the definition of happiness, and Aristotle refers to 'the *Ethics*' for it. As far as the passage itself goes, this might mean *Eth. Nic.* I. 6, 1098^a 16; if the other examples did not make it impossible. The emphasis on 'the realization *and perfect exercise* of virtue' is, however, a sign of the true state of affairs. This formulation occurs in *Eth. Eud.* II. 1, 1219^b 2, bound up with the determination of happiness. It is the standing definition in the earlier *Politics*, cp. VII. 8, 1328^a 38.

[3] The verbal parallel to *Eth. Eud.* VIII. 3, 1248^b 26, is clear at first sight, whereas there is no absolutely convincing correspondence to *Eth. Nic.* III. 6, 1113^a 15 ff.

by the quotation in 1334ᵃ 40 ff., where the thoroughly characteristic story of the Spartan view of virtue is taken from *Eth.
Eud.* 1248ᵇ 37 ff., as it is also in II, 1271ᵇ 4 ff. The *Eudemian*
distinction between genuine virtue and the spurious Spartan
kind necessarily assumed special importance for Aristotle when
he was laying the foundations of his archetypal state. Moreover, its connexion with 1332ᵃ 21 ff. is so close as to prove that
all three places refer to the same paragraph of the *Eudemian
Ethics*. In 1332ᵃ 21 we read: 'This also has been determined in
accordance with ethical arguments, that the good man is he
for whom, because he is virtuous, the things that are absolutely
good are good.' *Eth. Eud.* 1248ᵇ 26 runs: 'A good man, then, is
one for whom the natural goods are good', followed by the
reason, on which Aristotle is relying in this passage of the
Politics. There is also a quotation from the original *Ethics* in
the third book of the *Politics* (1278ᵇ 20 ff.). In contrast to this
dependence of the earlier books of the *Politics* on the *Eudemian*
version there is not a single demonstrable trace of their depending on the *Nicomachean*.

Another part of the early sketch of the ideal state enables us
to determine its date more accurately by means of an entirely
different approach. This part is Book II, which contains the
criticism of the earlier writers of Utopias, its chief attraction
being the criticism of Plato, far the most detailed that we have
from Aristotle. Besides the genuine Utopias he discusses Sparta
and Crete, which were regarded by Greek political theorists of
the fourth century as having exemplary constitutions (εὐνομού-
μεναι πολιτεῖαι). He also discusses Carthage.[1] In their present

---

[1] Book II as a whole is early, but the much discussed concluding chapter
may be an exception in date as well as in other respects. Aristotle there gives
a catalogue of lawgivers, and determines the characteristic or ἴδιον of the
statesmanship or writings of each. Scholars have always recognized that its
connexion with the preceding book is loose. If it were originally intended for
its present position it would be hard to see why Plato and Phaleas are discussed
a second time. For this reason Wilamowitz rejects 1274ᵇ 9–15 (*Aristoteles und
Athen*, vol. i, pp. 64 ff.). But obviously the catalogue of lawgivers arose independently and was added to the book subsequently, as I have shown in *Ent.
Metaph. Arist.*, p. 45. The tendency to collect all possible individual cases, and
the method of examining characteristics, suggest that it belongs to the late
period, when Aristotle was using similar methods in the description of nature.
The importance of the study of characteristics in Hellenistic science, for
example in ethnography, is well known.

form these chapters must have been written shortly after 345, since the departure to Crete of Phalaecus, the Phocian mercenary captain, is mentioned as having recently occurred;[1] but in substance they are older, for the *Protrepticus* denies that Crete or Sparta 'or any other such' is an exemplary constitution in the very same way. These states are there described as 'human states', the imitation of which can give only a human construction, and never anything enduring and divine.[2] Moreover, the material that Aristotle uses must surely have been collected before his stay in Assos and Mytilene, when Plato was working on the *Laws* and Spartan and Cretan institutions were a favourite subject of discussion in the Academy. The new information about Crete came from the history of Ephorus, and appeared simultaneously in *Politics* II and in the spurious Platonic dialogue *Minos*, which was probably written shortly after Plato's death.[3] We do not know Aristotle's authority for the Carthaginian constitution, but at any rate he had examined this also long before the collection of constitutions was made. In these studies he was guided by the idea of a standard. As in the *Protrepticus*, his purpose was to show that the best state does not occur anywhere in reality. The notion of the norm or ὅρος, which retires to the background in the *Nicomachean*, but which we have found still influential in the original *Ethics*, is nowhere so consistently applied as in the account of the ideal

[1] *Pol.* II. 10, 1272^b 20, where *pace* Newman (op. cit., vol. ii, p. 360) πόλεμος ξενικός means not a foreign but a mercenary war, as Fülleborn and Oncken have already pointed out. The former meaning is later Greek. [The Oxford translation follows Newman.—Tr.]

[2] Iambl. *Protr.*, p. 55, l. 17.

[3] It is not possible to decide with certainty the old controversy whether Aristotle used Ephorus for the tradition about Crete or contrariwise. What is excluded, of course, is that Ephorus used Aristotle's *Cretan Constitution*; the collection of constitutions was made much later, for Ephorus's work was known to Callisthenes, who went to Asia with Alexander in 334 (see Wilamowitz, *Aristoteles und Athen*, vol. i, p. 305). That Aristotle should have used Ephorus for his criticism of Cretan affairs in *Pol.* II. 10, during the latter half of the forties, is not at all impossible in itself, either chronologically or otherwise, since he was still far from the real study of particulars that characterized his latest period. On the other hand, in the early VII. 14, 1333^b 18, he speaks of Thibron's work on the Spartan state, and of 'all those who have written about the Lacedaemonian constitution', and hence he may have had local sources for Crete as well. The nature of the inferences about Crete is, however, so similar in Aristotle and in Ephorus, and so modern, that one would prefer to suppose that a historian like Ephorus was their originator.

state, and this is yet another reason for placing this account in the same period as the *Eudemian Ethics*.[1]

The criticism of Plato's *Republic* is very important for our knowledge of the contrast between Aristotle's nature and Plato's because it is not buried in abstract epistemological formulae; it was probably finished, together with the main body of the account of the ideal state, before the *Laws* appeared, which happened while Aristotle was in Assos. The account was then completed, while the impression created by this work was still fresh. This can be detected throughout. In fact, the actual criticism of the *Laws* itself seems to have been written rather hastily. As is well known, it contains all sorts of inaccuracies that suggest superficial reading. Aristotle's remains included copious extracts from the *Laws* as well as from the *Republic*; they were undoubtedly made for critical purposes. At this time he lacked the patience to form an exhaustive judgement on the work as a whole. He approached it with his opinions more or less made up beforehand, thinking himself already beyond it and therefore not bound to listen with an open mind. In spite of many correspondences in detail he was conscious of following another principle. All the more, however, did its powerfully realistic method of treatment compel him to make frequent isolated references to it, usually of a critical kind, of course. For example, 'we must not overlook the fact that even the number that Plato now proposes for the citizens[2] will require a territory as large as Babylon, or some other huge site, if 5,000 persons are to be supported in idleness, together with their women and attendants, who will be a multitude many times as great'.[3] His general opinion is: 'The discourses of Socrates . . . always exhibit grace, originality, and thought', but whether they are right is another question.

[1] A few examples must suffice. In many passages the meaning of the word ὅρος vacillates between norm as essence (the necessary determination of the essence) and norm as end. In Book VII, the actual outline of the ideal state, I have noted the following examples: 2, 1324b 4; 4, 1326a 35–36; 1326b 23 and 32; 1327a 6; 7, 1327b 19; 13, 1331b 36 (ὅρος directly synonymous with σκοπός, τέλος); 15, 1334a 12; σκοπός is also frequent: 2, 1324a 34; 13, 1331b 27 and 31; 14, 1333b 3 and 13. Books II, III, and VIII also use this conception of the norm often (Bonitz, *Ind. Arist.* s.v., does not do justice to this meaning of ὅρος): II. 6, 1265a 32; 7, 1267a 29; 9, 1271a 35; III. 9, 1280a 7; 13, 1283b 28; VIII. 7, 1342b 33 (cp. also 6, 1341b 15).

[2] Τὸ νῦν εἰρημένον πλῆθος. The Oxford translation involves another interpretation.—Tr.   [3] *Pol.* II. 6, 1265a 13.

It is significant that one of his criticisms of Plato's ideal states is that they take no account of foreign affairs. Plato constructs his state in a perfectly empty space. As to the brutal conflicts that arise in actual political existence, he either imagines them removed or—what would be worse—never thinks of them at all. It was certainly a clever and accurate observation 'that the legislator ought to have his eye directed to two points, the people and the country', but what about the neighbouring states? Since there are always neighbours, and since it is impossible to live the ideal existence isolated and undisturbed, whether one is an individual in a state or a state in the community of states, it is necessary to have a military organization adjusted not merely to the circumstances of one's own land but also to the nature of foreign countries.[1] The state must not merely meet the foe bravely in case of invasion, as Plato demands, but also prevent all other powers from desiring to attack it. Aristotle is just as sharp as his master in condemning the glorification of power and empire as the ultimate aim of the state; he denies that the people should be organized exclusively for the sake of war, and that the state should concentrate onesidedly on this single way of developing its powers. The characteristic part of his view, however, is what he adds to this. The necessities of foreign politics force the state into the struggle of conflicting national interests, and are liable to give it a direction different from that dictated by its ethical end.

What led him as a Platonist to this change of view? Clearly it was not theoretical reflections, but personal contact with actual foreign politics. The *Philippics* of Demosthenes would hardly have this effect on a mind like Aristotle's, though they began before he left Athens. On the other hand, continuous intercourse with a practical politician like Hermias of Atarneus must have given a new impulse to his political thinking, just as he in turn convinced Hermias of the necessity of ethical aims in politics. His account of the ideal state was completed in Assos and shortly afterwards.

No Greek state of the period was more dependent on 'neighbouring countries' than that of Hermias. Its unstable equilibrium, with Philip's military nation reaching out powerfully

[1] *Pol.* II. 6, 1265ª 18 ff.

on the European side of the Hellespont, and the Persian empire jealous of its overlordship on the Asiatic bank, demanded unremitting vigilance of eye and ear. And it is remarkable how the un-Platonic idea of the necessity for armaments, along with the fear of powerful and hostile neighbours, pervades the whole account.[1] In an interesting passage Aristotle attacks Plato's peculiarly Spartan idea that towns should not be fortified.[2] He declares that in view of modern siege-weapons and the new inventions in artillery this is an old-fashioned prejudice, although perhaps it was justifiable when one was surrounded only with enemies weaker than oneself, as Sparta used to be, and not with opponents of crushing superiority. This fits the situation of Hermias, who had, in fact, strongly fortified Atarneus, and was afterwards actually besieged by the Persians without success. And the other passage already mentioned refers explicitly to an earlier siege of this place.[3] It is obvious that here Hermias himself was the source of information. After objecting to Phaleas, as he had to Plato, that he takes no account of the necessity for an energetic foreign policy and for military armament in his description of the ideal state, Aristotle demands that domestic politics also, in which most of these theorists are unfortunately too exclusively interested, shall always be conducted in the closest connexion with external affairs. Above all, one must avoid amassing wealth large enough to excite the attacks of more powerful enemies and too large to be defended by its owners. In this respect the proper standard was set up by Eubulus of Atarneus, the predecessor of Hermias, who had previously been a banker. He said that 'a more powerful neighbour must have no inducement to go to war with you by reason of the excess of your wealth'; and when Autophradates, the Persian satrap, proposed to besiege him in Atarneus he invited him to calculate the cost of the siege, taking into account the length of time required. He declared himself ready to leave Atarneus at once for this amount, and so brought him to realize that the expense of the project would have been out of all proportion to its importance. Autophradates made the calculation and desisted from the siege.

---

[1] *Pol.* II. 7, 1267^a 19; II. 9, 1269^a 40; and VII. 11, 1330^b 32.
[2] *Pol.* VII. 11, 1330^b 32 to the end of the chapter.
[3] *Pol.* II. 7, 1267^a 19–37.

Thus the local colour of Atarneus is reflected in the early picture of the ideal state. Such a whimsical treatment must have been written before it was besieged for the second time by the same frightful enemy, before the death of Hermias had dimmed the amusing memory of the sly tricks of old Eubulus, his teacher in statecraft, and shattered the private happiness of Aristotle and his family. In this passage we seem to be listening to the actual conversations, while Hermias calls the attention of the Platonist, whose mind is open to all impressions, away from the ideals and towards the facts. Hermias's efforts in this respect, and his voluntarily taking the advice of the philosophers at Assos and changing his tyranny into a more moderate constitution, are reflected in the high value accorded to this mode of government in Aristotle's outline of the ideal state, and in his explicit limitation of the city's size and territory.

I conclude with a word or two about the character of Aristotle's method in constructing an ideal state. The foundation, which he lays in Book III, is the famous division of all possible constitutions into six, three true and three degenerate (παρεκβά-σεις). He takes over this normative attitude from the political works of his Academic period, to which he expressly refers in the passage where he develops his sixfold classification. Chapters 6 and 7 of the third book are essentially nothing but extracts from those works. Here the course of his development is especially plain. Plato had described the various types of constitution in the last part of the *Republic*. In the *Statesman* this led to the construction of a systematic conceptual scheme of true and perverted constitutions. Aristotle's methodical and architectonic trait led him to fasten on this point, as also did the fact that the *Statesman* appeared during his most receptive years as a member of the Academy. For these reasons his study of Plato's political doctrines is concerned mainly with this work, although it seems that from the first he emphasized the economic and social aspects of the various constitutions more than the purely formal ground of the classification. The influence of its derivatory, conceptual, and constructive method appears chiefly in the fact that he does not make his ideal state simply grow out of the earth, as Plato does in the *Republic* and the *Laws*, but develops it from a complete classification of constitutions according to their value. This enables him to introduce into the question of the best state, so far as the subject allows, the apodictic strictness that was essential to his nature. He is always striving for precise conceptions.[1] His ideal state is logical in framework; it is a piece of thought-construction in which the state is based rigidly on its fundamental elements and conceptions. He is very little interested in the vivid and realistic exposition of detail that makes the *Laws* living and effective. In the seventh book, for example, the discussion of a point as important as land and population is scarcely more than a bare enumeration of the various necessary conditions. The same is true of the sketchy section on the fundamental conditions (ὧν οὐκ ἄνευ) of the existence of the state.[2] Plato's sovereign legislative art of building the state becomes in Aristotle, in accordance with his principles, a scientific deduction, no longer purely Platonic in anything except its aim, which remains the knowledge of the absolutely standard constitution.

Aristotle looks to experience to confirm his conceptual constructions, but this is something entirely different from the empirical method of the later books, which contain the mere morphology of the actual state. It is prior to that not merely as the whole is prior to the part or the end to the means, but because biographically speaking it is an earlier and less developed stage of his political theory. Apart from many famous isolated remarks, its special nature and value lie mainly in its deliberate employment of the method of derivation. Aristotle's greatest creative power, his sense of concrete form, his ability to see the Idea moving in the flux of the living, reached its maturity only in his last period, when he wrestled successfully with the unlimited material of particular phenomena. At that time,

---

[1] In this classification every constitution is a fixed conception. Aristotle is still far removed from the idea of the later books of the *Politics*, that there may be various sorts of oligarchy and democracy, varying greatly in value, according to the nature and combinations of the various parts of the state. For this reason it is not probable that the development of the various forms of monarchy at the end of III belongs to the book in its earliest shape, that is, to the account of the ideal state as written during the forties, especially as it is also considered in IV. A more exact analysis would have to determine how Aristotle regarded the transition from III to IV when he was introducing Books IV—VI, and how far he altered the conclusion of III on that account.

[2] *Pol.* VII. 4, 1326ᵃ 5, and VII. 8, 1328ᵇ 2 ff.

however, the framework and comprehensive form of his *Politics* had long been fixed, and into it the new matter had to go, though it almost burst it. No wonder men have not felt themselves bound by this synthesis, but entitled to use whatever parts appealed to them and supported their own positions. Nevertheless, it is not a true estimate of Aristotle's achievement to take from his political or his ethical construction nothing but its rich experimental material, as the empiricist so often does, or to think, with the normative theorist, that one is justified in regarding it as a secondhand ideal of the Platonic type. The great, the new and comprehensive feature in Aristotle's work is his combination of normative thought, which had led him to set up a fresh ideal state better adapted to reality, with a sense of form capable of mastering and organizing the multiplicity of actual political facts. This sense of form kept his striving for the absolute standard from leading to stiffness, and revealed to him a thousand kinds of political existence and methods of improvement; while his stern grasp of the end preserved him from the relativity so easily induced by abandoning oneself indifferently to the comprehension of all that is. In both respects, and in the union of the two, he may well serve as the pattern of the mental and moral sciences to-day.

CHAPTER XI

THE ORIGIN OF THE SPECULATIVE PHYSICS
AND COSMOLOGY

IN Aristotle's scientific works it is considerably harder than in those that are strictly philosophical to come at the essential nature of his development. Little can be said about the details of the growth of his scientific thought; and presumably even the most searching inquiry into the composition of these writings, and the comparison of all details, would not overcome this misfortune, although we can say with perfect certainty that in view of the intensity of his research his progress was perhaps more astounding in this field than in all others, and that here, far more even than elsewhere, he must be understood through his development if we are really to grasp him in his individuality. It would be absurd to suppose that there is nothing to be discovered but relatively unimportant details, such as the gradual increase of his vast mass of material and the date of that particular draft of his lectures which happens to have been preserved. We have already pointed out that there are important differences in physical doctrine between the dialogue *On Philosophy* and the work *On the Heaven* (p. 153). We have found him gradually emancipating himself from the presuppositions of the mythical interpretation of nature, which always retained a powerful influence over the Greek mind, and had received fresh impetus from Plato's theory that the stars have souls. To examine this effort more accurately by means of copious examples would certainly be of the greatest interest for the history of Aristotle even as a philosopher, for it would bring the immanent tendencies of his thought clearly to light. The mere order in which he devoted himself to the different parts of nature would give us a curve which would be something quite other than a series of accidental points along the course of his biography—so much can be confidently affirmed beforehand, since we are dealing with the mind of an Aristotle. Up to the present, however, we have unfortunately not attained this insight, and therefore we must here confine ourselves to what our inquiries have already revealed to us.

It is necessary to begin with a warning against the perpetually recurring attempt to determine the temporal order of Aristotle's scientific works by means of their forward and backward references. Such references constitute a chronological criterion only when they contradict each other or the actual outline of a work, and when these contradictions are supported by other observations concerning the subject-matter itself. Now the works on natural science display a rigid system of references, and Zeller believed that his view of the order in which they were written could be based on this system.[1] According to this view the *Analytics* envisages the *Physics* as something not yet written, whereas the *Metaphysics* and the *Ethics*, together with most of the other scientific works, quote it or presuppose it; from which it is inferred that the *Physics* was written between the *Analytics* on the one hand and the *Metaphysics*, *Ethics*, and so on, on the other, a conclusion further supported by the fact that it does not itself quote or presuppose any of these latter works. The order of composition would therefore be *Physics*, *On the Heaven*, *On Coming-to-be and Passing-away*, *Meteorology*; and this appears to be confirmed by the *Meteorology*, which lists the other works as having preceded itself in precisely this order.[2] For the present we may disregard Zeller's further inferences about the *History of Animals*, the work *On the Soul*, and the other writings on organic nature. We have here one of those deeply rooted misunderstandings to whose ineradicable influence we owe the fact that scholars have mostly believed that any exact determination of the order of composition was impossible on principle. What this method gives us is at best only the order that Aristotle at the close of his literary activity believed to be demanded by the nature of the subject-matter or by pedagogical considerations; it will never give us a glimpse of his development or even of the mere order of the composition of particular works. We can no more raise a chronological structure on the series of references in the physical writings than we can argue from a mention of the *Ethics* in the *Politics*, or of the *Politics* in the *Ethics*, or of the *Ethics* in the *Metaphysics*, to the priority of the work in

[1] Zeller, *Aristotle and the Later Peripatetics*, p. 158. Cf. L. Spengel, 'Über die Reihenfolge der naturwissenschaftlichen Schriften des Aristoteles', *Abh. d. Münch. Akad.*, vol. v, pp. 150 ff.   [2] *Meteor.* I. 1, 338ᵃ 20.

question or of its content, without carefully examining the form of the quotation and the way in which it is used, and taking account of the possibility that the version referred to is earlier or later than the one that has come down to us. The supposed chronological order is nothing but the general scheme—perhaps a thoroughly late idea—into which at the end of his researches Aristotle forced the mass of his detailed inquiries. It agrees with the order as given in the best manuscripts,[1] and that this is factual and not temporal has presumably never been doubted. We must beware of confusing temporal with systematic priority, as it is easy to do, and of equating the time when an idea received literary form with the time when it first occurred to the philosopher.

The value of bearing all this in mind would previously have been purely theoretical, since the dates of composition of the *Metaphysics*, *Ethics*, and so on, were themselves unknown, and all the writings that we possess were supposed to have been crowded together in the last period. The inquiries of the foregoing chapters have altered this, however, and hence it is important to steer clear of a procedure that has thus far avoided contradictions only because it has not been applicable at all. On the other hand, however, we cannot altogether dispense with the references to the scientific works in the other writings, because the nature of the subject excludes all or practically all references to contemporary history, and because the development of Aristotle's method here does not fall into such sharply distinguished periods as are given for instance by the break with Plato's doctrine in the *Ethics* and the *Metaphysics*. When we use these references, therefore, we must first examine them carefully.

Of all the references to the *Physics* there is only one group that really has chronological significance, namely those in the oldest parts of the *Metaphysics*. We have shown that the first book of the *Metaphysics* was written shortly after Plato's death, at a time when its author was still a Platonist. For the teleological doctrine of the four causes, on which Aristotle bases

---

[1] For further details about the order of exposition in the lectures, so far as concerns the works following the *Meteorology* on anthropology and organic nature, see my article 'Das Pneuma im Lykeion', *Hermes*, vol. xlviii, p. 38. For the order see Arist. *de an. mot. et de an. inc.*, p. viii, Jaeger.

metaphysics, this book simply refers to the *Physics*, without giving any arguments for the exhaustiveness of the classification. This is not an isolated quotation such as could be imagined away without hurting the context, and therefore might have been added later. There is a whole series of passages in which Aristotle keeps on returning to the fact that his historical survey of the doctrines of earlier thinkers throughout confirms the theory of the four causes as stated in the *Physics*.[1] The whole first book of the *Metaphysics* rests on this presupposition, and would collapse if the aetiology of the *Physics* were not behind it in every line. This is incontrovertible proof that not only the second book of the *Physics*, which sets out the theory of the causes, but a complete series of investigations falling under the general notion of 'physical works' (φυσικά), was already in existence about 347. This is further confirmed by the isolated references in the *Metaphysics*[2] and above all by the general nature of this work, since its whole philosophical conception presupposes the *Physics* and develops out of it. Two of the foundations of Aristotle's first philosophy belong to *Physics*, and they are the most important of all, namely the distinction between matter and form and the theory of motion. From these two presuppositions he derives the necessity of the first mover, and even that pair of conceptions by means of which motion is linked up with form and matter, namely potency and entelechy, is not foreign to the *Physics*. The idea of interpreting nature in this teleological fashion, and its expression in the *Physics*, arose in the atmosphere of the Academy and under Plato's eye. It must be assigned not to Aristotle's latest but to his earliest stage.[3]

---

[1] *Metaph.* A 3, 983^a 33; 7, 988^a 21 and ^{b} 16; 8, 989^a 24; and 10, 993^a 11.

[2] Of the places where the *Metaphysics* appeals to the *Physics* the most important for our question are naturally those occurring in the parts that can be shown to be the oldest, that is to say, the beginning of the earlier investigation into the reality of the supersensible (M 9, 1086^a 23), and the laying down of the whole system of physical conceptions in Book Λ, 1–5.

[3] Gercke's statement that the *Physics* was written or completed after Aristotle had founded his school, and therefore in his latest period (Pauly-Wissowa, *Realenz. d. Klass. Alt.*, vol. ii, c. 1045, l. 38, under 'Aristoteles'), rests on an obvious piece of carelessness. The assassination of King Philip is not mentioned at all in the passage to which he refers, *Physics* II. 23 (*sic*), or in other words no such passage exists. He is confusing the *Physics* with the *Rhetoric*, which mentions Philip at II. 23, and then once more mixing up this mention with the well-

That is not true without qualification, however, of our present version of the *Physics* in its whole extent. This work resembles the philosopher's others in containing both early and late material. The present position of the seventh book is not due to Aristotle himself at all, for in content it comes too close to the other parts of the *Physics* in which the problem of motion is also discussed.[1] That it belongs to the oldest part, and arose at a time when he did not yet regard the theory of Ideas as simply exploded, is more than probable.[2] Like the *Metaphysics* and the

known reference to Philip's death in *Pol.* V. 10, 1311ᵇ 2. I draw attention to this only because its occurrence in such an authoritative position is likely to lead many readers astray. It is true that our version of the *Physics* belongs to the latest period, but the reasons that Gercke gives for this fact do not prove it (even the fact that it was written after the *Analytics* cannot possibly prove it as late as this), and anyhow this is a question merely of revision and has no significance whatever for Aristotle's philosophical development.

[1] Eudemus omitted it in his paraphrase of the *Physics* (see the preliminary remarks on Book VII in the commentary of Simplicius, vol. ii, p. 1036, in Diels), which shows that it did not belong to the collection entitled *Physics* that Aristotle himself put together and bequeathed to his disciples. This, however, naturally does not prove that the work was completely unknown in the Peripatos. It was, in fact, like some of the books of the *Metaphysics* that were originally handed down independently, preserved as being an important historical document, but having, in view of the 'great and comprehensive theorems' of the last book—to use Simplicius's expression—scarcely any practical value. It appears to have been the generation of Andronicus, with its pious desire to produce a complete collection, that first incorporated it in the *Physics*. Simplicius compared the two versions in which it is preserved without being able to discover any differences of content worth mentioning. He is right in pointing out, however, that the proofs of the first mover in Book VII stand on a lower level than those in Book VIII, and presumably this is the reason why Aristotle replaced it with the latter. Cp. E. Hoffmann, *De Aristotelis Physicorum libri septimi origine et auctoritate* (Berlin, Diss., 1905).

[2] *Phys.* VII. 4, 249ᵇ 19–26, is difficult and requires interpretation. Since Simplicius no one has tried to explain it if we except the translation by Prantl (Leipzig, 1854, p. 367), who did not understand the train of thought. In the fourth chapter Aristotle shows that the various sorts of motion, for example qualitative alteration (ἀλλοίωσις) and locomotion (φορά), are incommensurable. The idea of equal velocity (ὁμοταχές) can be applied only to specifically similar and commensurable motions. For example, qualitative motions can be compared with each other, and quantitative motions can be compared with each other. In the first example we speak of the likeness or unlikeness (ἀνομοιότης) of the qualitative alterations; in the second we speak of the equality or inequality (ἀνισότης) of the quantitative motions. Inequality arises from the 'greater or smaller' of the quantitative motions when they are compared together, unlikeness from the 'more or less' of two qualitative alterations when they are compared. There is another kind of motion that concerns the substance and not merely the quality or quantity, namely becoming and perishing. Two becomings can be compared in point of velocity only when we are concerned with two things of the same species (ὁμοειδῆ), as, for example, men. Speech has no

Ethics the *Physics* is a compilation of at least two parts, each of which again consisted of several monographs. These two parts, *On the First Principles* and *On Motion*, are always carefully distinguished, not merely in the works *On the Heaven* and *On Coming-to-be and Passing-away*, but also in the last book of the *Physics* (VIII). This book is really no part of the *Physics*, for it quotes passages from these two parts with the formula 'as we have previously shown in the *Physics*'.[1] Presumably it was originally, like the books *On Substance and Being*, which originally stood outside the *Metaphysics* (that is, before it), one of the inquiries that Aristotle reckoned as half physics and half metaphysics, and as

category, however, that can pregnantly express the nature of the difference between two becomings, and Aristotle therefore asks to be pardoned for merely speaking of their 'difference' (ἑτερότης) in a general and colourless manner, and for not being able to mention any pair of correlatives, like more and less in qualitative alteration and greater and smaller in locomotion, that would make it clear that the distinction here is neither intensive nor extensive, but something different. Then follows the remark that is important for the chronology: *if* the substance with whose becoming we are concerned is a number (as Plato and the Academy supposed), then the difference in velocity between the becomings of two substances is to be regarded as the arithmetical difference between two *numbers of the same species* with regard to the more and the less. There is, however, no common term for this difference in velocity. The last sentence is corrupt, but its meaning obviously is that there is also no term corresponding to 'more and less' and 'greater and smaller' to describe the two becomings that are being compared. Now the statement that the substances whose becomings are compared must be of the same species (ὁμοειδεῖς) follows from the whole argument of the fourth chapter, but what is the sense of this demand in the case of the numbers? We must remember that according to *Metaph.* M 7, 1080^b 37 ff., one of the main difficulties of the theory of Ideal numbers was the question whether the monads of which they are composed are perfectly commensurable like those of arithmetic, or whether every 'first number', the first dyad, triad, tetrad, and so on, is composed of monads of a special kind, so that only the monads inside a particular number are commensurable and 'of the same species' (the expression occurs in A 9, 991^b 24). The phrase 'of the same species', therefore, proves that in our passage Aristotle is still contemplating the possibility that substance may be a number, which he elsewhere combats. Otherwise one might think that we have here only an example intended to make the meaning concrete, as Simplicius does when he doubts whether Aristotle refers here to Ideal numbers or merely to the view that the nature of everything depends upon a particular numerical relation of its parts; but the assertion that the numbers must be 'of the same species' excludes the latter interpretation, for, if it is not obvious in itself that they must, the reference can only be to the Ideal numbers. If so, the character of the arguments in Book VII, which Simplicius calls 'weaker or as Alexander [more correctly] says more verbal' (op. cit., p. 1036, l. 12), will be best explained by supposing that in the course of the years Aristotle perfected them more and more. For another indication of the early origin of Book VII see above, p. 44, n. 1.

[1] See Bonitz, *Ind. Ar.* 98^a 27.

providing the transition from the one to the other.[1] Its temporal position can be determined by its treatment of the theory of the movers of the spheres, which is not worked out in so decidedly unified a fashion as in the later version in Book Λ of the *Metaphysics*.[2] Yet we can clearly recognize that Book VIII is intended to give a very careful re-establishment of the theory of the first mover on a physical basis, and to defend it against all sorts of objections that had already been brought from the astronomical side, probably by Callippus.[3] Fairly certainly, therefore, it was not written until the time of Aristotle's greatest power; and since even then it was not yet a part of the *Physics* (and hence presumably never at all during its author's life), the *Physics*, as we know it, did not yet exist as a whole. This is supported by the fact that the *Metaphysics* quotes as 'physics' the two works *On the Heaven* and *On Coming-to-be and Passing-away*. At that time, therefore, this word did not mean our *Physics*, but a larger group of independent monographs. Among its oldest parts were that on the first principles, to judge from the first book of the *Metaphysics*, and that on matter and form, to judge from Book N of the same work; that is to say, the first two books of our *Physics*. We may suppose, however, that in substance these works go back as far as his Platonic period, although certain passages, such as the mention of the Lyceum in Book IV, reveal later revision of the details.[4] For the history of Aristotle's philosophical development the date of completion is more or less unimportant compared with the discovery that the speculative character of what is called the *Physics* in the narrow sense is connected with its directly Platonic origin. It was worked out as part of a Platonic theory of the world, and stands on the same ground. This is especially clear when we come to the problems of concrete detail in the books *On the Heaven*, which are also referred to in the oldest parts of the *Metaphysics*.[5] The beginning of the first of these books must be early in essence,

---

[1] *Phys.* VIII. 1, 251ᵃ 5, on the eternity of motion: 'We must consider, then, how this matter stands, for the discovery of the truth about it is of importance, not only for the study of nature, but also for the investigation of the First Principle.'

[2] The proof that chapter 8 of Book Λ of the *Metaphysics*, with its theory of the movers of the spheres, is a later addition is given below in chapter XIV.

[3] *Phys.* VIII. 6.   [4] *Phys.* IV. 11, 219ᵇ 21.

[5] See Bonitz, *Ind. Ar.* 101ᵃ 7.

since it places triumphantly at the start of the whole course of lectures the young Academician's own discovery that there is a fifth element, the ether. As we have already shown, this theory is older than the books *On Philosophy*, which are based on it, and is necessarily connected with the first beginnings of the theory of the unmoved mover and the heavenly bodies.[1] The form that Aristotle gives to his theory of ether in the first chapters *On the Heaven* is later than the account in the exoteric work (above, p. 154). The view previously held, that in the dialogue he did not express his real opinion, but rather gave a poetic embellishment of it, is untenable; for what he preserves in his work *On the Heaven* is precisely the point that was supposed to be poetic, the theory that the heavenly bodies have souls.[2] The difference between the two comes in the physical theory of the natural motion of simple bodies, and in its connexion with the theory of weight, which is established in a wholly different manner in the dialogue. At this point we realize only too clearly what important matters are hidden from us by the dearth of source-material. Nevertheless, the disposition of the books *On the Heaven* does at any rate enable us to observe how Aristotle's cosmology arose out of Plato's. We know the latter directly only from the *Timaeus*, behind which lie the far-reaching Pythagorean speculations of the school; and it is therefore very important that this work of Aristotle's allows us a glimpse of the discussions that went on about the subject in the Academy.

That this is true of the problem of ether has already been shown. It connects directly with the *Timaeus*, and we find it

[1] For the origin of the theory of ether see the exhaustive discussion of Eva Sachs, *Die fünf platonischen Körper* (Berlin 1917). She, too, comes to the conclusion that the readiness with which Plato's followers accepted the theory shows that it arose in the Academy, and Aristotle therefore put it forward before Plato's death. Compare what was said above about the relation between the *Epinomis* and the dialogue *On Philosophy*, p.144, n. 2.

[2] *De Caelo* II. 12, 292ᵃ 18: 'We have been thinking of the stars as mere bodies and as units with a serial order indeed but entirely inanimate; but we should rather conceive them as enjoying life and action.' The expression recalls the dialogue *On Philosophy* and Plato's famous remarks in the *Laws*. According to *De Caelo* II. 8, however, it is the spheres, and not the stars on them, that move themselves, and this, taken strictly, implies that it is the spheres that have souls (or have movers as in *Metaph*. Λ 8), and not the stars as in the dialogue *On Philosophy*. It is only after a long examination, however, that Aristotle here decides that only the spheres and not the stars move themselves, so that here too we have a development of his earlier view.

reflected in the writings of all Aristotle's fellow-students. But the question whether there can be an infinite body, whether the world is finite or infinite, and whether there is only one world or more—a very important question for Aristotle's metaphysics, since the existence of the first mover depends on it—must also have been discussed by the astronomers in the Academy while Plato was still alive, and answered by Aristotle in accordance with his own view, which was that the world is one, eternal, and finite. He tries to prove not merely that there actually is only one heaven but also that there could not be more than one. It may seem otherwise, because every form (εἶδος) that is realized in matter usually exists in a number of specifically identical (ὁμοειδῆ) examples. Actually, however, it makes no difference to the result whether we regard the form as transcendent, that is, as an Idea, or as inseparable (obviously some of the Platonists were trying to fasten on this point);[1] for in this question one must not start from the form at all, according to Aristotle, but from the matter. Since the cosmos includes all matter there cannot be any other world besides. The argument seems somewhat naïve, but for him it is not really absurd, because by 'the heaven' he means, as he at once goes on to say, not merely the outermost sphere, or the region of the highest elements, in which the heavenly bodies move, but the comprehensive All, which is to be thought of as corporeally plastic, but never as *actu infinitum*. This plastic ball exhausts all the matter that there is. Outside it there is in fact not even place or time or void, much less bodies. The transcendental (τἀκεῖ) and supramundane is therefore not in space nor in a place; time does not age it; nor is there any sort of change in that realm beyond the outermost sphere. But let us allow Aristotle to speak for himself. His words breathe here a ceremoniousness unusual in the treatises.[2]

[1] The passage is interesting because in it the theory of Ideas and Aristotle's view that the form is immanent stand side by side as equally justifiable possibilities: 'Any shape or form has, or may have, more than one particular instance. On the supposition of Ideas such as some assert, this must be so, and equally on the view that no such entity has a separate existence. For in every case in which the essence is in matter it is a fact of observation that the particulars of like form are several or infinite in number.' (*De Caelo* I. 9, 278ª 15.)

[2] *De Caelo* I. 9, 279ª 17. I follow Bernays in giving the Greek and the translation side by side.

φανερὸν ἄρα ὅτι οὔτε τόπος οὔτε κενὸν οὔτε χρόνος ἐστὶν ἔξωθεν· Διόπερ οὔτ' ἐν τόπῳ τἀκεῖ πέφυκεν, οὔτε χρόνος αὐτὰ ποιεῖ γηράσκειν, οὐδ' ἐστὶν οὐδενὸς οὐδεμία μεταβολὴ τῶν ὑπὲρ τὴν ἐξωτάτω τεταγμένην φοράν, ἀλλ' ἀναλλοίωτα καὶ ἀπαθῆ τὴν ἀρίστην ἔχοντα ζωὴν καὶ τὴν αὐταρκεστάτην Διατελεῖ τὸν ἅπαντα αἰῶνα· καὶ γὰρ τοῦτο τοὔνομα θείως ἔφθεγκται παρὰ τῶν ἀρχαίων. τὸ γὰρ τέλος τὸ περιέχον τὸν τῆς ἑκάστου ζωῆς χρόνον, οὗ μηθὲν ἔξω κατὰ φύσιν, αἰὼν ἑκάστου κέκληται. κατὰ τὸν αὐτὸν Δὲ λόγον καὶ τὸ τοῦ παντὸς οὐρανοῦ τέλος καὶ τὸ τὸν πάντα χρόνον καὶ τὴν ἀπειρίαν περιέχον τέλος αἰών ἐστιν, ἀπὸ τοῦ ἀεὶ εἶναι εἰληφὼς τὴν ἐπωνυμίαν, ἀθάνατος καὶ θεῖος. ὅθεν καὶ τοῖς ἄλλοις ἐξήρτηται, τοῖς μὲν ἀκριβέστερον τοῖς Δ' ἀμαυρῶς, τὸ εἶναί τε καὶ ζῆν. καὶ γὰρ καθάπερ ἐν τοῖς ἐγκυκλίοις φιλοσοφήμασι περὶ τὰ θεῖα πολλάκις προφαίνεται τοῖς λόγοις ὅτι τὸ θεῖον ἀμετάβλητον ἀναγκαῖον εἶναι πᾶν τὸ πρῶτον καὶ ἀκρότατον· [ὃ] οὕτως ἔχον μαρτυρεῖ τοῖς εἰρημένοις. οὔτε γὰρ ἄλλο κρεῖττόν ἐστιν ὅτι κινήσει (ἐκεῖνο γὰρ ἂν εἴη θειότερον) οὔτ' ἔχει φαῦλον οὐθέν, οὔτ' ἐνδεὲς τῶν αὐτοῦ καλῶν οὐδενός ἐστιν. καὶ ἄπαυστον Δὴ κίνησιν κινεῖται εὐλόγως· πάντα γὰρ παύεται κινούμενα, ὅταν ἔλθῃ εἰς τὸν οἰκεῖον τόπον, τοῦ Δὲ κύκλῳ σώματος ὁ αὐτὸς τόπος ὅθεν ἤρξατο καὶ εἰς ὃν τελευτᾷ.

It is clear then that there is neither place, nor void, nor time, outside the heaven. Hence whatever there is, is of such a nature as not to occupy any place, nor does time age it; nor is there any change in any of the things that lie beyond the outermost motion; they continue through their entire duration unalterable and unmodified, living the best and most self-sufficient of lives. As a matter of fact, this word 'duration' possessed a divine significance for the ancients, for the fulfilment that includes the period of life of any creature, outside of which no natural development can fall, has been called its duration. On the same principle the fulfilment of the whole heaven, the fulfilment that includes all time and infinity, is 'duration'—a name based upon the fact that it *is always* —duration immortal and divine. From it derive the being and life that other things, some more or less articulately but others feebly, enjoy. So, too, *in its discussions concerning the divine, popular philosophy* often propounds the view that whatever is divine, whatever is primary and supreme, is necessarily unchangeable. This fact *confirms what we have said.* For there is nothing else stronger than it to move it—since that would mean more divine—and it has no defect and lacks none of its proper excellences. Its unceasing movement, then, is also reasonable, since everything ceases to move when it comes to its proper place, but the body whose path is the circle has one and the same place for starting point and goal.

'The discussions of popular philosophy' means the dialogue *On Philosophy*, the only one that discussed the theological problem and examined its relation to the question of the eternal circular motion of the firmament. The final words are a more or less verbal quotation from the argument of this dialogue, as preserved by Simplicius in his commentary on the passage; he expressly describes the dialogue as the source to which Aristotle's reference applies. Strangely enough, Bernays, who discussed this passage of Simplicius acutely,[1] confined his attention to the reference, and failed to observe that the whole of the passage immediately preceding it, quoted above, can be recognized by its style as a piece of literary prose taken from the same dialogue. Even the beginning of the tenth chapter, which immediately follows, does not read like an ordinary lecture, though here only isolated traces of another style can be pointed out. Anyhow we must expect Aristotle during his early period to introduce free reproductions of large portions of his literary works not merely into his political, metaphysical, and ethical, but also into his scientific, lectures. The dialogues, of course, did not often mention scientific matters. In the third book *On Philosophy*, however, he had discussed (see p. 140 above) the question whether the heaven is eternal, and argued against Plato's view that, while it will have no end, it had a beginning. We may therefore conjecture some dependence on that dialogue precisely in the last part of the first book *On the Heaven*, which follows the part quoted above, and in the beginning of the second, because the very same question is here discussed—'whether the cosmos is uncreated or created and imperishable or perishable'. In essentials this inquiry is, like that of the dialogue, a running polemic against Plato's *Timaeus*, which is explicitly mentioned.[2] Now the beginning of the second book is so completely alien in style and method to Aristotle's usual pedagogical procedure that the only possible explanation is that here, too, he is reproducing parts of the third book *On Philosophy*. Our lack of materials renders direct proof impossible; but since we have shown conclusively by numerous examples that such borrowing does occur, and since we know that there is a long extract from this book a few pages earlier, there can presumably be no doubt about the origin of the present passage.

---

[1] Bernays, *Die verlorenen Dialoge des Aristoteles*, p. 110.
[2] *De Caelo* I. 10, 280ᵃ 28. Cf. 279ᵇ 32.

Ὅτι μὲν οὖν οὔτε γέγονεν ὁ πᾶς
οὐρανὸς οὔτ' ἐνδέχεται φθαρῆναι,
καθάπερ τινές φασιν αὐτόν, ἀλλ' ἔστιν
εἷς καὶ ἀΐδιος, ἀρχὴν μὲν καὶ τελευτὴν
οὐκ ἔχων τοῦ παντὸς αἰῶνος, ἔχων
δὲ καὶ περιέχων ἐν αὑτῷ τὸν ἄπειρον
χρόνον, ἔκ τε τῶν εἰρημένων ἔξεστι
λαβεῖν τὴν πίστιν καὶ διὰ τῆς δόξης
τῆς παρὰ τῶν ἄλλως λεγόντων καὶ
γεννώντων αὐτόν· εἰ γὰρ οὕτως μὲν
ἔχειν ἐνδέχεται, καθ' ὃν δὲ τρόπον
ἐκεῖνοι γενέσθαι λέγουσιν οὐκ ἐνδέχεται, μεγάλην ἂν ἔχοι καὶ τοῦτο ῥοπὴν
εἰς πίστιν περὶ τῆς ἀθανασίας αὐτοῦ
καὶ τῆς ἀϊδιότητος· διόπερ καλῶς ἔχει
συμπείθειν ἑαυτὸν τοὺς ἀρχαίους καὶ
μάλιστα πατρίους ἡμῶν ἀληθεῖς εἶναι
λόγους, ὡς ἔστιν ἀθάνατόν τι καὶ
θεῖον τῶν ἐχόντων μὲν κίνησιν, ἐχόντων δὲ τοιαύτην ὥστε μηθὲν εἶναι
πέρας αὐτῆς, ἀλλὰ μᾶλλον ταύτην
τῶν ἄλλων πέρας· τό τε γὰρ πέρας
τῶν περιεχόντων ἐστί, καὶ αὕτη ἡ
κυκλοφορία τέλειος οὖσα περιέχει τὰς
ἀτελεῖς καὶ τὰς ἐχούσας πέρας καὶ
παῦλαν, αὐτὴ δὲ οὐδεμίαν οὔτ' ἀρχὴν
ἔχουσα οὔτε τελευτήν, ἀλλ' ἄπαυστος
οὖσα τὸν ἄπειρον χρόνον, τῶν δ'
ἄλλων τῶν μὲν αἰτία τῆς ἀρχῆς, τῶν
δὲ δεχομένη τὴν παῦλαν. τὸν δ'
οὐρανὸν καὶ τὸν ἄνω τόπον οἱ μὲν
ἀρχαῖοι τοῖς θεοῖς ἀπένειμαν ὡς ὄντα
μόνον ἀθάνατον· ὁ δὲ νῦν μαρτυρεῖ
λόγος ὡς ἄφθαρτος καὶ ἀγένητος, ἔτι
δ' ἀπαθὴς πάσης θνητῆς δυσχερείας
ἐστίν, πρὸς δὲ τούτοις ἄπονος διὰ τὸ
μηδεμιᾶς προσδεῖσθαι βιαίας ἀνάγκης,
ἣ κατέχει κωλύουσα φέρεσθαι πεφυ-
κότα αὐτὸν ἄλλως. πᾶν γὰρ τὸ
τοιοῦτον ἐπίπονον, ὅσῳπερ ἂν ἀϊδιώ-
τερον ᾖ, καὶ διαθέσεως τῆς ἀρίστης
ἄμοιρον, διόπερ οὔτε κατὰ τὸν τῶν
παλαιῶν μῦθον ὑποληπτέον ἔχειν, οἵ
φασιν Ἀτλαντός τινος αὐτῷ προσδεῖ-

That the heaven as a whole neither came into being nor admits of destruction, as some assert, but is one and eternal, with no end or beginning of its total duration, containing and embracing in itself the infinity of time, we may convince ourselves not only by the arguments already set forth but also by a consideration of the views of those who differ from us in providing for its generation. If our view is a possible one, and the manner of generation which they assert is impossible, this fact will have great weight in convincing us of the immortality and eternity of the world. Hence it is well to persuade oneself of the truth of the ancient and truly traditional theories, that there is some immortal and divine thing which possesses movement, but movement such as has no limit and is rather itself the limit of all other movement. A limit is a thing that contains, and this circular motion, being perfect, contains those imperfect motions which have a limit and a goal, having itself no beginning or end, but unceasing through the infinity of time, and of other movements, to some the cause of their beginning, to others offering the goal. The ancients gave to the Gods the heaven or upper place, as being alone immortal; and our present argument testifies that it is indestructible and ungenerated. Further, it is unaffected by any mortal discomfort, and, in addition, effortless; for it needs no constraining necessity to keep it to its path, and prevent it from moving with some other movement more natural to itself. Such a constrained movement would necessarily involve effort—the more so, the more eternal it were—and would be in-

σθαι τὴν σωτηρίαν· ἐοίκασι γὰρ καὶ
τοῦτον οἱ συστήσαντες τὸν λόγον τὴν
αὐτὴν ἔχειν ὑπόληψιν τοῖς ὑστερον·
ὡς γὰρ περὶ βάρος ἐχόντων καὶ
γεηρῶν ἁπάντων τῶν ἄνω σωμάτων
ὑπέστησαν αὐτῷ μυθικῶς ἀνάγκην
ἔμψυχον. οὔτε δὴ τοῦτον τὸν τρόπον
ὑποληπτέον, οὔτε διὰ τὴν δίνησιν
θάττονος τυγχάνοντα φορᾶς [διὰ]
τῆς οἰκείας ῥοπῆς ἔτι σῴζεσθαι
τοσοῦτον χρόνον, καθάπερ Ἐμπε-
δοκλῆς φησιν. ἀλλὰ μὴν οὐδ' ὑπὸ
ψυχῆς εὔλογον ἀναγκαζούσης μένειν
ἀΐδιον· οὐδὲ γὰρ τῆς ψυχῆς οἷόν τ'
εἶναι τὴν τοιαύτην ζωὴν ἄλυπον καὶ
μακαρίαν. ἀνάγκη γὰρ καὶ τὴν
κίνησιν μετὰ βίας οὖσαν, εἴπερ
κινεῖσθαι πεφυκότος τοῦ πρώτου
σώματος ἄλλως καὶ κινεῖ συνεχῶς,
ἄσχολον εἶναι καὶ πάσης ἀπηλλαγ-
μένην ῥᾳστώνης ἔμφρονος, εἴ γε μηδ'
ὥσπερ τῇ ψυχῇ τῇ τῶν θνητῶν ζῴων
ἐστὶν ἀνάπαυσις ἡ περὶ τὸν ὕπνον
γινομένη τοῦ σώματος ἄνεσις, ἀλλ'
ἀναγκαῖον Ἰξίονός τινος μοῖραν κατέ-
χειν αὐτὴν ἀΐδιον καὶ ἄτρυτον.

εἰ δὴ καθάπερ εἴπομεν ἐνδέχεται τὸν
εἰρημένον ἔχειν τρόπον περὶ τῆς
πρώτης φορᾶς, οὐ μόνον αὐτοῦ περὶ
τῆς ἀϊδιότητος οὕτως ὑπολαβεῖν
ἐμμελέστερον, ἀλλὰ καὶ τῇ μαντείᾳ τῇ
περὶ τὸν θεὸν μόνως ἂν ἔχοιμεν οὕτως
ὁμολογουμένως ἀποφαίνεσθαι συμ-
φώνους λόγους.

ἀλλὰ τῶν μὲν τοιούτων λόγων ἅλις
ἔστω τὰ νῦν.[1]

consistent with perfection. Hence we must not believe the old tale which says that the world needs some Atlas to keep it safe—a tale composed, it would seem, by men who, like later thinkers, conceived of all the upper bodies as earthy and endowed with weight, and therefore supported it in their fabulous way upon animate necessity. We must no more believe that than follow Empedocles when he says that the world, when its motion became faster because of the whirl, kept itself [suspended] all this time only by means of its own equilibrium. Nor, again, is it conceivable that it should persist eternally by the necessitation of a soul (world-soul). For a soul could not live in such conditions painlessly or happily, since the movement involves constraint, being imposed on the first body (the heaven), whose natural motion is different, and imposed continuously. It must therefore be uneasy and devoid of all rational satisfaction; for it could not even, like the soul of mortal animals, take recreation in the bodily relaxation of sleep. An Ixion's lot must needs possess it, without end or respite.

If then, as we said, the view already stated of the first motion is a possible one, it is not only more appropriate so to conceive of its eternity, but also on this hypothesis alone are we able to advance a theory consistent with popular divinations of the divine nature.

But of this enough for the present.[1]

It scarcely needs to be proved in detail that the style of this chapter is quite other than that of Aristotle's scientific prose.

[1] By these words, with which he resumes his ordinary lecturing style, Aristotle himself clearly tells us that the preceding passage belongs to 'another genus', and one which does not strictly fit the sober scientific mode of treatment prevailing elsewhere in this work.

The choice of high-sounding words that do not occur elsewhere
in these level plains, the noticeably solemn and elevated tone,
the wealth of rhetorical devices, the ornamental parisosis, chias-
mus, and antithesis, the bold images, such as that of Plato's
world-soul bound like Ixion to the perpetually turning wheel of
the heaven, the ringing doublets, like 'a limit and a goal' (τὰς
ἐχούσας πέρας καὶ παῦλαν), 'a lot without end or respite' (μοῖραν
ἀΐδιον καὶ ἄτρυτον), 'the immortality and eternity of the
world' (εἰς πίστιν περὶ τῆς ἀθανασίας αὐτοῦ καὶ τῆς ἀϊδιότητος),
'uneasy and devoid of all rational satisfaction', 'painlessly and
happily', 'the ancient and truly traditional theories', 'involve
effort and be inconsistent with perfection', above all the artificial order of the words, like the prose of Plato's later dialogues,
and the careful avoidance of hiatus, give to this passage a tone
and dignity fitting only to a dialogue. At the end it becomes
particularly clear that in their original connexion the purpose of
those physical ideas was mainly religious and metaphysical.
We have seen, in fact, that the 'symphony' between the physical
study of the imperishable heavens and what Aristotle beautifully and very Platonically calls the voice of God within us is a
conjunction characteristic of the third book *On Philosophy*. The
merely dialectical nature of the argument, which starts from the
respect due to the views of the ancients, from religious traditions, and from the probable (εὔλογον), also reveals its source.

This gives us a *terminus post quem* for the composition of the
existing version of the books *On the Heaven*. It was written after
the dialogue *On Philosophy*, and therefore at the earliest one or
two years after Plato's death. It was probably not much later
than this, however, for the whole point of view is that of the
later Academy.[1] The cosmic theories of the Pythagoreans,
which were so often blindly accepted in this circle; the belief
that the heaven and the earth are spherical in form; the doctrine

---

[1] Its wide divergence from the dialogue *On Philosophy* as regards ether,
which proves that this dialogue is its *terminus post quem*, since it can be taken
only as a correction and not as a previous stage of the view there given, might
seem to make against supposing that the *De Caelo* followed too closely on the
dialogue. We have, however, found Aristotle making generous use of his exoteric
works only in the treatises belonging to the middle period, which were still fairly
near to them in time; and we must therefore suppose that the work *On the Heaven*
mainly arose, or that the first draft of it was sketched out, during his middle
period, and that revisions, some of them drastic, took place during his later years.

of the spheres; the doctrine of their harmony, which Aristotle is as concerned to disprove as he is to get a clear and detailed physical picture of the way in which they may move the stars; the problems of the shape and rotation of the stars, which Plato had mooted; the fact that the astronomical catalogues of the Babylonians and Egyptians are obviously still a new discovery; the controversy, so momentous for subsequent history, about the position and motion of the earth in the universe, in which Aristotle decided that it is spherical, but, in view of the lack of convincing evidence that it moves, must remain in the centre of the universe, in accordance with the reigning view of the nature of gravitational phenomena; the indivisible lines of Xenocrates; Plato's theory of the elements as mathematical corpuscles; the problem of weight, with which the Academy struggled in vain—this whole richly developed world of physical speculations, a variegated structure made up of many special problems strung together, often apparently without much system, can be understood only historically, by reference to the soil that bred it, the Academy.   Aristotle's ideas were not put on paper in this shape until after 347, but they were formed while he was still in the Academy, in the course of discussion with Plato and his companions.[1]

[1] The date of the *Meteorology* is difficult to determine. The treatise *On Coming-to-be and Passing-away*, to which must be added the third and fourth books *On the Heaven*, proceeds very definitely along the same speculative lines as the *Physics* and the treatise *On the Heaven*. Its polemic concerns Plato's reduction of the four elements to mathematical figures (ἐπίπεδα), and the atomic theory of Leucippus and Democritus. The *Meteorology*, on the other hand, plunges into detail. Although the distinction between a general and a special portion is essential to the plan of Aristotle's works on nature, and although these works accordingly include both, yet, in view of the *Politics* and other writings, there can be no doubt that the empirical material came later, and was collected gradually, and often reacted upon his conceptual philosophy. We must not therefore date the *Meteorology* too early. Ideler's reasons for putting it before Alexander's expedition to Asia (*Arist. Meteor.* vol. i, p. ix) are not cogent. There is little to be inferred from the fact that Aristotle, following Herodotus, correctly believes the Caspian Sea to be an inland one, whereas Alexander's expedition came to the false conclusion that it connects with the North Sea, a view which thereafter prevailed until modern times; for even the *History of Animals*, which is certainly later, takes its accounts of Egyptian animals not from the reports of eyewitnesses but from Hecataeus of Miletus (Diels, *Hermes*, vol. xxii; the correspondences between the *History of Animals* and Herodotus were remarked by the great Cuvier in his *Histoire des sciences naturelles*, vol. i (1841), p. 136; cp. A. von Humboldt, *Kosmos*, vol. ii (1847), p. 427, n. 95). The fact that the *Meteorology* mentions the burning of the temple

We cannot here undertake to give a general estimate of Aristotle's philosophy of nature (we shall attempt to do so in the last part of this book); it must suffice to bring out the main facts about the course of his development as such. Our picture of the early appearance of the fundamental, i.e. cosmological and speculative, parts of his theory of nature, the *Physics* and the work *On the Heaven* with their appendix *On Coming-to-be and Passing-away*, is confirmed by the apparently late origin of the works *On the Parts* and *On the Generation of Animals*. These are based on the exact observation of detail. They are the most perfect and most characteristic things that he produced in the sphere of natural science. In contrast to them his physics and cosmology, with their conceptual and abstract discussions of the general principles of nature and of the world at large, are much nearer to Plato not only in the problems that they discuss but also in method, for they are examples of the careful and critical development of Plato's doctrines that characterizes Aristotle's middle period, the time when he wrote his account of the ideal state and his theological ethics and metaphysics. His continuous polemic against details of Plato's natural philosophy must not blind us to the fact that these criticisms arise precisely out of his greater nearness to Plato here, not out of distance from him. It is true that the things he is most concerned to bring out are the collapse of the invisible world of Ideas erected by Plato as the paradigm or pattern of the visible cosmos, his own dislike of mere speculation without the support of experience, and his sceptical attitude towards several of the bursts of unverifiable cosmological fancy into which many Academies had been led by their taste for Pythagorean philosophy; but we have only to put together his *Physics* and Plato's *Timaeus*, and contrast them both with the mechanical view of the world put forward by Democritus, or the purely mathematical theory of the heavens suggested by Eudoxus, to see that he stands wholly on ground prepared by Plato, and that his works on physics and cosmology are essentially discussions within the Academy.

at Ephesus (356) with the words νῦν συνέβαινε (III. 1, 371ᵃ 30) gives us only a *terminus post quem*, for this νῦν is known to be very ambiguous and to allow a wide margin. Whereas the expression 'we have only met with two instances of a moon-rainbow in more than fifty years' (III. 2, 372ᵃ 29) does not seem to fit a young man even if we do not take the first person literally.

PART THREE
MATURITY

CHAPTER XII

ARISTOTLE IN ATHENS

IN the year 335/4 Aristotle returned to Athens after an absence of thirteen years, not having seen it since the death of his master. Alexander's accession to the throne had put an end to the opportunities for direct influence at the court of Macedon. The young king must indeed have offered him an honourable leisure, together with the means for prosecuting research, and no one will believe that at a moment when he needed experienced advice more than ever he purposely removed from his neighbourhood the man who up to then had been his tutor in statesmanship, and who continued to sharpen his political conscience down to the time of the Asiatic expedition;[1] but the rhythm of their lives had become too divergent now that Alexander, in order to save a throne that tottered under every new incumbent, was hurrying from campaign to campaign, and fighting for recognition now in the Balkans and on the Danube, now in Greece. We do not know whether Aristotle remained at the court up to the moment of his return to Athens, or had previously withdrawn for a considerable period to his paternal property in Stagira. The latter is indicated by a fragment of a letter, the genuineness of which, however, is much to be doubted, since it suggests the stilted devices of the rhetorician rather than Aristotle's easy manner, which was celebrated in antiquity as the ideal epistolary style.[2] That he kept up some continuous relation with the court is also suggested by the fact that he did not return to Athens until Alexander crossed to Asia Minor.

Immediately after Alexander's accession (336) there had been a rising in Athens under the leadership of Demosthenes, who had been out of politics since Chaeronea, and the example had been

---

[1] For the conjecture that Aristotle wrote the work *On Monarchy* on the occasion of Alexander's accession see above, p. 259, n. 3.

[2] Frg. 669 in Rose. 'I went from Athens to Stagira because of the Great King, and from Stagira to Athens because of the great cold.' In itself, however, the natural thing to suppose is that Aristotle spent his time in study at Stagira whenever he was not required at the court; see above, p. 115. n. 1, on Theophrastus' stay in Stagira.

followed by his friends throughout Greece. Alexander's prompt suppression of the 'rebellion' seemed to have restored peace and obedience, until the report that he had been killed while campaigning on the Danube caused the nationalist party to rise once more (335) and proclaim freedom and autonomy.[1] Once again they were very quickly sobered. Alexander stormed Thebes and razed it to the ground, a warning to the other Greeks. Only with the utmost difficulty did Athens escape the degrading order to deliver up Demosthenes and all the nationalist leaders. These persons now disappeared from the public scene. The feeling against Macedon grew considerably less tense. Alexander withdrew in October, 335. In May, 334, he crossed into Asia Minor and defeated the Persian satraps on the Granicus.

About this time Aristotle came to Athens as the flower of Greek intellect, the outstanding philosopher, writer, and teacher, the friend of the most powerful ruler of the time, whose rapidly rising fame raised him with it even in the eyes of persons who stood too far from him to understand his own importance. His intention to return to the place of his growth may have been developed during his last years in Macedonia, when he was living in the retirement of research. It was his recollection of Plato that made him see in this return something more than a mere outward condition of any really wide influence. He thereby announced himself publicly to all the world as the successor of Plato. It is true that the Academy was estranged from him. After the death of Speusippus (339/8) the members had chosen Xenocrates as their head.[2] For Aristotle it was out of the question to re-enter a society now led by a former companion of such different intellectual interests, anxious though he was to preserve a good external understanding with that venerable man. We do not in fact hear of any quarrel (probably many persons attended lectures in both places), but from this moment the Academy surrendered the lead to the new school, which Aristotle opened first in the corridors of the palaestra in the Lyceum, and afterwards presumably outside it in a nearby space, with suitable rooms, in front of the gate of Diochares in the east of the town, a spot that had been a meeting-place of sophists

[1] Arrian I. 7, 2: 'promising freedom ⟨and autonomy⟩, ancient and noble names.' [2] *Ind. Acad. Hercul.*, col. vi, p. 38 (Mekler).

for decades. So long as Aristotle remained within the walls of Athens that dethroned queen of cities was once more, and for the last time, the intellectual centre of the Hellenic world, the metropolis of Greek learning. When he and Theophrastus died it was all over. Thereafter the centre of gravity lay in Alexandria. Aristotle the non-Athenian in Athens, at once the intellectual leader of the nation and the stronghold of Macedonian influence in what had formerly been the leading city of the Attic empire—that is the symbol of the new age.

Aristotle founded his new home of learning under the protection of his powerful Macedonian friend Antipater, whom Alexander had left behind as regent and commander-in-chief in Macedon and Greece. It is much to be regretted that we have lost his correspondence with this important man, who seems to have been more intimate with him than any one else after the death of Hermias. Since Antipater came from a totally different environment, and was no scholar, their friendship must have been based on some profound kinship of character. This explains how a relationship that began in the court of Philip, at a time when Aristotle was in high favour with the king and with Alexander, could outlast Alexander's fickle kindness and forge a lifelong bond that did not let Antipater go even when his philosophical friend was dead. Aristotle appointed him the executor of his last wishes in his will. The few remaining fragments of their letters speak the language of unhesitating mutual trust. We may infer that Aristotle and his circle were at one with the political intentions of Macedon, since during the years 334/23 Antipater was governing the domestic affairs of Greece with authority virtually absolute.

The Macedonian party at Athens, which was particularly strong among the rich, could now come forth into the open without danger. Mutual distrust had assumed frightful proportions among the citizenry, and it was still easy for the nationalists to stage and win oratorical contests like that between Demosthenes and Aeschines about the crown, and thereby to get the masses temporarily on their side. They were powerless, however, against the Macedonian lances, and they no longer had the support of the educated, to whose indifference, in fact, the shipwreck of Demosthenes' efforts was mainly due. To the intellectual

circles it was a distinct gain to have the moral support of a
school directly connected with the Macedonian administration.
Popular orators like Lycurgus and Demosthenes could not
prevail against the ethical and intellectual ascendancy of the
new arrivals, and could not impute treachery or corruption to
men who were not Athenians. It was nowhere possible to con-
vict them of directly political purposes; their influence in educating a new group functioned more through their tacit rejection
of Demosthenic nationalism than through any political programme. With his fine sensibility for such things Aristotle always
carefully avoided touching the sore spot of Athenian pride, or
letting fall any sharp remark about Demosthenes and his party,
objectionable as they doubtless were to him. Not until years
later does the Lyceum dare to reveal its private opinion in the
biting expressions of Theophrastus and of Demetrius of Phalerum on the style and delivery of Demosthenes as a popular
orator. Aristotle was not, of course, shortsighted enough to hold
Demosthenes responsible for the war of Chaeronea, as Aeschines
and his followers did. The only remark of his that is preserved
about Demosthenes rejects this view—but nothing could be
falser than to make this a reason for supposing that he had some
understanding of Demosthenes' position. The group of intel-
lectuals in the Lyceum, though not in the least cosmopolitan,
were resigned, all the more so because they had no confidence
in Alexander's almost fantastic reconstructions of the world,
and refused to consider fraternization of races or fusion with
Asiatics. Aristotle stood over the Greek nation like a troubled
physician at the bedside of his patient. Demosthenes and the
nationalists could not understand an attitude thus rooted in the
recognition of the bitter truth. They saw in Aristotle's school
a Macedonian secret-service bureau.[1]

There is no school of learning of which we have so complete
a picture as the Lyceum. The very lectures that were given
there are mostly preserved to us in the writings of Aristotle.

---

[1] This was certainly Demosthenes' view. Only he did not dare to say it
aloud, as his nephew Demochares did when defending the decree of Sophocles
(307/6). This decree abolished the pro-Macedonian schools of philosophy after
the liberation of Athens by Demetrius the Besieger. For the slanders about
Aristotle and his followers in the fragments of Demochares see Baiter-Suppe,
Or. Att., vol. ii, pp. 341 ff.

Athenian law forbade foreigners to acquire land in Attica, and yet later on we find Theophrastus in possession of a property consisting of a large garden containing a sanctuary of the Muses (in accordance with the precedent of the Academy), an altar, and several lecture-rooms.[1] It was in one of these rooms that the maps (γῆς περίοδοι) were set out on boards (πίνακες). The other instruments of learning, such as the library, must have been there too. In the Museum were a statue of Aristotle and other oblations. Demetrius of Phalerum, the pupil of Theophrastus, gave him this land to be his own property (ἴδιον), although he was a metic. This must have been an act of special legal significance, for it was contrary to the constitution. Since even under Aristotle the school possessed a great deal of material, and in particular a collection of books that can have been housed only in a large building, we cannot avoid the conjecture that the property later given to Theophrastus was precisely that on which Aristotle himself had taught. Demetrius preserved it for the school because the memory of the founder clung to that plot of ground. The actual gift, however, must have been made out in Theophrastus' name, since in his will he bequeathes the Peripatos to the school with these words. 'The garden and the walk and the houses adjoining the garden, all and sundry, I give and bequeath to such of our enrolled friends as may wish to study literature and philosophy there in common, since it is not possible for all men to be always in residence, on condition that no one alienates the property or devotes it to his private use, but so that they hold it like a temple in joint possession and live, as is right and proper, on terms of familiarity and friendship.'[2]

These beautiful words show that the spirit that Aristotle had planted in the school was still living there. Their common life was regulated according to definite rules. As a symbol of their community they had regular monthly social gatherings, either to eat or to drink. Later, in the will of Strato, we find listed along with the library the tableware for the banquets, linen, and drinking-cups.[3] These must have become more complete with each succeeding generation; for during the leadership of Lyco

---

[1] Diog. L.V. 39. The society therefore formed a fraternity (θίασος) dedicated to the cult of the Muses.

[2] Diog. L. V. 52.   [3] Diog. L. V. 62.

there were complaints that the poorer students could no longer take part in the feasts, because there was too much luxury. Aristotle himself wrote codes for the drinking and for the feasting (νόμοι συμποτικοί and νόμοι συσσιτικοί), as Xenocrates and Speusippus did for the Academy. These regulations played a not inconsiderable part in the philosophic schools.[1]

The lectures were also regulated. Tradition informs us that Aristotle gave his more difficult and philosophical lectures in the morning, and that in the afternoon he spoke to a larger public on rhetoric and dialectic. In addition to his there were lectures by the older disciples, such as Theophrastus and Eudemus. We do not hear of many disciples of Aristotle by name, but what Greek is there who wrote during the next hundred years on natural science, on rhetoric, on literature, or on the history of civilization, and was not called a Peripatetic? Lavish as the grammarians are with this title, it is easy to see that the intellectual influence of the school soon extended over the whole Greek-speaking world. We find scarcely any names of Athenians among the famous Peripatetics; a large part of the students must have come from other cities. In the Lyceum Plato's communal life or συзῆν became a university in the modern sense, an organization of sciences and of courses of study. The students, though still calling themselves 'friends', following Plato's pleasant custom, were constantly coming and going, because, as Theophrastus says with a trace of resignation, 'it is not possible for all men to be always in residence'. One thing, however, remained common to the new school and to the Academy: its inner order was, just like the idea of the Platonic community, an expression of the quintessential nature and mind of its creator. The organization of the Peripatetic school is a reflection of Aristotle's nature, the act of a single guiding mind whose will lives in its members.

We usually do not make sufficiently clear to ourselves that Aristotle was not one of those great philosophical authors who bequeath their work to posterity in literary form, and really begin to live only when they are dead, since the written word works for them. The series of literary works in Plato's style that

[1] For the external organization of the Peripatetic society and the election of officers see Wilamowitz, *Antigonos von Karystos*, p. 264.

he published during his earlier years was apparently mostly completed by the time he began to teach at Athens; at any rate the more important dialogues belong to a much earlier period, and it is hardly to be supposed that during these years he once more occupied himself by the way, in a more or less playful manner, with composing little conversations. He was now more than ever absorbed in teaching. The treatises that we possess are the groundwork of his living influence on his pupils. In the *Phaedrus* Plato tells us that the written word is useless in the transmission of real scientific knowledge. We have believed only too long that we could disregard this view, fundamental though it be to the comprehension of the dialogues; and only now do we begin to see that it has its basis in the actual relation obtaining between literary production and oral teaching in Plato's Academy, and that every general view of the dialogues that does not see them on the background of this comprehensive pedagogical activity represents a displacement of the centre of gravity.[1] With Aristotle the situation is different once again. Here we have a gradually increasing paralysis of the desire for literary creation, until finally he is wholly wrapped up in teaching. The vast sum of his life is to be found neither in the treatises nor in the dialogues. It lies in his living influence on his pupils, rooted not in Plato's Eros but in the desire to know and to teach. When separated from their creator and his voice the treatises could not and did not produce any independent effect. Even the Peripatetic school was unable to understand them once the immediate pupils of Aristotle were no longer there to interpret, and on the early Hellenistic age this giant mass of knowledge and reflection had an amazingly insignificant influence. Not until the first century before Christ were the treatises disinterred, but even then the Greek professors of philosophy in Athens did not understand them.[2] When the laborious work of the commentators, continued for centuries, had once more rendered visible these mighty thought-structures, which had come within a hairbreadth of being lost to posterity for ever, Aristotle at last began to be for the second time the master of the schools. At last people began to understand that they must not confine themselves to such of his writings as shone with the

[1] See my *Ent. Metaph. Arist.*, p. 140. [2] Cic. *Top.* I. 3.

crown of literary fame, but must learn to see the real man at work in the unpublished treatises, in order to catch the last shimmer of the individuality of a mind so niggardly towards posterity and so profuse towards its own surroundings. Thus Aristotle has become, quite contrary to his own intention, the teacher of all nations. This mission to all times and places stands in vivid contrast to his personal influence and desire, which displayed the genuine Greek concentration on the here and now, and focused all his powers on his immediate circle. Teaching like Aristotle's has never been seen again. To the Greeks it was something absolutely new, and, with the age of the great philosophic schools just beginning, it started a new epoch. Stoics, Epicureans, Academics, all laid more weight on oral teaching than on literary self-expression.

Aristotle's relations with Alexander cannot be traced to the end. The memoir *On Colonization*, with its dialogue-like subtitle *Alexander*, proves that they continued unbroken down to the time when the king was establishing cities in Egypt and Asia. They cannot, however, have remained unaffected by the fate of Callisthenes, which overtook him in the year 327.[1] This nephew of Aristotle's had been his pupil during his stay in Assos and also at Pella. Afterwards, immediately before Alexander's departure for Asia, he had helped him to draw up the list of Delphic victors. He then joined the king's headquarters, with the approval of his uncle. From the beginning it was undoubtedly his intention to record the king's deeds. His glorification of Alexander in the work that he dedicated to him, like his panegyric on Hermias, betrays the fact that his interest in his subject was not that of the true historian, but was rather of a personal nature. He thought himself into Alexander's mind with philosophical persistence, but he did not always reach the undistorted truth. He was no student of human nature. He was a scholar of fine literary taste, a philosopher with a keen intelligence, and not without talent as an orator, especially in extempore speaking, but as Aristotle himself declared he was devoid of natural common sense. Although he was a personal adherent of the king, and constantly defended him in his history against the opposition of the old Macedonian nobility, who dis-

---

[1] See Jacoby on 'Callisthenes' in Pauly-Wissowa, vol. x, c. 1674.

trusted his policy towards Asiatics, he nevertheless managed, by an untimely display of philosophic dignity on the question of obeisance, to bring upon himself the unfortunate suspicion of conspiracy with that very opposition, and thus to incur the displeasure of the king. His position at the court had presumably always been isolated, since he belonged neither to the party of the Macedonian military nobility nor to the Greek literary scandalmongers who swarmed at headquarters, but depended exclusively on the personal favour of the king. When that was withdrawn he was helpless against the intrigues of the rest. It is now certain that the men immediately surrounding the king afterwards thought it expedient to conceal some of the circumstances attending Callisthenes' fall. His guilt was by no means established by normal process of law, and his execution was one of the autocratic acts that Alexander committed at that time, when the extreme tension of his mental and physical powers sometimes led to volcanic outbursts of terrible passion even against his nearest friends. Though we may draw the veil of pity over these inhumanities they could not but cloud Aristotle's memory of the king and extinguish the feeling for him in his heart. He tried to preserve his spiritual balance by being just, inexorably just even with regard to the shortcomings of his nephew. The filthiness of human nature insisted on believing in antiquity that Alexander's early death was due to poison administered at the instigation of Aristotle. That was not the philosopher's character, but the cup of kingly friendship had certainly been embittered by a poisonous drop.

Aristotle's stay at Athens still depended solely on Alexander. When in the year 323 the news came of the latter's death, this time no one would believe it ; but when it was finally confirmed there was no holding the nationalist party. The sole protection of the friends of Macedon had been Antipater, but he, too, like Aristotle, had lost the confidence of the king during the last years, and was at that moment on the march through Asia Minor towards Babylon. He had been bidden to the court, to remain for the future under the king's eye. Aristotle avoided the sudden overflow of nationalist hate and the attacks of the Demosthenic party by fleeing to Chalcis in Euboea. The parental property of his dead mother was there, and there he remained during the following months until his own death. An affection of the stomach from which he suffered put an end to his life shortly afterwards, in his sixty-third year. It seems that he was aware of the approach of death, for the will that we possess was drawn up in Chalcis.[1] He was not spared the news that the Delphians, who had accorded him honours for his list of Pythian victors, were revoking them now that his royal patron was dead; but even the confusions of this time could not permanently disturb the peace of his soul, specially sensitive though he was to man's misfortunes.[2]

A word about his private life during these last years. His guardian Proxenus and his fostermother had long been dead. He had adopted their son Nicanor and made himself a father to him. Nicanor was an officer on Alexander's staff. In the year 324 the king sent him to Greece as the bearer of an important message. He it was who had to announce to the Hellenes assembled at Olympia for the national festival that Alexander claimed divine honours. By his will Aristotle bequeathed to Nicanor the hand of his daughter Pythias, who was still a minor, a child of the long dead Pythias. After the death of his wife he had taken a certain Herpyllis into his house, by whom he had a son called Nicomachus. In his will he is careful to provide faithfully for them all, and also for his students. There is something affecting in the spectacle of the exile putting his affairs in order. He is constantly calling to mind his home in Stagira and the lonely house of his parents far away, the figures of his foster parents, his only brother Arimnestus, whom he lost early, and his mother, whom he could picture only as he had seen her when a child. His desire is that his mortal remains be not divided from the bones of his wife Pythias, as was also her last wish. Between the lines of the sober practical dispositions in this last document we read a strange language, such as is not to be found in the wills of the other heads of the Peripatetic school,

[1] It speaks of Chalcis and Stagira as being the only possible places for Herpyllis to live, and does not mention Athens (Diog. L. V. 14). It also regards as uncertain where Aristotle is to be buried (V. 16), which would undoubtedly have been different if the arrangements had been made at Athens during quiet times.

[2] Frg. 666 in Rose (letter to Antipater): 'About the voting at Delphi and their depriving me of my honours my feeling is that I am sorry but not extremely sorry.' The tone of this fragment is very genuine.

which are also preserved. It is the warm tone of true humanity, and at the same time the sign of an almost terrifying gulf between him and the persons by whom he was surrounded. These words were written by a lonely man. A trace of this remains in an extremely moving confession that he makes in a letter of this last period, words that have an inimitably personal fragrance. 'The more solitary and isolated I am, the more I have come to love myths.' Within the noisy house there sits an old man living entirely to himself, a hermit, to use his own expression, a self withdrawn into itself, a person who in his happy moments loses himself in the profound wonderland of myth.[1] His austere and reserved personality, carefully hidden from the outside world behind the immovable ramparts of learning, here reveals itself and raises the veil of its secret. As with most ancient person-alities, we know just enough of Aristotle's to realize that we cannot really know anything about it. So much, however, we do see, that this full life was not exhausted, as a superficial eye might suppose, by all its science and research. His 'theoretic life' was rooted in a second life, hidden and profoundly personal, from which that ideal derived its force. The picture of Aristotle as nothing but a scientist is the reverse of the truth. This was precisely the age in which the self began to be emancipated from the chains of the objective side of life, when it felt more con-sciously than ever before that it could not be satisfied with external creation alone. At this time the private side of life withdrew from the turmoil of action into its quiet corner and made itself at home there. The private side of individuals also awoke and locked the door against uninvited guests. The absolutely objective form in which Aristotle always presented himself to the outside world was already based on a conscious separation of personal from externalized activities. Only a little later the rapidly swelling torrent of subjectivity burst its dam

[1] Frg. 668 in Rose. According to Aristotle myth and philosophy are closely connected. This was a problem that he took over from Plato. *Metaph.* A 2, 982^b 17: 'A man who is puzzled and wonders thinks himself ignorant. Hence even the lover of myth is in a sense a lover of Wisdom, for the myth is composed of wonders.' It is of course one thing to see elements of philosophy in the love of myth, and another when the philosopher, as Aristotle does in this fragment, indulges himself by returning at the end of his long struggle with the problems to the half-hidden, illogical, obscure, but suggestive, language of myth.

and swept all fixed objects away into the rhythm of its own inward movement.

The bust that recent research recognizes as being really Aristotle's shows a very individual head.[1] The artist has done his work in a somewhat conventionally refined manner, but in spite of that it has a speakingly vivid personality. As in the famous head of Euripides, the thinker is revealed by the hair hanging over the powerful forehead in thin and sparse locks. The artist has not stopped, however, at such more or less typical features in his effort to grasp his subject's individuality. From the side we are struck by the contrast between the chin jutting out beneath a tightly closed mouth, giving an expression of indomitable energy, and the critical, contemplative, perfectly level gaze of the eyes, directed towards some fixed point outside the man and strangely unconscious of the passion and movement portrayed in the lower half of the face. The intensity of that penetrating vision is almost disquieting. The whole countenance gives an impression of highly cultivated intelligence, but from the very first instant this is subordinate to the expression of strained and earnest attention that embraces all the features. The control of the intellect is evident throughout. Only round the mocking mouth there plays a shadow of suffering—the sole element of the involuntary that this visage reveals.

In conclusion we may place here a translation of his will. It transports us directly into the human atmosphere in which he lived.[2]

'All will be well; but, in case anything should happen, Aristotle has made these dispositions. Antipater is to be executor in all matters and in general; but, until Nicanor shall arrive, Aristomenes, Timarchus, Hipparchus, Dioteles and (if he consent and if circumstances permit him) Theophrastus shall take charge as well of Herpyllis and the children as of the property. And when the girl [his daughter Pythias] shall be grown up she shall be given in marriage to Nicanor; but if anything happen to the girl (which heaven forbid and no such thing will happen) before her marriage, or when she is married but before there are children, Nicanor shall have full powers, both with regard to the child and with regard to everything else, to administer in a manner worthy both of himself and of us. Nicanor shall take charge of the girl and of the boy Nicomachus as

[1] Studniczka, *Ein Bildnis des Aristoteles*, Leipzig, 1908. (Dekanatsprogramm.)

[2] Diog. L. V. 11. R. D. Hicks's translation (Loeb Classical Library).

he shall think fit in all that concerns them as if he were father and brother. And if anything should happen to Nicanor (which heaven forbid!) either before he marries the girl, or when he has married her but before there are children, any arrangements that he may make shall be valid. And if Theophrastus is willing to live with her, he shall have the same rights as Nicanor. Otherwise the executors in consultation with Antipater shall administer as regards the daughter and the boy as seems to them to be best. The executors and Nicanor, in memory of me and of the steady affection which Herpyllis has borne towards me, shall take care of her in every other respect and, if she desires to be married, shall see that she be given to one not unworthy; and besides what she has already received they shall give her a talent of silver out of the estate and three handmaids whomsoever she shall choose besides the maid she has at present and the man-servant Pyrrhaeus; and if she chooses to remain at Chalcis, the lodge by the garden, if in Stagira, my father's house. Whichever of these two houses she chooses, the executors shall furnish with such furniture as they think proper and as Herpyllis herself may approve. Nicanor shall take charge of the boy Myrmex, that he be taken to his own friends in a manner worthy of me with the property of his which we received. Ambracis shall be given her freedom, and on my daughter's marriage shall receive 500 drachmas and the maid whom she now has. And to Thale shall be given, in addition to the maid whom she has and who was bought, a thousand drachmas and a maid. And Simon, in addition to the money before paid to him towards another servant, shall either have a servant purchased for him or receive a further sum of money. And Tycho, Philo, Olympius, and his child shall have their freedom when my daughter is married. None of the servants who waited upon me shall be sold but they shall continue to be employed; and when they arrive at the proper age they shall have their freedom if they deserve it. My executors shall see to it when the images which Gryllion has been commissioned to execute are finished, that they be set up, namely that of Nicanor, that of Proxenus, which it was my intention to have executed, and that of Nicanor's mother; also they shall set up the bust which has been executed of Arimnestus, to be a memorial of him seeing that he died childless, and shall dedicate my mother's statue to Demeter at Nemea or wherever they think best. And wherever they bury me, there the bones of Pythias shall be laid, in accordance with her own instructions. And to commemorate Nicanor's safe return, as I vowed on his behalf, they shall set up in Stagira stone statues of life size to Zeus and Athena the Saviours.'

CHAPTER XIII

THE ORGANIZATION OF RESEARCH

ARISTOTLE'S second stay in Athens was the culmination of his development. It was his maturity; he completed his doctrine and functioned as the head of a great school. Since scholars have long recognized a connexion between the extant writings and his activity as a lecturer, while on the other hand they have supposed that only during this last period was he actually lecturing, they have naturally concluded that all the treatises were composed during this time, and have swallowed without misgiving the awkward consequence of their inference, namely that the whole composition must have been crowded into the short space of thirteen years. We cannot put the reigning view more briefly than it has been expressed by Zeller, who is still reckoned an authority on these questions: 'If, then, the view already indicated as to the destination of these texts for his scholars, their connexion with his teaching, and the character of their cross-references be right, it follows that all of them *must* have been composed during his final sojourn in Athens'.[1]

Our inquiry into the sojourn at Assos has made it unnecessary to say more about the untenability of this view, and it also makes it possible to get a clearer notion of the special significance of Aristotle's last period within his whole development. Now that we have succeeded in determining the spirit and direction of his work during the middle years, we see that the last phase, that in Athens, was very clearly distinguished from the preceding. Bold speculation and extensive empirical investigation, which according to the previous view were both compressed into a narrow space in the last period, now become separated in time. The foundations of his philosophy were complete by the middle

[1] Zeller, *Aristotle and the Earlier Peripatetics*, vol. i, p. 155. Cf. Bernays, *Die Dialoge des Aristoteles*, p. 128: 'All the surviving works belong to the last period of Aristotle's life; and even if the little that has been ascertained about their chronological relations to each other were ever to be increased by fortunate discoveries, the nature of their content excludes all hope that even the earliest of them could ever be early enough to show us Aristotle still working at his system; at all points it presents itself to us as complete; nowhere do we see the builder building.'

period—taking 'philosophy' in the narrow sense in which it is always used by the expositors, and therefore excluding his gigantic researches in the sciences of nature and of man. He began his philosophical development by following Plato; he then went on to criticize him; but in his third period there appeared something totally new and original. He turned to the empirical investigation of details, and by consistently carrying out his conception of form he became in this sphere the creator of a new type of study. For the present we will not ask what is the relation between this line of work and the philosophy of the preceding stage, nor how far the one completes the other and how far it goes beyond it. We must begin by establishing the fact as such, namely that while the central philosophical disciplines only received during this period certain alterations characteristic of the spirit of the new direction that his work was taking, it was the wide field of nature and history in which he was really productive. The main proof of this lies in the recently discovered papyri and inscriptions; but their necessary consequences for the history of his development have not yet been drawn.

An honorific inscription dug up in the year 1895 records the decision of the Delphians 'to praise and crown' Aristotle and his nephew Callisthenes in gratitude for their having established a complete list of the winners at the Pythian games from the earliest times to the present.[1] Such a list had of course necessitated very extensive researches among the archives, researches which must have been significant for the history of culture and literature as well. In this work Aristotle was, so far as we can see, breaking new ground. It cannot have taken place very early in view of the co-operation of his nephew, who had been his disciple at Assos and at Pella (above, p. 318); nor yet after 334, when Callisthenes went to Asia with Alexander. It was probably in connexion with his history of the Sacred War that Callisthenes obtained access to the archives of the Delphic priests, in order to study the sources for the struggles and negotiations with the Phocians, which could not be done elsewhere. That the actual date of the *List of Pythian Winners* was about 335/4, shortly before Callisthenes' departure for Asia, is shown by the mason's

[1] Dittenberger, *Sylloge*[3], p. 485.

bill for cutting a stone record of this list, which is preserved and bears the name of the Delphic archon Caphis (331/0). It was a laborious piece of work, amounting, by recent calculations, to a tablet of about 60,000 words. It can be none other than the list of Aristotle and Callisthenes, the chiselling of which apparently continued through several years.[1] It follows that this list was drawn up towards the end of the Macedonian period or at the beginning of the Athenian.

To the same period belong Aristotle's great antiquarian researches into the competitions at the great Dionysia and the Lenaea, and his *Didascaliae*, records of the dramatic performances at Athens, which later formed the framework of the chronology used by the Alexandrine historians of literature for their history of the classical theatre, and are still the foundation of all we know about the dates when the pieces were played. These researches, fundamental for the history of Greek literature, were undoubtedly suggested by Aristotle's philosophical study of the problems of poetics. The immense collection of material comes after the philosophical study, for the lost dialogue *On Poets* certainly goes back to early days. Here again the new element is the amplification of conceptual treatment by means of the study of historical and chronological detail. These researches can only have been made on the spot, in the archives of the archon, and therefore either prior to the death of Plato or after 335. The analogy of Aristotle's other works of this sort, however, clearly indicates that they belong to the late period, and it is very obvious of itself that the preliminary investigations, which would have been impossible without the permission of the government, were made in connexion with the civic reform of the theatre that Lycurgus, the maker of the new stone theatre at Athens, undertook towards the end of the thirties.[2] Just as he arranged for state copies of all the old

---

[1] Cf. Homolle in *Bulletin de correspondance hellénique*, vol. xxii, p. 631.

[2] Aristotle's interest in the development of the main literary forms, especially tragedy and comedy, which the post-Aristotelian Peripatetics extended to further classes (as appears from Horace, *Ars. Poet.* 73, 275), is revealed in the fragments of his *Victories* preserved on an inscription (C.I.A. II. 971), which mention the first performance of κῶμοι or revels. Unlike the *Didascaliae* this work arose not out of Aristotle's interest in the history of the theatre but merely out of the Athenian state's official interest in the persons and tribes of the winning backers and producers. Hence it clearly proves the connexion between

tragedies and monuments to the classical masters, as well as providing for regular revivals of their plays, so must he have been the man who set up in stone at the back of the Porch, behind the theatre of Dionysus, the record of all dramatic competitions since the end of the sixth century. The catalogues of Aristotle's writings also mention a work comparable to the list of Pythian winners on the winners at the Olympian games, following in the path first trodden by the sophist Hippias of Elis. Of this nothing is known. Presumably it was directly suggested by the Pythian list; if so it must also belong to the second stay in Athens.

It can be shown, as we have previously remarked, that the same conclusion is probably true also of that tremendous undertaking, the collection of 158 constitutions. The sole time when the philosopher could command the external aids necessary for such an extensive work, which must have employed a very large number of researchers, was while he was head of a great school within which he could train fellow-workers suited to his purpose. The sojourn at the court of Pella is not a conceivable alternative, for, while he had financial support there, he could not have found the necessary assistants. *The Constitution of Athens*, which was recovered at the beginning of the nineties and forms the first book of the collection, coming from Aristotle's own pen, gives in the specially copious material of Attic history an example of the method to be adopted throughout the whole work. The temporal references show that it was not published before 329/8.[1] The work on the other constitutions, of which, thanks to

---

these researches and Lycurgus' civic reform of the theatre. On the *Didascaliae* see Jachmann, *De Aristotelis Didascaliis* (Dissertation), Göttingen, 1909.

[1] For some time after the discovery of the *Constitution of Athens* much unnecessary dust was raised about its date as well as about its genuineness. Torr detected the truth at once in his 'Date of the Constitution of Athens' (*Athenaeum* No. 3302, cf. *Classical Review*, vol. v, 3, p. 119). The date of composition is limited in the backward direction by the mention of the archon Cephisophon (329/8), and forwards by the mention in chapter 46 of the building of triremes and quadriremes but not of quinqueremes, which, however, are spoken of in C.I.A. II. 809 d 90 as existing and are there taken over from the previous official year. It follows from this inscription that the decision to build quinqueremes, of which Aristotle is unaware, must have been taken at the latest in 326. Hence the *Constitution of Athens* was written between 329/8 and 327/6. See Wilamowitz, *Aristoteles und Athen*, vol. i, p. 211, n. 43. I pass over the completely mistaken attempts to put the work back into the fifties.

unusually numerous fragments, we still possess a variegated picture, cannot therefore have been done before Aristotle's last years, if, indeed, it was completed at all during his life.

With this colossal compilation, the result of careful and detailed work based on local source-material, Aristotle reached his point of greatest distance from the philosophy of Plato. The individual is now almost an end in itself. The same character appears still more clearly in the purely literary and philological *Homeric Problems*, the number of the books of which, as collected by the editors, was probably six; they lead up to Alexandrian interpretation and criticism, and together with the foundation of poetics, of the chronology of literature, and of the study of the personality of poets, they have made Aristotle the creator of philology, which his pupil's pupil, Demetrius of Phalerum, afterwards carried over to Alexandria. We can prove that the Δικαιώματα πόλεων or *Pleas of the Cities* also belongs to this late period (and thus make it fairly probable that the *Barbarian Customs* does so too) by means of a fragment mentioning the expedition of Alexander of Molossus to southern Italy, where he met his death. Aeschines in his speech on the crown refers to this death as being a very recent event, and hence it falls at the end of the thirties, 330 being the year usually assigned.[1]

The above-mentioned works represent a scientific type of exact research into the real world that was something absolutely new and pioneer in the Greek world of the time. Even Democritus cannot be compared with it. Freed from the Platonic way of thinking, Aristotle herewith became the hero of the line of universal inquirers that began with the Alexandrine philology of Callimachus and Aristarchus and has perpetuated itself every few centuries since the Renascence in isolated outstanding figures such as Scaliger. He far surpasses all his successors, however, in the originality of method that enabled him to foreshadow the science of future millennia—the method of applying the principle of form to the details of reality, the idea of the uni*form*ity of nature—and in the complexity of genius by which

[1] Arist. frg. 614 in Rose. Aesch. *Ctes.* 242. The expedition of Alexander the Molossian is mentioned in the *Pleas* as a historical example, and is obviously already past. The *Customs*, with its ethnological, antiquarian, and mythological interest, should belong to the same period of study. It is the counterpart of the *Constitutions*.

he spanned not merely the history and theory of culture but also the opposite hemisphere of natural science.

In natural science, again, the work of his last period reveals him as the master not so much of philosophy as of 'history' in the Greek sense of the word, which includes the detailed study of nature and natural life as well as the knowledge of human events. We have been accustomed of old to take his scientific works as all of a piece, and to put the *History of Animals*, and the books on the *Parts* and on the *Generation of Animals*, into the same series as the *Physics*, the work *On the Heavens*, and that *On Coming-to-be and Passing-away*. We should certainly hesitate, however, to assert that the *Problems* were early, since the collection as we have it is not identical with Aristotle's at all, but in part the property of his disciples, who were the immediate continuators of the detailed research inaugurated in the Peripatos. This makes it very probable that even the genuinely Aristotelian problems belong to the late period, as is indicated also by the richness of their material and the variety of their special interests. It is really perfectly obvious in itself that the celestial mechanics of the work *On the Heavens*, together with the speculative treatment of the fundamental conceptions of 'physics', were Academic in origin, as we have shown them to be, whereas this absorption in details, most of them utterly unrelated to philosophy, does not fit the period of speculation. But we must go farther still. The *History of Animals* itself belongs in intellectual structure not to the conceptual type exemplified by the *Physics* but to the same level as the collection of constitutions. As a collection of material its relation to the books on the *Parts* and on the *Generation of Animals*, which work upon it and inquire into the reasons of the phenomena that it contains, is exactly the same as that of the collection of constitutions to the late, empirical books of the *Politics*. It provides them with a substratum. Hence it is with the *History of Animals* just as with the *Problems* ; this work shows the clearest traces of different authors; the last books are by younger members of the school, who appear as continuing, completing, and even correcting and criticizing, the work of the master. Probably the task was organized just like that of collecting the constitutions, the work being distributed among various persons right from the start. What part Aristotle himself took in it can hardly be determined with certainty now. The description of the vegetable world, which is very closely connected with that of the animal, was assigned to Theophrastus, who carried it through on his own. It can scarcely be true, as has sometimes been asserted, that the *History of Animals* would be conceivable apart from the discoveries made by Alexander's expedition. The information it contains about the habits of animals at that time unknown in Greece, such as elephants, presupposes the experiences of the march to India, and there are certainly numerous other passages where the influence of this enormous extension of Greek knowledge is still concealed from us. How great was the profit of the Asiatic expeditions to Theophrastus' botany is made clear in Bretzl's admirable though not final work.[1] Thus all indications point to a late date for the origin of the philosopher's zoological works. We must not project this whole organization of specialized research backwards into the Academy; that would give a completely illusory picture. It has been shown above that the *Resemblances* of Speusippus, though mainly concerned with plants, did not contain botanical studies in the manner of Theophrastus but material for the method of division by genus and species as recommended by Plato in his later days in the *Sophist* and the *Statesman* and as actually practised in the Academy merely for the sake of the logic of classification and not out of any interest in particular things and the conditions of their lives.[2] We can clearly detect, in Aristotle's

---

[1] M. Bretzl, *Botanische Forschungen des Alexanderzugs*, Leipzig, 1903.

[2] In the first book *On the Parts of Animals*, which contains a general methodological introduction, the significance of which for the aim of Aristotle's latest researches must be evaluated hereafter, he contrasts his point of view in detail (cc. 2–4) with the Academic method of division. The principle of dichotomy as put forward by Plato in the *Sophist* and the *Statesman* and afterwards applied to particular natural kinds by his disciples, especially Speusippus, is there sharply criticized both from the standpoint of logic and also as being useless in the construction of a real zoology, if one is to avoid tearing related species asunder. It is true that even in the early *Topics* (VI. 6, 144^b 32) he criticizes certain superficialities of Academic division from the logical point of view, but this sort of contradiction had already arisen within the Academic circle itself, as he tells us there. The criticism in the *Parts of Animals* and at other places in the zoological works is totally independent of this. It arose out of his own long-continued positive concern with the actual animal kingdom, and is the upshot of his efforts to wrest a new classification from the facts themselves. The incompleteness of this 'system', which has often led to the denial of its

History of Animals and Theophrastus' *History of Plants*, the influence of the schematism of this method; but to suppose that its real achievement lay in the classification of animals and plants would be wrong. It was far less important in the development of natural science than the fact that here for the first time the observation and description of the individual and its life-history was being taken absolutely seriously. It is just here that the achievement of Aristotle and his school was so vast, in spite of several blunders which, in view of the multiplicity and various worth of the sources he had to use, were inevitable while the method was in its infancy. The *Meteorology* will also belong to this period as a whole.[1] The book on the cause of the Nile's floods, the genuineness of which can no longer be doubted, is a particularly interesting case of a special problem in this sphere. We can almost see Aristotle at work during this period when he communicates to his fellow-workers the results of the latest observations from the upper valley, and ends his account with the exclamation: 'The Nile floods are no longer a problem, for it has actually been observed that rains are the cause of the swelling.'[2]

Very closely connected with the studies of organic nature and living things is the set of inquiries that Aristotle undertakes in his work *On the Soul* and in the group of anthropological and physiological monographs attached thereto. The mere fact that he attaches to psychology the doctrines of perception and colour, of memory and recall, of sleep and waking, of dreams, of breathing, of the motion of living things, of longevity, of youth and age, of life and death, reveals a consistently physiological attitude; the starting-point of this series of studies is necessarily psychology, because the soul is here conceived as the principle of life,

---

existence, is due to its late appearance in Aristotle's development as a thinker. See Jürgen Bona Meyer, *Aristoteles' Tierkunde, Ein Beitrag zur Geschichte der Zoologie, Physiologie und alten Philosophie* (Berlin, 1855), pp. 53 and 70 ff.

[1] See above, pp. 307–8.

[2] I am convinced by Partsch's excellent article 'Des Aristoteles Buch über das Steigen des Nil', *Abhandlungen der sächsischen Gesellschaft der Wissenschaften* (philosophisch-historische Klasse), vol. xxvii, p. 553, Leipzig, 1910. The original form of the conclusion translated in the text is preserved by Photius (οὐκέτι πρόβλημά ἐστιν. ὤφθη γὰρ φανερῶς ὅτι ἐξ ὑετῶν αὔξει, see Partsch, p. 574), and is characteristic of Aristotle; cf. *Metaph.* H 6, 1045ᵃ 24, 'the question will no longer be thought a difficulty'.

which is thereafter pursued through all its characteristic manifestations. All sorts of traces indicate that the series only
gradually attained to its present completeness.[1] The conjunction of these more general physiological preliminaries with the
zoological works to form a comprehensive picture of the organic
world, as we now have it, gives us an artistic pedagogical structure which did not appear in this form until the last period.
The question is how far the psychology itself shares in the general
development that we have already sketched, and whether we can
discover any data for the construction of a chronology of this
work and of the so-called *Parva Naturalia*.

In this connexion the third book *On the Soul*, which contains
the doctrine of *Nus*, stands out as peculiarly Platonic and not
very scientific. This doctrine is an old and permanent element
of Aristotle's philosophy, one of the main roots of his metaphysics. The treatment of it in this work goes deeply into
metaphysics. On and around it the psycho-physical theory of
the soul was subsequently constructed, as it appears, without,
however, bridging the gulf between the two parts whose intellectual heritages were so different. It might be objected that
this twofold character pervades Aristotle's whole philosophy
and must have been inherent in it from the beginning. Against
this view it must be said that the doctrine of *Nus* was a traditional element inherited from Plato, who, however, had no
psycho-physics or only slight beginnings of one, and that, while
we find a developed theory of *Nus* even in the earliest works of
Aristotle of which we can have exact knowledge, as is consistent
with the general speculative tendency of his first Platonizing
philosophy, we do not find any trace of empirical psychology in
those works. The latter pursuit is entirely his own invention.
Hence it is certainly not an accident that his ethics, for example,
is built on a very primitive theory of the soul, namely the
division of it into a rational and an irrational part. This venerable doctrine, appearing in Aristotle as early as the *Protrepticus*,
is simply Plato's. For practical reasons he left it undisturbed
in later days, although his psychology had advanced a long way
in the meantime and he no longer recognized parts of the soul

[1] See Brandis, *Griechisch-römische Philosophie*, vol. ii b 2, pp. 1192 ff., and
my article 'Das Pneuma im Lykeion', *Hermes*, vol. xlviii, p. 42.

at all. In ethics it remained convenient to work with the old ideas, and no errors followed serious enough to vitiate the ethical result; Plato's old system was ingrained in the foundations of his ethics for good and all. Nevertheless he thinks it necessary to apologize for thus simplifying his problem.[1] The structure of his ethics would probably have been different if, when its foundations were being laid, his psychology had already reached the level at which we know it. This contrast of levels can still be pointed out in definite details. The way in which the *Eudemus* develops Plato's theory of Recollection, and the belief in personal immortality as we find it there and even in the dialogue *On Philosophy* (that is, even at the beginning of the middle period), are incompatible with the psycho-physics of the work *On the Soul* as it has come down to us. They presuppose the persistence after death of precisely that part of human consciousness which according to the philosopher's later view is bound up with the body.[2] Moreover, we have to recognize that the ethics of the middle period, with its theological notion of clairvoyance and of prophecy, is still on the same level as the dialogue *On Philosophy*, whereas the work *On the Interpretation of Dreams*, which belongs to the series of physiological inquiries attached to the books *On the Soul*, represents a complete break with this Platonizing view. The state of mind here is completely non-ethical and purely scientific; and more important than the fact that Aristotle rejects his previous view is the method on the basis of which he rejects it. He even introduces considerations drawn from the psychology of animals, a clear sign of the changed spirit of this new and completely unmystical attitude.[3] Now the

[1] In the *Eudemian Ethics* Aristotle is still confidently basing his doctrine of virtue on the old schematic division of the soul into 'two parts that share in reason' (II. 1, 1219^b 28), just as he does in the *Protrepticus*, which he is here following word for word (see above, p. 249). On the other hand, the corresponding passage of the later version (*Eth. Nic.* I. 13, 1102^a 23 ff.) apologetically insists that the statesman and the practical man, in order to judge questions of virtue correctly, need a minimum (only that!) of psychological knowledge. 'To refine further is perhaps more laborious than the matters in hand demand. Moreover, some points concerning virtue are sufficiently explained in the esoteric works, and they should be consulted.' Then comes the doctrine, traditional at this point, of the rational and the irrational parts of the soul, but with a short reference to the problematic nature of the conception of 'parts of the soul'. Accordingly this phrase is purposely avoided in what follows.   [2] See above, pp. 50 ff.

[3] In this extremely interesting essay Aristotle tries to give a natural explanation

new spirit is sovereign throughout the first two classical books of the psychology, with their theory of sense-perception and the accompanying view of the soul as the entelechy of the organic body. The doctrine of *Nus* could never have given rise to this. Equally epoch-making are the researches in the short physiological works. It is not a bold inference, but simply an evident fact, that they belong to the same late stage of development as the work *On the Interpretation of Dreams*, which is inserted among them as a monograph on a problem inherited from Plato.[1] In content, in method, in date, and in general outlook, this whole complex of researches belongs with the great works on the parts and generation of living things. Even if, therefore, the present version of the third book *On the Soul* is uniform and contemporary with the other two and the *Parva Naturalia* (on which I hazard no opinion, because the materials for a decision are lacking), that cannot alter the fact that the ideas about *Nus* are earlier, while the method and the execution of the rest is later and belongs to another stage of development—in fact, to another dimension of thought.[2]

Another and no less important creation of Aristotle's later days was the foundation of the history of philosophy and the sciences, a great collective work, encyclopaedic in dimensions yet uniform in outlook, whose monumental structure first made

of the phenomenon of dream-divination by means of psycho-physiology. He does not deny that we sometimes have prevision of the future in the dream-state, but he does now deny that this prevision proceeds from metaphysical regions. Against the belief in dreams sent by a god there is the fact that neither wise nor good men are accustomed to have such dreams, but often precisely morally inferior persons who happen to be physically disposed to them, and also the fact that animals too have dreams (a reference to the *History of Animals*, IV. 10, 536^b 28). He shows the connexion between what we dream and the subconscious or conscious impressions of the waking life, and examines in detail the causes of the distortion of images in dreams. For divination in the dialogue *On Philosophy* see above, pp. 162 ff., and in the original ethics above, pp. 240–241.

[1] It is not illuminating to suppose that Aristotle could have adopted the standpoint of scientific psychology in other matters at a time when he was still cherishing the mystical view of divination, and that just on this one point conservative Platonism was still causing him to compromise. On the contrary, his change of view about divination was simply the logical expression of a change in his whole manner of regarding psychic life.

[2] Although the *Parva Naturalia* deal only with the general physiological conditions of life, and do not enter into details, their frequent mention of principles of classification usual in the zoological works shows clearly that they are based on these empirically ascertained 'divisions'.

visible to sense that living unity of knowledge which the Peri-patos embodied. On a view of the world-process such as Aris-totle's the history of the gradual advance of human knowledge is the grand final theme of learning. With it science attains the stage of an historical understanding of the inner teleological law of its own being, just as it might that of a plant or an animal. It is astounding how he executed this task. It far exceeded the powers of a single person, and had to be divided among several workers, like the description of political forms or that of organic nature. Theophrastus was allotted the history of the physical and—in the modern sense—metaphysical systems, which he portrayed in eighteen books. In discussing the development of those two modes of thought, inseparably connected in ancient times, he gave a systematic arrangement to all the problems from Thales and the 'physiologists' down to his own age. Enough fragments of the work still exist, most of them recovered from the late doxographers, to enable us to estimate the compre-hensive nature of the comparative history that he produced. It could not have been carried out without the aid of Aristotle's library, the first considerable collection of books that we know of on European soil, and the documentary trustworthiness of the personal researches on which it rested made it antiquity's last word on the subject. In later times it was frequently con-tinued and carried down to the then present, selections were chosen from it, its contents were compressed into the most various forms, until in late antiquity, diluted to the utmost and rendered as far as possible mechanical, it was made into an introductory textbook for beginners. Besides the *Opinions of the Physicists* there was Eudemus' history of arithmetic, geometry, and astronomy, and presumably also his history of theology. The former in particular was an authoritative work throughout antiquity, and most of the later statements about the history of ancient mathematics go back to it. There was also a history of medicine, which Menon was commissioned to write ; an extract from it has recently been restored to us on a newly discovered papyrus. This whole work on the history of knowledge can have arisen only in that late period when the first attempts at a history of philosophy, as we find them in the early *Metaphysics* A, were continued on the grand scale of the *Constitutions*, and when specialized inquiries in the field of organic nature had established communication with the sphere of medicine.

Under the leadership of Theophrastus the Peripatetic school further cultivated its relations with the more famous of the contemporary schools of medicine, such as that at Cnidus, and later on that at Alexandria. Dynastic confirmation was given to these relations by the marriage of Aristotle's daughter Pythias to Metrodorus, a representative of the Cnidian school, who taught at Athens—no doubt in the Lyceum—where the great physician Erasistratus was his student. It can be shown that in his writing Aristotle makes constant use of medical literature, not merely of the Hippocratic kind that flourished in Cos, but even more of the Pneumatic physicians of the Sicilian school (Philistion, Diocles), and this proves that these studies were pursued in the Lyceum in connexion with physiology and anthropology. Then, too, was collected the pedagogical material treated in the medical work *Dissections*, to which Aristotle often refers in the zoological writings. This book was an illustrated, atlas-like work, for figures and drawings are expressly mentioned. The fact that such equipment was needed for object-lessons shows that there were regular courses of lectures in anatomy and physiology, which was not so in Plato's Academy. Plato's medical studies in the *Timaeus* and his relations with Philistion were isolated events. Here again the real organizer, the man who made empirical investigation an end in itself, was Aristotle.

To us moderns the scientific study of minutiae is no longer unfamiliar. We think of it as the fruitful depth of experience from which alone genuine knowledge of reality flows. It needs a lively historical sense, such as is not often found, to realize vividly at this time of day how strange and repellent this mode of procedure was to the average Greek of the fourth century, and what a revolutionary innovation Aristotle was making. Scientific thought had to forge step by step the methods that to-day are its securest possession and most commonplace tool. The technique of the orderly observation of particulars, methodically pursued, was learnt from the exact modern medicine of the end of the fifth century, and in the fourth century from the astronomy of the orientals with their century-long catalogues and records. Earlier students of the philosophy of nature had

not gone beyond the divinatory explanation of isolated striking phenomena. What the Academy had added was, as has been
said, not the collection and description of particulars, but the
logical classification of universal genera and species. Plato
in his later years had, of course, insistently demanded that we
should not stop half-way in our classifications, but carry on the
divisions until we came to the indivisible, for the sake of the
exhaustive completeness that alone could lend certainty to
the method; but he was referring only to the species, not to the
sensible appearances. His indivisible still remained a universal.
The first person to investigate the sensible as the vehicle of the
universal ('immattered form') was Aristotle. This aim was a
new one even in comparison with the empiricism of the older
medicine and astronomy.

He needed unspeakable labour and patience to lead his hearers
into the new paths. It cost him many efforts of persuasion and
many biting reprimands to teach the young men, who were
accustomed to the abstract play of ideas in Attic verbal duel-
ling, and understood by a liberal education the formal capacity
to handle political questions with the aid of rhetoric and logic,
or at best perhaps the knowledge of 'higher things' (μετέωρα)—
to teach them to devote themselves to the inspection of insects
and earth-worms, or to examine the entrails of dissected animals
without aesthetic repugnance. In the introduction to his work
On the Parts of Animals he initiates his hearers into this kind
of study with an acute exposition of the method, and depicts
in an impressive manner his new joy in the art of nature and in
the newly discovered world of secret orderliness.[1] We reproduce his words here in order that they may receive the attention
due to them in the history of the mind as Aristotle's profession
of his new ideal of studying the individual. He speaks of the
very different attractions of high speculation in the Platonic
sense and of the empiricism recommended by himself. He tries
to be fair to both, but we can feel on which side lay, if not his
heart, at any rate his scientific interest, when he was trying to
impress these ideas on his disciples. They were written at a
time when the metaphysical and conceptual attitude of his
early decades, though still forming the constructive framework

[1] *Part. An.* I. 5, 644^b 22.

of his general view, no longer held any place in his creative
activity.

'Of things constituted by nature some are ungenerated, imperishable,
and eternal, while others are subject to generation and decay. The
former are excellent beyond compare and divine, but less accessible to
knowledge. The evidence that might throw light on them, and on the
problems which we long to solve respecting them, is furnished but scantily
by sensation; whereas respecting perishable plants and animals we have
abundant information, living as we do in their midst, and ample data
may be collected concerning all their various kinds, if only we are willing
to take sufficient pains. Both departments, however, have their special
charm. The scanty conceptions to which we can attain of celestial things
give us, from their excellence, more pleasure than all our knowledge of
the world in which we live; just as a half glimpse of persons that we love
is more delightful than a leisurely view of other things, whatever their
number and dimensions. On the other hand, in certitude and in completeness our knowledge of terrestrial things has the advantage. Moreover, their greater nearness and affinity to us balances somewhat the
loftier interest of the heavenly things that are the objects of the higher
philosophy. Having already treated of the celestial world, as far as
our conjectures could reach, we proceed to treat of animals, without
omitting, to the best of our ability, any member of the kingdom, however
ignoble. For if some have no graces to charm the sense, yet even these,
by disclosing to intellectual perception the artistic spirit that designed
them, give immense pleasure to all who can trace links of causation, and
are inclined to philosophy. Indeed, it would be strange if mimic repre-
sentations of them were attractive, because they disclose the mimetic
skill of the painter or sculptor, and the original realities themselves were
not more interesting, to all at any rate who have eyes to discern the
reasons that determined their formation. We therefore must not recoil
with childish aversion from the examination of the humbler animals.
Every realm of nature is marvellous: and as Heraclitus, when the
strangers who came to visit him found him warming himself at the
furnace in the kitchen and hesitated to go in, is reported to have bidden
them not to be afraid to enter, as even in that kitchen divinities were
present, so we should venture on the study of every kind of animal
without distaste; for each and all will reveal to us something natural and
something beautiful. Absence of haphazard and conduciveness of everything to an end are to be found in Nature's works in the highest degree,
and the resultant end of her generations and combinations is a form of
the beautiful.

'If any person thinks the examination of the rest of the animal kingdom an unworthy task, he must hold in like disesteem the study of man.
For no one can look at the primordia of the human frame—blood, flesh,
bones, vessels, and the like—without much repugnance. Moreover, when
any one of the parts or structures, be it which it may, is under discussion,
it must not be supposed that it is its material composition to which
attention is being directed or which is the object of the discussion, but

the relation of such part to the total form (μορφή). Similarly, the true object of architecture is not bricks, mortar, or timber, but the house ; and so the principle object of natural philosophy is not the material elements, but their composition, and the totality of the form, independently of which they have no existence.'

The words read like a programme for research and instruction in the Peripatetic school. They explain to us the spirit that reigns in the works of Aristotle's followers, though these men placed metaphysics even more in the background than he does here, until it was expressly banished by Strato in the second generation. The later development of the school can in fact be understood only through the almost exclusively empirical interest here expressed by Aristotle in his old age, just as Plato's disciples attached themselves wholly to his later views. Aristotle is not, of course, proposing the complete excision of metaphysics and celestial physics. On the contrary, this very passage shows that the lectures on the animal world were preceded by some in that sphere. It is impossible, however, to mistake the complete change in his mood and the displacement of his inner centre of gravity as compared with the time when he thought of himself primarily as the reviver of Plato's supersensible philosophy and the pioneer of a new speculative knowledge of God. In his work on metaphysics this study appears, in the true Platonic fashion, as the only exact science because the only one based on pure *Nus* ; and though he called it, when he was writing the original metaphysics, a science vouchsafed only to divine knowledge, he was at the same time expressing his proud confidence that reason cannot be too highly thought of by man, and that nothing in reality is hidden from its power. How different sounds the language of his old age ! He no longer speaks of the world of appearances as more knowable to us but to be contrasted with the essence of reality, which is more knowable naturally. He justifies metaphysics now by means of the everlasting longing of the human heart to penetrate the mysteries of the imperishable and invisible world, and is ready to content himself with the merest corner of that hidden truth, while the precedence as real science (ἡ τῆς ἐπιστήμης ὑπεροχή) is now clearly assigned to empirical research. This is the praise of devotion to the small, the confession of allegiance to the study that fulfils its highest achievements in the *History of Animals*, the collection of *Constitutions*, the history of the theatre, and the chronicle of the Pythian competitions.

The spiritual bond between the work and purpose of these years and the reformed Platonism of the forties is his peculiar conception of 'immattered form', which in the passage quoted he sets up as the real aim of the study of nature. This idea, from being the object of an ontological theory of knowledge, came year by year to be rather a living instrument of the most varied researches. It now appears, therefore, not with the significance of a metaphysical principle—taking 'metaphysical' not in our sense but in Aristotle's—but as the direct object of conceptually interpreted experience. In the same way the notion of purpose, which is connected with it, is not in itself a metaphysical conception for Aristotle, but is simply read off from experience. The sphere of applicability of the notion of form, therefore, extends far beyond the immanent essences of his metaphysics, the latter being restricted, properly speaking, to the entelechies of natural things. He explains it in the passage quoted by means of the analogy of artistic form. Through this analogy his conception of form can be applied to the structures of human culture, which are partly of a purely artistic kind, and partly on the borderline between conscious spiritual creation and the spontaneous work of nature; of the latter kind are the state and all the forms of human society and manners of life. By his notion of form he bridges the contrast between pure thought and the empirical study of individuals, between nature and art. His empiricism is not a mechanical amassing of dead material, but the morphological articulation of reality. He organizes and overcomes the manifold (ἄπειρον) of appearances, which Plato simply passes over, by ascending from the smallest and most insignificant traces of organic form and order to more comprehensive unities. Thus he builds up out of experience the total picture of a world whose ultimate efficient and final cause is once more a highest form, the form of all forms, creative thought. According to Plato the spiritualization of man's whole life could be attained only by turning away the mind from appearances to the archetype; according to Aristotle it is in the end identical with the specialization of knowledge as here understood. This is because every new discovery of a form, be it that of the lowest insect or amphibian or of the tiniest part of human art or speech, is a step onward in the task of making mind supreme over matter and thus 'giving meaning to reality'. There is nothing in nature, even the most worthless and contemptible, that does not contain something wonderful within itself; and he whose eye with glad astonishment discovers it is akin to the spirit of Aristotle.

CHAPTER XIV

THE REVISION OF THE THEORY OF THE PRIME MOVER

IN Aristotle's last period there was another pregnant alteration in his theology, obviously made in connexion with the
final revision of the *Metaphysics*. On this occasion the oldest
part of this study, and that in which his Platonic heritage most
persistently asserted itself,[1] namely the theory of the unmoved
mover and of its relation to the celestial revolutions, underwent
a change. As has been shown,[2] the actual elaboration of the
theological portion was never completed in the final version,
but there remains a considerable passage that was intended to
form part of it, and was subsequently inserted by the editors
into Book Λ, to which in subject it belongs.

From its apparent lack of all external relation to the rest
Bonitz inferred that Book Λ is not the intended conclusion of
the *Metaphysics* but an independent treatise, and must be
assigned to an earlier date.[3] We have confirmed this inference
in another way by revealing the connexion of Book Λ with the
earliest version of the *Metaphysics* and the form there given to
the doctrine.[4] Against this early dating, however, there stands
the mention of Eudoxus' pupil Callippus in chapter 8.[5] Little
as we know about this famous astronomer and his dates, it is
extremely improbable that he met Aristotle before the latter's
second stay in Athens. The only fixed point in his chronology
is the great reform of the Attic calendar, which he was invited
to undertake by the Athenian government.[6] The new era, which

[1] Above, pp. 141 ff.
[2] Above, p. 223.
[3] Bonitz, *Comm. in Ar. Metaph.*, p. 25. Cf. above, p. 219.
[4] Above, pp. 219 ff.
[5] As was pointed out by Apelt in his review of my 'Ent. Metaph. Arist.',
Berliner philologische Wochenschrift, 1912, c. 1590.
[6] His date is briefly discussed by Boeckh in his *Vierjährige Sonnenkreise d.
Alt.*, p. 155, which, however, does not make use of the passages in the *Metaphysics*. For his era see the article in Pauly-Wissowa under the heading
'Kallippische Periode'; it is a fault that there is no article on Callippus himself
in this encyclopaedia. He deserves a separate study. As yet there is not even
a collection of the remains of his teaching.

is usually called after him, began in 330/29. He must therefore have been working in Athens for a considerable period about this time, and naturally he would renew the relations established by Eudoxus with the learned circles in the city. This is proved, with as much certainty as any one could wish for, merely by the way in which Aristotle speaks of him in Λ 8. He could not have reported as he does on the changes proposed by Callippus in the sphere-system of Eudoxus unless he had discussed these questions with the astronomer himself in the school circle. It was in fact, as will become clear hereafter, precisely these discussions, that is to say, the direct stimulation that he received from the astronomical side, which first incited Aristotle to work out the doctrine of the movers of the spheres. The imperfect tense that he uses when speaking of Callippus' alteration of the Eudoxian system admits of two explanations only: either it merely means that Aristotle owes his knowledge of these hypotheses to previous oral discussions with Callippus, or it also implies that at the time of writing Callippus was no longer alive. Since Aristotle also uses the imperfect in speaking of Eudoxus, who is known to have been long dead and with whom again Aristotle was personally acquainted, the most probable conclusion is that both were true of Callippus as well.[1] All the later must be the date of chapter 8. It must come during Aristotle's last time at Athens, and presumably after 330.[2] This conclusion is extremely impor-

---

[1] *Metaph.* Λ 8, 1073^b 17: 'Eudoxus *used to suppose* that the motion of the sun or of the moon involves, in either case, three spheres. . . . Callippus *used to make* the position of the spheres the same as Eudoxus did, but while he *used to assign* the same number as Eudoxus did to Jupiter and to Saturn, he *used to think* two more spheres should be added to the sun and two to the moon, if one is to explain the observed facts.' Aristotle uses similar language when speaking of views put forward by Plato in oral discussion, for ex., Λ 9, 992^a 20: 'Plato even *used to object* to this class of thing as being a geometrical fiction, and *used to give* the name of principle of the line—and this *he often used to posit*—to the indivisible lines.' The express addition of 'often' here is decisive for the understanding of this imperfect, and we must supply it in the passage about Eudoxus and Callippus. For the imperfect as the expression of the oral tradition of a school see for ex. *On the Sublime* III. 5 (and Wilamowitz's comment thereon in *Hermes*, vol. xxxv, p. 49, n. 2). Similar are the reminiscences of the Academy in *Metaph.* Z 11, 1036^b 25 (the younger Socrates), and *Eth. Nic.* X. 2, 1172^b 9–20 (Eudoxus). Antiquity's knowledge of the reasons for Callippus' alterations in the Eudoxian system was based on the oral tradition of the Lyceum as preserved by Eudemus (see his frg. 97, p. 142 in Spengel).

[2] According to Simplicius *In Arist. de Caelo* (p. 493, l. 5, in Heiberg) 'Callippus of Cyzicus, after studying with Polemarchus the friend of Eudoxus, came

tant for Aristotle's development. Either this chapter was written at the same time as the rest of Book Λ, and then all our conclusions about the antiquity of the form given to the doctrine in that book (above, p. 221) would totter, or our proof that the earliest *Metaphysics* had a distinct form of the doctrine holds good of Book Λ also, and then chapter 8 must be not an original element but a later insertion.

While the doctrine of Book Λ incontrovertibly belongs to the earlier conception of metaphysics, sharp eyes have been equally certain ever since the days of antiquity that chapter 8 is not an organic member of its surroundings but a foreign body. It remains, however, to give the real proof that what isolated critics have always suspected is actually so. Whereas others have usually taken their start from the astronomical content of the passage, we will begin with the style.

Book Λ is an outline of a lecture, not intended for the use of other persons at all (above, p. 219). It contains only the main points, sketchily put together, sometimes merely jotted down one after the other with a recurring 'Note, next, that . . .', and bare of all stylistic polish in detail.[1] The greatest difficulties of interpretation come in the first or physical part, which provides the foundation for the doctrine of the first mover; but even the second part, in which this doctrine is expounded, is not much more readable, which in view of the fundamental importance of the subject has always been found extremely distressing. Everything is left to the actual delivery. There is not the slightest reason to fear that in his lectures Aristotle spoke the sort of Greek that some readers, knowing none but these parts

to Athens after the latter and spent his time with Aristotle correcting and supplementing the discoveries of Eudoxus'. That this was not the Academic period, but the time when Aristotle was head of a school, follows not merely from the express separation of this stay of Callippus from the celebrated Athenian sojourn of Eudoxus (in 367), but also from the description of him as a pupil not of Eudoxus but of Eudoxus' pupil Polemarchus. Otherwise, moreover, we should not have merely Aristotle mentioned as his collaborator but rather Plato. All this points to the period of Callippus' reform. Simplicius must have obtained his information from a learned tradition (Eudemus' history of astronomy, apparently consulted in Sosigenes, see Simplicius, op. cit., p. 488, l. 19), for it cannot be deduced merely from the passage in the *Metaphysics*.

[1] See *Metaph.* Λ 3, 1069ᵇ 35 and 1070ᵃ 5, and the linking of arguments with ἔτι, καί, ἅμα δέ, ὁμοίως δέ, or ἢ καί, mainly in the early chapters but also, for ex., in chap. 9, 1074ᵇ 21, 25, 36, 38, 1075ᵃ 5 and 7, and chap. 10, 1075ᵃ 34, ᵇ 14, 16, 28, 34,

of him, reverence with respectful awe as genuine Aristotelian
brevity. How he really spoke is shown by chapter 8, which in
contrast to the rest of the book is fully written out. In consequence its style is so strikingly distinct from that of its context
that we must seek a reason for this phenomenon.

In chapter 8 Aristotle discusses the question whether there
is only one essence such as the unmoved mover, or a considerable number of them, so that they form a class. He begins with
some remarks on the history of the problem of determining the
number of the first principles with mathematical exactitude.
He then puts forward the theory that, just as the heaven of
the fixed stars requires an eternal unmoved mover in order
that it may move, those other complex motions executed in the
heavens by the planets each require their own unmoved mover.
This is because the stars are by nature eternal, and therefore
their motion presupposes some other eternal which must possess
independent being exactly as they do in accordance with the
principle that only substance (οὐσία) can be prior to substance.
For each star we must assume as many movers as it executes
motions; and since the system of Eudoxus, which Aristotle has
adopted, assumes a special sphere to each motion, this means
that there must be precisely as many unmoved movers as there
are spheres. It is for astronomy, not for metaphysics, to calculate the number of these spheres, but of course this does not
mean that astronomy has anything to do with the assumption
of unmoved movers. The latter is purely metaphysical in origin.
Aristotle does, however, transgress the bounds of metaphysics
when he enters into the calculations of the astronomers and tries
to show—as it is the main purpose of his discussion to do—that
neither the system of Eudoxus nor the revised form of it put forward by Callippus suffices to explain all the planetary motions.
Eudoxus had arrived at 26 spheres. Callippus raised the number
to 33. Aristotle with his hypothesis of 'counteracting spheres'
increased it to 47 or 55.

This survey of the main content of the astronomical chapter
will suffice to show that it is incompatible with its context not
merely in its style of writing but also in its 'style' of method.
The theology of the two preceding chapters breathes an entirely
different spirit. The unmoved mover there discussed moves the

heavens by itself, and through the medium of them, which move themselves, it moves this world of things whose motion is purely external to it.[1] The seventh chapter examines the character and essence of the highest principle. It is immaterial mind, pure act, serene and blessed life free from all interruption. Aristotle ascribes to it an eternal unmoved essence (οὐσία) that transcends all that is perceptible to sense. It can have no size or extension; it is an indivisible unity, impassible and unchangeable. In view of these essential properties the highest principle is declared to be God, for by the conception of God we understand an essence that is eternal, living, and most perfect. Now all this applies, according to Aristotle, to *Nus*. *Nus* is not only the eternal and most perfect thing; 'the actuality of thought is life'. This derivation of the Absolute is of course so concise and so far from exhaustive that it at once raises a series of questions to which Aristotle gives no answer, but the train of thought radiates a force, generated by religious experience, that carries one away. We are irresistibly driven on to the question of the ninth chapter: what is the content of this activity of *Nus* and what relation obtains between the content of its thought and its perfection? If it thinks nothing it is at rest, and hence at the most a potency, not a pure activity; if it thinks something other than itself it thinks something less perfect than itself, and thereby diminishes its own perfection. Thus Aristotle leads his hearers in one flight to the conclusion that necessarily follows from the conception of divine (that is, of the most perfect) being: thought thinks itself, and in this creative act it eternally enjoys its own absolute perfection.

Chapter 8 interrupts this continuous train of thought and breaks it into two parts. Remove it, and chapters 7 and 9 fit smoothly together. After reading chapter 8, on the other hand, it is impossible to take up again the speculative meditation broken off with chapter 7. From soaring flights, from Platonic religious speculation, we plunge headlong down to the monotonous plain of intricate computation and specialized intelligence. Simplicius was right when he said that such a discussion belonged rather to physics and astronomy than to theology;[2]

---

[1] *Metaph.* Λ 7, 1072^a 24. Cf. *Phys.* VIII. 5, 256^b 14 ff.
[2] Simpl. *In Arist. de Caelo*, p. 510, l. 31.

for it loses itself entirely in subsidiary matters, and shows far more interest in ascertaining the exact number of the spheres than it does understanding of the fact that this grotesque multiplication of the prime mover, this army of 47 or 55 movents, inevitably damages the divine position of the prime mover and makes the whole theology a matter of mere celestial mechanics. Hence Simplicius transferred his explanation of this astronomical passage to his commentary on the *De Caelo*, and it has been a favourite subject for astronomers from Sosigenes to Ideler.[1] Valentin Rose, however, when he wished to transfer the whole of Book Λ from the *Metaphysics* to the *Physics* made the mistake of appealing not merely to chapter 8 but also to the equally physical character of the fifth chapter of the first part.[2] He failed to see that Aristotle needed a foundation for his doctrine of the prime mover, and that originally the theology was built up directly and quite externally on the theory of physical 'substance'. The only real stumbling-block, therefore, is the astronomical interpolation, and before banishing the whole book on that account it is surely more reasonable to examine where the chapter itself properly belongs. Lasson's procedure in taking the whole astronomical passage out of the text into a note was far better, as he thus restored the connexion between the seventh and ninth chapters.[3] It is in fact an insertion that can have been made only by the editors of Aristotle's remains. In subject it is certainly closely connected with the question of the prime mover; but the minuteness with which it treats a

[1] Sosigenes in Simplicius, op. cit., p. 498, ll. 2 ff.

[2] Valentin Rose, *De Aristotelis librorum ordine et auctoritate*, p. 160. He considers that the basing of theology directly upon a preceding physical inquiry—which he truly sees to be characteristic—is the product of some post-Theophrastean Peripatetic who had 'already' conceived the 'false' notion of metaphysics as the science of 'the things that come after physical things'. He holds, naturally, that the metaphysics of 'substance' is the only genuine Aristotelian doctrine. Thus he puts things exactly the wrong way round; in reality the stage of development that we have in Book Λ comes before the metaphysics of 'substance'.

[3] *Aristoteles' Metaphysik*, translated into German by Adolf Lasson (Jena, 1907), pp. 175–6. Lasson contented himself, however, with removing the middle part of the chapter, $1073^b 8$–$1074^a 17$, which contains the actual calculation of the number of the spheres, while retaining the beginning and end. In so doing he failed to perceive the indivisible stylistic and material unity of the whole. The middle portion carries the beginning and end along with it. Moreover, his reason for his action was merely to help the student; he did not perceive the historical origin of the break in the train of thought.

subsidiary problem is so utterly excessive in an isolated lecture confining itself entirely to the main outlines that it must have been written for another, more detailed connexion. In view of this agreement between the criterion of style, the interruption of the train of thought, and the internal contradiction between the late origin of the astronomical part and the ancient character of the book as a whole, it is an extremely probable conjecture that the interpolation is not due to Aristotle himself.[1] The editors proceeded here just as they did in other parts of the *Metaphysics*. Now since the point that Aristotle reached in working out the later version of the *Metaphysics* was precisely the threshold of theology, it seems obvious that we have in the eighth chapter of Book Λ a piece of the new version of this final part. We observe that here again Aristotle was not in the least content with his original view; even in the last revision he reconstructed the whole theory of the movers of the spheres.

As we have previously discovered in the dialogue *On Philosophy*, the theology of Aristotle's earlier stage knew nothing of this theory. Since the ether had not yet become the element that 'by nature' moves in a circle, and the stars moved simply through the will of the star-souls, we must suppose that at that time Aristotle's idea was just that the heavenly bodies themselves have souls, and that he did not think it necessary to posit a number of movers for each one of them, corresponding to the number of its spheres (above, pp. 141–142). At that time, therefore, his only deviation from Plato's view lay in supposing an unmoved mover above the first heaven, which, being eternal, produced the eternal motion of the world. By this theory he overcame the notion of a self-moving world-soul, whose motion, like that of all the other self-moving things known to us in experience, had a beginning. Since, however, he had apparently always assumed, with Eudoxus, the existence of spheres for the wandering stars,[2]

---

[1] This, however, in no way demonstrates the spuriousness of the chapter, which for a long time some critics have thought they must assume, because they recognized its incoherence with the rest; for ex., J. L. Ideler (the son) in his *Aristotelis Meteorologica*, vol. i, pp. 318 ff. The father did not make this mistake; see 'Über Eudoxos', *Abhandlungen der Berliner Akademie* (historisch-philosophische Klasse) 1830, pp. 49 ff.

[2] See *De Caelo* II. 9, 12, esp. 293ᵃ5–8. Aristotle there expressly says that the heavenly bodies have souls—they possess 'action' and 'life', 292ᵃ18–21—but these souls belong not to the spheres but to the stars themselves, which 'we

it followed by analogy from his doctrine of the first mover that each of these circular motions (φοραί) beneath the outer heaven must also have its own mover; for if there were only the first mover we should expect all the other spheres to move in the same path as that of the fixed stars. This objection is made by Theophrastus, who places the questions of celestial mechanics in the centre of his fragment on metaphysics.[1] Even at that time there were still Aristotelians who clung to *one* mover. And Theophrastus shows us why, for he continues: 'If that which imparts movement is different for each moving body and the sources of movement are more than one, then their 'harmony as they move in the direction of the best desire' (ὄρεξις ἀρίστη) is by no means obvious. And the matter of the number of the spheres demands a fuller discussion of the reason for it; for the *astronomers'* account is not adequate.' He then reveals the difficulty concealed in Aristotle's conception of desire and impulse (ὄρεξις and ἔφεσις), namely that it presupposes a real soul; and criticizes the exclusion of the earth from the system of cosmic motions. If circular motion is the most perfect it is surely astonishing that the earth should have no part in it. Such an assumption presupposes either that the force of the first mover does not reach as far as the earth or that the earth is not susceptible to it. In any case—and here Theophrastus comes very close to the modern view—the question is transcendental (οἷον ὑπέρβατόν τι καὶ ἀζήτητον). *Metaphysics* Λ 8 is an attempt to draw the real consequences of applying the unmoved mover to all the spheres. Theophrastus' book is an echo of the new doctrine, which was being discussed during Aristotle's old

falsely take to be mere bodies and soulless monads in space'. He is speaking therefore not of the movers of the spheres, but of Plato's theory of star-souls, which we have shown from the dialogue *On Philosophy* that he believed in early days. We have proved above (see pp. 299 ff.) that the fundamental doctrines of the books *On the Heaven* are early in origin. The recognition of 'action' and 'life' in the stars is also connected with the Platonic view.

[1] Theophrastus, *Metaphysics*, p. 310 Brandisii: τὸ δὲ μετὰ ταῦτ' ἤδη λόγου δεῖται πλείονος περὶ τῆς ἐφέσεως, ποία καὶ τίνων, ἐπειδὴ πλείω τὰ κυκλικά, καὶ αἱ φοραὶ τρόπον τινὰ ὑπεναντίαι, καὶ τὸ ἀνήνυτον καὶ οὗ χάριν ἀφανές. εἴ τε γὰρ ἐν τὸ κινοῦν, ἄτοπον τὸ μὴ πάντα τὴν αὐτὴν (SC. κινεῖσθαι κίνησιν)· εἴ τε καθ' ἕκαστον ἕτερον (SC. τὸ κινοῦν ἐστιν) αἵ τ' ἀρχαὶ πλείους, ὥστε τὸ σύμφωνον αὐτῶν εἰς ὄρεξιν ἰόντων τὴν ἀρίστην οὐθαμῶς φανερόν. τὸ δὲ κατὰ τὸ πλῆθος τῶν σφαιρῶν τῆς αἰτίας μείζονα ζητεῖ λόγον. οὐ γὰρ ὁ γε τῶν ἀστρολόγων (SC. λόγος ἱκανός ἐστιν). Then follows the criticism of the notion of ἔφεσις or ὄρεξις ἀρίστη, an element of Aristotle's Platonic period which he always retained (cf. pp. 152 ff. above), even when he had abandoned the star-souls.

age. He agrees with Λ 8 in taking the theory of the first mover mainly as a physical doctrine; but he reflects still more clearly the difficulties into which the multiplication of the first principle plunged Aristotle's metaphysics.

Aristotle himself asks to be excused, in Λ 8, for entering a sphere that is beyond the bounds not merely of philosophy proper but even of demonstrative necessity. He will not speak of 'necessity' at all, but merely of the 'probable'.[1] This merely probable character contradicts, however, the original conception of metaphysics as a study far surpassing physics in exactitude, and Aristotle only makes the contrast more sensible when he excuses himself by remarking that anyhow astronomy is the closest related to philosophy of the mathematical disciplines.[2] How far the empirical method of this pronouncement of the 55 movers is from that of the old *Metaphysics* appears especially in the remark that the verification of these assertions must be left to specialized science. The purpose of the whole account is therefore simply to give an idea of the matter (ἐννοίας χάριν). This expression sounds alarmingly like fiction. The phrase 'to give some notion of the subject' really means just what Aristotle says the Platonists did when they assumed a certain origin of numbers merely—to quote their own expression—'for the sake of theorizing', not, therefore, as a judgement about any reality. Assuming then the correctness of the theory of the spheres and of the number of them as calculated, what he wishes to show is that the number of the first principles must be definite and precisely determinable. Obviously it was a special science, namely astronomy, that set him to extending his theory of the first mover. It taught him that the hypothesis of a single uniform ultimate motion was too primitive to account for the

---

[1] *Metaph.* Λ 8, 1074ᵃ 14: 'Let this, then, be taken as the number of the spheres, so that the unmovable substances and principles also may probably be taken as just so many: the assertion of *necessity* must be left to more powerful thinkers.' Cf. also 1074ᵃ 24, 'it is reasonable to infer this from a consideration of the bodies that are moved'. For the exactitude of the science of the immaterial see α 3, 995ᵃ 15 ff.

[2] *Metaph.* Λ 8, 1073ᵇ 3: 'In the number of the movements we reach a problem which must be treated from the standpoint of that one of the mathematical sciences which is most akin to philosophy—viz. of astronomy.' His reason is that astronomy, in contrast to the other mathematical disciplines, deals with an actual and moreover with an eternal reality—which certainly sounds extremely weak.

complications of the actual heavenly motions, and that the calculations of the number of the spheres undertaken by the school of Callippus offered the possibility of precisely determining the number of the first principles.

Aristotle's adoption of this new road, while it does honour to his unbending sense of fact, involved him in inextricable contradictions. They are so clear and obvious on the surface that it would be absurd to try to soften them. During the later days of antiquity, when much labour and great acuteness was bestowed on the interpretation of Aristotle's philosophy, Plotinus gave a decisive criticism of this theory, in which he developed the doubts raised by Theophrastus.[1] He first deprecates the method of mere probability, which Aristotle was obliged to admit because he could not attain to certainty. He then argues that even the probability is in poor shape; for, if all the spheres are to make up one unified world-system, the many unmoved movers which think themselves should rather have one single aim, the first mover. The relation, however, of the many movers to the first is wholly obscure. Either all these intelligible essences must arise from the first, and must, just as the spheres which they move fit into the outermost sphere and are governed by it, be contained in the highest *Nus* as its objects, which would give an intelligible world like Plato's; or each of them must be an independent principle, and if so there is no order or structure among them, and they cannot explain the symphony of the cosmos.

A further counter-argument of Plotinus' is that if the movers are all without body, how can they be many, since no matter attaches to them as principle of individuation? This objection is taken from Aristotle's own assumptions, and had in fact occurred to him. In the middle of the eighth chapter of Book Λ there is a remarkable passage that will not merge with its context as far as the thought is concerned. Even a superficial reading of it shows that it necessarily destroys all that is said in Λ 8 about the multiplicity of unmoved movers. 'Evidently there is but one heaven. For if there are many heavens as there are many men, the moving principles, of which each heaven will have one, will be one in form but in *number* many. But all

[1] Plotinus, *Enneads* V. 1, 9.

things that are many in number have matter; for one and the same definition, e.g. that of man, applies to many things, while Socrates is one. But the primary essence has not matter; for it is complete reality. So the unmovable first mover is one both in definition and in number; so too, therefore, is that which is moved always and continuously; therefore there is one heaven alone.'[1] The singleness of the heaven is here proved by an indirect method. If there were more than one, the first principle of each of them would be only generically identical with those of the others, while individually (ἀριθμῷ) distinct, as, for example, in the genus man, where the individual men coincide in form, but are many in number. Whereas the conception of man is common to all individuals of this genus, Socrates and the others are each a particular real unity, since every time that the conception of man joins itself as form to matter another individual arises. The first essence (τὸ τί ἦν εἶναι τὸ πρῶτον), the highest mover that guides the heaven, is an exception. It is pure entelechy and has no matter. That is to say, this highest form is not a genus appearing in several exemplars. It has no connexion with matter, which is the principle of individuation. In the highest of all forms unity of form and real singleness coincide. Hence that which it moves, the heaven, also occurs once only.

In the first place, it is clear that Plotinus' argument against there being many movers is nothing more than an application of the principle here laid down by Aristotle to the question of the intelligences of the spheres. If matter is the principle of individuation, as Aristotle teaches here and elsewhere, either the movers of the spheres cannot be immaterial, since they form a plurality of exemplars of a genus, or Aristotle refutes himself by retaining his doctrine of immateriality, since this excludes individual multiplicity. In either event he falls into contradiction with the presuppositions of his own philosophy. The fact is that the form of forms, the unmoved mover, is in origin an absolutely unique being, and its peculiar qualities are such that any duplication destroys the presuppositions of its own conception. The same conclusion follows from the proof in the *Physics*, where Aristotle infers the uniqueness of the unmoved mover from the continuity and unity of the world's

[1] *Metaph.* Λ 8, 1074ᵃ 31 ff.

motion. The commentators admit that they cannot explain this difficulty.[1]

If, however, we consider the passage from a linguistic point of view, the first glance shows that it is foreign to its context. With its first words, 'evidently there is but one heaven', another style begins, and with the last word of the insertion, 'therefore there is one heaven alone', it ceases again. It is the same short-hand style as obtains in the rest of Book Λ, and contrasts sharply with the impeccable language of chapter 8. That the passage is an insertion is also clear from the fact that it disturbs the gram-matical connexion. In the next sentence, 'our forefathers in the most remote ages have handed down to their posterity a tradition, in the form of a myth, that they are gods and that the divine encloses the whole of nature', the plural 'that they are gods' refers to nothing.[2] To learn who 'they' are we have to go ten lines back, where we are told that the end of every movement is one of the divine bodies that move through the heaven. The words 'divine bodies' lead directly to the reflection (1074^b1) that the men of old were right to think them gods and to believe that the divine is something that encloses the whole of nature. The intervening argumentation, deducing the singleness of the heaven from the immateriality and uniqueness of the first mover, is a later and in fact a critical addition, for it implicitly contains the refutation of the assumption that there are more movers than one. Aristotle must have noted it against this passage as a piece of self-criticism; his faithful editors introduced it into the text; and the keenest thinkers of posterity have racked their brains to understand how an Aris-totle could have involved himself in such contradictions.

[1] Bonitz, op. cit., p. 512; Schwegler, *Die Metaphysik des Aristoteles*, vol. iv, p. 280. Rose (op. cit., p. 161) regards the passage as the addition of a disciple, because in *De Caelo* I. 9 Aristotle proves the uniqueness of the first heaven on physical grounds; but in the same work (8, 277^b 9–10) Aristotle says that the point can also be proved by means of the *Metaphysics*, and this proof would not be discoverable in the latter work were it not preserved for us in the passage in question, Λ 8, 1074^a 31–39. It only fits, however, the earlier *Metaphysics*, which knew nothing of movers of the spheres—the same situation as when *De Caelo* was written—and not the doctrine of Λ 8. There are no demonstrable additions by disciples to the text of the *Metaphysics*.

[2] As Rose observed, op. cit., p. 161. [The Oxford translator writes 'these bodies' precisely in order to make the reference clear. The Greek is merely οὗτοι—Tr.]

The original idea of the unmoved mover was a unified and self-consistent conception. The later application of the same principle to the other spheres was also all of a piece, but it did not agree with the earlier system. Aristotle began to feel doubts about it arising out of the assumptions that had formed the basis of the original notion of the one unmoved mover. When, therefore, we see that this very part, the theory of the immaterial first principles, is lacking in the final version of the *Metaphysics*, and that instead of it we have only a makeshift, namely an early lecture (Λ) together with a single piece of the new theory (chapter 8) which still shows clearly that precisely in the last period of his life Aristotle was wrestling with these problems anew and failing to solve them—when we see this we shall presumably no longer think that the state in which the material has come down to us is due merely to the malignity of historical chance. Obviously his growing tendency to treat philosophical problems in the manner of the special sciences, working together with the ferment of the new ideas in cosmology, as we found them in Theophrastus, had shattered the self-confidence of the more or less Platonic speculations of his theology and driven him to attach himself increasingly to empirical science. In thus surrendering metaphysics to the special sciences he began a new era. Consistency on the empirical side made him inconsistent with his speculative foundations. This contradiction in his thinking, which he no longer had the force to overcome, is simply the result of the deep-seated inexorable logic of his whole development, and that must reconcile us to him. Incidentally, he made a mistake, according to the astronomers, in calculating the number of the spheres and got two less than he should have. He was moving here in a less familiar region. This error adds to the probability that chapter 8 is only a preliminary version, brought to light from among his papers. There can be no doubt, however, that it comes from Aristotle himself. It does not come from Theophrastus, for, whereas his term for the counteracting spheres was not ἀνελίττουσαι but ἀνταναφέρουσαι, only the former expression occurs in our chapter. Eudemus in his *History of Astronomy* assumes the problem as well known in Peripatetic circles.[1]

---

[1] This disposes of Rose's conjecture, op. cit., p. 161. For the expression

We possess two other works that throw light on the advance of the school in tackling the problem of the prime mover. The first is the essay *On the Motion of Animals*, whose genuineness I have shown in detail on an earlier occasion, after the doubts raised against it had long held the field.[1] This examines in particular the mechanics of animal motion. In order to change its place every living thing requires a fixed fulcrum, against which the limb that is making the movement supports itself. If only one limb of the body is to move, as the lower arm or leg, this fulcrum may be within the body itself, so long as it is outside the limb that is being moved, as in these examples the elbow or the kneejoint. If, however, the whole body is to move it must have a fixed point lying outside itself in order to push off. For land-animals the earth serves as resistance, either directly or indirectly; for those that swim the water; for those that fly the air. In the second, third, and fourth chapters of the work Aristotle examines the analogous problem in the motion of the universe. He there discusses a recent hypothesis, agreeing with its inventor that there must be an unmoved first principle and that this cannot possibly be either inside or a part of the moving vault of heaven,[2] for then the heaven would either stand quite still or break up. He disagrees with him, however, when from this reflection he deduces that the poles of the world's axis have a certain force, because they are the only conceivable points of rest in the heavenly sphere, and thus seem to present themselves as the only fixed points suitable for a mechanical explanation of the world's motion. Against this Aristotle holds that a mathematical point as such cannot possess physical reality or extension, far less exert force. Moreover, even if these two points did have some force, they could never produce a single unified

---

ἀντανφέρουσαι σφαῖραι see Simplicius, *Comm. in Arist. de Caelo*, p. 504, l. 6 (Heiberg). Pseudo-Alexander, following the astronomer Sosigenes, notices Aristotle's miscalculation in his *Comm. in Ar. Metaph.*, pp. 705, l. 39,—706, l. 15 (Hayduck). Eudemus gives Callippus' reasons for increasing the numbers of the spheres in frg. 97 (p. 143 Sp.).

[1] 'Das Pneuma im Lykeion', *Hermes*, vol. xlviii, pp. 31 ff.

[2] *De Animalium Motu*, c. 3, 699[a] 17. Notice the distinction that Aristotle draws between the representatives of this supposition and the inventors of the myth of Atlas. He is not attacking the same view twice over. Rather he mentions the mythical version merely to show that this modern view has had forerunners.

motion like the heaven's; and he expressly tells us that the author of the hypothesis assumed *two* poles. The question is connected with the problem whether the heaven could be destroyed.[1] If, for example, we were to assume that the earth is the required fulcrum, as being the centre of the world, then, apart from the fact that the fulcrum must not lie within the moving body and therefore not within the universe in this case, we should have the further difficulty of explaining how the inertia of the earth, which must be thought of as a limited quantity, could suffice to counterbalance the force of the world's axis acting against it. The latter must inevitably exceed the inertia of the earth, and hence force it out of its place in the centre of the universe. All these difficulties are removed if we suppose that outside the circling heaven there is an unmoved cause of motion such as Homer conceived Zeus to be when he makes him say to the Gods (VIII. 21–22. 20):

> You could not push from heaven to earth
> Zeus the highest of all, even if you laboured exceedingly
> And all gods and all goddesses took a hand.

The way in which Aristotle here again makes use of a myth in a philosophical question is characteristic of him. Not only does he derive his own principle from Homer both here and in Book Λ of the *Metaphysics*; he also attempts to see a revival of the myth of Atlas in the view, which he here attacks, of the earth as the fulcrum of the world's axis.[2]

The hypothesis that the motion of the universe requires an unmoved fulcrum, that the two poles serve as such, and that they are therefore the unmoved first principle of the motion of the heaven, is clearly astronomical in origin. It takes account of Aristotle's demand for a prime mover, and yet purposely avoids every metaphysical theory and seeks rather for a purely mathematical explanation within the world as given. We may suppose that some astronomer of the Eudoxian kind, such as Callippus, had taken up this sort of attitude towards the bold metaphysical inferences that Aristotle had thought it necessary to make from Eudoxus' theory of the spheres. The unknown astronomer tried

---

[1] *De Animalium Motu*, c. 4, esp. 699ᵇ 28 ff. See also 3, 699ᵃ 31 ff.
[2] See *Metaph.* Λ 8, 1074ᵇ 1–14; 10, 1076ᵃ 4. For the myth of Atlas see *De Animalium Motu*, 3, 699ᵃ 27 ff, and also the previous note but one.

to obtain, for the first time, a clear idea of the mechanical implications of the motion of the heaven, and in so doing he took his departure from the known kinds of motion and their laws. This way of looking at the thing was undoubtedly new to Aristotle. His own unmoved mover had been teleologically conceived, and moved the world by pure thought. The fact that he here at once adopts the attitude of the new natural science, just as he did in the question of the number of the movers, shows very clearly how much he vacillated in his last period about the nature of the fundamental problem of metaphysics. In his work *On the Motion of Animals* he tries to show that even from the point of view of modern celestial mechanics the unmoved mover standing outside the universe offers the only conceivable solution. Even now, of course, his mover does not become a 'force' of a physical kind; but he speaks of its being touched by the moving cosmos[1] as if there really were a spatial and physical relation between the two, and then destroys the point of his own acutely formulated problem by a transition to the intelligible world, namely the notion of the first principle moving the universe purely as an object of thought. Theophrastus takes account of this attempt also in his metaphysical fragment, and actually quotes the same Homeric lines in the same connexion, or rather assumes that they are familiar in this connexion.[2]

Whereas the work *On the Motion of Animals* does not mention the theory of the movers of the spheres, we have in Book VIII of the *Physics* a document belonging to the period of doubt, when Aristotle, though seriously considering the possibility of extending the principle of the prime mover to the planetary spheres, still hesitates to draw this consequence. As we have shown above,[3] the book is one of the latest parts of the

---

[1] *De Animalium Motu*, c. 3, 699[a] 15: 'it must touch something immovable in order to create movement.' Correspondingly in c. 4, 700[a] 2, 'and all gods and all goddesses set hands to it', where the comparison extends to setting hands to it as well as to the immobility of Zeus. Nevertheless this point always remained uncertain. In *De Gen. et Corr.*, I. 6, 323[a] 31, where he is speaking of physical contact (ἀφή), Aristotle says, 'so that if anything that is itself unmoved moves something else, it would touch the thing moved but nothing would touch it'. He seems to have dropped this self-contradictory idea later (see Zeller, *Aristotle and the Earlier Peripatetics*, vol. i, p. 408).

[2] In *De Animalium Motu*, c. 4, 699[b] 36 ff., Aristotle quotes lines VIII. 21–22 and 20. On p. 311, l. 11 (Brandis), of his *Metaphysics* Theophrastus quotes VIII. 24 in the same connexion.   [3] p. 299.

Physics. In content it occupies a middle place between physics and metaphysics, for it develops the theory of the unmoved first principle as far as that is possible inside and with the methods of physics. In the sixth chapter Aristotle shows the necessity of the hypothesis of a prime mover. Behind the exposition we glimpse the possibility of assuming a larger number of such movers, but he purposely avoids connecting this question with the proof of the prime mover, since the latter is naturally not simplified by the 55 planetary movers which it entails. Hence we find only a brief hint at the beginning of chapter 6 (258ᵇ 10): 'Since there must always be motion without inter-mission, there must necessarily be something, *whether one thing or a plurality*, that first imparts motion, and this first mover must be unmoved.' The expression 'whether . . . or' (εἴτε . . . εἴτε) is Aristotle's ordinary way of indicating that behind his formulation lies another problem, of which he assumes that his hearers are aware, but which he wishes to exclude at the present time.¹ Such a problem is usually one of the controversies of the school. This passage therefore makes it certain, as we had already discovered from Theophrastus, that even after the discussion of the planetary movers had begun there still remained in the Peripatos adherents of the theory that there is only one first principle of motion. This is again confirmed in what follows, where it becomes clear that Aristotle was not himself the leader in extending the earlier theory, but rather yielded unwillingly to the arguments of others. Let us first examine the connexion (258ᵇ 12 ff.).

Although there are some unmoved principles of motion and some self-moving beings that are not of eternal duration, this is not for Aristotle any disproof of the necessity of the first, absolutely unmoved, and eternal mover; for there must be a cause of motion that produces the continuous coming-to-be and

¹ For example in the *Protrepticus* (Iambl. *Protr.*, p. 39, l. 4, in Pistelli): 'whether fire or air or number or some other natures that are the first causes of the others.' By the last he means the Ideas. These words were written while the Academy was still debating about the theory of Ideas. See further *Metaph.* A 9, 991 ᵇ 18: 'And man himself, whether it is a number in a sense or not, will still be a numerical ratio of certain things.' The parenthetical insertion refers to a question that was burning at the time when Book A was written, whether the Ideas are numbers or not. In each passage Aristotle is referring to oral discussions in the school.

passing-away of those non-eternal unmoved beings, together with all change whatever, and this principle cannot be identical with any one of the other movers mentioned; it is transcendent and embraces them all. We may translate the important words (259^a 3 ff.).

'Nevertheless there is something that comprehends them all, and that as something apart from each one of them; and this is the cause of the fact that some things are and others are not and of the continuous process of change; and this causes the motion of the other movers, while they are the causes of the motion of other things. Motion, then, being eternal, the first mover, *if there is but one*, will be eternal also; *if there are more than one, there will be a plurality of such eternal movers. We ought, however, to suppose that there is one rather than many, and a finite rather than an infinite number.* When the consequences of either assumption are the same, we should always assume that things are finite rather than infinite in number, since in things constituted by nature that which is finite and which is better ought, if possible, to be present rather than the reverse; *and here it is sufficient to assume only one mover*, the first of unmoved things, which being eternal will be the principle of motion to everything else. The following argument also makes it evident that the first mover must be something that is one and eternal.'

In the words that I have italicized Aristotle returns to the alternative left open in the first sentence of the chapter, 'whether [the first mover is] one thing or a plurality'. He does not definitely say, however, as he does in *Metaphysics* Λ 8, that we must apply the principle to all the spheres, but doubtfully adds: 'if there is but one; if there are more than one, there will be a plurality of such eternal movers.' His sole hint as to how we can decide lies in the observation that we should assume a single mover rather than many, and, if we assume many, a finite rather than an infinite number. According to his teleological conception of nature, and according to the Platonic view in which he shared, mathematical definiteness and limitation is the chief attribute that we must demand from the highest reality and the first principles. He does not dare, however, to conclude with certainty that there can be only one principle of this sort; he merely says that the assumption of oneness is preferable to that of plurality. Whether there may not nevertheless be a plurality of movers he will not decide. It sounds like an attempt to comfort himself; and he reveals which of the two views he favoured in writing these words when he concludes the digression with the sentence: 'it is sufficient, however, to assume only *one* mover, the first of unmoved things, which being eternal will be the principle of motion to everything else' (that is, to the souls of terrestrial creatures). Its eternity is here made the distinguishing mark of the prime mover, the foundation of its character both as prime and as the origin of the others.

On the assumption of a plurality of movers it is not easy to say how Aristotle thought of their relation to the revolution of the outer heaven. Everything that is suggested about it in this chapter sounds rather provisional. Lines 259^b 1–20 explain why it is impossible to follow Plato, who, however, is not named, in placing at the head of the world's motion, on the analogy of the beings that have souls, something that moves itself, a world-soul. The motion of all the self-moving creatures that experience acquaints us with has a beginning at some time; the motion of the world, however, cannot be imagined to have begun at a definite instant, for then it would have passed into reality out of pure potency, whereas all merely potential being may just as well *not* be. If, therefore, we assume that the heaven moves itself as Plato would have it, it still requires something absolutely unmoved outside itself as the original cause of its motion. Moreover, a self-moving thing is always at the same time *accidentally* moved, even if *by nature* it is unmoved, as souls are in bodies; whereas the highest principle must not be moved even accidentally.

After writing this Aristotle appears to have thought of the objection (259^b 28) that then neither would the movers of the planetary spheres present an exact analogy to the prime mover, although they persist unmoved so far as moving their own spheres is concerned, because, inasmuch as these spheres are diverted from their own motion by that of the outer heaven and carried along in the path of the fixed stars, their movers must be accidentally moved along with them, that is to say, the place of their movers must be changed. He establishes, in a hastily written final sentence, this difference between earthly creatures, which though unmoved move themselves accidentally through changing the place of their bodies, and the intelligences of the heavenly spheres, that the latter are accidentally moved not by themselves but by something else, namely the outer heaven. How this helps to prove their immobility is not clear;

presumably it is merely an attempt to establish any sort of specific difference between terrestrial and celestial movers. It certainly does not lessen the gap between the highest and the planetary movers, for, if the latter are accidentally moved by something else through the attraction of their spheres into the revolution of the outer heaven, this spatial conception inevitably presupposes that they do not transcend their spheres like the prime mover, which is outside the world, but are immanent in them like souls. Simplicius objects to this inference without giving reasons, but Alexander of Aphrodisias was justified in making it.[1] At any rate no other interpretation is possible on the basis of this passage alone. The sphere-souls would then be a transitional stage between the original purely Platonic doctrine of star-souls in the dialogue *On Philosophy* and the transcendent sphere-movers of *Metaphysics* Λ 8; for although even in the latter chapter (whose comparative lateness follows from the mere degree of definiteness with which it sets out the new doctrine) these movers are not expressly described as 'separated', which is all the more striking since every other characteristic of the first mover is assigned to them, we must nevertheless suppose that Aristotle here regarded them as existing apart. He says that they precede the substance of the spheres, and must therefore be of the nature of substance themselves;[2] such a mode of expression does not fit the relation between soul and body, for according to Aristotle the soul is not a substance prior to the substance of the body. It is clear, therefore, that in the long run he was unable to be satisfied with the doctrine that the sphere-movers are accidentally moved by the first heaven, and therefore decided to hold that the planetary movers are also transcendent. This got rid of the external contradictions on one side. At the same time, however, it plunged him into the flood of difficulties involved in his new account of the relation between the other movers and the

[1] Simpl. *In Arist. Phys.*, vol. ii, pp. 1261, l. 30—1262, l. 5, in Diels.

[2] *Metaph.* Λ 8, 1073ᵃ 32: 'Each of these movements also must be caused by a substance both unmovable in itself and eternal. For the nature of the stars is eternal just because it is a certain kind of substance, and the mover is eternal and prior to the moved, and that which is prior to a substance must be a substance. Evidently, then, there must be substances which are of the same number as the movements of the stars, and in their nature eternal, and in themselves unmovable, and without magnitude, for the reason before mentioned.'

highest *Nus*, which ultimately threatened the foundations of his theology.

These indications in this chapter of the *Physics* of a plurality of unmoved guiders of the stars are obviously mere subsequent additions. Aristotle inserted them at the time when the school was beginning to discuss the extension of his theory of the unmoved mover, when there was still not much more than the bare possibility of deciding for a larger number of planetary movers. The passages in question are three.

The first is 258^b 10. Here grammatical reasons suggest that the parenthesis 'whether one thing or a plurality' is to be regarded as an addition. If we hold it to be original, the following words, 'it is not necessary that each of the things that are unmoved but impart motion should be eternal, so long as there is just one such thing',[1] must be about the movers of the spheres, to which 'whether one thing or a plurality' refers. This, however, gives no sense, as was observed by Simplicius, who tacitly substitutes the souls of terrestrial creatures as subject. That they must be the non-eternal unmoved movers whose existence Aristotle allows is not merely clear from what follows[2] but necessary in itself, for the movers of the stars, if they are to be assumed at all, must be as imperishable as the stars themselves. Thus the parenthesis actually upsets that contrast between the one eternal and the many perishable movers which is just Aristotle's point. Moreover, the words do not fit well in the sentence into which they have been introduced, for it is hard to imagine how we can argue from the continuity of the heavenly motion (which is all he is talking about both here and in what precedes and in what follows) to the existence of an unmoved eternal mover 'whether one thing or a plurality'. As a marginal note they are comprehensible; in the text they disturb the strict train of thought.

The second passage, $259^a 7$–13, is an equally improvised

---

[1] The Oxford translation differs here, but not in anything essential to the present point.—Tr.

[2] In what follows Aristotle often describes them as 'things that move themselves' (as in 258^b 24, 259^a 1, 259^b 2 ff., and ^{b} 17) and uses this expression as synonymous with the technical term 'unmoved but imparting motion'. In 259^b 2 he expressly mentions 'the animal kingdom and the whole class of living things'.

reference to the possibility of several movers. 'Motion, then, being eternal, the first mover will be eternal also (if there is but one; if there are more than one, there will be a plurality of such eternal movers).' As the words stand they are remarkably tautological, for all that can be meant is: if there are several movers, there is more than one eternal principle. If Aristotle had merely wished to state the principle that every continuous eternal revolution, whether that of the outer heaven or that of some other sphere, presupposes an unmoved eternal mover, without going into the question how many such revolutions and movers there are, he would have expressed himself more or less in this way: 'If there is a plurality of continuous revolutions, there is also such a mover for each one of them.' This, however, is just the consequence that he still shrinks from drawing, as the conclusion of the insertion shows: 'it is sufficient to assume only *one* mover.' In *Metaphysics* Λ 8 he is concerned only to ascertain the number of the spheres and thereby of the movers, while the principle, that there is a mover for every sphere, is established. Here, on the other hand, it is precisely this question of principle that has to be decided, whether we can get on with *one* mover instead of many. That is why he intentionally speaks in such an obscure and indecisive fashion: if motion is eternally continuous there must be an eternal mover—if there is only one mover; if, however, there are several there are also several eternal things, that is to say, they must of course be eternal also . . . however, one is enough. In style too the passage from 'if there is but one' onwards gives the impression of a subsequent addition. Finally, Aristotle could hardly have continued as he does if the suspected words had always stood in their present position (259ᵃ 15): 'We have shown that there must always be motion. That being so, motion must also be continuous, because what is always is continuous, whereas what is merely in succession is not continuous. But further, if motion is continuous it is *one*, and it is *one* only if the mover and the moved that constitute it are each of them *one*.' This must have been written when Aristotle, in inferring from the continuity of the motion to the mover, was still thinking of the motion of the world in its totality; for if he meant only that there are as many movers as there are continuous motions the parenthetical question whether there is one mover or more would have no point, and there would be nothing to say except 'There is a number of unmoved movers corresponding to the number of the spheres'.

The third passage that owes its existence to an addition is $259^b 28-31$, at the end of the series of proofs. Aristotle's original intention was to make the contrast between the world-spirit and the individual souls of the terrestrial realm as great as possible. The idea of the world-spirit had undeniably been obtained from the analogy of the souls of living things, but that was only the more reason for giving especial prominence to its outstanding and exceptional position. Apart from its intellectual characteristics, this appears in its *absolute* immobility. The souls of living creatures, while unmoved in themselves, move themselves indirectly when they move the body so that it changes its place. This is not true of the prime mover, which we must posit as the cause of the eternal continuous motion of the universe; in its absolute transcendence it remains unmoved both in itself and accidentally. Now when Aristotle came to introduce the sphere-souls he could not exempt them from all motion as he had the prime mover, for, though unmoved in themselves, they are carried along by the outer heaven with their spheres. In order, however, that they might not sink to the level of terrestrial 'souls', he inserted this passage ($259^b 28-31$), which nevertheless, as we showed above (p. 361), cannot conceal the fact that he is here introducing a new principle that does not harmonize with the contrast between the self-moving earthly souls and the absolutely unmoved spirit of the world. For the rest, the addition was intended to be hypothetical just like the two others; it was merely to recognize the *possibility* that the spheres have movers, nothing more.

The later Peripatetics, who knew the final form of the doctrine of the sphere-movers from *Metaphysics* Λ 8, necessarily interpreted these additions to the *Physics* in accordance with it. They were bound to assume that here also Aristotle had the same point of view, and to read it into this chapter. In general they were able to carry this out with the help of the further assumption that Aristotle wished to explain here only the principle of the relation obtaining between continuous revolution and unmoved mover, and not to raise the question of the special

nature and number of the movers of the spheres; but there is
one passage on which this view inevitably came to wreck. At
the end of the chain of argument we read as follows (259^b 20).
'Hence we may confidently conclude that if a thing belongs to
the class of unmoved movers that are also themselves moved
accidentally, it is impossible that it should cause continuous
motion. So the necessity that there should be motion continuously requires that there should be a first mover *that is
unmoved even accidentally*, if, as we have said, there is to be in
the world of things an unceasing and undying motion.' That
the correct reading was εἶναί τι Δεῖ τὸ πρῶτον κινοῦν ἀκίνητον
καὶ κατὰ συμβεβηκός, which remains only in one little-noticed
manuscript, is clear from Simplicius, whose interpretation of the
passage presupposes it.[1] Only the highest and transcendent
mover is unmoved accidentally as well as in itself, not the
sphere-souls, as Aristotle himself says in the interpolation
259^b 28–31. If then only the prime mover is in question here,
how could the interpreters also discover the doctrine of the
sphere-movers in the passage? So far were they, however, from
supposing Aristotle could ever have thought otherwise that they
simply corrected the passage and made it mean exactly the
opposite by inserting a negative. The false reading 'and not
unmoved accidentally' has made its way into all the better
manuscripts, although it is not even linguistically intelligible
and the real meaning is exactly repeated at 258^b 15.[2]

Fortunately tradition has preserved for us the way in which
the first generation of Aristotle's followers dealt with the riddle
presented by this chapter of the *Physics*. Eudemus partly

---

[1] Simpl. *In Phys.*, vol. ii, p. 1260, l. 11 (Diels). Cp. the *apparatus criticus* and
Diels 'Zur Textgeschichte der arist. Physik', *Berichte der Berliner Akademie*,
1882.

[2] Cp. 258^b 13: 'The following considerations will make it clear that there
must necessarily be some such thing, which, while it has the capacity of moving
something else, is itself unmoved and exempt from all change [as Simplicius
correctly reads; the manuscripts give 'unmoved in respect of all external
change'], which can affect it neither in an unqualified *nor in an accidental sense.*'
These words correspond to those at the end of the whole argument in 259^b
20–28. The two together enclose the series of proofs and thus show that this
whole chapter is concerned solely with the highest moving principle. The false
reading μὴ κατὰ συμβεβηκός occurs at 259^b 24 in all the manuscripts except H,
although some one has erased the μή in E (Parisinus), either because he had
looked at Simplicius' commentary or because his own reflections had revealed
to him that the logic of the argument requires its removal.

paraphrased the *Physics*, and partly reproduced it word for word, in a large work of several books apparently intended for lectures. In doing so he often gave more precise expression to doubtful passages, and sometimes added new arguments or made other additions, none of which can count as his own property. For the most part he simply brought the *Physics* up to the state in which the problems were at the time of Aristotle's death. This is perfectly clear in our passage. During the time just before the master's death the theory of the prime mover had been expanded into the theory of the movers of the spheres. Eudemus looked in vain in this chapter of the *Physics* for a definite explanation that there is a plurality of unmoved movers. The last of the arguments for the existence of an unmoved mover seemed rather, as we have seen, to exclude altogether the possibility of a multiplication of this principle. In his paraphrase Eudemus therefore inserted into Aristotle's argument, 'since there must necessarily be continuous motion, there must also be the unmoved first mover', the words 'for each revolution', that is, for each of the spheres.[1] He thus read into Aristotle's statement the doctrine that its author had finally recognized as the true one. He was justified in considering it the authentic one, and he saw in the words of the *Physics* a formulation that no longer accorded with Aristotle's most advanced view. He could not help seeing, naturally, that the elevated style of the 'undying and untiring motion' in this passage makes it fundamentally impossible to suppose that it refers to anything but the motion of the first heaven and the God who causes it; the whole pyramid of arguments in the last book of the *Physics* culminates in this idea. It is in fact, like many other formulations in this work, one of the evidences that its first

---

[1] Simpl., op. cit., vol. ii, p. 1262, l. 16, in Diels (Eudemus, frg. 80, p. 105, l. 5, in Spengel): 'Having shown first that there is always motion, and that it has neither a beginning before which it was not nor an end after which it will not be, and next that the prime mover "*in each motion*", *as Eudemus adds*, must be unmoved both in itself and accidentally . . .' This recapitulation of the content of the sixth chapter of *Physics* VIII refers, as far as Eudemus' addition is concerned, to the words (259^{b} 22–24): 'So the necessity that there should be motion continuously requires that the first mover (!) should exist and be unmoved both in itself and accidentally.' How Eudemus reconciled himself to the fact that his addition openly contradicts Aristotle's own explanation, according to which 'immobility both in itself *and accidentally*' belongs only to the highest mover, remains obscure.

draft dates from an early period. Eudemus and his fellow-students, therefore, knew this when they asserted their authentic interpretation; but the consciousness that Aristotle's surviving papers are the deposit of a process of evolution was obviously lost soon afterwards.

CHAPTER XV

ARISTOTLE'S PLACE IN HISTORY

THE name of Aristotle suggests impersonality, timelessness, intellectual sovereignty over the whole world of abstract thought throughout long stretches of history, and scholastic idolatry. In order to assimilate him entirely to their own world the Middle Ages erased his individual characteristics and made him *the* representative of philosophy. The greatness of such an attitude towards the matter that he represents is undeniable, and he himself aimed at the matter and not at the person, at eternal truth and not at historical learning; but the days when he was identified with truth itself have passed. His historical importance as the intellectual leader of the West is certainly not lessened by the fact that the evolution of independent philosophical achievement in European culture has taken the form of a five-hundred-years' struggle against him. Seen from the modern point of view, however, he is now merely the representative of the tradition, and not a symbol of our own problems or of the free and creative advance of knowledge. We attain a fruitful relation to him only by a detour, by historical knowledge of what he meant to Greek culture and philosophy, and of the special task that he fulfilled in his century. This fate befalls every great spirit who obtains historical survival. He must be detached from his historical roots and neutralized before he can become accessible to posterity. Only history can then answer the further question when the point has been reached where this 'living' influence changes to the opposite, so that nothing but a return from the tradition to the sources and to the real historical meaning of his life can save him from intellectual death. Even to-day we cannot easily agree whether Aristotle has reached this point, since the scholastic philosophy lives on among us as a world in itself. The present book, at any rate, arises out of an historical attitude towards him—which, however, does not necessarily make it useless to those who think fundamentally otherwise, for without deepening our understanding of Aristotle as an historical person we cannot even get a full grasp of the special nature and depth of his influence on posterity.

I propose therefore to conclude my discussions by applying the historical results of this book to the place of Aristotle in the intellectual movement of his century. Up to the present the inner connexion between his philosophical form and the great problem that Plato propounded to the scholarship of Greece has been made evident mainly in his criticism of the Ideas and in the evolution of particular conceptions. This examination of particular conceptions is the special task of the philosophical interpretation of Plato and Aristotle. The philological history of development, on the other hand, while requiring and further-ing this philosophical interpretation, does not find its ultimate aim in the history of problems as such, but sees therein only the special form taken by the whole intellectual progress of the nation in the philosophical sphere. To ask how far philosophy led or was led in this progress is idle. The question can hardly be decided even if one takes the whole culture of a period into account, because one erroneously supposes that only the content of consciousness really matters, and fails to see the significance of the formulation given to this content by philosophy. What follows attempts to understand the organic significance of Aris-totle's philosophy within Greek culture purely through itself and its historical circumstances, abstracting from the material content of the particular disciplines and concentrating attention solely on the historical nature of his problem and its intellectual forms.

I. ANALYTICAL THINKING

Aristotle's huge achievement in logical inquiry shall be touched on here only so far as it characterizes the whole spirit of his philosophy. In it the analytical power of his thought obtained classical expression. The way was prepared for it by certain discoveries in elementary logic contained in the theory of Ideas, and by the epistemological and methodical trait in Plato; but the *Analytics* and *Categories* sprang from another root than Plato's invariably concrete and objective thought. Modern research has successfully attempted to show that a large number of logical propositions occurring in undoubtedly early works such as the *Topics* and the *Categories* (above, p. 46) arose in the Academy and were simply taken over by Aristotle, and a comparative analysis of the elementary logic of Plato's dialogues, carried into the smallest details, would confirm and enlarge this result, as our examination of the *Eudemus* has shown ; but Aristotle is the first person in whom we find real abstraction. It took possession of all his thinking. Here is not the place to examine the first appearance of the abstract and its gradual emergence in Greek thought, nor to show how it unfolded itself more and more clearly out of Plato's Idea. It was reserved for Aristotle's powers of observation to grasp it wholly in itself, with its own peculiar laws. In his untiring research into the logical properties and relations of the categories and of the forms and presuppositions of scientific inference we can detect the investigator of later years, seeking to span in its entirety the whole realm of logical fact. He constructs his new discipline as a purely formal act, and expressly tells us that for him logic, like rhetoric, is not a theory of objects and so not a science (φιλοσοφία), but a faculty (Δύναμις) and a technique. He separates it rigorously from the question of the origin of conceptions and thoughts in the soul, and thus from psychology, and regards it purely as an instrument of knowledge ; but for this very reason he joins his doctrine of the syllogism to his theory of objects to make a self-supporting theory of knowledge, the basis of which is the inquiry into the so-called axioms. This does not justify us in speaking of a metaphysical logic. He had broken up the old ontologic—the only form of logic known to Pre-Aristotelian philosophy—once and for all into the elements Word (λόγος) and Thing (ὄν). The bond between them had to be restored somehow, and this was done by means of the conception of formal cause, which was at once conception and thing, ground of knowing and ground of being. This may not seem a satisfactory solution—it was historically conditioned by Aristotle's realism—but it is very far from the projection of logical conception, judgement, and inference, into the real as Hegel teaches it.

It is necessary to realize the tremendous influence of the analytical attitude on the intellectual form of Aristotle's philosophy, for it determines every step that he takes. In his works everything is the most perfect, polished, logical art, not the rough-and-ready style of modern thinkers or scholars, who frequently confound observation with inference and are very poor in conscious nuances of logical precision. Because we no longer have feeling or time for this art, and because we are more or less innocent of the finer cultivation of thinking as ancient dialectic understood it, our modern interpreters of Aristotle do not display an excessive amount of it in their commentaries. In this respect we could learn a good deal from the ancient expositors, who—at any rate those who do not belong to the decline— follow every step of the method with the conscious interest of the artist in thinking. The fact is that the thinking of the fourth century is in the same case as its speech; both are closed worlds to the ordinary person of to-day; only the pale glimmer of a notion of them ever penetrates his consciousness. Whatever attitude we take towards this conscious technical cultivation, we have in it a part of the essence of the fourth century, to which we always feel ourselves intellectually very close because the names of Plato and Aristotle have a direct significance for us. From that to real understanding, however, is another long journey.

The significance of this analytical habit of mind in the actual treatment of problems can be followed step by step, for example in the *Ethics*, where the fruitful but problematic equations into which conceptions were forced by the older speculation (such as 'virtue = knowledge') give way for the first time to a real analysis of the growth of ethical motives and of the forms of ethical action and will. This is by no means simply 'psychologizing' ethics; the starting-point is always an exact logical inquiry into the meaning of particular words and conceptions, together with a sharp delineation of their applicability. As an example we may take the analyses in *Nicomachean Ethics VI* of philosophic wisdom, *phronesis*, *Nus*, scientific knowledge, art, understanding, good deliberation, and cleverness. The psychological delicacy with which he here takes apart the knotted mass of conceptions contained in Plato's *phronesis* is a very great advance along the path from the blank Idea of the Good to an ethics of will and intention; and it would never have been possible but for his conceptual analysis, which provided him with a theory of meaning, based on language, from which his sympathetic psychological comprehension could take its start.

The example also shows clearly that when so examined Plato's 'conceptions' at once dissolve into their component parts and are then irrevocably lost. How much *phronesis* included according to him—the Idea as object and the contemplation of the Idea as the process of knowledge, theoretic recourse to the knowledge of the Good and the practical fulfilment of sentiment and action by means of this vision, in short, the whole 'philosophic life'. Aristotle reduces it to the meaning corresponding to ordinary speech; it becomes 'ethical insight' and is then only one element among many in the analysis of the moral *ethos*. In the same way Aristotle's thinking differentiates between Plato's theory of being and his theory of knowledge. The Idea, the palpable intelligible unity of the manifold, which was at once ethical ideal, aesthetic form, logical conception, and essential being, in an as yet undivided unity, breaks up into 'universal', 'substance', 'shape', 'what-it-was-to-be-so-and-so', 'definition', and 'end', none of which conceptions comes anywhere near it in comprehensiveness. Aristotle's 'form' (εἶδος) is the Idea (ἰδέα) intellectualized, and is related thereto just as his *phronesis* is to Plato's. Everything that Plato's spirit touched has a certain plastic roundness, than which nothing more strenuously resists the analytical urge of Aristotle's thought, which is to Plato's as the anatomical diagram is to the plastic human form. Perhaps this shocks the aesthetic and the religious man. Anyhow it is characteristic of Aristotle.

The execution of this principle was the birth of science in the modern sense. We must not forget, of course, that the phenomenon not merely possesses this esoteric significance but is also a symptom of the whole intellectual development. Within the history of Greek thought Aristotle stands decidedly at a point of transition. After the tremendous achievement of Plato's philosophy, in which the antique power of myth-making was imbued with the fructifying logical intelligence to an unprecedented degree, the world-picturing creativeness of the old days began apparently to fail, and to succumb to the preponderance of the scientific and conceptual attitude. The man who clinched this inevitable historical development was Aristotle, the founder of scientific philosophy. It is characteristic of philosophy, or at any rate of Greek philosophy, that this act did not become the start of a new and fruitful philosophical development, but was simply a high point through which it passed, and which remained attached to the name of Aristotle. The mechanical outward form of his art of *Analytics* was indeed taken over by Hellenistic philosophy, and pursued right down to scholasticism; but his analytical spirit, far from descending upon it, found its food in positive science. The foundation of scientific philosophy became the direct cause of the final separation of science from philosophy, because in the long run the Greeks could not endure the intrusion of the scientific spirit upon their efforts to picture the universe.

The peculiar form through which the analytical thought of scientific philosophy mastered both the real world and its intellectual heritage was the method of division, inference, and dialectic. Hypothesis played only a subordinate part, and was consistently used only in connexion with division. Hellenistic science did not possess the practical prerequisites for making fruitful use of this method, especially experiment. All division orders as well as distinguishes; it delimits the range and content of conceptions and the applicability of methods, and thereby leads indirectly to the general conceptual arrangement of things that we call system. Aristotle has always been reckoned the systematizer *par excellence*, because under the influence of his thought philosophy was divided into a series of independent disciplines combined into a unity by their common intellectual purpose. The first attempts, however, at making philosophy systematic in this way occur in the Academy in Plato's later view, when in the *Philebus* he distinguishes physics as 'second philosophy' from the study of the Ideas, which Aristotle afterwards called 'first philosophy'. That ethics, too, had already asserted its independence within the Academy is shown by Xenocrates' celebrated trichotomy, logic, physics, ethics, which established an epoch in Hellenistic philosophy.

Those very Stoic and Epicurean systems, however, clearly show that Aristotle's and Plato's 'systems' lacked the main feature of the type—they were not closed. It is no accident that they were unfamiliar with the technical term σύστημα, which aptly describes the constructive character of the Hellenistic pictures of the world, self-sufficient, emphasizing totality, and far removed from living research. The soul of Aristotle's thought is not putting together (συνιστάναι) but dividing (διαιρεῖν), and that not as a principle of construction but as an instrument of living research. Hence his 'system' remains provisional and open in every direction. No passage can be cited in which he even lays down the limits of the main disciplines unambiguously and definitively, and those who marvel at the systematic articulation of his philosophy cannot even say into what parts it divides. The celebrated division into theoretical and practical and productive, with the division of the first into theology and mathematics and physics, is nowhere realized and does not embody his actual system; it is a merely conceptual classification. At the level of development at which he wrote those words it signified merely a geometrical *locus* for the leading part played by metaphysics in philosophy. Moreover, the particular disciplines as such always opposed the greatest difficulties to the attempt at a completed systematization, as is only too intelligible now that we know how Aristotle's writings attained their form. Arising out of indefatigable work on specialized problems, they always present a disparate picture if we examine their systematic structure in detail. In this respect the *History of Animals* is the same as the *Metaphysics* or the *Politics*. Outlines of a systematic arrangement, often introduced only during the subsequent labour of welding the parts together, are carried only half through or remain entirely unfulfilled. To produce an external architectonic was not the original idea of this builder and therefore none can be 'reconstructed', any more than the treatises with their overlapping layers can be made into a smooth literary whole.

If we dismiss this sense of system, namely an edifice of dogma, there remains only that analytical power of separating and ordering which is systematic in a very different sense. System will now mean not the outwardly visible façade, the construction of a totality of knowledge, lifeless and dogmatic, out of the multiplicity of particular discoveries and disciplines,[1] but the inner

---

[1] This Hellenistic notion of the systematic is strikingly developed by Sextus Empiricus (*Adversus Logicos* I. 198, 3 ff.) on the basis of his—mainly Stoic—

stratification of fundamental conceptions, which Aristotle was the first to bring to light. When he flings the net of the categories over reality, then selects from them the independent 'this-something-or-other' (τόδε τι), declares it the 'substance' of philosophic thought, and so descends the pitshaft of this conception, in order to lay bare in it one after the other the levels of matter, form, essence, universal, potency, and act, that is certainly systematic thinking. By this analysis the mere 'this-something-or-other' is differentiated into the form which determines matter, and in which universal conceptual thinking grasps the essence of the real, the latter being related to matter as act to potency. The same fundamental conceptions persist like subterranean strata through several disciplines. Thus the conception of form penetrates psychology and logic and all the special sciences, while it also belongs to physics and metaphysics, that is, to theoretic philosophy. The doctrine of *Nus* runs through metaphysics, ethics, psychology, and analytics. These common intellectual themes hold the disciplines inwardly together. The unity does not arise, however, from any intentional assimilation of the parts to each other; it is the original kernel out of which the multiplicity has grown. Plato's Idea was ethics, ontology, and theory of knowledge, in one. The method of division dissolved it into several disciplines; but in accordance with Plato's striving for unity Aristotle built up beneath them a conception corresponding to the Idea, a conception common both to reality and to knowledge, which united the multiplicity at its root.

Nevertheless each special sphere retains its tentative and inquiring character, never achieving satisfaction in the external form of completeness and unimpeachable construction, always improving itself, overthrowing what it had previously set up, and looking for new paths. If there is any totality for which Aristotle strives it is a totality not of finished knowledge but of problems. This may be illustrated by our conclusions about his ethics. According to Plato's statement of the problem happiness consisted either in virtue or in pleasure or in *phronesis*. The *Philebus* shows how the problem of pleasure,

sources. Truth is here conceived as a 'fixed' scientific system (ὡς ἂν ἐπιστήμη καθεστηκυῖα συστηματική) and the latter is characterized as a congeries of many things (ἄθροισμα ἐκ πλειόνων).

for example, made itself independent in his philosophical inquiries and formed a realm of its own, touching the questions of *phronesis* and virtue and happiness only tangentially. The same thing happened to the realms of *phronesis*, virtue, friendship, and happiness. They all appeared frequently in the Academy, and always as relatively independent subjects of inquiry, as is shown by the titles of the works of the members. Plato's dialogues give a faithful picture of the sets of problems thus rendered independent. Aristotle collects together all the problems bearing on ethics (τὰ ἠθικά), and, without curtailing the free play of the particular sets, gradually subjects them all to a tighter methodical yoke within the framework of this originally loose unity. The unification never prospered sufficiently, however, to allow a 'systematic' justification of the appearance of the problems *On Friendship* in the eighth and ninth books of the *Nicomachean Ethics*, for example, or to make the double discussion of the problem of *Pleasure* in Books VII and X explicable through considerations other than editorial. Where we can see somewhat deeper into the origin of the writings, as in the *Metaphysics* and the *Physics*, we observe towards the end of the process an increasing effort to reach such a unified structure, although it is never completely successful. Only the history of his development can clearly reveal the roots and the meaning of what we may call Aristotle's 'system'. The Hellenistic systems are connected with his late work, but they take their departure from the external impression and make primary that which was secondary to him. They dogmatically construct a fixed picture of the world out of 'valid propositions', and in this safe shell they seek refuge from the storms of life.

II. SCIENCE AND METAPHYSICS

All the lines of Aristotle's philosophy run together in his metaphysics, while it on the other hand stretches out into all other disciplines. It expresses his ultimate philosophical purposes, and every study of the details of his doctrine that does not start from this central organ must miss the main point. To form a correct judgement on its nature and accomplishment is not easy, if only because of the hindrance arising from the prejudice attached to the name. The period during which

Aristotle's philosophy held dogmatic sway ended with the break-up of metaphysics as a branch of knowledge and thus demolished his creation. Since then we involuntarily regard him as the leader of the dogmatists, the antipode whom Kant overcame, and think we do him a service by preferring the non-metaphysical parts of his philosophy and putting him in a more positivist light. Yet he was never a positivist even in the days when research preponderated. The living significance of his metaphysics cannot be appreciated from the point of view of modern critical philosophy, but only in relation to the problems of his own time. When we look at it in the latter way we find that it is really founded on a critical purpose. His aim was to purge the philosophical consciousness of its mythical and metaphorical elements and to work out the strictly scientific foundations of a metaphysical view of the world that he took over in its main outlines from Plato. In other words, it was his interest in a particular method that led to this influential construction.

His metaphysics arises out of that inner tension between intellectual conscience and longing for a religious view of the world which constitutes what is new and problematic in his philosophical personality. In the earlier cosmologies of the Greek physicists the mythical and the rational elements interpenetrate in an as yet undivided unity. From the historical point of view it is an abuse of language, not in the least excused by its frequency, to call these philosophies metaphysical systems because they contain elements that are metaphysical in our sense. In this sense, naturally, Aristotle's *Physics* would also have to be called metaphysical, and yet precisely this example makes the historical absurdity of this anachronistic description as clear as daylight. Its application to the Presocratics would be sensible only if it were meant to express that in founding metaphysics as an independent science Aristotle's aim had been just precisely to make these dogmatic and mythical elements in the cosmologies of his predecessors the conscious centre of philosophical thought, whereas previously they had insinuated themselves unperceived. There is somewhat more justification for using the expression of Plato's world of Ideas. Here it indicates the entry into philosophical consciousness of the invisible and intelligible, and especially the objective side of the

Ideas as being a higher sort of reality, not to be apprehended by experience. With this is connected in the later phase of Plato's development the religious problem of teleological theology, which became the starting-point of Aristotle's metaphysics. Even this use of the modern conception is, however, strictly speaking unhistorical—although we continually fall back into it against our will—and hinders the true understanding of Aristotle's real achievement. Metaphysics arose in his mind, and it arose out of the conflict of the religious and cosmological convictions that he owed to Plato with his own scientific and analytical mode of thinking. This inner disunion was unknown to Plato. It was a consequence of the collapse of the procedure on which Plato had based the knowledge of his new supersensible reality, and in which for one instant exact science and the most ecstatic enjoyment of the inexperienceable had seemed to coincide without remainder. When this concrete unity of myth and logic fell to pieces Aristotle carried away as a *depositum fidei* the unshakable confidence that in the Platonic creed of his youth the inmost kernel must somehow or other be true. The *Metaphysics* is his grand attempt to make this Something that transcends the limits of human experience accessible to the critical understanding. Because of this profound and previously unrecognized community of problems with the philosophers of religion in medieval Christendom, Jewry, and Islam, and not through a mere accident of tradition, he became the intellectual leader of the centuries following Augustine, whose interior world was enlarged far beyond the limits of the Greek soul by their tension between faith and knowledge. The history of his development shows that behind his metaphysics, too, there lies the *credo ut intelligam*.

The study of his development also allows us to see more clearly the new conception of method on which this philosophy reposed. Up to now the reigning view has been that the word 'metaphysics' owes its origin merely to the order accidentally given to his writings in some complete edition of the Hellenistic age—Andronicus is usually suggested—and that it does not express the Aristotelian view of the real situation. In truth, however, this word, which was surely coined by some Peripatetic earlier than Andronicus, gives a perfectly just picture of the fundamental aim of 'first philosophy' in its original sense. Whereas

Plato had fixed his gaze from the very first moment on the highest peak of the world of Ideas, and believed that all certainty was rooted directly in knowledge of the invisible and intelligible, Aristotle's metaphysics is construed on the basis of physics, thus taking the opposite direction. The highest monad, after having been to Plato the most exact norm and the most certain object of the mind, came to be for Aristotle the last and most difficult of all problems. We usually overlook the fact that his commonest description of the new discipline is 'the science that we are seeking'. In contrast to all other sciences it starts not from a given subject-matter but from the question whether its subject-matter exists. Thus it has to begin by demonstrating its own possibility as a science, and this 'introductory' question really exhausts its whole nature.

From the very beginning Aristotle is certain that the science that we are seeking is possible only if there are either Ideas or some 'separated' intelligible reality corresponding to them. In spite of his critical attitude, therefore, he escapes no more than Plato did from the notion that all real knowing presupposes an object lying outside consciousness (ἔξω ὂν καὶ χωριστόν) which it somehow touches, represents, or mirrors. As we have said, this realism is nothing specifically Aristotelian, but universal among the Greeks. Ancient thinking never got beyond the confused notion of the relation between knowledge and its object indicated by these pictorial expressions. Within these historical limits, however, Aristotle's *Metaphysics* represents a state of the problems whose relation to Plato's ontologic corresponds pretty exactly to that of Kant to the dogmatic rationalism of the eighteenth century. The question, Is the science that we are seeking possible? has for him the objective meaning, Is there this supposed supersensible reality? while for Kant it has the methodological meaning, Are there *a priori* synthetic judgements? without which the traditional metaphysics was inconceivable. The fact that ancient criticism—*sit venia verbo*—bears the realistic, while modern bears the idealistic, signature, must not prevent us from detecting the inner similarity of the historical situations. Both thinkers represent extreme points in the chains of development to which they belong, and have therefore had no posterity, except for a revival following on long misunderstanding and ending in formalism. The really living evolution passes over or goes behind the metaphysical aspect of Kant or Aristotle, disregarding, with a onesidedness that is sometimes sensationalist and at other times rationalist or mystical, the scientific precision and fineness that both thinkers gave to the problems. Hence Aristotle is the only Greek thinker with whom Kant could talk on an equal footing, and whom he could try to overcome. For the rest, while Kant's position is based exclusively on his transcendental criticism of the apprehending consciousness, the foundation of Aristotle's critical realism is his physical system, together with a critical analysis, starting from the objects of experience, of the conception of being.

Metaphysics is based on physics according to Aristotle in the first place because it is nothing but the conceptually necessary completion of the experimentally revealed system of moving nature. The prime task of physics is to explain motion, and one of Aristotle's main objections to the theory of Ideas is that it does not do so. In making this objection he is setting up a definite type of natural science as a classical model, namely the method of constructing hypotheses invented by Eudoxus, which explains a complicated set of facts by referring it to the most simple principles—in this instance to the mathematical construction of all planetary motions from simple circles. 'To save the phenomena' is the methodological ideal of metaphysics. It has to elicit the ultimate grounds of experience from the facts themselves and from their inner law. To this end it must, indeed, overstep the bounds of immediate experience at one point, but it must not hope for more than to bring to light the presuppositions that lie in the facts themselves when rightly interpreted. The reference of animal motion to the eternal cosmic motion and of the latter to the motion of the outermost circle was for Aristotle a fact that the natural science of Eudoxus had placed beyond all doubt. It represented a degree of mathematically accurate experiential knowledge never before attained in this sphere. On the presuppositions of Aristotelian physics this system of motions had to find its coping-stone in some ultimate cause. The inference to a prime mover was thus suggested by nature itself.

Aristotle anchors this branch of knowledge still more firmly

in physics by means of his analysis of the conception of substance. He thereby gives to the idea of an ultimate cause of all
motion a more definite shape as the highest and final form in the
realm of natural forms. The starting-point of his theory of being
is the world of perceptible appearances, the individual thing
of the naïvely realistic consciousness. Was there any way of
apprehending this individual being? The earlier physics had in
fact possessed no such means. Its theory of the elements and of
motion did indeed offer much information about the components
of 'all things' and the forces active within them, but it obtained
this information by pure speculation. The technical analysis of
an individual thing into its material elements, as modern natural
science understands it, was just as impossible for Democritus
with his highly developed atomic theory as it had been for earlier
and still more primitive physicists. In the last and highest stage
of its development Plato's philosophy embraced as the object of
scientific knowledge (ἐπιστήμη) the whole hierarchy of Ideas as
developed through the dialectical art of division, from the most
comprehensive genus down to the lowest and not further divisible
species (ἄτομον εἶδος); but all that lay on the hither side of the
Ideal world, where it bordered on that of experience, was indeterminate (ἄπειρον), the object of mere opinion, and not truly real.
Plato's indivisible is not yet Aristotle's individual, an immanent
form linked with matter (ἔνυλον εἶδος). Earnestly though Plato
wrestled with the question of opinion in his last period, he
could not pass from the Idea to a grasp of the individual being of
experience. Physics to him was merely a heap of 'likely myths'.

This is where Aristotle's critique begins. His aim is all along to
make the Idea capable of producing knowledge of appearances.
This was, to him, synonymous with the demand that the things
of sense shall be accessible to concepts, for as a Platonist he
held that only through the universal are knowledge and science
possible. He stands in the middle of the change undergone by
the theory of Ideas in Plato's later years, which brought with it
the first thorough elucidation of the logical side of the Idea, as
the universal and the conception, and of its importance for knowledge. The same process rendered the ontological side of the Idea
problematic. Aristotle considered it axiomatic that nothing
universal possesses independent existence. From his point of

view Plato's later theory of Ideas appeared as a hypostatization of the universal, to which he opposed his doctrine of the determination of matter by form. This doctrine really abolishes the 'things' of naïve realism by making them conceptual. The object of sense-experience can come to the knowledge of the thinking subject only so far as it becomes a conceptual form; on the other hand it *is* only so far as it is form. The complete determination of reality by the forms of the understanding and by the categorial multiplicity of their conceptual stratification is rooted not in transcendental laws of the knowing consciousness but in the structure of reality itself. Herein is concealed a serious problem, which we must not overlook, but Aristotle's whole purpose is to grasp the individual through the Idea, a procedure, however, which was conceivable to him only by supposing that through the Idea one grasped that in the thing which it really was (τὸ τί ἦν εἶναι). Matter is the remnant, the non-existent, in itself unknowable and alien to reason, that remains after this process of clarifying the thing into a form and a conception. This nonexistent neither is nor is not; it is 'not yet', that is to say it attains to reality only in so far as it becomes the vehicle of some conceptual determination. Hence no matter is just matter, as the physicists supposed; it is matter for this definite form, but apart from this form and considered in itself it is already somehow informed. Nothing absolutely formless and indeterminate 'is' at all. The conception of ultimate matter, absolutely unformed and undetermined, while a limiting conception of our thinking, does not characterize any substantial reality. Everything is form, but form itself becomes the matter of a higher form. Thus Aristotle's view of being drives us on towards an ultimate Form that determines everything else and is not itself determined by anything. His physics of immanent forms attains its goal only in the transcendent Form of his metaphysics.

In this way form comes to explain motion as well, of which neither Democritus nor Plato had been able to give a scientific account from their points of view. The aim of Aristotle's theory of motion is to invent a logic of it. He tries to make it accessible to conceptual thought, just as he does particular material things, by discovering in it some form or determinateness through which it can be explained. He therefore confines it within a fixed framework, for where all is motion and flux, and nothing is fixed and enduring, science loses its rights. According to his physics this enduring element is to be found in quality and in form as the end of motion, not in quantity itself. In the first place, he lacked the technical means for making exact quantitative measurements or determining the quantitative conditions of qualities, so that research could not advance in this direction. Above all, however, he saw that in the cosmos motion took place in fixed forms and within fixed limits. The apparent caprice and lawlessness of the motions of life on the earth, which is very small in comparison with the world as a whole, could not in any way prejudice the magnificent picture of the upper and imperishable part of the universe. Here, again, Eudoxus' theory of the spheres assumed fundamental importance for Aristotle's view of the world. In the concert and continuity of the eternal revolution of the stars, as assumed in that hypothesis to account for the appearances visible in the sky, there was something purposeful and instinct with form that could not possibly be derived from the mechanical presuppositions of the contemporary theory of gravity. For the most part the physicists had had recourse to the idea of a cosmogonic vortex which set the world in motion, but as men increased their knowledge of the orderliness and invariability of the phenomena the notion of a mechanical cosmogony retreated more and more into the background, in fact it seemed to be nonsense. Aristotle went even farther than Plato in this matter. The latter had at any rate attempted to conceive what the creation of the world must have been on the assumption of Eudoxus' astronomy, when he made the beginning not chaos but the reason that orders things. Aristotle, however, breaks completely with this Anaxagorean ordering or διακόσμησις by Mind when he declares the heavenly bodies and the heaven itself to be everlasting and uncreated and derives their motion from internal formal or final causes.

With reference to motion the form is the entelechy (ἐν-τελ-έχεια), inasmuch as in its form each thing possesses the end of motion realized within itself. For the heavenly bodies this is their eternal circular revolution, but Aristotle carries over the principle to earthly things as well, thus working out Plato's teleology in every part of his world of forms. The motion of earthly things appears to be, in Platonic language, disorderly or ἄτακτος, but on closer inspection we discover that the fundamental principle of change in the organic world is the same as it is in the heavens, namely locomotion, to which all kinds of motion are to be referred. Locomotion here serves the special laws of organic coming-to-be and passing-away, which in their turn depend on the form. The entelechy of beings that come to be and pass away is the height of this organic development. In them form appears as an orderliness and determinateness building from within and unfolding itself from the matter as from a seed.

We have always supposed that this latter meaning of 'entelechy' is the original, and that the conception was first developed in the case of organic life and from thence transferred to other spheres by a generalization—that it means, therefore, something vitalistic or biological like the modern 'life-force'. This assumes that Aristotle possessed from the beginning the complete mastery of zoology and biology that he displays in the *History of Animals*, and that he more or less *saw* this principle in the object during his researches. Recently we have come to believe that the conception of biological development was his real achievement, which is a thoroughly vicious modernization. The meaning of 'entelechy' is not biological; it is logical and ontological. In every kind of motion Aristotle's gaze is fastened on the end. What interests him is the fact, not that something *is coming to be*, but that *something* is coming to be; that something fixed and normative is making its way into existence—the form.

> Creative Power, that works eternal schemes,
> Clasp you in bonds of love, relaxing never,
> And what in wavering apparition gleams
> Fix in its place with thoughts that stand forever!

The notions of potency and act, which also are usually derived from the process of organic life, are indeed occasionally illustrated by Aristotle with the example of the seed and the developed organism, but they cannot really come from this sphere. They must be taken from human power or δύναμις, which now remains latent and now becomes active (ἔργον), attaining its end (entelechy) only in this activity (ἐνέργεια). It is still more unhistorical to look on the star-souls as a consequence of extending to the whole of reality the supposedly vitalistic or even animistic *forma substantialis*, as is done by those interpreters who then consistently go on to suppose that Aristotle ascribed a soul to the inorganic also and thus make him a panpsychist.

The higher we ascend in the cosmos, the more purely the motion expresses the form that is its end. As a whole the motion of the world is the effect and expression of a form that is absolute and free of all matter. This form completes the reaction from Pre-Platonic physics, in which the world arose out of chaotic matter and was explained by mechanical causes. Reality is in its determinateness and in its essence necessarily what it is. It cannot be explained from mere possibility and chance, for then it might as well not be or be otherwise. There must be form at the head of motion, and the highest form must be pure act, through and through determination and thought. This thought cannot think anything more perfect than itself, for as the end of the motion of the whole world it is necessarily the most perfect thing existing, since everything aims towards it. Nevertheless, the thought that thinks itself is not a merely formal self-consciousness devoid of content, an absolute ego in Fichte's sense. In Aristotle's teleology substance and end are one, and the highest end is the most determinate reality there is. This substantial thought possesses at one and the same time the highest ideality as conceived by Plato and the rich determinateness of the individual, and hence life and everlasting blessedness. God is one with the world not by penetrating it, nor by maintaining the totality of its forms as an intelligible world within himself, but because the world 'hangs' (ἤρτηται) on him; he *is* its unity, although not in it. As each thing strives to realize its own form, it realizes for its part that infinite perfection which as a whole is God.

Aristotle's attempt to make the exact thinking that Plato had discovered, the conception and the form, bear fruit in knowledge of the sensible world, could consist only of a conceptual apprehension of nature and its essence; it could not at first assist our insight into the material causes. It thus created a philosophy of nature, resting on a basis that was 'metaphysical' in our modern sense. Aristotle's own intention was the opposite. He believed that his teleological explanation of nature had done away with ᵗthe earlier physics, which derived all that occurs from material and mechanical causes. While recognizing these lower causes he subordinated them to the formal and final causes. Matter and force are not 'nature'. They are nature's handymen; she herself is the builder proceeding according to an inner plan and idea. Natural necessity as the Atomists understood it is of course the indispensable condition of nature's activity as of man's techniques, but to the interpreter of nature it remains, as Plato had already laid down, a merely secondary cause (συναίτιον). The farther Aristotle went in positive research in the course of his life, the deeper he had to penetrate in the investigation of the special material constitution of individual things. So long, on the other hand, as his physics remained in the sphere of conceptual discussion, the relation between the secondary and the final cause gave him little difficulty. The spurious fourth book of the *Meteorology*, which contains the first ancient attempt at chemistry, illustrates how this relation becomes problematic to a follower of Aristotle as soon as he turns to the question of the constitution of matter. Democritus' atomic theory and his conception of the void instantly reappear as working hypotheses, without at first endangering the fundamentally teleological character of physics. The author of the fourth book of the *Meteorology* belongs to this transitional stage.[1] Strato goes farther and drops teleology and metaphysics along with it, rebuilding Aristotle's physics on a Democritean base. He transfers the 'craftsmanship' of nature to matter and its qualities. It has been suggested that he is the author of this book, which would then be an early work in which the doctrine of his master struggled with atomist conceptions; but we do not need the famous name in order to understand the direction of the development revealed in this interesting work. Teleological physics penetrated from Plato's later days into Aristotle's first period and became the groundwork of the latter's philosophy. It found fruitful soil for its principle in the investigation of the animal and vegetable kingdoms. When it came to the examination of inorganic matter, on the other hand, the principle of form failed in the long run, and the atomist point of view reappeared of its own accord.

[1] For what follows see J Hammer-Jensen, *Hermes*, vol. l, pp. 113 ff.

Aristotle's interest in method rules in his further development also, as when he afterwards inserts between the *Physics* and the *Metaphysics* a special connecting inquiry into the continuity and eternity of the world's motion and into circular motion, which takes us right to the threshold of metaphysics and shows that physics without metaphysics is a trunk without a head. The fundamental idea of the later metaphysics is also an idea about method, namely to prefix to theology a doctrine of substance in general and thus expand metaphysics into a study of the various meanings of being. The theory of supersensible being, whose subject-matter was distinct from that of physics, now becomes a study of the nature, as being, of the very subject-matter that physics looks at from the point of view of motion. Thus the two original fundamental subjects of metaphysics—the physical subject of the first mover and the metaphysical subject of the supersensible—retreat into the background, and instead of them there appears the new subject of the morphology of being. One can detect in this the characteristics of Aristotle's later universal science of reality, beginning to have its effect on metaphysics and receiving here an ontological and axiomatic foundation. The suppression of speculation in favour of factual research also left its traces, as we have seen, on the later treatment of the question of the prime mover. The conceptually necessary complement of the body of physical doctrine, the principle on which everything depends, now becomes very like a mere cosmological hypothesis in character, and the impossibility of confirming it like other hypotheses through experience is immediately felt to be an incurable defect.

This interest in the method tended to repress Aristotle's interest in picturing his philosophy. It was not given to him to create striking symbols of the content of his view of the world like Plato's myths and similes. He must have felt this himself; once, in his first account of his own philosophy, the manifesto *On Philosophy*, he tried to give pictorial form to his new attitude towards things in a variant of the simile of the Cave in Plato's *Republic* (above, p. 163). The simile of the ascent of the subterranean men to the vision of the eternal orders and forms of the cosmos strikes us as a fine and individual version of the Platonic original, but dependent upon it to the last; and the relation between his attitude towards the world and Plato's leaves the same impression. It is as though he were absolutely presupposing it and turning at once to his own methodical argumentation and analysis. Only in isolated passages do we suddenly become aware, almost with astonishment, of the living presence of a felt whole behind the subtle network of conceptions. It remains latent like the driving religious force that lies behind the *Metaphysics* without ever coming forward and directly confessing itself. This is why both reveal themselves only in the indirect forms of conceptual thinking and of the method he uses to wrestle with them, and why the force of his philosophy as a religion and as a world-view has come alive in history only where men have not been merely seeking aesthetic intuitions but have themselves known something of this heavy struggle. Let us nevertheless attempt to make his world pictorially visible to ourselves.

Aristotle introduced the logically discrete character of Plato's Ideal world into the visible world as well. According to Plato the happiest image of the world of appearances is the Heraclitean flux of all things, in which certain enduring islands appear. Aristotle did not look at nature so; for him it was a cosmos in which all motion revolved around the fixed centres of abiding forms. Nevertheless, he does not, as one might expect, foist upon the living reality the rigid hierarchy of a world of abstract conceptions; his forms work as the constructive laws of all becoming. What we feel in them most of all, however, is the separateness of accurately determined logical unities. The image in which he pictures his world is τάξις or order, not συμφωνία or harmony. What he wants is not a sounding polyphonic concord, however natural this feeling may have been to a Hellenistic Greek, but the organized common labour of all forms for the realization of a superordinate Thought. To express this view of the world he invented, for once, a happy simile—the tactical motion of the warriors in an army, through which is executed the plan of the unseen general. Compared with the 'breath penetrating all things' of the Stoic monism it is a classic world of plastic forms and contours. The members of this realm lack contact and dynamic reaction upon each other. This feature, foreign to the 'harmoniously unified' world of imperial philosophy, is what Plotinus had in mind when he desiderated some contact between the prime mover and the forms of the movers of the spheres. The same is true of the whole realm of forms in Aristotle's cosmos, though their law is embodied most purely and beautifully in that of the spheres.

'The things that change imitate those that are imperishable.' The coming-to-be and passing-away of earthly things is just as much a stationary revolution as the motion of the stars. In spite of its uninterrupted change nature has no history according to Aristotle, for organic becoming is held fast by the constancy of its forms in a rhythm that remains eternally the same. Similarly the human world of state and society and mind appears to him not as caught in the incalculable mobility of irrecapturable historical destiny, whether we consider personal life or that of nations and cultures, but as founded fast in the unalterable permanence of forms that, while they change within certain limits, remain identical in essence and purpose. This feeling about life is symbolized by the Great Year, at the close of which all the stars have returned to their original position and begin their course anew. In the same way the cultures of the earth wax and wane, according to Aristotle, as determined by great natural catastrophes, which in turn are causally connected with the regular changes of the heavens. That which Aristotle at this instant newly discovers has been discerned a thousand times before, will be lost again, and one day discerned afresh. Myths are the lost echoes telling of the philosophy of lost ages, equal in value to our own; and some day all our knowledge too will be only a hoary myth. The philosopher, standing upon the earth in the centre of the universe, embraces within the limits of thought a cosmos itself bounded by fixed limits and enclosed in the ethereal ball of the outer heaven. The philosophic *Nus*, when gazing from the peak of human knowledge upon the eternal rhythm of the whole, divines something of the pure unsullied happiness of the world-spirit perduring unmoved in contemplative thought.

The old geometrical cosmos of the Greeks was differentiated but not broken by Aristotle's picture of the world. The new ideas of the fourth century were introduced into its typical outlines. Reality is now seen from within; it is no longer solid, but to a certain extent transparent. Aristotle completes the reception of Platonism into the ordinary Greek picture of the world. The perspective is indefinitely extended both in space and in time by the astronomical and historical inquiries of the century. In its finiteness Aristotle's world is identical with Plato's; but the contrast between the two realms, which gave the last-named its special mood and spiritual impetus, is gone, and now the visible cosmos itself shines with Platonic colours. The Greek picture of the world has attained its maximum of unified harmony and completeness. Yet all this moves the spirit of the philosopher not from the aesthetic and emotional side, but merely so far as it can be conceptually established by strict science. Although this singularly beautiful picture collapsed long ago, science is still wrestling with the problems and methods that were developed by means of it. In them, and not in the picture as such, lies the real ἐνέργεια or activity of its genius.

III. THE ANALYSIS OF MAN

The foundation of ethics as a science was profoundly affected by the fact that Socrates had brought the question of moral *knowledge* to the forefront and that Plato went farther in this direction. We are accustomed to consider that personal conscience and intention is the essential problem, and hence we tend to look on Socrates' alien way of putting the question as an historical condition of his thought, concealing what was in reality a question not of consciousness but of conscience. However justifiable it may be to make the great phenomena in the history of the Greek mind clearer to ourselves by translating them into the corresponding categories of our day, it involves the danger of missing the real achievement of Greece. This achievement lies not in religious prophecy nor merely in the thorough radicalism with which they applied morality to life, but in their apprehension of the objectivity of ethical values and of the objective position of the ethical element in the universe as a whole. Socrates was not indeed an ethical theorist, he was merely seeking the road towards virtue and away from his aporia of ignorance; but this very starting-point contains the seed of the conclusion towards which the development that he inaugurated was to strive, the foundation of 'ethics'. The question 'What *is* the good or the just?' is not that of a prophet but that of an inquirer. Passionately though it affirms the good, what it puts first is the discovery of the nature of what we call good; and ignorance of this is the real distress that it expresses. That the greatest moral leader of Greece should be so much concerned with objectification and the apprehension of the right shows that the Greeks could attain their highest moral achievement only in the creation of a philosophy of morals. This is why the question of subjective intention and 'performance', of the education of the will, takes second place with Socrates and is treated by him in a way that—however much we may talk around it—cannot satisfy us. For him, as for Plato, this question was not so much the sole guiding purpose as simply the presupposition of the question that they really did feel intensely, namely what is the essence of the good. The road to knowledge was long for them; on the other hand, that knowledge would ensure action seemed almost self-evident.

The development from Socrates to Aristotle has been represented as a process of increasing alienation from the former in the course of which his practical moral teaching was gradually reduced to theoretical form, and this is how it really appears if one looks on Socrates as investigating the nature of conscience and spreading a gospel of moral freedom; in other words, if one ascribes to him the modern Protestant and Kantian attitude.[1] From our point of view, however, the actual course of events was the inevitable process of progressively objectifying the morally right, and was due to the essential nature of the Greek spirit, not to the accident of particular personalities. Only this process could overcome the old traditional morality, which was steadily disintegrating, together with the complete subjectivism that accompanied the disintegration. The striving for objectivity was certainly born from the practical aporia of a powerful and militant moral personality, but its own nature compelled it to develop by allying itself to philosophical thought, in which it found the instrument of obtaining its end—or more correctly, by calling into existence a new philosophical movement, which created new instruments for itself. The movement took a

[1] Cf. Heinrich Maier, *Sokrates, sein Werk und seine geschichtliche Stellung*, pp. 516 ff. and 577 ff.

different course with each Socratic, according to whether he approached Socrates externally with sophistical problems already in possession of his mind, and used him merely to enrich his material without grasping the core of his problem in its suprapersonal significance, or, recognizing the new and pioneering element in him, as Plato did, seized on this point and developed it with originative force.

Scholars commonly regard it as another merely historical accident that Plato made his great discovery of the moral Ought, to use modern terms, in the form of an Idea, that is, a supersensible essence having a higher reality; and we excuse this roundabout method by pointing to the artistic requirements of the Greek spirit. Yet here again merely to claim superior knowledge and precipitately impose our own 'more advanced' point of view is not enough. The very feature that to us seems roundabout or wrong was the necessary historical presupposition of the recognition of the real nature of the thing itself. The discovery of the objective spiritual values, whether moral or aesthetic or logical, and their abstraction in purified form from the jumbled chaos of moral and aesthetic and logical assumptions always occurring in human souls, was possible only because of the objectifying, shaping, formative vision with which the Greeks approached all things, even the intellectual, and to which they owe their species of philosophy and art. Other peoples have experienced great moral elevations, but for a philosophic account of morality as a value in its pure form the Greeks and Plato had to come into the world. The Idea, when it dawned on the Greek mind, appeared to be by natural necessity an objective reality, independent of the consciousness in which it is reflected. And since it had come as the answer to the Socratic question 'What is so and so?' it also possessed the attributes of the object of logic, the conception. This is the only way in which it was possible, at that non-abstract level of thought, to recognize two of the essential properties of the moral Ought, its incontestability and its unconditionality. Plato must have thought, as he discovered the Idea, that he was for the first time attaining a real understanding of the essence of Socrates' lifework; it had been the erection of a higher intellectual world of unshakable ends and aims (τέλος, ὅρος). In the transcendental vision of the

Good in itself, not to be derived from any sense-experience, the Socratic search now attains fulfilment.

Plato is fond of putting his philosophical recognition that the pure Good is the only morally valid motive of human action in the form of the popular Greek search for the highest good or best life. To the numerous suggestions that had already been made, including more or less all the goods of the world, he opposed his own, 'that a man becomes happy when he becomes good'. Only the good man can use the world's goods rightly, and hence it is only for him that they are goods in the real sense of means to the Good. He, however, is independent of them, and carries happiness within himself. Thus Plato banishes eudaemonism and the ethics of goods, the foundations of every popular Greek view of life. Like a true Greek, however, he recalls them in the same instant, though in changed and elevated shape. The vision of the Good in itself is the fruit of a lifetime of fervid toil. It presupposes the soul's gradual familiarization with the 'Good itself'; it is revealed only to him who is really seeking wisdom, and then only at the end of a painful intellectual road passing through all the methods of argument (μέθοδοι λόγων). Unlike mechanical knowledge it cannot be transferred from one person to another. The best life is therefore the 'philosophic' life, and the highest Good is the inner happiness of him who truly apprehends the Good.

Thus Plato became not merely the theoretical discoverer of morality, but also the creator of a new ideal of life, although he left the common morality standing as a lower level beside philosophic virtue. In the course of his later development the philosophic life became more and more religious in character, as the thought of God took the place of the Idea of the Good as the measure of all measures. Through all phases of his development, however, his chief concern remained the problem of objective values and norms. Life 'with reference to the end' included in itself the impulse to strive for the end. Plato was, in fact, overwhelmingly impressed by the newly discovered objective world of pure values and by the new sureness that it imparted to life.

Aristotle's early dialogues are full of a tremendous ardour for Plato's philosophic life, but at the same time even as early a book as the *Protrepticus* clearly shows the limits of the influence that could be exerted on civic reality by this exclusive ideal of intellectual aristocracy. The attempt to impose it on the whole life of the nation could only lead to a complete renunciation of reality, since reality showed itself unable to adopt it. The tendency to renounce the world, together with a pitchblack pessimism about its goods and a pitiless criticism of its unintellectual society, is strikingly obvious in Aristotle's early work. Against this foil his metaphysico-religious optimism stands out all the more clearly, shining over all the worthlessness and all the misery of this world, striving with the pure intellect beyond this realm of appearances towards the beckoning goal of immortal life. The lasting impression that Aristotle received from this Platonic view of things cannot be doubted by any one who has followed its influence through his later development, but we must also bear in mind the background that is hidden from us by this typical Academic view. In this school began the movement that culminated in Aristotle's ethics, and even his dialogues betray something of the penetrating conceptual analysis that brought it into being. Men sought to understand the high ideal of the philosophic life by means of the nature of the human spirit itself, and in so doing, although they might at first, owing to the lack of analytical psychology, seem to find confirmation of their belief in the primacy of the knowing mind over the other parts of the soul, they at any rate stumbled on the problem of the different 'parts' of the soul, and on the task of doing justice to the irrational parts also, that is to say, of including them in the process of assimilating the spirit to God. In the *Philebus* as in the *Protrepticus* other 'lives' appear besides the philosophical, and an attempt is made to relate them. A question like that of the part played by pleasure in the pure philosophic life leads to the investigation of the motives of moral action; and the pedagogical idea of Plato's old age, which was to train up the young to the good by accustoming them early to feel pleasure in the good and displeasure at the bad, is already close to Aristotle's ethics, according to which an act is good only when accompanied by joy in the good. The problem of character must also have been worked out in the Academy, since Xenocrates divided philosophy into logic, physics, and ethics or the study of character. Plato's later dialogues show signs of a theory of the will and of moral responsibility, which proves that Aristotle was not the first person to attain a philosophical mastery of this question so much discussed in Greek criminal law. When Aristotle examines and rejects definitions of such words as choice, happiness, and pleasure, he probably takes them all from discussions in the Academy. The intellectualization of Plato's early metaphors and the inauguration of ethics as a separate study were already in full swing in that school. Aristotle is merely the Platonist who carried out these tendencies with the greatest definiteness.

Aristotle was not a moral lawgiver in Plato's manner. This was neither within the compass of his nature nor allowed by the advance of the problems. Though his ethics was at first saturated with the idea of the divine norm, and regarded all life as the service and knowledge of God, even in his earliest work the new element reveals another direction, namely the analysis of the forms of the moral life as they actually are. He abandons Plato's theory of virtue for a theory of living types, adequate to the rich variety of the moral life in all conceivable manifestations, including economics, society, class-relationships, law, and business. Between this realistic study of civic life, and the lofty ideas handed down from Plato's religious philosophy, which form the framework of the whole, there is great tension. Although Aristotle explains the types of the just man, the brave, the proud, the liberal, and the magnificent, by means of a single formal conception of virtue, the principle of the proper mean, and although he develops his types not by pure description but by a dialectical construction in which every feature is logically connected with the others, the content is taken from experience and the types themselves arise from factual relationships as they are actually given. The introductory discussion of the fundamental nature of virtue is orientated with regard to the question of moral intention and its cultivation. This was a decided step forward; the essence of moral value is now developed out of the subjective self, and the sphere of the will is marked off as its peculiar realm. This really gives the virtue of character pre-eminence over that of the intellect, and hence the larger part of the discussion is devoted to it, although Aristotle is still far from making a fundamental division between the two. The theory of ethical virtue now becomes to a certain extent an ethics within ethics, and determines the name of the whole. From Aristotle alone we should no longer see why the theory of intellectual virtue comes into ethics at all, if we did not know that to Plato (and to Aristotle in his youth) it had been the very centre, the science of the highest objective value. Even in his later days Aristotle connected the highest end of human life with the divine end of the world, and hence made ethics culminate in theoretical metaphysics; but his main emphasis then lay not on the apprehension of this eternal norm, but on the question how human individuals can realize this norm in will and action. As in ontology he made Plato's Idea bear fruit in the apprehension of the world of appearances, so in ethics he made the will of the moral individual adopt the transcendental norm and thus objectify itself. The norm when thus internalized of course loses its character of universal validity, for there is no imperative that is binding on all men equally, except a purely formal generalization devoid of content. Aristotle's aim is to unite the idea of complete obedience to the norm with the greatest individual variety. The moral personality is 'a law to itself'. In this guise the idea of personal moral autonomy, which was foreign to Plato, enters Greek consciousness for the first time.

The two main parts of Aristotle's ethics, the ethical doctrine of morality based on the good will and the metaphysical doctrine of the contemplation of God as our norm, evince a tendency to rid themselves of each other more and more in the course of his development. The actual 'ethic' or theory of character, which in the original *Ethics* was closely bound up with the theological culmination, afterwards becomes independent and finds a principle of its own in practical moral insight. Aristotle finally abandoned altogether the attempt to carry Plato's primacy of theoretical reason into the sphere of everyday ethics. He had, of course, watered down Plato's 'wisdom' and '*Nus*' into pure 'theoretical reason'; and the necessity for a sharp distinction between civic and metaphysical ethics is a direct result of the intellectualization of these conceptions, which to Plato meant both the knowledge of the good and the actual goodness of the soul. Thus Aristotle preserved the fundamentally critical character of his philosophy in ethics too. The result was a tremendous enlargement and refinement in psychological comprehension of the moral self, and the compression of 'intellectualism' and the metaphysical element into a very small space. As in metaphysics, however, so in ethics he remains ultimately a Platonist, there in that he explains the world of experience teleologically by reference to a highest inexperienceable end, here in that he recognizes, beyond ordinary civic morality and the realm of practical action and will, a life passed in contemplating the eternal, which in his estimate unconditionally deserves the palm, and stands on a higher level even from the ethical point of view. In the *Nicomachean Ethics*, however, he makes the morality of civic life independent of this theology. They are two separate worlds differing in rank. The appearance of the 'theoretic life' at the end of the work means now, not that all earthly change must be 'made immortal' as far as possible, but that above the world of practical morality there is a higher. Thus Aristotle builds the Platonic world of his youth into the actual world, and gives it the highest position therein, the place from which the light of the eternal shines upon this world. This juxtaposition of the two 'lives' has always been felt to be in some way personal and dependent on the philosopher's own experience. It does not possess the radical consistency either of Plato, who finds only the philosophic life worth living, or of Kant, who breaks once and for all with the primacy of theoretical reason and declares the moral will to be the highest thing in the world. Both in ethics and in metaphysics Aristotle goes a little way with Kant, but something in him makes him shrink from the final conclusion. Neither the self-sufficiency of pure natural science nor the self-confidence of the mere will to fulfil one's moral obligations satisfied his sense of reality and of life. Plato's transcendent world would not let him go, and he was conscious that in introducing it he had added a new portion of reality to the old Greek structure of the world. Only so can we explain why his *Nus* takes on an almost mystical gleam in the theological parts of his metaphysics and ethics. This summit of human contemplation comes directly out of Plato's intellectual realm into Aristotle's world of facts, and gives to his view of life its peculiar modern tension and two-sidedness.

In politics, which we will here touch on only briefly, the inner stratification is the same as in ethics and metaphysics. In fact, the historical development is particularly clear in this field. From the standpoint of the history of the mind the decisive problem in Plato's politics lies in that strict unconditional subordination of the individual to the state by which he 're-stored' the genuine old Greek life. In the fourth century this life had long been disrupted by the preponderance of commercial forces and interests in the state and in the political parties, and by the intellectual individualism that became general during the period. Presumably every intelligent person saw clearly that the state could not be healed unless this individualism could be overcome, at least in its crudest form as the unbounded selfish-ness of each person; but it was hard to get rid of when the state itself was inspired by the same spirit—had, in fact, made it the principle of its actions. The predatory politics of the end of the fifth century had gradually brought the citizens round to these new ways of thinking, and now the state fell a victim to the egoistic idea, impressively pictured by Thucydides, that it had itself made into a principle. The old state with its laws had represented to its citizens the totality of all 'customary' stan-dards. To live according to the laws was the highest unwritten law in ancient Greece, as Plato for one last time sadly represents it in his *Crito*. That dialogue shows the tragic conflict of the fourth century sharpened into conscious absurdity; the state is now such that according to its laws the justest and purest man in the Greek nation must drink the hemlock. The death of Socrates is a *reductio ad absurdum* of the whole state, not merely of the contemporary office-holders. In the *Gorgias* Plato measures the Periclean state and its weaker successors by the standard of the radical moral law, and arrives at an uncon-ditional condemnation of the historical state. When he goes on in the *Republic* to sacrifice the life of the individual completely to the state, with a one-sided strictness intolerable to the natural feelings of his century, his justification lies in the changed spirit of his new state. The sun that shines in it is the Idea of the Good, which illuminates its darkest corners. Thus the subordination of all individuals to it, the reconversion of emancipated persons into true 'citizens', is after all only another way of expressing the historical fact that morality had finally separated itself from politics and from the laws or customs of the historical state; and that henceforth the independent conscience of the individual is the supreme court even for public questions. There had been conflicts of this sort before; what is new is the proclamation of a permanent conflict. Plato's demand that philosophers shall be kings, which he maintained unabated right to the end, means that the state is to be rendered ethical through and through. It shows that the persons who stood highest in the intellectual scale had already abandoned the actual ship of state, for a state like Plato's could not have come alive in his own time, and perhaps not at any time.

Aristotle retains Plato's external subordination of ethics to politics, but with him, too, the real strength lies in the former, and from it he derives the norm of the best state and the content of the 'best life'. To his sense of reality, however, this starting-point presents insoluble difficulties, which lead, at the very beginning of the earlier sketch of the ideal state, to the first clear formulation of the profound conflict concealed in Plato's state. In politics, too, Aristotle lives not in the Ideal world but in the tension between Idea and experience. The actual political life of his time, however, does not allow him to find any way of relaxing this tension. In metaphysics and ethics he keeps the door to Plato's world open, in spite of his immanent point of view, and he can do so because that world is actual within himself. In politics, on the other hand, the 'best state' remains a mere Utopia, and shows all too clearly that along this road the most one can attain to is a mere educational institution. Incidentally, Aristotle did indeed formulate the problem of power clearly—he appends it to Plato's notion of the state as a sort of question-mark—and also explain that not all 'mastery' is fundamentally bad; but he did not reach a satisfying solution, and in that advanced stage of general Greek culture a practical solution was no doubt altogether impossible.

The problem of the state was wholly unmanageable. The Greeks' theoretical awareness of their own political life attained its highest point, like the conscious nervous nationalism of the Demosthenic party, at a time when the Greek city-state had begun to decline. It was a form that had lived its life out, and it now succumbed to societies of a cruder sort that still retained their vigour. In his sketch of the ideal state Aristotle turns immediately to the significant question whether to escape from the state be not the only possible aim, and begins his analysis of actual political life by declaring that, with regard to reality, there is nothing for the philosopher to do but contribute his superior knowledge of the conditions of each particular constitution to the correct treatment of political disorders as they arise. This attitude of resignation is typical of the intellectual personalities of the time, even of the practical statesmen, who one and all approached the state with a certain detachment and whose politics always remained a sort of experiment. This detachment and the consciousness of it went furthest with Aristotle, because, himself without a state, he lived as an objective observer in a great state in the throes of dissolution, and had mastered the tremendous wealth of forms and possibilities. The only effective community that still had a strong hold on the Greeks of his time was civil society with its firm notions of education, demeanour, and urbanity. Significantly, he counts this not as a political force but as part of the permanent ethical make-up of personality, and therefore his discussion of it appears in the *Ethics* in the form of special 'virtues'. The outer and inner support of the old morality had been the laws of the state; that of the modern was the objective forms of society. There is no abstract ethical individualism in Aristotle—even the Stoics and Epicureans kept far from that extreme, in spite of the cosmopolitanism of the former and the ideal friendship of the latter—but his *Politics* shows with crass realism that society itself is only a small group of favoured persons, dragged hither and thither and maintaining a precarious existence in the universal struggle for money and power. Hellenistic ethics finally came to rest in the notion of inward freedom, which only occasionally appears in Aristotle; this confirmed for good and all the individual's independence of state and society. Within Aristotle's ethics this self-sufficiency exists only for the man who shares in the 'theoretic life', and even for him only on certain conditions; but this increased sensitiveness to man's dependence on 'fortune' and external circumstances is itself precisely an expression of that longing for inward freedom, and that sense of the moral dignity of personality, which are characteristic of the whole age.

IV. PHILOSOPHY AS THE UNIVERSAL SCIENCE

Aristotle's philosophy represents the difficulties that his age felt about the universe, expressed with the highest art of methodical thought. His scientific research, on the other hand, is more, and extends far beyond the vision of his contemporaries. To see this side of his achievement in a false light, by applying to it the standards of modern science and factual knowledge, is only too easy, and has been done again and again, every time that he has engaged the attention of the representatives of the specialized branches of science or the historians of the positive sciences. Perhaps, however, we may venture to hope that to-day the *naïveté* of all such comparisons is clear even to those who have not been schooled by historical thought, and that we are relieved of the obligation to examine them. Here we may not only exclude the question of the correctness of Aristotle's detailed observations, but also omit to give any precise account of his epoch-making achievement as an inventor of methods, since our concern is only to evaluate the significance of his researches as a sign of the evolution of philosophy.

The enlargement of Platonic 'philosophy' into universal science was a step forced on Aristotle by his high estimate of experience and by his principle that speculation must be based on perceptible reality. Nevertheless, it took place only gradually, for, though he was by nature a scholar from the beginning and stood out as the great reader among the abstract Platonists—the story that Plato called him so is true in essence at any rate—the intellectual attitude of his first or transcendental period is incompatible with his subsequent unreserved devotion to the endless world of facts. From theoretical insight into the necessity of bringing experience within the sphere of philosophic thought, for the logical establishment of a conception of being approximating to the world of appearances, it is still a long way to the collection and elaboration of a gigantic mass of facts purely for their own sake ; and where we possess detailed insight into Aristotle's development we can still see clearly how once he set foot on this road he was driven step by step farther along it. One example must suffice. The celebrated sketch of the development from Thales to Plato in the first book of the *Metaphysics* is strictly philosophical in intention; its purpose is to derive the four principles on which Aristotle bases metaphysics, that is to say, it is not historical, as has often been supposed, but systematic. It compresses and distorts the facts for the sake of what he wishes to extract from them. In his later period this account was enlarged into a general history of the sciences. It went far beyond its original systematic purpose and became an independent science, governed solely by its concern for the material. The collection of constitutions is rather different; at any rate in theory this factual research remained a part of politics, its relation to which is certainly closer than that of the history of the sciences to metaphysics. Even in politics, however, the advance from mere bookish scholarship and from the principle of respecting experience to the working-up of all that constitutional material is an immense step and takes us beyond the bounds of philosophy proper.

Every other example would serve to convince us in a similar way that in spite of the inner consistency of this evolution it involved a momentous displacement of the centre of gravity in the direction of positive research. The conceptual philosopher became a scientist who explained the whole world in universal fashion. Philosophy to him was now the name of the sphere of the sciences as a whole. When the word was coined it meant in the first place every kind of study or intellectual interest, and in a narrower sense the search for truth and knowledge. The first person to give it a permanent terminological significance was Plato, who needed, to describe *his* kind of knowing, a word that expressed at once the unattainability of the transcendental goal of knowledge and the eternity of the struggle towards it, the suspension between ignorance and 'wisdom'. Never, however, had it meant the established unity and present totality of all knowledge. Such an idea had never entered any one's brain at all. In Aristotle it did not take the form of attempting to justify the collection and organization of all existing sciences in one school by means of some attempt at external systematization. He was not an encyclopaedist. This is shown by the fact that, though it may have been his theory to do so, he did not actually adopt in his 'philosophy' the older independent sciences such as mathematics, optics, astronomy, and geography. Only medicine got in and was industriously pursued, because and so far as it offered a fruitful field for the actualization of Aristotle's morphological ideas. Those other studies did not do so, and thus the exceptions show that the astounding totality of Aristotle's science is an organic growth from the central point of his philosophy, the notion of form. This notion determined the limits of what his philosophy could master. As he developed his 'form' changed from a theoretical conception of being to an instrument of applied science, a morphological and phenomenological study of all things. He thus put philosophy in a position to attain a scientific grasp of the whole of reality. It ruled over all the provinces of knowledge to an extent that has never since been equalled. We must, however, keep on insisting that the cause of this fact is that his philosophy possessed the power of creating sciences, so that new ones were always springing forth from its lap, such as the biological, morphological, and physiological study of nature, or the biographical and morphological sciences of culture. Mere logic or formal systematic could never enable philosophy to maintain such a place in science, still less could an arbitrarily dictated view of the universe.

The relation between science and world-view is the problematical point in Aristotle's philosophy. There are two sides to it, since science rests on principles that have to be established not by itself but by philosophy, while on the other hand philosophy is built up on the basis of scientific experience. He believed that with this conception of thought and experience he could make Plato's philosophy into critical science; for, although he does not distinguish philosophy and science by different names, the starting-point of his criticism of all earlier philosophy is a firm conception of what constitutes science. Even within his own philosophy he recognizes that the factual knowledge of the special sciences is scientific in a superior degree, not because of its greater exactitude (for this belongs rather to conceptual thinking) but because of its impregnable reality—the problem whether the supersensible is real gave rise to all kinds of uncertainty in the other sphere. Aristotle's intellectual world presents a unified appearance from without, but it carries within itself a conscious discord in the fundamental idea that philosophy and science tend to diverge, in spite of his efforts to bring them together by conceiving philosophy in the narrower and higher sense of the word as the necessary conclusion of the study of reality. Greek science had always received strong stimulation from that metaphysical attitude towards the world which is the driving force of philosophy, and each had furthered the other during their development. Once on the summit, however, they found themselves in conflict. Aristotle restores them to unstable equilibrium. This instant represents the high point of the common part of their development.

In Post-Aristotelian times neither philosophy nor science was able to maintain itself on this height. Science needed freer play than philosophy gave it. Its results often rendered doubtful the methods and principles of explanation that philosophy had provided it with. On the other side, the cultured classes, who had lost their religion, needed a metaphysical view of the world, and thus tempted philosophy to renew its bold speculative flight ; and we have to admit that in trying to satisfy this longing it was only obeying the impulse of self-preservation. Compared with Aristotle's critical attitude Stoicism and Epicureanism look like dogmatism and the collapse of scientific philosophy. They took over his logical technique and developed the content of some of his metaphysical views, mixing them with older primitive ideas; or they renewed Pre-Socratic physics as Epicurus renewed Democritus, and built up an ethical ideal of life on that foundation. The centre of gravity lay in metaphysics and ethics ; real research was not prosecuted at all. After the third generation the Peripatos assumed the same practical tendency, although it could not compete with the Stoics and the Epicureans in this field ; the result was the regrettable collapse of the school after Strato. That great investigator clearly shows, however, the only path that the movement initiated by Aristotle could take under the circumstances. During his period Peripatetic research was already in touch with Alexandria, where the soil was more favourable than in Attica to the development of the positive sciences, and where the keen wind of reality was blowing. Alexandrian science is the spiritual continuation of Aristotle's last period. There the link between science and philosophy was definitely broken; the infinitely refined technique of Ptolemaic research dispensed with the stable intellectual centre that Aristotle's detailed work had possessed in his great spiritualist view of the universe. On the other hand, the most important discoveries of ancient science are due to this separation, which was a necessary liberation of research. It was now that medicine and natural science, together with exact philology, attained their greatest flowering. They were represented by figures like Aristarchus, Aristophanes, Hipparchus, Eratosthenes, and Archimedes. From the standpoint of Aristotelian philosophy and science, of course, all this is but half of the intellectual realm; but the desire for a metaphysical view of the world, and the desire for scientific strictness, never came together again in the ancient world. Aristotle is classical in spite of his lateness just because he united them, although even in him research and explanation preponderate over the formation of world-pictures.

High as Aristotle's ideal was in itself, what is still more wonderful is its realization in the mind of a single man. This is and will remain a psychological marvel, into which we cannot penetrate deeper. The word 'universality' describes only his astounding power of spreading himself over all fields of reality, and his tremendous capacity for assimilation, both of which were attainable only in a period conscious of technique; but what is far greater is the intellectual range that included both the contemplation of supersensible essences by pure *Nus* and a knifelike keenness of the conceptual understanding and a microscopic accuracy of sensible observation. This phenomenon becomes more comprehensible if we observe in the course of Aristotle's development that originality and power of assimilation balance each other, but even so his leaning towards metaphysics and his highly developed capacity for inward experience remain something unique in the spiritual make-up of a pronounced observer and discoverer. In spite of the many layers of his mental world there is a great unity about it because all his powers are developed only so far as they serve as instruments for the objective contemplation of reality. His *Nus* lacks Plato's world-transforming power, his conceptual thinking the solid practical bulk of dogmatism, his observation the turn for inventions and technical improvements; the three are united in one single task, the apprehension of what is. His whole creativity is exhausted in the continual production of new instruments for the service of this work.

The presupposition of this complete devotion to the contemplation of the world is the objectivity, to the ultimate spiritual depths of which we cannot penetrate, in which everything that Aristotle put out is steeped, and which he bequeathed to Hellenistic science. We have already remarked that it is not to be confused with impersonality, but is a suprapersonal form of the mind. It is as far removed from the artistic objectivity with which Plato in his writings clothes his spiritual passion to transform human life, as from that Thucydidean kind which escapes the pains of a frightful historical fate by regarding it as the necessary course of events and turning it into political knowledge. In those two Attic writers the struggle for objectivity is the reaction of a self that concentrates on sovereign values and is passionately interested in life. In their cases we ought to speak of objectification rather than simple objectivity. The objectivity of Aristotle is something primary. It expresses a great serenity towards life and the world, which we look for vainly in Attica from Solon to Epicurus. It is to be found rather in Hecataeus, Herodotus, Anaxagoras, Eudoxus, and Democritus, much as these men differ from each other. There is something peculiarly contemplative and non-tragic about them. Aristotle, too, possessed that world-wide Ionian horizon, of whose soul-liberating breadth the brooding Athenians had no inkling. At the same time the essence of the Attic spirit had a profound influence upon him as it had upon Herodotus; it gave to his comprehensive ἱστορία or inquiry its unity and strictness of principle. Through these gifts he became, what it was not vouchsafed to any of the Ionian contemplators of the universe to be, the compelling organizer of reality and of science.

DIOCLES OF CARYSTUS

A NEW PUPIL OF ARISTOTLE

THE great man whom I wish to introduce is probably not only un-known to most of my readers as a pupil of Aristotle but is also likely to be a complete stranger to them. That he did not live in the beginning of the fourth century B.C., as has been generally assumed up to the present time, but was one of the outstanding members of the Peripatetic school a hundred years later is the thesis of a recent book of mine entitled *Diokles von Karystos* (Berlin, 1938) which is a continuation of my book on Aristotle.[1] I shall give my reasons for this thesis as far as it is possible within the limits of the present chapter.[2]

I

Although Diocles may still be unknown to the historians of philosophy, he is by no means unknown to our historians of medicine. He used to be called 'the second Hippocrates' by the Athenians[3] of his age and enjoyed a high reputation among the Greek physicians of later centuries who preserved through frequent quotations more than one hundred printed pages of his lost writings. This somewhat meagre evidence forms the basis of our investigations. But since we cannot attribute with certainty even to Hippocrates any of the numerous books which are preserved under his name, we are in the case of Diocles in a comparatively favourable situation. The longest of his fragments contains about nine pages.[4] This is almost what the

---

[1] *Diokles von Karystos. Die griechische Medizin und die Schule des Aristoteles* (Berlin, W. de Gruyter & Co., 1938). viii+244 pp. Cf. also my 'Vergessene Fragmente des Peripatetikers Diokles von Karystos. Nebst zwei Anhängen zur Chronologie der dogmatischen Ärzteschule', in *Abhandlungen der Preussischen Akademie der Wissenschaften*, Jahrgang 1938, Phil.-hist. Klasse, No. 3, pp. 1–46.

In the second of these publications I have made several additions which confirm and enlarge, and, on some minor issues, modify the conclusions of my book on Diocles. Hereafter I shall refer to the book as *Diokles*, and to the article above mentioned as *Vergessene Fragmente*.

[2] This chapter is reprinted, with permission, from *The Philosophical Review*, vol. xlix (1940), pp. 393–407.

[3] Cf. *Diokles*, p. 4, n. 4.

[4] Max Wellmann, *Die Fragmente der sikelischen Ärzte Akron, Philistion und des Diokles von Karystos* (Berlin, 1901), frg. 141. (I shall quote the fragments of Diocles only by their numbers in Wellmann's collection.)

ancients would call a book (βιβλίον), and it should be sufficient to form an impression of his style, method, culture, and personality, which can be verified by the rest of the fragments.[1] The fragments have been collected by Max Wellmann, one of the pioneers and acknowledged authorities in Greek medicine, a field which was only penetrated by classical scholars with modern historical and philological methods towards the end of the nineteenth century. Wellmann's collection of the fragments was published in 1901. It is part and parcel of a collection of the fragments of the Sicilian school of medicine (late fifth and early fourth century) to which, according to Wellmann, Diocles belongs.[2] Wellmann's book was a first attempt to reconstruct the history of Greek medicine during the century after Hippocrates' death, in which it reached the culminating point of its scientific development.

We call this period, according to ancient tradition, the dogmatic school. Its first and greatest representative was Hippocrates (second half of the fifth century). Galen and Celsus mention as his successors Diocles of Carystus, Praxagoras of Cos, Herophilus of Chalcedon, and Erasistratus of Ceus. Diocles, they say, flourished *after* Hippocrates but *before* Praxagoras and the others.[3] Pliny, too, says that Diocles was the second great figure of the dogmatic school, second, in time and in fame, to Hippocrates only.[4] Unfortunately we do not know exactly when Praxagoras lived. He was the teacher of Herophilus, who flourished under Ptolemies I and II at Alexandria in the 80's of the third century and later. Erasistratus was the last of the series, his *floruit* being put by Eusebius in his *Chronica* in 258.[5] If Herophilus flourished in the 80's and 70's of the third century, his teacher Praxagoras must have been the leader of the Hippocratic school at Cos about 300, or not much later. If Diocles' *floruit* as given by Galen, Pliny, and Celsus is correct, the problem arises as to where in the long interval between Hippocrates and Praxagoras (between 400 and 300) Diocles is to be put. Wellmann and other scholars thought that

[1] The extensive portion preserved from Diocles' book on diet, cf. p. 407, n. 4, was incorporated by U. von Wilamowitz in his *Griechisches Lesebuch* (Berlin, 1902), vol. ii, pp. 277 ff., as a masterpiece of Greek scientific prose and as one of the most colourful pictures of the daily life of a Greek citizen in Athens' classical period. At the same time it offers a graphic example of Diocles' medical art and method and the principles on which it rests.

[2] Cf. p. 407, n. 4. The book was published as the first volume of a collection of the fragments of the Greek physicians. But a second volume has never appeared.

[3] Cf. Ps. Gal., *Introd.*, c. 4 (frg. 3, Wellmann, op. cit.) ; Gal. iv. 731 Kühn (frg. 16) ; Celsus, praef. 2 (frg. 4).

[4] Plin. *Nat. hist.* xxvi. 10 (frg. 5), 'qui [Diocles] secundus aetate famaque extitit'.

[5] Cf. the chronology of the physicians of the dogmatic school, *Vergessene Fragmente*, pp. 36 ff., Anhang I.

the 'second Hippocrates' must unquestionably have lived *immediately* after the first Hippocrates. Diocles often refers to writings of our Hippocratic corpus without quoting them. As a rule he does not quote authors at all, thus making it very difficult to determine his time.[1] Besides the Hippocratic influence, Diocles is strikingly dependent upon the Sicilian school in many characteristic details and for his fundamental theory of the *pneuma* as the source of organic life. The main figure of that school was Philistion. Wellmann therefore linked Diocles with Philistion as well as with Hippocrates. Since Plato proves to be largely dependent upon Philistion's theory in his *Timaeus* and the second Platonic letter mentions a planned trip of Philistion from Syracuse to Plato's Academy in Athens, Wellmann believed that Philistion and Diocles were contemporaries of Plato's earlier years and put them in the first third of the fourth century.[2] This has generally been assumed to be the case, although doubts have been occasionally expressed during the last fifteen years.[3]

When I had to deal with Diocles for the first time, shortly after I had completed my doctor's dissertation, I did not dare to question the accuracy of such authorities as Wellmann and Fredrich. I tried to pursue the doctrine of the *pneuma* and its influence on Aristotle's physiological and zoological theories and, in accordance with the prevailing view, presupposed that Diocles and Philistion were Aristotle's sources in the same way as they were supposed to be the sources of Plato's physiology.[4] When I returned to Diocles some decades later with a somewhat greater experience, I saw at once that the idiom of this brilliant author does not belong to the time when Plato's earliest works were written, but that it is characterized by all the traits of the Greek language spoken at the beginning of the

[1] For an important exception to this rule cf. infra, p. 411, n. 4. I do not begin, however, with these quotations, because they are not given in a literally-preserved direct fragment of Diocles, but occur in an excerpt made by a later ancient physician.

[2] Wellmann, op. cit., pp. 66 ff. He had a predecessor in C. Fredrich, *Hippokratische Untersuchungen* (Berlin, 1899), pp. 171 and 196. Wilamowitz, loc. cit., thinks of the same date.

[3] Cf. *Diokles*, pp. 13 ff. I have shown there also that, long before these modern doubts were expressed, V. Rose in a short remark of his almost forgotten book *Aristoteles Pseudepigraphus* (Leipzig, 1863), p. 380, had placed Diocles after Aristotle. In *Vergessene Fragmente*, p. 11, I have added two more scholars who wanted to place Diocles later, in the third century B.C.— I. A. Fabricius, *Bibliotheca Graeca* (Hamburg, 1724), vol. xii, p. 584, and I. L. Ideler, *Aristotelis Meteorol. Libri IV* (Leipzig, 1834), vol. i, p. 157. However, both had but very scanty information about Diocles, and that attenuates the authority of their statements. For this reason Fredrich and Wellmann did not even mention these predecessors, and consequently their view was entirely obliterated, like that of Rose, for several decades.

[4] *Hermes*, vol. xlviii (1913), p. 51.

Hellenistic period (about 300). I have dedicated many pages of my book to an intense analysis of his style and language, but I do not think it feasible to repeat them here. Diocles' style, moreover, is full of the philosophical terminology of Aristotle.[1] His fragments give abundant evidence of his perfect training in, and command of, Aristotelian methods of thought and argument.[2] Since the fragments of his various works show no difference in this regard, the influence cannot be due to a late and occasional acquaintance with Aristotle. It penetrates everything. Diocles thus must have flourished when the Peripatetic school was at its height, i.e. about the end of the fourth century. He cannot have been *much* earlier than Praxagoras.

There are many other indications favouring this late date. Diocles is mentioned for the first time in Greek literature by Theophrastus, who quotes him as an authority for a mineralogical problem in his book *On Minerals*, which was written between 315 and 288. The imperfect which he uses in this quotation seems to indicate that he has known him personally and that Diocles was known to the Peripatetic circle.[3] Diocles' work on diet was dedicated to a certain Plistarchus. Wellmann never asked who this man was. Beloch, in a short footnote of his *Greek History*, asks whether he was a Macedonian prince, brother of Cassander and one of the younger sons of Antipater.[4] This is, indeed, highly probable. Antipater was Alexander's man of confidence, whom he entrusted with the administration of Macedonia and Greece during the long years of his absence in Asia. Aristotle had

[1] For these stylistic and philological arguments I must refer to *Diokles*, pp. 16–59. The Aristotelian element, as soon as it is recognized as such, at once establishes a *terminus post quem* for our chronological considerations. It goes without saying—and even the ancient critics of style have pronounced this as a methodical rule for every such attempt to attribute a document to a certain individuality or period—that the single symptoms which indicate the origin of that document from a certain time do not prove much if isolated. They are indicative of one individual stylistic character or period only when visualized in their entirety. The scholarly observer reaches his conclusions not by summing up single impressions of more or less significance, but by one unified impression based on many details.

[2] Cf. infra, pp. 414 ff., where I have compared Diocles' method and basic concepts with Aristotle.

[3] Theophr. *De lapidibus*, 5. 38 ὥσπερ καὶ Διοκλῆς ἔλεγεν. No one has doubted thus far that Theophrastus is quoting the Carystian and not another Diocles, even though Diocles was supposed to have lived a century earlier. This identification is confirmed now, since we find so many other indications that Diocles must have been a Peripatetic of Theophrastus' own environment. That Diocles the physician should have been also a mineralogist and as such be quoted by his Peripatetic colleague must, of course, shock the modern specialist. but Diocles was also a meteorologist and botanist. Cf. infra, pp. 413 ff., and p. 423.

[4] J. Beloch, *Griechische Geschichte*, vol. iii, I², p. 413, n. 2, and *Diokles*, pp. 62 ff.

met Antipater when he was the educator of Alexander at King Philip's court, and from that time until his death Antipater remained his most intimate friend. Aristotle appointed him in his will as general executor. He and his son Cassander were the protectors of the Peripatetic school after Alexander's and Aristotle's deaths. Plistarchus became king of Lycia and Caria after the battle of Ipsus in 301. Almost all the Hellenistic kings were protectors of science and philosophy. The dedication of scientific works to princes and other powerful men is a custom which begins shortly before Alexander's time[1] and throws much light upon the relations of philosophical schools and politics. Moreover, in one of Diocles' books the cucumbers of Antioch were recommended.[2] *Antioch was founded in the year 300 B.C. Thus Diocles wrote his book in the third, not in the beginning of the fourth century.*

If he was still alive in the third century, how long did he live? Here I have to make some additions to my own book.[3] There I still acquiesced in the view of my predecessors who had occupied themselves with the quotation of Diocles in Theophrastus' book *On Minerals*. They believed that the imperfect, 'Diocles used to say', must mean that he was dead at that time. Aristotle speaks in the same way of Plato when he quotes his oral statements after his death. When he quotes Plato's dialogues, he always writes 'Plato says'. But although the imperfect *may* mean that the person quoted is now dead, it does not *necessarily* mean this. It may mean only that the person who formerly used to belong to the circle of Theophrastus did not live any longer in that community. I am inclined to think that Diocles was not dead when Theophrastus quoted him in this way but had been absent for some time. First there is a polemic of Diocles against Herophilus in an excerpt of his theory on the nature of the *sperma*.[4] As I have said, Herophilus flourished during the 80's and the 70's of the third century, under the first and second Ptolemy in Alexandria. This can very well be reconciled with the chronological tradition that Diocles' own flourishing *preceded* that of Praxagoras

---

[1] Isocrates dedicated one of his works to Nicocles, king of Cyprus, another to King Philip of Macedon. Aristotle dedicated his *Protrepticus* to Themison, prince of Cyprus. Whether his book *On Monarchy* was dedicated to Alexander the Great, we do not know, but at any rate it was offered to him.

[2] Frg. 125 (Ath. II. 59 a).

[3] Cf. for the following arguments *Vergessene Fragmente*, pp. 14 ff.

[4] Cf. Wellmann, op. cit., p. 208. Diocles quotes in that passage from Herophilus, Diogenes of Apollonia, and Aristotle. Wellmann assumed that these names were inserted later, at least that of Herophilus and Aristotle, because he thought that Diocles lived earlier than they, but he was inconsistent enough to think that the name of Diogenes was genuine, because he had lived in the fifth century, i.e. before Wellmann's date of Diocles.

and Herophilus. The flourishing or *akmé* of a man means, according to the usage of Greek chronologists, the fortieth year of age. If Diocles flourished shortly before or about 300, he may have lived until 260 or so, provided he reached his eightieth year. That he lived to an old age is manifest from the will of Strato, Aristotle's second successor in the leadership of the school. He mentions a Diocles as one of the leading authorities of the Peripatetic school to whom he entrusts, as executors, the permanent care of his will and of the school.[1] Strato appointed as his successor a young man named Lyco, who kept this post for forty-four years, thus ensuring the continuity of the school. But Strato explicitly adds in his will that he had consulted the others before deciding on Lyco, who was not a prominent scholar but only a brilliant teacher and speaker. The others, however, had declined to become his successor, 'because they were either too old or too busy'. Strato died in 270 or 269. If Diocles had attended Aristotle's lectures during the master's last years and if he were born about 345, he could have reached his prime about 300 and would have been over seventy when Strato died. He was thus one of those Peripatetic authorities who were 'too old' for the leadership of the school.

Now there is a fragment of one of Diocles' books in which Galatia in Asia Minor is mentioned as the homeland of certain vegetables.[2] Galatia was named after the Gauls who invaded Asia Minor in the 70's of the third century and settled in that part of the peninsula to which they subsequently gave their name. This may have happened soon after, during the 70's or 60's of the third century.[3] We cannot trace Diocles' lifetime farther than that (1) because of the ancient tradition that his *floruit* preceded that of Praxagoras, Herophilus, and Erasistratus[4] and (2) because Theophrastus and Strato already knew him

[1] Diog. Laert. V. 62; cf. *Vergessene Fragmente*, 13. Strato seems to have quoted extensively Diocles' gynaecological work and adopted his elaborate medical theory of the hebdomadic periods of the development of the embryo and the human body. Cf. the large excerpts, frg. 177, and the new information from a Neo-Platonic source, which I added in *Vergessene Fragmente*, pp. 19–34.

[2] Frg. 125 (Ath. II. 59 a). This is the same passage in which Diocles mentions the good cucumbers of Antioch. Cf. supra, p. 411.

[3] Professor Felix Staehelin of Basle, Switzerland, author of *Geschichte der kleinasiatischen Galater* (Leipzig), in a letter to me expressed the view that the name 'Galatia' came up soon after the Galatians settled in that part of Asia Minor. He thinks it happened in the 70's of the third century B.C. At any rate, this historical allusion is in harmony with the fact that Diocles is named in the will of Strato the Peripatetic (died in 270).

[4] Professor D'Arcy Thompson in his comments on my *Diokles, Philosophical Review*, vol. xlviii (1939), pp. 210 ff., seems to have overlooked this fact. Even though he is ready to admit that I am correct in placing Diocles about a century later than he had been placed thus far, Professor D'Arcy Thompson feels encouraged to go even farther down with Diocles' lifetime. But, as I said before

as an outstanding authority. If he was considered as a possible candidate for the leadership of the Peripatos by Strato, his name must be engraved along with that of Theophrastus, Eudemus, and Strato as one of the great characters of that astounding group of scholars and scientists who represent the school of Aristotle.

There exists under the name of Diocles a didactic letter to King Antigonus on prophylaxis of inner diseases.[1] It has been rejected as unauthentic because Diocles was supposed to have lived a century earlier. It strictly resembles the style of the larger fragments and evidently belongs to the beginning of the Hellenistic era. It mentions the great age of the king, who, according to all we have said, can be only Antigonus I.[2] He was about eighty years of age when he became king in 305, and died in the battle of Ipsus in 301. In this letter the author appears not only as a medical authority, but also as a meteorologist. Diocles was a universal mind, as were all those Peripatetic scholars. He was at once a physician, botanist, and meteorologist. His connexion with Theophrastus becomes better understood when we read that he wrote not less than three works on botany, with special regard to the dietetical and pharmacological use of plants. From the fragments of these books modern historians of botany have reconstructed a pre-Theophrastean system of plants. This system

(cf. above, p. 408), Diocles' *terminus ante quem*, as given by the unanimous testimony of three ancient experts on the history of Greek medicine (Celsus, Pliny, and Galen), does not permit us to go farther down with Diocles' flourishing than shortly before that of Praxagoras (about 300). This fact, and the Aristotelian terminology of his medical language, place Diocles' flourishing towards the end of the last third of the fourth century B.C.—i.e. between the opening of the Aristotelian school, 335, and the flourishing of Praxagoras, 300.

[1] It is preserved in the ancient medical author Paulus Aegineta at the end of Book I and reprinted in *Diokles*, pp. 75 ff., where I have discussed it at length.

[2] D'Arcy Thompson, loc. cit., thinks that perhaps the old Fabricius, loc. cit., was right in referring Diocles' *Letter to Antigonus* to King Antigonus Gonatas (second half of the third century B.C.). But when Fabricius ventured his conjecture in the year 1724, he did not know then the many other testimonia on Diocles which we now read in Wellmann's collection, nor those which I added to them. We must take Fabricius' surmise for what it is—a mere improvisation. I do not see how to reconcile it with the rest of our tradition. For example, how shall we explain the origin of the ancient tradition (Galen) that Diocles wrote the first systematic work on anatomy, if he had lived after Herophilus and Erasistratus, both of whom wrote great anatomical works and appear to be more advanced than Diocles in this respect? And how could the characteristic formula of Pliny originate, who terms Diocles 'the second in time and in fame' (after Hippocrates), *secundus aetate famaque*, if in reality he was the fifth and last in the series of famous dogmatic physicians? This objection has been made already by Eduard Zeller, *Philosophie der Griechen*, vol. iii, 2³, p. 916, to the earlier chronology of Fabricius and Ideler, who placed Diocles under Antigonus Gonatas.

is now broken down. In the same way zoologists have reconstructed a pre-Aristotelian system of animals from Diocles' classification of the animals in his work on diet. In reality Aristotle does not depend upon Diocles' zoological system, but Diocles naturally takes advantage of Aristotle's systematic zoology for his dietetic purpose.[1] Galen reports that Diocles was also the first to write a special work on anatomy.[2] This is apparently in connexion with Aristotle's anatomic dissections, the ἀνατομαί. Some decades ago a papyrus containing medical data was excavated in Egypt. The editor, Professor Gerhard of Heidelberg, was inclined to attribute the work, several columns of which are preserved, to Diocles for stylistic reasons. The authorities silenced him because they said there were many Aristotelian terms in the treatise and it resembled Aristotle's *Problemata*. In this they were absolutely correct. But they did not see that all the fragments of Diocles are full of Aristotelian concepts, as we have noted. From our point of view their objection is an argument *for* Diocles' authorship of the papyrus and not *against* it.

II

I have enumerated a number of historical and philological arguments, but I will not detain the reader any longer with details. Instead, I shall discuss some more philosophical problems offered by the text of Diocles' fragments.[3] The author differs from the writers of the Hippocratic treatises by his awareness of the logical and philosophical problems involved in his medical conclusions. He often limits the factual statements which he uses as premises for practical advice by

[1] D'Arcy Thompson, loc. cit., tries to minimize somewhat the congruencies between Diocles' and Aristotle's systematic classification of the animals which had aroused the attention of zoological and philological scholars before me, but which were interpreted by them as proving Aristotle's dependence upon Diocles because of the then prevailing chronology which made Diocles earlier than Aristotle. Cf. *Diokles*, pp. 167–80. D'Arcy Thompson suggests, for instance, that Diocles could have studied the various sorts of fish, mentioned in his work on diet, at the Athenian fish-market without reading Aristotle. This sounds very convincing, especially if we neglect the order in which Diocles enumerates them. But Diocles, who has studied Aristotle in so many other fields thoroughly, as will be shown, would not be likely to neglect the zoological works which were closest to his interests, and the man who, in botany, had a systematic mind, and wrote three books on plants from his medical point of view, must have dissected also all sorts of animals for his anatomical purposes. Incidentally, the very fact that he judges the structure of the human womb from the dissections of mules (frg. 29) proves that he belongs to the pre-Alexandrian period of anatomy.

[2] Frg. 23.

[3] For this reason, I shall not deal here with Diocles' medical and botanical views, for which I must refer to my book.

saying συμβαίνειν εἴωθε, 'it usually happens', instead of 'it is so'. Though this is not entirely alien from Hippocrates, in Diocles this phrase is comparatively frequent. Its frequency signalizes a new methodical consciousness. The word εἴωθε, which I have translated by the adverb 'usually', is frequent in Aristotle. It is connected with his doctrine of experience. He distinguishes three grades of certainty in knowledge: that which is necessary (ἀναγκαῖον), that which usually occurs (ὡς ἐπὶ τὸ πολύ), and that which is only accidental (συμβε-βηκός). Mathematical propositions are necessary; physical premises belong mostly to the second class, that which 'usually happens'. The expression is most frequent in Aristotle's ethical, political, physical, and zoological writings, i.e. in those parts of his philosophy which are largely based on experience.

Keen observation of the frequency and regularity of physical or social phenomena was the way in which Aristotle and his pupils tried more and more to determine that which they called τὸ κατὰ φύσιν, i.e. that which is according to nature. Aristotle used to speak of the κατὰ φύσιν originally in a Platonic sense. In Plato it had a strictly teleological and normative meaning. It was that which *ought to be according to nature*, and 'nature' meant the Platonic idea, which is the pattern of things. But later in Aristotle and in Theophrastus (e.g. in his book on the causes of the plants) the κατὰ φύσιν is applied likewise to pathological phenomena which occur with a certain regularity. Thus empirical observation of that which usually happens becomes the only methodical way to determine what is 'according to nature'. In this sense even a disturbance of the normal process of growth in a plant or an animal may be called 'according to nature', if it frequently or usually occurs under certain conditions of climate or weather or even disease and, in this way, proves to be 'normal'. This is a development of meaning which seems rather natural in sciences largely concerned with pathological phenomena. Medical pathology must have given the first impulse towards a development of the Platonic concept of nature in this direction. Even Aristotle in the works of his earliest period does not consider the symptoms of the degenerated forms of government as normal, but calls the present conditions of real states on earth παρὰ φύσιν, i.e. contrary to nature, because they do not correspond to the ideal. More and more, however, the pathological phenomena come to the foreground as realistic observation in Aristotle's mind gets the upper hand. According to the medical patterns, a pathology of political and social life and a pathology of animals and plants are developed.

In spite of this increase of the realistic element in Aristotle's school, we must point out two things: (1) Even in Plato there was from the beginning a keen interest in the pathological changes of nature.

Plato's *Republic* for the first time develops a system of degenerative forms of the best state. We also know that Plato's philosophy was largely influenced by the medical pattern to which he refers so often. (2) In spite of the general trend towards an extension of observation to pathological phenomena, Aristotle never gives up the teleological foundation of his system, although he and Theophrastus are quite aware of its difficulties in questions of detail. Thus we are not astonished to see in Diocles a physician who sticks determinedly to a teleological view of nature. I do not mean to say that this was absolutely new, and that Hippocratic medicine was as decidedly anti-teleological as modern historians of medicine seem to think. A physician who, like the author of *Epidemics* V, considers himself only a humble assistant of the powers of nature when he tries to cure a patient of illness,[1] cannot be termed an anti-teleologist, even if he does not pronounce the word *telos*. It is true, however, that teleology is not an axiom which the Hippocratic writers apply systematically to all phenomena. We may say only that there is an unmistakable tendency in some of the Hippocratic books towards a teleological approach to nature, even though it remains undeveloped.

For this thesis, which on this occasion I can maintain only in a dogmatic form, I hope to give full evidence in the future. Diogenes of Apollonia in the fifth century was also a teleologist, but in a different way.[2] He is the typical rationalist who tries to prove that nature acts throughout like an intelligent artist and must be interpreted according to the rules of human mechanics and art. This type also left its mark on some of our Hippocratic writings and on Aristotle. But Diocles is a follower of the specifically Aristotelian teleology.[3] He knows the Aristotelian concepts of potentiality and act and applies them, e.g. to the hygiene and ethics of sexual life. His teleological approach to nature makes him accentuate the discipline of dietetics more than any other part of medicine. Medicine becomes from his point of view largely the education of the healthy man; it is no longer only the cure of the ill. In this it resembles Plato's and Aristotle's philosophies, which are the dietetics of the human soul. Plato, in the *Gorgias*, ranks the legislator higher than the judge and the teacher of gymnastics higher than the physician. This shows that Plato was still far from an idea of medicine which is above all dietetics, the care of the healthy. In his time the care of the healthy was still merely up to the gymnast. The gymnast never lost that position

---

[1] Cf. a Hippocratic sentence, like the famous νούσων φύσιες ἰητροί, i.e. it is the patient's own nature which really cures the illness.

[2] Cf. Willy Theiler, *Geschichte der teleologischen Naturbetrachtung bis auf Aristoteles* (Zürich, 1925), pp. 25 ff. [On Hippocrates see *Paideia* III. 27 ff.]

[3] Cf. *Diokles*, pp. 51 ff.

entirely in Greek civilization, but somewhat later he had to share it with the physician when medicine developed a carefully worked out system of diet.

Diocles displays a detailed programme of daily life which gives a unique picture of Greek culture about the year 300 B.C. As does Aristotle's ethics, the diet of Diocles presupposes a type of man who belongs to the upper class of human society. He who wishes to live according to his rules must be equipped with material means. The whole of hygienic life is put in the framework of the regular gymnastic activities which formed the main part of the daily work of a Greek gentleman in the forenoon as well as in the afternoon. Diocles does not give only a few rules for summer and winter like the Hippocratic author *On the Healthy Life*, nor does he only enumerate long lists of food or drinks or exercises like the author of the four books *On Regimen*. He gives a rounded picture of daily life from early rising to bedtime, a true Peripatetic *bios*. It is a *bios*, to be sure, in the medical sense of the word. But the attitude which this physician takes with regard to diet is almost an ethical one. His dietetics is, so to speak, the ethics of the body.[1] This idea cannot have been very far from the Greek mind, after Plato and Aristotle had parallelized over and again the virtues of the soul and the virtues of the body. The concept of virtue or *areté* means in Greek the highest excellence or perfection of everything, not just our moral virtue. Moral virtue was a particular case of a general law of perfection which pervaded nature as a whole. Aristotle incessantly refers in his *Ethics* to the biological and medical example. Diocles, on the other hand, regiments the life of the human body by a standard similar to that of the Aristotelian mean. We must not forget that Aristotle's idea of the right mean and the two vicious extremes of excess and deficiency was originally taken from medicine. Aristotle compares the individual moral action of the virtuous man with the individual treatment given to a patient by his physician. It cannot be regulated by general rules. The Hippocratic author *On Ancient Medicine* describes the art of the physician as a στοχάζεσθαι, a conjectural aiming at a target.[2] So Aristotle calls the moral act a στοχάζεσθαι, an aiming at the right mean between the vicious extremes of the too much and the too little, of excess and deficiency. Diocles applies this criterion systematically to the diet of the healthy. His main concept is the ἁρμόττον, 'the appropriate'. It is synonymous with the concept of πρέπον, 'the suitable'. These concepts presuppose the idea that the nature of everything bears in itself the rules according to which it should be treated. Both concepts appear now and then before Aristotle, to be sure, but

[1] Cf. *Diokles*, pp. 45 ff. (Diocles' theory of diet and Aristotelian ethics).
[2] Cf. ibid., p. 46.

they were generalized by him. In Aristotle's philosophy they became dominant, especially in his ethics and aesthetics. Diocles transferred them to dietetics. They, too, reveal his teleological view of nature. The main rule of diet is to do nothing against nature, but everything in accordance with nature. This is what Diocles means by adapting oneself to nature. He very often gives his rules in the stereotyped form of βέλτιόν ἐστι, 'it is better'. Aristotle's philosophy distinguishes four causes, among which the final cause is the highest and most important. Aristotle often criticizes the former natural philosophers for the reason that they neglected this cause. They did not see that most things in nature are as they are because it is *better* for them to be so. Diocles calls the whole discipline of dietetics *Hygieina*. From this word, which became general in later ancient medical systems, the modern term 'hygiene' is directly derived. It is shaped on the pattern of Aristotle's philosophical disciplines, for he called them by adjectives in the plural of the neuter, e.g. *Ethica*, *Politica*, *Analytica*.

In the first book of his treatise *On Diet*, Diocles discussed, obviously at the outset, the problem of medical method, with special regard to aetiology. Fortunately Galen has preserved the original words.[1] Those people, Diocles says, who believe that they must in every case determine the reason why a thing is nourishing or why it is laxative or uretic or producing another effect of this sort, apparently do not know, first, that this is often unnecessary for medical practice and, second, that many things which exist (in Greek we have here the philosophical word ὄντα) are, so to speak, like principles (ἀρχαί) according to nature, in that they do not admit a further regress to the cause. Moreover, physicians are wrong sometimes when they take as a premise that which is unknown and not agreed upon and improbable and believe this to be a sufficient determination of the cause. We need not pay attention to those physicians who give aetiological explanations of this sort and who feel obliged to define the cause of everything, but we should rather put our confidence in those things which have been observed by experience (ἐμπειρία) over a long period of time. We ought to seek a cause only when the nature of the subject allows it, provided that our statement about it will in this way attain a higher degree of knowledge and certainty.

I ought perhaps to discuss first the passage preceding these words. There Diocles points out that we cannot always reduce similar effects to the same cause as his predecessors often had done in their aetio-

---

[1] Gal. *De alimentorum fac.*, vol. vi, p. 455 Kühn. The more recent edition of Helmreich gives several slight improvements of the text. For the following analysis of this interesting methodological fragment, I refer to my book, pp. 25–45.

logical zeal to derive all phenomena with which the physician is concerned from a few primary causes. Nor can we say, he continues, that things which have the same taste or odour or temperature or anything of the sort must have the same effects. Things which are similar *in this sense of the term* very often have dissimilar effects, as can easily be shown. It is not true that everything is laxative or uretic or has any other such power because it is warm or moist or salty or the like. The sweet and the sharp and the bitter and all the rest of these qualities do not have the same effects, but according to Diocles we had better say that 'the whole nature' is the cause of the fact that, when we apply each of them, certain effects usually happen.[1]

The author of the Hippocratic book *On Ancient Medicine* had already expounded with remarkable zeal the belief that those medical schools are wrong which believe that they must make medicine into an exact art or science by adopting one of the systems of Ionic natural philosophy and deriving everything from one principle or a few principles.[2] They are too much impressed by philosophy. We ought never to forget that these philosophical principles are mere hypotheses and speculations and cannot give any certainty whatever to a physician who has to give a patient the treatment he needs when his life is in danger. The only firm ground on which he can stand is experience. Diocles agrees with this Hippocratic author; and so one may ask: What is the use of calling him an Aristotelian and a philosophical mind? But here we see how the Aristotelian philosophy comes in. The protest of the Hippocratic author against philosophy is a protest against natural philosophy of the Pre-Socratic type. He himself calls it the type which Empedocles and that sort of people have introduced.[3] But philosophy when driven out by the front door soon comes in again by the back door in other clothes. This time it is dressed in the coat of the logician and methodologist.[4]

When Diocles rejects the conclusion from similar biological effects of the same cause, because similar things *of this sort* need not necessarily produce the same effects, he applies Aristotle's new method of distinguishing the various meanings of every concept (the method of the πολλαχῶς λεγόμενα, which we know best from Book Δ of the *Metaphysics*). There and in Book I Aristotle enumerates various

[1] From the point of view of the most recent development of modern science, it is characteristic of the situation in which Diocles finds himself that medicine and natural science as a whole are inclined to surrender the method of mechanical explanation of the single phenomena and take an attitude which we now call *ganzheitlich* or 'holistic'.

[2] Hippocrates, *De vet. med.*, c. 1 ff., and especially c. 20.

[3] Ibid., c. 20.

[4] It is merely ignorance of history to think, as many historians seem to do, that Hippocrates eliminated philosophy from medicine once and for all.

meanings of the concept of the similar (ὅμοιον). Only in the less exact usage of rhetorical instruction does Aristotle adopt the general statement that similar effects are produced by similar causes.[1] In metaphysics, however, i.e. in strictly philosophical environment, he first distinguishes the various meanings of the similar. This method became necessary at the moment when various branches of scientific thought met one another in one and the same philosophical school. Then it was realized that the concept of the similar which is used by the mathematician when he speaks of similar triangles or parallelograms, and which is defined by Euclid in the first axiom of the sixth book of the *Elements*, is totally different from the 'similar' which the physician is thinking of when speaking of similar causes and effects. In Aristotle's distinction of the four meanings of 'similar' we can still recognize that this was the reason for his attempt at differentiation. The first of the four meanings in Book I of the *Metaphysics* is apparently meant to be a definition of the mathematical concept of similarity.[2] It is the similarity of two rectangular figures which are not identical in their concrete essence, comprising form and matter, but in their form. Also the second meaning is referred to an identity of form. It occurs in things which admit a 'more or less' (e.g. physical qualities like 'warm'), but which actually have the same degree of the quality in question. Third, we call similar those things which have the same quality (e.g. white colour), but have it in two different shades (e.g. tin and silver). Fourth, we call similar such things as have more identical than different qualities. It is obvious that Diocles' statement that similar biological effects need not be produced by the same causes is based on a similar distinction. There is an essential difference between things which are identical in their form (i.e. substantially) and things which have only one quality in common. Things which have in common the quality 'warm' need not produce all the same effect, e.g. on digestion or urination. Diocles' statement is, of course, very short. It does not refer explicitly to Aristotle's logical theory. But this was neither needed nor usual. No Peripatetic philosopher ever mentions Aristotle when he discusses, applies, or criticizes the doctrine of the master. But after having proved that Diocles was an Aristotelian from his terminology and his membership in the Peripatetic school, there can be no doubt that he knows and presupposes in this classical methodological chapter the Aristotelian doctrine of the various meanings of scientific concepts. Diocles throughout pays much attention to the question of synonyms for diseases, medical plants, &c., and when he says, for example, that we speak of motion as moving and motion as moved, he certainly is

[1] Ar. *Rhet.* I. 4, 1360ᵃ 5.   [2] Ar. *Met.* I. 3, 1054ᵇ 3.

Aristotelizing, and there is no Hippocratic writer who ever speaks in this way. I would rather say that he rejects in the Hippocratic way unnecessary and unproved hypotheses in medicine; but he proves this maxim by the new Aristotelian logic.

We observe the same keen consciousness of the logical implications of every medical statement in the following words, in which he rejects the seemingly scientific demand of some medical schools to determine the cause of everything. The whole paragraph is tinged by Aristotelian terminology. When Diocles speaks of certain facts beyond which we cannot advance in the series of causes and which we therefore have to accept as principles, he does not mean principles in the Pre-Socratic sense of the term, i.e. real causes, but the *principles of knowledge* from which, according to Aristotle, all other knowledge in every field is derived.[1] We must admit that such a discussion is unique in medicine even in classical antiquity. It was possible, I dare say, only in the Peripatetic school. There, not only a general philosophical consciousness of all methods of human knowledge was developed, but it penetrated every branch of science and scholarship. Aristotle teaches that these first principles are undemonstrable and immediate (ἀναπόδεικτα and ἄμεσα). They are arrived at in a different way in every field. In mathematics, which doubtless gave the first impulse to this development by formulating a number of such axioms, they are reached by direct perception (αἴσθησις). In physics the principles are attained by induction from experience. In ethics they rest on habituation, i.e. on experience of another sort than that used in physics.[2] We may term it an inner experience, which results in shaping a permanent attitude or habit.

It is in the *Nicomachean Ethics* that Aristotle indicates most clearly the way in which we attain knowledge of these principles and how we should behave with regard to the question of scientific method. There he states, with regard to the methodical ideal of the Platonic school of treating ethical problems in a mathematical way, that we ought not to ask for mathematical exactness when the nature of the object does not allow it. He thinks it the sign of true scientific culture (παιδεία) to know just how much we should demand in every field of knowledge.[3] In ethics and politics we must be content with a

---

[1] Ar. *Met.* B. 1, 995ᵇ 7, and elsewhere, distinguishes the principles of being and the principles of knowledge (apodictic principles). The principles of being or real principles (water, fire, and the like) were the object of all the investigations of the Pre-Socratic philosophers. In Aristotle, therefore, the principles of knowledge are the new discovery. We must keep that in mind when we find them discussed by Diocles. Cf. my analysis of this problem, *Diokles*, pp. 42 ff.

[2] Ar. *Eth. Nic.* I. 7, 1098ᵇ 3, and J. Burnet, *The Ethics of Aristotle*, Introduction, pp. xxxiv ff.

[3] Ar. op. cit. I. 1, 1094ᵇ 19 ff.

typical way of description, and we must not ask for necessary conclusions when we can hope to attain only a knowledge of what usually happens or what is usually right. This resembles, of course, the situation in medicine. Diocles, in his methodological fragment, follows the thoughts of Aristotle, and even his words, so closely that we cannot escape the conclusion that he had the pattern of the *Nicomachean Ethics* before his eyes when he formulated his opinion. We have already pointed out that he conceives the discipline of dietetics as a medical counterpart of ethics. It is, therefore, not so far-fetched when he extends this analogy even to the methodological situation of both sciences. On the contrary, after Plato and Aristotle had referred so often in their ethical treatises to the parallel situation in medicine, it was very natural for a man of Diocles' many-sided philosophical culture to take advantage for medicine of the refinement of ethical methods which was reached by Aristotle.

Aristotle and Diocles likewise demand that we start not with unknown and doubtful premises but with that which is known to us and agreed upon. Both say that we must not ask for a cause where the facts as such are the last evidence which we can attain. Diocles' remarkable formulation, that the facts in such cases are, so to speak, like principles according to nature, means the same as the formulation by Aristotle expressed by the famous words in the *Ethics* on the 'that' and the 'why' (ὅτι and διότι). When we have attained, he says, certain fundamental facts by moral experience, it is not necessary to ask for the causes of these facts, for he who has the facts also has the principles, or can grasp them easily.[1] Also Diocles' other argument, that a knowledge of the cause is often not needed for medical practice, is to be found in the methodical introduction of the *Nicomachean Ethics*.[2] Aristotle there warns us not to exaggerate our methodical demands because there is a difference between the mathematician and the architect. Both of them want to determine in their field the right angle, but the geometrician investigates the nature and the qualities of this mathematical conception as such, whereas the architect determines it only as far as it is wanted for his work. Aristotle here thinks it to be the higher degree of philosophical knowledge to be aware of the limits which are drawn by the nature of our object, rather than to waste our time in aiming at unattainable methodical ideals. We ought not to take the *parergon* more seriously than the *ergon*. It is more philosophical for a discipline like ethics to be aware of its practical character than to aim at becoming an exact theoretical science. This idea is transferred to medicine by Diocles. And in this sense he considers medicine as a part of the whole of

---

[1] Ar. op. cit. I. 7, 1098ᵃ 33 and I. 2, 1095ᵇ 6.
[2] Ibid. I. 7, 1098ᵃ 26 ff.

human knowledge or science, which the Peripatetic school called philosophy. In his letter to King Antigonus Diocles claims that title for his medical art.[1] The way in which he penetrates it with a philosophical consciousness of method and combines it with a universal study of nature justifies this name.

The letter to King Antigonus, which I have given back to Diocles, illustrates from still another side his interest in the methodical problem. It likewise illustrates the contribution which a philosophically conscious physician was able to make to the Peripatetic discussion of the problem of scientific method. Diocles is going to write for his royal patient a medical vade-mecum or catechism in the form of a letter of only a few pages. The old man, in whose hands lay at that time the destiny of the world, was about eighty, as I have said. Diocles wants to tell him about the best way to prevent serious illness. This is a point of view different from dietetics, although it also involves prescriptions on diet. Prophylaxis is about to develop into a special discipline. Diocles calls it a theory of how diseases originate and how we can find help against them. This depends largely upon our awareness of the fact that there are certain *signs* indicating in advance the coming illness and upon our ability to take advantage of these signs. Diocles' refined sense of comparative methodology makes him observe at once the essential identity of the nature of such signs in pathology with those signs by which, for example, meteorological observation predicts atmospheric changes and the coming storm. This practical meteorology had up to that time been developed mostly by experts of navigation, as Diocles mentions. In addition, he mentions some 'people of many-sided experience'. We think of Peripatetic scientists of encyclopaedic knowledge like Theophrastus who has written a whole treatise on meteorological signs which has been preserved. Diocles himself is a meteorologist, as I can prove by a meteorological fragment which I recently discovered and which may belong to his lost book *On Fire and Air*.[2] So he must have been familiar with the meteorological use of those signs which had been taken over from the old nautic tradition by the modern Peripatetic scientists. They adapted this method to their scientific purposes and tried to learn something from it for their philosophical analysis of experience. The Peripatetics made use of the sign, for example, in the new discipline of physiognomics about which a treatise has been preserved under the name of Aristotle. It certainly

---

[1] Cf. *Ep. ad Antig.* I (*Diokles*, p. 75).

[2] Cf. *Vergessene Fragmente*, pp. 5–10. The title of Diocles' book *On Fire and Air* is listed by Wellmann, op. cit., p. 117. The new fragment deals with the process of combustion (ἐκπύρωσις) in the highest region of the air in the universe.

belongs to the Peripatetic school. The author investigates the relation between physiognomic sign and character. The method is strictly
empirical and based on the observation of similarities in our experience and on certain constant conjunctions from which we infer like
similarities and conjunctions in the unknown. Stoics and Epicureans
developed the concept of sign or *semeion* more generally, in its logical
significance, and built on this basis an epistemological theory which
they called semeiotic, the Stoics in a rationalistic way, the Epicureans
in a more empirical sense. But the roots of this development lie in
the Aristotelian school and in Greek medicine. Aristotle treats the
syllogism from signs at the end of the prior Analytics. He illustrates
it by examples taken from medical prognosis and adds a whole chapter on the special question as to whether scientific physiognomics is
possible. If we had Diocles' lost book on prognosis, we would perhaps
know more about his methodological theories. At any rate, we look
here into Aristotle's school and see something of the background of
his logic. This logic did not stand in a vacuum. Aristotle's logic is
the logic of the sciences which were in existence in his time, and it in
turn gave a new impulse to the sciences, as we learn from Diocles.

If our conclusions are sound, as I think they are, we have succeeded in reconstructing an important but hitherto unknown part
of Aristotle's school and philosophy which had disappeared, together
with the ideal of scientific life from which this school had sprung.
Medicine was one of the most authoritative and respected members
of the large family of sciences united in the Peripatos. The medical
department of the Peripatetic school had in Diocles its greatest representative. Metrodorus belonged to it. Erasistratus, like Diocles one
of the greatest medical figures of all times, studied in it. The influence
of Diocles on Praxagoras of Cos, in his main theories as well as in
many details, was noted long ago, but it remained unexplained since
almost a century lay between them. Now we suddenly see that
Praxagoras was a contemporary, only a little younger than Diocles.
Since Praxagoras was the head of the Hippocratic school, his dependence upon Diocles means that about twenty years after Aristotle's
death the Hippocratic school at Cos was under the dominating influence of the medical department of Aristotle's school. Herophilus, the
head of the new medical school at Alexandria during the reign of
Ptolemies I and II, was a pupil of Praxagoras. He developed anatomy,
on which Diocles had written the first systematic work, and enriched
it by many new discoveries. He also developed the dialectical and
logical element in medicine, which Diocles had introduced, and therefore was called the dialectician. It was a pupil of his who founded the
empirical school of medicine in the late third century.

The Peripatetic biologists all adhered to the theory of the *pneuma*, which was Diocles' fundamental idea in physiology and pathology. The fact that Theophrastus and Strato are linked very closely with Diocles' medical theory has seemed rather strange heretofore, but now becomes easily understandable, as does the important part which the theory of the *pneuma* plays in Stoic psychology and physiology and even in Stoic metaphysics. It goes back to the Sicilian school of medicine and was adopted by Plato and Aristotle.[1] In Aristotle's school it experienced a renaissance in Diocles' medical system and was blended by him with elements of Hippocratic and Cnidean medicine, for, like Aristotle's philosophy at large, Diocles' medicine is characterized by a strongly synthetic tendency. It unites within itself the historical schools of Greek medicine and tries to link them into greater unity. It is this new historical and synthetic consciousness which gives Diocles his key position in the history of Greek medicine. Furthermore, it makes it clear why it was this generation which produced the first history of medicine in the work of Meno. He obviously belonged to the same medical department of the Aristotelian school. The work was not written by Aristotle himself, as traditionally believed in classical antiquity, but under his guidance, as were Theophrastus' history of the earlier physical systems, and Eudemus' famous works on the history of geometry, astronomy, and theology. When large excerpts from Meno's history of medicine were discovered some decades ago, the most difficult problem which scholars had to face was the picture which he gives of Hippocrates.[2] He represents him as a pneumatic and this misrepresentation seemed hardly understandable. For us it no longer offers a serious problem. Meno, Diocles, and the Peripatetic school obviously saw the history of medicine in the light and perspective of their own theory. They tried to find the first indications of it in Hippocrates and this is only an evidence of their high regard for this great physician.

[1] Cf. my article 'Das Pneuma im Lykeion' in *Hermes*, vol. xlviii, p. 51.

[2] Edited by H. Diels in *Supplementum Aristotelicum*, vol. iii, p. 1 (Berlin, 1893). On Meno's picture of Hippocrates, cf. H. Diels, *Hermes*, vol. xxviii, p. 407.

ON THE ORIGIN AND CYCLE OF THE PHILOSOPHIC
IDEAL OF LIFE

THE memory of the earliest Greek thinkers lived on in the literature of the succeeding centuries through the permanent association of their names with particular opinions and questions, while their writings, in so far as they left any, went early to destruction. But besides this doxographical tradition, as it is called, which was committed to writing and sifted in the works which Aristotle's school devoted to the history of philosophy, and above all in Theophrastus' great *Opinions of the Physicists*, there survived also another sort of remembrance of them, sprung from an entirely different source. From this point of view the earliest figures in the history of philosophy were not persons who held more or less primitive and long superseded views on all sorts of strange questions, but the venerable archetypes and representatives of the form of intellectual life that is characteristic of the philosophic man in all ages, and that seemed to be incorporated with special purity and impressiveness in its earliest pioneers. This tradition had only general and typical traits to tell of those old thinkers, and therefore found expression characteristically in the form of anecdotes and apophthegms. But, as these typical traits became connected with the names of individuals who were thus known and identified, there arose alongside the impersonal tradition of their opinions a picture of the earliest philosophers that compensated the later centuries for their lack of all information about their human personalities, and was often taken for genuine historical tradition. These stories are related to us by later philosophers, from Plato on, with reverence and wonder.

Originally, however, they certainly arose in part from a wholly different motive, namely the people's amazement at a new type of man, the unworldly and withdrawn student and scholar who expresses himself in these anecdotes with paradoxes and freakish peculiarities. Such is Plato's story of Thales falling into a well while observing the sky, and being mocked by a witty Thracian servant-girl—that is to say, by the most uneducated sort of person a Greek could imagine— because 'he wants to discover what there is in the sky, but he doesn't even see what is lying at his own feet'.[1] Herds of cattle devoured the crops of Democritus, says Horace in his *Letters*,[2] while his quick mind roved far away from his body. In the division of his rich paternal

[1] Plato, *Theaet.* 174 A (Diels, *Vors.*⁵ 11, A 9).

[2] Horat. *Ep*. I. 12, 12 (and the parallel passages in Diels, *Vors.*⁵ 68, A 15).

inheritance his brothers led him by the nose, because he wished to be paid in cash in order to make long journeys. He was not given the full worth of his share, and what he did receive he spent on his travels to Egypt and to the Chaldees. While his father was alive he used to shut himself up in a little garden-house that was sometimes also used as a stable. He entirely failed to notice one day that his father had tied up an ox for sacrifice there, and remained peacefully under the same roof with it until the beast was fetched to the slaughter and Democritus' attention was drawn to his remarkable society.[1]

That stories of this sort were by no means merely the expression of a deep and sympathetic admiration of unusual intellectual concentration, but also give the folk's mocking view of absentminded scholars, is sharply brought out in the case of Thales by the complement that Aristotle gives us to the anecdote of the astronomer who pitched into the well. This is the tale of a smart business manœuvre that Thales carried through with brilliant success in order to show those who despised science that one can make a lot of money with meteorology if one sets one's mind to it. Expecting an unusually good olive harvest, he hired all the presses in the country round; when the great harvest arrived and no one had a press, he leased them to their owners at a high price.[2] Aristotle, with his usual keen critical sense, remarks that this is obviously a typical story, attributed to Thales merely because he was known to be wise. He also correctly describes the purpose of the attribution: to make it palpably evident that the truth is not that science is useless but that scientists are not interested in using it to enrich themselves. The typical character of many of these stories comes out above all in the fact that they are told of several persons. Thus Anaxagoras is also supposed to have neglected his inheritance, like Democritus; when his relatives called him to account, he replied: 'Look after it yourselves', and with these words he freely handed over to them all his goods and chattels, in order to be able to live for study alone.[3] Here the anecdote has taken on a more affecting character, instead of the good-humoured mockery that colours the Democritean version. The distracted philosopher, absentmindedly letting his cattle devour his grain, has become a great and independent spirit who consciously despises external goods and heroically rejects them. The same spirit informs an apophthegm in which Anaxagoras, asked what he lives for, gives the proud answer: 'To observe and study the sun and the moon and the sky.'[4] Equally

---

[1] Demetrius, in *Men of the Same Name*, according to Diog. IX. 35–6 (*Vors.*[5] 68, A 1).

[2] Arist. *Pol.* I. 11, 1259[a] 6 (*Vors.*[5] 11, A 10).

[3] Diog. II. 7 (*Vors.*[5] 59, A 1).

[4] Diog. II. 10 (*Vors.*[5] 59, A 1). The utterance occurs in another form in

heroic are the utterances that tradition ascribes to him when he was condemned by the Athenian court and when his son died. They are meant to show that the heart of the true student is not in perishable things, not even in the highest human goods, in civilized life and wife and child.[1] The anecdote that Anaxagoras, when accused of not caring for his country, pointed to heaven and cried: 'I care greatly for my country', is intended to bear witness to the complete withdrawal of the philosopher from that political life in which the Greek of the classical period was wholly absorbed.[2]

The time and place at which these stories arose are obscure. For those which, like the anecdote of the absentminded astronomer, express the feeling of the masses rather than the opinion of an individual, we have absolutely nothing to go on. With the last mentioned tales, however, the situation is somewhat different. These owe their coinage entirely to men of a definite class, men who were themselves full of the *ethos* of what was later called the 'theoretic life', and made themselves a sort of symbol for it in the striking utterances of the wise men of old. And this implies that, at the time when these anecdotes arose, the 'theoretic life' was not merely being lived by isolated exceptional men following their natural instinct, but had already become a conscious philosophical ideal. But this can certainly not be said of the earlier Pre-Socratic philosophers of nature. The ideal of the 'life' dedicated to knowledge was created by Plato, whose ethics describes several opposed types of 'life' and culminates in the 'choice of the best life'.[3] In itself, indeed, it is perfectly possible that a student like Anaxagoras, living in such an exclusively political society as the Athens of Pericles, should come to realize the

---

Arist. *Eth. Eud.* I. 5, 1216ᵃ 11. We are to understand in the same way the purposely obscure answer of Anaxagoras to the question: Who is the happiest man?: 'None of those whom you suppose, but someone who would seem absurd to you.' Cf. Arist. *Eth. Eud.* I. 4, 1215ᵇ 6 (*Vors.*⁵ 59, A 30).

[1] Diog. II. 13 (*Vors.*⁵ 59, A 1).

[2] Diog. II. 7 (*Vors.*⁵ 59, A 1).

[3] In an Academy address that is charming and full of feeling (*Vita Contemplativa*, Ber. Heidelb. Akad. 1920, 8), Franz Boll has set down a series of representatives of this 'life', beginning with Thales, Heraclitus, and Anaxagoras. Plato and Aristotle are merely touched on. Their influence on later men receives more of its due. Boll was far removed from the question that forms the starting-point of our examination: How far are our reports of the earlier thinkers and their 'life' a real historical tradition? When they ascribe the conscious ideal of the 'theoretic life' to Pre-Socratic philosophers, is that historically credible or is it a mere reflection of a later 'life' ethics? The whole tradition needs to be re-examined from this point of view, now that the development of philosophical ethics and 'life' doctrine from Plato to Aristotle and his pupils has been put in the right light. This gives us a fixed point that is also a focus for the history of the origin of the tradition concerning the history of philosophy. This, then, must be our starting-point.

separateness of his detached existence. Euripides already commended the quiet life of the student of nature, removed from the political machinery,[1] and depicted in his *Antiope* the tragic conflict between the 'musical' and the practical man.[2] But Plato was the first to introduce the theoretical man as an ethical problem into philosophy and to justify and glorify his life. Seen from Plato's position, the existence of this type in earlier times either had to appear as a mere paradox, a curiosity of human nature lacking all moral basis, or else the early representatives of this type, like Thales and Anaxagoras, had to be posthumously provided with Plato's legitimation and Plato's moral and emotional views of the 'theoretic life'. The latter can be shown to have been what occurred. All stories that make the older philosophers conscious followers of the ideal of the 'theoretic life' either come directly from Plato's school or arose soon afterwards under the influence of the Platonic ideal. The effect of the Platonic philosophy in forming tradition, and of its direct heir the Peripatetic school, would repay a connected examination. But the result is a foregone conclusion: the whole picture that has come down to us of the history of early philosophy was fashioned during the two or three generations from Plato to the immediate pupils of Aristotle. Along with the philosophy of these two schools it has remained a foundation-stone in the historical structure of our culture. And one of the most instructive examples of this rule is the reflection of the ideal of life as conceived during this flowering of Greek philosophy in the picture of the old Pre-Socratic thinkers and their 'life'. We are even still in a position to see that the great and apparently irreconcilable contradictions in the traditional account of the early thinkers are a necessary consequence of the fluctuations to which men's views of the 'best life' were subjected in the time from Plato to Aristotle and his pupils. To understand the development of the ethical problem, and of the 'life' problem in particular, during this period, is to clear up the creation of our tradition concerning the lives of the earliest philosophers. The present inquiry must therefore begin with the significance of the 'life' problem for the Platonic philosophy, and follow its development in some detail. First I must recall certain fundamental points from my *Aristotle* and carry them farther.

[1] Eur. frg. 910 Nauck.

[2] Plato in *Gorgias*, 484 E and 485 E ff., makes Callicles quote lines from *Antiope* as part of his campaign against a onesidedly philosophical life. It is true that Euripides depicts Amphion as a musical rather than as a scientific man. But the similarity lies in their being both unpolitical, and so Plato could make Callicles use against Socrates the lines of Zethus against Amphion. (Plato, although he believed in the political mission of Socrates, never denied that his teacher was an unpolitical man in the sense of ordinary party politics.)

The pure θεωρίη or 'theory' of the early physicists arose in Ionia. It was one of the most remarkable flowers of that late Ionian culture which was rendered increasingly unpolitical by the predominance of the mercantile atmosphere and later by foreign rule, and which by its great individual freedom facilitated the appearance of the type within the civic community of the *polis*. The down-to-earth Attic mentality with its tight political organization of life left no room for such special activities of individuals. Down to Plato's day and beyond it remained as unfriendly and reserved towards pure science as did later the Roman senatorial class. This hard earth was bound to give rise to the social tragedy of the 'unpolitical person', which Euripides first brought to light. The tension between the duties of a citizen and the leisure of a student, between action and knowledge, was here logically bound to increase into an enmity towards science on the part of the pure political man and a flight from politics on the part of the philosopher. Here alone, too, on Attic soil could Plato venture his profound attempt to reconcile the theoretic life and the political life without compromise, by giving science and philosophy a new subject, namely the state, and by making the highest norms and laws of social action their chief problem, on whose solution hung the welfare of the 'state itself'. In his earliest writings, where he presented Socrates to his contemporaries as the one true statesman whom they needed, because he had turned their eyes to the decisive question of the knowledge of the highest norm,[1] we find admittedly as yet no trace of the ideal of the theoretic life as Plato later proclaimed it. In those days his ideal both of *logos* and of 'life' was still embodied exclusively in Socrates; and there is the most obvious contrast between Socrates and the type of the unworldly pure scientist, the 'mind astronomizing and geometrizing', as set up for model in the famous digression in Plato's *Theaetetus*.[2] But Socrates' moral problem was for Plato a problem of knowledge from the beginning. Within the question of the right moral insight, of *phronesis* as Socrates had said in accordance with the prevailing Greek usage, was hidden the still deeper question of the essence of knowledge in general and of the true nature of being; and the detour through these fundamental questions, which Plato believed he must take in order

[1] See my *Platos Stellung im Aufbau der griechischen Bildung* (Berlin, 1928), p. 40 of the separate edition.

[2] Socrates is by no means lacking in 'theoretical' traits, although he likes most to be where people are thronging, in the wrestling-school or the market-place. But though Boll, op. cit., p. 9, refers to his neglect of his domestic affairs and his withdrawal from common politics, or to his 'I shall not cease from philosophizing' in the *Apology* (29 D), there is a great gulf between Socrates' sort of reflective concentration and the type of scholar depicted in *Theaetetus* (173 E). See above, p. 15.

to answer the Socratic question, led him more and more into a general doctrine of knowledge and being, and compelled him to add to his structure of theoretical science even the branches of mathematics and astronomy that he found existing. So *phronesis* was filled with the contents of this *sophia*, and out of the Socratic *aporia* and *elenchus* there grew a 'theoretic life' devoted to the purest research. In *Theaetetus*, where the alliance between philosophy and mathematics is specially prominent, Socrates sings a veritable hymn to the life of the student, and paints an ideal picture of this life in colours borrowed from the type of the astronomer and mathematician. That is the context in which Thales is cited as the perfect example of a philosopher unconcerned about practical and political life, and the story is told how he fell in the well while observing the stars. It is strange that this praise of geometry and astronomy is here sung by Socrates, whom Plato had once in the *Apology* made to say that of such high matters he understood neither much nor little but just precisely nothing.[1] It is clear that Plato himself was aware that with this latest picture of Socrates in *Theaetetus* he had reached the limit of what artistic freedom could justify in the way of transforming the historical Socrates. The new ideal of the theoretic life, and the type of pure speculative science on which it was based, demanded some other symbol, some other *archegete* than Socrates, who had hitherto been the leading figure in Plato's dialogues. And so in the *Sophist* and the *Statesman*, the two works written after *Theaetetus* and linked therewith, the leaders of the discussion are the two venerable representatives of Eleatic dialectic, Parmenides and Zeno; and Socrates has to be content with a subordinate role. Similarly in *Timaeus* the figure of the Pythagorean of that name is made the spokesman of Plato's cosmology. The ideal of the theoretic life, as realized in Plato's Academy at that time, was proclaimed in a work by the young Aristotle, the *Protrepticus*, which I have assessed in detail in a previous chapter.[2] It shows the changed attitude of the Academy to Socrates and his problems, that 'metaphysics', which was then for Plato's school the central question, and which had not yet obtained a precise name of its own, is indicated in the *Protrepticus* by the following circumlocution: 'the science of truth, as introduced by Anaxagoras and Parmenides'. Evidently the names of the old thinkers are here used simply as a substitute for pure theoretical philosophy, as whose representatives they were reckoned in this circle.[3] As I showed, too, the Academy also gave rise to that picture of Pythagoras, so determinative for later antiquity, which first takes

---

[1] Plato, *Apol.* 19 D.
[2] See the chapter on the *Protrepticus*, above, pp. 80 ff.
[3] Arist. frg. 52 (p. 59, 3 Rose).

form for us in the well known story told by Plato's pupil Heraclides of Pontus. He said that Pythagoras was the first to use the words 'philosophy' and 'philosopher' and to explain the nature of the philosopher by means of the famous comparison with the 'pure' spectators of the games at Olympia. The comparison depends on the ambiguity of the word θεωρεῖν, which means both watching a spectacle and contemplation and research in the 'theoretical' sense. Since Aristotle in the *Protrepticus* also compares the activity of the student absorbed in pure science to the gaze of the θεωροί or on-lookers at Olympia, it is clear that this analogy for the theoretical life had become classical in the Academy. The retroactive attribu-tion of this ideal of philosophic life to Pythagoras as its founder is con-nected with the high esteem in which the Academicians held this man and the Pythagoreans; for they came more and more to see in them the real historical pattern of their own mathematicizing philosophy. It is a useless labour of love to want to save this pleasant story for the historical Pythagoras, to whom at just this time an abundance of apocryphal traits and anecdotes was attributed, and about whose life and utterances a whole literature of a purely legendary character arose in a short period.[1] We do better to follow the example of Aris-

---

[1] See my *Aristotle*, above, p. 98. Burnet, *Early Greek Philosophy*[4], p. 98, seems inclined to consider Heraclides' story historical, and to carry back to Pythagoras the doctrine of the three 'lives' (the 'apolaustic', the 'political', and the 'theoretic') which it presupposes, and which we find in Aristotle's two *Ethics*. But neither the name of Heraclides, who was a byword for romancing, nor the story itself speaks in favour of this. The doctrine of the 'lives' is found in Aristotle as well as Heraclides, and they both owe it to the Academy (see Plato's *Republic* IX, 581 c ff.). Nor does the tale contain any other 'Pytha-gorean' element that points at all beyond the Platonic doctrine. When Cicero (*Tusc.* V. 9; other accounts in Diog. VIII. 8, Iambl. *Vit. Pythag.*, p. 58) tells us that Heraclides' account included the feature that, as celebrants come from various cities to take part in the great Greek panegyris, so men have wandered into this life from another one, that is nothing but Plato's well known doctrine of the soul. We cannot infer from it that the doctrine of the three 'lives' was Pythagorean, on the ground that the transmigration of souls is a demonstrably Pythagorean view. Certainly there was a 'Pythagorean way of life', in the same sense as there was an 'Orphic way of life'; but that is something quite different from a division and classification of 'lives' such as we find in Plato and Aristotle. The 'lives' are three because there are three τέλη or purposes in life in which according to Plato and Aristotle various men place their happi-ness, namely either pleasure or virtue or *phronesis*. It is therefore not an acci-dent that they are three, and not an accident that they are precisely these three. They correspond to the three systematic foundation-pillars of Platonic–Aristotelian ethics. This is very clearly expressed in Aristotle's *Eudemian Ethics* I. 1, 1214[a] 30: 'Happiness and blessed living would reside in three things most, the three that seem to be most desirable. For some say that *phronesis* is the greatest good, some virtue, and some pleasure.' (The same in Aristotle's *Protrepticus* in Iambl. *Protr.*, c. vii ff.; see my *Aristotle*, above, pp. 65 ff.) On this trinity of the objects of choice Aristotle then expressly proceeds to construct

totle, who avoids using the name of Pythagoras and prefers merely to speak of the contemporary 'so called Pythagoreans', because he believes that it is no longer possible to obtain trustworthy information about the real Pythagoras. On the other hand, he himself, in his dialogue *On Philosophy*, made use of the seven sages for the prehistory of philosophy—for we can hardly interpret otherwise the report that he there regarded them as 'sophists', naturally in the good sense of the word.[1] Indeed, the Academy even extended the conception of the 'theoretic life' to the Egyptian priests. Aristotle says in the early first book of his *Metaphysics* that they were the first to devote themselves to pure science, because their profession gave them leisure. And the *Epinomis* of the Platonist Philip of Opus, which undertakes to fit the 'theoretic life' as an appendix into the political structure of the *Laws*, sees the direct predecessors of this ideal in the astrologers of the Chaldees. Thus did the Academy during Plato's last decades create the historical framework that fitted its 'life'.[2]

There runs through the *Epinomis* a deep resignation that this 'life' is reserved for a very few exceptional persons. The same mood informs the but little earlier seventh letter of Plato, that great manifesto of his old age in which he for the last time took a stand on the question that had concerned him all his life, the question of the relation between politics and philosophical knowledge. The fundamental inner readiness to convert the thoughts of philosophy into creative action, and to take part in the life of the state, remained even in these last years of Plato's the same as it had been at the beginning of his intellectual course, notwithstanding the shipwreck that his favourite pupil Dion had suffered in Syracuse in the first serious attempt to realize the Platonic Ideas. But it was now impossible not to notice a strong tension between this originally all-controlling aim

the three 'lives' (*Eth. Eud.* I. 2, 1215ᵃ 35). The trinity of pleasure, virtue, and *phronesis*, is in him connected with Plato's doctrine that the soul has three parts, from which he derives the three 'lives' and the three sorts of pleasure (*Republic* IX, 580 D ff.). Apocryphal Pythagorean literature later naturally attributed the trichotomy of the soul also to Pythagoras or the Pythagoreans (along with nearly everything else), and even people like Posidonius, not to mention uncritical believers like Iamblichus or Porphyry, took such forgeries for genuine. Had I possessed a complete view of this sort of literature when I wrote my *Nemesius* (pp. 63 ff.), I should have treated these 'testimonies' to the Pythagorean origin of the trichotomy of the soul with less ceremony. I am glad, however, that even then I did not blindly trust them. Recently A. E. Taylor, in his commentary on Plato's *Timaeus*, p. 497, has come out again for a Pythagorean ancestry of this doctrine.

[1] According to Arist. frg. 3 Rose, the seven sages occurred in the dialogue *On Philosophy*. Rose is therefore probably right in referring to the same dialogue the statement, in *Etymol. M.* s.v. σοφιστής, that Aristotle called the seven sages 'sophists'.

[2] Arist. *Metaph.* A 1, 981ᵇ 23; *Epin.* 986 E.

of his philosophizing[1] and the actual dedication of his old age entirely to pure theoretical study. Thus gradually arose a set of problems which were inherited by Aristotle in their full gravity, and which threatened the essential unity of scientific knowledge and practical action that had been since Plato's Socratic period the presupposition of his research and therefore a foundation-pillar of his idea of the 'theoretic life'. Plato's personal development and the inner tendency of Platonic science worked in the same direction. The passionate Socratic drive for knowledge was aimed, to speak Platonically, purely at the 'vision of the Idea of the Good'; and action was to Socrates identical with the knowledge of the Good. Plato's early philosophy had then pressed still more determinedly towards participation in actual life and in the state. But in the course of Plato's development the drive towards knowledge had immeasurably extended its range. Late Platonic science did indeed appear to have developed quite organically out of the Socratic seed, by a process of constantly incorporating richer theoretical content; but its field was no longer exclusively political ethics as it had been in the writings down to the *Republic*. Ethics had become a mere 'part' of philosophy, co-ordinate with logic and physics;[2] and when Plato in his old age lectured 'on the Good', he understood by that mathematics and metaphysics and heaven knows what else, but definitely not a doctrine of the goods of human life, as Aristotle used afterwards to tell his students, according to the well known report of Aristoxenus, who heard him. That Plato's philosophy, originally very close to life, had changed into pure theory is symbolized by the story that the announcement of the old subject 'On the Good' attracted great crowds of hearers, but that general disappointment reigned as soon as Plato began to lecture on numbers and lines and the highest One which is the Good.[3]

The ideal of the theoretic life did not at first appear to be threatened by this development. On the contrary, it seemed that pure science, as the late Plato understood it, was triumphing over the onesidedly

[1] See my address 'Die griechische Staatsethik im Zeitalter des Plato', in *Humanistische Reden und Vorträge*, p. 105; and 'Platos Stellung im Aufbau der griechischen Bildung', op. cit., p. 158.

[2] It was so in Xenocrates' well known division of philosophy (frg. 1 Heinze), which held for the later Plato too. Aristotle was not the first to differentiate philosophy in this way.

[3] Aristoxenus *Harmon*. 30 Meibom (p. 44, 5 Marq.): 'as Aristotle always used to tell happened to most of those who heard Plato give his lecture on the Good: everyone came expecting to learn something about those recognized human goods such as wealth, health, strength, and in general some wonderful happiness; but when it became plain that his discussion was about mathematics and numbers and geometry and astronomy and finally that Good is One, I think it seemed an absolute paradox to them. Thereupon some of them despised the matter and others condemned it.'

practical tendency of Socrates. Aristotle was the first to bring this tendency to complete victory; he enlarged Plato's 'doctrine of Ideas' into a universal science of being founded on experience. In a certain sense he is an even purer representative of the theoretic life than Plato. The difficulty for this new science was to take care that it did not, in the course of its unimpeded development on the theoretical side, lose its root connexion with Socratic–Platonic ethics; for it was precisely its services to actual living that had given the theoretic life according to Plato its moral dignity and its sacred rights. Aristotle's philosophic being was rooted, even after he had given up the doctrine of Ideas, far too firmly in the *ethos* in which he had grown up in the Academy for him to sacrifice one jot or tittle of Plato's belief in the educational and moral mission of science, and he had himself proclaimed it in the *Protrepticus*. Though he separates ethics from metaphysics and makes it a special discipline, at the decisive point he connects the two together as Plato did: he holds fast to the significance of intellectual cultivation and knowledge for the moral culture of the personality. He assigns the theoretic life the highest rank both in the state[1] and in the orders of the moral world; and the individual human being's happiness, the aim of human striving, is achieved on his view not in moral perfection or at any rate not in that alone, but only in the full development of the intellectual powers of human nature.[2] In the end, indeed, exactly like Plato, he makes specifically moral insight dependent on the knowledge of the ultimate source of reality. The primacy of the theoretical over the practical reason is his enduring Platonic conviction. And this is not only because intellectual activity (νοῦ ἐνέργεια) is independent of the sensuous side of human nature and of our external needs, and constitutes a portion of the eternal blessedness of God carried within ourselves, of the omniscience that timelessly knows itself; it is also because moral knowledge is also positively imbued and coloured with the metaphysical world-view of the scientifically thinking man.[3]

[1] Aristotle, *Pol.* VII. 2–3, discusses the aim of the best state and the education of its citizens, and adopts a position on the question whether the best life is the political and practical or another (meaning the theoretic life). He rejects each of the extremes, both the view that only the political life is manly and free, and also the withdrawal from politics on principle and the complete rejection of every sort of rule as mere tyranny. To him the 'theoretic life' is by no means synonymous with the '*xenic* life' or life of the alien, but is at the same time 'practical' in the highest sense Philosophers and men of knowledge are creative, for him, in that they are 'architects with their thoughts' (see esp. 1325^b 14–23).

[2] Happiness in the highest sense is secured only by the theoretic life, according to *Eth. Nic.* X. 7, 'and in secondary degree the life according to the other sort of virtue'. In the next chapter this subordination of ethical to intellectual virtue is established in more detail.

[3] The independence of the mind from man's sensuous nature, in contrast to

But at this point there arises for Aristotle a problem that did not exist for Plato in such sharpness. It throws an abrupt light on the inner difficulties that Aristotelian Platonism has to contend with here. Although the moral and scientific spheres touch each other, and the latter leads into the moral, this happens only at one point, whereas in Plato the moral was still completely contained in the scientific. Science has now separated itself into numerous disciplines; and each one of them is striving for independence from the whole. Metaphysics or ontology has also separated itself, once in Plato the totality of the philosophic consideration of the world, but now only the queen of the sciences, also called 'theology'. And it is this science that is pre-eminently intended, science as world-view, wherever Aristotle lets the ethical sphere come into contact with the theoretical. Nowhere else is this so clearly expressed as in the earliest form that we possess of Aristotle's *Ethics*, the version edited by Eudemus, at the end of which we read that the natural goods of life are moral goods for man only so far as they help him to serve and know God. The knowledge of God is thus the way to the true service of God and the criterion of earthly values, which hold their value in fee from its value.[1] But now does this mean that the whole gigantic structure of particular theoretical knowledge, built up by Aristotle in his system and culminating in theology, is presupposed here and is therefore an indispensable condition of the correct moral conduct of life? To put the question is to perceive that, while this is in a certain sense so for the philosopher, who in his metaphysical survey of the whole can fit the totality of knowledge into a unity, it can hardly be so for the mere specialist with his gaze fixed only on a limited area, and the man morally active in the affairs of life can absolutely not be thought of as depending on such a condition in his decisions. Every attempt to determine the power of theoretical reason over moral insight, of *sophia* over *phronesis*, more exactly in detail than is done in that decisive passage of the *Eudemian Ethics*, must inevitably lead to a weakening of this power and a strengthening of the relative independence of the moral sphere from 'theory'.

ethical virtue, whose whole sphere is nothing but the relation of the impulses to reason, is emphasized in Aristotle's *Eth. Nic.* X. 8, 1178ª 16–22. From this it follows that the theoretic life is also less dependent on 'external provision' than the practical; see from 1178ª 24 to the end of the chapter. With regard to practical and moral thought and action being shot through with *sophia* and 'theory', compare the differences between the two *Ethics* in what follows.

[1] Arist. *Eth. Eud.* VIII. 3, 1249ᵇ 16: 'Therefore whichever choice and possession of natural goods will produce the most contemplation of God, whether goods of the body or wealth or friends or any other, that is the best and this is the finest standard; and whichever either by defect or by excess prevents one from serving and contemplating God, that is bad.' See my *Aristotle*, above, p. 243 and the whole preceding section.

Plato had attached moral insight, the *phronesis* of Socrates, to the contemplation of the Idea of the Good. They were conflated to such a degree that the concept of *phronesis*, which in ordinary usage was purely ethical and practical, came in Plato always to include the theoretical knowledge of the idea, became, in fact, finally synonymous with expressions that had long meant nothing but pure knowing and contained no relation to the practical, such as *sophia*, *nus*, *episteme*, theory, and the like. This Platonic sense of the word *phronesis* is still to be found in the early Aristotle. It appears in his *Protrepticus*, where it means the theoretical science of being, or metaphysics, and where Anaxagoras and Parmenides are named as typical representatives of 'this *phronesis*'.[1] In the *Eudemian Ethics*, *phronesis* is still often the name for the intellectual organ of the theoretic life; and Anaxagoras is cited as the prototype of a life of pure *phronesis* because he devoted himself entirely to the astronomical study of the sky.[2] On the other hand, in the sixth book of the *Nicomachean Ethics*, the later version of Aristotle's ethics, we find this Platonic conception of *phronesis* critically broken up into its original elements; the expression is narrowed to mean only practical moral insight, and all theoretical content is removed from it. Aristotle now recommends *sophia* as the proper word to indicate theoretical knowledge of reason; he explains that *phronesis* concerns only human affairs, but *sophia* also divine affairs and the whole cosmos; that is why we call Anaxagoras, Thales, and such people, *sophoi*, but Pericles and people of his sort *phronimoi*.[3] *Sophia*, he says, studies only the general, like all true science. *Phronesis*, on the other hand, concerns itself also with the application of general moral knowledge to the particular practical case.[4] Thus politics, which once in Plato had not merely been the

---

[1] On the development of the conception of *phronesis* see my *Aristotle*, above, pp. 83 ff.

[2] See *Eth. Eud.* I. 4, 1215ᵇ 1 and 6; I. 5, 1216ᵃ 11 ff. On the conception of *phronesis* and its significance in the *Eudemian Ethics* see my *Aristotle*, above, pp. 236 ff., 239 ff.

[3] *Eth. Nic.* VI. 7, 1141ᵇ 2: 'From what has been said it is clear that *sophia* is both science and intuition of the things that are most valuable by nature. Hence men say that Anaxagoras and Thales and such persons are *sophoi* but not *phronimoi*, when they see them ignorant of their own advantage, and they say that the things which these men know are exceedingly marvellous and difficult and divine, but useless, and that they do not seek human goods. But *phronesis* concerns human affairs and matters that can be deliberated. For good deliberation is, we say, the most essential function of the *phronimos*.' 1140ᵇ 7: 'Hence we think that Pericles and such men are *phronimoi*, because they can see what is good for themselves and for men; and we think that household-managers and statesmen are persons of this sort.' Clearly Aristotle is here arguing against his own earlier and still purely Platonic statements in the *Protrepticus* and the *Eudemian Ethics*.

[4] *Eth. Nic.* VI. 7, 1141ᵃ 9 ff., and 5, 1140ᵃ 24 ff.

ruling science but also included all human knowledge within itself, is relegated to a lower level, together with its subordinate ethics; for its organ is *phronesis*, as much in legislation as in politics in the narrower sense. Since man is by no means the highest being in the world, ethics and politics are by no means equivalent to the highest science.[1] The separation of metaphysics from ethics that Aristotle carried through is here clearly observable. That is not indeed any devaluation of the theoretic life, rather a heightening of its intellectual rank; but the higher the sky the less it touches the earth; and that is why in the *Nicomachean Ethics* it is not easy to discover what precisely, apart from the intellectual precedence of the theoretic over the practical life, the inner dependence of moral virtue on scientific knowledge consists in.[2] Modern scholars have made acute inquiries into this matter. But the result is negative; and the mere fact that Aristotle fails to make any positive utterance on the question is significant of the weakness of the connexion between the doctrine of virtue and character proper and the picture of the happiness of the theoretic life that crowns the whole at the end.[3] The whole of the *Nicomachean Ethics* contains no sentence like that which, at the end of the *Eudemian Ethics*, makes knowledge of God the measure of all moral evaluation.[4] The position is perfectly clear. The preferred status of the speculative life is indeed preserved unchanged in the *Nicomachean Ethics*; ever since Aristotle's young days, when he had sent his *Protrepticus* into the world while still a pupil of Plato, that had remained the unmoving pole of his philosophical life. But the dependence, also taken over from Plato, of the doctrine of character and virtue upon theoretical philosophy and theology, has progressively disappeared. The tendency of Aristotle's own development is, on the contrary, always to increase the division between the practical and the theoretical spheres; and the weight of his own scientific con-

---

[1] *Eth. Nic.* VI. 7, 1141ᵃ 21: 'It is absurd to think that politics or *phronesis* is the best, since man is not the best thing in the cosmos.'

[2] See my *Aristotle*, above, pp. 239 ff.

[3] L. H. G. Greenwood, *Aristotle, Nicomachean Ethics, Book Six* (Cambridge, 1909), pp. 82 ff., after a very subtle examination of all utterances bearing on this point in the *Nicomachean Ethics*, came to the correct conclusion that we remain condemned to mere conjectures about it.

[4] Greenwood's statement, 'Actions are good, according to Aristotle, in proportion as they lead to the θεωρητικὸς βίος as the end' (op. cit., p. 82), only fits the relation of moral virtue to the contemplation of God as formulated in the final sentences of the *Eudemian Ethics*. To the *Nicomachean Ethics*, on the other hand, applies what he says on page 83: 'He probably followed to some extent the feelings of the ordinary man in attributing to moral actions an independent goodness of their own, and would allow the πολιτικὸς βίος to possess a certain rationality and value even though it should ignore or contemn the θεωρητικὸς βίος altogether.'

tribution to ethics lies in his genial development of that part of it whose preponderance has given the whole its name, to wit, the doctrine of character and the system of the moral virtues.[1] It is true that he also still recognizes the 'intellectual virtues', that is, the spiritual and intellectual education of man, as the second pillar of the value of the personality; he even gives in the sixth book of the *Nicomachean Ethics* a detailed analysis of these purely intellectual powers and capacities of man.[2] But this analysis is connected with the very inquiry that led him to separate the intellectual side from the specifically ethical. Rather than aiming at positively preparing for, and connecting to the doctrine of virtue, the doctrine of the

---

[1] See my *Aristotle*, above, p. 396 and frequently.

[2] The distinction between moral and intellectual virtues in Aristotle's ethics had already been made by Plato, so that what we have here is an Academic doctrinal tradition. This has apparently not yet been noticed; and I did not notice it myself until, during a seminar on Plato's *Cratylus* in the winter term of 1926–7, I discovered that there is a definite principle in the ordering of the etymologies of the technical terms that come after the names of the gods and of physical conceptions (such as 'sun', 'moon', 'stars', 'lightning', 'fire', 'air', 'ether', and so on). First come *phronesis, noesis, episteme, synesis, sophia.* After the mention of the 'good' there follow 'justice' and 'courage'. 'Temperance', the third virtue usually listed as a typical example of the 'ethical' virtues, is inserted after *phronesis* and *noesis* as a sort of annotation, because it is interpreted as meaning the preservation of *phronesis* (σωτηρία φρονήσεως) and could therefore be dealt with in passing here. The conceptions such as *phronesis, noesis, sophia, synesis*, and so on, are very closely connected with 'justice', 'temperance', and 'courage'. Both sets fall under the common conception of 'virtue'. Whereas the latter are the 'moral virtues' in Aristotle's sense, the former correspond precisely to the 'intellectual virtues' of the sixth book of the *Nicomachean Ethics*. It follows that Plato had already analysed the conception of virtue into a *phronetic* and an ethical element, and determined the various kinds of the virtues of *phronesis* and of *ethos* by his method of division. This is an important point for our view of the development of Aristotle's ethics, which in other respects, too, operates at every step with established Academic doctrines and conceptions. Significantly, however, Plato, unlike *Nicomachean Ethics* VI, did not yet regard *phronesis* as a mere species of intellectual virtue but as the genus of this whole class. That is proved by *Philebus* 19 A, where we read that one must grasp *phronesis* (and pleasure) not merely as one but also as many in its various forms; and this is presented as the great achievement of the method of division that has just been described. There follow in *Philebus* 19 D the same species of *phronesis* as in *Cratylus* 411 D ff. and *Nicomachean Ethics* VI. This corresponds exactly to the view and terminology of the early Aristotle in the *Protrepticus* and the *Eudemian Ethics* (see my *Aristotle*, above, pp. 82 and 239). This whole Platonic and early Aristotelian terminology and determination of the place of *phronesis* among the intellectual virtues is being attacked by Aristotle in the sixth book of the *Nicomachean Ethics*. The early date which is at present favoured for *Cratylus* seems to me hard to reconcile with its differentiated doctrine of virtue; but that is only one of many evidences that cannot be discussed here. A thorough re-examination of this difficult dialogue from the standpoint of our present knowledge of Plato is an urgent need and is being undertaken.

theoretical life which we read at the end of the *Nicomachean Ethics*, it enlarges the gulf between this originally central part of Aristotle's ethics and the doctrine of virtue proper. Thus it provides a striking confirmation of our proof of the progressive loosening of the tie connecting the theoretic life with the kernel of Aristotle's ethics.

The picture here drawn of the development of Aristotle's ethics is confirmed by the further transformations of the problem in the Peripatetic school. Unfortunately the ethical writings of Aristotle's chief pupils are lost to us. Our most important source, the sole ethical work of the period that survives nearly complete, is the so called *Great Ethics*, handed down under Aristotle's name, the work of some Peripatetic who lived not before the scholarchate of Theophrastus.[1] The way in which the author reproduces the ideas of

[1] This is the established view since Spengel's famous discussion of the three *Ethics* in the Munich Academy. After Kapp and I had shown the genuineness of the *Eudemian Ethics*, Hans von Arnim in a whole series of writings has recently defended the genuineness of the so called *Great Ethics* (which, of course, is the smallest) and interpreted it as the earliest and most original of the Aristotelian *Ethics*, without, however, producing the smallest conviction. I must entirely associate myself with the critical rejection of his view by two such proven experts in the study of Aristotle's ethics as Professor E. Kapp in his two articles (*Gnomon*, 1927) and Professor J. L. Stocks in Manchester (*Deutsche Literatur-Zeitung*, 1927). It is, after all, not the first time that learned experts in old masters have confused the copy and the original. Arnim's only partisan that he will value is Schleiermacher in his Berlin Academy lecture. Schleiermacher was certainly a high and sensitive mind; but his services concerning Plato were due to philosophical and artistic congeniality, not to historical vision; on the contrary, as a pupil of the Halle rationalists he had no eye for Plato's development, and his authority postponed our historical knowledge of it for decades. He succeeded no better with the *Great Ethics*. He strangely thought it the only genuine one, rejecting the two genuine ones because only the *Great Ethics* came up to his Kantian ideal of a true ethics. He thought that it did not, like the other two *Ethics*, make morality depend on theoretical reason, but left the theoretic life aside. But that is precisely the main argument for its spuriousness. Now that we can clearly survey the development from Plato through Aristotle to the latter's pupils in its particular stages, and grasp the strict inner necessity of this intellectual process, it ought not to be hard to see that the *Great Ethics* fits in only here (after the *Nicomachean*), and necessarily here. The fact is that Arnim has simply not entered into the new way of comparing different stages in the history of a problem, as Stocks rightly emphasized. Let it be here extended to the *Great Ethics* for the present problem as a substitute for any further refutation of Arnim's arguments. For his method seems to me to strain out gnats and swallow camels. This way of approach will be carried out for the whole of the *Great Ethics* by my pupil Richard Walzer in his forthcoming book (Volume VI of *Neue Philologische Untersuchungen*), which I must naturally touch on in the single point that I am here discussing. That the *Great Ethics* dates itself by using as example Neleus, the favourite pupil of Theophrastus and inheritor of his library, in the same way as Aristotle in his writings had used Neleus' father, his friend and fellow-scholar Coriscus, escaped Arnim's notice. Wilamowitz acquainted him

Aristotle's ethics abbreviated and clarified, mostly in close dependence on the *Eudemian* but also using the *Nicomachean* version,

with it in *Hermes* for 1927; and drew the correct conclusion that the *Great
Ethics* is not to be placed before the time of Theophrastus. Arnim's objection
(in *Hermes* for 1928) that Neleus heard Aristotle (the late Aristotle!) and therefore did not enter the School under Theophrastus, misses the main difficulty:
as I have shown in *Entstehungsgeschichte*, &c., p. 34, and in *Aristotle* (above,
p. 256), Aristotle's habit of citing Coriscus as an example obviously goes back
to the time when Coriscus was himself present at the lecture, which was soon
after Plato's death and in Assos and Scepsis, whither Coriscus had returned
according to Plato's sixth letter a considerable time previously. Particularly
do the witty allusions of the *Eudemian Ethics* to Coriscus give the most
vivid impression of actuality and presuppose that the listeners have personal
acquaintance with the man. That in a still earlier lecture on ethics, which
the *Great Ethics* would be, according to Arnim, Aristotle would have mentioned the ungrown son of Coriscus (who presumably was attending the
lecture?) and only later come to make the father, the old friend of his youth,
his standing example, is absurd and chronologically impossible. On the contrary, the isolated mention of Neleus can be explained only by the assumption
that the use of his father Coriscus as example had at some earlier time been
common form in Aristotle's school. And that fits into the post-Aristotelian
period only. The post-Aristotelian origin of the *Great Ethics* is also indicated
by numerous technical terms foreign to Aristotle and introduced by Theophrastus, which Walzer will collect. As an example of the sort of thing one can
point to the un-Aristotelian, spurious books of the *History of Animals*, whose
origin in particular cases can still be illuminated more precisely by such study
of words. But, apart from all these proofs, the non-Aristotelian origin of the
Great Ethics is indicated above all by its language at every step. It is, of course,
like all Peripatetic prose, dependent on the diction of Aristotle; but it betrays
itself as later by a multitude of Hellenistic symptoms. Some of these shall be
listed here. They positively offer themselves to every connoisseur of Aristotle's
language. The *Great Ethics* uses forms which during Attic times and in Aristotle
are not yet used or at any rate appear only as quite isolated exceptions. Thus
we have the future εἰλήσομεν once in *Top.* I. 18, 108ᵃ 28, otherwise only in the
spurious *Rhet. ad Al.* 36, 1441ᵇ 29, but in the *Great Ethics* 1182ᵃ 4 εἰλήσομεν,
1208ᵃ 26 εἰλήσω, 1183ᵃ 16 and 17 εἰλήσει; the aorist εἰλῆσαι *only* in *Gr. Eth.*
I. 1, 1182ᵃ 5, 8, 1186ᵃ 10, II. 10, 1208ᵃ 35, εἰλήσας 1208ᵃ 31, but nowhere in
Aristotle except for one place in the spurious *Probl.* (XIX. 42, 921ᵇ 26), which
are themselves of later origin. οἴδαμεν occurs only once in the whole Aristotelian corpus (*Anal.* IV. 8, 93ᵃ 25), but in the *Gr. Eth.* at 1199ᵃ 32 and 35, i.e.
twice in a smaller space. οἴδασι, 1190ᵇ 24, otherwise only once in the spurious
On Marvellous Reports 119, 842ᵃ 2. εἴδομεν used as a present = ὁρῶμεν (with
subordinate clause ὅταν θέλωμεν) 1213ᵃ 21; ὑγιῇ 1201ᵇ 28 (Arist. writes ὑγιᾶ);
and more of the like. It is known that the use of ὑπέρ for περί, which is common
in Hellenistic Greek, occurs in Aristotle only in vanishingly few places; but
in the *Great Ethics* it is the rule. For the author to come forward with 'I'
is un-Aristotelian, but common in other learned literature, e.g. in the Hippocratic corpus; in the *Gr. Eth.* 1181ᵇ 28 τὴν ἐπωνυμίαν Δικαίως Δοκεῖ ἄν μοι ἔχειν,
1169ᵇ 9 ἀλλ' ἐρεῖ μοι, τὰ ποῖα Διασάφησον, &c. Characteristic is also the lively,
direct address, more like the diatribe style, where the opponent imagined by
the speaker says 'you'. With this compare the constantly occurring 'he says'
as a means of introducing the adversary's objections, 1198ᵇ 11, 1200ᵃ 19, 21,

agrees entirely with the usual method of handing down doctrines in the close-knit Greek schools of philosophy, even to the peculiar mixture of dependence and freedom towards the doctrine of the founder. We cannot doubt that the method of the later Peripatetic commentators is ultimately derived from those ways of handing on the

1208ᵃ 25, 27, 1212ᵇ 38, 1213ᵃ 1, 6, &c. A particularly vivid imaginary dialogue of this sort in the 'you' and 'I' style is, for example, 1208ᵃ 20: 'But perhaps someone would say: "When the passions are in what state (ὅταν πῶς ἔχωσι!) do they not prevent it, and when are they in that state? For I don't know." That sort of thing is not easy to say; the physician cannot say it either, when he tells you to give barley-gruel to the feverish person. "How shall I recognize fever?" (Read αἰσθάνωμαι.) When, he says, you see him looking pale. "And how shall I know pallor?" There the physician must use his judgement. For if, he says, you don't have in yourself the power to perceive such things, you can't know.' There is nothing like this regular school-jargon in the whole of Aristotle. The striving for palpable sensual clarity does not fit Aristotle's reserved and objective manner. It occurs throughout the *Great Ethics*. Characteristic of the work is also the author's favourite trick of interrupting himself with an insistently didactic 'Why?', 1182ᵇ 32, 1183ᵇ 11, and often. Similar are the 'What then?, someone will say', 1185ᵃ 23; 'Yes' 1190ᵃ 37, 1208ᵃ 20. Very commonly the author uses a subject in the neuter plural with a verb in the plural, 1194ᵇ 32, 1197ᵃ 37, ᵇ 33, 1200ᵇ 26–7, 1201ᵃ 3, 1206ᵇ 12, and often. The terminology of the school is already characteristically sprawled out in him; he says not only 'the best' or 'the good', but also 'the best good', as well as 'the final end' and the like. He is un-Aristotelian also in his slovenly habit of redundantly repeating words, especially after a parenthetic subordinate clause, as in 1183ᵃ 29: 'Yet they think they must, when they speak about the good, must speak about the idea'; or immediately thereafter, ᵃ 33: 'Not that the political science or faculty, about which we are now speaking, it does not inquire about this good'; 1196ᵃ 1: 'And if the person towards whom it bids him act, if he does not act towards this person, he wrongs him'; 1198ᵃ 8: 'Nor is the reason and nor is the choice quite completed'; 1204ᵇ 21: 'Nor are these . . . pleasures are not processes'; 1206ᵇ 26: 'But the passions do not, if they receive a start from reason towards noble things, they do not necessarily follow'; similarly μή . . . οὐκ 1195ᵃ 1 instead of οὐκ . . . οὐκ. The use of 'you' = 'one', which is not usual in Aristotle though common in the rest of scientific literature, occurs 1197ᵇ 16 'for you would not separate', with which only the 'you will find' in the spurious *Categories* is comparable. 1185ᵃ 30 'Whatever you throw in . . . if you do not throw in . . . for if you throw in . . . if you do not throw in'. The regular use of ἦν = 'was' for ἐστίν = 'is' is characteristic, 1182ᵇ 29, 1185ᵃ 13, 1194ᵃ 20, and often; even in the form 1196ᵃ 6: 'But perhaps this was not true and it is impossible for a man to wrong himself' (where ἦν should not be emended to ἦ); also the regular οὐκέτι = 'no longer' instead of οὐκ = 'not'. Redundance occurs also in 1203ᵃ 11 'to whom nothing of any good sort belongs', and in 1204ᵇ 21 the addition of the demonstrative pronoun αὗται, which comes several times, and 1204ᵃ 1 μὲν οὖν ἄρα. This list could be substantially increased. I see no trace of an attempt by von Arnim to explain the linguistic peculiarities of the *Great Ethics*, or even to face the fact that the author writes such an abnormal Greek. Even if the train of thought in the *Great Ethics* did not betray the same etiolated and scholastic deadness, its linguistic condition would be enough to exclude all serious discussion of its genuineness among philologists.

doctrines of the school that established themselves in the very first generations after Aristotle. This can still be made plain by the example of Theophrastus' fragment on metaphysics, or of Eudemus' physics; and we have recently become able to do so even for so obscure a period of the Peripatos as the late second century B.C.; for the excerpts of the Pseudo-Ocellus have preserved pieces of a Peripatetic lecture of this time, actually a paraphrasing reproduction of Aristotle's work *On Coming to be and Passing away*.[1] In giving his personal nuance to the fixed doctrines of the school which he inherits, the author of the *Great Ethics* often uses the form of the *aporia*, as Aristotle before him had done with regard to the traditional doctrine of the Academy, which his own exposition often simply followed.[2] His omissions and his emphases, however, also frequently reveal his own attitude to the questions he deals with, questions which he often completely fails to understand in the sense they originally had for Aristotle. This appears particularly in the peculiar difficulties that Aristotle incurred because his intellectual progress compelled him to be perpetually settling accounts with Plato. The anchoring of ethics in the theoretic life was precisely such a Platonic legacy that caused no slight difficulty to the author of the *Great Ethics*.

The end of the *Great Ethics* is unfortunately lost. It breaks off in the middle of the treatment of friendship, to which, as we know, the *Nicomachean Ethics* adds as tenth book a (second) discussion of pleasure and the doctrine of the theoretic life. We cannot say whether the *Great Ethics* once ended in the same way; it is not at all necessary, for particularly in structure it leans more on the *Eudemian Ethics*,

[1] The remains of the physics of Eudemus are brought together in the collection of his fragments by Leonhard Spengel. The metaphysical fragment of Theophrastus was last edited by Usener [now by Ross and Fobes, Oxford, 1929.—Tr.]. On Pseudo-Ocellus' use of pre-Andronican Peripatetic interpretation of Aristotle's *On Coming to be and Passing away*, see R. Harder, *Ocellus Lucanus, Text und Kommentar*, Berlin, 1926, pp. 97–111 (Volume I of my *Neue Philologische Untersuchungen*).

[2] Just one example of this. In *Eth. Nic.* VI. 1, 1138^b 20–34, Aristotle says that the 'right mean', of which he had spoken in determining the essence of ethical virtue, is 'as the right *logos* says', but this determination is not clear enough and needs to be made more precise. In II. 2, 1103^b 31, we learn that the definition of the morally good habit as 'in accord with the right *logos*' is universally admitted (κοινόν) and can be immediately assumed, but will later require more precise determination. Finally, we hear in VI. 13, 1144^b 21, that 'now everybody', when he defines virtue, adds the phrase 'in accord with the right *logos*', which naturally refers to the Academy, whose pupils often diverged on such questions. The ideal task of research, no longer possible in detail, is to separate the Academic basis of every Aristotelian conception and doctrine sharply from the individual modification that Aristotle made in it. The same holds for the relation of the *Great Ethics* to Aristotle, except that here both originals are preserved to us.

and it reproduces the end of that. This end, the sections on the relation between happiness and good fortune, and on true *calocagathy*,
is a sort of parallel to the doctrine of happiness at the end of the
Nicomachean Ethics; but it is also characteristically different therefrom. For this reason it is not probable that the *Great Ethics*, which
adopts this end of the *Eudemian Ethics* (though it transfers it to
before the treatment of friendship), originally also adopted the end
of the *Nicomachean Ethics*, the description of the theoretic life.[1]
That would not correspond to its attitude to contemplation and the
intellectual virtues, which is in other respects also fairly negative.
In reproducing the end of the *Eudemian Ethics*, the doctrine of good
fortune, the author of the *Great Ethics* significantly omitted the
metaphysical element, the '*divine* good fortune', which was so
thoroughly essential to the late-Platonic attitude of the *Eudemian
Ethics*.[2] Similarly from the treatment of *calocagathy*, also borrowed
from the end of the *Eudemian Ethics*, he omitted the relation to the
contemplation of God and to the theoretic life. The starting-point
of the *Eudemian Ethics* has also dropped out, the question of happiness and the choice of a 'life', where the theoretic life is described as
one of those open to choice, and the solution of the problem of happiness by this means is thus prepared from the beginning. In view of
what we have ascertained about the weakening of the connexion
between the theoretic life and the central part of ethics in the *Nicomachean Ethics*, it cannot astonish us that this process, which we can
follow from Plato and Aristotle's early *Protrepticus* on through the
Eudemian to the *Nicomachean Ethics*, should reveal itself in the
Great Ethics in its most advanced stage. It is the process of the
increasing dispossession of the metaphysical and intellectual element
(historically speaking, the Platonic element) from Aristotle's ethics.
Aristotle himself never went so far as to abandon this Platonic legacy
that had been so decisive for his attitude of research and his ideal of
science. But his pupils were sometimes more Aristotelian than Aris-

---

[1] *Gr. Eth.* II. 8 on good fortune and II. 9 on *calocagathy* are attached to the
doctrine of pleasure and its significance for happiness (II. 7). The two chapters
are exactly parallel to chapters VIII. 2 and VIII. 3 of the *Eudemian Ethics*.
The parallelism of these two sections to the last book of the *Nicomachean
Ethics* is strengthened when we make them follow the section on pleasure, as
they do in the *Great Ethics*; for the tenth book of the *Nicomachean Ethics* also
begins with a discussion of pleasure. A special discussion of the theoretic life
need not have followed even in the *Eudemian Ethics*, for which that life is the
centre of motion. It is practically out of the question in the *Great Ethics* owing
to the removal of this whole part II. 7–9 from the end of the whole to before
the discussion of the intellectual virtues.

[2] The late-Platonic doctrine of divine fortune urgently needs a separate
examination, before it can be assigned its right place in the history of the
problem of *tyche* or fortune among the Greeks.

totle; and the distance of the philosophical situation of the *Great Ethics* from Plato impresses itself very sharply in that work from the first page on. With this is connected the fact that the emancipation of ethics from the theory of Ideas, to which the two genuine *Ethics* of Aristotle devote so much space and on which they found it necessary to spend such great pains, is assumed as an established fact by the *Great Ethics* right from the beginning, in the short historical retrospect with which it opens. There Pythagoras and Plato are blamed because neither of them understood how to keep ethics independent of metaphysical speculations: one confounded the question of virtue with number-metaphysics, the other with the theory of Ideas and ontology. Socrates is praised because he kept himself free from this intermingling.[1]

The absolute selfevidence of the emancipation of ethics from metaphysics for the author of the *Great Ethics* from its opening sentences on must naturally reveal itself especially in his treatment of the so called intellectual virtues, and of the question of the relation between *sophia* and *phronesis*. In the early Aristotle (*Protrepticus*, *Eudemian Ethics*) *sophia* and *phronesis* were, in full accord with Plato's view, not yet strictly distinguished, because moral insight was rooted in the knowledge of the highest good and the latter was immediately decisive for moral action. In the sixth book of the *Nicomachean Ethics* a sharp line was drawn between the two, as we have shown above. The *Great Ethics* goes one step farther. Although it adopts no radically divergent point of view, but here, too, gives the problem in a form externally true to Aristotle's ethics, yet that it goes beyond the *Nicomachean Ethics* is clear. In that work there is assumed from the beginning a perfect equality between the intellectual and the moral virtues, which is what makes it necessary to give an intensive argument for their explicit separation. The thoroughness with which *phronesis*, as specifically moral and practical reason, is there separated from pure theoretical *sophia*, the knowledge of the highest and most general principles, is due to the fact that this division of the realms was to Aristotle as a Platonist even in the last phase of his development by no means yet selfevident. It was he who had to achieve it; and the particular inquiry that was needed in order to separate the intellectual virtues and *sophia* from the doctrine of character itself indirectly gave them a new claim to be treated in ethics. This hybrid position of theirs had a certain inner justification to Aristotle because of the course of his development. The author of the *Great Ethics* finds it, in spite of his loyalty to the tradition, fundamentally incomprehensible and uncomfortable. When in the discussion of *phronesis* (I. 34), which corresponds to the sixth

[1] *Gr. Ethics* I. 1, 1182ᵃ 10–30.

book of the *Nicomachean Ethics*, he from the very first divides the
rational part of the soul (λογικόν) into a practically deliberative and
a scientifically apprehending part (βουλευτικόν and ἐπιστημονικόν),
he is assuming as fixed and solidified that essential distinction between
phronesis and *sophia* which was first achieved in the corresponding
section of the *Nicomachean Ethics*. In this he was following some
earlier Peripatetic who taught the same division, as is shown by the
excerpts from the ethical literature of the Peripatetic school in
Stobaeus (II. 117, 14 W.). He draws much farther-reaching consequences from this sharp distinction between *phronesis* and *sophia*
than Aristotle had. It means to him the complete emancipation of
phronesis from *sophia*. Yet he is in a sense only following logically
in the direction initiated by Aristotle when he expresses his wonder
that *sophia*, which he distinguishes from *phronesis* as being purely
theoretical knowledge, is not completely excluded from ethics: 'One
might puzzle and wonder why, when we are speaking of morals and
of some political inquiry, we mention *sophia*.'[1] So speaks a man
when confronted with an established tradition to which he externally
submits although he no longer really understands it. This is no great
philosophical wonder such as that which according to Plato is the
beginning of all wisdom. It is the schoolman's 'I wonder', at peculiarities of the tradition that are no longer grasped. For this author
the question of *sophia* has lost the actuality that it possessed for
Aristotle as a Platonist. To explain its introduction he has to think
up all sorts of scholastic subtleties. He comforts himself with the
reflection that it is really a sign of wide philosophical vision to take
notice of such secondary questions which do not strictly belong to
the subject; furthermore, ethics concerns the soul, and to the soul
belongs theoretical science also—and the rest of the foolish chatter![2]

At the time when the *Great Ethics* was written, the Peripatos was
actually weighing the doctrine that practical reason has the primacy
over the theoretical, and some were defending it. The *Great Ethics*
itself raises at the end of Book I the question whether *phronesis* be
not the real ruling force in the soul, 'as it seems and as is debated'.
That this refers to a real opponent of the Aristotelian view and is not
a mere invented *aporia* is also shown by the 'he says' which is used
to introduce an argument of the representative of this thesis. However, the *Great Ethics* does not turn so far away from Aristotle as to
subordinate *sophia* to *phronesis* and throw it completely out of ethics.
It is characteristic of the intermediate intellectual position of its
author that he does not draw this consequence to which his own
thought really presses, but holds fast to the tradition of the school
although he can no longer maintain it without reserve. He tries to

[1] *Gr. Eth.* I. 34, 1197^b 28–30.   [2] Ibid. 1197^b 30–5.

defend the orthodox Peripatetic view against the daring heresy of the pre-eminence of practical reason by means of a picture; and compares *phronesis* to the steward, whose position is that of a servant, whereas *sophia* corresponds in the intellectual economy of the soul to the master.[1] How much even in the *Great Ethics* the interest in *logos* or reason has in fact yielded to the importance of character and the emotions is shown by a sentence like the following, in which the author is summing up his view in conclusion: 'In general, not *logos*, as others think, is the beginning and guide to virtue, but rather the emotions.'[2] The 'others' to whom he here objects are of course primarily the creators of Greek ethics, Socrates and Plato; but Aristotle must here be reckoned as a Platonist too; he, too, is liable to the reproach of the *Great Ethics* that he assigned to the intellect a high significance in moral training. To give the passions their rights against *logos* means nothing else than that ethics, both theoretically and practically, must concern itself above all with *ethos* or character. The determination with which the author emphasizes this against Aristotle from the first lines onwards is connected with his systematic suppression of *logos* and the 'rational part of the soul'.

The chief argument of the *Nicomachean Ethics* for the pre-eminence

---

[1] Ibid. 1198^b 9 ff.; 'he says' ibid. 1198^b 11. At first sight one might think that this *aporia* meant just the same as *Eth. Nic.* VI. 7, 1141^a 21: 'For it is absurd to think that politics or *phronesis* is the best, since man is not the best thing in the cosmos.' But that is merely a rejection of the Socratic–Platonic notion of *phronesis* in its ambiguity. Since the word *phronesis* originally referred only to human affairs, Aristotle could not adopt it as a designation for the highest intellectual faculty even in the extended sense, including *sophia*, that the later Plato had given it. He was compelled to restore *sophia* to its rights, as being the highest form of rational knowledge, because its subject is the divine. But that installation of *phronesis* as of the highest importance which *Gr. Eth.* I. 34, 1198^b 9, attacks is in its turn a polemic directed against this Aristotelian supremacy of *sophia*. That it is not Plato's conception of *phronesis* that is here meant follows from the fact that one can never say of Plato that he questioned the primacy of *sophia* and declared that *phronesis* 'instead' is the ruling element in the soul. On the other hand, what *Eth. Nic.* says in the place mentioned fits him exactly: he believed politics or *phronesis* to be the best, not indeed because he thought 'man the best thing in the cosmos' as Aristotle there expresses it, but because the subject of politics and *phronesis*, the Idea of the Good, was to him definitely the highest thing both in the human world and in the cosmos. The struggle between *phronesis* and *sophia* for first place could not begin until Aristotle had separated them again, and politics was no longer one with metaphysics as in Plato. While Aristotle decides for *sophia* because its object is the higher, his adversary, against whom the *Great Ethics* is arguing, champions *phronesis* because it 'cares for all', that is, has the supreme authority in practice, whereas *sophia* merely wishes to remain in its study as undisturbed as possible. But precisely this seems to the author of the *Great Ethics* the more distinguished. To him, therefore, *phronesis* is merely the housekeeper and not the mistress of the soul.

[2] *Gr. Eth.* II. 7, 1206^b 17.

of *sophia* and the theoretic life over the life of practical activity, namely the inference from the intellectual activity of the divine mind to the highest and most valuable form of human existence, is also dropped by the *Great Ethics*. That agrees with the effort to keep aloof from everything metaphysical. But obviously it also represents a concession to some opponent who maintained that the activity of Aristotle's God, contemplating only himself, is emphatically not the highest conceivable, any more than such a contemplation of self would be the highest and most valuable state for a man. That the author of the *Great Ethics* took the objection seriously is shown by his himself applying the argument to the question of the selfsufficiency of the happy man, and warning us to beware of a hasty analogical inference from the selfsufficiency of God to what is worthy of mortal man's endeavour.[1]

If, then, our author found the seat of human virtue so decidedly and exclusively in character, we must ask ourselves whether he could still speak of intellectual virtue at all in addition to ethical virtue? Would not the concept of *areté* have to take on for him the meaning, originally strange to a Greek, of our word 'morality'? One would expect it. In fact, however, we find, here as in his relation to the question of *sophia*, rather doubt and hesitation than sharp finality in thought. We even meet with direct contradictions in his statements on the point. Aristotle had handed down to him the doctrine that it is a mark of the conception of *areté* that an action or habit is 'praised'. So, when he introduces the division of the soul into the rational and the irrational part, and attaches to this the distinction between the ethical virtues (as courage and temperance) and the intellectual virtues (as intuition, wisdom, memory, &c.), he firmly sets aside the intellectual virtues as only incidental to ethics, in

---

[1] *Eth. Nic.* X. 8, 1178b 7–23: man believes that God enjoys perfect happiness. Yet it is not credible that God is active in affairs or exercises any kind of moral activity, be it courage or generosity or justice or prudence. All that is completely unworthy of God. If we remove action of this sort from a life, there clearly remains as content nothing but pure thought. God's activity and blessedness is therefore to be conceived as theoretical activity (θεωρητικὴ ἐνέργεια). Hence for man, too, the happiest way of life is that which most resembles this divine existence (cf. *Metaph.* Λ 7, 1072b 25). The *Great Ethics* is concerned with an opponent of this argument in II. 15, 1212b 37. It appears to take no stand towards his objection, so far as concerns the activity of God (see 1213a 7: 'let us put aside the question what God will contemplate'); but that the author admits it so far as concerns the inference from God to man follows from 1212b 33: 'The analogy customarily drawn from God in the discussions is neither right there nor would it be useful here.' Thus he rejects the doctrine of the selfsufficiency of the happy man, and with it the identification of human happiness with the temporal enjoyment of the thought-activity that God enjoys eternally.

accordance with his high estimate of ethical virtue. Our action receives praise, he says, only when it concerns ethical qualities; no one is praised on account of the superiority of his mind, as being wise or penetrating or anything of that sort.[1] That is the opposite of what Aristotle teaches in the parallel passage of the *Nicomachean* and the *Eudemian Ethics*. We are told there that man is praised on account of the qualities of his mind as well as those of his character.[2]

To Aristotle the conception of *areté* was not yet narrowed to the meaning 'virtue', as it was for common speech and for the way of thinking natural to the author of the *Great Ethics*, who is here directly controverting Aristotle.[3] The only strange thing is that he is not so consistent as entirely to deny the character of virtue to intellectual qualities such as *phronesis* and *sophia*; but, the farther he advances and the deeper he thinks himself into his model, the more confused he becomes about the denial he had so energetically announced. Not only does he calmly retain the traditional classification of *phronesis*, *sophia*, understanding, &c., as virtues. He plainly contradicts himself in his detailed discussion of them (I. 34) in reference to the sixth book of the *Nicomachean Ethics*. For he there asserts repeatedly, and even seeks to prove in form, that one is also praised for valuable intellectual qualities, and why.[4] Even stranger to him

---

[1] *Gr. Eth.* I. 5, 1185^b 5: 'In the rational [part of the soul] arise *phronesis*, shrewdness, *sophia*, quickness in learning, memory, and the like. In the irrational part arise the virtues, as they are called, temperance, justice, courage, and whatever other aspects of character seem praiseworthy. For we are called praiseworthy on account of these. But no one is praised on account of those belonging to the rational part. No one is praised because he is wise or because he is prudent or because of any such quality.'

[2] *Eth. Nic.* I. 13, 1103^a 4: 'Virtue is also divided by this distinction [of the rational and irrational parts of the soul]. For we call some of them intellectual and some moral—*sophia* and understanding and *phronesis* intellectual, liberality and temperance moral. When we are talking of character we do not call a man wise or understanding but gentle or temperate, but we praise the wise man also for his habit. Praiseworthy habits we call virtues.' Similarly *Eth. Eud.* II. 1, 1220^a 5: 'There are two kinds of virtue, the moral and the intellectual. For we praise not only the just but also the understanding and the wise.'

[3] In *Gr. Eth.* I. 5, 1185^b 5, he makes the distinction: in the rational part of the soul arise *phronesis*, *sophia*, and the like (obviously speaking vaguely on purpose); in the irrational part arise 'the virtues, as they are called'. Though he immediately afterwards relapses into the Aristotelian usage and speaks of 'virtues of the rational part', it is quite clear that this point of view is really strange to him. That is why he tries to distinguish them from the real virtues, the ethical ones, at least by this mark, that they do not receive praise.

[4] It is probably impossible to explain this contradiction as long as we assume that both sides of it arose from the independent thinking of the author. Just as in I. 34 he is taking the sixth book of the *Nicomachean Ethics* as his model, so in the contradictory passage I. 5, 1185^b 5 ff., he has obviously copied some other Peripatetic who rejected the hypothesis of intellectual virtues or at any

than the conception of intellectual 'virtues' is naturally Aristotle's view that there are 'virtues' not only of the rational and irrational parts of the soul but even of the 'nutritive' part. The tradition of the school and the wording of Aristotle's *Ethics* compel him to mention this peculiar view; but he obviously expects no sympathy for it from his hearers or readers, and declares that the question whether such a kind of virtue is to be assumed had best be dropped from ethics.[1] As little as he grasps the culmination of Aristotle's ethics in metaphysics when he asks what *sophia* is doing in morals, does he understand its anchoring in the teleological system of nature when he can no longer grasp human virtue as the next level above the virtue of plants and animals.

One gets definitely the impression that the *Great Ethics* is tacking apprehensively between the steep contradictions that rent the Peripatetic school asunder during the generation of Aristotle's earliest pupils. They concerned precisely the point on which we have found the author vacillating between independent criticism and pupillary fidelity to the tradition, namely the determination of the value of the theoretic life and the 'intellectual virtues' in elevating human life, and their place in ethics. We still know the name of the enemy within the gates who attacked Aristotle strongly and rejected his high estimation of the theoretical life; it was Dicaearchus of Messene. Tradition makes him in this matter the polar opposite of Theophrastus, who, as Aristotle's successor in the direction of the school and his truest adherent, but also undoubtedly out of his innermost convictions as a researcher, held fast to the doctrine of the primacy of the theoretic life. The controversy between him and Dicaearchus must have been celebrated, for in Cicero's time the contention

rate denied that they were praiseworthy. It is believed that the influence of this man is also to be traced in the avoidance of the Aristotelian technical term 'intellectual virtues' in the *Great Ethics* (cf. the Peripatetic writers on ethics in Stob. II. 137, 19; but to the contrary 118, 1, and 145, 17). Later Peripatetic ethics, of course, regards the intellectual 'virtues' as not properly and the ethical 'virtues' as properly so called. This departure from Aristotle begins in the *Great Ethics*; or at least that is where we can first demonstrate it.

[1] *Gr. Eth.* I. 4, 1185[a] 23: 'What, then, someone may say, does this part of the soul also have a virtue?' And [a] 26: 'Whether or not there is a virtue of this part is another question.' On the contrary, *Eth. Nic.* I. 13, 1102[b] 2 ff.: 'The virtue of this part [i.e. of the nutritive faculty of the soul] seems to be not human but common.' *Eth. Eud.* II. 1, 1219[b] 38: 'Hence the virtues of the nutritive and growing part are not virtues of man.' In both places Aristotle is working on the assumption that the view that the nutritive part has its own peculiar virtue is perfectly current. The astonished question of the *Great Ethics* reminds one in its Epigonic nature of the author's astonishment at the introduction of *sophia* into ethics (I. 34, 1197[b] 28). His way of putting the question aside is similar to his way of putting aside the problem whether God thinks of himself, II. 15, 1213[a] 7.

between the theoretical and the practical lives for the first rank was still attached to these two names.[1]

Dicaearchus was the Peripatetic who declared that not *sophia* but *phronesis* is the ruling power in the human soul; that follows necessarily from the fact that he found the essence of man in action, not in contemplation.[2] He must have severed the connexions that Aristotle, following Plato, had held to exist between moral action and the knowledge of the highest questions, and reached the logical conclusion of which we hear the echo in the author of the *Great Ethics*: 'One must wonder what *sophia* has to do with ethics', since the latter concerns character and action.[3] He must have put *logos* after character in significance; and we can also be confident that he completely denied the quality of virtue to the intellectual powers and confined this conception to ethical and political action. And who but he can have been capable of that argument, most heretical for a Peripatetic, which the author of the *Great Ethics* cites as very remarkable: the famous conclusion (of Aristotle) must be false, to the effect that God can have no other object of thought than himself, because he can think only the most perfect and there is nothing more perfect than he. Since even a man who was entirely occupied in the contemplation of himself would be blamed as a heartless being, the idea of a God who contemplates himself is absurd.[4]

The dissolution here proclaimed of Aristotle's conception of the world and of God is based on an argument at the bottom of which

---

[1] Cic. *Ep. ad Att.* II. 16: 'Now I have definitely decided that, since there is such a controversy between your associate Dicaearchus and my friend Theophrastus, yours far preferring the practical life to everything and mine the theoretical, I will appear as having paid my dues to both of them. I think I have adequately satisfied Dicaearchus, and I am now turning to the school that not only allows me to rest but rebukes me for not always resting. So let me address myself, dear Titus, to those famous studies, and return at last to what I should never have left.'

[2] Above, pp. 446–8.

[3] Above, p. 446.

[4] Theophrastus, of whom one might think in this connexion, appears, however, to be out of the question. In his metaphysical fragment he obviously regards God's activity, and his influence on nature and on the motions of the spheres in particular, exactly as Aristotle does in *Metaph.* Λ 7. The highest principle is 'immovable in itself'; it causes the motion of other beings through another sort of influence, namely their 'appetite' for the best. For this they need soul and thought, from which appetite takes its start. All the more, therefore, is the primary being to be conceived as mind, and as the thought and will for the most perfect, which, however, it itself is in its perfection. The expression, 'the primary and most divine being, desiring all the best things', does not in my opinion contain anything that goes beyond Aristotle's doctrine. God thinks himself as the best there is, and he must also will this goodness of his. On the other hand, if we do away with God's thought of himself we alter the object of the divine will also and give it another direction.

lies the ultimately indemonstrable value-equation: Life is action. The selfcontemplation of the Aristotelian *Nus* had to cease being the most sublime ideal of human and divine life as soon as its earthly model, the theoretic life of the philosopher, was no longer capable, in the actual feeling of contemporary persons, of justifying this high claim against other ways of life. Aristotle himself had already taught that the theoretical life has pre-eminence over the practical only because the philosopher at the same time occupies the highest level of creative activity: he is the 'architect' of the intellectual and social world.[1]

The more theoretical, in our sense of the word, science became in the course of this development, the more it turned away from life, the less could it wholly appropriate Aristotle's ideal of the theoretic life. Through its onesidedness it gave prominence to the antithesis, the ideal of the practical life. Dicaearchus showed the followers of Aristotle that they were definitely not the highest flowering of humanity, and that history nowhere offers us such a supremacy of mere intelligence above creative action.

At this point our inquiry turns back to its beginning, the ancient tradition about the 'life' of the earliest philosophers. Owing to the radical change in the philosophic ideal of life they suddenly appeared in a wholly new light. Dicaearchus himself wrote *Lives of the Philosophers*. Isolated fragments of them are preserved, concerning precisely the earlier thinkers; and they show clearly how the author's ethical view is everywhere reflected in his view of the past. The earliest representatives of philosophy are obviously for him, too, the representatives of an ideal by which to measure the philosophers of his own time. Whoever, like Dicaearchus, saw the end in active living for human society would inevitably come either to despise all study altogether, or to oppose to the onesided life of contemporary philosophy the picture of a greater past in which thought had really still possessed the power of constructive action. When one looked at the scanty accounts of the earlier thinkers from this point of view, there appeared, in addition to that devotion to pure contemplation which Plato and Aristotle had emphasized exclusively, a close connexion with public life, which was strange to contemporary thinkers and had not been called attention to. These men had really fulfilled in their 'lives' the ideal of Aristotle that the bearers of the highest thought should be at the same time the 'architects' of active life. It was clearly incorrect of Aristotle in the dialogue *On Philosophy* to interpret the seven sages in modern guise as 'sophists'. Precisely these revered personages, who had continued to live in the mind of the Greek folk down to the present time, incorporated the most

[1] *Pol.* VII. 3, 1325[b] 23.

complete unity of thought and action. They were lawgivers and men of politics, so Dicaearchus declared;[1] and he must have found his view confirmed not merely by Solon and Pittacus, but also by Thales, for example, whom Plato had made a pure representative of the theoretical life. Evidence for his view was easy to collect from the best historical sources, and also from the realm of anecdotes. Tradition connected Thales with the greatest technical achievements of navigation and astronomy. According to a report preserved in Herodotus, he was an engineer in the service of King Croesus when the latter led his army against the Medes; and by a special device was able to show how to divert the river Halys and lower its level, in order to put the Lydian army across it without bridge or boat.[2]

Though Herodotus as a rationalistic critic doubted the trustworthiness of the report, Thales obviously was to the Greek people in general a practical man rather than an otherworldly scholar. As statesman, too, he had taken part in the life of the Ionian cities; for Herodotus has heard of his advice to the Ionians to make a common parliament and place it on the island of Teos, which lay in the middle of the Ionian cities, and to subordinate the previously independent cities to this central control as members of a unified state. This tradition gives him a political reputation reaching far beyond his own city; and it is certain, though not expressly handed down to us, that Dicaearchus did not let this and similar traits escape him.[3]

In the tradition of late antiquity concerning the earlier thinkers we find reports of this kind, and completely opposite traits intended to prove that the great sages were absorbed in science and uninterested in practice, occurring side by side, for the most part quite peacefully, as befits the compilatory character of Diogenes and the sources akin to him.[4]

[1] *Fragm. Hist. Graec.* vol. ii, p. 243 Mueller (frg. 28). Diog. I. 40: 'Dicaearchus says they were neither wise men nor philosophers, but lawgivers and men of understanding.'

[2] The crossing of the Halys, Herod. I. 75 (*Vors.*[5] 11, A 6). That the Peripatos adopted the tradition of Thales' astronomy is shown by Eudemus frg. 94 Spengel. It occurs already in Herod. I. 74.

[3] Herod. I. 170 (*Vors.*[5] 11, A 4). Diog. I. 25 (*Vors.*[5] 11, A 1) ascribes to Thales also the political advice to the Milesians to reject the alliance offered to them by Croesus, which saved them later when Cyrus was at war with Croesus.

[4] Thus immediately after the story of Thales' political advice (see the previous note) we read that Heraclides of Pontus (frg. 47 Voss) made Thales, obviously in the same sort of way as he made Pythagoras himself tell of his previous incarnations (Diog. VIII. 4), say of himself that he was an individualist and lived for himself (μονήρης καὶ ἰδιαστής). That, of course, fits only the theoretic life. One is reminded of Aristotle's description of himself as 'solitary and isolated' (αὐτίτης καὶ μονώτης, frg. 668 Rose), on which Demetrius remarks in interpretation: 'the isolation indicates a more individualistic habit', &c. (τὸ μὲν γὰρ μονώτης ἰδιωτικωτέρου ἔθους ἤδη ἐστί κτλ.). That explains the

We may with great probability suppose, what we can still directly prove in the case of the seven sages, that the reports which make the early philosophers lawgivers, politicians, and practical men, were first introduced into the stream of the tradition by Dicaearchus. Such are the accounts emphasizing the active part taken in political life by Anaximander, Parmenides, Zeno, Melissus, and especially Empedocles.[1]

Thinkers of the type of Anaxagoras and Democritus naturally fell into the background for Dicaearchus as definitely as they had occupied the middle position for the adherents of the contemplative life. Their practical cosmopolitanism made them necessarily unattractive to him. For Heraclitus it was not difficult to reveal the political side

---

association of μονήρης with Ἰδιαστής in Heraclides. Perhaps Aristotle actually had the latter in mind. To Heraclides Thales was just as selfevidently a typical representative of the theoretic life as was Pythagoras, of whom he relates the conversation with the tyrant Leon of Phlius (see above, p. 432).

[1] Anaximander led a colony from Miletus to Apollonia on the Pontus (*Vors.*[5] 12, A 3). Parmenides gave laws to his fellow-citizens (ibid. 28, A 1 = Diog. IX. 23). Zeno was a fanatical partisan of freedom and a member of the conspiracy against the tyrant Nearchus (others give the name as 'Diomedon' or 'Demylus'); he maintained his political attitude on the rack (*Vors.*[5] 29, A 1 = Diog. IX. 26; 29, A 6–7). Melissus was a statesman and led the Samians in the war against Pericles as naval commander (*Vors.*[5] 30, A 1–2). The tradition is particularly detailed about Empedocles' political activity (ibid. 31, A 1, Diog. VIII. 63 ff.). This goes back to the historical activity of Timaeus, whom we shall meet below as the transmitter of the Dicaearchan tradition about the political activity of Pythagoras. The accounts themselves are certainly in part older than Dicaearchus. Thus the one about Parmenides' lawgiving is quoted from the *On Philosophers* of Speusippus, who was probably looking for a precedent for Plato's similar efforts. But there must once have been some individual historian of philosophy who presented the thinkers systematically in the light of their political and practical life and collected the reports of this kind; and such an interest in the practical life of the philosophers in particular is not likely to have existed in any one but the man who found the greatness of the earlier thinkers in their practical influence above all, and dealt with them only for this reason—Dicaearchus. It is not for nothing that we find this member of the earliest Peripatos not, like Theophrastus, Eudemus, and Meno, among the doxographers, but interested only in the lives of the philosophers. But what is called 'biography' did not arise out of mere interest in individuality as such. It sought in the life of the individual representatives the expression of the type, of that which philosophical ethics understood by βίος or 'life', and the varieties of which it developed. Whether, and how far, the collection of politically active philosophers and their deeds in Plutarch, *Adv. Colot.* c. 32, goes back directly or indirectly to Dicaearchus cannot be determined. The list embraces the philosophers down to Aristotle and Theophrastus, but it lacks precisely the seven sages and Pythagoras, who are known to have been important for Dicaearchus. And that he would have mentioned Theophrastus as a representative of the political life is improbable, especially as the reason that Plutarch gives for him as for Aristotle proves little, and both of them seem to be added more for the sake of completeness.

in his thought, and to show that he was not a pure physicist, although he felt himself detached from the political life of his own city. The philosophy of Socrates and Plato had a directly political intention. Dicaearchus seems, however, to have regarded the ideal type of philosophical reformer and lawgiver as being realized in Pythagoras rather than in Plato. Through the work of the Peripatetics and of the Academy Pythagoras had long been in the centre of philosophical interest; and concerning him there flared up now an all the more vivid strife of opinions, the more vaguely and ambiguously his image flickered in the oral tradition.

In the middle and the second half of the fourth century B.C. the name 'Pythagorean' referred to two entirely different groups of men. When Aristotle speaks repeatedly of the 'so called Pythagoreans' he means the scientific circle of Archytas of Tarentum, with whom Plato had had personal intercourse. He seems, however, to have possessed no definite indications as to how far back this tradition went in southern Italy, still less to have considered it permissible to refer its beginnings to Pythagoras himself, after whom the circle named itself. But another sort of men also called themselves 'Pythagoreans', men whose peculiar way of living is often mocked in the Middle Comedy, and must therefore have been known to the people at that time. This was a strictly ascetic and pious order that derived its religious symbols and ideas from Pythagoras and honoured him as the founder of a religion and a worker of miracles.[1]

Quite early, in the fourth century at latest, we find these two conceptions of Pythagoras at war with each other; and naturally the two groups, which then, at any rate, had nothing in common and therefore might have existed peaceably side by side, were driven by their description as 'Pythagoreans' or 'Pythagorists' into controversy as to which were the descendants of the genuine Pythagoras and whose attitude was the truly Pythagorean one. Archytas' mathematical and astronomical school appears not to have followed that commandment to abstain from meat and some other foods that was sacred to the other party; and presumably it was they who introduced the version according to which Pythagoras did not preach abstinence. To them also must be due the assignment of certain of their fundamental scientific notions and of particular mathematical and physical propositions to the person of Pythagoras.[2]

[1] See the fundamental discussions of Erwin Rohde in his classical article 'Die Quellen des Iamblichus in seiner Biographie des Pythagoras' (*Kleine Schriften*, vol. ii, pp. 102 ff.). Rohde explains the existence of the two movements as due to a split in the school, and thus makes them to have been both united in the personality of Pythagoras. Similarly J. Burnet, *Early Greek Philosophy*[4], p. 86. The evidence of the Comic poets is collected in Diels's *Vors.*[5] 58, E, p. 478.

[2] The representative of this worldly conception of Pythagoras is Aristoxenus;

These scientific students could not but find it distasteful to think of their founder as a wandering medicine-man and miracle-worker. Their conception was best suited by the picture of Pythagoras as the founder of the theoretic life, a picture which we first came across in Heraclides of Pontus. But how was one to explain the fact that men of such different types derived their ideals of life from one and the same founder? This problem was by no means solved by the two conflicting conceptions of Pythagoras' personality. Not until Dicaearchus put forward his point of view did it seem to clear up. To Dicaearchus it was easy to see in the archaic thinker not a mere theorist in the modern style, but a lawgiver and founder of states, who made both religion and knowledge serve creatively in the establishment of life.

We do actually find in our late and entirely legendary tradition about the life of Pythagoras, whose chief representatives, the Neo-Platonists Iamblichus and Porphyry, reproduce at second or third hand old sources like Aristoxenus, Heraclides, and Dicaearchus, a third picture in addition to those of the student and the miracle-monger, namely that of the lawgiver and founder of states. Although it is quite uncritically intermingled with the other two, some thoroughly characteristic traits are expressly referred to Dicaearchus, and they confirm Erwin Rohde's conjecture that Dicaearchus made Pythagoras into an ideal picture of the practical life as he himself taught it and tried to realize it in his own person.[1] In doing this he must have been especially encouraged by the example of the Pythagorean Archytas, who was also statesman and student both.[2]

From Dicaearchus comes our tradition that when Pythagoras arrived at Croton in South Italy he was commissioned by the council to give educational political addresses to the men, the women, and the children, of the city. And although Aristoxenus preceded Dicaearchus in declaring that Pythagorean ideas had had a great influence on political relations in southern Italy and Sicily, we can show that Dicaearchus adopted this view and tried to establish it more exactly in detail. The political conception of the influence of Pythagoras found especially welcome fuel in the tradition that the order suffered a violent catastrophe because of its growing political unpopularity and the master fled to Metapontum.[3] But now the political inter-

---

and in this he was following, according to Gell. IV. 11, 7 (*Fragm. Hist. Graec.*, vol. ii, p. 273 Mueller = Aristox. frg. 7), the view of his Pythagorean scientific friends (cf. Rohde, op. cit., p. 108).

[1] See Rohde, op. cit., p. 110. In modern times Dicaearchus' view has been revived by Krische, *De societatis a Pythagora conditae scopo politico*, 1830.

[2] See George Grote, *History of Greece*, vol. iv, p. 405.

[3] For Dicaearchus on the various speeches of Pythagoras at Croton, see Porphyry's *Vit. Pyth.*, §§ 18, 19. The wording of the speeches is given by Iamblichus, *Vit. Pyth.*, §§ 37–57, from another source, in which these speeches

vention of Pythagoras in Croton on his arrival in southern Italy would have come without any transition after the miracle-hungry were freely invented from the indications given by Dicaearchus (see Rohde, op. cit., p. 132, who infers that Timaeus originated the speeches). Dicaearchus frg. 31, Mueller, also presupposes that Pythagoras intended political reforms; for it says that, when Pythagoras in his flight from Croton came to Locri, the Locrians sent messengers to the frontier to tell him that they valued his wisdom, but they had no objection to their laws and no intention of altering the existing condition of the state, so would he please direct his steps elsewhere. The account of the legislative influence of the Pythagoreans on the cities of Sicily and southern Italy differs in Porphyry, § 21, and Iamblichus, § 130 (the latter repeated § 172 with only minor variations). As an intermediary source for what Dicaearchus had said about the addresses to the Crotoniates, Porphyry used Nicomachus (§ 20), and obviously borrowed from him also the section on the legislation of the Pythagoreans in the cities of Sicily and Magna Graecia, which follows immediately and is very closely connected with the preceding both logically and verbally. Nicomachus got this section (§ 21) not from Dicaearchus but from Aristoxenus, i.e. from a source of equal age and value. Porphyry himself says this in § 22, so far as concerns the political influence exerted on the Lucanians, Messapians, Peucetians, and Romans, that is, the surrounding barbarians; from which it follows that it is also true of the previously listed Greek cities of Magna Graecia and Sicily. Now Porphyry, following Aristoxenus, tells us that the Pythagoreans gave laws to Croton, Sybaris, Catana, Rhegium, Himera, Acragas, Tauromenium, and other cities, and he ascribes all of these laws to two supposedly Pythagorean persons, Charondas and Zaleucus. Iamblichus, on the other hand, reports (§ 130) that Charondas gave laws to Catana; for Locri he names a certain Timares (or Timaratus, § 172) in addition to Zaleucus; for Rhegium, obviously basing himself on copious local traditions, he begins with the οἰκιστής or founder Thucles (see Thuc. VI. 3, 3), and names a whole list of persons who were connected with changes in the constitution, § 130 Phytius, Helicaon, Aristocrates, and in § 172 (where Thucles is missing) Theaetetus also. It cannot be that Aristoxenus' original version contained these same details and Porphyry (or his intermediary Nicomachus) merely made careless excerpts. Iamblichus must be here following some source other than Aristoxenus and Porphyry. That Aristoxenus' version was old and intact is evidenced by Aristotle's catalogue of lawgivers, which, as I have previously shown (*Entsteh. d. Metaph.*, p. 45, and *Aristotle*, above, p. 285), is a subsequent appendix to the second book of the *Politics*. We read there (1274ᵃ 22) that Zaleucus was lawgiver to Locri, and Charondas was lawgiver to Catana 'and the other Chalcidian cities in Italy and Sicily' (Porphyry's language is less precise; but he obviously means the same, when he designates Zaleucus and Charondas together as the originators of all lawgiving in Sicily and southern Italy.) For Iamblichus' local tradition about the lawgivers of Rhegium we must therefore seek some other source than Aristoxenus; and in the circumstances that can only be an author as well informed about the neighbouring city as the Messenian Dicaearchus, who is one of Iamblichus' sources and also, as was shown above, often one of Porphyry's in addition to Aristoxenus. The erudition of Aristotle's catalogue of lawgivers about Zaleucus and Charondas, which gives them so much wider an influence than do Dicaearchus and Iamblichus, is certainly drawn from Aristoxenus, for he wrote early while this appendix was added to the book quite late. He tells us in Iambl., § 233, that he heard the story of the devotion of the two Pythagoreans, Damon and Phintias (known to us from Schiller's ballad *Die Bürgschaft*), from the mouth of the

account of his study-travel in Egypt and the East, and would have
lacked all motive in the history of his youth and education, had not
Iamblichus and Pompeius Trogus inserted between his return from
these long journeys and his arrival in southern Italy a further journey
to Crete and Sparta, with the object of studying the laws of Minos
and Lycurgus.[1]

This version, which is obviously a subsequent attempt to make a
place for the political element in the course of Pythagoras' education,
derives his social pedagogical ideals from the model of the two classical
Dorian constitutions. Since it is a necessary presupposition of the
intervention of Pythagoras in Croton as depicted in Dicaearchus'
account of his addresses there, we are compelled to assume that the
journey to Crete and Sparta also comes from Dicaearchus. And this is
rendered the more probable by the analogy of his conception of Plato.

In a passage of Plutarch which, I think, is usually incorrectly understood, we read that Plato obviously amalgamated Lycurgus no less
than Pythagoras with the teaching of Socrates, as Dicaearchus
believed.[2] This interpretation of Plutarch's words assumes only a

---

tyrant Dionysius himself, 'when he had lost his throne and was teaching letters
in Corinth'. (He was driven out of Syracuse by Dion in 354.) The tale is perfectly credible and thoroughly in the manner of Aristoxenus; elsewhere, too, he
takes pleasure in such personal reminiscences (see above, p. 434, n. 3, and
also his story of his father Spintharus' charming reminiscence of Archytas,
Iambl., op. cit., § 197). For the rest, the present case teaches us that Dicaearchus, as a learned Peripatetic, did not simply pick his political conception of
the earlier thinkers out of the air, but everywhere drew from good sources.
Thus, in regard to Pythagoras, he was obviously preceded by Aristoxenus, with
whom he had ties of friendship and to whom he was probably indebted for
suggestions in political theory too. (Similarly by Speusippus in regard to the
political activity of Parmenides, see above, p. 454.)

[1] Iamblichus, op. cit., § 25, mentions the journey to Crete and Sparta only
briefly after his long account of those in Egypt and the East; but that it was
equally firmly rooted in the earlier tradition is shown by Pompeius Trogus
(Justin, *Epitome*, XX. 4): 'Returning thence he sought out Crete and Lace-
daemon, in order to ascertain the laws of Minos and Lycurgus, which were
famous at that time. Having learned all these things, he came to Croton. . . .'
There follow the addresses to the Crotoniates as according to Dicaearchus (cf.
Porph., § 18). But Justin obviously knows their content already and reproduces it in catchword style. The decorative development of Dicaearchus'
account and the free composition of the addresses must therefore have already
existed in the source of Pompeius-Justin. Rohde showed that its originator
was Timaeus, who therefore made use of Dicaearchus (*Kleine Schriften*, vol. ii,
p. 132). This is also evident because Timaeus, as an historian, was positively
obliged by the style of his genre to invent speeches freely. Timaeus was much
used by Pompeius Trogus. That the story at the end of the chapter on Pythagoras (the conversion of Pythagoras' house into a temple, Justin, XX. 4, 18)
goes back to Timaeus is shown by Porphyry, op. cit. 4, and is the most important evidence for Rohde's hypothesis.

[2] Plut. *Quaest. Conviv.* VIII. 2, 2 (frg. 27 Mueller): ἀλλ' ὅρα μή τί σοι προσῆκον

small change in the text, without which it would mean: Plato mixed
Socrates with Lycurgus, and not merely, as Dicaearchus believed,
with Pythagoras. The speaker in Plutarch's dialogue would then be
expressing this as his own view and as an addition to that of Dicaearchus. Mere fiddling with the construction of the sentence will
hardly get us near the truth; but what the sense demands seems to
me clear. Dicaearchus was precisely the historian of philosophy who
had everywhere brought the political side into prominence. There
was no need to quote him for the opinion common throughout antiquity that Plato's philosophy was a mixture of Socratic and Pytha-
goreanism. That was in Aristotle, and had been the universal
conviction of the Platonic and Peripatetic school from the beginning.[1]
The special nuance that Dicaearchus added to this conventional view
can only lie in the asserted relation of the theoretical philosopher to
the practical statesman and lawgiver, in which naturally he was
thinking especially of Plato's *Laws*. That the great political thinker
should find his model in Lycurgus' expert creation is characteristic
of Dicaearchus' mind in two ways. He regarded Sparta as realizing
that mixed constitution in which he saw the ideal state. (That
Plutarch is referring to the mixed constitution seems to me to be
clearly revealed by his next sentence, and to confirm the present
interpretation of the passage.)[2] But especially Dicaearchic is the

ὁ Πλάτων καὶ οἰκεῖον αἰνιττόμενος λέληθεν, ἅτε δὴ τῷ Σωκράτει τὸν Λυκοῦργον ἀναμιγνὺς
οὐχ ἧττον ἢ τὸν Πυθαγόραν, ⟨ὡς⟩ ᾤετο Δικαίαρχος. 'But don't you think that
Plato is hinting at something that concerns you nearly and you have overlooked it, when he mixes with Socrates not merely Pythagoras but also
Lycurgus, as Dicaearchus thought?' The insertion of ὡς is due to Osann, the
only one who has looked at this textual question correctly in its intellectual
connexion with Dicaearchus' view as a whole, in the reconstruction of which
he has acquired the highest merit. Bernardakis adopted ὡς into the text.
Mueller declares that he cannot see why ὡς is necessary, which naturally
abolishes the reference of Dicaearchus to Lycurgus. So M. Fuhr before him,
Dicaearchi Mess. quae supersunt, Darmstadt, 1838, p. 58.
    [1] Instead of further witnesses I will quote for this merely Aristotle, *Metaph.*
A 6, 987ᵃ 29: 'After the above philosophies came the work of Plato, which in
most respects agreed with these men, but also had some peculiarities distinct
from the philosophy of the Italians.' Particularly close was the relation of the
other Platonists to the Pythagoreans, especially Speusippus, Xenocrates,
Heraclides, and Philip of Opus. In saying that Plato made use of Pythagoras,
Dicaearchus, of course, must have meant that he made use of the Pythagorean
school, since there were no writings by Pythagoras. His assertion is therefore
none other than the prevailing opinion in the Academy and the Peripatos.
Plutarch could never have fallen into quoting this particular man for that
purpose, especially with the cautious expression 'Dicaearchus *thought*', as if it
were a conjecture and not the most well known historical fact. Plato's relation
to the Pythagoreans has recently been examined by E. Frank and shown to be
very positive (*Plato und die sogenannten Pythagoreer*, Halle, 1923).
    [2] Dicaearchus, frgs. 21-3 Mueller. Cf. Fuhr, op. cit., p. 29. Polybius adopted

view that the norms and arrangements of human life are never and nowhere originally created by theoretical philosophy, but have always been the work of the states and their lawgivers; and that all philosophers have drawn their ideas from this historical reality. We read these views in the introduction to Cicero's main work of political philosophy, in which Dicaearchus' opinions continue to exercise an influence in numerous other ways too.[1]

This is the background that teaches us how to understand Dicaearchus' effort to bring Plato close to Lycurgus; and it makes it as good as certain that the relation which the tradition in Iamblichus and Pompeius Trogus sets up between Pythagoras and the laws of Minos and Lycurgus is also derived from Dicaearchus' view.

Here we conclude. The peculiar phenomenon from which our discussion began, the contradictory lights in which the tradition puts the life of the earlier philosophers, now as theoretical and now as practical, has revealed itself as a reflection of the development of the ideal of the philosophic life from Plato to Dicaearchus. This development with its various stages was mirrored in men's view of the past. It is no new discovery that all genuine history, if it is not mere raw material but a formed intellectual picture of the past, receives the decisive stimuli for its shaping and its selection of facts from the effective inner centre of the life of the beholder. The picture of history is therefore shaped anew by every new age. That is doubly true of the Greeks, to whom history was never the mere ascertainment of what had once happened, but always took shape in the mind of the historian through some ideal that informed him or some great

---

both Dicaearchus' doctrine of the mixed constitution and the Lycurgan state as its classic example, VI. 3, 8, and VI. 10. Plut. *Quaest. Conviv.* VIII. 2, 2 (p. 719 B) characterizes the Lycurgan state quite clearly in accordance with Dicaearchus' conception of Sparta as a constitution compounded of democracy, aristocracy, and kingship, so that it is perfectly clear that this was the ground on which Dicaearchus had asserted that Lycurgus influenced Plato. They wanted to make a constitution that took as its basis not the external mechanical equality but the proportional equality (*suum cuique*) of men, which alone fits a 'temperate oligarchy' and a 'constitutional kingship'. Since equality in whatever form constitutes the democratic element, we have here the three elements of Dicaearchus' ideal state.

[1] Cic. *De Rep.* I. 2, 2: 'Everything that philosophers have said, if it is well and truly said, was begotten and confirmed by those who have given laws to states.' That this and the following sentences derive from Dicaearchus can only be asserted here without further proof. I hope soon to be able to give the proof in another connexion; but the thing is really evident enough in itself. For the superiority of political to philosophical activity Cicero, op. cit. I. 7, 12, quotes the example of the greatest philosophers, who—like Plato—devoted themselves at any rate to the *problem* of the state, and especially of the seven sages, who, he says, were almost all immersed in political life. Here, too, he is drawing on Dicaearchus (cf. frg. 28 Mueller).

and general insight that it revealed to him. The tradition concerning the personalities and ways of living of the earlier thinkers, largely anecdotal and legendary, often purely oral, provided a plastic material almost waxy soft for the expression of the changing wish-pictures of philosophical ethics. If the whole value of this tradition lay only in its store of so called historical facts, we should have to resign ourselves to its being slight, as our own examination of its vicissitudes has shown ; but it remains important for all times because of the store of ideas that its various creators have immortalized in it.

The philosophical movement, whose reflections in the traditions about the earliest thinkers we have followed, presents a train of thought possessing remarkable necessity. Each step of the way follows inevitably from the preceding, and their order could not be changed without distorting the direction of motion into a zigzag. The sequence constitutes an independent section of the development of Greek culture. We do its importance less than justice if we regard it only as a piece of more or less insignificant history of the philosophical schools. It is necessary not merely in that the individual viewpoints follow logically one from the other, but also in that the possibilities inherent in the human mind are exhaustively revealed in them. At first we find Socrates and Plato linking the moral world to the philosophical knowledge of being. Then in Dicaearchus' practical ideal, life and ethics are entirely withdrawn again from the rule of high philosophical speculation and restored to independence, and the daring wing of speculative thought is pinioned. With it fades the power of the ideal of theoretic life. When we meet it thereafter it is always the world of 'pure science' and contrasted as such with the life of practice. Or else we find lame compromises such as the so called 'synthetic life' or βίος σύνθετος, which is actually a mere external juxtaposition of the theoretical and practical lives. Not until the destruction of scientific philosophy and metaphysics by scepticism could the theoretic life achieve renewal, now in the religious form of the contemplative life, which has been the monastic ideal since Philo's work of that name. It is worth noticing that the Romans, when they incorporated classical Greek philosophy into their culture, left the ideal of the philosophic life behind. There were indeed always individual personal believers who joined in the poet's praise:

Felix qui potuit rerum cognoscere causas.

But, when Cicero in his books *On the State* undertook to give Greek philosophy a fixed place in the whole of Roman culture, he could combine the political spirit of his people with Greek science only by disregarding his deep reverence for Plato and Aristotle and adopting Dicaearchus' ideal of the political life.

INDEXES

1. SUBJECTS

2. PERSONS

3. THE WRITINGS OF ARISTOTLE AND PLATO

1. ARISTOTLE

2. PLATO

4. GREEK WORDS AND PHRASES

PRINTED IN GREAT BRITAIN
AT THE UNIVERSITY PRESS, OXFORD
BY VIVIAN RIDLER
PRINTER TO THE UNIVERSITY